EMPIRE, AUTHORITY, AND AUTONOMY IN ACHAEMENID ANATOLIA

The Achaemenid Persian Empire (550–330 BCE) was a vast and complex sociopolitical structure that encompassed much of modern-day Turkey, Syria, Jordan, Israel, Egypt, Iraq, Iran, and Afghanistan and included two dozen distinct peoples who spoke different languages, worshiped different deities, lived in different environments, and had widely differing social customs. This book offers a radically revised approach to understanding not only the Achaemenid Persian Empire but imperialism more generally. Drawing on a wide array of textual, visual, and archaeological material, Elspeth R. M. Dusinberre shows how the rulers of the empire constructed a system flexible enough to provide for the needs of different peoples within the confines of a single imperial authority and highlights the variability of their responses. This book examines the dynamic tensions between authority and autonomy across the empire, providing a valuable new means of considering imperial structure and development.

Elspeth R. M. Dusinberre is Associate Professor in the Classics Department at the University of Colorado Boulder. She has published articles in the *American Journal of Archaeology*, *Ars Orientalis*, *Anatolian Studies*, and the *Annual of the American Schools of Oriental Research*. She is the author of *Aspects of Empire in Achaemenid Sardis* and *Gordion Seals and Sealings: Individuals and Society*.

Empire, Authority, and Autonomy in Achaemenid Anatolia

Elspeth R. M. Dusinberre
University of Colorado Boulder

CAMBRIDGE UNIVERSITY PRESS

CAMBRIDGE
UNIVERSITY PRESS

32 Avenue of the Americas, New York, NY 10013-2473, USA

Cambridge University Press is part of the University of Cambridge.

It furthers the University's mission by disseminating knowledge in the pursuit of education, learning, and research at the highest international levels of excellence.

www.cambridge.org
Information on this title: www.cambridge.org/9781107577152

© Elspeth R. M. Dusinberre 2013

This publication is in copyright. Subject to statutory exception and to the provisions of relevant collective licensing agreements, no reproduction of any part may take place without the written permission of Cambridge University Press.

First published 2013
Reprinted 2015
First paperback edition 2015

Printed in the United States of America

A catalog record for this publication is available from the British Library.

Library of Congress Cataloging in Publication data
Dusinberre, Elspeth R. M.
Empire, authority, and autonomy in Achaemenid Anatolia / Elspeth R. M. Dusinberre.
   p. cm.
Includes bibliographical references and index.
ISBN 978-1-107-01826-6 (hardback)
1. Turkey – History – To 1453.   2. Achaemenid dynasty, 559–330 B.C.   I. Title.
DR481.D87   2013
9 39′.2–dc23   2012007852

ISBN 978-1-107-01826-6 Hardback
ISBN 978-1-107-57715-2 Paperback

Cambridge University Press has no responsibility for the persistence or accuracy of URLs for external or third-party Internet Web sites referred to in this publication and does not guarantee that any content on such Web sites is, or will remain, accurate or appropriate.

for Edward

CONTENTS

List of Figures and Tables	page xi
Preface	xvii
Abbreviations	xxi

1	INTRODUCTION	1
	Assessing Achaemenid Anatolia	1
	Background: Core–Periphery and Tempered Sovereignty	3
	Deriving a New Model	3
	An "Authority–Autonomy" Framework of Interpretation	4
	A Brief Overview of Achaemenid History	8
	Anatolia	15
	Urartu	17
	Phrygia	19
	Lydia	22
	Southwestern and Southern Anatolia	24
	Western Coast of Anatolia	25
	Chapter-by-Chapter Overview	26
	Divide and Conquer, or Conquer and Unify?	30
2	GOVERNING ANATOLIA	32
	Part I: Administering Anatolia	33
	Satraps and Satrapies	34
	Taxes and Tribute	35

Contents

Lydia and Cilicia	42
Roads	47
Part II: Combining the Practical and Ideological	49
Assertions of Royal Power: The Progress of Xerxes	50
Paradeisoi as Power Statements	54
Assertions of Achaemenid Power: Dascylium	56
Assertions of Achaemenid Power: Altıntepe	59
Assertions of Achaemenid Power: Nonsatrapal Sites	60
Governing Anatolia via Cultural Impositions? Religion and Language	63
Archives	65
Authority and Style among the Elite	69
Messages of Authority and Style among Non-Elites	71
Coins	72
Co-opting the Local Elite	76
Royal Gifts	79
Summary	81

3 Controlling Anatolia, Guarding the Empire — 83

The Military in Achaemenid Anatolia	85
Textual Resources	85
Visual Resources	93
Archaeological Evidence of Fortification Installations	94
Summary	107
Catalogue of Achaemenid Military Presence in Anatolia	108

4 Eating and Drinking with Class and Style — 114

Feasts Fit for a King	114
Dining and Status in Persia	119
Feasting and Human Society	122
Eating Utensils and Dining Behaviors	125
Value-Laden Cups of Precious Metal	128
Value-Laden Cups of Clay	136

5 Dealing with the Dead — 141

Lydia	142
Rock-Cut Tombs	142
Cists	144
Tumulus Tombs	145
Mortuary Inclusions from Sardis	151

Contents

Grave Markers	158
Unique Structures	165
Pyramid Tomb	166
Taş Kule	166
Temple Tomb	167
The Western Seaboard: Ionia and Mysia	168
Clazomenian Sarcophagi	168
Grave Stelae	170
Hellespontine Phrygia	171
Granicus Valley Tumuli	172
Grave Stelae	174
Pillar Tomb	175
Central Anatolia: Highland Phrygia, Cappadocia	176
Black Sea Coast	179
Armenia	181
Southeast	183
Cilicia	187
Pisidia	188
Lycia	189
Pillar Tombs	190
Sarcophagi	195
Rock-Cut Tombs	197
Tumulus Tombs	197
Temple Tombs	199
Caria	201
Summary	206

6 Worshiping the Divine — 207

Continuity of Cults	209
Mother Goddess	209
Apollo	220
Anatolian Storm God	222
Malija	222
Hero Cults	222
Accretion of Cults	225
Artemis at Sardis and Ephesus	226
The Sanctuary of Zeus at Labraunda	230
Conversion of Cult? The Altar to Cybele at Sardis	234

Contents

	Introduction of Non-Anatolian Cults	234
	Royal Cult	241
7	EDUCATING THE YOUNG AND OLD	245
	Educating the Persian Elite	245
	Art and Education	248
	Ideology	250
	Religion	252
	Language	253
	Gender Matters	254
	Accounting	256
	Summary	258
8	EMPIRE AND IDENTITY IN ACHAEMENID ANATOLIA	259
	Identity and Status	259
	Identity and Ethnicity	260
	Identity and Religion	263
	Identity and Administration	263
	Authority and Autonomy in Achaemenid Anatolia	266
Notes		273
Bibliography		315
Index		367

FIGURES AND TABLES

FIGURES

1	Impression left by cylinder seal from Sardis	*page* xx
2	Achaemenid Anatolia; Syria and Assyria shown for context	2
3	Achaemenid Empire	5
4	Achaemenid Empire; author's drawing	6–7
5	Statue of Udjahorresne	10
6	Oblique view of the central Iranian plateau toward the southeast	12
7	Apadana at Persepolis	14
8	Anatolia	15
9	Anatolia, through a fish-eye lens	16
10	The mountains of Urartu	17
11	Eastern Anatolia, looking northwest (Urartu from the Assyrian perspective)	18
12	Mount Ararat, above Lake Van	19
13	North central Anatolia, looking south across eastern Phrygia	20
14	Gordion's Citadel Mound in the Middle Phrygian period	21
15	The Aegean coast, looking east across Lydia	22
16	Sardis in August	23
17	Caria, Lycia, and Pamphylia, looking east	24
18	Pamphylia and Cilicia, looking north across Cappadocia	25
19	The Achaemenid Empire, through a fish-eye lens	26
20	Different subject peoples of the realm, from Persepolis	29
21	Achaemenid Anatolia; author's drawing	30–1
22	Achaemenid Anatolia	38
23	Lydian Delegation (Delegation VI), eastern stairway of Persepolis Apadana	41

Figures and Tables

24	Anatolia from the Greek perspective	42
25	Cilician coastal plain and Taurus Mountains, looking west	47
26	Royal Road from Ephesus to Mosul	48
27	Bisitun	50
28	Trilingual Inscription of Xerxes at Van	51
29	The Rock at Van	52
30	Plan of Pasargadae; author's drawing	56
31	Architectural elements from the first and second building phases at Dascylium	58
32	Altıntepe	60
33	The Mosaic Building at Gordion: paved forecourt, rectangular colonnaded porch with mosaic, and throne room (?)	61
34	Gordion Seal 100, modern impression	62
35	Dascylium Seals 2, 3, and 4	67
36	Seals from Sardis	68
37	Seals from İkiztepe; author's drawing	68
38	IAM 4581, from Sardis	69
39	Seals carved with iconography of authority in Achaemenid koine styles from Sardis	70
40	Seals from Gordion	72
41	Tiarate head coins	75
42	Athenian tetradrachm and tiarate head coin	76
43	Proskynesis before the king, from Persepolis	77
44	The king's horses and a Skudrian (?) horse from Persepolis	78
45	Sites of Achaemenid military authority in Anatolia	84
46	Warrior images on Achaemenid Anatolian-style seals	94
47	Western Anatolia, looking east: Sardis	95
48	Sardis, sites of Achaemenid-period remains	96
49	Northwestern Anatolia, looking southeast: Dascylium	98
50	Southern Anatolia, looking north: Meydancıkkale	98
51	Meydancıkkale; author's drawing	99
52	Meydancıkkale gate and Building A; author's drawings	100
53	Meydancıkkale Persepolitan reliefs; author's drawing	101
54	Western Anatolia, looking east: Şahankaya	102
55	Şahankaya	102
56	Fire bowl at Şahankaya	103
57	Servants with banquet (?) supplies, palaces of Darius and of Xerxes at Persepolis	121
58	Late Phrygian / YHSS 4 vessels from Gordion	126
59	Rhyton, Achaemenid bowl, round-bottomed bowl, and phiale	129
60	Spouted table amphorae and cups, from the Apadana at Persepolis	130
61	Persepolis Fortification Seal 535*	131

Figures and Tables

62	Clear glass cups from Mylasa; author's drawing	133
63	Bronze mirror from Sardis	134
64	A ceramic skyphos and two ceramic Achaemenid bowls from Sardis	135
65	Elite male figure from the west wall at Karaburun II	136
66	A ceramic Achaemenid bowl from Sardis	137
67	Achaemenid bowls from a deposit at Sardis	138
68	Plan and section of Tomb 813	143
69	Bathtub sarcophagi from a rock-cut tomb at Sardis	144
70	Tumuli at Bin Tepe	146
71	Reconstruction of tumulus chamber at Lâle Tepe	147
72	Figures from Harta	148
73	Objects from İkiztepe	149
74	Selected items from the sarcophagus burial at Sarıkız	150
75	Selected items from Gökçeler	151
76	Gold foil clothing appliqués from Sardis	152
77	Beaded necklace from Sardis	153
78	Gold earrings and an ivory figurine from Sardis wearing similar earrings	154
79	Seals with Neo-Babylonian and Greek imagery from Sardis	154
80	Gold seal ring from Sardis, apparently that of a seventeen-year-old girl	155
81	Two seal rings from Sardis, Tomb S 16	155
82	Gold seal ring and pyramidal stamp seal from Sardis, Tomb 811	156
83	Two seals and a pendant from Sardis, Tomb 18	156
84	Doorstones from İkiztepe	158
85	Anthemion stele fragments from Sardis	159
86	Banquet stele from Sardis	161
87	Grave stelae from Ödemiş and Hayallı	162
88	Grave stele from Manisa; author's drawing	162
89	Grave stele from Tire	162
90	Grave stele from Gökçeler	163
91	Pyramid Tomb at Sardis	165
92	Taş Kule	166
93	Banqueting pediment from Sardis	167
94	Clazomenian Sarcophagus, ca. 480–470	169
95	Polyxena Sarcophagus; author's drawing	172
96	Silver ladle and phiale from the Kızöldün burial	173
97	Sarcophagus from Çan in the Granicus valley	174
98	Two examples of grave stelae from Hellespontine Phrygia	175
99	Items from Tumulus A at Gordion	177
100	Stele from Altıntaş	178

101	Painted beams from Tatarlı	179
102	Silver from Sinope	181
103	Silver vessels "from Erzincan"	183
104	Deve Hüyük Grave Group 1; author's drawing	185
105	Deve Hüyük Grave Group 15; author's drawing	186
106	Deve Hüyük Grave Group 20; author's drawing	187
107	Gold foil clothing appliqué from Silifke	188
108	Stele from Delipınar; author's drawing	189
109	Reconstructed pillar tomb at Xanthus	191
110	East side of the Harpy Tomb	192
111	Audience scene from Persepolis	193
112	The Inscribed Pillar at Xanthus	194
113	The Sarcophagus of Payava	195
114	The theater group at Myra	196
115	Kızılbel southwest corner, departure scene	197
116	Kızılbel south wall, Gorgons and Pegasus	198
117	The Nereid Monument	200
118	Erbbina (?) under a parasol, from the Nereid Monument	201
119	Mausoleum at Halicarnassus, reconstruction	202
120	Two slabs of the Amazonomachy frieze, from the Mausoleum	202
121	Artemisia II (?) and Mausolus (?)	203
122	Rhodian silver didrachm of 400–333	204
123	Mausolus (?)	205
124	Relief of Matar from Ankara	210
125	Midas Monument	211
126	The main step monument at Midas City	214
127	Marble temple sculpture from Sardis	216
128	Stele from Sardis with Artemis and Cybele	217
129	Silver coin of Ephesus, fifth century, with bee and incuse	218
130	Construction at Ephesus and Didyma; author's drawing	220
131	Statue from Achaemenid-period Didyma	221
132	Relief from Building G at Xanthus	223
133	Xanthus Building G detail and the king's horse from the Apadana at Persepolis	224
134	The altar to Artemis at Sardis	227
135	Coin of Mausolus; author's drawing	230
136	Sanctuary of Zeus at Labraunda	231
137	Andron B at Labraunda	232
138	Sphinx from Labraunda	233
139	Persian ritual: Cappadocia and Dascylium	238
140	Tarsus stater, struck under Pharnabazus (379–374); author's drawing	239

Figures and Tables

141	Tarsus stater	239
142	Tarsus stater; author's drawing	240
143	Seal of Gobryas, impressed on Persepolis Fortification Tablet 688; and seal from Sardis	241
144	Issus stater, struck under Tiribazus; author's drawing	241
145	Stater of Myriandrus and obol, 361–334; author's drawing	242
146	Cylinder seals from Gordion and Sardis	243
147	Impression of a rock-crystal pyramidal stamp seal from Tomb 5(A) at Sardis	251
148	Glass Seals 56, 188, 44, 90, 112, 192, 205, and 75 from Gordion	264
149	Glass seals from Dülük Baba Tepesi	265
150	Achaemenid Empire	271

TABLES

1	Regions and Rulers of Achaemenid Anatolia	*page* 36
2	Peoples and Tributes of Achaemenid Anatolia	40
3	Mints of Achaemenid Anatolia	74

PREFACE

Why Bother?

"Why should people care about this book?" a scientist friend recently asked me. The answers to this are not limited to the simple "because it's so interesting!" – which was my first response. The subject matter is interesting: how imperialism worked in the Achaemenid Empire; how people were folded into the empire; how that affected their lives and the ways they defined themselves; what differences and similarities are observed across the Anatolian peninsula and what explains those trends. Some of the artifacts recovered are exceptionally beautiful, a feature that conveys little information to a scholar but makes them a great pleasure to look at – this surely had an impact on their use and resonance in antiquity, even as it does today. Beyond this, though, I think it is important to understand how this ancient empire functioned – and not only because it can help us understand other ancient empires and the ways they were similar to or different from the Achaemenid. The book also matters because imperialism is scarcely a thing of the past.

Many of the problems people face in a situation that requires interaction with an empire remain fundamentally similar even if solutions to those issues change with time, geography, and cultural background. The actions of imperial authority in Achaemenid Anatolia, the ways people living in Anatolia reacted to or took on aspects of authority within an imperial context, the impact the empire had on how people lived and expressed themselves: these are important and valuable in analyzing modern societies too. Understanding autonomy and the situations in which people act autonomously within an empire matters as much as understanding the actions and motivations of top-down authority. When and where was autonomy granted by authorities? When did a person or group of

Preface

people act autonomously without the authority to do so? What were the effects of these actions? It is extraordinary that enough material concerning Anatolia in the Achaemenid period is preserved that we can consider these behaviors in antiquity. If we wish, it can allow us a glimpse into our own lives as well.

A Note on Evidence

An enormous amount of evidence exists concerning Achaemenid Anatolia. It includes literary documents, archives, and inscriptions in Anatolia and elsewhere. The residua of satrapal palaces have been unearthed, and so has the everyday detritus of non-elite people. Mortuary assemblages, structures, and art have been found across Anatolia. Sculptures, sealstones, paintings, and terracottas afford glimpses into people's lives and priorities. Sealed bullae attest to archives, military structures show us the army, temples indicate gods, and coins demonstrate ideology and practice combined in a single artifact. Ceramic assemblages indicate people's dietary behaviors and how they developed; comparing the assemblages used by living people with those interred with the dead can illuminate ideologies. Because I have organized this book by behaviors and actions rather than by material or region, these different categories of evidence are repeatedly revisited to shed light on each issue. This is important because sometimes we have little direct evidence for, say, the co-option of local elites into the new imperial authority, but by combining the understanding gained through the study of Greek historical texts, mortuary sculpture, the architecture of power, and imagery on sealstones we can get a sense of what was happening and how.

There is currently more evidence for considering the lives of the elite in Achaemenid Anatolia than the non-elite, and this book reflects that bias. For instance, published mortuary material showcases the elite. Even a cemetery like Deve Hüyük, not one exclusively of the wealthy, is skewed in publication toward its more "valuable" contents (metals and jewelry rather than potsherds and skeletons), those being the materials for which people were willing to pay at the time it was dug. Recent excavations in Turkey are beginning to rectify this bias, but as yet the material is not fully available for study. This book therefore necessarily considers the lives and deaths of the elite in greater detail than those of the non-elite, although I have made every effort to include as much non-elite material as possible. The nature of the evidence varies according to place. Little mention is made in textual sources of Paphlagonia in the Achaemenid period, for instance, although there are archaeological remains. Grave stelae are common in some parts of Anatolia and so far unseen in others. Evidence for religious practice in Achaemenid Armenia is hard to find, although much evidence exists in other parts of the peninsula; evidence related to domestic architecture is hard to find in the published literature at all. Greek literary sources have a great deal

Preface

to say about Lydia. The coins of Cilicia have been particularly well published. Intensive and extensive regional studies have been conducted in parts of Lydia and Hellespontine Phrygia, with recent exemplary publications. Tombs with painted interiors have been published from Lydia, northern Lycia, and southwestern Phrygia. Gordion has had its entire ceramic assemblage discussed in detailed publications, by excavators who were already familiar with Iranian as well as local and Greek assemblages. These exigencies have an impact on what we can say about different areas. I have tried to weave together as much information as possible, to explore particular behaviors and to trace some of those issues to which different Anatolian regions found similar or sometimes different responses.

Writing This Book

My love affair with Achaemenid Anatolia began during my first season excavating at Sardis, just after I graduated from college, when a sherd turned up in my trench of a cup shape I had never seen before, painted with narrow horizontal stripes in lively white and red. When the project director, Crawford H. Greenewalt, jr., next came by I asked him what it was. "That," he said, "is a sherd of the so-called Achaemenid bowl." I was hooked. This feeling was reinforced in the following months when I began graduate school and took first a course on ancient Near Eastern archaeology and then a seminar on Achaemenid art with Margaret Cool Root. The clincher was the moment in February that year when Greenewalt sent me a picture of the impression left by an Achaemenid-period cylinder seal from Sardis (IAM 4581) and then allowed me to write my seminar paper on it for Root. I love that seal; it still makes my heart go pitter-pat every time I see an image of it. From that study came first an appreciation of Achaemenid art and then a fascination with the ideology and practice of the Achaemenid Empire. The years I have spent working in Turkey since have served only to increase my love of Anatolia and interest in Achaemenid imperialism. This book is thus the culmination of twenty years of research.

Research and writing were made possible thanks to an ACLS/SSRC/NEH International and Area Studies Fellowship, a Loeb Classical Library Foundation Fellowship, and a University of Colorado Graduate School Faculty Fellowship. A series of three-dimensional digital maps with exceptional resolution were made by Professor Karl Mueller of the Department of Geological Sciences at the University of Colorado Boulder; their creation was funded in part by a University of Colorado Faculty Research Fund, a University of Colorado Dean's Fund for Excellence Grant, and a University of Colorado Kayden Research Award. I wish I could thank adequately all those who have helped me with their thoughts and expertise; they include Catherine Alexander, Annalisa Azzoni, Tomris Bakır, Elizabeth Baughan, John Boardman, Pierre Briant, Nicholas Cahill,

Preface

1. Impression left by cylinder seal from Sardis. IAM 4581. Courtesy Sir John Boardman.

Olivier Casabonne, Henry Colburn, Hasan Dedeoğlu, Keith DeVries, Edward Dusinberre, William Dusinberre, Susanne Ebbinghaus, Margherita Facella, Mark Garrison, Jennifer Gates-Foster, Crawford Greenewalt, Sebastian Heath, Wouter Henkelman, Robert Henrickson, Deniz Kaptan, Şehrazat Karagöz, Vahap Kaya, Halim Korucu, Noel Lenski, Marjorie McIntosh, Michael Metcalfe, Margaret Miller, Jacob Morton, Karl Mueller, İlknur Özgen, Andrew Ramage, Christopher Roosevelt, Brian Rose, Kenneth Sams, Heleen Sancisi-Weerdenburg, StJohn Simpson, Peter Sommer, Gil Stein, Matthew Stolper, David Stronach, Lâtife Summerer, Geoffrey Summers, Mikhail Treister, Christopher Tuplin, Michael Vickers, Mary Voigt, Matthew Waters, Emily Wilson, Bahadır Yıldırım, Cem Yücesoy, and Paul Zimansky. I am particularly indebted to Amélie Kuhrt, Margaret Cool Root, and the two reviewers for Cambridge University Press, who provided comments on various drafts of this book. Any errors that remain are my own.

ABBREVIATIONS

Achaemenid Texts

DB	Bisitun Inscription
DNb	Lower register of Darius's tomb at Naqsh-i Rustam
DNe	Names of peoples at Naqsh-i Rustam
DPd	Terrace Inscription of Darius at Persepolis
DPe	Terrace Inscription of Darius at Persepolis
DPf	Terrace Inscription of Darius (in Elamite) at Persepolis
DPg	Terrace Inscription of Darius (in Babylonian) at Persepolis
DSf	Foundation Inscription of Darius at Susa
XPh	"Daiva" Inscription of Xerxes
XV	Inscription of Xerxes at Van
PF	Persepolis Fortification Tablet
PFS	Persepolis Fortification Seal
PT	Persepolis Treasury Tablet
PTS	Persepolis Treasury Seal

Classical Authors

Ael. *De nat. anim.*	Aelian, *De natura animalium*
Ar. *Acharn.*	Aristophanes, *Acharnians*
Arist. *Analyt. post.*	Aristotle, *Analytica posteriora*
Arist. *De mundo*	Aristotle, *De mundo*
Arist. *Rhet.*	Aristotle, *Rhetorica*
Arr.	Arrian, *Anabasis*

Abbreviations

Cic. *De senect.*	Cicero, *De senectute*
Cic. *Poet. frag.*	Cicero, *Poetica fragmenta*
Ctes.	Ctesias, *Persica*
Curt.	Quintus Curtius Rufus, *Historiae Alexandri Magni*
Dem.	Demosthenes
Dio. Sic.	Diodorus Siculus, *The Library of History*
Hdt	Herodotus, *The Histories*
Hell. Oxy.	Hellenica Oxyrhynchia
Hom. *Il.*	Homer, *Iliad*
Isoc.	Isocrates
Nepos *Alc.*	Cornelius Nepos, *Alcibiades*
Nepos *Dat.*	Cornelius Nepos, *Datames*
Plut. *Alc.*	Plutarch, *Alcibiades*
Plut. *Alex.*	Plutarch, *Alexander*
Plut. *Artax.*	Plutarch, *Artaxerxes*
Plut. *Mor.*	Plutarch, *Moralia*
Polyaen.	Polyaenus, *Strategemata*
Ps.-Arist. *Oec*	Pseudo-Aristotle, *Oeconomicus*
Strabo	Strabo, *The Geography*
Thuc.	Thucydides, *History of the Peloponnesian War*
Xen. *Ages.*	Xenophon, *Agesilaus*
Xen. *Anab.*	Xenophon, *Anabasis*
Xen. *Cyr.*	Xenophon, *Cyropaedia*
Xen. *Hell.*	Xenophon, *Hellenica*
Xen. *Oec.*	Xenophon, *Oeconomicus*

Collections of Inscriptions

FGrH	*Fragmente der griechischen Historiker*
FHG	*Fragmenta historicorum Graecorum*
IG	*Inscriptiones Graecae*
OGIS	*Orientis Graeci inscriptiones selectae*
SEG	*Supplementum epigraphicum graecum*
SIG	*Sylloge inscriptionum graecarum*
TAM	*Tituli Asiae Minoris*

Books/Series

Achaemenid Impact	I. Delemen, ed., *The Achaemenid Impact on Local Populations and Cultures in Anatolia (Sixth–Fourth Centuries B.C.)*, Papers presented at the International Workshop Istanbul, 20–21 May 2005, Istanbul 2007

Abbreviations

AchHist	*Achaemenid History*
AES	Archaeological Exploration of Sardis
AMS	Asia Minor Studien
AOAT	Alter Orient und Altes Testament
L'archéologie de l'empire achéménide	P. Briant and R. Boucharlat, eds., *L'archéologie de l'empire achéménide: nouvelles recherches*, Persika 6, Paris
BAR	British Archaeological Reports
CAH	*Cambridge Ancient History*
CANE	J. Sasson et al., eds., *Civilizations of the Ancient Near East*, New York, 1995
DJD	Discoveries in the Judaean Desert
EncIr	*Encyclopedia Iranica*
MDP	Mémoires de la délégation en Perse
OBO	Orbis biblicus et orientalis
OIP	Oriental Institute Press
SAOC	Studies in Ancient Oriental Civilization
SIMA	Studies in Mediterranean Archaeology
TSTS	Toronto Semitic Texts and Studies
UCPCS	University of California Publications in Classical Studies
UMMAA	University of Michigan Museum of Anthropological Archaeology
VAB	Vorderasiatische Bibliothek

Journals

AA	*Archäologischer Anzeiger*
AASA	*Annali di Archeologia e Storia Antica*
AASOR	*Annual of the American Schools of Oriental Research*
AbhBerl	*Abhandlungen der Königlichen Akademie der Wissenschaften zu Berlin*
ACSS	*Ancient Civilizations from Scythia to Siberia*
ActArch	*Acta Archaeologica*
ActIr	*Acta Iranica*
ActSum	*Acta Sumerologica*
AfO	*Archiv für Orientforschung*
AHB	*Ancient History Bulletin*
AJA	*American Journal of Archaeology*
AJAH	*American Journal of Ancient History*
AJPh	*American Journal of Philology*

Abbreviations

AJSemL	*American Journal of Semitic Languages and Literature*
AmAnt	*American Antiquity*
AmAnth	*American Anthropologist*
AMI	*Archäologische Mitteilungen aus Iran*
AMT	*Archaeological Method and Theory*
AnatAnt	*Anatolia Antiqua*
AnatSt	*Anatolian Studies*
ANES	*Ancient Near Eastern Studies*
ANSNNM	*American Numismatic Society Numismatic Notes and Monographs*
AntCl	*L'antiquité classique*
AntJ	*Antiquaries Journal*
AntK	*Antike Kunst*
AnzWien	*Anzeiger der Österreichischen Akademie der Wissenschaften, phil.-hist. Klasse*
ARA	*Annual Review of Anthropology*
ArchEph	*Archaiologike Ephemeris*
ArkeoAtlas	*Arkeo-Atlas Dergisi*
ArsAsia	*Ars Asiatiques*
ArsOr	*Ars Orientalis*
ARTA	*Achaemenid Research on Texts and Archaeology*
AS	*Arkeoloji ve Sanat*
AST	*Araştırma Sonuçları Toplantısı*
AthMitt	*Mitteilungen des Deutschen Archäologischen Instituts, Athenische Abteilung*
AW	*Antike Welt*
AWE	*Ancient West & East*
BAI	*Bulletin of the Asia Institute*
BASOR	*Bulletin of the American Schools of Oriental Research*
BASP	*Bulletin of the American Society of Papyrologists*
BCH	*Bulletin de correspondance hellénique*
BMCR	*Bryn Mawr Classical Review* (http://bmcr.brynmawr.edu/)
BSA	*British School of Archaeology at Athens*
BSFN	*Bulletin de la societé française de numismatique*
CA	*Classical Antiquity*
CAJ	*Cambridge Archaeological Journal*
CAnth	*Current Anthropology*
CDAFI	*Cahiers de la délégation archéologique française en Iran*
CP	*Classical Philology*
CR	*Classical Review*
CRAI	*Comptes rendus de l'Académie des Inscriptions et Belles-Lettres*
CSCA	*California Studies in Classical Antiquity*

Abbreviations

DHA	*Dialogues de l'histoire ancienne*
EA	*Epigraphica Anatolica*
EW	*East & West*
HSCP	*Harvard Studies in Classical Philology*
HZ	*Historische Zeitschrift*
IAMY	*İstanbul Arkeoloji Müzesi Yıllığı*
IEJ	*Israel Exploration Journal*
IJAIS	*International Journal of Ancient Iranian Studies*
IrAnt	*Iranica Antiqua*
IstForsch	*Istanbuler Forschungen*
IstMitt	*Mitteilungen des Deutschen Archäologischen Instituts, Abteilung Istanbul*
JA	*Journal asiatique*
JAS	*Journal of Archaeological Science*
JCS	*Journal of Cuneiform Studies*
JdI	*Jahrbuch des Deutschen Archäologischen Instituts*
JEA	*Journal of Egyptian Archaeology*
JEOL	*Jaarbericht Ex Oriente Lux*
JESHO	*Journal of the Economic and Social History of the Orient*
JFA	*Journal of Field Archaeology*
JGS	*Journal of Glass Studies*
JHS	*Journal of Hellenic Studies*
JMA	*Journal of Mediterranean Archaeology*
JNES	*Journal of Near Eastern Studies*
JPolPhil	*Journal of Political Philosophy*
JRAS	*Journal of the Royal Asiatic Society*
JRS	*Journal of Roman Studies*
JSA	*Journal of Studies on Alcohol*
KF	*Kleinasiatische Forschungen*
KST	*Kazı Sonuçları Toplantısı*
LAAA	*Liverpool Annals of Archaeology and Anthropology*
MDAFI	*Mémoires de la Délégation Archéologique Française en Iran*
MDAIK	*Mitteilungen des Deutschen Archäologischen Instituts, Abteilung Kairo*
MesArch	*Mesoamerican Archaeology*
MIAA	*Material Issues in Art and Archaeology*
MJBK	*Münchener Jahrbuch für bildende Kunst*
MKKS	*Müze Kurtarma Kazıları Semineri*
NAPR	*Northern Akkad Project Reports*
NC	*Numismatic Chronicle*
OAJ	*Oxford Art Journal*
OCTS	*Oriental Carpet and Textile Studies*

Abbreviations

OJA	*Oxford Journal of Archaeology*
ÖJh	*Jahreshefte des Österreichischen Archäologischen Instituts*
OpAth	*Opuscula atheniensia*
PAPhS	*Proceedings of the American Philosophical Society*
PCPS	*Proceedings of the Cambridge Philological Society*
QDAP	*Quarterly of the Department of Antiquities in Palestine*
RA	*Revue archéologique*
RAN	*Revue archéologique de Narbonnaise*
RBibl	*Revue biblique*
RdÉ	*Revue d'égyptologie*
REA	*Revue des études anciennes*
REG	*Revue des études grecques*
RhM	*Rheinisches Museum*
SM	*Schweizer Münzblätter*
StIr	*Studia Iranica*
StTroica	*Studia Troica*
TTK	*Türk Tarih Kurumu*
TürkAD	*Türk Arkeoloji Dergisi*
ZA	*Zeitschrift für Assyriologie und vorderasiatische Archäologie*
ZÄS	*Zeitschrift für Ägyptische Sprache und Altertumskunde*
ZDMG	*Zeitschrift der Deutschen Morgenländischen Gesellschaft*
ZPE	*Zeitschrift für Papyrologie und Epigraphik*
ZVS	*Zeitschrift für Vergleichende Sprachforschung*

ONE

INTRODUCTION

Assessing Achaemenid Anatolia

In the middle of the sixth century B.C.E., the kingdoms of Anatolia were abuzz with rumors of imminent upheaval. The new king of Persia, Cyrus II, had consolidated the Median and Persian peoples and was amassing his forces in the northwest part of his territories, high on the Anatolian plateau near the headwaters of the Tigris and Euphrates Rivers.[1] The king of Lydia, legendarily wealthy Croesus, held control over much of western and central Anatolia from his seat at the ancient Lydian capital, Sardis. Hearing of the activities of Cyrus, he realized that the borders recognized for the past forty years might no longer hold. Might he cross the eastern edge of his kingdom, at the Halys River, and annex new territory to his lands?[2] He sent to the prophetic priestess of Apollo at Delphi for advice. "If Croesus crosses the Halys," intoned the oracle, "he will destroy a mighty empire"; and so Croesus crossed the river that marked the boundary of his kingdom and invaded the Persian Empire with joyous confidence – only to learn it was his own empire that would fall.[3]

The annexation of Anatolia to the Achaemenid Empire, the workings of the imperial administration, the responses of the newly subject populace, and the impact of imperialism on the peoples of Anatolia form the focus of this study. Our knowledge of the Achaemenid Empire's workings has grown tremendously thanks to recent scholarly work and intensive archaeological investigation. This book seeks to develop two aspects of study of the Achaemenid Empire and, indeed, of ancient imperialism in general:

1. It provides an overarching discussion of Anatolia when it was part of the Achaemenid Empire. Anatolia works well as an isolatable, coherent segment of the empire. The name designates a large geographic area but does not

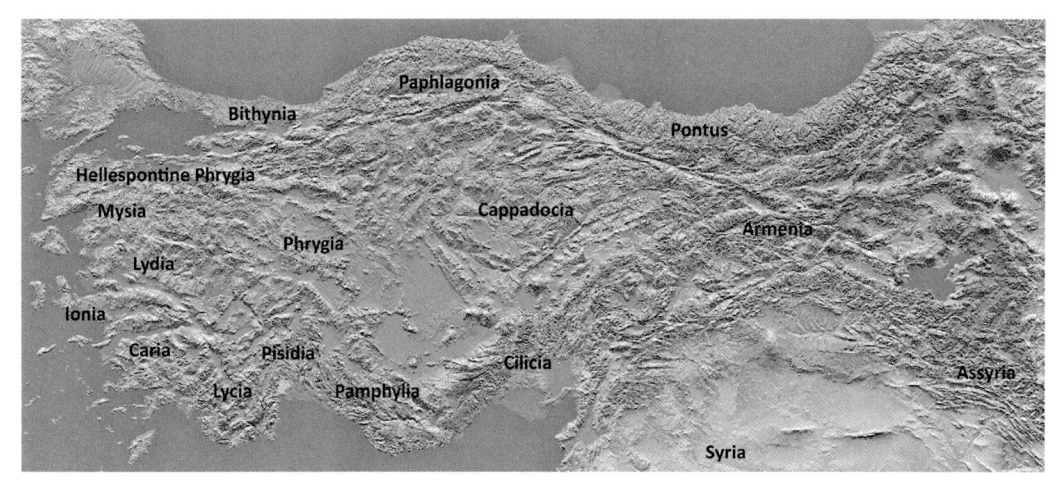

2. Achaemenid Anatolia. Syria and Assyria shown for context. Courtesy Karl Mueller.

correspond to an Achaemenid political entity or concept. It was inhabited before the Persians arrived by varied populations with long-standing histories and traditions, most of them speaking a variety of Indo-European languages. Its geographic, geologic, agricultural, and climatic diversity is very great; in this way it functions as a microcosm of the empire as a whole. I have used the modern boundaries of Asiatic Turkey to define the area of this study.

Anatolia has been the focus of much high-quality archaeological research over the past 150 years. We thus know much about the region, but its full Achaemenid history has not been considered before in a single venue except as collected articles by different authors.[4] Previous research on the area has tended to focus on specific geographic regions or a specific issue. This study departs from others in attempting to provide an overarching discussion of this prosperous, important, and well-researched but undersynthesized region of the empire: What was going on across the entire Anatolian peninsula?

2. This book also proposes a new model for understanding ancient imperialism, which I call an "authority–autonomy" model. It explores the complex relations between imperial authority and various aspects of authority and autonomy within the empire. It allows us to remove ourselves from the limiting geographically determined models (e.g., "core–periphery"), world-systems models, or models following North American notions of "spheres of influence" that have dominated the discourse so far. Instead, this interpretive framework conceives of the empire as a web of relations that includes geographic factors but is not determined primarily by locale. It recognizes the fact that different social groups (e.g., priests, the military) may have exercised particular sorts of authority and autonomy. It explains features of the empire such as the tremendous difference in mortuary treatments combined with a simultaneous similarity in the mortuary inclusions of the elite. The authority–autonomy model represents a shift in the way we might think about the Achaemenid Empire or, indeed, empires in general.

Introduction

Background: Core–Periphery and Tempered Sovereignty

Discussion of the Achaemenid Empire has been dominated by core–periphery models, with an occasional nod at world-systems analysis. These approaches have not, however, formed satisfactory models for understanding the empire. It is clear that the various satrapies, or administrative regions, of the empire were not affected solely by their proximity to the imperial heartland or by geographic proximity to each other, as "core–periphery" would suggest. Indeed, defining particular areas as discrete and coherent "peripheries" has proved challenging and idiosyncratic. Although it is clear that different areas of the empire adopted and adapted different aspects of Achaemenid ideology to fit their local needs and traditions, it is also clear that factors other than geographic ones were often the most important organizing principles.

In beginning this work, I considered the idea of tempered sovereignty to replace and refine the standard core–periphery model. Tempered sovereignty involves the notion that certain nations or regions might operate with some, often circumscribed, sovereignty of various sorts within an overarching sovereign state. I was particularly interested in those aspects of local sovereignty that might preserve the vitality of distinct cultural communities within the empire.

The language of inquiry within this approach ultimately proved unproductive for my purposes. "Sovereignty" is a term so grounded in European political theory that it requires engagement with modern notions like nation and nationality that actually confuse salient issues of imperialism in antiquity. Moreover, each modern field has its own definitions and bibliography: the word "sovereignty" introduces definitional murkiness to an interdisciplinary study. Sovereignty as an idea seemed insufficiently nuanced to enhance the study of imperialism.

Deriving a New Model

The new authority–autonomy model proposed here examines primary issues at stake within an empire. The line of inquiry is clear: to consider the imperial authority's point of view. What matters to the imperial administration, and does the administration try to enforce consistency in these areas? The variability in response allows us to see the point of view of the people on the ground. The approach can be surprisingly clear and straightforward.

The question "what matters to the imperial authority?" seems simplistic, but it has interesting ramifications. The most obvious approaches to the question are the following:

1. to look at the archaeological and textual evidence and see what it suggests, expecting that great variability means the imperial authority had little

vested interest in a given matter, whereas great conformity means a present and guiding imperial hand; and
2. to consider what might matter most to the administration and see whether the material evidence bears that out.

Thus the approach can be multidirectional, beginning from the evidence and determining where great consistency, and hence matters of great imperial concern, lie or beginning from suppositions about matters of imperial importance and seeing whether the evidence supports that.

A major element is the empowerment of local populaces: variability may suggest that the imperial administration did not care about something, or it may suggest just the opposite. A particular matter might be of such importance that it could become a meaningful way for a local populace to resist imperial domination. Thus the fabric of this inquiry has imperial authority as its warp, but its weft is autonomous agency. Particularly interesting is the variability in *types* of autonomy. Autonomy may be local, with geographically conscripted responses to the imposition of imperial authority. But autonomy may also spread across an issue regardless of geography: autonomy may emerge in a whole category of behavior, such as funerary customs or the education of children.

An "Authority–Autonomy" Framework of Interpretation

I use the term "authority" here to mean power with a claim to legitimacy, the justification and right to exercise that power.[5] Many different kinds of authority exist. In the Achaemenid Empire these included political, legal (authority based on the formal rules and established laws of a recognized sociopolitical entity), religious, military, craft-based (authority of the more skilled over the lesser in crafts such as farming as well as those such as carpentry), educational, bureaucratic or organizational, financial, and familial, as well as that informal authority of leadership that generally arises when humans group together (usually based either on traditional authority, deriving from established customs, habits, and social structures, or on charismatic authority, deriving from the personal traits of an individual).[6]

What distinguishes authority from coercion or force is its legitimacy.[7] Leadership, persuasion, and influence play an essential role in manufacturing and sustaining legitimacy. When these qualities are lacking, more charismatic leaders are likely to foment social movements or outright revolutions against standing authority. Thus for a sociopolitical entity to remain secure, a leader must have acknowledged legitimacy of power in the eyes of the populace as well as military leaders, the administration, and those running the political apparatus.

Within this network of authority, groups or individuals possess agency. Such agency can run counter or parallel to perceived authority. Successfully allowing

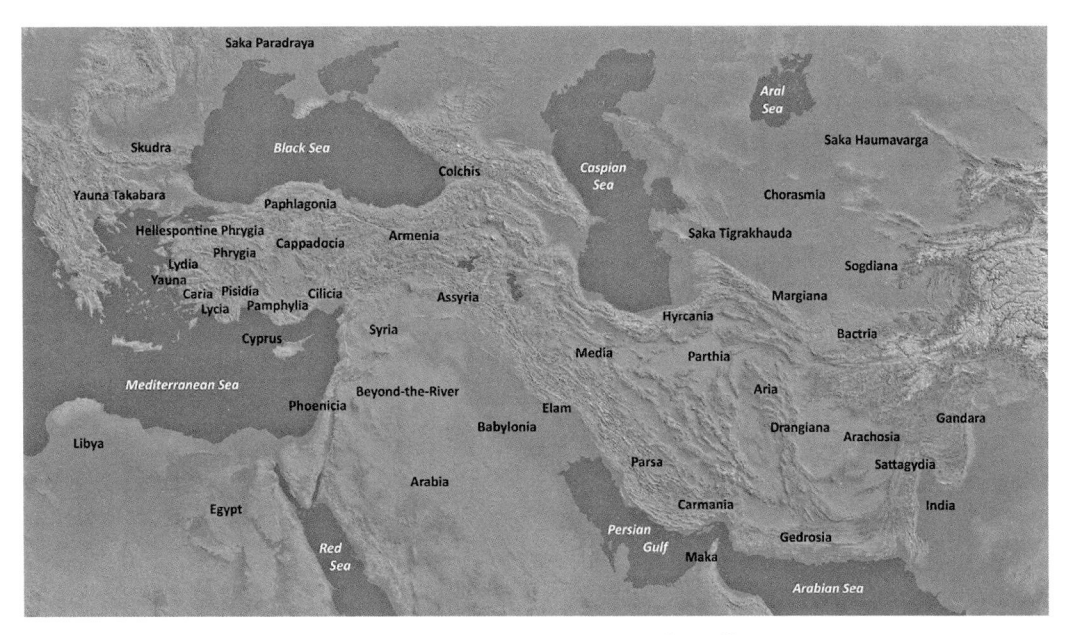

3. Achaemenid Empire. Courtesy Karl Mueller.

for or even implementing autonomous agency is a key element of long-lasting social structures such as the Achaemenid Empire.

Human behaviors were the great organizing feature of the Achaemenid Empire, often, if not always, transcending geographic boundaries. I have thus organized this book by issues rather than by regions or artifact category. The book cannot be an encyclopedia of all archaeological and textual finds in the separate regions of ancient Anatolia, but it considers as much of the archaeological and other evidence as possible to help us understand how the Achaemenid Empire worked. When I have foregrounded particular evidence, it is because that evidence is typical of an issue or serves as an especially illuminating case study. For instance, although the discussion does not include every example of a sealstone or seal impression found in Anatolia that might date to the Achaemenid period, it seeks to articulate the patterns that those seals demonstrate and to describe individual seals that serve as exemplars of or, sometimes, deviations from those patterns.

This chapter includes a brief historical overview of the Achaemenid period, focusing on imperial activities in the center of the empire and its western edges. It summarizes political events, rather than social history, and is based primarily on texts – in this context, I will not constantly question the reliability or frailties of such evidence, but many of the literary sources are Classical Greek and Roman texts and are therefore quite naturally skewed toward western Anatolia.[8] The chapter then turns to look at Anatolia: Who was already living there when Cyrus II arrived, and what kinds of societies made up its complex variety of

EMPIRE, AUTHORITY, AND AUTONOMY IN ACHAEMENID ANATOLIA

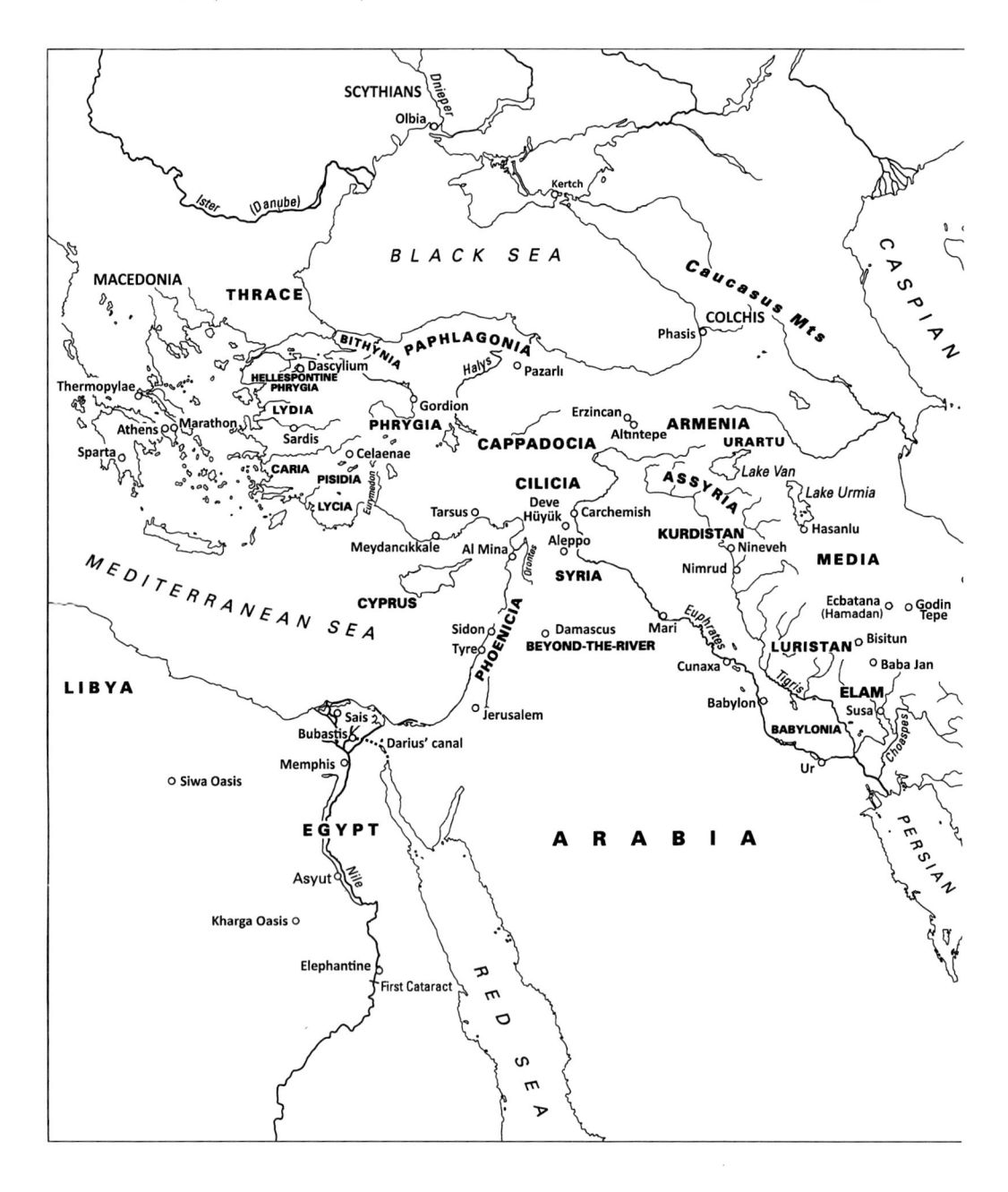

INTRODUCTION

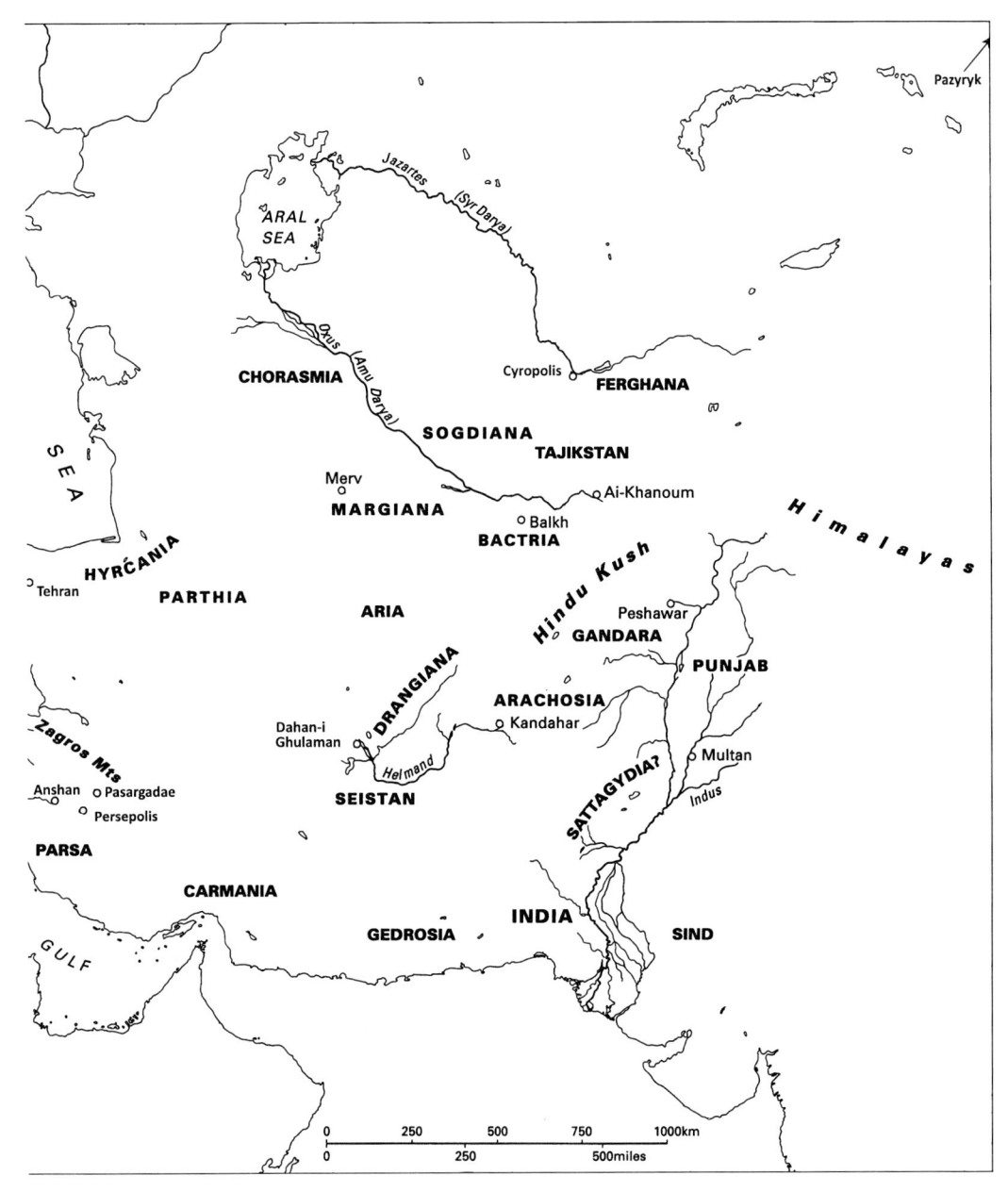

4. Achaemenid Empire. Author's drawing, after Miller 1997.

cultures? Many of the issues faced by the Achaemenid administration across the empire were encountered in Anatolia, and the opening chapter of this book therefore attempts to provide a glimpse into its diversity. The chapter ends with an overview of the book as a whole.

A Brief Overview of Achaemenid History

The Achaemenid Persian Empire (ca. 550–330) was a vast and complex sociopolitical structure founded by Cyrus II (the Great) that centered on southwest Iran and lower Mesopotamia, the area of its genesis in the western Zagros Mountains when Cyrus united the Persians and Medes under his leadership.[9] Under Darius I (522–486) the empire reached its greatest extent, stretching from the Aegean Sea to the Indus River, from Egypt to the modern Central Asian Republics. Although there were subsequent fluctuations in territorial control, there were no major losses apart from Egypt (and that temporary). The empire encompassed within its boundaries twenty-three distinct subject peoples, who spoke different languages, worshiped different deities, lived in different environments, and had widely differing social customs. The Achaemenid dynasty was to devise a method of hegemony that would allow these various peoples to function within the confines of the new imperial authority, to construct a system of empire flexible enough to provide for the needs of different peoples and ensure their ability to operate as part of the system of the new Achaemenid Empire.

Recent historical studies of the Achaemenid Empire have emphasized its complexity, its strengths, the multiple avenues for its investigation, the ways in which various sources may balance and correct each other, and the situations of those living outside the imperial centers.[10] The historical overview presented here cannot provide the kind of richness such specialized studies offer but seeks to present a summary, focusing on the Achaemenid kings and the political and military events that characterized their reigns – my goal is to provide a framework for the discussions that make up the rest of the book. If I privilege the western part of the empire, particularly Anatolia itself, this is a result of both the focus of this book and the nature of our sources.

According to traditional versions of history, Cyrus became king of the Persians in 559 and defeated Astyages, the king of Media, in 550. Perhaps in 547 or 542 Cyrus conquered Lydia and became overlord of most of Anatolia.[11] Either before or after this conquest, he added Bactria and Sogdiana to the empire; in 539 he conquered Babylon. Sometime before 530 he founded a new palace and garden site in southwestern Iran at Pasargadae. In 530, according to one tradition, he was killed in Central Asia during a campaign against the Massagetae.

Cyrus's construction at Pasargadae established certain trademarks of Achaemenid imperial architectural and artistic rhetoric for centuries to come.[12]

Introduction

"Palaces" characterized by many-columned halls and formal gardens with symbolically charged layouts, watered via elaborate channels, and spatial layouts emphasizing open air and movement set Pasargadae apart both from normal life and from the palaces of earlier Mesopotamian kings. In addition to the architectural articulations of the landscape, the art forms that adorned certain doorjambs set the scene for later Achaemenid developments, in some cases drawing on earlier iconographies (such as the figure clad in an Assyrianizing fish costume, carved on the jamb of the southeast doorway of Palace S)[13] or in others creating new forms (such as the four-winged "genius" with the unusual composite crown from Gate R).[14]

Cyrus was succeeded by his son Cambyses, who consolidated the eastern Mediterranean and added Egypt to the empire in 525. The written sources for Cambyses' actions in Egypt highlight certain difficulties of Achaemenid history. The Greek historian Herodotus in Book 3 of the *Histories* is hostile, portraying Cambyses as a brutal foreign invader, a despotic and paranoid ruler with pretensions of grandeur and no sensitivity to local concerns. The autobiographical, hieroglyphic inscription on a statue of an Egyptian naval commander named Udjahorresne, almost certainly from Sais, paints a different picture, however: according to this contemporary source, Cambyses tried to forge links with local elites and install them in symbolically important if not politically powerful positions.[15]

Cambyses seems to have drawn on the knowledge and support of the local elite to facilitate acceptance of his rule and to learn how best to fill the role of a king in local terms.[16] He is said to have died in Syria in 522, apparently while on his way back to the great capital cities of the empire. His throne was taken over (either before or after his death – the chronology is opaque) by a man named Bardiya. In September 522 the throne was usurped by a Persian nobleman named Darius.[17]

Darius circulated various versions of his accession to the throne. According to the great trilingual inscription and relief sculpture at Bisitun above the east–west road through the Zagros near modern Hamadan, his assumption of the throne was followed by numerous revolts across the empire as local personages, including individuals claiming to be such important figures as Phraortes of Media and Nebuchadnezzar of Babylon, sought to take power into their hands.[18] These revolts were swiftly suppressed. According to Herodotus, Darius then reorganized the empire, creating different administrative regions governed by satraps who were responsible for collecting taxes as well as administering their provinces.[19] Under Darius I and his generals, new territory, including parts of Scythian territory, was added to the empire, until it reached its largest size. In 499 various Ionian city-states revolted unsuccessfully against their Achaemenid overlords, and in 490 an Achaemenid force landed on the peninsula of Attica at the plain of Marathon, where it was defeated by the Greeks.

5. Statue of Udjahorresne. 22690. © Vatican Museums.

Herodotus's characterization of Darius consistently has him out for profit, usually at odds with the natural harmony and balance of the world.[20] Conversely, Darius portrayed himself as solely responsible for the harmony and balance of the world.[21] The triumph of Truth over the Lie, of Light over Dark, and the benefits that his rule brings to his subjects form key parts of Darius's imperial rhetoric and that of his successors in inscriptions and in art. Thus DPd, one of four trilingual inscriptions Darius displayed on the palace terrace wall at Persepolis, proclaims:

§1. 1–5. Great Ahuramazda, the greatest of gods – he created Darius the King, he bestowed on him the kingdom; by the favor of Ahuramazda Darius is King.

§2. 5–12. Saith Darius the King: This country Persia which Ahuramazda bestowed upon me – good, possessed of good horses, possessed of good men – by the favor of Ahuramazda and of me, Darius the King, does not feel fear of (any) other.

Introduction

§3. 12–24. Saith Darius the King: May Ahuramazda bear me aid, with the gods of the royal house; and may Ahuramazda protect this country from a (hostile) army, from famine, from the Lie! Upon this country may there not come an army, nor famine, nor the Lie; this I pray as a boon from Ahuramazda together with the gods of the royal house. This boon may Ahuramazda together with the gods of the royal house give to me![22]

Darius built a great new palace at Susa, founded deep into the tell, claiming and putting an unmistakable Achaemenid stamp on this most important ancient capital.[23] He created a new palatial complex at Persepolis in southwestern Iran: a raised terrace with a treasury, a palace, and an audience hall. These were adorned with images proclaiming his ideology of empire, notably in the reliefs on the stairs of the new audience hall, or Apadana, which showed the twenty-three distinct peoples and Persians bringing gifts to a central image of the king enthroned. These images are not simply reality-based representations of tribute assessed to specific regions, but represent new royal agendas of diversity within unity and the peaceful cheer enjoyed by the subject peoples of the realm.[24]

In addition to establishing imperial rhetoric, Darius drew on earlier administrative traditions to organize a complex governing system. The Persepolis Fortification Archive illustrates certain key aspects of imperial administrative practices under Darius.[25] Excavated from within the fortification wall on the terrace at Persepolis, it includes roughly twenty thousand clay tablets dating to the years around 500. It records disbursements of foodstuffs and beverages to people engaged in imperial business at and around Persepolis, and its tablets bear impressions left by the personal or administrative seals of the people involved. The archive includes both individual transactions and summaries, in multiple languages, with thousands of different seals represented. The overwhelming majority are inscribed in Imperial Elamite, while somewhere around eight hundred are written in Aramaic; at least one each is written in Greek, Phrygian, Akkadian, and Old Persian cuneiform. Thousands of the tablets are without inscription but bear seal impressions. The seals display a wide variety of styles and images, demonstrating the degree of choice available to individuals.[26] The complexity of the Persepolis Fortification Archive highlights the investment made by Darius in establishing a flexible and workable foundation for imperial administration.

Darius's son Xerxes (486–465) succeeded to the throne and put down a revolt in Egypt and two in Babylonia.[27] He continued his father's policies: he resumed work on the palace terrace at Persepolis and set out to conquer Greece. The latter attempt proved unsuccessful (in 480/79), despite a promising beginning, and Xerxes returned to Asia, where he further consolidated the empire and saw to its security. His efforts probably included dividing the enormous province of Babylonia into two: "Babylonia," the areas east of the

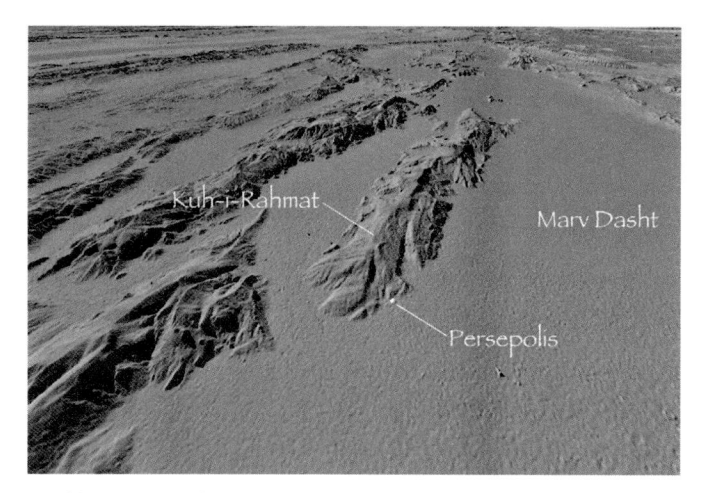

6. Oblique view of the central Iranian plateau toward the southeast. Persepolis is situated near water, in a fertile valley at a place where north–south and east–west routes intersected. Courtesy Karl Mueller.

Euphrates as far north as Carchemish, and "Beyond the River," the lands west of the Euphrates, including much of Syro-Palestine.[28] He seems also to have divided the Anatolian province of Lydia into two, separating the northern part off as Hellespontine Phrygia.[29] During Xerxes' reign, the Athenian-led Delian League gained control of various Achaemenid strategic positions and defeated the Achaemenid military at the battle of the Eurymedon River off Pamphylia in 467/6.[30] Xerxes and his heir, Darius, were murdered in 465 in a court plot that remains obscure to us.[31] Another son, Artaxerxes I, became king and enjoyed a long reign (465–424/3).

At the beginning of Artaxerxes' rule, the Athenians moved into Levantine territory and supported the revolt of Egypt under a local leader, Inarus, in 460–454.[32] Artaxerxes sent a general named Megabazus to Egypt, who crushed the revolt – including the Athenians – and established new fortified garrisons.[33] The missions of the Hebrew courtiers Ezra and Nehemiah to Jerusalem may have formed part of Artaxerxes' efforts to consolidate the western parts of the empire; Athenian efforts to take Cyprus were unsuccessful, and it may be that the "Peace of Callias" between the Athenians and the empire was concluded at this time.[34]

Under Artaxerxes I and his son Darius II (423–404) the empire remained stable and powerful, the wealthiest and most powerful sociopolitical entity on earth. Its effects were profound even on people living outside its formal boundaries; for instance, the Athenians adopted and adapted numerous Achaemenid institutions and habits, while to the north the Cadusians maintained a relationship of alliance with Persian authorities, and far to the east the nomadic chieftain burials at Pazyryk included luxury goods that show cultural interaction with

Introduction

and adaptation of Achaemenid court images and ideology.[35] In western Anatolia, the Persians supported a revolt of Samos against Athens in 440 and took advantage of the failed Athenian attempt to conquer Sicily (414/13) to begin levying tribute again from the Ionian cities of Asia Minor.[36] Persian gold supported the Spartans and their conquest of the Athenians in 404.[37] Perhaps in an effort to control the rivalry between the satraps of western Anatolia, Darius II sent a younger son named Cyrus to the western front with special powers to take control of the situation.[38]

Darius II was succeeded by his eldest son, Arses, who took the regnal name Artaxerxes II Mnemon (405/4–359/8) in what seems to have been a smooth transfer of power. Egypt revolted against Achaemenid rule in 404 under a leader named Amyrtaeus; this revolt was eventually successful and led to Egypt's temporary independence from Achaemenid rule (it was reconquered in 342/1).[39] At the same time, Artaxerxes' younger brother Cyrus put together an army in Sardis to revolt against his brother. This attempt was efficiently wiped out in 401 and Cyrus killed at the battle of Cunaxa; Artaxerxes II's rule was secure.

His was a lengthy reign, the longest of all the Persian kings, marked by peace in the empire. His military and political successes include the important "King's Peace" with the Greeks in 387/6, which returned to the king's power all the city-states of Asia Minor, and the squelching of a series of rebellious satraps in western Anatolia during 367–362. Artaxerxes II continued construction at the central Achaemenid capitals, including the building of a tomb at Naqsh-i Rustam near Persepolis, work at Ecbatana, and the construction of a new palace at Babylon.[40] He was interested in ways to link religion to a tightened adherence among Persian diaspora – including, perhaps, mandating worship of the goddess Anahita in various parts of the empire and introducing human-shaped statues to her cult.[41] Inscriptions dating to his reign show that the version of Mazdaism practiced by the Achaemenid elite included explicit worship of Mithras and Anahita, in addition to Ahuramazda "and the other gods who are."[42] Plutarch portrays Artaxerxes II as a generous king who was accessible to his subjects, a courageous warrior who shared the hardships of his soldiers, and a loving husband.[43]

Artaxerxes II was succeeded by his son Artaxerxes III Ochus (358–338), under whom Egypt was successfully reannexed to the empire and revolts in Phoenicia quelled.[44] A letter he wrote to the Athenians in 355 may have moved them to accept defeat in the Social War – if so, it demonstrates the Achaemenid kings' continued involvement in Greek affairs. At Persepolis, Artaxerxes III built a tomb above the palace terrace instead of at Naqsh-i Rustam with the other royal tombs.[45] He added a stair to the Palace of Darius and may have been the one who moved the original central panels of the Apadana staircase to their enshrinement in Courtyard 17 of the Treasury.[46] Artaxerxes III died of natural

7. Apadana at Persepolis. P56997. Courtesy of the Oriental Institute of the University of Chicago.

causes, probably in September 338.[47] He was succeeded by his son Artaxerxes IV Arses (338–336).

Artaxerxes III's death was followed by upheavals in the empire, including the revolt of Egypt and perhaps of Babylonia. Shortly after Artaxerxes IV's accession to power, Philip of Macedon began massing his forces on the other side of the Hellespont, and in the spring of 336 he invaded Asia Minor. Indeed, Artaxerxes IV scarcely had time to settle the reins of rule in his hands before he was killed in the summer of 336, perhaps by a powerful court figure named Bagoas or perhaps by the satrap of Armenia, a man named Artashata, who now became king under the name of Darius III Codomannus (336–330).

Darius III seems to have been a strong king and a man of great personal bravery, who reunited the empire and whose generals pushed Philip of Macedon's soldiers out of Asia Minor. It was his bad luck that Philip's son Alexander succeeded to the throne of Macedon and invaded the Achaemenid Empire in 334, an invasion that was to end in the death of Darius III in 330 and the demise of the Achaemenid dynasty.[48] The numerous Achaemenid ruling strategies and aspects of imperial organization that Alexander and his successors maintained testify to the health and robust nature of the Achaemenid Empire at the time of its conquest.[49]

Introduction

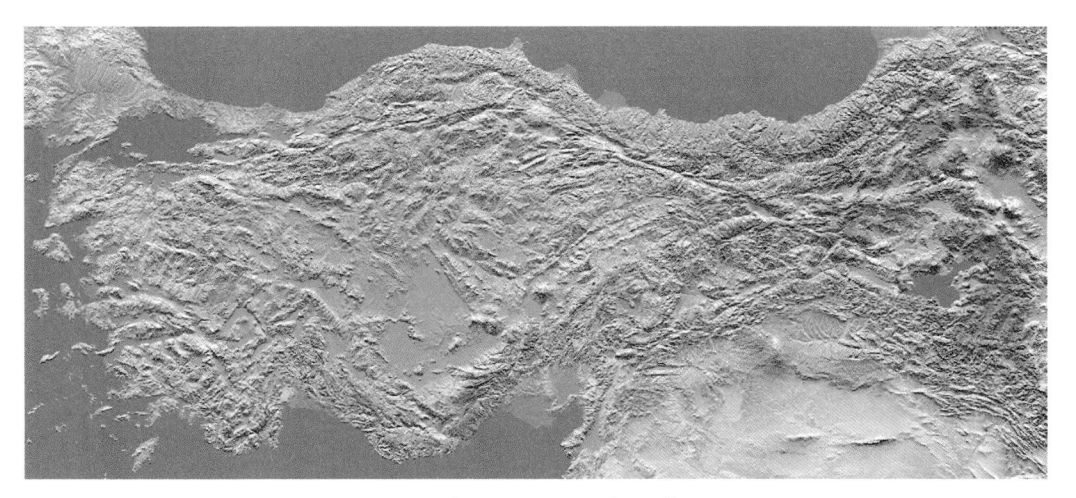

8. Anatolia. Courtesy Karl Mueller.

Anatolia

We turn now briefly to consider Anatolia as a populated space. When Cyrus II and his army made their way into these lands, what and whom did they encounter? How did the places and the people who lived there affect Achaemenid governing policies and practices, and how did the new imperial presence affect the lives of those people? The short overview presented here seeks to set the stage in geographic and human terms for the discussion to follow.

Anatolia consists of a high central plateau with fertile river valleys and coastal plains surrounding it, reaching from the Black Sea mountain range in the north to the Taurus Mountains in the south. Eastern Anatolia is mountainous and the source of the headwaters to the Euphrates, the Tigris, and the Aras Rivers. It is also the location of the vast Lake Van and Mount Ararat, Anatolia's highest point, at 16,946 feet.[50] Anatolia's varied landscapes result from complex geological processes and plate shifts that still cause earthquakes and volcanic eruptions. The Bosphorus and Hellespont are the product of fault lines, as is the strike-slip line visible in the map here as a long valley running across the north of the peninsula from east to west; a second fault line running from the east down toward the southwest shows the southern edge of the plate as it moves gradually west into the Aegean.[51]

The coastal parts of Anatolia bordering the Mediterranean and Aegean Seas have a temperate Mediterranean climate, with hot dry summers often above 86°F and mild wet winters averaging a little below 34°F. Conditions in the higher, drier interior are harsher; the mountain ranges close to the coast give the Anatolian plateau a continental climate with strongly contrasting seasons and severe winters. Temperatures of −22°F to −40°F can occur in the eastern mountains, with snow on the ground for as many as four months of the year.

9. Anatolia, through a fish-eye lens. Courtesy Karl Mueller.

Precipitation across Anatolia averages around 15 inches per year, with more rain falling at lower elevations and less at higher. The driest regions are the Konya and Malatya plains, where annual rainfall is often less than 12 inches per year. May is generally the wettest month, and July/August the driest.[52]

The peoples who inhabited Anatolia at the time of Cyrus's arrival were equally varied. Several important states developed in the first half of the first millennium B.C.E., including various small Neo-Hittite principalities in the southeast, some of which were incorporated into Assyria and its successor state, the Neo-Babylonian Empire, and also Urartu in the east, Phrygia in the central zone, and Lydia in the west. The regions of Lycia and Caria are not as well attested in textual sources before the sixth century, and the peoples of Cilicia and Pamphylia were loosely, if at all, confederated before the Achaemenid period. The larger states, Urartu, Phrygia, and Lydia, undoubtedly interacted with the great Mesopotamian empires in political, economic, and cultural ways. Urartu is probably best known, thanks to extensive archaeological explorations and the recovery of Urartian inscriptions as well as Assyrian material attesting to intense interactions. Phrygia and Lydia are occasionally mentioned by the Greeks and by Near Eastern historical sources, and excavations at their capital cities of Gordion and Sardis, plus regional archaeological surveys, add to our knowledge of these areas. The following overview will give some idea of the people and sociopolitical situations Cyrus encountered in Anatolia.

Introduction

10. The mountains of Urartu. Courtesy Manfred Schweda, www.thisfabtrek.com.

Urartu

Urartu was centered in the mountainous area around Lakes Van, Urmia, and Sevan and flourished from ca. 840 to 585 (?); its territory was very large (perhaps around 200,000 km^2) and its geographic features high and varied.[53] It included territory now partly occupied by modern Iran and Armenia as well as Turkey. The Urartian Kingdom was ruled by a single dynasty from 825 on and seems to have had a centralized political organization overseeing a decentralized system of distribution, with vast grain storage centers to hold the products of the fertile irrigated soil around the great lakes. Lake Van has a high soda content and Urmia a high sodium content; thus although they are full of fish, their water cannot be used to irrigate plants. Urartu owed its fertility to the large number of smaller streams emptying into the lakes out of the mountains around them. To this feature it also owed part of its ability to remain independent from Assyria, as it was impossible for the Assyrians to cut off their water source.[54]

Amélie Kuhrt describes the Assyrian impression of Urartu as preserved on the bronze temple gates of Shalmaneser III at Balawat: "Fortresses set on mountain peaks are shown being burnt by the Assyrian army; Assyrian soldiers cut down fruit trees and wheel away gigantic storage jars. At the same time the horrendous physical obstacles that the soldiers had to overcome are illustrated, with Assyrian soldiers heaving their horses up and down the sheer mountains."[55]

We have some sense of the living conditions in Urartu. Tremendous amounts of raw material (copper, silver, iron) made the Urartians justly famous for their

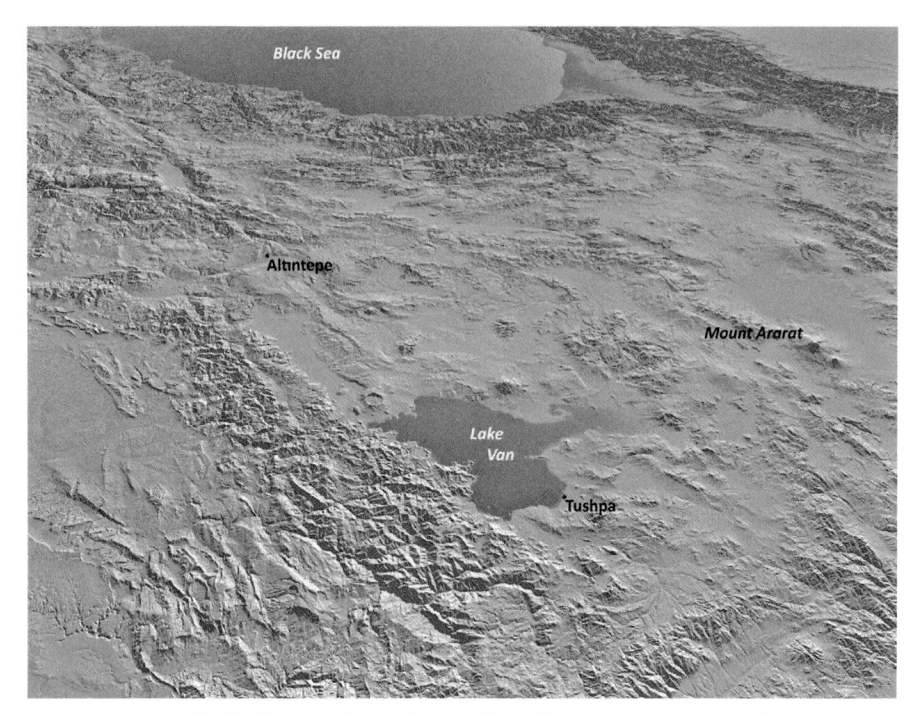

11. Eastern Anatolia, looking northwest (Urartu from the Assyrian perspective). Courtesy Karl Mueller.

metalwork. The Assyrian king Sargon II gives an account of his campaign in 714 that includes descriptions of waterworks sponsored by the Urartian king near the city of Ulhu, the fertility of the land, the large number of healthy animals, elaborate dwellings, strong fortresses, and wine flowing like a river.[56] The Urartians presumably practiced seasonal transhumance to shelter animals indoors during the bitter winters. Their hardiness was a necessary correlate of their living conditions; when Xenophon passed through the area soon after 400, he was overwhelmed by the physical and climatic hardships of the territory:

> The houses were underground structures with an aperture like the mouth of a well by which to enter, but they were broad and spacious below. The entrance for the beasts of burden was dug out, but the human occupants descended by a ladder. In these dwellings were to be found goats and sheep and cattle, and cocks and hens, with their various progeny. The flocks and herds were all reared under cover upon green food. There were stores within of wheat and barley and vegetables, and wine made from barley (beer) in great bowls.[57]

The last certain mention of the Urartian state is an Assyrian description of an embassy to the court of Assurbanipal in 643. The Neo-Babylonian king Nabopolassar (626–605) apparently undertook military operations along the Urartian frontier.[58] By 585, according to Herodotus (1.74), the Medes held

Introduction

12. Mount Ararat, above Lake Van. Courtesy Cem Yücesoy.

some sort of hegemony over all the lands east of the Halys River – and significantly, the revolts in Urartu referred to in the Babylonian version of the Bisitun Inscription of Darius lack named leaders but are undertaken simply by "rebels." These points suggest that the Urartian state had ceased to exist by this time. Its history between 643 and its reappearance as the Achaemenid province of Armenia remains unclear.

Phrygia

To the west of Urartu was the state of Phrygia. It seems to have developed sometime after the collapse of the Hittite Empire; the extent of its territorial control is uncertain and much debated.[59] Its primary center was Gordion, but by the eighth century its control extended east of the Halys River to include many of the areas previously held by the Hittites and south far down into Cappadocia, as well as west to Afyon. Its most recognizable features include magnificent sculpted rock faces, such as those at Midas City and Arslankaya, and great burial tumuli covering wooden chambers within. The Phrygian capital, Gordion, has been extensively excavated since 1950 and provides us with our most detailed evidence concerning Phrygian culture.

At the moment, the Early Iron Age is known at Gordion from limited excavation on the eastern half of the Citadel Mound.[60] It seems likely that it was at

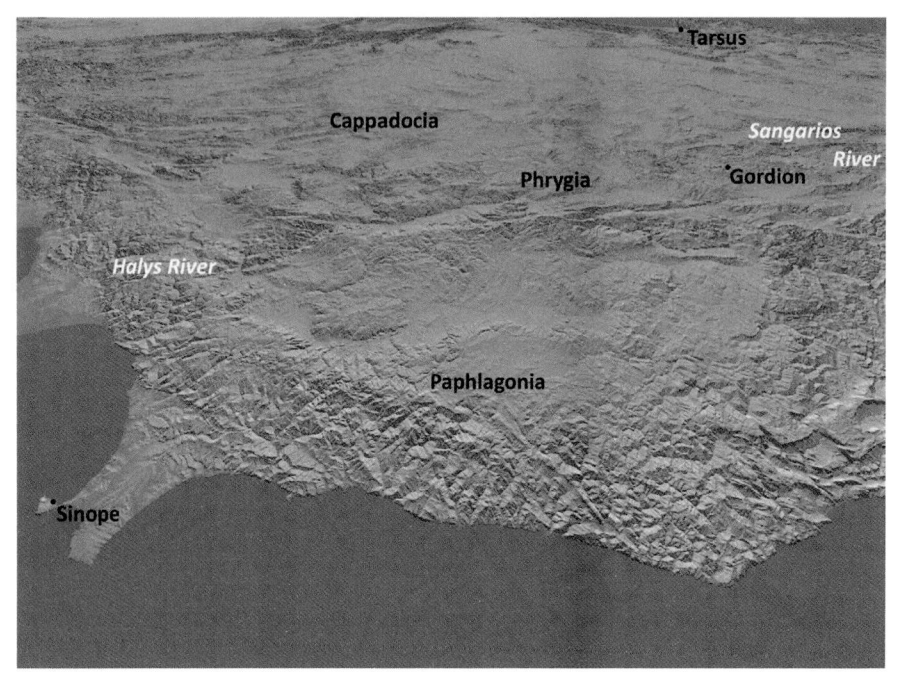

13. North central Anatolia, looking south across eastern Phrygia. Courtesy Karl Mueller.

some point during the Early Iron Age that the Phrygians – a group of Phrygian-speaking Indo-Europeans who probably came into Anatolia through Thrace – first arrived at Gordion and settled in the area. The archaeological evidence suggests "renewed or continuing influxes of people and ideas over time and perhaps not all coming from the same precise area."[61]

In the Early Phrygian period (950–800), the site of Gordion saw massive building projects, culminating in a vast fortified complex now generally called the Old Citadel.[62] The artifacts found within them show that each of the famous megarons on the Citadel Mound served as an independent production unit, with multiple tasks going on that were reduplicated from one building to the next; the rooms served primarily for food and textile production. The mound demonstrates a flourishing society in the Early Phrygian period that supported a wealthy elite and seems to have had cultural connections, as judged by material evidence, with others in Anatolia – especially to the east and southeast.[63]

Gordion was consumed in a conflagration around 800.[64] Extraordinarily, the New Citadel of the Middle Phrygian period (ca. 800–540) was laid out on the same plan as the Old Citadel.[65] A fill of sterile clay was laid over the destroyed buildings, and the rubble foundations for the ashlar buildings of the New Citadel were laid as the fill rose. The ashlar blocks used to build the superstructure of the walls were multicolored and probably very striking.[66] The plan of the new buildings correlates with that of the Old Citadel almost exactly, and it may be that the function of the buildings also paralleled that of their predecessors.[67]

Introduction

GORDION
MIDDLE PHRYGIAN CITADEL

0　　　　　　　　　　100 m.

1973 HEMANS, CUMMER　　　　1:500 SCALE
1979 LIGHTBODY, SMITH, BELL

14. Gordion's Citadel Mound in the Middle Phrygian period. © Gordion Archaeological Project.

Gordion in the Middle Phrygian period was larger in size and probably population than earlier, an increase that may reflect the growing extent of the Phrygian Kingdom altogether.[68] Middle Phrygian pottery is found over a vast area of central Anatolia, at least as far east as Alişar and Alaca Höyük and as far west as Afyon.[69] The city on the mountain at Kerkenes Dağ also dates to this time period and attests to extensive Phrygian control over this part of Anatolia.[70] The annals of Sargon II of Assyria (721–706) mention a Mita of Mushki, now generally identified with Midas of Phrygia; the redating of Gordion's destruction level brings the Phrygian tumuli and Gordion's most famous king into the glorious New Citadel phase with its colorful ashlar buildings.[71] This was King Midas of the Golden Touch – indeed, the fact that the Phrygians in this period made some items from brass, not just bronze, may perhaps account for the legend.[72]

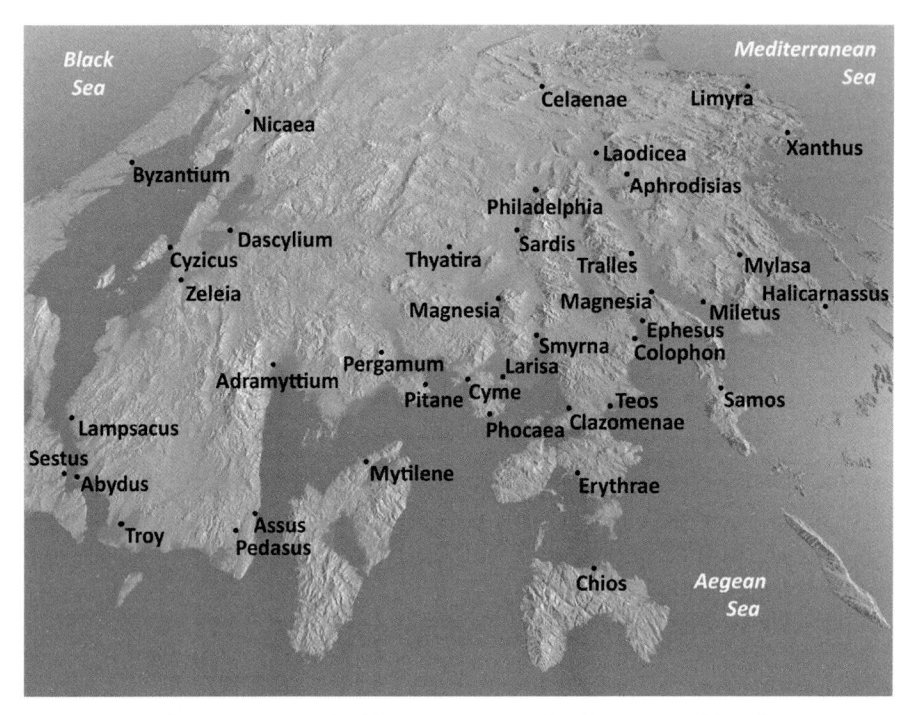

15. The Aegean coast, looking east across Lydia. Courtesy Karl Mueller.

Archaeological evidence suggests that toward the end of the Middle Phrygian period, around 575–550, Gordion was conquered by Lydians coming from the west. They brought with them a taste for merrily colored pots and perhaps also the scented oils thought to have filled the characteristically shaped lydions.[73] Bowls that appear to be of Iranian origin or inspiration have also been discovered in a deposit at the site that dates to ca. 550. Thus the end of the Middle Phrygian period, the years right before Cyrus arrived in central Anatolia, saw a time of mixed ethnicities and influences at Gordion, a time when conquest and commerce brought different peoples and ideas to this ancient city and the local populace responded with various degrees of enthusiasm to the presence and habits of foreign conquerors.

Lydia

Lydia, with its capital city at Sardis, made up much of western and northwestern Anatolia by the time Cyrus arrived in the mid–sixth century. The Middle Lydian period is usually defined as the time when Sardis was ruled by the Mermnad kings, from Gyges (ca. 680) to Croesus (ca. 560).[74] During this time Lydia extended its territory and control, conquering Greek cities on the Aegean coast, forging links with Greek sanctuaries, and expanding north, south, and east. The Lydian language is related to the Hittite–Luwian group but remains poorly understood.[75]

Introduction

16. Sardis in August. Photo author.

The lushness of the Hermus River valley is partly to thank for Sardis's legendary wealth in antiquity, but the metal deposits of the Tmolus mountain range added to the already rich resources of the area.[76] The image the Greeks entertained of Mermnad Lydia as a land of unparalleled wealth influenced their descriptions of the Orient ever after.[77] For the Greeks of the seventh and sixth centuries, Sardis was wealthy, embraced by the gold-bearing Pactolus; it was the abode of tyrants and of priests of Cybele, of learned and skilled men, of warriors and charioteers, and of horses.[78]

Literary sources for the history of Lydia begin in Greece with the first Greek literature: the *Iliad* mentions the beauty of the area and the skill of its inhabitants as early as the eighth or seventh century.[79] The Mermnad dynasts and their capital city are mentioned sporadically by Greek lyric poets and by Near Eastern sources. Seventh-century Assyrian records mention Gyges as the king of Lydia, a land so far away that it had previously been unknown to the kings of the expanding Neo-Assyrian Empire.[80] In these records, it is clear that Gyges is seeking an alliance in the face of the Cimmerian invasion. Thus a connection between Sardis and eastern lands was established by the mid–seventh century.

For the most part, Greek authors are concerned with the expansionist desires of the Lydian rulers, who extended the borders of Lydia until by the end of Croesus's reign all of Anatolia west of the Halys, and much of the southwest, were under Lydian control.[81] Croesus constructed an alliance, including Babylonia, Egypt, and Sparta, against the Persians. His was seemingly a vibrant international court that, according to Herodotus, was visited by wealthy statesmen like Alcmeon as well as philosophers and politicians

23

17. Caria, Lycia, and Pamphylia, looking east. Courtesy Karl Mueller.

like Solon. No doubt craftspeople also poured into Sardis to work for such a wealthy patron; the fruits of Croesus's artisans astounded the Greeks when he dedicated some of them at Delphi.[82] Croesus also patronized the Temple of Artemis at Ephesus, contributing at least some of its columns, and work in ivory and paint provides glimpses of the exceptional sophistication of Lydian artwork.[83]

Southwestern and Southern Anatolia

The regions of southwestern and southern Anatolia (Caria, Lycia, Pamphylia, Cilicia) remain shrouded in mystery before the Achaemenid period. One author sums up what we know:

> As noted earlier, we have no significant evidence for settlement in Lycia before the end of the eighth century at the very earliest. Remains of buildings on the acropolis of Xanthus (modern Günük), Lycia's most important city, may date back to this period. Prior to the sixth century, Lycia seems to have had few contacts with the outside world. We have no information about the history of Lycia until the middle of the sixth century when Herodotus tells us that the Lycians, along with the Cilicians further to the east, were the only people not conquered by the Lydian king Croesus during his campaigns in Asia Minor.[84]

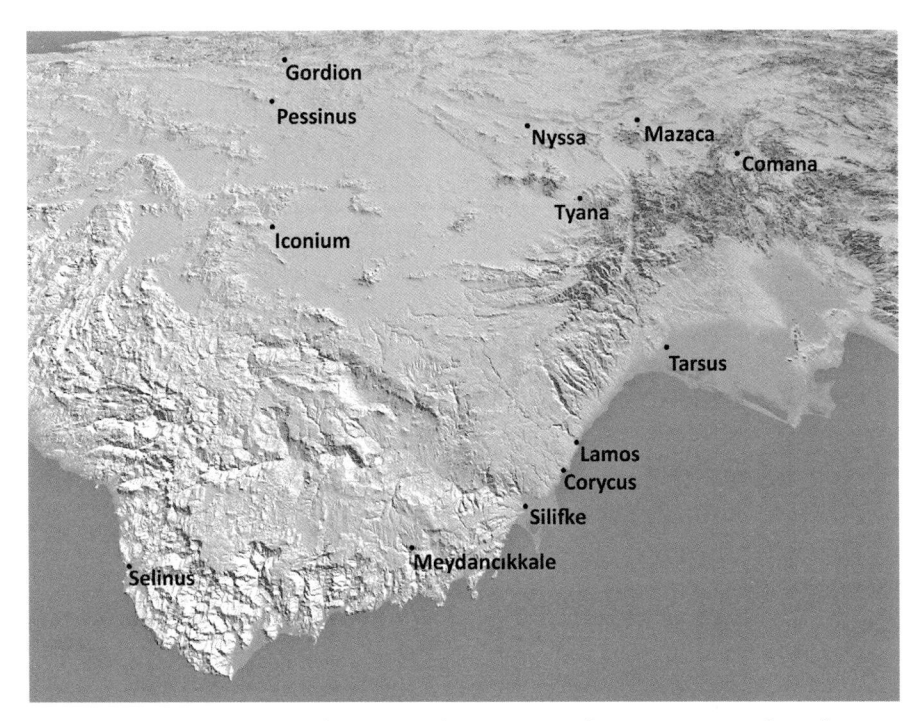

18. Pamphylia and Cilicia, looking north across Cappadocia. Courtesy Karl Mueller.

Although there is but scanty archaeological evidence so far, there is some continuity between later Lycian language and place names and those of the Late Bronze Age; this suggests that the Lycian people had remained in place and possibly insubordinate the entire time.[85] The inhabitants of these mountainous areas, with limited littorals and plunging hillslopes, harsh valleys, and meager agricultural resources, lived in isolated settlements with hilltop fortifications and stone-built dwellings.[86] They were often determined fighters, some by land and others by sea, who acquired an international reputation as mercenary soldiers or pirates.[87] It is not surprising that Croesus left the Lycians of southwestern Anatolia unconquered; it is more surprising that Cyrus and his generals bothered to include these regions in the Achaemenid Empire when they annexed Anatolia.[88]

Western Coast of Anatolia

The Aegean seaboard was heavily populated by a polyethnic mix of peoples inhabiting the Ionian colonies of East Greece. These cities were largely Bronze Age Greek colonies. Greek-speaking, and with political and other power often held by Greeks, the cities formed their own nation-states with regionally specific traditions but seem to have shared a certain cohesive identity as Ionian Greeks.[89] Thus "Ionia" corresponds more to an idea than a geographic region.

19. The Achaemenid Empire, through a fish-eye lens. Courtesy Karl Mueller.

Their control of harbors was key and contributed to the significant wealth enjoyed by some in the years before they were annexed to the empire by Cyrus's general Harpagus. Heavily fortified against siege, situated in defensible areas with good land around them, drawing on Greek and Anatolian expressions of religion, art, and politics, accumulating the wealth and population to establish new colonies themselves, the cities of Anatolia's western seaboard thrived before the Persian arrival in the area.

This brief overview of Anatolia demonstrates the challenges Cyrus and the subsequent Achaemenid kings faced in governing their empire. It was only through a complex mix of authority exerted and autonomy allowed or wielded that the empire could survive. The steps taken by the Achaemenid administration bound the lands and people of Anatolia firmly together and serve as testimony to the Achaemenid Empire's variety, thoroughness, and success.

Chapter-by-Chapter Overview

Chapter 2, "Governing Anatolia," deals with fundamental issues of governance in Achaemenid Anatolia. It has two primary divisions: the first considers the logistics of governance (administrative regions, taxes, the histories of two particular geographic areas as case studies) and the second looks at ways in which

INTRODUCTION

Achaemenid authority combined practical and ideological considerations in its execution. The chapter addresses basic issues of politics and infrastructure, including taxation, roads, the architecture of power, imperial statements in art, and the inscriptional evidence that allows us to reconstruct power hierarchies such as land-granting systems or political-religious issues. It thus considers the logistics of governance through its practical efforts and effects and its symbolic or semiotically charged impact. It ends by considering the role of local elites in solidifying the Achaemenid administration of Anatolia.

Many previous discussions of the Achaemenid army have followed the issues of interest delineated by Greek sources, including the different peoples that fought in it and the garments that adorned their bodies. Some important work in Anatolia has drawn on literary sources to consider military deployment, however, while other archaeological work has investigated garrison sites. Chapter 3, "Controlling Anatolia, Guarding the Empire," considers Achaemenid military sites in Anatolia as a whole, tying them into the literary testimonia and visual evidence that fill out our understanding of the Achaemenid army in Anatolia.

Given the similarity across the board of elite paraphernalia and iconography, it comes as no surprise to find a notable similarity among precious-metal drinking vessels across the Achaemenid Empire, as shown in Chapter 4, "Eating and Drinking with Class and Style." The so-called Achaemenid bowl and the animal-protome rhyton clearly both served as signifiers of elite drinking behaviors in Anatolia. Metal examples in bronze, silver, and gold plate are remarkably consistent across Anatolia in their form and surface decoration; they reflect central Achaemenid iconography and style in overt ways that certainly were played out in drinking behaviors as well.

Recent research demonstrates that ceramic Achaemenid bowls, not only silver ones, were popular almost everywhere in Achaemenid Anatolia. What makes the issue interesting is their tremendous standardization of shape, fabric, and surface treatment. They demonstrate craft specialization and, probably, centralization or at least nucleation of production. This conformity suggests that it mattered to the imperial authority. Anthropological work examining the social importance of feasting and the impact of feasting behavior as a reflection and an agent of social change lends sense to this observation. To have something as important as communal drinking involve specifically imperial wine-drinking cups, with associated wine-drinking behaviors, brings this important social activity into the framework of imperial acculturation for both the elite and the non-elite. Standardized drinking behaviors encouraged people to share habits in an essential communal activity that participated in, created, and reified imperial authority.[90]

Chapter 5, "Dealing with the Dead," concentrates primarily on the tombs of the elite. It takes as its point of departure the observation that elite mortuary structures and markers are tremendously variable across Anatolia, while the artistic decorations and mortuary inclusions interred with their occupants are not. It is clear that the imperial authority did not mandate mortuary behaviors. The remarkable cohesion of elite grave goods, however, demonstrates particularly strongly that signaling membership in the Achaemenid elite allowed for little deviation. An interesting corollary of this is that it is virtually impossible to determine the ethnicity of an elite person: people signaled their identity with an emphasis on status rather than ethnic background. Thus the mortuary deposits of the Achaemenid period allow us a singularly clear glimpse into shared elite identity, even as the mortuary structures themselves often proclaim geographic or cultural autonomy.

To make the point clear, this chapter departs from the others in being organized by region. It begins in Lydia and makes its way clockwise around Anatolia, examining both the form and the contents of tombs. The behaviors of the living society that are illuminated by this study demonstrate the sharp distinctions that could occur within an authority–autonomy model, where people have significant autonomy and personal agency in some decisions and apparently little in others.

A great deal of material has been published that relates to religious belief and practice. Architectural remains such as temples or altars allow us to consider the kinds of tensions and interplay between local and imported deities across the peninsula. Numismatic evidence provides another means of examining religious belief and practice, and so do sealstones. Chapter 6, "Worshiping the Divine," returns to behavior categories, examining instances of the continuity of cults, the syncretism of cults, a possible example of conversion of cult, and the introduction of non-Anatolian cults, including, perhaps, a form of royal cult. The discussion will, I hope, raise questions and introduce nuance into our consideration of an authority–autonomy model, as the evidence for religious belief and practice in Achaemenid Anatolia is exceptionally complex and does not neatly fit any one interpretive framework.

Chapter 7, "Educating the Young and Old," represents a new direction in Achaemenid studies; it opens an avenue of exploration and provides controversial material for enriching scholarly discourse. Because the subject is so complicated and new, I intend this chapter not to offer a definitive discussion but rather to present some issues, define a few basic problems, suggest approaches, and posit initial interpretations.

There have as yet been found no schoolrooms, textbooks, or copybooks in the Achaemenid Empire, much less in Achaemenid Anatolia, although there are indications of scribal training elsewhere. Thus the chapter must take an indirect approach to understanding education. It begins with an overview of elite education and then turns to that of the non-elite. We can see education at work in the development and continuance of artistic schools, including those for seal carvers, sculptors, and potters. Education in an empire can mean teaching people about pre-imperial or local customs and traditions, or conversely it can

Introduction

20. Different subject peoples of the realm, from Persepolis. P22263. Courtesy of the Oriental Institute of the University of Chicago.

mean instructing people in new behaviors linked to the new imperial authority. Another form of education can be deduced from looking at the army, in which men were educated in warcraft, in teamwork, and in loyalty to the Achaemenid Empire. Language continuity or change may also provide information on education. Archives enable us to learn about accounting practices and the kind of education necessary to keep accounts. Finally, the chapter explores the role of education at temples, places where people practiced (and were educated in) not only religious behaviors but also behaviors to do with banking and law.

Chapter 8, "Empire and Identity in Achaemenid Anatolia," considers the ways in which the authority–autonomy model sheds light on interactions between Anatolia and the imperial heartland. It focuses on questions of identity, for Achaemenid Anatolia provides multiple examples of individuals or groups of people defining themselves in different ways under different circumstances. The discussion in this chapter is couched within the context of the imperial rhetoric surrounding localized and specified ethnicity; the dynamic tension between imperial rhetoric and that of specific Anatolian cultures provides rich ground for interpretation and discussion.

Divide and Conquer, or Conquer and Unify?

This book does not consider imperialism primarily in terms of ethnicity, geographic region, or artifact category. Thinking instead in terms of behavioral categories allows us to consider all of these aspects of imperialism, but it changes the emphasis of discussion. Empires cover geographic space, but what lies at their heart is the interaction among people. Imperialism in its expansionist phase must develop into a stabilizing and restructuring phase if an empire is to last.[91] Retaining authority in the hands of an imperial administration (or warrior class, or priest class, or other select group) requires the participation not only of those wielding power but of those on the receiving end as well. It is clear that the Achaemenid Empire was so successful for so long – despite its vast territory and exceptional diversity, as this study of Anatolia begins to highlight – because of the complex interweaving of authority and autonomy.

Introduction

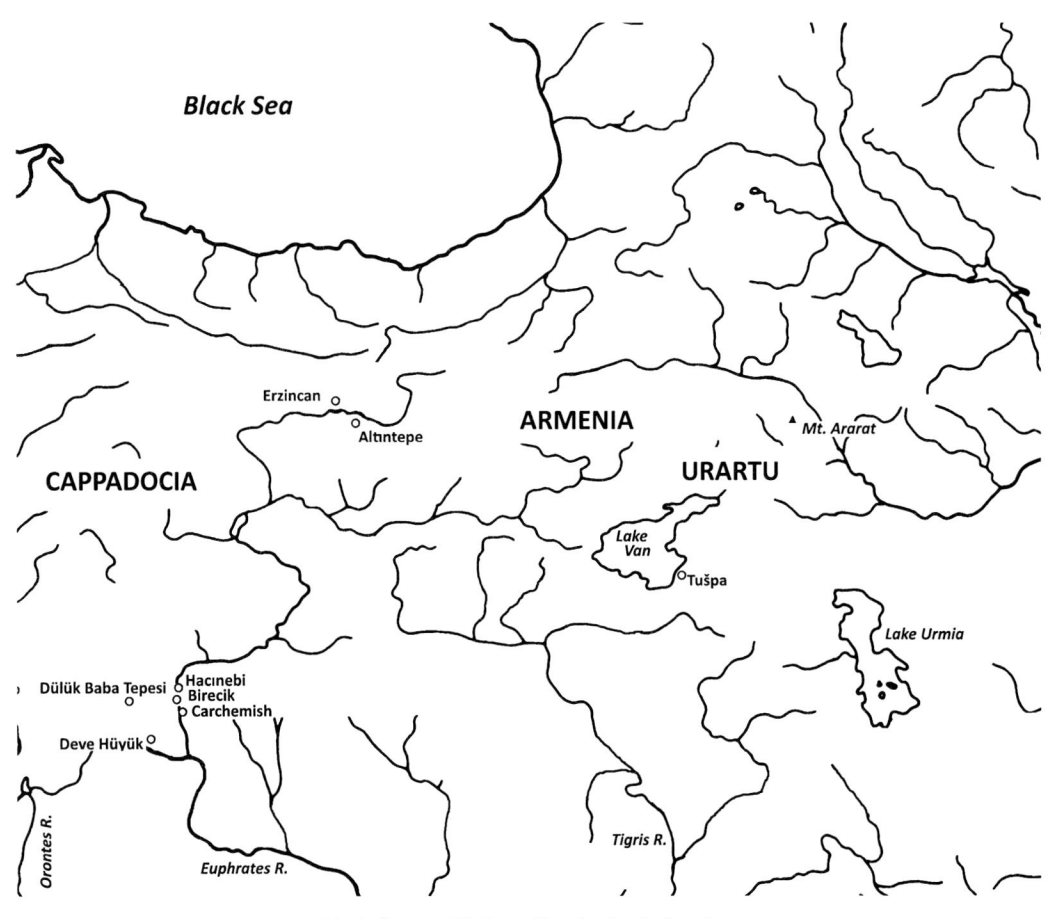

21. Achaemenid Anatolia. Author's drawing.

When the Achaemenid imperial administration exerted its authority, it did so in a way that was occasionally overt, as in the deployment of the military, occasionally manifested largely through local elites, as in the propagation of imperial ideology, and occasionally subtle but far-reaching, as in the change of drinking behaviors to reflect participation in the new empire. Different kinds of authority were employed by various groups of people, such as priests in practicing religion and educating acolytes, or families in burying their dead in ways hallowed by local tradition. These aspects of authority were possible because of the autonomy allowed by the imperial administration and practiced by individuals or groups. Thus the tricky balance between imperial might and personal agency, the balance that allowed for the smooth, continued existence of the empire with few revolts and successful tax collection, could persist. It is this balance between authority and autonomy, most clearly seen in the way humans act and interact, that defines the success of an empire and allowed Achaemenid Anatolia to prosper.

TWO

GOVERNING ANATOLIA

Achaemenid authority was exerted overtly in the governance of the Anatolian provinces. What aspects of governance mattered most to the imperial administration? What choices were made in terms of tribute, politics, roadways? What elements of governance were practical, what were symbolic, and what might function as both? How did the local populaces respond?

Top-down examples of power demonstrate various means the imperial administration employed to exert and reify its authority, as well as specific expressions of that authority. The first part of this chapter begins with a discussion of imperial administrative divisions, including the various satrapies and satraps of Anatolia – its regions and local rulers – as a way to consider the logistics of government. It then discusses taxes and tribute from the different provinces. The chapter then examines two satrapies in Anatolia as case studies: Lydia, a frontier zone that faced frequent disruption through interaction with the Greeks, had to be governed in a more controlled way than Cilicia, which seems to have enjoyed considerable autonomy. Focusing on the actions of the Achaemenid administrative elite shows the ways in which the satrapies were bound through their governance to the central imperial authority. This discussion ends with the road system, which functioned both as a physical avenue for the movement of goods, people, and messages and as a symbolic representation of imperial power.

The second part of the chapter addresses various ways in which ideology and governing might be combined, using examples of architecture and actions that served both practical and symbolic purposes. It begins with five undertakings of Xerxes that show the range of approaches a king might pursue in marking and perpetuating his authority. Imperial power statements form the next focus of the chapter's investigation: Persian formal gardens, or paradeisoi, and the satrapal structures at Dascylium and Altıntepe. Gordion, a nonsatrapal site, and the finds excavated there show that assertions of Achaemenid power could be as overt in this city as they were at satrapal headquarters.

The ideologically laden logistics of governing Anatolia mattered too; for instance, religious expression and the use of different languages might function – or not – as avenues for exerting imperial power.[1] Archives and archival practices, including the visual imagery on the seals used to ratify documents, illuminate the role of artistic iconography and style as potent conveyors of authority-laden messages as well as the authority-driven behaviors they accompanied. Coins, like seals, might serve a dual function as objects with practical administrative and economic significance and as ideologically charged visual tools. Governing Anatolia clearly involved a complex network of allegiances and affiliations that could be signaled via visual messages as well as played out in the practical use of seals and coins.

A key element of Achaemenid authority was the participation of the elite in administration. Of interest here is the degree of conformity found across Anatolia in the ways people signaled membership in the elite. Co-option of the local elite and an emphasis on proclaiming elite identity (rather than, say, ethnic identity) were apparently key features of Achaemenid administrative practice and imperial authority.[2] In connection with this aspect of governing Anatolia, and bringing the discussion full circle to the behaviors of the Persian kings, the chapter ends with the topic of royal gifts and the roles they might play in solidifying the interactions of those participating in the polyethnic Achaemenid administration.

Part I: Administering Anatolia

Anatolia in the Achaemenid period was divided into various satrapies, or administrative units.[3] The satrapies included at one time or another Armenia, Cappadocia, Hellespontine Phrygia, Greater Phrygia, Lydia, Caria, Lycia, and Cilicia.[4] Their borders are rather unclear and seemingly impermanent; Lydia, Phrygia, and Cappadocia were apparently all subdivided at various points. The same uncertainty applies to our terminology. The use of the word "satrap" and the derived verb in Greek is unspecific; it is applied haphazardly in Classical texts to people wielding some kind of command and did not have a circumscribed meaning of "provincial governor."[5] It is, however, this meaning of the term that I use in this work.

A key element of establishing and retaining imperial authority in Anatolia involved creating regional governing centers and administrations that would remain loyal to the central authority while exercising a degree of local autonomy. The royal capitals, newly founded at Persepolis and Pasargadae and with new palaces built at the ancient cities of Babylon and Susa, were reflected and extended by regional capitals in the various satrapies.[6] In many cases, the new rulers continued using old centers of control as administrative centers, often recast with accoutrements reflecting Achaemenid courtly milieux. These were generally strategically located for trade or warfare and often already had in place administrative hierarchies or apparatuses appropriate for the area.[7]

The empire was not run simply by a central administration that radiated power and authority from its core, but rather each province was run along parallel lines. The satrapal capitals functioned very much like the royal ones. Provincial taxes, paid in kind and in precious metals, were collected and stored there before being redistributed to local garrisons and to others working for the administration or before being sent to the imperial treasuries.[8] The satraps lived in elaborate residences, often in palaces taken over from previous rulers.[9] They kept archives of official correspondence, as well as records of regional bureaucracy.[10] The satrapal capitals of Anatolia were linked to the royal centers in Mesopotamia and Iran and to each other by an extensive network of roads that supported rapid travel; way stations at one-day intervals made it possible for messengers traveling on official business to obtain food, drink, and fresh horses.[11] Travel was monitored, and strategic points on the roads were guarded by armed soldiers.

Satraps and Satrapies

The word "satrap" comes from the Old Persian word xšaθrapāvā (protector of the province) – xšaθra meaning "realm" or "province," and pāvā meaning "protector." In Greek, the word was rendered as σατράπης. The satraps were heads of administration in their provinces – generally, it seems, Persian nobles installed in alien territory but sometimes people drawn from local populaces. Although most of the historically attested satraps were male, it is clear that women could occasionally wield real power in the Achaemenid Empire. Mania, a governor of Hellespontine Phrygia, is probably the best-known example of a female administrator in Anatolia, along with two rulers of Caria named Artemisia; the first led her ships in battle against the Greeks at the battle of Salamis in 480, while her descendant was co-ruler of Caria with her husband and brother, Mausolus, in the mid–fourth century.[12] Women might hold vast tracts of land in the center of the empire, without being themselves satraps: Darius I's wife Irtashduna (Artystone) is an example, as is the "royal woman" Irdabama, both known from the Persepolis Fortification Archive.[13] In the absence of widespread evidence for women holding power in Achaemenid Anatolia, however, I will refer to satraps as "he" henceforth. This initial section sets the stage for understanding some of the issues faced in governing; further details about specific satraps and their actions will follow later in the chapter.

The duties of a satrap were complex, and they depended to a certain extent on the region governed. He collected the taxes, controlled local officials and the subject tribes and cities, and served as local magistrate for both civil and criminal cases.[14] He was responsible for the safety of the roads and had to quell brigands and rebels. He had to maintain a well-equipped, well-trained, loyal army to protect the land; he had to exact taxes and might need the army's assistance.

A satrap had to balance the requirements of the king with those of the people in his satrapy.[15] Although the army might give him power to obtain taxes from those who were otherwise unwilling to pay, it could be effective only where the ability to pay existed.[16] The satrap had to ensure the productivity of the land in order to collect taxes; this required maintaining a sufficiently high level of capability among the people tending the land that they might husband it to good effect. Thus the satrap needed always to calculate the ability of his subjects to send the appropriate amount of tribute to the king now, balancing it with the need to produce tribute again in the future.[17]

Greek historical sources provide us with information about the names and dates of satraps in (north)western Anatolia, particularly during those times when these governors were in direct conflict with various Greek forces (much of the Achaemenid period, it must be said). Our information for other parts of Anatolia is significantly different in nature, being primarily archaeological rather than textual; what texts there are tend not to follow Greek historical narrative traditions or are very late in date. Indeed, balancing the type and amount of information available is central to any attempt to understand Achaemenid Anatolia.

Table 1 summarizes our current knowledge of rulers' names and years. The substantial blanks that reflect our lack of knowledge of political-historical events in certain areas are perhaps as illuminating as our detailed knowledge of other areas, as they demonstrate times and places for which certain types of written records do not exist. I have omitted from this table the northern coast of Anatolia along the Black Sea, as there is at this point insufficient evidence to determine the degree to which it was ruled by Achaemenid Persia.[18] Some areas, such as Hellespontine Phrygia, Caria, Lycia, and Cilicia, seem to have experienced times during which their rulers were part of a hereditary dynasty. Other areas, such as Lydia and Cappadocia, apparently saw more direct (even interventionist) control by the imperial administration. This may have been the result of imperial suspicion about regional loyalty, a feature that led to less autonomous familial continuity in their oversight but perhaps a more consistent degree or type of interaction with the imperial authority.

Taxes and Tribute

Imperial income was linked to human resource management, land management, production, control, and trade; the role that satraps played in the creation and flow of taxes was crucial. The sources available on Achaemenid taxation are

Table 1. Regions and Rulers of Achaemenid Anatolia

Lydia[a]	Hellespontine Phrygia[b]	Cappadocia[c]	Caria	Lycia	Cilicia	Armenia
Tabalus and Pactyes (540s)	Pharnouchus (540s–535)		Satraps established now?[d]			
Oroetes (ca. 525–520?)	Mitrobates (ca. 525–522)	Part of Greater Phrygia during reign of Darius I[e]		Lycia in first satrapy; dynasty begins?[f]		Tushpa capital of thirteenth satrapy?[g]
Artaphernes I (ca. 513–492)	Megabazus (500–492)	Ariaramnes (in 515/14)[h]	Lygdamis		Oromedon (late 6th c.?)	
Artaphernes II (492–450s)	Megabates (479–477)		Artemisia (in 480)	Kuprlli I (early 5th c.)		
	Artabazus I (479–468?)			Kuprlli II (ca. 465–430)	Syennesis[i] (in 480)[j]	
Pissouthnes (450s–ca. 420)	Pharnabazus I (460–430)		Lygdamis (460s–450s)[k]	Kheriga (ca. 430–?)		
	Pharnaces (430/29–413)					Orontes I and Tiribazus (423–359)[l]
Tissaphernes (ca. 416–407)	Pharnabazus II (413–ca. 387)				Syennesis (in 401)	
Cyrus the Younger (407–401)						
Tissaphernes (401–395)		Spithridates (early 4th c.)[m]	Hecatomnus of Mylasa (391–377)[n]	Arttumpara / Pericles (early 4th c.)		
Tithraustes(?) (395–394)						
Tiribazus (ca. 391–ca. 374?)	Ariobarzanes (ca. 387–367)		Hyssaldomus?	Erbbina (early 4th c.)[o]		
Autophradates (ca. 374?–362?)	Artabazus II (ca. 367–350s)	Datames (374?–360s)[p]	Mausolus (377–353)[q]			

36

Rhosaces (by 343/2)		Timades (360s)[r]		Mausolus (358–353)	Mazaeus (361–336)	Artashata (later Darius III) (?–336)
Spithridates (334)	Arsites (by 336–334)	Ariarathes (?) (340s?–331 and later)[s]	Artemisia (353–351)	Pixodarus[t] (341/40–336/35)		Orontes II and Mithraustes (in 331)[u]
			Idrieus (351–344)			
			Orontobates (334)			

[a] Roosevelt 2009: 26–30; Kuhrt 2007: 882.
[b] Bakır 2007: 168; Kuhrt 2007: 882.
[c] Pamphylia seems to have belonged in part to Cappadocia and in part to Cilicia during the Achaemenid period. The boundaries of Cappadocia and Cilicia are uncertain; an excellent overview is Facella 2009: 390–1. See also Çokay-Kepçe and Recke 2007. The lack of Pamphylian (or indeed Cappadocian) names included here of course reflects not the quality of these scholars' work or the work of others in the area, but the nature of the evidence available. As Çokay-Kepçe and Recke 2007: 87 summarize: "Pamphylia was obliged to pay taxes and to contribute soldiers to the Lydian king Croesus until it fell under the hegemony of the Persians following the defeat of the Lydians in 547/6 B.C. For the Classical period, we find Perge among other Pamphylian cities on the contribution lists of the Delian League. Diodorus Siculus (15.90.3) informs us that the Pamphylians took part in the revolt of the satraps around 360 B.C. This shows that Pamphylia remained in the sphere of Persian hegemony until the arrival of Alexander the Great."
[d] Xen. *Cyr.* 7.4.7. Against this see Ray 1995: 1186, following Hdt. 5.115 rather than Xenophon.
[e] Casabonne 2007: 105.
[f] Bryce 1995: 1163.
[g] Tarhan 2007: 120.
[h] Ctes. 16.
[i] "Syennesis" is a Greek rendering of the word that means "king."
[j] This king served in the Persian navy and married his daughter to a Carian, Pixodarus. Hdt. 5.118.
[k] Lygdamis was said to have put to death the poet Panyassis, who was either the uncle or cousin of Herodotus and whose death was the immediate cause of Herodotus's exile from Halicarnassus (Ray 1995: 1188).
[l] Xen. *Anab.* 3.5.17, 4.4.4; Petit 1990.
[m] I include this ruler of Pamphylia under Cappadocia rather than Cilicia, although this may be misleading.
[n] Ray 1995: 1188.
[o] Bryce 1995: 1168.
[p] Briant 2002: 650.
[q] Hornblower 1982.
[r] Summerer 2003: 18, 2005: 149. Tuplin 2007: 25 raises doubts about this. Casabonne 2007: 103 argues persuasively it was at this date that the province of Cappadocia was divided into two parts.
[s] Arr. 3.8.5 calls him Ariaces. For Ariarathes, see Briant 2002: 743; Dio. Sic. 18.3.1, 16.1.
[t] Kuhrt 2007: 704 n. 2.
[u] Arr. 3.8.5.

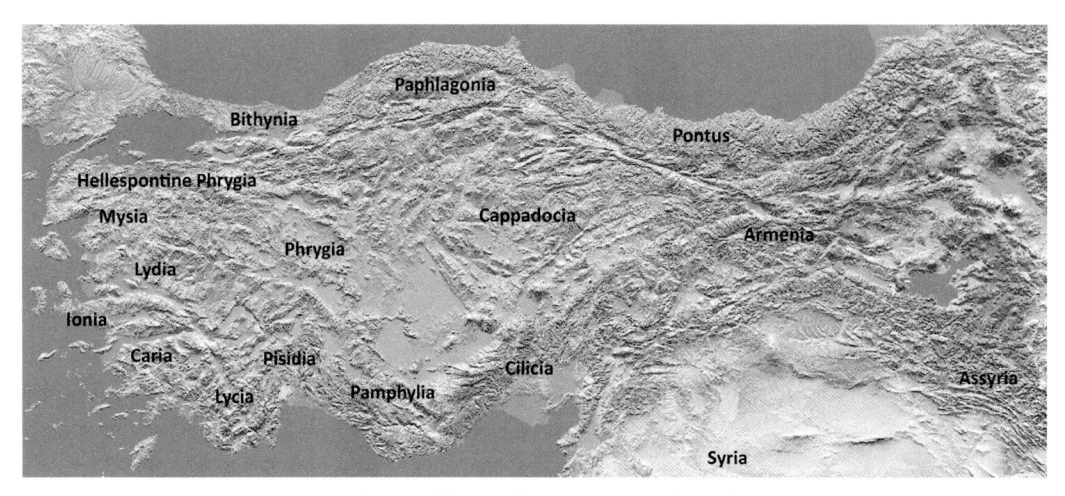

22. Achaemenid Anatolia. Courtesy Karl Mueller.

fragmentary and complicated. An early Hellenistic text describes basic principles of management in the Achaemenid Empire:

> There are four types of administration that can be distinguished (we shall see that the others fit with them): royal, satrapal, civic, private.
>
> Of these the largest and most straightforward is the royal, [the largest and most complicated the satrapal], the most varied and easy the civic, the smallest and most varied the private. Clearly they share many features; but the specific nature of each we should examine. Let us look first at the royal administration. It has complete power, and has four concerns – coinage, goods going out, goods coming in and expenditure.
>
> Now for each of these. In the matter of coinage, the question is what kind to issue and when; as for goods going out and goods coming in, once received from the satraps as revenue, when and how it is best to dispose of them; and with respect to expenditure, what should be removed and when, and then whether the cost should be settled with coined money or merchandise instead.
>
> Secondly, the satrapal. It concerns six types of income: [from land, from the products peculiar to a region, from trade, from dues, from herds, from other things]. Of these, the first and most important is income from the land; this is what is sometimes called *ekphorion* and sometimes *dekate*. The second is what is peculiar to a region – as it might be gold here, silver there, copper, or whatever the product might be. The third is that which comes from trading stations. The fourth derives from the dues imposed on land and markets. The fifth comes from herds, called *epikarpia* and tithe. The sixth comes from individuals, known as the poll-tax and craftsman tax.[19]

A tribute system of some sort must have existed in the empire's earliest years, but it seems likely that Darius I reorganized it and perhaps tightened measures for ensuring regular payment.[20] The tribute lists offered by Herodotus seem overall to provide an accurate assessment of the payments levied on different provinces of the empire.[21] Because they are translated into metal equivalents (silver for most areas, gold for India), they obfuscate the diversity of income detailed by the author just quoted, but they provide a rough outline nonetheless. Table 2 summarizes the tribute supplied by various Anatolian provinces to the king. The sources are arranged chronologically, left to right. I include the Apadana reliefs here as a symbolically charged imperial declaration of gifts brought to the king to balance the later, also charged declarations of Classical authors (note that all emphasize elite masculine power display in the form of horses).

Other sources provide us with direct or indirect information about some of the ways in which these figures were broken down. For instance, the terms *ekphorion* and *dekate* may refer to two different systems of calculating revenue, the former referring to a rate set by the government on the basis of estimated agricultural productivity and the latter being levied as a tithe on an actual harvest.[22] The Mnesimachus Inscription, engraved on a wall of the Temple of Artemis at Sardis, dates to the early Hellenistic period and probably refers to Achaemenid land-tenure systems. It suggests that annual tribute was levied at the rate of $\frac{1}{12}$, on the basis of a fiscal unit of one gold mina per parasang (a unit of length related to distance traveled over a particular period of time, probably roughly equal to 3 miles).[23] Three distinct categories of dues are assessed in this inscription: land (*komai, kleroi, oikopeda*) and men (*laoi*); dues rendered in silver and labor; and products (wine, produce, fruits).[24] Land was held by gift of the king, who could give it to whomever he pleased, whenever he pleased; a person who held the land could give it to someone else, so long as he continued to provide payment to the king.[25]

A recent study compares the Mnesimachus Inscription with two Aramaic inscriptions in Lydia and suggests that estates in western Anatolia were centered on large houses perhaps occupied by the estate owners and their families.[26] The estates included vineyards, gardens and orchards, and fields. Larger estates included outbuildings for laborers (slaves?), as well as livestock and farm equipment, and may have had settlements of tenants who worked estate lands perhaps as sharecroppers.[27] These estates served as residences and work areas for food processing and craft production.[28] The Mnesimachus Inscription shows that the estate owner garnered revenues in the form of labor, money, agricultural goods, and wine vessels.

This raises questions about the nature of produce and production and brings us back to taxes. Royal revenues apparently included various items: furniture, textiles, and works of art as well as coined money, if we are to believe accounts of what Alexander found at Susa.[29] Indeed, one author's suggestion that the regions of the empire paid "what each land produced" and thereby provided for all the needs of the imperial administration is supported by a tablet from

Table 2. Peoples and Tributes of Achaemenid Anatolia

Nome	Peoples	Tribute acc. to the Apadana reliefs[a]	Tribute acc. to Herodotus	Tribute acc. to Strabo	Tribute acc. to Arrian
I	Ionians, Magnesians in Asia, Aeolians, Lycians, Milyans, Pamphylians				
	Ionians	Vessels, clothing, honey (Delegation XII)	400 talents		
	Carians (?)	Shield, spear, horse-drawn chariot (Delegation XXI?)			
II	Mysians, Lydians, Lasonians, Cabalians, Hytennians		500 talents		
	Lydians	Vessels, arm rings, horse-drawn chariot (Delegation VI)	360 talents		
III	[Hellespontine] Phrygians, Thracians of Asia (i.e., Bithynians), Paphlagonians, Mariandynians, Syrians (i.e., Cappadocians)				
	Cappadocians	Horse, clothing (Delegation IX?)		In addition to the silver tax, 1,500 horses, 2,000 mules, and 50,000 sheep[b]	
	Aspendus				Horses[c]
IV	Cilicians		500 talents and 360 white horses		
	Armenians	Horse, vessel (Delegation III?)		20,000 foals[d]	

[a] For the identifications here, see Roaf 2004; Delegation XII emended apud Root 2007.
[b] Strabo 11.13.8.
[c] Arr. 1.26.3.
[d] Strabo 11.14.9.

23. Lydian Delegation (Delegation VI), eastern stairway of Persepolis Apadana. P29002. Courtesy of the Oriental Institute of the University of Chicago.

Babylon describing the diverse tax levied on a soldier: beer, sheep, flour, barley, and silver.[30] The special provisions of Anatolia probably included mineral and metal resources as well as pigments.[31]

Other contributions to the imperial administration were also expected, just as those to local estate owners such as Mnesimachus were expected of tenants. Documents record labor obligations to the imperial authority, including transport service, work on canals, road clearing and maintenance, and other assignments.[32] One onerous duty was supplying the royal table, as will be discussed in Chapter 4.[33] Trade was taxed in addition to land, produce, and labor. This is demonstrated by a Babylonian text recording a tax on river traffic and the Aramaic palimpsest papyrus from Elephantine detailing shipping in and out of Egypt, recording taxes levied on ships coming from or going to the Levant and southwestern Anatolia; these include entry and exit dues, tax on itemized cargoes, and possibly even a poll tax.[34] Slave sales were also taxed.[35]

Taxes paid to the imperial authority served multiple functions. Not only did they fill the royal coffers, but they were important indicators of the great diversity, size, and wealth of the empire. This is demonstrated by the interest shown in antiquity in the variety of goods coming to the imperial treasury. Ancient sources emphasize the multiplicity of nations paying tribute to the king and the diversity of items for which they were responsible, even as they emphasize the unifying principle of taxation. In this way the revenue coming to the administration served a symbolic function as well as a practical one, underscoring an essential element of Achaemenid ideology: *e pluribus unum*. Moreover, the need to pay taxes regularly served as a reminder of imperial authority. Kuhrt sums this up:

> The system of taxation drew the empire's subjects together into a web of obligations to the central power. It made its presence manifest through

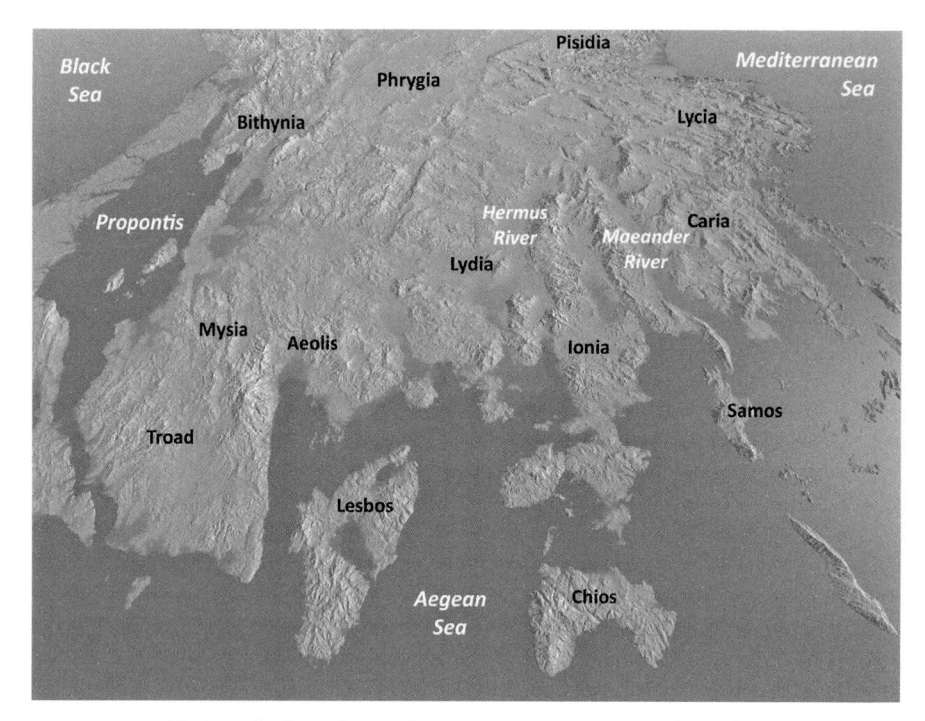

24. Anatolia from the Greek perspective. Courtesy Karl Mueller.

settlement, call-up duties, crown officials managing local resources and tax collectors. It allowed the government to reach into the very heart of local systems, with manpower, production and enterprise all focussed on, and profiting from, meeting supra-provincial requirements.[36]

Lydia and Cilicia

Two satrapies in Anatolia may provide a sense of the administrative options explored by the imperial authority. They demonstrate two different approaches to governing in Achaemenid Anatolia, two ways of trying to ensure a steady flow of taxes and acceptance of Achaemenid authority. Lydia and Cilicia demonstrate the degree of variety inherent in imperial administrative strategy.

Wealth and Disruption: Lydia and Interactions with Greeks

Because the Greeks wrote at length about their neighbors in Lydia, a great deal of information exists about the political and military history of this area insofar as it involved interactions with Greeks. The following account of Achaemenid Lydia highlights the complexity of governing western Anatolia and the multiple obligations satraps had to fulfill as they balanced the needs of king and local people, the threat of invasion by Greeks, and their own desire for power and wealth.[37]

Governing Anatolia

The primary concerns of the king in appointing satraps at the Lydian capital, Sardis, were to bind the region to himself, to balance the power of other western Anatolian satraps, and to fend off foreign invasions. Sardis was wealthy, fortified, distant from Persia, and close to Greece. Its satraps were consistently appointed by the king – and Persian in ethnicity. There was no reflection at Sardis of the hereditary satrapy at Dascylium: in Lydia, the king took a more interventionist approach to establishing satraps. Sometimes Sardis's governors were close family members of the king, but this could be a dangerous strategy as Sardis's wealth and defensibility allowed the possibility of autonomy or indeed rebellion. A man too close to the royal throne might use Sardis as a base to launch an attempt on that throne. A brief overview of the Sardian satraps highlights this balance of authority and autonomy.

The first, left behind by Cyrus, was a Persian man named Tabalus.[38] He directed an administration that apparently included many Lydians; the Lydian Pactyes was "in charge of the gold of Croesus and the other Lydians."[39] After an abortive Lydian uprising led by Pactyes, however, Cyrus took reprisals against those who had aided him and appointed another Persian, Oroetes, as satrap.[40] Oroetes had expansionist tendencies: he was responsible for killing Polycrates, Greek tyrant of Samos, and perhaps adding Samos to Achaemenid territory.[41] Around 522, Oroetes rebelled against the provincial boundaries and moved against the Cappadocians to the east. He also had the Persian Mitrobates, satrap of Dascylium, and his son Cranaspes killed. These exploits made Oroetes the most powerful man in western Anatolia.

Darius took the throne in 521 and, according to Herodotus, directly afterward had Oroetes removed from his position – a wise move on the part of a usurper who wished to prevent another from achieving the same success.[42] The king secured the area by appointing his brother satrap at Sardis; Artaphernes defended the walled acropolis at Sardis from the ravages of the Ionian Revolt (499–494) and helped squash the uprising.[43] Thus the first fifty years of Sardis's history as satrapal headquarters were defined by the desire for territorial control: the Lydians attempted to regain control of their old capital; the satrap sought to take control of larger tracts of land, including, perhaps, one of the Greek islands; the Ionian city-states fought to acquire control over the seaboard and hinterlands. With this kind of armed tension in the area, communication and loyalty between satrap and king were of paramount importance.

Artaphernes' measures in assessing taxes and military obligations in 493, involving a careful survey of land, were a crucial aspect of governing Anatolia.[44] They stayed in effect through the entire fifth century and may also have been the basis for the tribute exacted by the Athenians from those Ionian city-states that joined the Delian League.[45] That the military obligations established by Artaphernes were honored may be seen in the lists of peoples in the Achaemenid army that invaded Greece.[46]

Royal intervention at Sardis was great. Both Darius and Xerxes used the city as a base for their forces before and during combat with Greeks in 490 and 480, a time when Artaphernes' son, Xerxes' cousin Artaphernes II, was confirmed as satrap.[47] Xerxes spent the winter of 479 at Sardis and may have enhanced its great fortification wall while there.[48] The problematic Peace of Callias, a treaty that may or may not have been signed in the mid–fifth century after the Battle of the Eurymedon River, purports to have given autonomy to the Ionian city-states on the Aegean coast, but it is unclear whether it in fact ever existed. If so, it reduced the responsibilities of the satrap of Lydia until 412/11.[49]

Following Artaphernes II, sometime after 450, another member of the royal family was satrap: Pissouthnes, possibly grandson of Darius I and son of Hystaspes II, who assisted the Samians when they revolted against Athens in 440.[50] He was replaced during the turbulent years of Darius II by a man named Tissaphernes, perhaps a distant relative.[51] Tissaphernes is portrayed by Thucydides as a cheater, a liar, one who could not be trusted.[52] If viewed from his own side, however, he may be seen as a brilliant diplomat who kept the Greeks at each other's throats and in 412/11 led them to sign a treaty that granted back to the king all the land in Asia Minor that had been his – effectively undoing the depredations of the Ionian uprisings and all the uncertainties in the years around them.

Ironically, the resolution of conflict between Greeks and the Achaemenid Empire in western Anatolia allowed the satrap of Sardis to turn his attentions inward, toward power in the empire itself. In 407, Darius II appointed his younger son, Cyrus, to be satrap of Lydia, Greater Phrygia, and Cappadocia (an enormous area) and relegated Tissaphernes to Caria and Ionia.[53] This act afforded great power and wealth to one of Darius's sons even as it removed him from central imperial oversight and authority. Did the king want Cyrus to practice ruling? Did he wish him far away? Did he trust him to balance any threat Tissaphernes might pose and bind western Anatolia more securely to the central administration? Whatever the reasoning, it is clear that appointing one's own brother as satrap of Sardis was a more successful political move than appointing two sons to different areas of the empire: when Darius II died, Cyrus used his satrapal headquarters as a base to launch a revolt against his brother, the new king.

Cyrus's preparations were stealthy. He sponsored exiles in various cities and wooed people coming from court; when Sparta offered ambivalent support, he recruited mercenaries in cities of European Greece rather than Anatolia.[54] In 404, his father died and the Spartans won a decisive victory over the Athenians. Cyrus amassed his troops, nominally to lead them against Tissaphernes in Pisidia (as he claimed to the Greek mercenary troops in his service).[55] In 401, he led the same troops to Babylonia instead in an effort to overthrow his brother Artaxerxes II, king since 404.[56] The attempt to consolidate Anatolia by sending a scion of the royal family to govern it had failed: the resources of western

Anatolia proved too tempting and enabling to one who himself wished to warm the throne of Persia.

Tissaphernes, who had traveled in person to warn the king of Cyrus's approaching army, was reinstated in his previous position, perhaps even with expanded territories under his control.[57] His first acts at the beginning of the fourth century make it clear that he wished to govern with overt allegiance to the central imperial authority; thus when the Ionian cities refused to pay tribute, he ravaged the territory of Cyme and besieged the city.[58] The spring of 399 saw the renewal of hostilities between Greeks and the Achaemenid troops in western Anatolia.[59] A tumultuous few years followed, with Spartan-led troops warring against those of the satraps. When Tissaphernes was defeated by the Greeks outside Sardis in 395, he was replaced by Tithraustes, a man whose military victories on land were bolstered by a decisive Achaemenid naval victory at Cnidus in 394 that was led by the Dascylium-based Pharnabazus.[60]

Tithraustes was recalled by the king and replaced with an old friend and adviser, Tiribazus, who was granted the satrapy and some form of overarching military command.[61] With Tiribazus, the Spartan king Antalcidas finally agreed to a peace treaty: the Spartans would withdraw from Anatolia, and all the Greek cities of the Anatolian mainland would pay tribute to the Achaemenid Empire, leaving the islands and European Greece autonomous and free of tribute obligations.[62] Although the king initially rejected the treaty, three years later, in 386, he agreed to it. Tiribazus was confirmed in his command at Sardis, while Pharnabazus was wedded to one of the king's own daughters.[63] The satrapies of western Anatolia were thus linked firmly to the king in Persia, an essential element of maintaining authority in this frontier zone.

Lydia had but short respite from combat, however: the "satraps' revolt" broke out in 361, and it had surely been brewing for several years before its eruption.[64] Epigraphic evidence from Anatolia and Egypt demonstrates that this so-called revolt probably consisted of a series of local uprisings rather than a concerted and unified effort.[65] The revolts were all put down, the local satraps replaced. No surviving records detail happenings in Lydia in the next few decades. When its leaders surrendered Sardis to Alexander without a fight in 334, this was surely another example of people in authority wishing to retain control over these fertile lands. It seems that balancing the authority and autonomy of the satrap at Sardis was a particularly difficult task for the king: the wealth of the area sparked the desire of many, both within the empire and without, to control it for themselves. The region's political and military history was defined by the struggle for authority.

This brief summary elucidates the efforts to which the Achaemenid administration went to bind the westernmost satrapies closely to the central authority and the degree to which the satraps themselves had flexibility in exercising authority in Anatolia. They consulted the king on various key questions of governance, but overall the amount of autonomy available to them was fairly great, so long as they ensured the regular input of tribute to the imperial coffers.[66] When something happened to disrupt that flow, the satrap was replaced by someone the king could trust personally. Thus personal ties linked satraps to the king and, often, to each other; how they dealt with the disruptive threat of the Greeks was left largely to them.

Wealth and Autonomy: The Case of Cilicia

Cilicia provides an alternative model of government; until 400, it may have been a semiautonomous region with a local king (the Syennesis), a tribute-paying province apparently without a Persian satrap. The tribute exacted from this wealthy province was the highest in Anatolia: 500 silver talents and 360 white horses per annum. The amount no doubt reflects the resources of silver, iron, and tin in the area, as well as the produce of its large and fertile plains. The autonomy of Cilicia, if real, was perhaps allowed because of its geographic situation: a broad and fertile coastal plain, with a continuation farther inland, is encircled by high and virtually impassable mountains. As one author summarizes:

> The area should be promising for information about trade, economy, and rural and urban life in the period 550–300 B.C. (as indeed for all periods). It includes two mountain chains (Taurus and Amanus), sources of timber and metals; a long coastline which in its eastern sector gives quick access to Upper Mesopotamia (the Fertile Crescent); a rich agricultural area (smooth Cilicia, today's Çukurova plain) with a city prominent in written sources (Tarsus); and a smaller but also fertile plain (the Amuq, or, in Turkish, Amik) dominated in the Bronze Age by important cities and in Hellenistic and Roman imperial times by the great city of Antioch. In addition, the Battle of Issos took place in this region – a distinction, although of little importance for the archaeological record.[67]

So far, archaeological excavations have produced little evidence for Cilician autonomy or governance in the Achaemenid period, although as we shall see other aspects of life are illuminated thanks in part to local coin issues discussed in Chapter 6. Our understanding of Achaemenid governing in Cilicia relies primarily on nonarchaeological sources.

Cilicia was the principal base for Mediterranean actions for a succession of Persian kings. Perhaps because of this importance, the naval and military presence in the area was extensive and led to a restructuring of the entire monetary system.[68] The capital of Cilicia in the Achaemenid period was Tarsus, where the Syennesis resided. Achaemenid imperial strategy in Cilicia maintained this figurehead, at least until 400 and perhaps after, and respected local political structures.[69] It seems that Artaxerxes II took on the responsibilities of these ancestral kings and united Pamphylia and Cilicia into a single province under more

25. Cilician coastal plain and Taurus Mountains, looking west. Courtesy Karl Mueller.

direct control of the king.[70] Several important sanctuaries prospered during the Achaemenid period: that of Artemis Perasia (or Cybele) at Castabala in the northeast, a sanctuary at Mazaca where fire was worshiped, and an oracle at Mallus. These sanctuaries were autonomous and gained international reputations.

Cilicia prospered during the Achaemenid period, and although its last Syennesis may have aided Cyrus the Younger at the end of the fifth century, it did not foster any revolts itself.[71] Indeed, it seems to have paid its vast tribute regularly without much demur. As an experiment in political autonomy, Cilicia was a success. Perhaps in part because of its example, the Achaemenid authority was willing to grant other mountainous provinces of southern Anatolia, Lycia and Caria, significant autonomy in the fourth century.[72] We cannot know just how much of this was due to the impossibility of imposing central authority on such rugged terrain, but the political autonomy of Cilicia at any rate seems to have meant neither a diminution of tribute paid nor an increase in violent unrest. Here the balance of imperial authority and regional autonomy worked.

Roads

An intricate web of roads bound Anatolia together and to the rest of the empire, providing an efficient system of communication that allowed the imperial authority to control conquered territories and maintain security, collect and transport

26. Royal Road from Ephesus to Mosul. After French 1998. Courtesy Karl Mueller.

produce and people, and provide an ever-present reminder of its power and potential. Herodotus gives a famous (and infamously vague) description of the road from Sardis to Susa, and the Persepolis Fortification Archive demonstrates that the entire empire was connected by a network of roads.[73] According to Herodotus, it was a three-month journey from Sardis to Susa by foot, quicker by horseback and very quick for official travelers who could draw on fresh mounts at official way stations.[74] These way stations made rapid travel possible and allowed messages to be sent by a swift courier system across thousands of miles of plains and mountains. The roads were in some places small trails that required a local guide to follow accurately, but the Royal Road was broad and "wheelworthy" for chariots or carts from Phrygia to Cilicia.[75]

The system of roads required its own administration, involving work teams specializing in road maintenance and construction, bridge builders, and surveyors.[76] Roads were guarded at key spots and patrolled to ensure safety for licit travelers.[77] The road network and checkpoints it included thus provided an infrastructure that linked the various regions of the Achaemenid Empire, keeping even the most distant areas in communication.

Kuhrt has summarized our knowledge of official travel along the Royal Road system:

> The texts from the Persepolis archive make it plain that official authorisation was needed to draw on the supplies at the stopping points along routes, and that such issues were carefully logged. Only one example of such a 'passport' ... has survived. The signatory addressed the officials in charge of the way-stations within their sub-provinces by name and specified what provisions, how much and for how long were to be issued to the traveller carrying the sealed letter of credit. The expenditures were noted and debited to the name of the authoriser. As the Persepolis material

shows, these records were collected (by the relevant provincial authorities) and the disbursements entered into account books, where the supplier's account was credited and that of the authoriser debited. We also learn that some travel parties and high-status individuals were escorted by official 'guides'. Presumably they would have provided protection and ensured that arrangements for the reception of travellers at the stopping points along the route were in place.[78]

The road must have had an impact on people's minds, as well as on ease of travel. This is significant, for an important part of governing involved reminding people of Achaemenid authority. The Royal Road would have played an essential role in this, through not only its physical but also its symbolic presence: it certainly served economic and administrative purposes, but its ideological function was also profound. Indeed, Herodotus claims the Thracians held the road by which Xerxes had traveled in such reverence that they neither plowed nor sowed it even down to his own time.[79] No doubt the engineering feat of its construction made an impression, and the traffic to and fro of those engaged in imperial business would have been a powerful reminder of imperial presence and workings not only for those near the roads but also for those who heard of it. In this way, akin to the collection of taxes, the Achaemenid road network fulfilled both practical and symbolic functions for the imperial authority.

PART II: COMBINING THE PRACTICAL AND IDEOLOGICAL

Thus even as Achaemenid bureaucracies were laid out and administrative networks put into effect, programs were established to support and promulgate the ideology of empire. A legitimizing ideology is an important factor in establishing imperial authority; without the participation of an empire's inhabitants in power relations, the legitimacy of authority dissolves.[80] Ideologies may be manifested in many ways to convey and reify central authority. Darius's inscription and sculpted relief at Bisitun provide an example – and when he had the text translated into various languages and disseminated, along with copies of the image, to locations throughout the empire, the authority-laden expressions of Bisitun took on yet greater power.[81] Using local languages was a strategy with profound symbolic as well as practical value.

Ideology may be manifested materially, through architecture and art as well as luxury and everyday goods.[82] Such expressions of imperial ideology are particularly important in maintaining imperial authority, as they can be widely disseminated and may draw on local traditions to couch authority in terms designed for a local populace. The Achaemenid administration often composed its imperial expressions in such a manner; references to time-honored regional patterns provided ways to legitimize the new regime at specific places.[83] Couching new ideology in familiar local forms also helped nullify the seeming remoteness of

27. Bisitun. © German Archaeological Institute.

foreign conquerors; in the multicultural milieux of the Achaemenid Empire, ideology had to be translated into the cultural discourses of the various populations participating in the system.[84]

Achaemenid ideological programs included the manipulation not only of texts and architectural forms, but also of visual culture. Official imperial iconography was translated into regional artistic syntaxes to make it intelligible to local viewing audiences. Imperially charged adaptation of images had a self-reflexive function as well, for appropriating and manipulating local iconographies and styles signified the incorporation of specific areas into the empire. In this way, differing artistic traditions within an imperial framework reinforced the authority of both local peoples and the empire, drawing on autonomous regional traditions to affirm imperial inclusion.

Assertions of Royal Power: The Progress of Xerxes

Occasional comments and actual remains exist that make it clear Achaemenid kings asserted their power in Anatolia overtly and impressively. These assertions served as specific references to individual kings in a manner rather different from that of the overarching imperial statements considered so far. Perhaps Xerxes provides the best example. His reminders of kingly hegemony were established across the Anatolian peninsula and showed remarkable diversity of approach and statement. I have selected five statements of Xerxes' royal power

28. Trilingual Inscription of Xerxes at Van. Courtesy Paul Zimansky.

to illustrate this point; this discussion is not exhaustive but demonstrates their variety and potency. They are (1) an inscription set up by Xerxes at Van; (2) a gold-encrusted plane tree in western Anatolia; (3) inscribed alabastra found at Halicarnassus; (4) a royal name seal giving the name of the king in Old Persian, used at Dascylium; and (5) a new palace at Celaenae.

(1) Above Lake Van, in the Achaemenid province of Armenia, a trilingual inscription was carved in cuneiform onto a rock face overlooking the ancient center of Urartian power and wealth. Boldly written in Babylonian, Elamite, and Old Persian, it proclaimed:

§1. A great god is Ahuramazda, the greatest of the gods, who created this earth, who created yonder sky, who created man, created happiness for man, who made Xerxes king, one king of many, one lord of many.
§2. I (am) Xerxes, the great king, king of kings, king of all kinds of people, king on this earth far and wide, the son of Darius the king, the Achaemenid.
§3. Xerxes the great king proclaims: King Darius, my father, by the favor of Ahuramazda, made much that is good, and this niche he ordered to be cut; as he did not have an inscription written, then I ordered that this inscription be written.
§4. Me may Ahuramazda protect, together with the gods, and my kingdom and what I have done.[85]

This inscription conveys many messages. Old Persian was apparently first written as a cuneiform script by Xerxes' father, Darius I, and was prominently displayed in imperial inscriptions at the new capitals of Pasargadae and Persepolis

29. The Rock at Van. Courtesy Paul Zimansky.

in Persia; this inscription at Van, one of the few instances of Old Persian found outside Iran, overtly extends kingly reach into the mountains and valleys of Anatolia.[86] The inscription's use of *only* Mesopotamian and Persian languages makes a strong statement about that reach: this is a conquering overlord, a foreigner of power, who now exerts authority over the ancient lands of Urartu. No attempt is made to translate the message into the local vernacular.

Given the lengthy history of warfare between Urartu and Assyria, this choice of languages is a blatant assertion of Achaemenid power over Armenia and of Achaemenid superiority to Assyria in military might. The Old Persian version takes up twice as much room as the Babylonian and Elamite ones – it is carved slightly larger, with more generous spacing between the characters. This may be intended similarly to convey a comment about the superiority of the Achaemenid Persians over the ancient Mesopotamian peoples. Such simple visuals were important, as the inscription is high on the Rock at Van and difficult to read from ground level.

For those who could read the words or to whom they were read aloud, the inscription carried additional meaning. Xerxes' opening mention of Ahuramazda affirms his connection to the religion of his father, using language that mirrors that used by Darius in imperial inscriptions in Persia. In his new inscription at Van, Xerxes affirms that his god is the greatest god, the creator god, and through his legitimating might Xerxes reigns.[87] In addition, Xerxes asserts in this inscription, he is the rightful ruler through descent. And he is a good king and a good son, finishing the work begun by his father: the inscription practically reiterates the campaign against Greece that was responsible for Xerxes' personal presence in Anatolia. The concluding words of the inscription echo those of Darius at Persepolis, but with the area for which protection is sought extended from the king's house to the king's *entire empire and the effects of his deeds*. It is thus clear that the inscription of Xerxes at Van is not a mildly risible description of filling an empty space; rather, it serves as a highly visible and exceptionally powerful royal statement of empire and authority, situated in a spot charged with historical meaning and kingly significance.[88]

(2) Certain assertions of royal presence and potency were related to actualized cultic performances. One of these, the alleged marking of a tree by Xerxes as he was on his way with the army to Greece, became most famous in the Greek literary tradition. Herodotus describes his actions:

> From Phrygia he passed into Lydia. Here the road divides, the left one going in the direction of Caria and the right one to Sardis. Xerxes went by this road and found a plane tree which, for its beauty, he adorned with gold and then entrusted to a steward who was immortal.[89]

Many ancient authors commented on this act, one of a series of deeds that punctuated Xerxes' progress through Anatolia.[90] Whether an instance of tree worship or an appreciation of beauty, the king's treatment of this plane tree and his establishment of its care made a strong statement of wealth and power to the ancient local populace, one that had a tremendous impact on the imagination of generations. Some of Xerxes' other performative acts, such as sacrificing a thousand cattle to Athena of Ilium while priests offered libations to the dead Trojan heroes, also left no permanent marker on the land but were sufficiently impressive to spectators that they, too, were still spoken of decades later.[91]

(3) Xerxes marked his passage in some instances by leaving his name on significant gifts. Offering as gifts the paraphernalia of banqueting, marked with the royal name, certainly formed a part of his interaction with local elites. This is shown by the discovery at Halicarnassus of alabaster alabastra, of which one bears the inscription "Xerxes, the Great King" in Old Persian, Elamite, Babylonian, and Egyptian.[92] These alabastra, presented by the king to forge and demonstrate close links with local elite, were clearly prized: treated as heirlooms, they were included in a foundation deposit more than a century later for the Mausoleum itself.[93] Indeed, close relations with the Persian royal family may have aided Mausolus and his family in their bid for power and contributed to their local authority.

(4) The presence of royal name seals of Xerxes used at the satrapal headquarters at Dascylium demonstrates another instance of the king's name marking his progress.[94] The archive itself will be discussed later; for now, what matters is the presence of two seals bearing the name of Xerxes represented by impressions on clay bullae at Dascylium (see Figure 35). It is significant that royal name seals, with their powerful connections to Persian royal court protocol and expression, turn up at those very Anatolian satrapal headquarters most remote from the imperial centers in Fars. The royal name seals at Persepolis were used not by the king himself but by important imperial administrative offices or officials; we should therefore expect to find royal name seals as part of the intricate and close

network binding the satrapal and other centers to the imperial administration across Anatolia.[95] Deniz Kaptan describes their significance at Dascylium:

> Seals bearing the name of the king were highly prestigious items in the Persian world and like those in Persepolis the Daskyleion royal name seals were most probably used as office seals. Their designs conspicuously reflected significant aspects of Achaemenid iconography. The textual information accompanying the Persepolis seal impressions indicates that certain individuals were granted authorization to use seals with the king's name. Because lightweight papyrus was widely used for writing in the empire, we are not so fortunate to know the names of the individuals who used the seals on Daskyleion documents for the simple reason that all the papyri carrying the bullae have long perished. However, thanks to the inscriptions reading the name of kings, we are able to explore the venues of design selection for these prestigious seals.... [The royal name seal] DS 3 displays in detail the iconography and style that were prevalent in the Persepolis court glyptic, and thus it has been classified as an outstanding example of the Achaemenid koine styles.... DS 3 is also the most frequently used one in the Dascylium archive. On 33% of the Daskyleion bullae this royal name seal was used.[96]

Such an overt iteration of royal name, imperial art, and imperial practice at the farthest reaches of the empire would have served to link the satrapal headquarters to the imperial palaces and simultaneously to voice imperial authority in the strongest and most explicit terms.

(5) Certain of Xerxes' power statements in Anatolia served to strengthen Achaemenid authority through interactions with local elites. Thus Xenophon says that Xerxes founded a citadel and a palace at Celaenae, augmented perhaps later by a paradeisos, or royal garden, on his way back to Persia after the unsuccessful Greek war.[97] A palace and acropolis were assertive statements of continued imperial power at this time, as well as practical edifices at the headwaters of the Marsyas River, a tributary to the great Maeander. After the defeat by the Greeks, securing this passageway from the Aegean to the Anatolian interior might well have seemed necessary. The situation of the buildings was also an appropriate reminder of kingly presence for the local elite, however; not only does Xenophon describe it as "large and well-favored," but it was sufficiently verdant, varied, and lush for someone (Cyrus the Younger?) to have founded a game park there as well. Xerxes' power statements in the western reaches of his empire were significant, memorable, and successful.

Paradeisoi as Power Statements

Celaenae was not the only place to have a paradeisos in Achaemenid Anatolia; from Greek sources it seems clear that more than one satrap established formal paradeisoi at Sardis, just as the satraps of Hellespontine Phrygia did at Dascylium.[98] The paradeisoi were probably variable, and there is as yet no archaeological evidence from Anatolia to suggest their appearance. According to literary sources, they could have been formal gardens or game parks, in each case with plants or animals that might have been imported from great distances.[99] Royal gardens planted with exotic flora and populated by unusual fauna, flourishing with agricultural land and orchards, were part of the earlier Near Eastern backdrop of imperial expression.[100] But the Achaemenid period saw two apparent innovations: the gardens were arranged with careful formality, and the concept was exported widely throughout the empire and even beyond.[101]

There is no evidence, textual or archaeological, suggesting pre-Achaemenid paradeisoi in Anatolia. The concept was a Persian import to Anatolia, and paradeisoi served as profound markers of Persian identity and authority.[102] As part of a widely spread manifestation of the tastes and preferences of the new leadership, they may have provided familiar surroundings and ease of mind to ethnic Persians in Anatolia, as well as a venue and avenue for local elites to partake of Persian lifeways. That they served as power statements may be indicated by the fact that at Sardis, at least, multiple satraps went to the trouble and expense of laying out and planting formal gardens.[103] These gardens combined the practical and ideological in their form.

The appearance of such gardens has been suggested by excavations at Pasargadae.[104] The order and formality of the gardens had ideological ramifications.[105] Pavilions with many columns formed an integral part of a series of formal rectilinear gardens, each with trees and shrubs laid out in straight lines. As when one moves past a modern vineyard planted in regiments of individual vines, walking or riding along the paths of such a garden would create a constant sense of linear rearrangement as new vistas opened down rows of plants or along diagonals. The gardens were irrigated by means of finely dressed stone watercourses. The placement of buildings and – as suggested by Pasargadae – thrones was carefully aligned to the garden beds.[106]

The ideology of power behind the strict alignment of the paradeisos at Pasargadae was profound, as the excavator comments:

> [T]he manner in which the central axis of the principal garden of Cyrus was made to fall directly in line with the permanent throne in the main portico of one of the two major palatial buildings at Pasargadae, Palace P, provides an unequivocal demonstration of the way in which, from the second half of the sixth century BC onward, a recognizable symbol of power at the apex of a garden design could be used to imbue a visual, axial avenue with potent indications of authority.[107]

The rectilinear nature of the garden may also be an articulation of the ideology inherent in the title "king of the four quarters." The unguarded, open

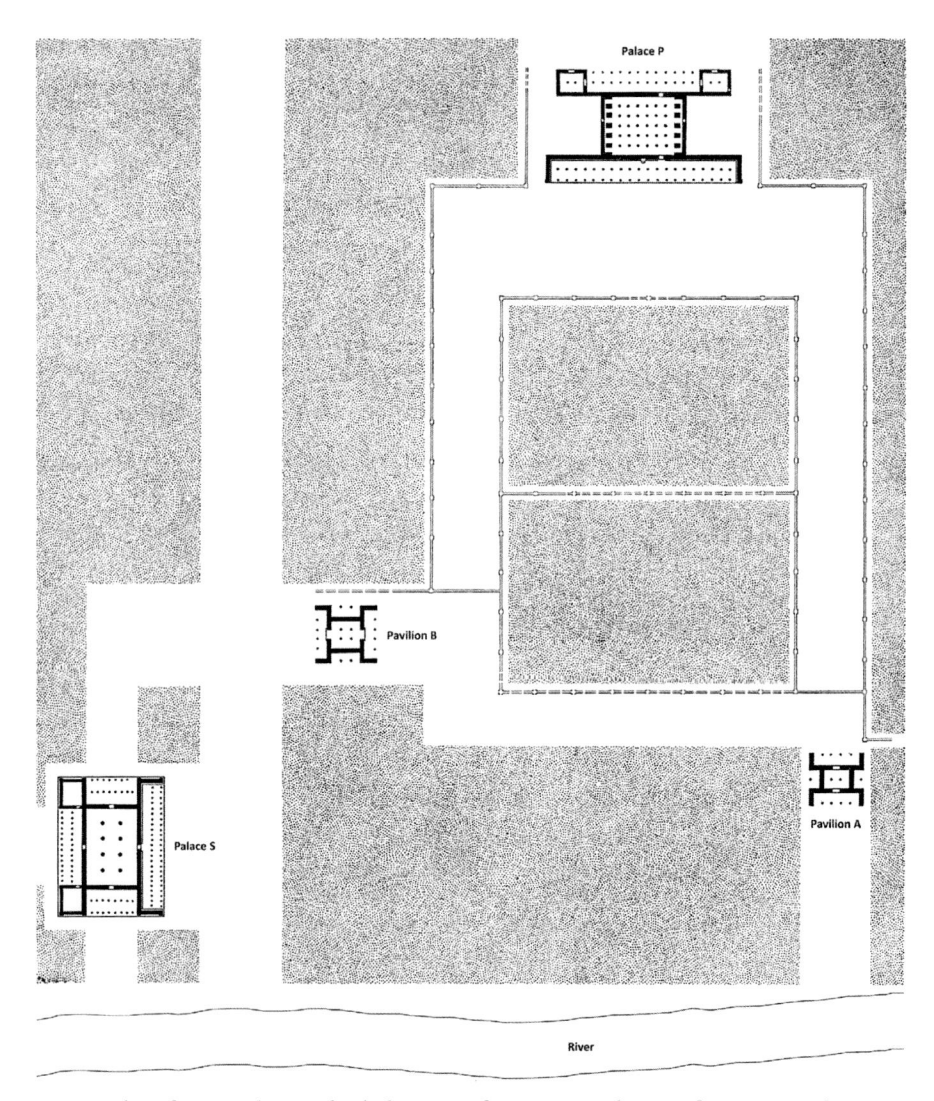

30. Plan of Pasargadae. Author's drawing, after D. Stronach 1978: figs. 3, 24, and 48.

paradeisoi may indeed have been intended to be microcosms of the Achaemenid Empire, ideally "a well-ordered, productive estate, free from external and internal disruption."[108] Thus the construction of paradeisoi was of profound ideological importance, and the role they play in Greek narratives demonstrates the impact they made on the mind of the foreign beholder. Paradeisoi reflected a recognizably Persian notion of civilization and empire.

Assertions of Achaemenid Power: Dascylium

Excavations at Dascylium have unearthed remains of what may be satrapal palaces. They give us a sense of imperial power statements made in architectural form in Anatolia. Such buildings served a dual purpose, like the Royal Road. On the one hand, they had a practical function, serving as structures where imperial business could be transacted and imperial concerns guarded or effected. On the other hand, they served to reflect and reify imperial administrative authority – local representatives and, by extension, the king himself.

The site of Dascylium had not been a local capital before the mid–sixth century and was probably chosen as satrapal headquarters for a variety of reasons.[109] Before the Achaemenid period, it had enjoyed close relations with the Milesian colony Cyzicus, which commanded tremendous economic potential through its situation on the Sea of Marmara and its high-quality Proconnesian marble. Dascylium itself was defensible and possessed a good visual catchment area. The proximity of the site to Lake Daskylitis with its rich bird life and abundant fish may also have made it attractive. And its location near the edge of the empire gave it symbolic as well as practical value. During the Achaemenid period, "the city held in its hand control as well as political and economic governance over the entire area of Thrace, the Bosphorus and Dardanelles, the Sea of Marmara (Propontis) and Hellespontine Phrygia."[110]

The Persians strengthened the extant defenses of the site when they established satrapal headquarters at Dascylium. The retaining terrace wall that surrounded at least part of the site was rebuilt or repaired several times during the Achaemenid period.[111] It shored up the sides of the mound at Dascylium, which seems to have been leveled and extended at the beginning of the Achaemenid period, perhaps to make room for satrapal edifices.[112] The terrace wall itself was lengthened and fortified during the Achaemenid period, with multicolored smooth-faced ashlar blocks and a gentle batter to its lower levels and a probable brick superstructure.[113]

During the time of the satrap Mitrobates and his son Cranaspes (the last quarter of the sixth century), a monumental building was constructed at Dascylium.[114] Indeed, during this time, building activity at the site flourished, with fragments of marble architectural molding demonstrating a desire to incorporate Greek decorative features. These included the use of blue-veined Proconnesian marble in an Ionian cyma, as well as other architectural elements.[115] The particular style of this molding links it to Miletus and Didyma, possibly indicating the presence at Dascylium of craftspeople from these sites, as well as the interest of the Achaemenid administration in Ionian masonry. Certainly it provides a direct link between this most remote satrapal residence and the royal structures of Cyrus in Persia itself, where overtly Ionian masonry techniques figured prominently; ostentatiously, flagrantly Ionian workmanship on display at Pasargadae and at Dascylium proclaimed the close connections between these administrative centers.[116] The incorporation of Ionian elements in imperial structures also drove home the authority of the Achaemenid administration over skilled craftspeople throughout the

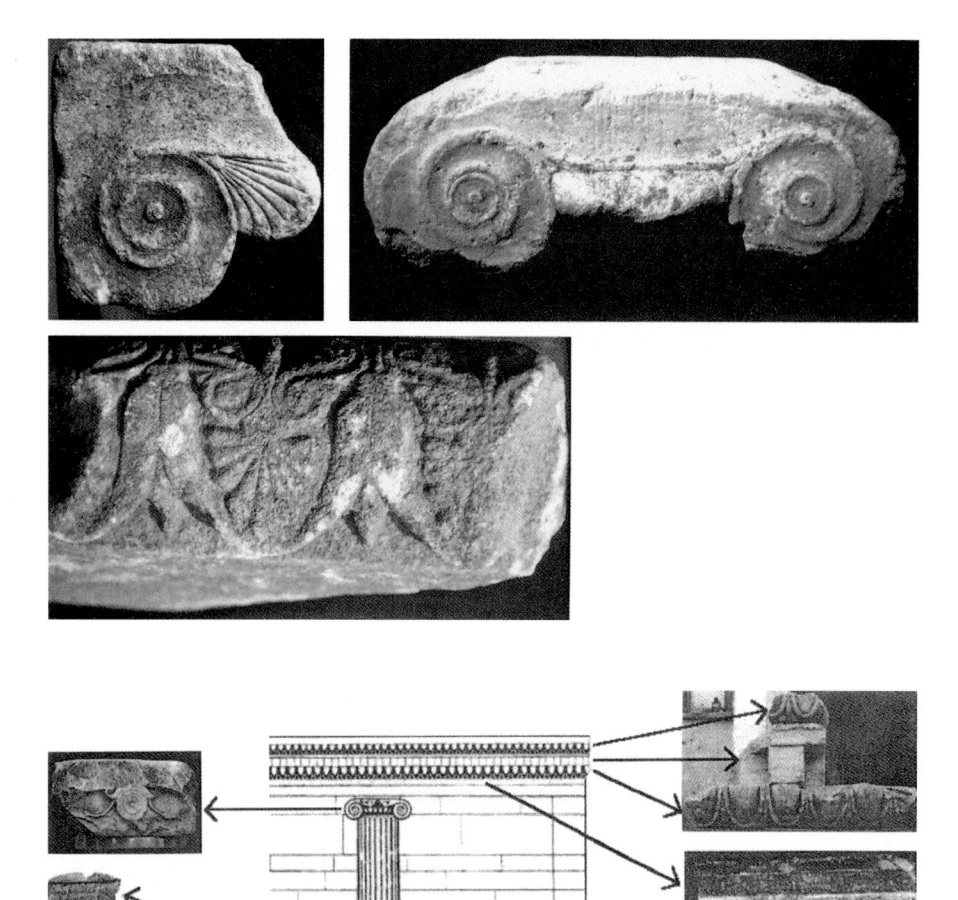

31. Architectural elements from the first and second building phases at Dascylium. After Erdoğan 2007. Courtesy Tomris Bakır.

empire, as well as its ability to move them from one place to another and command their labor.

A second great period of construction at Dascylium seems to have taken place in the fifth century.[117] A structure that has been identified as the archive building may date to this time, and remnants of monumental buildings in andesite and marble were reused in a later wall but attest to as many as ten different grandiose constructions during this period.[118] At least one monumental building was constructed in Dascylium during the rule of the satrap Artabazus I (477–465), and it is possible that the elegant marble architectural elements that date to this time even formed part of the satrapal palace mentioned in Greek sources.[119] Again, the fragments are notable for their overtly Ionian nature.

It is likely that other monumental buildings were constructed at the time that were *not* Greek in style, of course; the apparent preponderance of Greek architectural elements may partly result from our current understanding of dating and stylistic development.[120] It is nonetheless significant that so many examples of Greek architectural embellishment are to be found at this important administrative center. At one level, this makes sense for a site that had as many interactions with the Greeks as did Dascylium. At another level, it serves creatively to link Dascylium explicitly to Pasargadae, adapting regional styles for Achaemenid imperial expression. It reiterates in the most public way the ability of the Achaemenid authority to muster and marshal expertise and manpower from across the tremendous empire.

Assertions of Achaemenid Power: Altıntepe

The many-columned hall at Altıntepe, with its wall paintings showing a mounted deer hunt, is now thought by its excavators to have been built in the Urartian period and to have continued in use during the Achaemenid period.[121] Painted pottery provides clear evidence of use during the Achaemenid period, and the columned hall itself is thought to have served as satrapal headquarters for this part of Armenia.[122] A massive fortification wall at the site had lower courses of cyclopean masonry and Urartian spolia surmounted by a mudbrick superstructure, with buttresses every 11 m.[123] This vast and complicated site provides an example of an administrative building constructed before the Persian arrival, continuing in its earlier function during the Achaemenid period. Whether the painted deer hunt from horseback that adorned its interior was painted under Achaemenid hegemony or before, it provided a rich illustration of manly behaviors that were highly valued in Achaemenid Anatolia.

Geoffrey Summers has argued that Altıntepe's neighboring hill, Cimin Tepe, functioned as part of a larger important site in the Achaemenid period that was linked to Altıntepe.[124] He draws attention to the nine silver objects of the Franks Bequest presented to the British Museum in 1897, said to be "found near Erzincan" and, he comments, probably from one or more tombs associated with the settlements at Altıntepe and Cimin Tepe.[125] In addition to these artifacts, twenty silver bars were discovered in 1938 at a hill near Altıntepe, "most probably Cimin Tepe," which weighed a total of 15 kg and of which some were inscribed in cuneiform (language not stated).[126] The introduction of a new style of painted fine wares drawing extensively on Persian precedent confirms

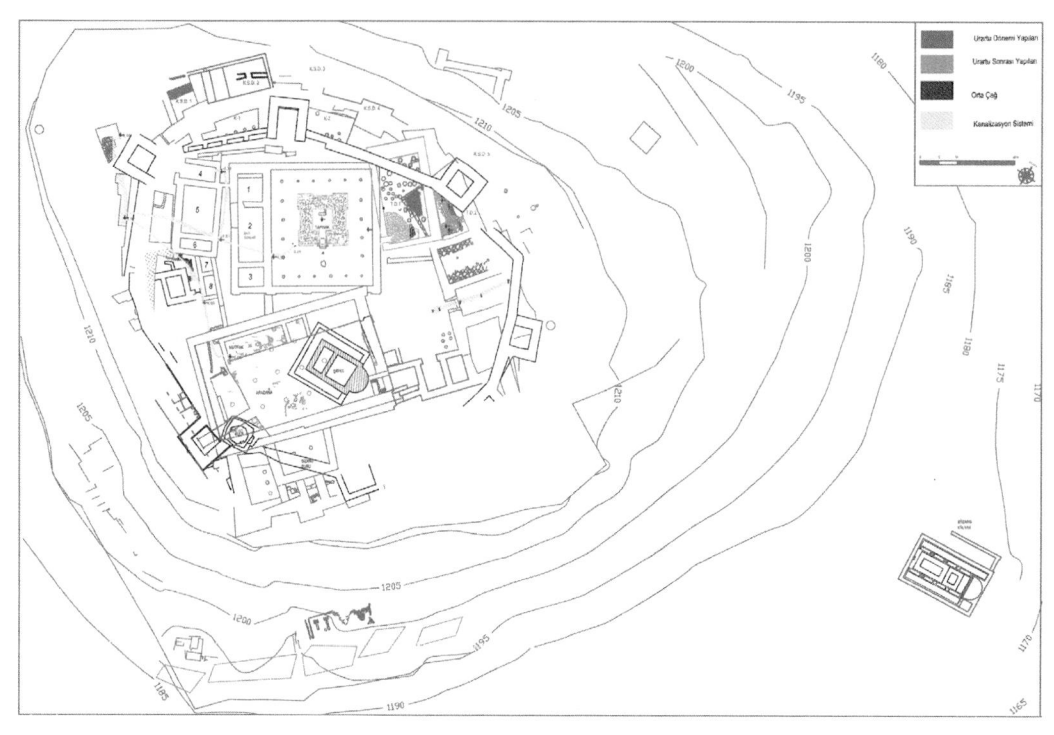

32. Altıntepe. Courtesy Halim Korucu. © Altıntepe Kazıları.

the sense of an elite site with powerful and strongly stated connections to elite expressions in the Achaemenid heartland.[127] Achaemenid Armenia displayed a close link to Fars itself, even as it adapted the usage of the Urartian site and great administrative building at Altıntepe.

Assertions of Achaemenid Power: Nonsatrapal Sites

What do we see when we turn to nonsatrapal sites in Anatolia? Gordion during the Achaemenid period was of secondary importance. It provides a clear example of Achaemenid imperial authority and serves as a case study for the kinds of things we might expect to find at second-tier cities of Achaemenid Anatolia. Gordion prospered at this time: it expanded to its greatest size during the Achaemenid period and saw increased interaction with other peoples both within and outside the borders of the Achaemenid Empire.[128] It may have been the residence of elite personages, a regional fortified setting that did not have the status of a satrapal center but still included certain markers of authority.

In May 1952, a red agate cylinder seal (2342 SS 100) was excavated from the Citadel Mound at Gordion.[129] It was found during the exposure of an elaborate Achaemenid-period structure, the so-called Mosaic Building.[130] With the seal

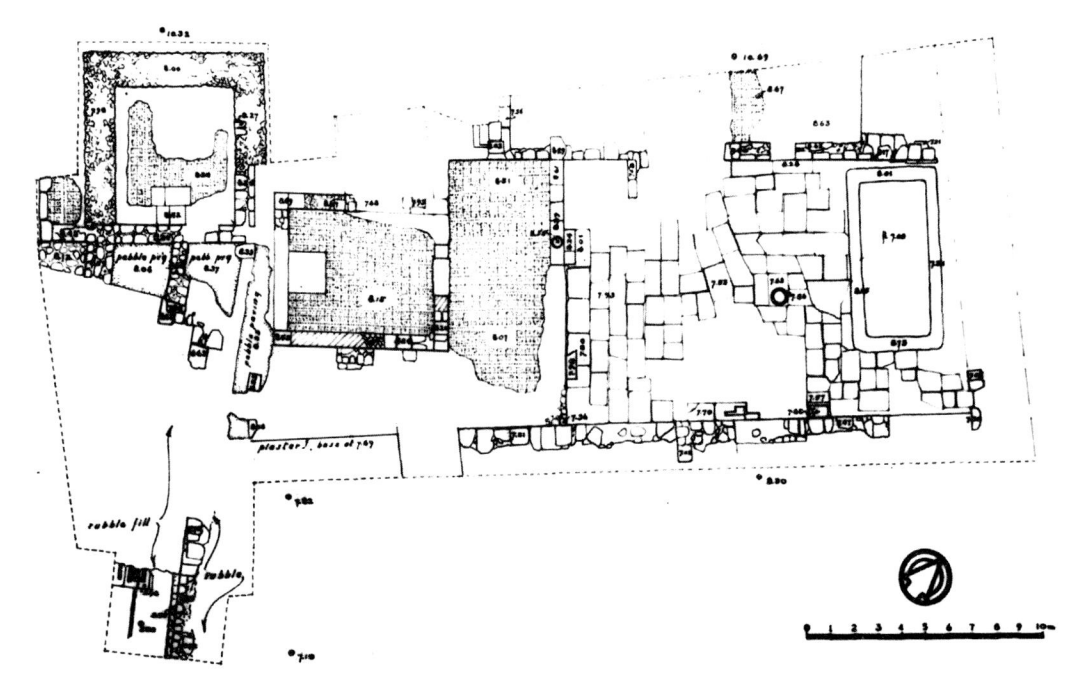

33. The Mosaic Building at Gordion. Paved forecourt at right; rectangular colonnaded porch with mosaic at center of plan; throne room (?) to left of that. © Gordion Archaeological Project.

were found architectural tiles of the Mosaic Building and potsherds dating to the fifth and the first half of the fourth centuries. The most recent date suggested for the building is the second quarter of the fifth century. The seal itself was probably carved sometime in the fifth century.[131]

The Mosaic Building was a grand one. The complex had a large (11 × 17 m) stone-paved forecourt with a stepped and colonnaded porch on one side that measured fully 4.25 × 12 m.[132] The porch was paved with a pebble mosaic, from which the building took its name, showing a geometric meander pattern in blue, yellow, and white. A door at the back of the porch led to a room in which most of the floor was paved in the same pattern. Matt Glendinning concludes his description of the room: "A square area against the back wall is void of mosaic, suggesting the presence of something like a throne dais, altar or statue base."[133] This is essential: this elaborate, decorated building served in an official, public capacity. Whether it was a religious site or a site of government, it was created on a plan not previously seen at Gordion and carefully articulated to maximize the impact of the figure at the back of the mosaic-floored room. This new imposition of an expensive building on the people of Gordion made a clear and explicit statement of power – of a new, non-Phrygian power.

The cylinder seal comes from a later, disturbed context, but the probable date of its carving places it as contemporary with the building itself.[134] The seal

Empire, Authority, and Autonomy in Achaemenid Anatolia

34. Gordion Seal 100 (2342 SS 100), modern impression. © Gordion Archaeological Project.

is of interest on a number of levels. It is the most elaborate Achaemenid-period seal found at Gordion, and the only inscribed one. It is inscribed in Aramaic, the administrative lingua franca of the Achaemenid Empire but not native to Phrygia. It shows heartland Achaemenid religious and kingly iconography, but it is carved in a style unknown at Persepolis, a style significant in Achaemenid Anatolia for its connections to the elite – as will be discussed later.[135] Its inscription says, "Seal of Bn', son of Ztw, (hyashana)"; the last word is perhaps an office.[136] These are Persian names; the use of Aramaic here may function as another prestige signifier.

Seal 100 thus adds to the sense gained from the Mosaic Building in providing insight into the cultural milieu at Gordion and the impact of Achaemenid imperial authority.[137] It demonstrates the presence of iconography from the imperial heartland, united with elite provincial style, at this site. It also confirms the sense gained from a change in sealing practices at Gordion during the Achaemenid period; a new administrative system was set in place at this time, one that relied on seals that could be linked to individuals.[138] Increased elaboration of seal imagery meant that individuals or offices could be recognized and held accountable for their actions, while simultaneously their seals offered an opportunity for expression of identity. Significantly, the visual expressions of the Achaemenid-period seals from Gordion show great variety within an overarching set of images closely linked to Achaemenid visual practices and ideology.

The finds from Gordion show that close attention was paid to establishing imperial authority at second-tier cities in Anatolia, not just at satrapal headquarters. New architectural forms and administrative practices and expressions were established that bound Gordion to Achaemenid authority. And this city enjoyed significant cultural exchange and the ability to exploit a wealth of resources under Achaemenid hegemony.[139]

A few other sites provide further glimpses into life in the Achaemenid period. The large building, or "Achaemenid palace," at Tille Höyük on the west bank of the Euphrates, in southeastern Anatolia, may have been built in the late sixth to early fifth century; its massive walls were coated in white plaster, and its ceiling was apparently supported by wooden columns resting on basalt bases in a manner that reflected the many-columned halls of Persia itself. As the building was thoroughly cleaned out in antiquity, however, it provides little evidence for human activity.[140] Tilbes Höyük, on the Euphrates near modern Birecik, has produced storage facilities for agricultural products in the form of silos and warehouses, as well as mortuary finds, including terracotta figurines of riders (typically associated with Achaemenid presence) and bronze jewelry.[141] These remains indicate a centralized authority, one that oversaw the collection and redistribution of the area's rich produce. These nonsatrapal but impressive sites thus alert us to significant Achaemenid presence and control over the fertile valley of the Euphrates and demonstrate the possibility that significantly more intensive and extensive authority was exerted over a more widespread area than we have previously realized.

Governing Anatolia via Cultural Impositions? Religion and Language

Interestingly, neither religious expression nor the use of specific languages, with the possible exception of Aramaic, seems to have been exploited extensively by the central imperial authority as an avenue of imposing power. Rather, these potentially ideologically charged avenues of communication were granted a great deal of autonomy. Religion is the subject of intensive investigation in Chapter 6, so the present discussion merely touches on it. What emerges most clearly is that religious expression does not provide a single impression: religious belief and practice were complex and do not neatly fit any one interpretive framework. In a way, they demonstrate the simultaneous flow of authority and autonomy, here practiced perhaps by religious leaders rather than by government officials. It is clear that there were times when local political figures attempted to use religious cults to increase their own authority. It is equally clear, however, that the Achaemenid administration did not effect any systematic conversion of cult to reify its own authority. In general, religion seems to have been a way for local populaces to exercise autonomy over a key aspect of their own culture and life systems.

A similar official approach to language seems to have pertained. Epigraphic evidence demonstrates that local languages were inscribed through the Achaemenid period. Particularly regional in language use were funerary markers, discussed in Chapter 5, which often were inscribed in a local language even when little evidence exists for an earlier epigraphic tradition and when significant evidence exists for the simultaneous use of an additional language.

The notion that Aramaic served as a koine is perhaps borne out by the presence of Aramaic inscriptions on seals, while a number of bilingual inscriptions suggest that Aramaic had status as a "powerfact" language, linking the inscriber with the might of imperial authority no matter what his ethnicity. Such is suggested, for instance, by the bilingual Greek–Aramaic inscription from Ağaca Kale in Cappadocia, which names an official of clearly Iranian heritage:

BYRT' *[Z' HQY]M[W]'*
RYRMN *B[R HRYWK/R'/T?]*
SYL*[----- W]BR 'H[B]*
HR*Y[WK/R'/T?]* BR 'RYRMN
ḤŠT*[RPNY' B'ND]*MN

[This] fortified city [they established] A-ryaramna *son [of Haryuka/Aryurat?]*
..?..[.......?...... *and]* the son be*[loved]* Hary*[uka/Aryurat?]*, son of Aryaramna sat[raps *to Andô]môn*.[142]

Neither Greek nor Aramaic was likely to have been the first language spoken by the Persians named, but the men use these languages explicitly in this Anatolian context. In this part of Cappadocia, indeed, it is possible that neither Greek nor Aramaic was the primary spoken language, period. Thus the languages of the inscription are seen to demonstrate appropriative linguistic power. The same may be said, perhaps, of the trilingual inscription from Xanthus in Lycia, where Aramaic serves as a satrapal summary or endorsement, while the Lycian and Greek versions might be placed in satrapal archives.[143] These inscriptions represent authority in languages of power; they are themselves an assertion of multicultural authority.

At this point we cannot know what the languages of imperial archives in Anatolia might have been. The multilingual evidence from Persepolis combined with the multiple languages used on seal inscriptions at Dascylium (discussed later) suggests that we should think of the imperial archives as incorporating various people with various backgrounds, using different languages in different ways.[144] In this manner, archival practice served as a microcosm of imperial authority and a notion of empire as well as a reflection of the reality of empire. The archives of the empire served to bind administrative centers and those they governed, both in logistical or practical ways and in the ideological notion of unity created by their diverse uniformity and expression of centralized authority.

Archives

A brief note on vocabulary: a sealing, or bulla, or clay tag means the entire clay object that preserves the impression of a seal (thus technically a sealed tablet is also a form of sealing, although it is never discussed in that way). A seal impression is the impression left by an ancient seal tool on the clay or other material. A seal is either the actual seal tool itself or the seal image as gleaned from its impressions known via a sealing.

Bookkeeping was an age-old tradition in Mesopotamia, and if the Persians had not developed the habit before the reign of Darius they certainly did by then. With record keeping so well established at Persepolis and elsewhere, it should come as no surprise to find remnants of archival practices at Dascylium, where the sealings demonstrate the presence of a satrapal archive even though they were not found in an archival context. Although other archives have not yet been discovered in Achaemenid Anatolia, Persian presence led to so much change in the quantity and quality of seals at multiple sites that we can be certain significant administrative changes took effect across the peninsula.[145]

A survey of four sites – three elite, one non-elite – will establish this point, with implications for the complexities involved in governing Anatolia. From the sealings found at the satrapal headquarters of Dascylium, the discussion will turn to the sealstones found at the satrapal headquarters of Sardis. Seals found in the elite graves at İkiztepe offer a different glimpse into the implications of seal use in Achaemenid Anatolia and connections between style and authority. As a contrast to these sites, Gordion provides us with a body of seals apparently belonging to and used by largely non-elite people. Thus we can gain a sense of the practical governance of Anatolia, emphasizing an artifact that served both as administrative tool and as representative of an individual or office with individual tastes and needs. The lack of precise chronology in this discussion reflects our current inability to fine-tune the dating of seals; style apparently bore specific meaning and cannot be used as a chronological indicator. The few other means available to us to begin establishing a viable chronology are still insufficiently secure to allow for certainty.

The Dascylium bullae are clay tags with seal impressions on one side and the impressions of papyrus fiber and string on the back of most; the fifty bullae without papyrus impressions have such a smooth flat surface that it has been suggested they were attached to leather or parchment, perhaps in groups of more than one on a single roll.[146] Some seals were more likely to be attached to such a leather roll than to papyrus.[147] Kaptan dismisses the notion that the bullae were attached to copies of royal letters and suggests instead:

> Since the documentation from the archives from the center and the provinces of the empire deals with local and communal issues, it is not hard to assume that the Daskyleion documents may have dealt with local/communal

bureaucratic and economic issues. As P. Briant noted (1986: 434–437) the archives in the satrapal residences stored copies of documents on regional bureaucratic activities, petitions sent to the satrap and his decisions on the local issues.

... Records of ... bureaucratic activities must have been kept in each local administrative center of the empire. When any payment or delivery was made from the treasury or any item was received by the treasury, the activity must have been registered. Thus it is not incongruous to assume that Daskyleion had a local storehouse/treasury from which local needs could also be transferred.... In addition to the payments of rations from the storehouse, the arrivals and receipts of taxes from the satrapal territory must have been registered in papyrus or parchment rolls enclosed by the sealed bullae. The most convincing assumption about the contents of the Daskyleion documents is that they recorded such bureaucratic activities and were sealed by the officials of the satrapy who held royal authorization.[148]

Because the sealed tags from Dascylium apparently ratified documents written on a perishable material such as papyrus or parchment, we cannot know the specifics of the archivists' record keeping. We can see that Dascylium, like Persepolis, included certain seals that apparently functioned as office seals, and we see very overt connections in iconography and style to Persepolitan glyptic art and relief sculpture in certain seals. Fully 74 percent of the seals impressed on the clay tags of the Dascylium archive bore imagery that has been called "Achaemenid koine or Persianizing" in style.[149] At the same time, people bearing seals with utterly different, often Greek imagery also ratified the documents – the wide-ranging options available to people at Persepolis in iconography and style are reflected in this satrapal site of Achaemenid Anatolia as well.[150] Some seals were inscribed with personal names or the royal name: people from a variety of ethnic backgrounds used various languages in their inscriptions, not infrequently employing a language with a different heritage to write the name.[151] The ethnicity of the names generally bore no connection to the style of the seal.

Almost half the sealings found at Dascylium present impressions of three royal name seals, two of Xerxes (DS 2, 3) and one of Artaxerxes (DS 4).[152] One of the seals of Xerxes (DS 2) is carved in the Achaemenid Court Style identified at Persepolis; DS 2, represented by but three impressions, is the only seal at Dascylium for which style and the ethnicity of the name match. The other two royal name seals draw on courtly imagery but render it in a different style, a recognizably western mode.[153]

As is usual, the royal name seals were not used by the king whose name they bear; indeed, the preponderance of DS 3, represented by 147 impressions, demonstrates that it was most likely an office seal rather than one belonging to any

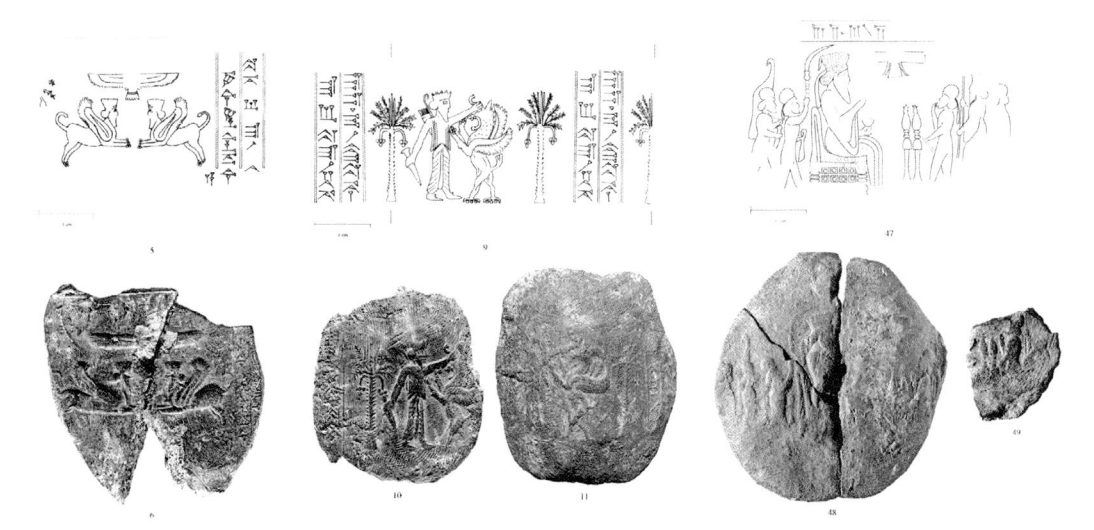

35. Dascylium Seals 2, 3, and 4. After Kaptan 2002. Courtesy Deniz Kaptan.

individual.[154] This seal and DS 4 are each represented by two almost identical cylinders intended to look exactly alike, rather than a single seal. DS 4 is particularly interesting, as it shows an audience scene that closely resembles the one on Darius's staircase at Persepolis, while slight differences in dress "among the attendants of the King may indicate that the seal-maker did not understand the intricacies of the Persepolitan dress code."[155]

The Dascylium archive thus shows record-keeping practices similar to those current at Persepolis, but the archive clearly functions as a local operation. As was the case at Persepolis, seal owners could make choices among multiple styles and images. Although we cannot be sure, it seems that the record-keeping practices of Persepolis were exported to Anatolia, and the seals represented by impressions on the Dascylium archive suggest that artistic flexibility and communication were potent features of this governing practice.

Other sites have not yet yielded archives, but the sealstones that have been found give an inkling of governance. Sardis had been the capital of Lydia and retained its administrative importance under Achaemenid hegemony as a satrapal seat. Its seals reflect its importance in the empire in some particularly interesting ways: they display official imperial iconography rendered in a collection of styles related to each other and not represented at Persepolis, with local tastes and preferences perhaps reflected in the selection of imperial images. The large number of seals found – thirty-four of them – is partly a reflection of the enormous number of tombs excavated at Sardis (well more than a thousand), the source of the seals found.[156] The very large number attests to the impact of the Achaemenid presence on the life and lifestyles of the elite.[157] Our inability to date the seals stylistically is significant: styles did not shift traceably over time

36. Seals from Sardis. Courtesy C. H. Greenewalt, jr.

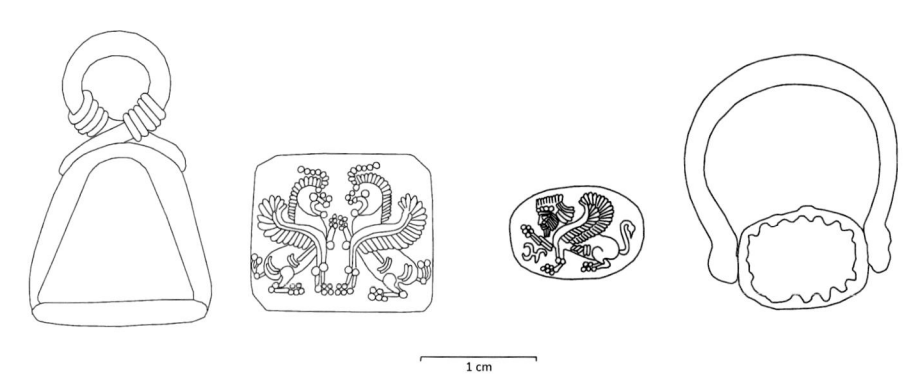

37. Seals from İkiztepe. Author's drawing, after Özgen and Öztürk 1996: 95, 98.

but seem, as we shall see, to have borne specific meaning that predicated against change.

Like those impressed on the archives at Persepolis and Dascylium, the seals from Sardis demonstrate a variety of choices available in iconography, style, shapes, and materials.[158] All of the seals excavated at Sardis have settings that show they were worn on the body in a visible spot. Many seals have particularly beautiful suspension devices, with elaborate attention to those qualities that enhanced their value as adornments. The highly visible nature of the seals underscores their importance as indicators of individuality: not only the image carved on a seal, but its very form could convey messages about the person using it. The seals excavated at Sardis demonstrate that – as at Persepolis and Dascylium – multiple artistic styles existed concurrently at this satrapal capital. Interestingly, most of the Sardian seals are carved in a related group of styles that are readily distinguishable from, say, Greek styles. The seals from Sardis carved in this linked group of styles almost all convey imperially meaningful Achaemenid iconography, indeed often iconography associated explicitly with high status.[159]

The seals found in the tombs at İkiztepe, on the border between Lydia and Phrygia, demonstrate the same processes of style, iconography, and display among elites who lived (or died) in a nonsatrapal site.[160] These seals, too, are

38. IAM 4581, from Sardis. Courtesy Sir John Boardman.

carved from semiprecious stones in various styles, so the emphasis on the imperial court and its imagery is meaningful. As Kaptan has shown, fully 60 percent of them evince overt connections to Achaemenid iconography.[161]

Other groups or individual seals and sealings demonstrate a similar phenomenon elsewhere in the peninsula, with seals displaying high-status imagery linking them to Persepolis but rendered in distinctive and recognizably linked styles that connected their users to authority.[162] Thus the elite of Anatolia, whether they were buried at satrapal sites or not, were woven into the intricate process and display of governmental authority by emblems of self and tools of power.

Authority and Style among the Elite

The imagery on these seals matters. It demonstrates the network of artistic and sociopolitical connections that united the Persian, and Persianizing, elite. Many of the seals are carved in a recognizable group of related styles, a newly composed and socially symbolic art of empire. They are characterized by flat broad articulations with undisguised use of the rotating drill to pick out and emphasize particular aspects of figures. Volumes are precise but generally unmodeled, and lines are clearly and broadly incised, often to indicate feathers, the borders between muscles (as in the haunches of the lion-griffins at İkiztepe), hair, bunched up cloth (as at the borders of a robe's sleeves), or elements of furniture that might otherwise have been less strikingly indicated by modeling. This collection of Achaemenid elite visual imagery, linked very closely through iconography and in a recognizable way through style, used to be characterized as "Graeco-Persian"; a current trend is to categorize the style as "Achaemenid Anatolian" or as the more fluid "Achaemenid koine."[163] The seals carved with such imagery form part of the strikingly cohesive and highly visible Achaemenid elite portable culture.

Empire, Authority, and Autonomy in Achaemenid Anatolia

39. Seals carved with iconography of authority in Achaemenid koine styles from Sardis. After C. D. Curtis 1925.

The homogeneity of iconographic discourse and linked styles in the seals has even greater significance when we consider the tremendous adherence within this group to imagery that links the elite of Anatolia directly to Achaemenid imperial iconography. The seals thus become a citation of power and authority, an affirmation of connections between the elite across the empire expressed in a visual performance linked to the new regime and its supporters. And the great beauty of the seals themselves suggests that they were meant to be seen as well as used, that theirs was a message to be proclaimed aloud. Indeed, their elegance certainly played a role in indicating and internalizing the new language of authority.[164]

The conclusion I draw from this is that the question "how do you signal membership in the Achaemenid elite?" was one to which a limited range of answers existed, although there was room for personal choice and taste. That is, this was a matter in which the Achaemenid authority had a vested interest. Indeed, it was an important question: co-opting local elites in order to make them feel cohesion with and loyalty to a new and different body (the new imperial administration) was no doubt a complicated matter. It was of consequence, if the political transformations that accompanied Achaemenid conquest were to have a lasting positive effect on local social structures.

Members of the Anatolian elite persistently chose to have their seals carved with Achaemenid court imagery. There was not one prescriptive style in which seals might be carved, but rather people chose from a visually distinctive group of related styles from which people might choose. This cohesion of iconography with expression in a variety of related styles, overtly signaling membership in the new polyethnic elite, demonstrates the care and concern the new authority felt for unified power and collusion.

Messages of Authority and Style among Non-Elites

The situation in Gordion during the time of Achaemenid hegemony was very different from that in Sardis or Dascylium, and its seals offer insights into a cross section of seal owners, ranging from those with very high status seals to others.[165] In the Achaemenid period, the use of seals at the site exploded. During the time of the Achaemenid Empire, fully twenty-nine seals and impressions were left at Gordion in deposits that have been uncovered by archaeologists – a tremendous increase over earlier numbers.[166] Unlike the earlier eras at Gordion, when the few seals found were crafted largely from local materials, during the Achaemenid period the stuff of which the seals were made is remarkably varied. Materials include glass, bone, ivory, agate, lapis lazuli, chalcedony, faience, rock crystal, meerschaum, and more. They come from all over, from as far east as Afghanistan and as far south as Egypt, from the wildly banded agate found near Sardis and from the heartland of the Achaemenid Empire itself. Given the mobility of craftspeople, patrons, and seals, we cannot say how many of these artifacts were created at Gordion itself, but no doubt some were imported.[167] The iconography that decorated the Achaemenid-period seals was as diverse as the materials available for use. Instead of the striations and nondescript imagery that characterize some of the sealstones from the pre–Achaemenid period and many of those from the post–Achaemenid period, the seals dating to the Achaemenid period at Gordion have instantly recognizable and often highly idiosyncratic imagery.

These seals situate Gordion solidly in the middle of glyptic practice throughout the empire, without providing any evidence that they were used by the elite alone. They give an idea of an Achaemenid administration at Gordion, a taste for Achaemenid visual culture, and a sense of the tremendous increase in options available to seal users; Gordion mirrors the kind of administrative practices known from Persepolis and Susa.[168] Gordion's seals demonstrate, if anything, a wider range of materials, styles, and imagery than do the seals of the elite from Sardis. Like the Sardian seals, these draw on the visual culture of the Achaemenid heartland, but seal users at Gordion also selected seals sporting Greek, Egyptian, and other images, and their seals were made of materials including but not limited to the semiprecious stones of Sardis and İkiztepe.

The seals and sealings of Achaemenid Anatolia demonstrate the connections that bound together the Achaemenid elite at its governing centers. They

40. Seals from Gordion. After Dusinberre 2005.

also demonstrate the strong impact of Achaemenid hegemony on second-tier cities in the empire. The number and variety of seals at Gordion show that its inhabitants took to using seals with verve, and they seem to have incorporated many aspects of Achaemenid administrative practice into their lives. The number and types of seals at Sardis and İkiztepe show that the ruling elite were using seals to effect the practices of Achaemenid administration in ways that indicated their internalization of the new visual language of authority. Elite authority is demonstrated in practice by the impressions of Dascylium's archive. The seals of Anatolian sites underscore some of the differences between their roles in the empire. But the seals also demonstrate the extent to which Achaemenid governing practices and ideologically charged iconography pervaded the empire.

Coins

An essential aspect of governance in Anatolia concerned minted money. Coins are objects with ideological as well as practical significance, widely disseminated, and of particular importance in Anatolia because of their potential impact on Greeks.[169] Although Lydia and some Greek city-states of Ionia certainly used minted coins earlier, the Achaemenid Empire contributed tremendously to the monetization of Anatolia.[170] Silver and bronze coins circulated widely by the end of the Achaemenid period, with mints in western and southern Anatolia particularly active (see Table 3). These coins and their gold counterparts were apparently used primarily to pay the military, and perhaps to contribute to taxes.[171] Their distribution and the wear they show demonstrate that the less valuable coins, at any rate, entered the public economy and served as a medium for exchange.

The most familiar coins of the Achaemenid Empire are the imperial issues, gold darics and silver sigloi. These coins bear on the obverse an image of a figure wearing the Persian court robe and dentate crown, carrying a bow and sometimes other weapons. The coins are hence generally designated "archers."[172] How well Achaemenid coins functioned as recognized signifiers of the Persian king's might is clear from Greek sources. When the Spartan Agesilaus withdrew from the Troad in 394, he is said by a very late source to have claimed he was driven from Asia by the king's thirty thousand archers.[173] It is the king's *gold* archers to which he refers, used by Artaxerxes II to foment revolt in Greece against Sparta.

The significance of the archer coins probably reflects more than the ideological importance of the bow in the Achaemenid assessment of virtue, as discussed in Chapter 7.[174] The earliest type of archer coin minted clearly suggests the idea of a *divine* figure holding a bow: only the upper half of the figure is portrayed, emerging from a crescent. The format recalls earlier Assyrian portrayals of the god Assur and contemporary Achaemenid images of Ahuramazda on seals and wall reliefs.[175] And yet the crenellated crown worn by the figure links him to representations of the king in an almost symbiotic association. The figure represents an image of divine kingship, in this case founded not in ancient Mesopotamian iconography but in the imperial ideology of the Achaemenids themselves.

In the fourth century the production of silver sigloi petered out; apparently these coins were increasingly replaced in western Anatolia by what have been considered issues by local satraps.[176] I believe that these new coins are not the result of growing satrapal independence and the establishment of new local satrapal mints, but instead conform to the symbolic import of the original sigloi. They bear an imperial statement of conflated kingship and divinity, like the other imperial issues, but couched in stylistic terms that would have increased their impact on local audiences. Thus they demonstrate continued governance of Anatolia in ways that bound the imperial administration together, serving as reiterations of imperial authority in their message as well as local autonomy in the artistic vocabulary used to express that message. A case study will serve to make this point: the "tiarate head" coins.

The so-called tiarate head series were silver and bronze coins minted in western Anatolia in the fifth and especially fourth centuries.[177] These coins bear on their obverse a bearded head, usually in profile, wearing the so-called tiara, or "Median" headgear, a soft cap with side and back flaps – the headgear a Persian warrior would wear into battle.[178] The style of the head is subtly modeled and highly veristic, with intricate plastic volumes showing the folds of the headgear

Table 3. Mints of Achaemenid Anatolia

Lydia	*Hellespontine Phrygia*	*Pamphylia*
Sardis	Abydus	Aspendus
	Achilleion (ca. 400–330)	Olbia
Ionia	Antandrus	Side
Clazomenae	Assus	
Colophon	Cebren	*Pisidia*
Ephesus	Dardanus	Etenna (ca. 400–330)
Erythrae	Gargara	Selge (ca. 400–330)
Leuce (ca. 400–330)	Gentinus (ca. 400–330)	
Magnesia ad Maeandrum	Gergis (ca. 400–330)	*Lycia*
Miletus	Hamaxitus (ca. 400–330)	Lycia
Naulochus (ca. 400–330)	Lamponeia	Phaselis
Phocaea	Neandria	
Phygela (ca. 400–330)	Ophrynium (ca. 400–330)	*Caria*
Priene (ca. 400–330)	Rhoeteium (ca. 400–330)	Astyra
Smyrna (ca. 400–330)	Scamandria (ca. 400–330)	Caunus (5th and 4th c.)[a]
Teos	Scepsis	Chersonesus (ca. 550–500)
Chios	Sigeium (ca. 400–330)	Cnidus
Samos	Thymbra (ca. 400–330)	Halicarnassus
	Zeleia (ca. 400–330)	Iasus (ca. 400–330)
Aeolis	Tenedos	Idyma
Autocane (ca. 400–330)		Lydae (ca. 400–330)
Cyme	*Bithynia*	Mylasa (satrapal issues)
Elaea	Astacus (5th c.)	Termera (only Archaic period)
Larissa Phriconis	Calchedon	Cos
Myrina (ca. 400–330)	Heracleia Pontica	Megiste (ca. 400–330)
Temnus (ca. 400–330)		Nisyros (ca. 400–330)
Tisna (ca. 400–330)	*Paphlagonia*	Camirus Rhodi (5th c.)
	Cromna	Ialysus Rhodi (5th c.)
Mysia	Sinope	Lindus Rhodi (5th c.)
Adramytteum (ca. 400–330)		Rhodes (ca. 400–330)[b]
Atarneus (ca. 400–330)	*Pontus*	Telos (ca. 400–330)
Cisthene (ca. 400–330)	Amisus (ca. 400–330)	
Cyzicus	Trapezus (ca. 400–330)	
Gabrium (ca. 400–330)		
Iolla (ca. 400–330)	*Cilicia*	
Lampsacus	Aphrodisias	
Parium	Celenderis	
Pergamum	Holmi (ca. 400–330)	
Pitane (ca. 400–330)	Issus (ca. 400–330)	
Placia (ca. 400–330)	Mallus	
Proconnesus (ca. 400–330)	Nagidus	
Teuthrania (ca. 400–330)	Soli	
Thebe (ca. 400–330)	Tarsus	

[a] Caunus's inclusion here is substantiated by Head, but based primarily on Konuk 1998.
[b] The coinage of Rhodes replaced the coinages of Camirus, Ialysus, and Lindus.
I am grateful to Henry Colburn, graduate student at the University of Michigan, for providing this table. Compiled from Head 1911.

41. Tiarate head coins. After Dusinberre 2003b.

and the configuration of facial muscles, and with great attention to detail in the carving of beards and eyes as well as long aquiline noses. It is a style that is essentially Greek.

The coins have often been called portraits, either of specific Persian kings or of the Persian satraps or local dynasts responsible for their issuing.[179] But these assignations are erroneous.[180] The heads are not portraits of specific individuals, but rather represent a composite of features in a general stereotyped image; in the words of one scholar, they are "more or less hellenized images of oriental rulers, idealized to almost divine dignity."[181] The heads on the tiarate coins represent generalizing and idealized portrayals of a Persian in military garb.[182] Unlike the archer coins, the tiarate head coins bear a figural reverse instead of a simple incuse punch. Some include on their reverse motifs of particular Greek cities – for instance, the owl of Athens or the kithara of the Chalcidicians.[183] But whereas the coins show the motifs of Greek cities, they are inscribed in Greek "of the King." The imagery, the style of carving, and the language of inscription leave little room for doubt that the intended audience of the coins was Greek.

The obverse of these coins conveys a message parallel to that of the coins they replaced. Sigloi and darics showed a figure representing both kingship and divinity, carrying his bow and spear far forth from the Persian heartland. On the tiarate head coins, too, we see a militant Persian figure. The Apadana reliefs at Persepolis show the peoples of the realm bearing significant gifts to the king. In particular, examples of the military costume are prominently – almost emphatically – displayed in the procession. This costume seems to have served specifically as a symbol of the king as warrior.[184] The same image is seen on the reliefs of the Nereid Monument in Xanthus, Lycia, in an Anatolian context (see Chapter 5). Just as weaponry was an important symbol of kingship, the military costume was significant. On the tiarate head coins, the garment is particularly charged. In addition to its symbolic value, it bears particular meaning for its local audience: those small-change soldiers on the edges of the empire who actually *saw* the king would have seen him as a warrior.

42. Athenian tetradrachm and tiarate head coin. After Dusinberre 2003b.

The coins also bear meaning within the imperial visual program of power and iconography. Repeatedly in Achaemenid art, images with age-old divine significance are altered so that the figure of a god is replaced by that of the king.[185] These coins take a Greek portrayal of godhead and replace it with the head of the Persian king; on Greek issues, a head on the obverse of an issue is always that of a deity. The heads of the tiarate coins are carved in a fully Greek style on the obverse of coins and are a numismatic emblem used in Greek contexts only to display gods. They show the head of kingship, associated with divinity by allusion to heads on Greek coins.

The significance of the tiarate head coins is intricate. The coins portray the king as warrior, reinforcing the relation of viewers to imperial authority. At the same time, they appropriate the iconography and artistic style of the Greek sphere to equate king with god. They are not portraits of a specific local governor, nor do they indicate rejection of imperial authority or an act of rebellion and assertion of sovereignty over regions of Anatolia. Instead, these coins represent a manipulation of visual culture to bear a complex message of authority. They form part of a consistent program of the Achaemenid kings to appropriate and rework local visual traditions to equate kingship with the divine, an imperial system of images built on local artistic environments.

Co-opting the Local Elite

It was not just satraps who created authority. An important part of governing Anatolia involved folding the local elite into the new regime. It is not clear how the Achaemenid administration first brought about the remarkable cohesion of the elite, but the consistency of manner in which people demonstrated their membership in the polyethnic elite of Achaemenid Anatolia – the consistency of portable elite culture – is striking. As will be explored in depth in subsequent chapters, the elite signaled their status in a great variety of ways: their clothing, their drinking and dining behaviors and apparatus, the imagery and style of their personal sealstones, the size and kind of mortuary structures

43. Proskynesis before the king, from Persepolis. P57121. Courtesy of the Oriental Institute of the University of Chicago.

they constructed and the nature of their mortuary inclusions, their adoption of Persianizing equipment like horse trappings and behaviors like public greetings, the gifts they exchanged to cement relations among one another, even architectural power statements. The meaning and significance of these behaviors led to great continuity across Anatolia.

In some instances, ethnic Persians themselves may have formed the elite. Nick Sekunda argued in 1988 that three large landowning families (his "dukedoms") in Hellespontine Phrygia were ethnically Persian and suggested that analogous social structures were to be found elsewhere in western Anatolia as well.[186] Although some evidence, such as the Sacrilege Inscription from Ephesus discussed in Chapters 6 and 7, demonstrates that names of a given ethnic background need not indicate that same ethnicity on the part of their holders, Sekunda's is a plausible scenario given what we know of landholding in Persia and of imperial colonization and consolidation in general. Historical texts provide clear evidence that Persians employed local elite leaders to govern and control regions of Anatolia, however, including Pythius of Lydia in the mid–sixth century and Zenis and Mania in the Troad late in the fifth.[187] Indeed, the very mix of ethnicities in the names of the Sacrilege Inscription demonstrates a mingling of ideas and sharing of cultural aspects across ethnicity in this part of Anatolia, as will be explored later.

Certain public behaviors in addition to dining, dressing, and displaying or using seals (all to be discussed in subsequent chapters) set the Achaemenid elite apart. Herodotus's famous description of Persians meeting in the streets (1.134) gives us an inkling of the sorts of behaviors for which we are missing evidence in the archaeological record: equals kiss each other on the mouth, near equals kiss on the cheek, and one of greatly inferior rank performs proskynesis to (i.e., kisses his own hand before) one of higher rank.[188] Such patterns of social behavior and clear differentiation of status would have been important in creating a bond between members of the elite.

44. The king's horses and a Skudrian (?) horse to show the right hand, from Persepolis. Note the difference in size and conformation of the horses, as well as the trappings and hairstyles. P28975, PS-65. Courtesy of the Oriental Institute of the University of Chicago.

Archaeological material provides insight into one highly visible elite indicator: horsemanship. The value placed in the Achaemenid period on fine horses, their breeding, training, and handling, was tremendous.[189] Margaret Miller has recently assembled evidence for Persian horsemanship in western Anatolia.[190] She has demonstrated that in addition to cosmetic changes in hairdressing (such as leaving forelocks and tails long but tied up to stay out of the way), rectangular saddle cloths and a new sort of bitted bridle were adopted during the Achaemenid period, as was the practice of guiding the horse in hand with one arm across the withers.[191] The archaeological discovery at Deve Hüyük of bronze bits and a horse bell of Persian type shows that the adoption of Persian equine practices and accoutrements was not limited to the western regions of the peninsula.[192]

These are not all ornamental expressions, designed to make someone look au courant; they had significant practical importance. The bridles and bits introduced to Anatolia in the Achaemenid period would provide the rider with tremendous control over the horse, particularly when combined with the positioning of head and neck shown in visual renditions. In marked contrast to Greek horses, these arch their necks over, bringing their noses to the vertical.[193] Such use of the forequarters enables the horse's back and abdominal muscles to engage more fully, letting it position its haunches deeper under itself and load more of its weight onto its hind legs. This allows a rider to control and employ the power of the hindquarters for stopping, starting, turning, or jumping – useful during a hunt or in battle. It also changes the pressure of the bit against the horse's jawbones, permitting more meaningful use of the reins and more subtle clues to the horse given through a rider's seat and legs rather than hands. This in turn frees up the hands, so that a rider can wield a sword or a spear effectively from horseback while communicating fully with a responsive mount. The bridles and bits of the Persians, combined with the training given their steeds in using their bodies, would have allowed them great control over the animals.

It is no wonder that this aspect of elite behavior was adopted enthusiastically by the men of Achaemenid Anatolia.[194]

Royal Gifts

With these aspects of elite behavior in mind, the nature of objects attested in the literary record as royal gifts takes on particular meaning. It was precisely in the areas of dining, dressing, and riding that gifts were most frequently made, in addition to revenues from tracts of land. Gifts were notable for their visibility as well as for the role they might play in social behavior. Royal gifts marked a recipient as valued, provided overt and recognizable signifiers of elite status, and ensured that the recipient behaved in a manner consonant with the Achaemenid elite. They were simultaneously a mark of favor and an avenue of social control.

Ostentatious gifting and display of gifts formed an essential part of communication between the king and elites, as well as among elites themselves.[195] This key element of Achaemenid social interaction has been much discussed, and its importance cannot be stressed too strongly.[196] I wish to touch on just a few aspects of the phenomenon here that relate closely to the Achaemenid elite in Anatolia.

Xenophon says of Cyrus the Great's gift giving (surely based on his own observations of Cyrus the Younger):

> Though he far exceeded all other men in the amount of the revenues he received, yet he excelled still more in the quantity of presents he made. It was Cyrus, therefore, who began the practice of lavish giving (*polydoria*), and among the kings it continues even to this day. For who has richer friends (*philoi*) to show than the Persian king? Who is there that is known to adorn his friends with more beautiful robes than does the king? Whose gifts are so readily recognized as some of those which the king gives, such as bracelets, necklaces, and horses with gold-studded bridles? For, as everybody knows, no one over there is allowed to have such things except those to whom the king has given them.[197]

This is quite a statement. Not only does the king accrue social capital from his gift giving, but his gifts are readily recognized even by those who did not witness the event. Thus the recipient also gains status through the favor granted him by the king. Greek authors agree that dress, jewelry, and bridles were recognizable royal gifts, and to these indicators of status we can add drinking cups of precious metal and dress weaponry.[198] Gifts might be used by their recipients in significant ways: early in the fourth century an Athenian named Demus who had received a gold drinking cup from the king expected to be able to use this mark of royal favor to gain "lavish hospitality and endless credit" across the empire.[199]

Pierre Briant offers a concise overview of dress and jewelry as royal gifts, with reference to further elite gift giving:

> Robes and jewelry are archetypal royal gifts frequently attested in the record. Xenophon's Cyrus often resorts to them. Before a major parade, he distributes Median robes to "those of the Persians and of the allies who held office.... And when he had distributed among the noblest the most beautiful garments, he brought out other Median robes, for he had had a great many made, with no stint of purple or sable or red or scarlet or crimson cloaks," in such a way that in turn those close to him distributed them to their friends (*Cyr.* 8.3.1–3). It seems clear that the different colors referred to a hierarchy defined by the king (cf. 8.1.40): some jobs at the central court carried the right (and no doubt the obligation) to wear special robes (Plutarch, *Alex.* 18.8 [*astandes*]). It is no less clear that wearing them permitted the recipients to vaunt themselves above other Persians. Thus Mithradates, overwhelmed with gifts after the battle of Cunaxa, never appeared in public without the robe and jewelry that Artaxerxes gave him. Hence this reflection by a eunuch – at once ironic, envious, and provocative: "A magnificent dress indeed, O Mithradates, is this which the king has given you; the chains and bracelets are glorious, and your scimitar (*akinakes*) of invaluable worth; how happy has he made you, the object of every eye!" (Plutarch, *Art.* 15.2). Likewise Artapates, the most faithful of Cyrus the Younger's scepter-bearers, "had a dagger (*akinakes*) of gold, and he also wore a necklace and bracelets and all the other ornaments that the noblest (*aristoi*) Persians wear; for he had been honoured by Cyrus (*etimeto hypo Kyrou*) because of his affection and fidelity" (Xen., *Anab.* 1.8.29). In Persian eyes, in fact, these robes and jewels were not baubles; they were the resplendent marks of the king's favor granted to them in return for services rendered. Wearing these ornaments meant accession to the rank of Persians most esteemed by the king.[200]

As Margaret Root has shown, "Median robes" are the garments worn by men on horseback in hunting and warfare.[201] Thus the gifts that might be given by the king, and as Briant suggests exchanged also by the elite, were highly visible and instantly recognizable. They held inherent value, but it was their social value on which Greek commentators focused – not just the fact that a silver dish weighed a Babylonian talent, but that it came overtly as a gift from on high.[202]

The Achaemenid authority made explicit use of gifts to solidify allegiance to the king and signify membership in the Achaemenid elite. The nature of these gifts was linked to behavioral patterns that defined the elite. For such gifts to be given, accepted, and used publicly in the correct ways both reiterated and reified active participation in the upper echelons of Achaemenid authority. In this way gift giving became a powerful tool in the peaceable and perpetuated governance of Achaemenid Anatolia.

Summary

It is clear from the discussion in this chapter that the kind of evidence concerning Achaemenid governing practices in Anatolia varies from region to region. Some areas provide archaeological material but nothing textual. Some aspects of behavior are attested only in the literary record. With such lack of evenness in the evidence, the consistent picture we gain of Achaemenid governance is all the more remarkable. The authority–autonomy model allows us to see this uniformity clearly. Under the umbrella of Achaemenid authority, regions were allowed significant autonomy in particular expressions of governance. Thus the wealthy provinces of Lydia and Cilicia were treated quite differently in terms of the role the central authority played in appointing local leaders, at least until Cilicia – like Lydia before it – showed signs of supporting revolt. At this point, central Achaemenid authority was more strictly enforced. Authority was strongly wielded in the political sphere if a province was held to be potentially dangerous. If like Hellespontine Phrygia or fourth-century Caria a region remained consistently loyal to the central administration, it was granted such great autonomy that its rulers could forge local dynasties for themselves and their families.

This balance between the concerns of the central authority and its willingness to grant local autonomy is seen repeatedly in the evidence concerning the governance of Anatolia. The newly built architecture of imperial power at Dascylium links local expressions to architectural formats in the Persian heartland. Altıntepe's architecture of authority demonstrates the co-option of the old by the new. Both emphasized imperial ability to move goods and craftspeople around, even as the buildings that housed overarching imperial authority drew on visual expressions of Anatolian elite masculinity for their embellishment.

Altogether, it is clear that the central Achaemenid authority allowed significant regional autonomy in local Anatolian governance so long as the central authority was appropriately respected and kept firmly in mind. Certain aspects of life showed real continuity from one place to another; thus buildings of administrative power might be expressed in a local idiom or not, but were linked to architectural models in Fars. The road system with its new level of consolidated infrastructure and the tribute structure would similarly have served as permanent reminders of Achaemenid authority. Record-keeping and seal-carving practices demonstrate the introduction of a more complex economic system, tracked according to new administrative techniques that required responsibility and accountability on the part of both individuals and offices. The wholehearted co-option of the elite, which involved their adoption of newly articulated behaviors and expressions, was considered to be essential in governance, it seems, on the basis of similarities that define those expressions across the peninsula and the lack of variability allowed. Indeed, as the rest of this book seeks to articulate, Achaemenid Anatolia demonstrates a delicate balance between authority and autonomy, the latter allowed whenever and wherever it did not conflict with the needs of the central administration.

THREE

CONTROLLING ANATOLIA, GUARDING THE EMPIRE

Evidence concerning the Achaemenid military in Anatolia is widespread and includes both literary and archaeological sources. This chapter begins with a discussion of military authority, imagining what one would expect to find as a result of extensive centralized military power and then considering the evidence to see whether it confirms that expectation. Greek and other literary sources reveal some aspects of the organization and deployment of the Achaemenid military, especially in western Anatolia. Excavated remains at the satrapal sites Sardis and Dascylium, the garrison site Meydancıkkale, and the watchtower site Şahankaya provide a look at the military from a wholly different perspective. A consideration of the cemetery at Deve Hüyük affords insight into those individuals who manned the military centers. An overview of other excavated sites in Anatolia and the empire as a whole provides context, while the catalogue of Achaemenid military sites in Anatolia at the end of the chapter will, I hope, be of use as a research tool.

The two things that have perhaps mattered most to any imperial authority are (1) preempting or suppressing revolts and (2) collecting taxes on time and in full. The absorption and conversion of local elites in Achaemenid Anatolia described in the preceding chapter, a co-option of hearts and minds in tandem with an imperial administrative structure and infrastructure, would have been helpful in both respects. Another feature of the Achaemenid Empire that no doubt played a role was the existence of a standing army.

A standing army creates challenges. These include logistical ones: providing food, weapons, and horses or vehicles and securing communication within and among military sites. They also include deeper ones: ensuring that the soldiers' primary loyalty is to their brothers-in-arms and the commanding authority rather than to the local populace. Thus soldiers in modern times, like diplomats,

Empire, Authority, and Autonomy in Achaemenid Anatolia

45. Sites of Achaemenid military authority in Anatolia. Courtesy Karl Mueller.

are generally moved frequently to ensure that the people with whom they have the closest ties are their own comrades. Their loyalty is remunerated by the primary controlling authority. Because of the high cost, only some troops are on a constant pay list, while additional trained soldiers are kept as reserves. And a single cohort of soldiers is often made up of people from different geographic origins to help reduce the likelihood that they will feel stronger allegiances to each other than to the commanding authority.

When soldiers are moved from one place to another, it is key that they be able to operate as fully functional warriors immediately upon arrival. They cannot be granted three weeks to get their feet under them and find their way around. Culture shock is not an option. One method for keeping soldiers operational despite frequent moves is to standardize military locations. Thus U.S. Air Force bases share similarities, not only within a country but from one country to another: soldiers know roughly what they will find at a new base and roughly where to find it.[1] Some societies, like the Roman Empire under Trajan or Hadrian, took this approach to great heights: standardized fort layouts provided military unity and eased soldiers' transitions from one place to another.

In Achaemenid Anatolia, I would anticipate the following. The imperial administration's need to prevent and/or suppress revolts, as well as its need for a mighty arm to back up its demands for taxes, would necessitate a standing army. Its soldiers would have to be responsible to and feel primary loyalty to the king himself rather than to local governors or others who might take advantage of soldiers' loyalty to them to incite an insurrection. Because maintaining a large standing army is very expensive, I would expect a core group of regular soldiers under central imperial control, with other (less formidable?) troops supported by local administrations; I might expect certain garrisoned troops on permanent pay and a thinly spread reserve that could be called up in case of need. The soldiers would have to be moved at times, to retain their loyalty to each other and the king instead of to local individuals. In order for these soldiers to retain full deployment capacity at very short notice in new locations, garrison sites would have to share certain features, so that soldiers would quickly feel at ease. Thus if this initial line of thinking is correct, I would expect to find recognizable Achaemenid-period garrisons that demonstrated at least some degree of standardization.

Four things, then, follow as logical military corollaries to this top-down aspect of the authority–autonomy model:

1. evidence for troops with direct loyalty to the top authority;
2. a standing force and a reserve, probably differentiated in terms of pay, weaponry, and living conditions;
3. evidence for standing troops being moved around or serving in areas other than their native lands; and
4. at least some continuity of form among garrison sites.

All of these turn out, indeed, to be the case in Achaemenid Anatolia.

The Military in Achaemenid Anatolia

Jutting above the hills of north central Lydia is the double-peaked rock outcrop of Şahankaya.[2] Nearby tumuli demonstrate Achaemenid-period occupation in the vicinity, and a slingshot bullet inscribed with the name of Tissaphernes demonstrates a military importance for the site by the late fifth or early fourth century. Fortification walls at Şahankaya were previously thought to be Hellenistic, but the most recent study of the site puts them earlier, into the late Achaemenid period.[3] A fourth-century (?) watchtower with a base roughly 8 m square dominates the highest point of the site and provides a visual catchment of the entire surrounding area of northern Lydia; "its intervisibility with Sardis and many other points in central and northern Lydia make it a very strategic place."[4] One curious feature, cut from bedrock on the top of the fortified stronghold but not at its highest point, is a square plinth roughly 2 m across and 30 cm tall, supporting a rounded protrusion of stone topped by a shallow basin; this has been called a "Persian-style fire altar."[5] A military outpost on a high rocky outcrop, Şahankaya commands the surrounding area and probably could communicate with other strategic points. Walled and with a watchtower, showing evidence of occupation and military use, the site provides a backdrop for the following discussion of Achaemenid military authority in Anatolia. We will return to it in greater detail later.

Textual Resources

Although Greek and other sources frequently mention Achaemenid soldiers and garrisons in Anatolia, two passages in Xenophon provide us with the most information for understanding the types and duties of military garrisons.[6] One of them (*Cyr.* 8.6.1–15) purports to describe Cyrus's institution of an imperial system after his conquest of Babylon. The other (*Oec.* 4.5–11) describes the organization of authority in the Persian military. It is not clear which text Xenophon wrote first, but together they give a sense of a landscape with fortified spots that housed soldiers and a thin but pervasive presence of troops on the ground throughout inhabited rural areas. These men thus essentially fall into two categories: standing troops and reserves.

The most important discussion of the Xenophon texts summarizes the relevant points of the *Cyropaedia* passage:

1. The existing situation, when Cyrus defeated Babylon in 539, was that there were soldiers (*phrouroi*) in the defeated cities (*poleis*) whose job was to protect the walls (*teikhe*);
2. Cyrus now proposes to send satraps to the defeated peoples (*ethne*);
3. The situation will then be that each group (*ethnos*) contains:
   (i) satraps
   (ii) various military forces 'belonging to the King,' described thus:
      (a) soldiers and leaders (*phrourarchs*) in the high places (*akrai*) and leaders (*chiliarchs*) of the guards in the surrounding areas (*hoi kata khoran phylakes*);
      (b) 'the guards (*phylakai*) in the high places (*akrai*) are the King's and the leaders (*chiliarchs*) of the guards (*phylakai*) are established by the King (*ek basileos*) and are registered with the King (*para basilei apogegrammenoi*)';
4. The satrap's duties include:
   (i) paying wages (*misthos*) to the soldiers (*phrouroi*),
   (ii) organizing cavalry and chariot forces from the Persians and allies,
   (iii) protecting the residents.[7]

There is no evidence that Cyrus himself organized such a scheme, but Xenophon says explicitly that he based his account on the system familiar to him at the end of the fifth century after his experiences in Anatolia.[8] It can be characterized as follows.

By the end of the fifth century, two distinct tiers of military authority existed. The king held ultimate authority, with direct control over two discrete groups of forces: soldiers and officers who were positioned in large numbers on defensible high places and officers in control of guards over the surrounding low-lying areas. These soldiers and officers were directly responsible to the king and registered as part of a military list kept by the king. Xenophon does not tell us to whom the guards in the low-lying territories were responsible, just that their officers answered to the king; he states explicitly that the soldiers concentrated in high places, like their officers, were the king's.[9] The passage has additionally been interpreted as suggesting garrisons of infantry on the inner citadels of walled cities, as well as (previously unfortified) defensible high places outside preexisting city walls.[10] Thus garrisoned troops and all major officers gave their loyalty directly to the king, the top tier of authority in the empire.

The second tier of authority, comprising the satraps, was responsible for paying the king's troops and the guards, for organizing those polyethnic troops who worked with horses, and for protecting those who lived in their own territories. The satrap paid the military's wages, perhaps drawn as a charge on his province's tribute.[11] In addition to recompensing the infantry positioned on high rocky places, a satrap had to pay and organize the horsed auxiliaries. These mounted troops played a key role in Achaemenid military control, not least because of their speed; horses need a significant amount of forage, so their dispersal through a wider area not only would have spread swift-footed military might, but would have had the practical effect of making it easier to feed them.[12]

Thus far we see a clear separation: like the guards and the troops, the satrap was loyal to the king. He was responsible for paying the wages of those troops. Presumably their responsibility to him is seen in the final part of the Xenophon passage: they helped him protect the local inhabitants in case of need (and provided the implicit threat of force necessary to collect taxes from those same inhabitants?). They clearly had the discretion not to obey the satrap's orders if they suspected him of insurrection, as shown by the elaborate sequence of subterfuges undertaken by Cyrus the Younger when he wished to lead troops against the newly enthroned Artaxerxes II.[13] Thus the satrap had some degree of autonomous authority over the troops, backed up by the fact that it was he who paid them and supported further by his role in putting together some of the troops himself.

Xenophon's *Oeconomicus* 4.5–11 adds nuance.[14] It has three sections: 5–7 (military dispositions), 8–9 (agricultural dispositions), and 9–11 (separation of commands). Xenophon establishes the king's concern with both agricultural and military matters and comments that separate officials exist for each; he suggests the king ensures that the land as a whole is protected by soldiers who are maintained thanks to successful cultivation of that same land. He differentiates between two types of military men: soldiers (*phrouroi*) and those who are armed (*hoplismenoi*). The parts of the passage that concern us can be summarized as follows:

1. The King
   (a) fixes for each leader (*arkhon*) the number of cavalry, archers, slingers and those who use wicker shields (*gerrophoroi*) to whom he is to give maintenance (*trophe*) – their purpose being protection of the surrounding area (*khora*) and repulsion of invaders – and
   (b) separately from these maintains (*trephei*) acropolis garrisons.
2. The leader (*arkhon*) "to whom this has been given as a charge" provides maintenance (*trophe*) for the soldiers (*phrouroi*).

3. The King institutes annual inspections of
    (a) the mercenaries (*misthophoroi*) and
    (b) "those who are under orders to be armed" (*hois hoplisthai prostetaktai*).
4. The inspector
    (a) leaves acropolis guards where they are but
    (b) collects everyone else to the mustering place (*syllogos*).
5. The officers under scrutiny are garrison officers (*phrourarchs*), officers of the guard (*chiliarchs*) and satraps. The good ones produce the correct numbers with good weapons and horses, the bad ones neglect the soldiers (*phrouroi*) or make profit for themselves.[15]

From the duties of the inspector it emerges that high places with guards are relatively rare and restricted in nature, so that they can be surveyed quickly, whereas the units in the surrounding areas are scattered, perhaps through various localities. As Christopher Tuplin notes, "The disposition of protective troops outside major urban centres does not involve maintenance of largish, compact bodies at a handful of sites which could be as conveniently visited and assessed as were the acropoleis. Xenophon's impression of the military security of the *ethne* seems, therefore, to be based upon a small number of fortified urban centres and a widely scattered and thinly spread militia."[16] Indeed, he continues, it is "tempting to think that the *misthophoroi* are garrisons resident within city-acropoleis whose only remuneration is their 'pay' (not necessarily all cash), while the others are groups resident in, and possessing at least the usufruct of parts of, the *khora*, though also in receipt of *trophe* – a distinction between straightforward mercenary garrisons and military communities."[17]

No evidence exists from Anatolia to elucidate how the surrounding areas and their inhabitants were supposed to maintain the troops, but Babylonian records may indicate the kind of obligations under which people served.[18] Particular sorts of communally held land allotments were required to furnish a certain number of troops, fully equipped, upon request. A similar system of government land grants on which military service was owed is attested in southern Egypt at the garrison on the island of Elephantine near Aswan and may have extended to other parts of the empire as well, including Anatolia.[19] Participating in the military could be costly; in 513, for instance, a horseman could be called up for three years and required to provide a mule and its upkeep, plus twelve light-armed men with equipment (clothing, blankets, travel bags, shoes, oil, salt, and cress).[20] Tenants of government land could take out loans, guaranteed by the usufruct of their land, to acquire the silver necessary to buy their military equipment if they did not have it on hand.[21] Or those who were wealthy enough could buy their way out of service altogether.[22]

The Aramaic documents from Elephantine do suggest that the soldiers drawing a salary, the *misthophoroi* of the Greek texts, were paid partly in kind and partly in cash.[23] They held property, sometimes in personal ownership and sometimes as land grants made to the garrison.[24] The soldiers of the garrison were considered formally distinct from the members of the city where they were stationed.[25] And although the soldiers were of various ethnicities, their highest officers were Persian.[26] Hence these documents add nuance and depth to our understanding of the situation and upkeep of garrisoned soldiers.

The land grants attested in Babylonian documentation correspond to the impression gained from Greek sources of the situation in northern and western Anatolia. Although probably neither Mysia nor Paphlagonia was a separate satrapy, both literary and epigraphic evidence attests to military establishments in these parts of Anatolia during the fifth century, a network of defensible positions and soldiers that held firm control over the land.[27] Thus the Persian Asidates had a large fortified estate in Mysia, peopled with slaves and dependents; the land around it is even described by one modern author as having been "populated with military colonists and garrisons and bristl[ing] with small forts."[28] Aeolis, too, in northwestern Anatolia, apparently included a network of small forts, commanded by the *phrourarch* of the surrounding areas in the Aeolid. Miller has suggested that increased population in the Granicus River valley in the fifth and fourth centuries as well as in the Caecus River valley, the lower Hermus, and the Maeander, may have been the result of security concerns, providing a sort of "buffer zone" for the empire. She continues, "The new concentration of sites may reflect strategic deployment of land grants, with their feudal requirement to generate troops."[29] These troops could be called up from a wide area in case of need, as demonstrated by Herodotus's description of the Persians holding land grants west of the Halys River who were mustered when the Ionians burned Sardis in 498.[30] In the Hellenistic period, the Cataonia plain in Cilicia was surrounded by garrisons (*phrouria*) on the mountains and was itself covered by a dense network of small fortified sites; although there is no good evidence concerning the Achaemenid landscape, garrisons and other forts may well have existed already.[31] We see, therefore, tracts of land cultivated by people responsible for maintaining troops that were to defend against invading armies and hold their region secure.

Further references in Xenophon and other sources elucidate another aspect of the troops: their ethnic makeup.[32] Of interest here are not the specific ethnicities of particular troops or the appearance of their arms and armor. Instead, I wish to explore the question of mobility of troops: Did they remain in one place for generations, and to whom were they loyal? Were troops who worked together of one ethnicity only, or did they come from a mix of backgrounds? What does this imply in terms of fighting strategies and communication?

The presence of Greek mercenaries in the Achaemenid army is well known. These men came from multiple city-states, including those at war or recently at war with each other, but they were expected to function as one military unit.[33] When disputes arose within the Greek division, it is possible that the men spoke and voted as separate polis blocks, but they might have functioned as individuals within the military unit. It is not clear whether the nationalities of various Greeks within the unit caused a sense of differentiation by background or allegiance within the unit, or whether they considered themselves amalgamated as ethnically "Greek" troops within the Achaemenid army in a manner that paralleled their function as a unit within that army.[34] It is clear, however, that a satrap could summon Greek mercenaries from various Greek towns (European as well as Anatolian) mustering under a Greek commander, and he could expect them to serve him as a unit in defense of Achaemenid land and authority.[35] It is also clear that satraps could move these troops around freely within their own territory and even to bordering areas, although amassing too many troops or moving too overtly toward the imperial capitals in Persia would be a cause for imperial concern. Greek commanders are attested at Mytilene, Samos, Miletus, Caunus, and Notion, as well as in Aeolis; Greek troops are mentioned in literary sources as serving at Notion, Miletus, Celaenae, and Caunus, serving in Ionian seaboard colonies, and populating Pharnabazus's "land by the sea" in Hellespontine Phrygia.[36] They were not, so far as we know, part of the established garrisons on high places. Thus these mercenary troops served away from their indigenous areas, with sworn loyalty to the king's own appointee, the satrap. They functioned as an isolable unit within a larger army, taking immediate orders from their own generals but serving under Persian commanders who were appointed by the king.

This is an important point. The highest commanders of the Persian army were, so far as we can tell, Persian.[37] Below a certain rank, commanders might be of other ethnicities. At least sometimes, the commander of a smaller group seems to have shared the ethnicity of that group, even as he reported to a higher officer who was Persian.

Evidence for the ethnicity of the garrisoned troops is problematic. Herodotus and Diodorus speak of "Persian" garrisons; the senior commanders were apparently Persian at Doriscus, Eion, Sardis, Gaza, Elephantine, and Memphis (of which only Sardis is in Anatolia).[38] The great majority of army commanders mentioned by Greek authors have Persian names, and they are often members of extensive noble families.[39] Non-Persians are rarely found as garrison commanders in Greek literature, aside from the occasional Greek, but the Elephantine papyri include company commanders with Babylonian names as well, so we should imagine a more diverse and complicated scenario than that painted by the Greek sources.[40]

There was significant ethnic mixing beyond Persians and Greeks in the Anatolian-based troops. Thus Greek sources mention Assyrians and Hyrcanians in Hellespontine Phrygia, "barbarians" in Aeolis, Carians at Caunus and Celaenae, "natives" at Syllion, Cilicians at the northern Syrian Gates, Babylonians somewhere in Asia Minor, and troops of various nationalities in Armenia.[41] Other sources demonstrate the presence in the Anatolian garrisons of Bactrians and Egyptians as well.[42]

Xenophon's description of a concentration of troops instantly available for local defense in the Caecus valley, mentioned earlier, is particularly illuminating.[43] The troops included not only forces answering to the local authority, but also Assyrian hoplites and eighty Hyrcanian cavalry – both of which he describes as "royal *misthophoroi*," or salaried soldiers – and eight hundred light-armed soldiers from Comania (the location of which is disputed), plus other troops, including cavalry.[44] Here are both tiers of the military, the wage-earning soldiers and the guards of the surrounding area, mustered within twelve hours of their summons and including people with a variety of ethnic backgrounds and fighting tactics – some of them very far indeed from their homeland.[45] The practice of moving soldiers applied to the garrison troops and may have applied to the troops in the surrounding areas as well; certainly it was a feature, in this instance, of the Achaemenid standing army.

How did these people communicate with each other? Interpreters might be employed for high-level communication – Tissaphernes had an interpreter to speak to Carian troops, while Cyrus the Younger's interpreter Pigres conveyed orders from the Persian officer to foreign undercommanders in their own languages.[46] It is possible, although I find no evidence for it, that Aramaic became widespread not only because of its use as an administrative language, but also because it had a role in military communications.[47] For now, we should probably imagine a military scene resembling polyethnic gatherings of humans in general: people mingling with those from other backgrounds, unified in a new setting that imposed shared customs, functions, schedules, expectations, living conditions, and (perhaps) diet, with the curious or linguistically gifted most likely to learn the histories of their comrades.

Communication between garrisons was a central feature of military efficiency. Achaemenid troops had multiple means to send information from one garrison to another. The Royal Road was famous for the rapidity of communication sent along it, but not all garrisoned soldiers lived near this information highway.[48] Signal fires were used to pass messages from height to height; they could summon help quickly and were used not only by formal garrisons but apparently also by those living in fortified strongholds in the surrounding areas.[49] Additional light and mirror signals were so swift in relaying news that it was said the king at his seat in Ecbatana or Susa could learn of goings-on across the empire the same day they occurred.[50] In addition, certain men were trained "in loud speaking and in breathing, and in the use of their lungs" to communicate by shouting.[51] A Hellenistic text describes aural signals that probably found their origin in the Achaemenid period:

> Although some of the Persians were distant a thirty days' journey, they all received the order on that very day, thanks to the skillful arrangement of the posts of the guard, a matter that it is not well to pass over in silence. Persia is cut by many narrow valleys and has many lookout posts that are high and close together, on which those of the inhabitants who had the loudest voices had been stationed. Since these posts were separated from each other by the distance at which a man's voice can be heard, those who received the order passed it on in the same way to the next, and then these in turn to others until the message had been delivered at the border of the satrapy.[52]

In sum, the textual evidence gives us an overarching sense of the following military makeup.[53] Anatolia was guarded by two distinct sorts of military men in the Achaemenid period. The soldiers who were garrisoned in high places, their officers, and the officers overseeing the surrounding area were all directly responsible to the king and registered by the king. Other soldiers, guarding the surrounding areas, were appointed by and presumably answerable to the local satrap (who, like the officers and soldiers of the garrisons, was appointed by and answerable to the king himself). All of these soldiers and officers were maintained by the satrap, with payment drawn from the produce of the region that they were protecting (a job for which the satrap was responsible). The soldiers garrisoned in high places drew a steady wage; those who were armed in the surrounding areas were apparently paid through some other system (probably via usufruct of the land).

We see a significant series of distinctions. Some soldiers lived in garrisons on high places, drew a steady wage, were on call and in their place continuously, and answered directly to the king. Other troops were more thinly scattered through the surrounding area, were paid in some way other than by means of a regular salary, had to be called up in order to be surveyed, and were apparently maintained by the satrap. According to Xenophon, moreover, the guards of the surrounding areas were light-armed and swift-moving troops with a wide variety of weaponry and assault tactics available; they included archers, slingers, wicker-shield bearers, cavalry, and charioteers. Xenophon describes each of these aspects in contrast to the troops in high places, so although he does not say so we may imagine that the permanently stationed soldiers were heavy-armed infantry. The other textual sources corroborate this picture.[54]

In addition to the distinctions between these formal dispositions, Greek literary sources provide clear evidence for the movement of troops. The ethnicities of soldiers are not always indicated with sufficient precision to say much; for instance, "barbarian" soldiers guarding Anatolia may have been serving in their native lands. But enough evidence exists to be certain that at least some of the

Achaemenid army served in places far removed from the soldiers' homelands. Moreover, troops within a single military jurisdiction could be drawn from multiple ethnic backgrounds.

It is therefore clear that the disposition of troops in Achaemenid Anatolia consisted of a regular standing army with direct loyalty to the king, garrisoned in high places variously distributed throughout the land, as well as auxiliaries who were held in reserve and distributed thinly through the surrounding areas.[55] Those soldiers were not always native but could be far from their places of ethnic origin; indeed, the standing army responsible for guarding a single territory was made up of troops with a variety of ethnic backgrounds. Thus from literary sources we learn that the first three military corollaries of top-down authority apply: we have evidence for troops with direct loyalty to the top authority; evidence for a standing force and a reserve, differentiated in terms of pay, weaponry, and living conditions; and evidence for troops being moved around to serve in areas other than their native lands.

Visual Resources

This brief discussion makes no attempt to catalogue all appearances of Persian warriors in the visual culture of Achaemenid Anatolia.[56] Instead I wish to remark briefly on the frequency of such depictions on portable items: seals and coins. A common representation of Persians in glyptic art reflects imperial ideology and shows the king engaged in heroic encounters with various animals or worshiping symbols of the Light.[57] When men other than the king but wearing Persian garb are shown in the figurative art of Achaemenid Anatolia, they tend to be depicted as hunters or warriors, often on horseback, often wielding or testing arrows or spears. Such representation would have borne great weight. The widespread presence of Achaemenid military authority in Anatolia ensured that people were familiar with the appearance of the Achaemenid army and explicitly Persian warriors. For a man to choose to portray himself as such via dress and other behavior was a power statement backed up by reality. It is even possible that such images were explicitly or unofficially condoned by the imperial authority.

The frequency of warrior imagery on objects of such wide circulation and visibility as coins and sealstones may have had multiple layers of meaning, layers that take on greater nuance when we recognize how few were the images of warriors slaying humans in the seal imagery of Persia itself.[58] The Anatolian figures were recognizably Achaemenid warriors. They could serve as a citation of power for an individual bearing the image on his sealstone or for the administrative authority minting the coins. They might unite the authority of government, military, and finance all in one object. They could refer to and be a reminder of a real state of affairs, the ongoing presence of Achaemenid military authority in

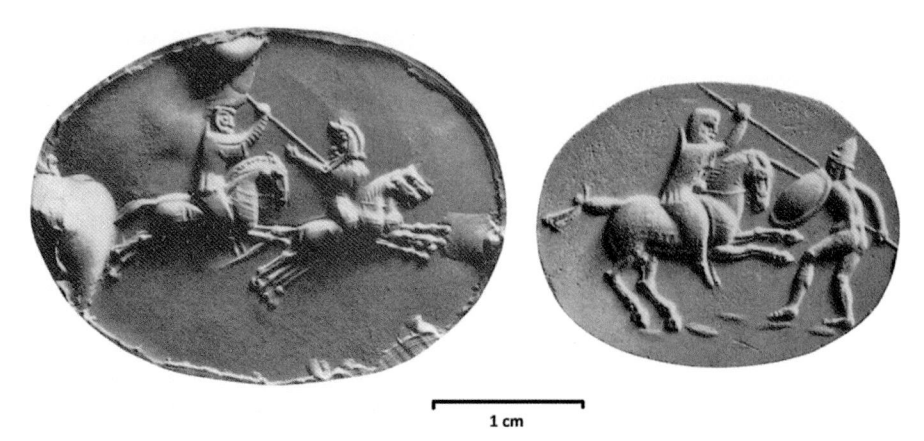

46. Warrior images on Achaemenid Anatolian–style seals. From Boardman 1970a, 2001: 882, 881. Photo R. L. Wilkins, courtesy Sir John Boardman.

Anatolia. They combine literal representations of warriors with the framework of imperial ideology that emphasizes skill in the art of weaponry.

The visual emphasis on Persians as hunters and warriors, horsed and with weapons to cast, surely has ideological as well as practical significance. Herodotus tells us that the chief proof of manliness for Persians was to be a good fighter, and the three things a Persian lad was taught were to ride, to shoot straight, and to tell the truth (see Chapter 7).[59] Indeed, it is of these very things that King Darius speaks when he claims (echoed word for word by his son Xerxes):

> As a horseman I am a good horseman. As a bowman I am a good bowman, both on foot and on horseback. As a spearman I am a good spearman, both on foot and on horseback.
>
> These are the skills which Ahuramazda has bestowed upon me and I have had the strength to bear them.[60]

The representations of Persian men as spearmen, bowmen, and horsemen in the art of Achaemenid Anatolia are charged with significance. They get at the very root of Persian manly self-image. It is no doubt because of this that they turn up so frequently in the art of death – on funeral stelae, on sarcophagi, and in tomb paintings (see Chapter 5).[61] Thus the very common portrayal of men in the garb of the Achaemenid military simultaneously reiterated Achaemenid military authority and reified Achaemenid manly virtues. For both public and private display, man-as-fighter was an essential part of the visual landscape of Achaemenid Anatolia.

Archaeological Evidence of Fortification Installations

Archaeological evidence in the form of well-preserved and neatly excavated fortified garrison sites in Anatolia that can clearly be dated to the Achaemenid period is still not common, but it is widespread and allows us to confirm and build on the picture gained from textual sources. Sites like Sardis, Dascylium, Meydancıkkale, and Şahankaya, as presented later, give us a sense of the physical aspect of the high places mentioned by Greek authors. Fortified cities and soldiers' cemeteries give us another glimpse into the military reality of Achaemenid Anatolia. And comparisons with excavated fortress or barracks sites elsewhere in the Achaemenid Empire allow us to re-create the military landscape of Anatolia to a significant extent.

Sardis

Sardis was protected in the Achaemenid period by multiple rings of walls.[62] Greek sources include information about the enormous, and partially excavated, fortification wall at various times in its history. Herodotus suggests that the walls were impregnable wherever they were guarded when Cyrus sacked Sardis; only a spectacular feat of mountaineering, scaling the steep and crumbly face of the acropolis, finally breached them.[63] At least part of the city extended beyond the fortification walls during the Achaemenid period and was therefore open to destruction by marauders such as Agesilaus;[64] one current theory suggests that the lack of extensive Achaemenid-period remains within the city walls may indicate a scattering of the population, with the exception of the garrison housed on the acropolis.[65] That acropolis was heavily fortified.

47. Western Anatolia, looking east: Sardis. Courtesy Karl Mueller.

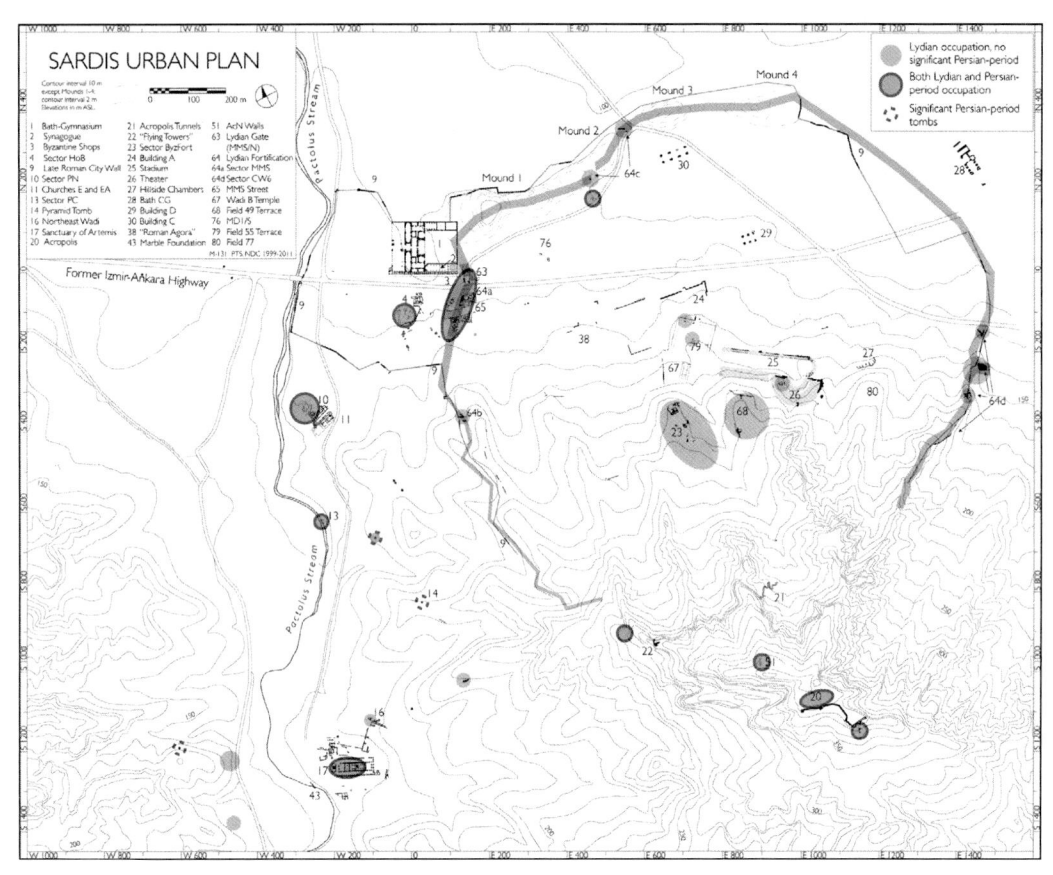

48. Sardis, sites of Achaemenid-period remains marked. © Archaeological Exploration of Sardis.

Herodotus's description of the revolt of the Lydian Pactyes, who besieged the Persian Tabalus on the acropolis of the city, demonstrates that the acropolis was fortified separately from the rest of the city at the beginning of the Achaemenid period.[66] This inner defense wall was apparently maintained, for Artaphernes successfully held the acropolis against the Ionians in 499 even though the lower city was destroyed before the reserve troops arrived from the surrounding countryside.[67] Multiple walls are also suggested by Aristotle: "The Athenians sailed with twenty ships to help the Ionians. And they marched to Sardis and took the entire area around Sardis outside the walls of the royal palace."[68] This type of city fortification, with rings of defense walls, is known from Near Eastern cities, including the Achaemenid capitals of Ecbatana and Persepolis.[69] By the time Alexander arrived at Sardis, fully three circuits of wall surrounded the garrison at its acropolis: "He climbed the acropolis where the Persian troops were garrisoned: and the place seemed secure to him, for it was very high and precipitous on all sides, and was guarded by a triple wall."[70]

The textual evidence is largely corroborated by archaeological evidence. Two sets of walls apparently in use during the Achaemenid period have been excavated at Sardis: a massive fortification around the Lydian city and further walls that served as terracing and/or fortifications on the lower slopes of the acropolis.[71] The fortifications of Sardis were enormous and carefully maintained. After the sack of the city by Cyrus, at least one of the Lydian city gates was thoroughly blocked. A stone-faced wall was constructed atop the remains of the partially destroyed Lydian mudbrick city wall along at least part of its extent, raising the height of the wall and presenting a smooth impenetrable face to potential attackers. Steeply sloping earthworks along the fortification wall and a glacis added to the defensibility of the site.

Sardis thus could serve as a safe base for launching military operations and as a citadel that might be held against insurrectionists. Its acropolis was triply fortified and served as a garrison for standing troops. That its garrison commander, Mithrenes, in consort with the local officials of Sardis, welcomed Alexander rather than trying to hold out against him was key to the Macedonian's lightning-speed success.[72] It is a pity that the rate of erosion at Sardis is such that no archaeological traces remain atop the acropolis to help us determine the disposition of its Achaemenid-period troops, but it is clear that this fortified acropolis, high above the lower city, remained defended by troops loyal to the king until the end of the Achaemenid Empire – and that the defection of the troops' leader was a key element in that end.

Dascylium

When Alexander arrived at Dascylium, the site is said to have been defended by a stronghold and a garrison.[73] The excavated remains at Dascylium demonstrate tremendous strengthening of the site in two major phases of construction during the Achaemenid period.[74] No physical evidence for a garrison has yet emerged, but the terrace wall that surrounds the mound was rebuilt in the first phase and suggests both that the habitable area grew during the Achaemenid period and that this area was defensible.[75] Thus the terrace wall both provided stable land for the increased building on the hilltop and – at least to the east and south – functioned as a defense for those raised structures. During the second phase of construction, dating perhaps to the end of the Achaemenid period, the terrace wall was extended to the southeast; it was apparently built quickly, as it incorporates blocks from as many as ten other buildings.[76] It seems that the high areas of the site, and possibly the lower town as well, were defensible. So far a lower town has not been investigated through excavation at Dascylium, although part of a large city fortification wall may have emerged to the east of the city mound.[77] This satrapal site may therefore have resembled Sardis, with a fortified acropolis defended by garrisoned troops, while the lower town was surrounded by fortifications but perhaps not defended with such vigor.

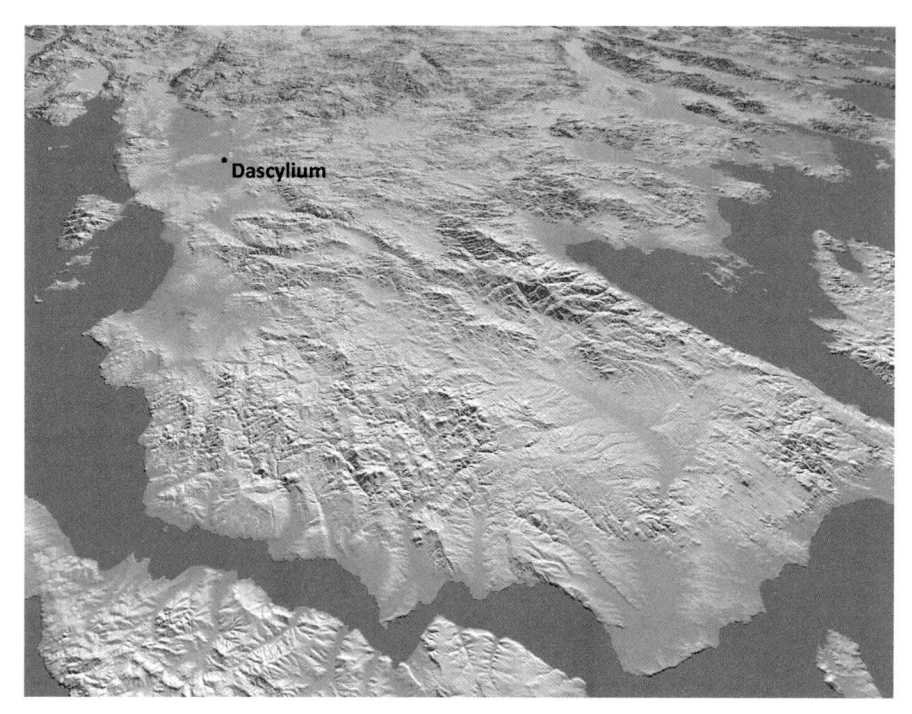

49. Northwestern Anatolia, looking southeast: Dascylium. Courtesy Karl Mueller.

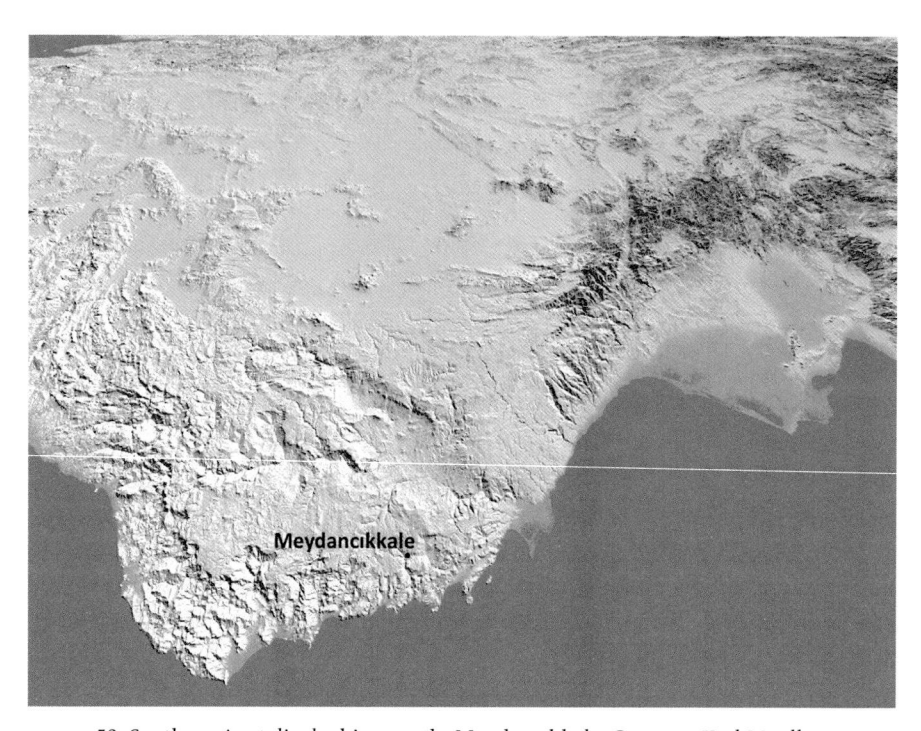

50. Southern Anatolia, looking north: Meydancıkkale. Courtesy Karl Mueller.

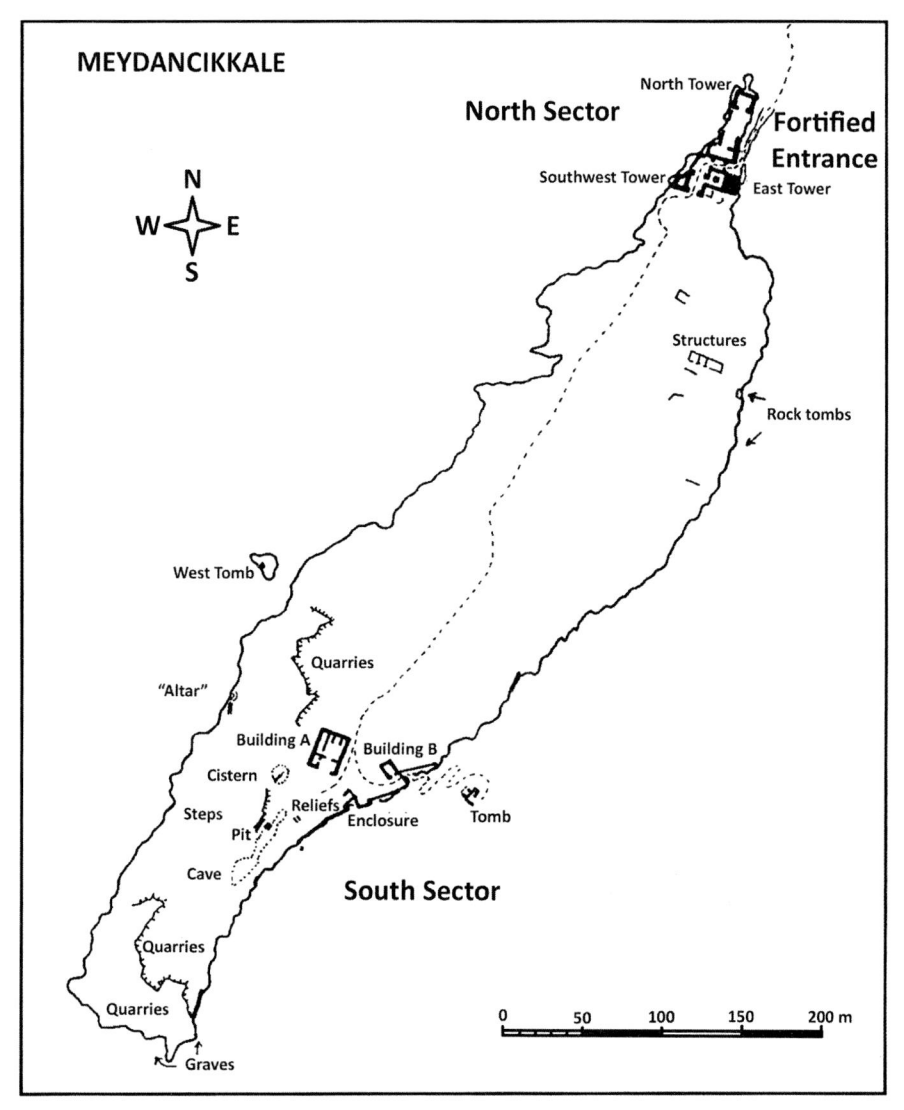

51. Meydancıkkale. Author's drawing, after Davesne and Laroche-Traunecker 1998: 19, fig. 3.

Meydancıkkale

Meydancıkkale is a fortress on a precipitous hilltop in western Cilicia, some 710 m long and 150 m across at its widest point, 710 m high, soaring above a landscape with streams rushing through steep gorges down from wooded hills and plateaus.[78] It juts above the surrounding countryside and overlooks hundreds of square kilometers. Remote from modern roads, it probably functioned as a fortified outpost from which the coast and timber-rich mountains could be patrolled.[79]

Achaemenid-period remains at Meydancıkkale are scattered; cultural deposits are rare, as each era of occupation sought firm foundations in bedrock and

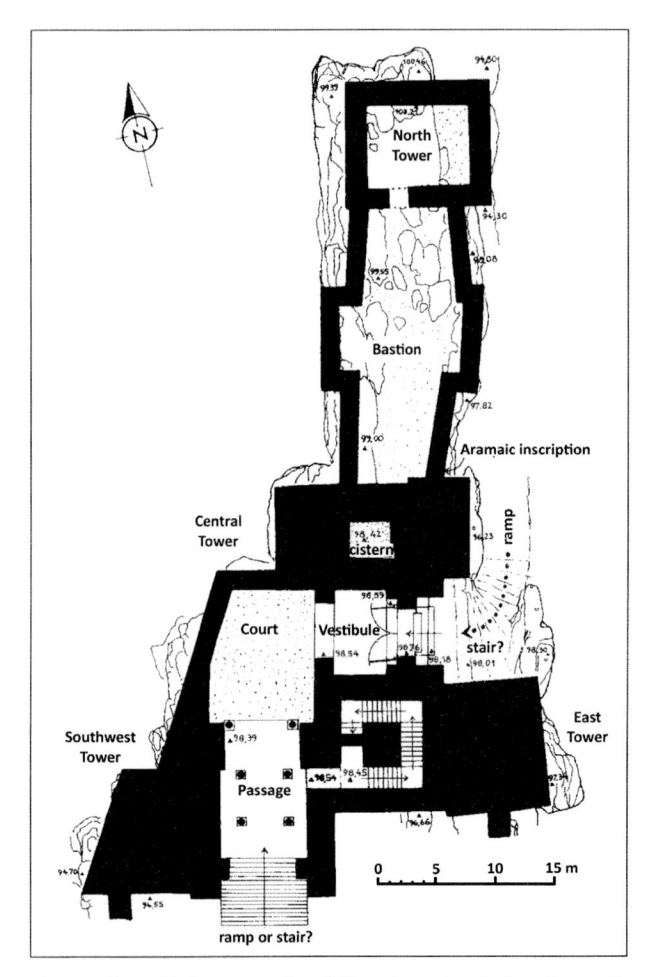

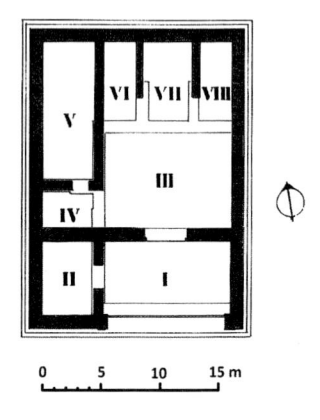

52. Meydancıkkale gate and Building A. Author's drawings, after Davesne and Laroche-Traunecker 1998: 142, fig. 20, and Davesne and Le Rider 1989: 8, fig. 2.

little was allowed to accumulate.[80] During the Achaemenid period, however, the site saw the construction of a massive fortified gate with three towers guarding its entrance, a cistern, and magazines.[81] Two Aramaic inscriptions dating to this period have been discovered; they give the ancient name of the city as KRŠBYRT, or "fortress of Kirshu," a site also named in Neo-Babylonian texts of the mid–sixth century.[82] Building A, a large and sumptuous building at the south of the site, is thought to be a Hellenistic construction on Achaemenid foundations; it resembles palaces on Cyprus and garrison buildings elsewhere, and its excavator suggests that it may have served as a prytaneion or administrative building.[83]

Perhaps it is from Building A that the sculpted blocks come that make Meydancıkkale so famous in an Achaemenid context.[84] These sculptures cannot

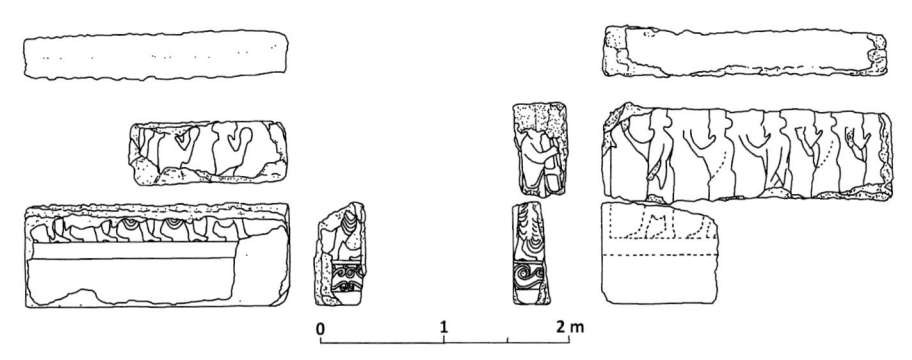

53. Meydancıkkale Persepolitan reliefs. Author's drawing, after Davesne and Laroche-Traunecker 1998: 306, fig. 15.

be closely dated stylistically, and the suggestion that they should be placed sometime between the end of the fifth century and the middle of the fourth seems safest for now.[85] At this fortified site, with its possible administrative building, have been found remains of a relief that recalls the Ionian tribute bearers from the Apadana at Persepolis. Bearded figures move to the left, wearing chiton and himation and with their hair in curls at the nape of the neck. They bear cups and other vessels in their upraised hands, proffering them in what may be intended as a gesture of homage.[86] A parallel relief includes men moving to the right; because it is not as well preserved, it is more difficult to reconstruct what these figures are doing, although they may be wearing Achaemenid court dress. Each block is finished at one end with a figure wearing Achaemenid court dress and apparently carrying a spear. These reliefs are charged with Achaemenid authority; their presence at Meydancıkkale is significant. A profound iteration of imperial authority, they would have served to remind soldiers holding the garrison on the high place of the king to whom they owed their loyalty and of the cohesion uniting the upper echelons of the military.

Şahankaya

We return now to Şahankaya with more nuanced understanding. A fortified high place like Meydancıkkale, Şahankaya too was off the beaten track but with a large visual catchment to the south. The mountains of northern Lydia are not particularly fertile, so it is unlikely that the outcrop at Şahankaya was fortified to protect agricultural produce. The site may have been developed to protect a route through the mountains or a particular resource of the area.[87] The "intervisibility with Sardis and many other points in central and northern Lydia" noted before establishes its importance as a communication hub as well, and its tremendous defensibility would have made it not only wise to establish a garrison on its summit but indeed foolhardy *not* to have done so.[88]

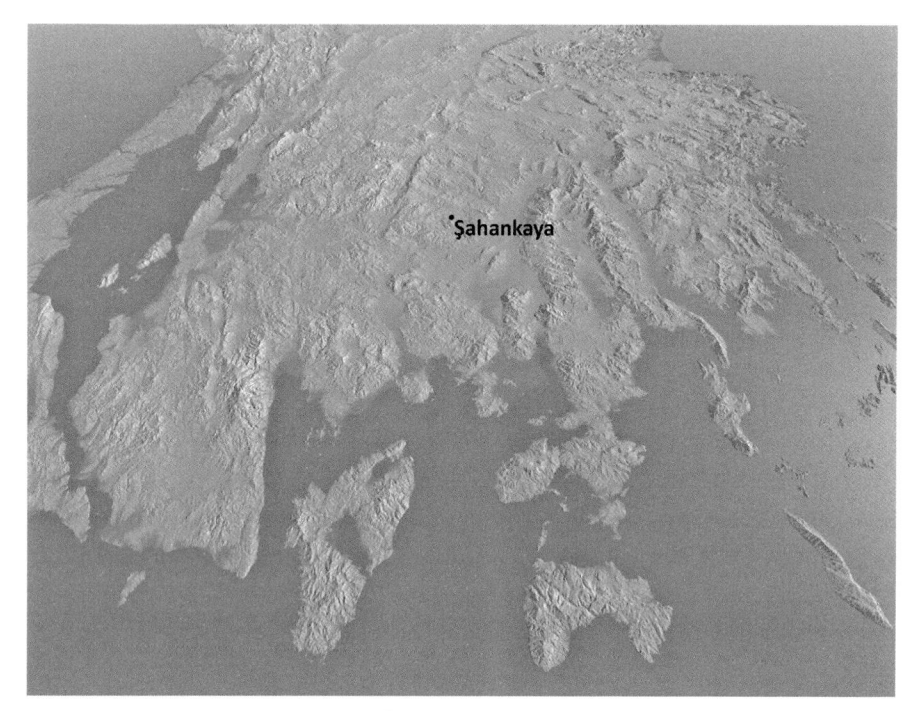

54. Western Anatolia, looking east: Şahankaya. Courtesy Karl Mueller.

55. Şahankaya. After Roosevelt 2009: fig. 5.6. Courtesy Christopher Roosevelt.

At Şahankaya, a fortified garrison of soldiers on a high place, the troops were apparently a Persian group called the Maebazanoe.[89] A lead slingshot bullet found nearby and bearing the legend, in Greek, "TISSAPHER.E" in raised relief confirms the presence of military action in the vicinity.[90] That this

56. Fire bowl at Şahankaya. After Roosevelt 2009: fig. 5.8. Courtesy Christopher Roosevelt.

mold-made bullet should carry the name of its sender in the language of its likely recipient seems to me a nice touch: the Greek who was presumably the intended target would have had no doubt about who was responsible for his wound. Elite Achaemenid remains from nearby tumuli demonstrate that personages of some importance lived, or at least died, at the site (see Chapter 5).[91] Of particular interest in a military context is the feature called a fire altar, after a parallel on a ledge southeast of Naqsh-i Rustam near Persepolis.[92] That example is unique in the corpus of fire altars published.[93] Indeed, the feature at Şahankaya makes me wonder if we should reconsider that at Naqsh-i Rustam.

Literary sources tell us that Achaemenid garrisons could communicate with each other via signal fires; with its tremendous visual catchment area, Şahankaya was an ideal place to house such a device. I suggest that the square plinth with a raised rounded hump emerging from it and a fire bowl in its center at Şahankaya forms the base for a fire signal. If this is true, rather than being a fire altar that "allowed ethnic Persian soldiers a familiar sacred outlet in a land that was otherwise completely foreign," this feature served as a locus for a signal fire that could be seen as far away as Sardis itself.[94] The situation of the parallel at Naqsh-i Rustam also commands a wide area; the "fire altar" there looks nothing like any other example, either excavated or rendered in visual resources. Perhaps that one, too, served as a signal fire to convey information in and out of the nearby administrative headquarters. In both cases, the situation of the fire basin, scooped out of solid rock but still raised above the land around it with a high outcrop of rock elevating the fire above the ground, is particularly important in lands that become so tinder dry by the end of summer that the least flying spark could ignite a blazing inferno. The combination of the visual catchment area and the care taken so that a large and highly visible fire would not set the lands around alight indicate to me very strongly that Şahankaya was the locus of a signal fire, part of the linked series of communications that unified the Achaemenid military forces of western Anatolia.

Şahankaya fits into a cohesive picture of garrisons in Achaemenid Anatolia. A fortified high place of strategic significance at a distance from the walled acropolis of Sardis, it served as a garrison site for soldiers brought from afar. At least some of those people were buried with all the trappings of the polyethnic Achaemenid elite. An exposed place for fires at the site most likely served as the base for a signal fire in case of an urgent need for communication. The fact that Şahankaya and Sardis are visible to each other may indicate that the latter suggestion was practical. Thus Şahankaya served as a fortified garrison on a high place in Lydia that helps link that at Meydancıkkale with the testimonia of literary sources to create a cohesive picture of this aspect of the Achaemenid army in Anatolia.

The Cemetery at Deve Hüyük

Completely different in nature is the archaeological evidence from Deve Hüyük located in southeastern Anatolia, right at the northern edge of the Syrian desert, in rich agricultural land near a branch of the Euphrates. The cemetery at this apparently unfortified tell site was exposed and looted in 1913, in connection with the construction of the Baghdad railway.[95] Two distinct types and periods of burial emerged, of which the second – consisting of inhumation rather than cremation graves – dates to the Achaemenid period, between 480 and 380.[96] These graves are generally considered to be the remains of a garrison force (to be discussed in greater detail in Chapter 5).[97]

Because the cemetery was looted and the material at hand today consists only of that deemed salable by the looters, the assemblages are biased toward the expensive and exotic. Even so, they provide rich material for study. Grave goods include imported Caspian pottery, coarse ware anthropomorphic lamps and a zoomorphic rhyton; fine ware Attic Greek vessels and two coins; Egyptian faience flasks and *wadjet* eyes; iron weapons, including the Persian short sword (acinaces) as well as quiver elements (gorytus), battle-axes (sagaris), arrowheads, and spearheads; horse bits and a horse bell; terracotta rider figurines; bronze phialae and Achaemenid bowls; and many other items to be discussed in Chapter 5. As Roger Moorey summarizes:

The inhumation cemetery at Deve Hüyük appears to have been opened some time in the first half of the fifth century B.C. for troops serving a military establishment somewhat set back from the river Euphrates, in an area rich enough agriculturally to support it and with good access to two Euphrates crossings, either down the Sajur valley or directly across country. Soldiers were buried there with certain distinctive arms and pottery; their womenfolk with personal ornaments and cosmetic articles differing little from finds of the period throughout Syro-Palestine. With the evidence of arms alone: *acinaces*, *sagaris* and *gorytus*, it may only be said that this is likely to have been a garrison of predominantly Iranian-speaking troops rather than local Syrians, whose traditional arms were different. The additional evidence of the crude anthropomorphic lamps strengthens the suggestion (and it may be no more) that some at least of them were drawn from the Caspian provinces, where the cist form of burial was also at home.[98]

On the basis of our growing understanding of Achaemenid military authority and practice, we can begin to contextualize the Deve Hüyük population in a military setting. Like garrisoned troops elsewhere in Anatolia, these men apparently included some at least who were brought to the site from lands far away, perhaps from Fars or even from the lands around the Caspian. Their weapons conformed to standard Achaemenid military practice and allowed them both to shoot from afar and to engage in hand-to-hand combat using a variety of techniques. Some had horses caparisoned with Persian bits and bells, although there is no evidence for cavalry per se at the site. Some had enough wealth to possess exotic fine ware or faience vases from Greece and Egypt, as well as bronze wine-drinking vessels of significant types (see Chapter 4).

Deve Hüyük thus provides us with an archaeological site of a very different nature than those considered already, one that supports and elaborates our understanding of Achaemenid military authority. Together with the textual and visual evidence, these sites allow us to see the workings of the Achaemenid army with surprising clarity.

Other Sites in Anatolia

Archaeological work in Anatolia provides still further information about Achaemenid military options, of which I mention only a few examples here. We learn, for instance, of watchtowers or platforms situated above communication routes or on high places with excellent overlooks, not only from textual sources but now also thanks to extensive regional survey:

> High-elevation sites overlooking communication routes include a settlement on the ridge of Kayapınar just west of Magnesia ad Sipylum, which is ideally suited to guard the access between western Lydia and Ionia

through a pass that today hosts a major highway connecting Manisa and Izmir. Just east of Magnesia ad Sipylum and on a rocky spur in the lower foothills of Mt. Sipylus was another such site: Yarıkkaya. With commanding views over the entire middle Hermus River valley and north to the Hyrcanian Plain, this site had control over at least two major communication routes. Sites in the Tmolus Range [which rises above Sardis to the south], too, were probably situated to control communications in and between the range and/or to overlook valleys to its north and south: Yılan Kalesi to the east overlooks the Cilbian Plain, and Kel Dağ to the west has more panoramic and controlling vistas ... over the surrounding valleys, especially the Cayster to the south.[99]

Even this one small part of western Lydia thus gives us a sense of the widespread nature of Achaemenid watchposts – again on high places – and the attention paid to controlling and defending not only communication routes in particular but also the fertile agricultural lands of the western empire in general.

Like Lydia, Lycia has been a focus of intensive archaeological study for decades. At such places as Limyra, Xanthus, and Latmus we see nucleated settlements, characterized by a fortified citadel on an acropolis and a lower town surrounded by a further fortification wall.[100] Walled fortresses in Armenia add to our sense of Achaemenid military strength and display in Anatolia, including those at Sultantepe and Altıntepe.[101] Additional walled buildings with towers, found with noticeable frequency in southwestern Anatolia, may resemble those Achaemenid outposts described by Greek authors in lands just to the north.[102] Intriguingly, it has been suggested that the emphasis on tower structures may have had not only practical use but also a symbolic purpose: if, as it seems, the corners of the Apadana at Persepolis are to be reconstructed as towers, then the presence of freestanding buildings with corner towers in the remotest reaches of the empire resonates with imperial as well as military authority.[103] Thus we see the combining of ideological and practical in the military statements of Achaemenid Anatolia.

Sites Elsewhere in the Achaemenid Empire

This cursory overview indicates the range of Achaemenid military sites excavated elsewhere, as comparanda for those in Anatolia. In Egypt, the garrison at Elephantine is superbly represented via Aramaic documents, but little if anything is known of its physical appearance.[104] Sinai has produced two Achaemenid-period fortresses at Tell el-Herr and a fortified residence at Tell Kedoua that demonstrate similarities to the types of sites found in Anatolia.[105] An Achaemenid fortress at Tell Defenneh in the Nile delta (mentioned also as the site of a Persian garrison in Hdt. 2.30) and one at Dorginarti in Upper Egypt complete our sense of excavated Achaemenid-period military remains from the Nile River valley.[106] What makes them exciting is the similarity they bear to the Achaemenid fortresses excavated in Palestine. These are characterized by a single building type, a fortress with thickened corner rooms that suggest corner towers, an open courtyard, thick exterior walls, and rooms of various sizes opening onto the courtyard.[107] Such plans are mirrored precisely in Achaemenid fortresses as far away as Central Asia as well.[108] Thus the excavated fortresses of other parts of the Achaemenid Empire flesh out our understanding of Achaemenid military practice and demonstrate the similarity of form posited at the beginning of the chapter. Evidence from Anatolia has not yet yielded such a plan, but given its pattern of occurrence elsewhere it can be safely proposed here, too – and perhaps sought.

Summary

> When [Xenophon and his comrades] reached the [estate and stronghold of Asidates, in Mysia], about midnight, the slaves that were round about the tower and most of the animals ran away, the Greeks leaving them unheeded in order to capture Asidates himself and his belongings. And when they found themselves unable to take the tower by storm (for it was high and large, and furnished with battlements and a considerable force of warlike defenders), they attempted to dig through the tower-wall. Now the wall had a thickness of eight earthen bricks. At daybreak, however, a breach had been made; and just as soon as the light showed through, someone from within struck with an ox-spit clean through the thigh of the man who was nearest the hole; and from that time on they kept shooting out arrows and so made it unsafe even to pass by the place any more. Then, as the result of their shouting and lighting of beacon fires, there came to their assistance Itamenes with his own force, and from Comania Assyrian hoplites and Hyrcanian horsemen – these also being mercenaries in the service of the King – to the number of eighty, as well as about eight hundred peltasts, and more from Parthenium, and more from Apollonia and from the near-by places, including horsemen.[109]

The overview of Achaemenid military authority in Anatolia presented here has demonstrated that the four elements we would expect to see indicating an imperial standing army are all to be found, and indeed it has elaborated our understanding of the military landscape. Troops of mixed ethnicities, some of them very far from their lands of origin, served together to control and protect Anatolia for the Achaemenid authority. Some of these troops were garrisoned soldiers; others formed a light-armed and mobile reserve. Garrisons were situated in walled cities and on fortified high places. High places also served as outlooks from which to control routes and watch over the land; signals conveying messages or summoning help could be sent rapidly from one lookout to the next.

Small freestanding fortified buildings served as protected areas and perhaps as watchtowers. The prevalence of towers in fortified buildings and possibly in the garrisoned fortresses offered improved surveillance and martial capabilities and may have had additional symbolic significance, linking these structures to the seat of imperial authority at Persepolis. Textual and archaeological evidence demonstrates significant military presence in areas of key importance and so many troops within a given area that hundreds of them could be called up for active service within twelve hours of receiving a message. Moreover, the visual record demonstrates the importance of warfare to the self-image of adult men in Achaemenid Anatolia. Thus the military arm of imperial authority in Achaemenid Anatolia was long, strong, flexible, well trained, well regarded, and eminently effective for hundreds of years.

Catalogue of Achaemenid Military Presence in Anatolia

Much of this material, including all textual examples, is drawn from Tuplin 1987b: 235–8. I have here included only those sites he listed as "core" sites, ones almost certainly garrisoned in the Achaemenid period. His catalogue also includes sites garrisoned in the Hellenistic period that were probably garrisoned in the Achaemenid period too, as well as sites mentioned as Achaemenid garrisons by significantly later authors.

Western Anatolia (General)

Unnamed	Dio. Sic. 11.60.1 (470s)
	phrourai along Asian coast
Unnamed	Polyaen. 2.19 (390s)
	phrourion/-arkhos, khorion, phylakes
Unnamed	Isoc. 4.163 (late 380s)
	phrouroi in western Anatolian cities

Hellespontine Phrygia

Dascylium	Hell. Oxy. 22 (17).3 (395)[110]
	okhuron khorion
	Arr. 1.17.2 (334)
	phrouroi
	Archaeological evidence for a city wall and terrace walls: Erdoğan 2007
Miletouteichus	Hell. Oxy. 22(17).3 (395)
	khorion
Unnamed	Xen. *Hell.* 1.1.24–5 (410)
	phylakes on the coast of Hellespontine Phrygia

Unnamed	Polyaen. 4.3.15; Strabo 587; Arr. 1.17.8 (late Achaemenid period)
	khoria of Memnon in the Aesepsus valley

TROAD

Cebren[111]	Xen. *Hell.* 3.1.10–11 (399)
	phrouroi, phylake, khorion
	Archaeological evidence for city walls
Cocylium	Xen. *Hell.* 3.1.10–11 (399)
	phrouroi
Colonae	Xen. *Hell.* 3.1.10–11 (399)
	phrouroi
Gergis	Xen. *Hell.* 3.1.10–11 (399)
	phrouroi
Hamaxitus	Xen. *Hell.* 3.1.10–11 (399)
	phrouroi
Ilium	Xen. *Hell.* 3.1.10–11 (399)
	phrouroi
Larissa	Xen. *Hell.* 3.1.10–11 (399)
	phrouroi
	Archaeological evidence for city walls
Neandria	Xen. *Hell.* 3.1.10–11 (399)
	phrouroi
	Archaeological evidence for city walls
Scepsis	Xen. *Hell.* 3.1.10–11 (399)
	phrouroi

AEOLIS, MYSIA

Antandrus	Thuc. 8.108; Dio. Sic. 13.41.4 (411)
	phroura/-oi, akropolis, phylake
	Xen. *Hell.* 1.124–5 (410)
	phylakes, phroure
	Archaeological evidence for city walls
Apollonia	Xen. *Anab.* 7.8.15 (400)
	Base of "oriental" troops and royal mercenaries, along with Comania, Parthenion
Comania	Xen. *Anab.* 7.8.15 (400)
	Base of "oriental" troops and royal mercenaries, along with Apollonia, Parthenion
Parthenion	Xen. *Anab.* 7.8.15 (400)
	Base of "oriental" troops and royal mercenaries, along with Apollonia, Comania

Unnamed	Polyaen. 6.10 (390s)
	phrourein/-arkhos, khoria
PHRYGIA	
Celaenae	Arr. 1.29.1; Curt. 3.1.11–12 (334/3)
	phylake, akra, arx
	Xen. *Anab.* 1.2.7
	erumna, akropoleis mentioned
Gordion	Hell. Oxy. 21(16).6 (395)
	khorion . . . kataskeuasmenon kalos
Leonton Cephalae	Hell. Oxy. 21(16).5 (395)
	khorion
LYDIA	
Blaunda	Dio. Sic. 13.104.3 (405/4)
	phrourion
Kayapınar	Possible military settlement: Roosevelt 2009:117
Sardis	Hdt. 1.153 (540s)
	Acropolis held by satrap
	Hdt. 5.100; Charon 62F5 (498)
	Acropolis, *teikhos* (held by satrap)
	Xen. *Anab.* 1.6.6 (403–401)
	Acropolis held by Orontes
	Donner and Röllig 1963: 60B (394 or 348)
	byrt'
	Arr. 1.17.3 (334)
	phrourion/-arkhos, akropolis, okhuron khorion
	Archaeological evidence for a city wall and terrace walls: Dusinberre 2003a: 47–56, 73–5; Ratté 2011
Şahankaya	Archaeological evidence for a fortified high place, with a fire bowl; tumuli with elite Achaemenid artifacts and a slingshot bullet inscribed "Tissaphernes" found nearby: Roosevelt 2009: 118–21, 240–2
Tmolus range	Watchtowers to the east (Yılan Kalesı) and south (Kel Dağ): Roosevelt 2009: 117
Yarıkkaya	Possible military settlement: Roosevelt 2009: 117
IONIA	
Colophon	Archaeological evidence for city walls
Ephesus	Arr. 1.17.9 (334)
	phrourountes
Miletus	Thuc. 8.84.109 (412/11)
	phrourion/-oi, phylakes

	Arr. 1.18.3 (334)
	phroura, phylake
	Archaeological evidence for city walls
Notion	Thuc. 3.34 (430–427)
	phrourein
Phocaea	Hdt. 1.165.2 (late 540s)
	phylake, phrourein
	Archaeological evidence for city walls
Unnamed	Xen. *Anab.* 1.1.6–7; 2.1–2 (403–401)
	phylakai, phrourarkhoi, akropoleis

CARIA, LYCIA

Caunus	Hell. Oxy. 20(15).1–2 (395)
	phrouroi
	Dio. Sic. 20.27.2
	One *akra* called *to Persikon*
Cnidus	Thuc. 8.109 (412–411)
	phrouroi
	Archaeological evidence for city walls
Halicarnassus	Dio. Sic. 15.90.3, 17.23.4; Arr. 1.23.3 (360s, 334/3)
	akropoleis, akrai
	Archaeological evidence for a fourth-century fortification: Hornblower 1982: 299–300
Hyparnae	Arr. 1.24.3 (334/3)
	phylake, akra, khorion okhuron
Iasus	Thuc. 8.29 (412)
	phrourein
	Archaeological evidence for city walls
Latmus	Archaeological evidence for city walls: Marksteiner 2005: 37
Limyra	Archaeological evidence for fortifications: Marksteiner 1997a, 1997b
Trysa	Archaeological evidence for fortifications: Marksteiner 2002b
Xanthus	Fouilles de Xanthus 6 (Paris 1979): 337
	byrt'
	Archaeological evidence for fortifications: Marksteiner 2002c
Unnamed	Dio. Sic. 11.60.4 (before 467)
	phrourai in Carian cities
Unnamed	Xen. *Hell.* 3.2.14 (397)
	erumata, phylakai

Unnamed	Dio. Sic. 15.90.3 (late 360s)
	Mausolus's realm made up of *poleis* and *erumata*
Unnamed	Arr. 1.23.8 (334)
	khoria (implicitly loyal to the king, by contrast to Alinda)
Unnamed	Archaeological evidence for fortified tower houses: Marksteiner 1996, 1999, 2005

PISIDIA, SOUTHERN ANATOLIA

Syllion	Arr. 1.26.5 (334/3)
	phroura, khorion
Unnamed	Dio. Sic. 17.27.3–4 (334/3)
	phrouria in southern Anatolia

CILICIA

Cilician Gates	Xen. *Anab.* 1.2.21–2 (401)
	phylattein
	Arr. 2.4.3 (334/3)
	phylakai
Kinet Höyük	Archaeological evidence for massive and elegant fortifications ca. 400: C. Gates 2005: 61–2
Meydancıkkale	Archaeological evidence for fortified gate, palatial building: Davesne and Laroche-Treunecker 1998 Davesne, Lemaire, and Lozachmeur 1987: 377
	byrt'
Unnamed	Hdt. 3.91 (6th–5th c.)
	phroureousa hippos
Unnamed	Xen. *Anab.* 1.2.24 (401)
	khorion near Tarsus (refuge)
Unnamed	Xen. *Anab.* 1.4.4 (401)
	teikhos, phylake, on Cilician side of Syrian Gates

CAPPADOCIA

Unnamed	Polyaen. 7.29.1; Nepos *Dat.* 10.2 (late 360s)
	phrouria, castella

ARMENIA

Altıntepe	Archaeological evidence for a fortified city: Fuensanta and Charvat 2005:164
Sultantepe	Archaeological evidence for a fortified city: Fuensanta and Charvat 2005:162
Tigra	DB 27 (522/1)
	dida, halmarrish, byrt'

Uyama   DB 28 (522/1)
                  dida, *halmarrish*

Royal Road
                  Hdt. 5.52 (6th–5th c.)
                  phylakteria on Halys River
                  (Phrygia–Cappadocia border), on
                  Cappadocia–Cilicia border (two), and in
                  Armenia

FOUR

EATING AND DRINKING WITH CLASS AND STYLE

What you eat and drink; how, when, and where you eat and drink; with whom you eat and drink – these behaviors have agricultural and trade implications, nutritional and health consequences, an impact on status and prestige, and the potential for cementing old traditions and social structures or introducing new ones.[1] They can be reaffirming or subversive, conservative or innovative; they can exploit readily accessible resources or demand those that are exotic or difficult to obtain. It is clear that the Achaemenid imperial authority not only recognized but also used all these features of food and beverages, from influencing the daily fare of the empire's inhabitants to presenting the tremendous feasts offered by its king. This chapter begins with a brief review of aspects of dining at the imperial capital at Persepolis, then examines current theoretical and methodological approaches to understanding dining behaviors in order to embed Achaemenid practice in a broader discussion, and finally turns to Anatolia to consider the eating and drinking of its elite and non-elite inhabitants during the Achaemenid period. Indeed, at this point Anatolian sites offer the most contextually diverse as well as secure, the most materially diverse, and the most quantitatively significant corpora for a study of drinking and dining behaviors in the Achaemenid Empire. Thus this topic is especially important to pursue and may offer a paradigm for questions to be asked of other regions. Anatolia bears witness to an active collaboration of the subject peoples with the ideology of universalism in the Achaemenid Empire.[2]

Feasts Fit for a King

Most of what has been written about dining in Achaemenid Persia focuses on the King's Dinner – in part because the Greeks commented on it and in part

Eating and Drinking with Class and Style

because modern authors, like ancient ones, are flabbergasted by the size and quality of the meal.³ Often ancient authors describe the eating and drinking of the king explicitly to create a contrast with their own more modest habits. A similar undercurrent underlies various modern discussions, and in this way it is obvious that the Achaemenid Persian use of dining for show and status was successful not only in antiquity but thousands of years after the empire's demise.

Indeed, the King's Dinner was impressive. Polyaenus preserves a list of items he claims was engraved on a bronze pillar, detailing the ingredients used to create the king's daily fare:

1.		Wheat flour, pure	400 ardabs
2.		Wheat flour, second class	300 ardabs
3.		Wheat flour, third class	300 ardabs
	Wheat flour, total for dinner		1,000 ardabs
4.		Barley flour, very pure	200 ardabs
5.		Barley flour, second class	400 ardabs
6.		[Barley flour, third class	400 ardabs]
	Barley flour, total for dinner		1,000 ardabs
7.		[? *Semidalis*	?]
8.		Groats made from *olyra*	200 ardabs
9.		Fine flour from *alphita*, for possets	200 ardabs
10.		Chopped cardamom, sifted fine	xxx ardabs
11.		*Ptisane* (treated barley?)	10 ardabs
12.		Mustard seed	⅓ ardab
13.		Sheep and goats (male)	400
14.		Cattle	100
15.		Horses	30
16.		Fattened geese	400
17.		Pigeons	300
18.		Various small birds	600
19.		Lambs	300
20.		Goslings	100
21.		Gazelles	30
22.		Today's milk	10 marrish
23.		Sweetened sour milk	10 marrish
24.		Garlic	1 talent
25.		Onions, pungent	½ talent
26.		*Phyllon* (silphium-fruit?)	1 ardab
27.		Juice of silphium	1 talent
28.		Oil of sweet apples	¼ ardab
29.		Posset from sour pomegranates	1 ardab
30.		Oil of cumin	¼ ardab
31.		Black raisins	3 talents
32.		Anise flower	3 minas
33.		Black cumin	⅓ ardab

34.	Seed of *diarinon*	2 kapetis
35.	Sesame, pure	10 ardabs
36.	*Gleukos* from wine	5 marrish
37.	Cooked round radishes in wine	5 marrish
38.	Capers in brine, from which they make sour sauce	5 marrish
39.	Salt	10 ardabs
40.	Ethiopian cumin	6 kapetis
41.	Dried anise	30 minas
42.	Celery seed	4 kapetis
43.	Sesame oil	10 marrish
44.	Oil "from milk"	5 marrish
45.	Terebinth oil	5 marrish
46.	Acanthus oil	5 marrish
47.	Oil from sweet almonds	3 marrish
48.	Dried sweet almonds	3 marrish
49.	Wine	500 marrish

(When he is in Babylon or Susa, he has half his wine from palms, half from vines.)

50.	Wood (*xyla*)	200 cartloads
51.	Wood (*hule*)	100 cartloads
52.	"Raining honey"	100 square blocks, weighing 10 minas each

(When the king is in Media, he distributes these things:)

53.	Safflower seed	3 ardabs
54.	Saffron	2 minas

(All of this for beverages and *ariston*)

He distributes:

55.	Wheat flour, pure	500 ardabs
56.	Barley flour, pure	1,000 ardabs
57.	Barley flour, second class	1,000 ardabs
58.	*Semidalis*	500 ardabs
59.	Groats made from *olyra*	500 marrish
60.	Barley for the animals	2,000 ardabs
61.	Chaff	10,000 wagons
62.	Straw	5,000 wagons
63.	Sesame oil	200 marrish
64.	Vinegar	100 marrish
65.	Chopped cardamom, fine	30 ardabs

All of the above is given to the soldiers (?)

This is what the King consumes in a day, including his *ariston*, his *deipnon*, and what he distributes.[4]

Athenaeus marveled at the quantity of food required for the king's meals: "One thousand animals are slaughtered daily for the king; these comprise horses, camels, oxen, asses, deer, and most of the smaller animals; many birds also are consumed, including Arabian ostriches – and the creature is large – geese, and cocks."[5] Herodotus emphasized not only the quantity of the king's culinary offerings to his supporters, but also the exotic and specialized nature of the king's own repast. For example: "When the Persian king goes to war, he is always well provided not only with victuals from home and his own cattle, but also with water from the Choaspes."[6] To drink this water was a royal privilege, and it was probably prized for its health-giving qualities.[7] Course after course came out for the King's Dinner, a method of presenting food wholly different from that of the Greeks.[8] Both in quantity and in quality, the king dined in superior, different, even extravagant ways that established and reaffirmed his great power and lofty status.

The ingredients listed by Polyaenus demonstrate some interesting points.[9] The lack of rising agents should not make us assume that all the flour was turned into unleavened bread, although of course it could have been baked into tortilla-like flatbreads that might serve as an eating utensil. The presence in the Fortification Archive of at least one tablet detailing thirteen different kinds of barley bread, flavored with various ingredients, allows us to imagine a great array of baked goods – a notion that is probably supported by the different grades of flour in Polyaenus's list.[10] Other tablets from the archive describe meats and poultry, various kinds of grain, wine, beer, fruit (including figs, grapes, pomegranates), oil and ghee, cheese, pastries, and honey – indeed, a great array of foods.[11] Meat and, especially, poultry were reserved for the royal table and for royal redistribution as gifts, as was honey.[12] Dairy was present as sweetened sour milk and cheese or as milk that would have to be cooked into puddings early on a hot day to remain edible by evening (unless used as soured milk). The food was not spicy, although enough flavorful ingredients were included that the meal would have had real piquancy in the hands of a skilled cook. The emphasis was on a combination of a few highly savory ingredients with a number of salty and sweet elements. I am fortunate enough to have sampled a meal created from the ingredients listed by Polyaenus, with duck as a base; it was indeed a mouthwatering feast fit for a king.

A vast amount of meat was served, from small birds to horses; the meats listed by literary sources should be considered to represent a range of options rather than those served every day, however, as lamb is seasonal.[13] Moreover, the enormous amounts should be interpreted within the context of redistribution; thus the huge quantities attested in the Fortification Archive that were occasionally disbursed on a single day (e.g., 1,333 fowls, PF 2034, or enough flour for 11,886 people, PF 702) need not indicate feasting consumption of the food on that day, but more likely the redistribution to retainers of food that may have been eaten over the course of more than one day.[14]

The workers required to turn these ingredients into a meal were numerous and impressive; a letter written by Alexander's general Parmenion after the battle of Issus, in which he made careful note of the king's baggage and attendants so they might be returned to him later, included the following list of those necessary for dining properly:

1.	Royal concubine musicians	329
2.	Garland makers	46
3.	Cooks	277
4.	Young kitchen helpers	29
5.	Cooks who specialize in dairy dishes	13
6.	Beverage preparers	17
7.	Wine strainers (or mixers?)	70
8.	Perfume makers	14
Total kitchen and banquet workers		79[15]

Athenaeus comments on the rituals required of these servitors: "All who attend upon the Persian kings when they dine first bathe themselves and then serve in white clothes, and spend nearly half the day on preparations for the dinner."[16] The king's meals were markers of prestige not only because of the foodstuffs involved but also because of the complexity and manner in which they were served.[17] Royal table wares and the mode of eating were a significant part of this, too, as will be discussed in detail later.

The Classical authors who described the king's meals commented also on the number of people they were meant to feed. Although the exact figures differ, the sources agree that the king fed a large number of retainers, soldiers, and other followers.[18] Thus the amount of each ingredient required for the meal was stupendous in its own right, and maximum public show and impact could be gained thanks to the sheer number of people who created, observed, and consumed the resulting feast. The cost of providing such a meal, which included not only food and drink but also differentiated settings for the king and his immediate entourage (hangings; a couch for the king, if not for his followers; drinking vessels of metal for the king and his elite followers, if not the soldiers), was vast – a fact that no doubt served to underscore the wealth of the king.[19] Indeed, Greek and Persian sources are in agreement on the importance they ascribe to the king's meals. As Wouter Henkelman summarizes, "It becomes evident that the Persepolis administrators, like the Greek historiographers, thought of the king's table as an *institution*, as a complex organisation with its own rules and hierarchy, with very specific needs and demands, and with its own administrators."[20]

How the king ate and drank was as important as how much and what. The prevalence at the Persian royal table of cups for drinking wine, made of silver and gold, was commented on repeatedly by the Greeks, to whom by the mid-fifth century the association of precious-metal wine-drinking vessels with the Persian elite had practically become a literary trope.[21] Excavated examples of such vessels demonstrate that they could be rendered large, so that they might comfortably hold a liter or even a liter and a half of wine.[22] The silver was very fine: that which has been analyzed is 97 to 99 percent pure.[23] And the metalwork was exquisite. With this kind of quality and elite association, it is no wonder that silver or gold wine-drinking vessels took on an explicit status and that when the king wished to insult a particular courtier he had him served his wine from a clay cup rather than a silver one.[24]

When the king traveled, the local citizens who provided him with his accustomed fare might find themselves crippled by the expense of creating but a single meal in the manner the king provided daily at home. Herodotus, describing Xerxes' procession through northern Greece in 480, says:

> The moment that word came from the officers who carried the king's commands, people in every town distributed their stores of grain and employed themselves for months on end in making barley and wheat flour, in buying up and fattening the best cattle they could find, and feeding poultry in coops and waterfowl in ponds, to be ready for the army when it came. In addition to this they ordered the manufacture of drinking cups and mixing bowls of gold and silver, and of everything else that is needed to adorn the table. All this, of course, was for the king himself and those who dined with him; for the troops in general the preparations were confined to food. On the arrival of the army, there was always a tent ready for Xerxes to take his rest in, while the men bivouacked in the open; but it was when dinnertime came that the real trouble for the unfortunate hosts began. The guests ate their fill and, after spending the night in the place, pulled up the tent next morning, seized the cups and table-gear and everything else it contained, and marched off without leaving a single thing behind.[25]

This description reflects the astounded response of the Greeks to the dining habits of the Persians, especially of the Persian king. Thus the passage demonstrates the role dining behaviors played in the negotiation of status relations.[26] The Persian king's dining reiterated his power and prestige on a daily basis and emphasized the authority exercised by the Achaemenid elite (in this case, the king) over subject peoples (in this case, the Greeks).

Dining and Status in Persia

The use of dining to affirm and cement status in Persia was not limited to the king. Herodotus contrasts the types of feasts offered by Persians of different degrees of wealth on their birthdays and ends with a comment that conveys Persian awareness of dining as a demonstration of prestige:

> The day in the year that each man values most is his own birthday, which he celebrates with a meal of particular magnificence. A rich Persian on his

birthday will have an ox or a horse or a camel or a donkey baked whole in the oven and served up at the table, and a poor man will have some smaller beast. The main dishes at their meals are few, but they have many sorts of side dishes, the various courses being served separately. It is this custom that has made them say that the Greeks leave the table hungry, because we never have anything worth mentioning after the first course: they think that if we did, we should go on eating.[27]

This passage shows three major things: (1) feasting was an explicit part of Persian behavior; (2) the kinds of food offered, and the ways in which they were offered, bore unequivocal connections to status and power; and (3) the specific social importance of dining behaviors was understood not only by Persians but also by those (like Herodotus) who came in contact with them. Thus dining behaviors provided a potent avenue for expressing authority or autonomy in the Achaemenid Empire and created obligations through reciprocal hosting. The king's table groaned under the weight of entertaining nobles and diplomats, many of whom were doubtless the very ones who provided for him when he and his entourage progressed through the empire. Indeed, precious vessels such as the famous silver phialae engraved with the name of Artaxerxes and similar uninscribed table wares were probably given by the king to personages feasting him around the empire as permanent reminders of royal feasting.[28] Thus the connections between dining and status and among individuals who dined together were strong.

Visual representations from Persia may provide additional evidence related to dining. At Persepolis, reliefs on the palaces of Darius and Xerxes show men bearing accoutrements of banqueting or ritual (the purpose is contested).[29] The Apadana reliefs could also act as a permanent reminder of incoming supplies for royally exotic and elaborate eating and drinking, even as the king's repast was a daily reminder of their outgoing flow.

The Persepolis Fortification Archive documents a highly developed system of distributing food to people at all levels, often as recompense for labor, and demonstrates that differentiated access to foodstuffs indicated social status. Fixed ration scales existed for certain ranking officials.[30] Thus the main overseer at Persepolis in the years around 500, Parnaka (an uncle of Darius I), received daily foodstuffs to the extent of 2 sheep, 90 quarts of wine, and 180 quarts of flour – no matter where he was. Darius's right-hand man, Gobryas, received even more.[31] There is every reason to think that they provided meals for others in their household or entourage from these disbursements.[32]

Quantity of food was equated with prestige at Persepolis, at all social ranks. Thus male laborers generally received higher rations than women engaged in the same work, unless the women were chiefs or overseers, in which case they received equivalent quantities or sometimes even more.[33] Boys were given more food than girls. Nursing mothers received a once-off ration of extra wine, twice

57. Servants with banquet (?) supplies, palaces of Darius (left) and Xerxes (right) at Persepolis. P28949 and P57675. Courtesy of the Oriental Institute of the University of Chicago.

as much if the child was a boy rather than a girl.[34] Skilled craftspeople received larger rations than unskilled laborers, including rations that were special in some way. David Lewis provides an overview:

> 1 and 1½ quarts of flour are near the norm, but there is evidence for very marked differentiation by skill, age and sex. To take a group of what appear to be garment-workers, with unintelligible specialities (PF 999), 3 males are on 45 quarts a month, 17 women on 40, 2 men and 36 women on 30, 3 women on 25, 15 mixed on 20, 2 boys and 1 girl on 15, 6 boys and 5 girls on 10, 2 boys and 5 girls on 5, but the boys and girls have no trade designation and are probably very young. There are odd commoners who get up to 60 quarts. In this social scale sheep rations are very uncommon and, when they come, they can be of the order of 1/9, 1/15, or even 1/30 of a sheep a month.... [The] ration-statements enable us to build up a remarkable picture of the size of operations involved ... the tablets have 15,376 people on the pay-roll, attached to 108 villages, over the period 509–494, [with] 8,728 in the 23rd year alone.[35]

The Fortification Archive thus provides evidence for a carefully regulated food system in Achaemenid Persia – food differentiated by quantity and quality based on type of work done and type of person receiving it.[36]

Even this brief overview of textual evidence for non-kingly dining in Persia demonstrates the extent to which food served as a marker of status. This was reiterated on a daily basis, for the loftiest elite as well as the lowliest worker. What one ate, and how much one had to eat of certain foods, was at least in some instances state-regulated and always bore a recognizable social consequence. That this consequence was evident not only to Persians but also to others is made clear by Herodotus's description of birthday feasts. Although state-regulated manipulation of eating may be unusual in complex societies, it is related to common human behaviors. In the Achaemenid Empire, dining functioned as an ongoing statement of relative social status within a community, renewing and re-creating obligations between people in ways that daily wove them together in intricately restated patterns.[37] It became part of the daily fabric of authority and autonomy.

Feasting and Human Society

Most scholarly studies focus on feasting in contrast to the consumption of daily fare. The focus of this chapter is therefore rather different, as it examines commensal behaviors on a "normal" scale rather than the extraordinary, often ritual or ritualized basis of feasting. Analysis of feasting behaviors and their consequences is nonetheless valuable because it helps embed the quotidian in a more nuanced discussion of dining behaviors.

In his seminal work, Michael Dietler differentiates between "entrepreneurial" feasts, "patron-role or redistributive" feasts, and "diacritical" feasts: entrepreneurial feasts are used to build up prestige; redistributive feasts are vast in quantity and legitimize or reiterate inequality in social/political power; diacritical feasts differentiate food and dining *behaviors* to naturalize and perpetuate concepts of differing social status.[38] Feasts, he claims, are an idealized representation of the social order but may be manipulated by individuals or groups "to alter or make statements about their relative position within that social order as it is perceived and presented."[39]

Others have demonstrated the ways in which feasts can be used competitively to generate debt and confer social leverage on their givers: by converting surpluses into proffered wealth and power, they create and perpetuate social inequalities.[40] Competitive feasting has obvious benefits for one seeking prestige: if a feast giver offers large quantities of food, his gesture cannot easily be emulated by others, so it is unlikely to go unnoticed (as Greek commentators on the King's Dinner demonstrate).[41] Interestingly, offering a different *quality* of food seems to be effective only if the feast giver already enjoys the high status that allows him "to set norms of cuisine or etiquette – in effect to create value."[42]

Value is complex. Foods associated with feasting are usually scarce and take a long time to prepare.[43] If an item is rare or difficult to produce – for example, a precious-metal vessel or a dining couch of imported ivory, hung with richly dyed and finely woven textiles – its value is intrinsic. Cultural constructs are also important in creating and defining value, however. Ceramic vessels that imitate metal prototypes may accrue value not because people think they are actually metallic, but because the imitations symbolically represent *both* the metal prototypes *and* their high-status social contexts.[44] Objects or food may also acquire value by association with valued attributes such as masculinity or with particular histories or customs.[45] Adult male game animals may thus be valued for more than their weight of meat – for an impressive rack of antlers, for instance.[46]

Eating and Drinking with Class and Style

In addition to table service and foodstuffs, the company kept is important. Eating with particular individuals may reinforce the cohesion of a small group of people by emphasizing shared traits and excluding other people. Conversely, commensality may involve a wider gathering of people who share various cultural assumptions and ideologies, yet who are otherwise divided by status or wealth, by obligation, or by other connections.[47] This point raises a difficulty in studying ancient value systems: food, table wares, and manners are as likely to gain value by association with those already of high status as to confer prestige on those using them.[48] It is precisely this that makes the study so important in considering imperial expansion and consolidation, however.

Because food and feasting are important elements in negotiating identity and power, they may provide rich material for studying gender relations. Preparing and consuming food are sexual and gendered performances in many societies, providing a way for men and women to define their masculinity and femininity.[49] Often, the power and prestige that feasting might provide have accrued to men even if women were largely responsible for food preparation and serving.[50] Women's participation in feasting, when it occurs, not only might reaffirm differences between genders but could offer both men and women an opportunity to engage in subversive public behaviors or forms of social/political commentary that might otherwise be impossible. Explicitly gendered roles might therefore be an important part of feasting.[51]

It is not surprising that alcohol has played a role in the social reaffirmation, identity creation, and incurring of debt that feature so strongly in commensality.[52] This undoubtedly has to do with the psychotropic features of alcohol and the way it can facilitate a sense of mutual understanding, of belonging to a group, of moving forward to positive endeavors with others.[53] As Oswyn Murray has pointed out, there is a close connection in human history between the social use of alcohol and the creation of a warrior elite.[54] The group drinking occasions that characterize many military societies, both ancient and modern, he suggests, "serve to establish and to reinforce power relationships among individuals of different rank, through a specially constructed ritual space where equality and status are in conflict: drinking customs relate to power structures."[55] The sense of community that alcohol can provide ties those dining together more tightly to the status differentiation marked at the same time by various prestige indicators: participation in value performance creates authority.

Alcohol returns us to Achaemenid Anatolia. Drinking and dining behaviors varied across Anatolia, of course; most interesting is the apparent degree to which they became homogeneous in the Achaemenid period. This observation is important because it applies not only to the male elite or to the elite in general, but – as far as we can tell – to people of all sorts. In the context of an authority–autonomy model, this is crucial. It seems that these most important social behaviors, dining and (especially) drinking, were recognized by the imperial authority as so germane to the ongoing functioning of the empire that they were consciously manipulated.

We do not know whether inhabitants of pre-Achaemenid Anatolia enjoyed a gendered Greek-style symposium, characterized by an all-male group that engaged in extensive drinking after a meal, with wine mixed with water in a communal krater and garland-adorned participants reclining on couches. "The [Greek] symposium has private, political, and cultural dimensions: it is the place of *euphrosyne*, of music, poetry, and other forms of entertainment; it is bound up with sexuality, especially homosexuality; it guarantees the social control of the *polis* by the aristocrats. It is a dominating social form in Greek civilization from Homer onward, and well beyond the Hellenistic period."[56] The women at Greek symposia were entertainers or slaves, not the good women of the house. As will become clear, Anatolia in the Achaemenid period saw rather different drinking and dining behaviors.

Ample evidence from Achaemenid Anatolia highlights the interfaces of drinking and dining with value. The rest of this chapter examines ways in which these social behaviors influenced identity formation. Public drinking was not always a gender-exclusive activity, as it was in Greece, but clearly included women as well as men in its performance of status and identity. Visual representations of women alongside men in the art of Achaemenid Anatolia suggest that women joined men in this semiotically charged activity, although their behaviors – sitting rather than reclining, perhaps using cups of a differentiated shape – set them apart in clearly gendered ways. Only men are shown reclining and raising a status-laden drinking cup, while women sit upright on chairs or the ends of couches, often lifting a fragrant object such as a blossom before them.[57] Certain buildings with spaces for multiple banqueting couches, labeled *andrones*, or "men's rooms" in Greek, suggest that public male dining was also a feature of Achaemenid Anatolia in some places and times. As a further indication of status, servants waited on elite diners.

The sources for understanding dining in Anatolia during the Achaemenid period are of a particular nature. Extensive publications of ceramic assemblages in use by an ancient living society are few; dietary analyses based on palynological (ancient pollens) or other paleobotanical remains (largely seeds) are also still rather rare. It is thus at this point impossible to offer a rundown of the Achaemenid-period diet for any region of Anatolia based on such data or to analyze differences between diet from one area to the next. However, there is quite extensive material evidence to shed light on drinking and dining *behaviors*. Several studies have examined ceramic and metal drinking vessels from individual sites. A relatively large number of metal drinking vessels have been excavated from tombs, allowing us to consider aspects of elite dining behaviors; additional ceramic vessels also come from mortuary contexts. Some sites and surface surveys have provided more extensive ceramic evidence as well, and a few exotic outliers such as the clear glass cups from Mylasa and Ephesus give a sense of the range of materials used. The following discussion outlines a basis for analysis in the hope that the finds of future excavations will refine it.

Eating Utensils and Dining Behaviors

One of the best ways to understand dining behaviors in Achaemenid Anatolia is to study excavated ceramic assemblages. Vessel shapes, firing techniques, and surface decoration can afford insight into the kinds of food and drink people consumed and the ways in which they did so, while the prevalence of certain shapes can give us an idea of popularity or frequency of use. From pots we can thus learn about table manners as well as diet – even when we have no botanical or textual remains to help us. Sometimes a ceramic assemblage demonstrates a deep-rooted tradition in eating and drinking, while at other times it provides evidence for innovation or external influence.

The only Anatolian site to have undergone in-depth analysis and comparison of pre-Achaemenid and Achaemenid ceramic assemblages, discovered through intensive controlled excavations, is Gordion.[58] A notable change occurred at the beginning of the Achaemenid period at Gordion, concentrated primarily in fine wares (those used for and visible during dining, perhaps particularly at the tables of the relatively wealthy). In the Middle Phrygian period, which lasted from ca. 800 to 550, the ceramic assemblage was characterized by standardized vessel types, sizes, and production sequences that demonstrated mass production. Fully 85 percent of the assemblage was fired in a reducing environment, and emphasis was on quantity rather than quality when it came to utilitarian wares.[59] The fine wares comprised black polished gray ware skeuomorphs of metal prototypes and showed great continuity with Early Phrygian wares; indeed, overall the Middle Phrygian assemblage was locally made and there were few outside influences on vessel types, wares, or forming sequences.[60] Even in elite contexts, imported ceramics were virtually absent.[61]

The Achaemenid, or "Late Phrygian," period (YHSS 4, ca. 550–330) affords a marked contrast to this. The utilitarian wares continued the earlier traditions in shape and rim types, although some new shapes "with possible foreign antecedents" appeared.[62] Interestingly, the firing techniques changed so that gray wares (reduction-fired) constituted only 60 percent of the common ware assemblage, while buff wares (oxidization fired) increased dramatically from 6.4 to 18.1 percent of the common wares. The fine wares demonstrate three major changes. First, the frequency of local fine gray wares decreased from 11.5 to 5.9 percent. Second, the remaining gray or black polished fine wares incorporated new shapes with Achaemenid parallels, including numerous shallow bowls and drinking cups. On local versions of the Achaemenid bowl, pattern burnishing mimicked the flutes of Achaemenid metal wares. Third, the frequency of buff

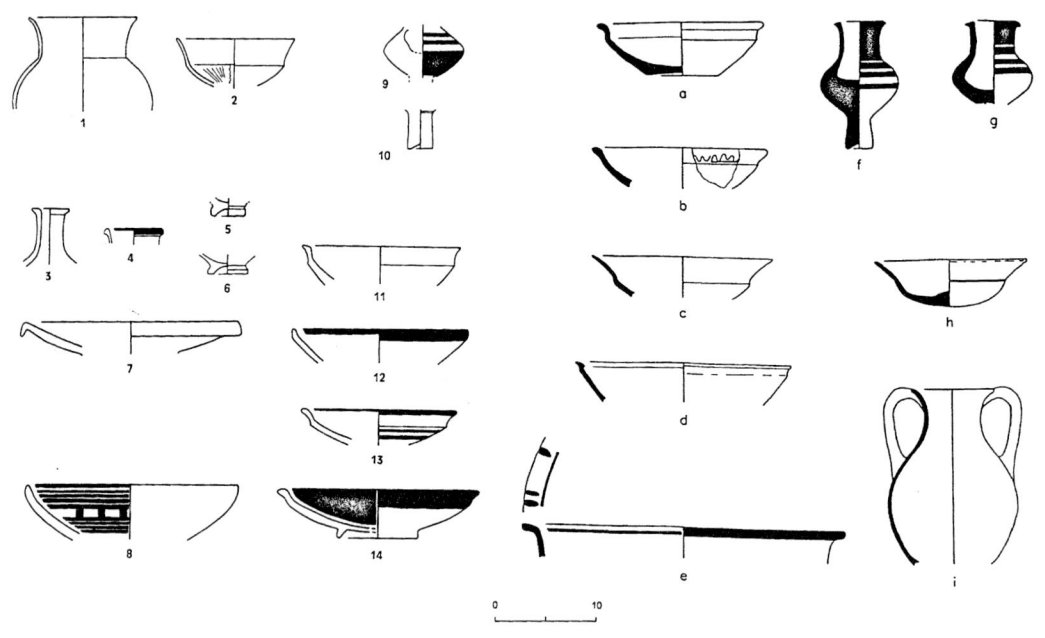

58. Late Phrygian / YHSS 4 vessels from Gordion. After Henrickson 1993: fig. 19 and Voigt et al. 1997: fig. 30. Courtesy Mary Voigt and Robert Henrickson. © Gordion Archaeological Project.

fine wares (unknown in the pre-Achaemenid deposits) was more than double the decline of the gray and polished wares (an increase of 11.6 percent vs. a decrease of 5.6 percent). Moreover, new forming and finishing techniques were introduced, and imported wares from several different areas appeared or became notably more common in the Achaemenid period.[63] The local fine ware tradition seems to have been partially abandoned, while potters incorporated new vessel shapes from other cultures – particularly Persian.[64]

Gordion's ceramic assemblage thus demonstrates a real change in vessel types and production during the Achaemenid period. This involved not only an increase in imports but a change in locally made pots to incorporate more vessels of distinctly Iranian or Greek shape, finished in ways that increased their resemblance to the foreign wares and reduced their similarity to the vessels of Phrygian tradition. Such changes were seen throughout the entire assemblage, but they were most notable in the vessels used for the serving and consumption of wine.

The satrapal capital of Sardis offers some comparison with Gordion, although its wares have not yet been as extensively published; Sardis has still to produce much in the way of datable Achaemenid ceramic assemblages. What follows is a brief summary of evidence excavated from a sequence of eight pits dating from ca. 500 into the Hellenistic period.[65] Achaemenid-period vessels for the preparation and consumption of food show striking differences from their earlier counterparts. Cooking pots were somewhat thinner walled than their pre-conquest counterparts and were fired harder; often they were fired red rather than gray, as had been common in the Lydian period.[66] The added grit might include somewhat more mica and less lime. Many of the pots had flat bottoms, so that they could stand alone, placed next to a fire rather than over it, as seems to have been customary in the earlier period.[67] Bread trays were thinner in the Achaemenid period than in Lydian times and were fired harder, a feature that would probably have produced a thinner, crisper bread.

Wine drinking was popular at Sardis in Achaemenid as in pre-Achaemenid times, and the Lydian-era column krater continued to be made through the Achaemenid period. These kraters showed greater angularity of rim and thinner walls and tended to be fired red rather than dark, although the decorative scheme and size remained otherwise similar to those of the Lydian period. Trefoil oenochoae and small pitchers suggest one means of serving wine at table. A change occurred in drinking cups, as hard-fired, red-slipped Achaemenid bowls supplanted the local skyphos; this will be discussed in greater detail later in the chapter.

The dishes from which people ate also changed. The stemmed vessels of the Lydian period fell into disuse and were replaced by a thin-walled bowl with a ring foot and an incurved thickened rim. The bowls with thickened rims for the most part took the place of the simple-rimmed early variety, although some continued to be made. Bowls of both types were slipped on the interior and partially slipped on the exterior, as far as half the bowl. Like the Achaemenid drinking bowl, the bowl with thickened incurved rim has an Iranian shape; it is ubiquitous in western Iran and Media from the late seventh century on.[68]

These changes in the ceramic assemblage suggest a possible shift in dietary habits in the Achaemenid period at Sardis, although more faunal and botanical evidence must be examined before this question can be settled satisfactorily. They also suggest a change in dining behaviors. Perhaps most provocative is the supplanting of Lydian stemmed dishes by bowls with inverted rims, an Iranian shape very similar to those of Achaemenid-period Gordion. Bowls are one of the most common vessel shapes in Media and western Iran, with a great number of vessels and variety of forms found.[69] With these food bowls and the Achaemenid drinking bowls represented in such number, the place settings of Achaemenid-period Sardis looked very different than the pre-conquest ones.

These two sites demonstrate significant changes in vessels used for eating and drinking during the Achaemenid period. Both sites include the introduction of specifically Iranian shapes and perhaps behaviors. Gordion's imported wares show that its sphere of interaction widened as it was incorporated into the empire; the quantity of Greek imports, for instance, skyrockets at the site after the Achaemenid conquest.[70] Although its assemblages have not yet been fully published, the ongoing studies of Dascylium's imported pottery also demonstrate an increase in foreign imports, both from European Greece and from elsewhere in western Anatolia.[71] A survey of Achaemenid-period pots from eastern Anatolia demonstrates a similar change in vessel shapes and firing techniques, again with an upswing in imported wares forming a significant element of the assemblages.[72]

All of this is thought-provoking and demonstrates major shifts in a semiotically charged area. We are fortunate to have additional sources of evidence for dining and drinking behaviors in Achaemenid Anatolia, however, most of it from mortuary contexts. Tombs have produced examples of precious-metal vessels and demonstrate a wide array of accoutrements associated with wine preparation and public drinking, including strainers and ladles, and even incense burners. They contain not only cups of Persian shape but also elaborate rhyta with the foreparts of animals as terminals. And representations of banqueters, including paintings from tombs as well as tombstones carved in relief, provide us with visual evidence for the ways these items were used and the importance the Anatolian elite placed on proper dining behaviors.

It is crucially significant that Achaemenid hegemony had such an impact on eating and drinking customs. That impact extended not only to the elite but, as the shifts in ceramic assemblages demonstrate, through all levels of society. Perhaps this is not surprising, for literary evidence supports the notion that differentiated dining was important to the Persians; but the degree to which the Achaemenid imperial authority changed dining and, perhaps particularly, drinking behaviors attests to its manipulation of this aspect of social identity. As Dietler points out:

> The nasty little secret of history is that states and empires are very fragile, volatile, and transitory – far more so than their buildings and monuments. They are a fluid *process* rather than a durable thing, and they depend upon constant hard work in the micro-political struggles of negotiation and legitimation to survive and operate. Crucially, governments must constantly reproduce a degree of consent in their populations, whether in the form of credible authority or cynical acquiescence, in order for the ephemeral idea of a state to persist. Material monuments and institutions provide arenas (of variable effectiveness) for this interpersonal activity to be carried out, but they do not replace it or make it redundant. Hence, practices such as feasting are every bit as important to the operation of states as they are to other forms of political organization.[73]

Value-Laden Cups of Precious Metal

Drinking played an important role in establishing and securing Achaemenid authority. The story mentioned earlier in which the king drank the water only of the Choaspes River suggests that the consumption of water could bear symbolic significance; but it was also presumably a common practice. The drinking

59. Rhyton, Achaemenid bowl, round-bottomed bowl, and phiale. ME 124081, ME 123256, ME 134740, and ME 1998-1-17. © Trustees of the British Museum.

of milk is suggested by the list of ingredients for the King's Dinner. We do not know whether fermented mare's milk was consumed, or fruit or vegetable juices, but they seem plausible. What is certain is that wine drinking played a role in the administration of the empire.

Herodotus famously commented that the Persians conducted any important discussions twice over, either first drunk and then sober or first sober and then drunk; for a decision to be adopted it had to be agreed upon both ways.[74] Significant evidence exists for the imbibing of wine and also (in places) beer.[75] Wine drinking played a role in the dissemination of imperial authority, as shown by the numerous receipts for wine in the Persepolis Fortification Archive, the decision-making process mentioned by Herodotus, and the banqueting imagery on various seals of the Fortification Archive.[76] On the basis of visual representations and the archaeological recovery of wine cups, we know that the consumption of wine abounded in Achaemenid Anatolia. It is notable and significant that the cups used for drinking are highly standardized and even prominently showcased in images and assemblages throughout Anatolia.

Drinking vessels of precious materials exhibit striking similarity across the empire. Particular cup shapes clearly signified elite status and indicated elite drinking behaviors. Achaemenid Anatolia has provided many of these: a deep cup with offset carinated rim (the Achaemenid bowl), the shallower phiale, often with an omphalos at its center and lobes or flutes on its sides, round-bottomed bowls that resemble ostrich eggs, and animal-protome rhyta in bronze, silver, and gold plate. They are remarkably consistent in their form and their surface decoration; they reflect central Achaemenid iconography and style in obvious ways. They were made according to standardized ideals and with a specified outcome. There is no doubt that the use of bronze, silver, and gold wine-drinking vessels was another way the elite of Anatolia signified their membership in and adherence to the polyethnic Achaemenid elite.

60. Spouted table amphorae and cups, from the Apadana at Persepolis. P29345, P23162, and P29347. Courtesy of the Oriental Institute of the University of Chicago.

This was a declaration of imperial authority expressed through elite practice that found emphatic iteration in the imperial heartland and seems to have been a significant element of establishing authority across the empire. The observation is underscored by the distinction afforded wine-drinking vessels in visual representations. The Apadana reliefs at Persepolis give great prominence to wine vessels in worked metal, including round-bottomed cups, Achaemenid bowls, and table amphorae.[77] Delegations from as many as twelve of the twenty-three different peoples bring these vessels to the king, offering them along with items of regional significance. What makes this so interesting is that some items, including animals and dress, clearly indicate the variety of peoples, creatures, and regional specialties of the empire. The wine vessels, however, are of the same recognizable style no matter who brings them, or from what corner of the empire. Persepolis demonstrates a clearly articulated ideology here: metal drinking vessels look alike no matter where the elite use them.

There are no rhyta represented on the Apadana reliefs or anywhere else in monumental form at Persepolis, nor are there any phialae. The overwhelming number of Achaemenid bowls represented therefore highlights their significance to the imperial authority and underscores their importance as markers of imperium in Anatolia. The delight that individuals might take in other imperially marked vessel shapes is demonstrated at Persepolis, however, by their representation on various seals used on the Fortification Archive, representations that give us an unusual opportunity to see how these vessels were really used in banqueting situations.[78]

The conformity of appearance of actual metal vessels excavated in Achaemenid Anatolia must be considered within a framework of imperial authority expressed

EATING AND DRINKING WITH CLASS AND STYLE

61. Persepolis Fortification Seal 535*. Courtesy Mark B. Garrison and Margaret Cool Root.

by the elite through their drinking vessels and behaviors. This is a clear example of the "diacritical drinking" mentioned earlier, by means of which people can signal and perpetuate their status and identity through behaviors. Even a few of the most commonly found drinking vessel shapes demonstrate the significance of the group in an elite context. That these same shapes were made from clay, presumably for non-elites, demonstrates the implications of the cups for understanding Achaemenid authority in Anatolia. Although the examples we have of drinking vessels made of precious metals are from tombs, textual evidence shows they were used by the elite in living society as well. The visual evidence introduces ambiguity to our analysis of behavior: it is certain that men drank from such vessels, reclining on their left sides, but it is not clear whether women, too, used cups of these shapes as they sat at banquets. The cups' inclusion in the tombs of, apparently, both sexes suggests that their use may not have been gendered, but for now the question remains open.

Susanne Ebbinghaus has demonstrated that the rhyton with animal foreparts, the shape of which combines elements of the animal-headed cup, the zoomorphic vessel, and the drinking horn, was devised for the Achaemenid court in the later sixth century.[79] Her comparison of these drinking vessels with earlier forms of animal-headed vessels, notably Neo-Assyrian, highlights the function and peculiar iconography of the Achaemenid rhyta. Through their use as ritually charged drinking vessels and prestigious gifts, she suggests, the habit of drinking from rhyta spread among the elites of the empire, simultaneously signaling the drinker's high status and his allegiance to the king.[80]

Rhyta provide an excellent starting point for this discussion because of the drinking behaviors they imply as well as their striking shape.[81] A true rhyton has a spout at its bottom that could be unstoppered, so the wine would shoot out (ideally) into the mouth of the drinker. Vessels of the same shape but without the spout were more closely akin to drinking horns – the vessels are frequently called rhyta because of their shape, but the manner of drinking from them was very different. Both types appear in Achaemenid Anatolia, made of precious metals and with protomes of real or fantastic animals. It is clear from visual representations that the vessel's shape was the most important signifier of its value. Either way, however, drinking from such a vessel involved wholly different etiquette than drinking from a traditional skyphos with handles and a ring foot. Rhyta are illustrated at Persepolis in glyptic art and in Anatolia in mortuary art; their use is overtly and exclusively associated with high-status drinking.[82] To my knowledge, the art of Achaemenid Anatolia shows only men drinking from rhyta or drinking horns. It is possible that this was a vessel shape with gendered significance.

More frequently found than the rhyta are two of the three shapes of drinking bowl, often made of bronze or silver, sometimes with gold appliqués: the Achaemenid bowl and the phiale.[83] Of these, the Achaemenid bowl seems to have borne particular significance at Persepolis in the authority-charged visual renditions of the Apadana reliefs. It is noteworthy that the Achaemenid bowl has no precedent in Anatolia before the arrival of the Persians. Silver versions of this shape and the phiale have been found across Anatolia, including in Lycia, Sardis, İkiztepe, Sinope, Erzincan, and Deve Hüyük. Although most of them were found in tombs, the discovery of a clear glass phiale at the Artemision at Ephesus adds to the literary and visual evidence demonstrating that precious cups not only were mortuary inclusions or used in living banquets, but could be so highly valued as to serve as dedications at sanctuaries.[84]

Two features of these wine-drinking cups combine to make them important in considering the role of drinking in the authority–autonomy model: their conformity in appearance and their apparently local production.[85] The standardization of their shape and ornamentation is crucial to their function as indicators of elite status. The conformity of elite metal wares across the empire demonstrates that they were designed to look alike, to adhere to a recognizable and specific format regardless of context or time. They not only symbolize but to some extent actually *create* the elite. The fact that they were made and used locally adds greatly to the significance of the recognition. These are not solely Persian imports, although some of them may have been; rather, some at least were made by local craftspeople.[86] They demonstrate the degree to which Anatolian elites and artisans adopted the new model of authority and assimilated Achaemenid drinking behaviors into their own practice. As Miller comments, this is a very charged matter, both geographically and notionally, for those seeking to imprint and convey their social identity.[87]

Value-laden metal drinking vessels and accoutrements of clearly Achaemenid persuasion have been found in tombs at the satrapal site of Sardis, which forms the beginning locus of our investigation.[88] These include a silver phiale with flutes and lobes that was found in a tomb along with a silver Achaemenid bowl; a second Achaemenid bowl from another tomb; a ladle with calf's-head terminal

EATING AND DRINKING WITH CLASS AND STYLE

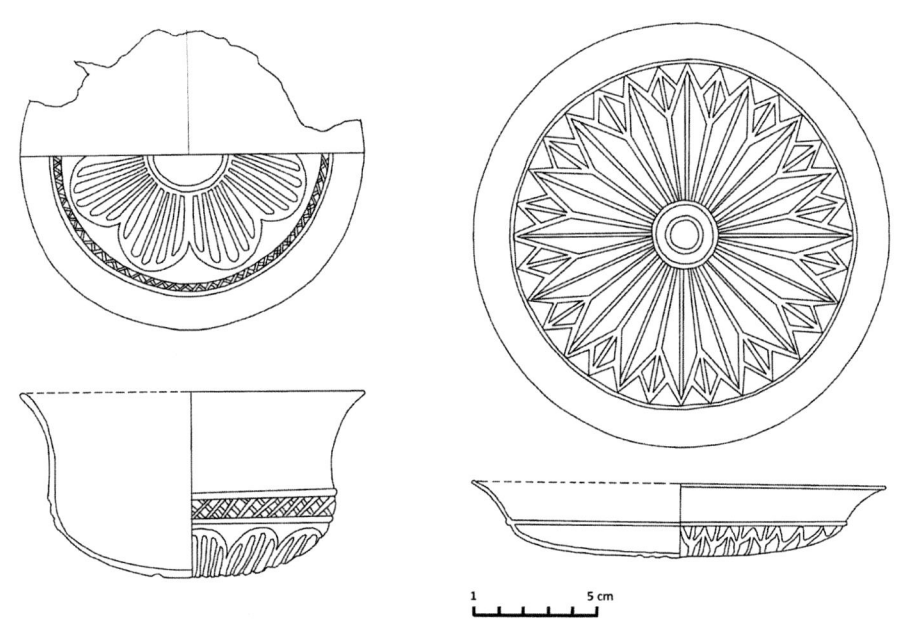

62. Clear glass cups from Mylasa. Author's drawing, after Yağcı 1995: pls. 1 and 2.

and a spouted dish found together; a fluted jar and three silver saucers from a different tomb; and two additional silver saucers from yet another tomb.[89] Perhaps also to be included with the banqueting paraphernalia is the bronze mirror with double-horse protome at its handle, found in the same tomb as one of the silver Achaemenid bowls and the silver phiale.[90] These drinking vessels, as well as the mirror, demonstrate strong connections with imagery of Achaemenid authority.

Metal examples of the traditional Lydian skyphos have not been found in Achaemenid-period Sardian tombs, but excavations in the city demonstrate that skyphoi continued to be made from clay and used through the Achaemenid period.[91] Were there clay examples in the Achaemenid-period tombs as well? Were there originally silver ones, which were found by tomb robbers before the modern excavations began and thus not retrieved by archaeologists? At the moment we cannot know, and it seems safest to assume that both cup shapes figured in Sardian drinking practices, whether of the living society or associated with mortuary ritual. What we can say is this: drinking out of a cup with no handle and a tippy bottom requires different practice than drinking out of a cup with handles and a stable base; to use these new cups, the elite had to alter their behavior.

Miller has demonstrated that balancing a small drinking bowl on three fingertips was a defining characteristic of drinking in appropriately authoritative ways, not only in the Persian heartland but indeed in the western Achaemenid Empire – and also has pointed out that insufficient evidence exists in western

63. Bronze mirror from Sardis. IAM 4572. Courtesy Yapı Kredi Yayınları.

Anatolia to determine how widespread the practice was.[92] My argument here relies less on that most semiotically charged of behaviors than on the actual *necessity* of changed interaction with a drinking cup that has no handles and no ring foot to its base, although a specific manner of holding the cup ties into the issue as well. The process of picking up, holding, drinking from, and setting down these cups was different from that with a skyphos (in my experience, it requires greater finesse to avoid spilling).[93] The presence of the Achaemenid bowls in Sardian tombs therefore demonstrates a shift in elite behavior. These bowls reflect a manner of drinking in Anatolia that was highly charged and filled with value because of its association with the elite, a manner of drinking

64. A ceramic skyphos and two ceramic Achaemenid bowls from Sardis. © Archaeological Exploration of Sardis.

so closely connected to elite behavior that it reified elite status and authority. Moreover, metal cups of these shapes have not been found only at the satrapal site of Sardis: they come from the Lydian–Phrygian border at Uşak, from northernmost Paphlagonia at Sinope, from the Armenian highlands at Erzincan, and from the agricultural plain of the Euphrates at Deve Hüyük.[94] Feasting in explicitly Achaemenid ways to mark the transition from life to death was a powerful comment on new manifestations of power, and its significance would not have been diminished by the presence of traditional local shapes alongside the new.

The importance of this liminal dining, feasting to usher the dead out of life, is demonstrated repeatedly in Anatolia. The presence of funerary couches in mortuary contexts, perhaps implying banqueting, has been well addressed by Elizabeth Baughan, who also points out the tremendous preponderance of banqueting vessels and other paraphernalia in the grave goods of Achaemenid Lydia.[95] Funerary feasting is demonstrated not only by the recovery of vessels from tombs, however, but also by the visual representations of the elite in mortuary contexts across much of Anatolia. Probably the most famous of these is the painted interior of a tomb at Karaburun, dating to ca. 470, showing elite manly pursuits: battle, a funerary cortege, and a reclining banquet scene.[96] The vessels (and manner of holding them) are prominently on display.

Banquet scenes are common on the mortuary relief sculptures of western and central Anatolia as well.[97] Several aspects of this are important for understanding Achaemenid authority in Anatolia. Feasting was associated with elite funerary behaviors, and the manner of feasting was explicitly portrayed. Reclining on his left elbow into stacked cushions, a male held a cup of recognizably Achaemenid shape in one hand. Accompanying him and often shown interacting with him were one or more females seated on the foot of the couch or on a chair or stool

65. Elite male figure from the west wall at Karaburun II. Courtesy Stella Miller-Colette.

near his head, often with their feet on a footstool. These women were generally veiled and raised a flower or other sweet-scented object before their noses. Proper elite feasting required assistance from servitors. And elite feasting was elaborate in the number and type of vessels necessary for drinking. The consistency of visual representation coincides with the consistency of actual metal vessels recovered from tombs and reiterates this essential aspect of elite signaling. What you drank, how you drank, with whom you drank – all of these mattered. All had value in demonstrating and perpetuating authority.

Value-Laden Cups of Clay

The elite drank enthusiastically out of wine vessels of precious metal in specific shapes, often made locally, that bore a close connection to the Persian court.[98] The Achaemenid elite thus participated in drinking behaviors that linked them to the king and to each other in overt and specific ways. It should come as no surprise that at least one of these cup shapes, the Achaemenid bowl, was produced in clay as well; it was apparently used by people of lesser status and thus demonstrates the introduction of elite behaviors – if not wealth – far down the prestige scale.

At Sardis the ceramic version of the Achaemenid bowl enjoyed tremendous popularity from the earliest datable Achaemenid deposits well into the Hellenistic period; indeed, it is the most common drinking cup found at Sardis from the moment of its first appearance in the archaeological record until the time it is supplanted by the molded bowls of the second century.[99] Recent research makes it clear that ceramic Achaemenid bowls were popular almost everywhere in Achaemenid Anatolia. This is relatively unsurprising, given the

66. A ceramic Achaemenid bowl from Sardis. © Archaeological Exploration of Sardis.

well-known phenomenon of less wealthy people imitating in clay the expensive metal vessels of the elite. The mere appearance of ceramic Achaemenid bowls in the archaeological record could simply be attributed to this behavior. What is interesting is the tremendous standardization of Achaemenid bowls across the empire. Their shapes differ very little. They are regularly made of highly levigated clay of the finest quality, sometimes apparently local but sometimes brought from farther afield and easily correlated to the finest vessels of big cities (without more extensive neutron activation analysis this correlation must rely on visual observation, but so far it is clear). They demonstrate craft specialization and, probably, centralization or at least nucleation of production.[100]

Achaemenid bowls at Sardis were fired harder and redder than was usual for Lydian wares, and with their instantly recognizable surface treatment of mottled red color they clearly stand out from the rest of the ceramic assemblage. Indeed, a single sherd of an Achaemenid bowl can be diagnostic of the shape. What makes this important is that neutron activation analysis establishes that the bowls were locally produced; the change in their firing was deliberate, and it specifically distinguished them from traditional local wares.[101] Moreover, they were widely exported: Miller has documented their retrieval from multiple sites in western Anatolia, including Harta and Lâle Tepe in Lydia, Karaburun and Hacımusalar in Lycia, and possibly Celaenae in Phrygia.[102] This is an overt example of the centralized production of a new, specifically Achaemenid wine-drinking shape, one with powerful elite associations, fired in a new manner that distinguished it from all other fabrics. The satrapal site of Sardis thus supplied clay cups with high-status and imperial connotations to other sites across much of western Anatolia.

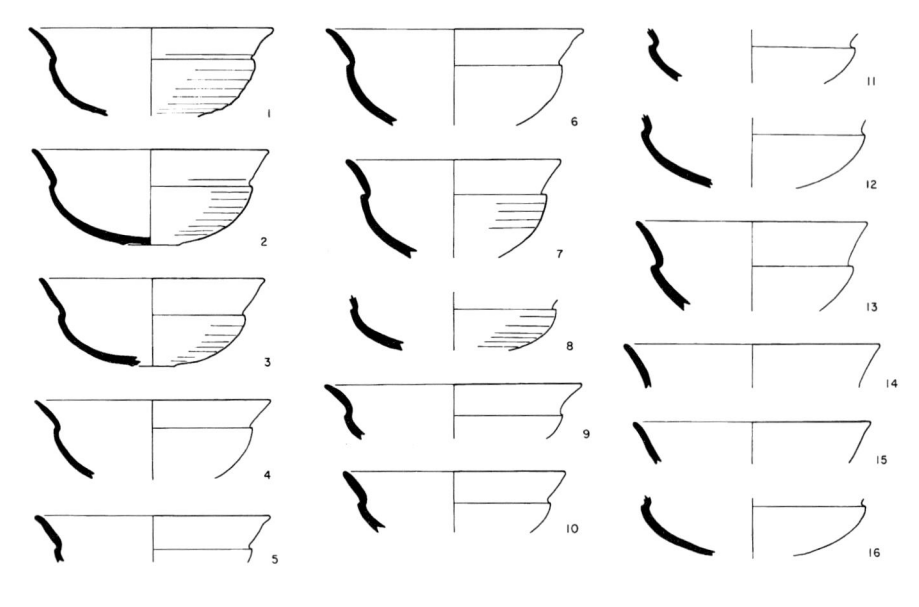

67. Achaemenid bowls from a deposit at Sardis. After Dusinberre 1999: fig. 4.
© Archaeological Exploration of Sardis.

Achaemenid bowls in the empire are consistently distinguished from earlier fine wares and other contemporary vessels by clay, firing technique, and surface decoration. They are fired thinner and harder than other wares, with finely levigated clay usually fired to a pale, pink, or red color but sometimes a fine dark gray or polished black with pattern burnishing to suggest toreutic decorations.[103] Examples of Achaemenid bowls from Anatolia that were not exported from Sardis also exhibit these characteristics. The vessels from Dascylium in Hellespontine Phrygia and from Phrygian Gordion at the north of the Anatolian plateau share essential features with those from the sites of southern Pamphylia.[104] Of great interest is the recent publication of fine wares from northern Armenia by Antonio and Claudia Sagona.[105] This area was described by Xenophon as a beer-drinking rather than a wine-drinking center, but the Assyrian description of Urartu as awash with wine, as well as the quality and popularity of Armenian wine in modern times, demonstrates that both beverages could be produced here.[106]

It is striking that Sagona and Sagona's study includes local Iron Age fine wares formed into the shape of Achaemenid bowls, fired pale red-gold or dark with burnished patterns like the Gordion material.[107] Altıntepe and the neighboring Cimin Tepe have produced not only very fine large examples of the Persian or Persian-influenced "Triangle Ware," but also drinking bowls fired buff with carinated offset rims.[108] This new shape, imported or made of local clay treated in a recognizably elegant manner, thus appears across all Anatolia – including those areas that produced beer as well as wine. In some cases, it seems, both a particular beverage and a cup shape and its associated drinking behaviors were highlighted. Given the significance of wine drinking in Persian society and modern understanding of the community-enhancing role that alcohol of all sorts plays in human society, this is an observation of fundamental importance.

Who used these cups? Andrew Ramage, in speaking of Achaemenid bowls from Sardis, reiterated the point that the earlier fine table wares of the Lydian period continued in use through the Achaemenid period, alongside the Achaemenid bowls.[109] This raises a crucial question. Were the Achaemenid bowls used by some, perhaps with a three-fingered hold, while the skyphoi were used by others? Might a group of people have used cups of both shapes, some perhaps holding the skyphoi in one way and others holding Achaemenid bowls in another way? That they are often found together suggests to me that the latter suggestion is more likely. This is exciting. While the elite drank from vessels of silver and gold, the non-elite drank from Achaemenid shapes of special clay. Because it is impossible to hold or use these vessels as one would a cup with handles and a foot, using them requires different drinking behaviors. This does not mean that everyone did it "right," with a three-fingered balance. But the new standardized shape, the manufacture of which may have been overseen by the Achaemenid authority, required a new hold and behavioral style. Thus down to the very lowest levels of society, even where people continued to use traditional shapes and behaviors, the new infiltrated. People across Anatolia were constantly engaged in drinking practices that united them to the new authority.

Judith Butler has analyzed the role of performance in creating and reifying societally determined roles.[110] She argues that what may seem natural coherences, such as gender or status distinctions, are actually culturally constructed through the repetition over time of stylized acts that establish the appearance and definition of a core "fact."[111] Thus gender and sexuality are grounded in gender performativity, rendered significant because of performance repetition or "iterability":

> Performativity cannot be understood outside of a process of iterability, a regularized and constrained repetition of norms. And this repetition is not performed *by* a subject; this repetition is what enables a subject and constitutes the temporal condition for the subject. This iterability implies that "performance" is not a singular "act" or event, but a ritualized production, a ritual reiterated under and through constraint, under and through the force of prohibition and taboo, with the threat of ostracism and even death controlling and compelling the shape of the production, but not, I will insist, determining it fully in advance.[112]

These performative acts need not be voluntary and indeed may be coerced by political or other agency.[113]

Although Butler's work focuses on gender roles, it is significant in the context of this discussion of drinking because of the importance it places on performance: what matters is not how you feel but rather how you behave. Performativity creates belonging. It creates a public connection regardless of the initial reason for performance: some may want to conform to particular behaviors, some may conform because they recognize the advantages of doing so, and some may have conformity thrust upon them, either because someone else makes them conform or because they have no other options. We cannot tell the motivational difference archaeologically. But when we understand the importance of performativity in creating and reiterating social roles, we see that the initial rationale for an individual's conformity to performative norms may have mattered greatly to that person, but it affects the cultural and political result of the person's actions very little. From the point of view of imperial authority in Achaemenid Anatolia, it was the performance that was key.

The conformity of Achaemenid bowls suggests that this feature was something that mattered to the imperial authority. The possible centralization, as well as standardization, of their production supports this notion. To have something as significant and pervasive as commensal drinking involve specifically imperial wine-drinking cups was important. The new shape, standardized across Anatolia, required that people change the way they handled their cups. The cups' overtly Achaemenid-associated appearance underscored their connection to the new imperial authority. That they involved people of all ranks in unifying behaviors of status and authority is tremendously significant. The sharing of drinking behaviors among people across Achaemenid Anatolia meant that they actively participated in establishing, legitimating, and perpetuating imperial authority. Thus eating and drinking became performative iterations of class and style, creating value and using behaviors to unite not only the elite but indeed all ranks of people within the empire.

FIVE

DEALING WITH THE DEAD

What mattered to the central authority, and what kinds of autonomy were allowed or exercised? Across Anatolia, mortuary treatment is tremendously variable. Even at a single site, we may observe multiple means of disposing of the dead. Some are buried in rock-cut tombs carved into cliff faces, others in simple unmarked cists, still others in chambers or sarcophagi heaped over with tumuli. Some have elaborate grave stelae or other markers. Some are entombed in temple-shaped mausolea or other distinctive structures built above the ground. Certain forms follow local traditions, while others demonstrate radical departures. Thus we see many different answers to the same question: What do you do with your dead? The answer to the question was apparently left open to those responsible for each corpse, for tending the spiritual and social demands of death within a family or community. The degree of variability in mortuary structure demonstrates that the Achaemenid imperial administration did not mandate how people disposed of their dead. In this area, people exercised considerable autonomy, and the agency of decision was, it seems, their own. Indeed, the frequently local, geographically bounded variability suggests that mortuary structures might serve as a way for local Anatolian populaces to claim adherence to pre-Achaemenid traditions and inheritances, to proclaim their local roots and non-Persian identities.

At the same time, however, mortuary inclusions demonstrate remarkable uniformity of social agenda and presentation in signaling membership in or allegiance to the imperial enterprise – particularly among those wealthy enough to be buried with prestige-laden items. These artifacts demonstrate that while mortuary *structures* showed great local variability, mortuary *assemblages* did not.

Across Anatolia, the status-signaling mortuary assemblages of the elite display an almost astonishing conformity of visible, semiotically charged material.

Silver, gold, and bronze drinking assemblages include vessels of the same shapes, apparently used for the same purposes. Jewelry in bronze, copper, silver, and gold is crafted in forms charged with imperial meaning and elite nuances. Semiprecious stones and enamel inlays are used in the same colors and ways in bracelets, earrings, and necklaces. Gold foil clothing ornaments share iconography linked to Achaemenid imperial might. Even horse trappings signal prestige.

Such displays of status through wealth expenditure are common in human societies, and their uniformity of expression in Achaemenid Anatolia is significant.[1] It demonstrates the cohesion of those displaying their membership in the authority-laden Achaemenid elite. An interesting aspect of this analysis has to do with the ethnicities of the elite. Mortuary contexts provide us with much of the information we have for considering the elite in Achaemenid Anatolia. Those of high status and authority were not strictly Persian in ethnicity. Indeed, it is difficult to ascertain the ethnicity of a given elite person on the basis of mortuary inclusions. It seems to have mattered more to people to signal "being elite" in their dress and dining than to signal "being Carian" or "being Phrygian" or "being Lycian."[2] Their mortuary structures, however, add nuance and complexity to ethnic signaling.

In order to make clear the connections and differences across the peninsula, this chapter departs from the others in being organized geographically. It begins with Lydia and moves clockwise, ending with that spectacular mortuary monument of Caria, the Mausoleum of Halicarnassus. With few exceptions, the evidence demonstrates the maintenance of local traditions in elite tomb construction but the incorporation of elite Achaemenid ideology into tomb decoration and mortuary inclusions.

Lydia

The number of Achaemenid-period tombs in Lydia makes it challenging to summarize them; the current discussion attempts to suggest the overall variety by surveying their most common forms and considering the artifacts retrieved from within them. External grave markers lead to a final consideration of a few uniquely extravagant forms.

Rock-Cut Tombs

Rock-cut tombs make up the majority of those excavated at Sardis: at least 1,154 graves.[3] Sardis's rock-cut tombs usually had a dromos leading to one or more rectangular chambers, often with a pitched ceiling. Benches, or klinae, might be found along the back and side walls. Bodies seem to have been placed directly on these klinae; some were also buried in sarcophagi, of which the most common

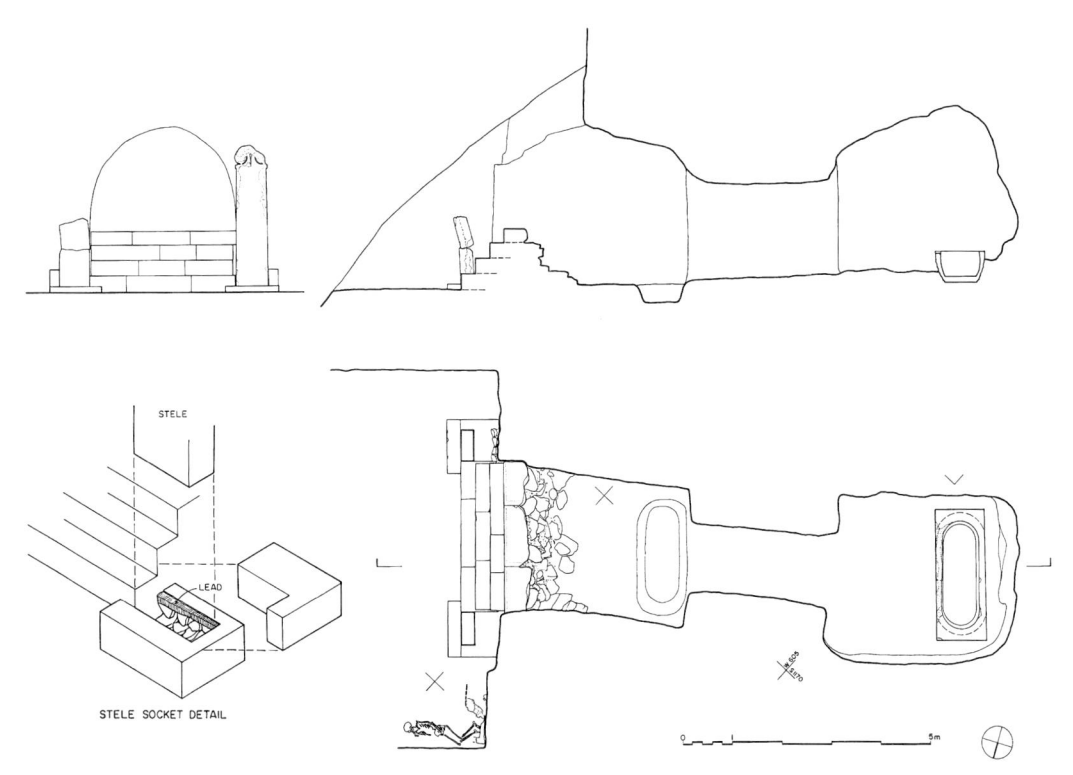

68. Plan and section of Tomb 813. After Greenewalt, Cahill, and Rautman 1987: fig. 24. © Archaeological Exploration of Sardis.

type was bathtub-shaped. It may be that those tombs with multiple interments are specifically Achaemenid in date.[4] Some of the rock-cut tombs, such as Tomb 813, were embellished with an elaborate facade: in the case of 813, two anthemion stelae flanked a limestone staircase at the tomb's entrance that led up to nowhere and therefore served a symbolic, ceremonial, or decorative function.[5] Rock-cut tombs are a clear example of a Lydian mortuary tradition continuing into the Achaemenid period, but the funerary stelae may be an Achaemenid-period introduction.

Similar tombs are known from rural Lydia as well as Sardis, although their documentation is scanty and establishing chronology remains difficult. They date from the late seventh or early sixth century on and represent a funerary tradition with local roots that continued through the Achaemenid period.[6] Rock-cut cemeteries dating to the pre-Achaemenid and Achaemenid periods are attested west of Sardis in the middle Hermus River valley, along the northern foothills of Mt. Sipylus, in the Hyrcanian plain, in the middle Phrygius River valley, in the Lycus valley, in the upper Caecus valley, in the central Tmolus mountain range, and in the Cayster valley.[7] Roosevelt has suggested that a tomb cut into a spur of limestone at Kahraman near Gelenbe may have provided an inexpensive way to imitate the freestanding tombs of Sardis.[8] At this time, there

69. Bathtub sarcophagi from a rock-cut tomb at Sardis. After H. Butler 1922: fig. 177. Courtesy Princeton University Press.

is no evidence that these tombs sought to evoke the Achaemenid royal tombs, nor do we know who was buried in them.

Cists

Residents of Achaemenid Lydia were also buried in cist graves and in sarcophagi, often bathtub-shaped and made of terracotta or marble.[9] The sarcophagi could be placed in rock-cut tombs, buried in tumuli, or simply buried in the ground. I do not discuss them at any length here; it is clear, however, that bathtub sarcophagi were common. A bathtub sarcophagus found at Susa, with much wealth inside, and the richly painted Clazomenian sarcophagi discussed later may suggest that they had elite associations even beyond the cost of their fabrication.[10]

The profiles of the Achaemenid Lydian marble sarcophagi are rather different than those elsewhere, but the connection is clear. At least one rock-lined cist grave dates to the Achaemenid period at Sardis, and we may postulate many, many more that have so far escaped archaeological detection.[11]

Tumulus Tombs

The most prominent form of mortuary treatment in Lydia was the tumulus tomb – indeed, more than six hundred have been documented.[12] They are earthen tumuli erected over built chambers that were generally constructed of ashlar masonry and (in Achaemenid-period tombs) with a symbolic false door and often a dromos as well, in which there have frequently been found remains of iron wheel bands that were originally, presumably, part of a funeral cart or a chariot.[13] Such tumuli were labor-intensive, expensive, visible monuments.[14] Many of them had stone, wood, or even bronze klinae in their chambers to hold the bodies of the dead.[15] By far the majority of the tumuli are situated on ridges or hilltops, where they attain visual prominence as well as a kind of symbolic dominance over the surrounding landscape; most of the tumuli were probably constructed between the mid–sixth and mid–fifth centuries.[16] At least some of them were topped with the aniconic markers that have been called phalli.[17]

Tumuli have perhaps been the most carefully explored of the tomb types at Sardis and yield information about funerary activities. Charcoal layers have been recovered from above the limestone ceiling beams of several built chamber tombs/tumuli, including at least one tumulus of the Lydian Kingdom (the Tomb of Alyattes) as well as smaller tumuli dating to the Achaemenid period.[18] These fires need not indicate the incineration of bodies – indeed, probably do not – but rather most likely represent some type of ceremony involving fire at the tomb site.[19] Pyres are attested in the ceremonies surrounding the use of tumulus tombs in both the pre-Achaemenid and the Achaemenid periods, and we may hypothesize the continuity of a Lydian funerary tradition into Achaemenid times.

In the Achaemenid period and probably in the Hellenistic, use of the tumulus cemetery at Bin Tepe across the valley from Sardis increased dramatically: of the approximately 150 tombs at Bin Tepe, only the three largest are fairly securely datable to the Lydian Kingdom. Those smaller tumuli that have been excavated may be dated on the basis of masonry techniques and other evidence to the Achaemenid period and later. The grave goods embrace Persian luxury accoutrements, as will be discussed later; they include dozens of gold foil clothing appliqués and other jewelry that conform to Achaemenid-period imperial iconography, including such features as stamped appliqués showing winged human-headed bulls and earrings with lion's-head terminals.[20] At least one tumulus had a chariot burial – complete with horse(s) – in its dromos.[21]

70. Tumuli at Bin Tepe. Author's photo.

Two tumulus tombs with built chambers provide an idea of the form and decoration of many: those at Lâle Tepe and at Harta. Lâle Tepe, 11 km west of Sardis, dates perhaps to the early fifth century and presents a chamber of ashlar limestone blocks with a gabled roof, a porch or small vestibule, and a dromos of ashlar, all covered with an earthen tumulus.[22] It contained several elaborately carved klinae painted with figural decoration, while the upper walls and ceiling were painted with geometric designs. The tomb had been looted, but ceramic finds recovered by archaeologists included oil flasks such as lydions and lekythoi, as well as bowls, cooking pots, and drinking cups. A recumbent lion statue was found above the dromos lintel.[23] A marble door between chamber and dromos was decorated with riveted bands carved in relief, with painted double-lyre decorations plus rosettes with six petals and six sepals, set within concentric circles, that are paralleled by rosettes painted on the klinae.[24] The klinae – one double couch and two single couches – were carved and painted to resemble wooden couches, including the careful articulation of a cushion or mattress.[25] The legs of the double kline, at the rear of the tomb, have volute capitals; its front edge is painted with a bud and lotus motif. A limestone slab beneath the rear kline is decorated with a meander pattern at top and a bottom border framing three date palms rendered in vivid green and black against a red background. The side klinae's legs are also richly decorated in sculpture and paint. This tumulus demonstrates the architectural and decorative elaboration of funerary monuments possible in Lydia at the time.

The tumulus at Harta, in northwest Lydia, takes us a step further in the interior decoration of its chamber, which includes life-sized humans painted on its ashlar walls and kline supports in the form of carved marble sphinxes.[26] Like Lâle Tepe, Harta has a dromos and porch leading to the chamber; a double

71. Reconstruction of tumulus chamber at Lâle Tepe. © Archaeological Exploration of Sardis.

kline at the back of the room was made of marble that contrasted with the tan of the walls' sandstone. The kline once had painted decoration, and the beardless sphinxes that formed its legs faced out into the chamber.

The tomb's wall paintings were vandalized by looters, but enough remains to see that they included a procession of figures and at least one wheeled vehicle.[27] The long robes worn by the men link them to the Ionians on the Apadana reliefs at Persepolis.[28] A horse and two wheels may have been depicted on another wall. Remains of a ceramic Achaemenid bowl and a black-slipped lamp were also recovered from the tomb. This chamber thus preserves evidence for funeral klinae with sphinxes rather than lions in an apotropaic position, painted processions with wheeled horse-drawn vehicles, and vessels for drinking.

By far the best-known and most extensively published tumulus tombs of Achaemenid Lydia are three tumuli near Uşak, the contents of which were published as the "Lydian Treasure" in 1996.[29] Their assemblages included rich collections of gold and silver, especially jewelry and drinking vessels, plus sealstones carved with specifically imperial Achaemenid imagery. The overwhelming majority of the finds from these tombs were associated with personal adornment and banqueting. They are recognizably Achaemenid in iconography, distinctively Achaemenid in shape, and laden with status. Not only the precious materials from which they were made, but also the form, iconography,

72. Figures from Harta. Courtesy Yapı Kredi Yayınları.

and style of the jewelry and vessels show that their users were elite. These relics of public behavior signify wealth and status, outward manifestations of elite authority. They provide a glimpse of the cohesion that characterized elite mortuary inclusions across Anatolia, of the construction of Achaemenid portable elite culture.[30]

Terracotta and marble bathtub sarcophagi are frequent inclusions in Lydian tumuli and rock-cut tombs. A bathtub sarcophagus was found in the Sarıkız neighborhood of Kendirlik about 10 m east of the Deliktepe A tumulus.[31] Within it were 370 gold items, including stamped appliqués for clothing (a human-headed winged bull wearing an upright tiara, half-circles with articulated segments, small and large eight-petaled rosettes, large four-petaled rosettes, lotus

73. Objects from İkiztepe. After Baughan 2010: fig. 16. Courtesy Yapı Kredi Yayınları.

buds, and lotus flowers) and jewelry (probably at least one necklace with pendant gold pomegranates and beads of now-missing colored glass). These items suggest that the occupant of the sarcophagus wore at least one necklace and either garments or a shroud richly decorated in gold, gold that linked the

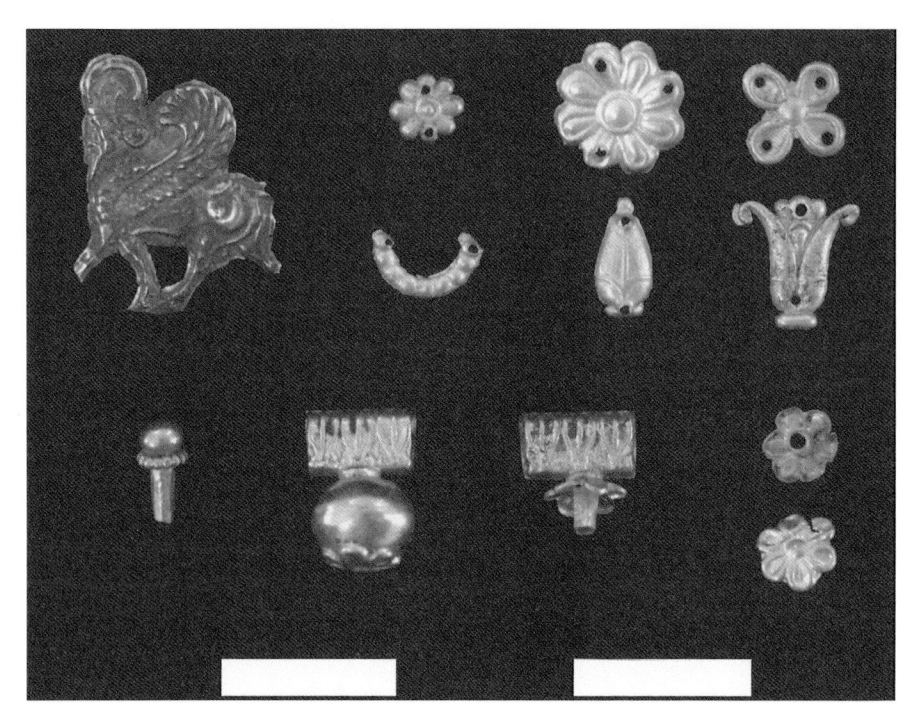

Empire, Authority, and Autonomy in Achaemenid Anatolia

74. Selected items from the sarcophagus burial at Sarıkız. MM6277–87. After Roosevelt 2009: fig. C.1. Courtesy Christopher Roosevelt.

deceased explicitly to Persepolis and perhaps also to Greek, western Anatolian, and Persian notions of blessed death.

Items recovered from one or more graves at Gökçeler near Şahankaya perhaps associated with the stele discussed later (see Figure 90) include bronze and silver mirrors, a golden ram ornament with embossed fleece, a gold boat-shaped earring, two gold rings, two silver bracelets with antelope-head terminals, two silver Achaemenid bowls (one with vertical flutes and one without), a silver ladle with antelope-head terminal, and a bronze cup. Here we do not see the abundance of gold-ornamented cloth that marked the sarcophagus at Sarıkız, but gold is still an important part of personal adornment for the deceased at Gökçeler. Significant are the drinking vessels, including not only elaborate cups but perhaps evidence for flavoring and certainly for serving ceremonies in the form of the ladle. This assemblage thus provides metal accoutrements for the kind of banqueting that is so abundantly illustrated on figural relief stelae.

Miller has demonstrated that the figured cups from the Uşak tombs were made locally even as they draw on the iconography of power current at Persepolis.[32] We cannot think of Achaemenid elite iconography simply as something made in Persia and exported; rather, the elite of Anatolia used authority-laden Achaemenid visual and behavioral vocabulary in their own expressions of power. The people living in Achaemenid Lydia – and, as we shall see, in

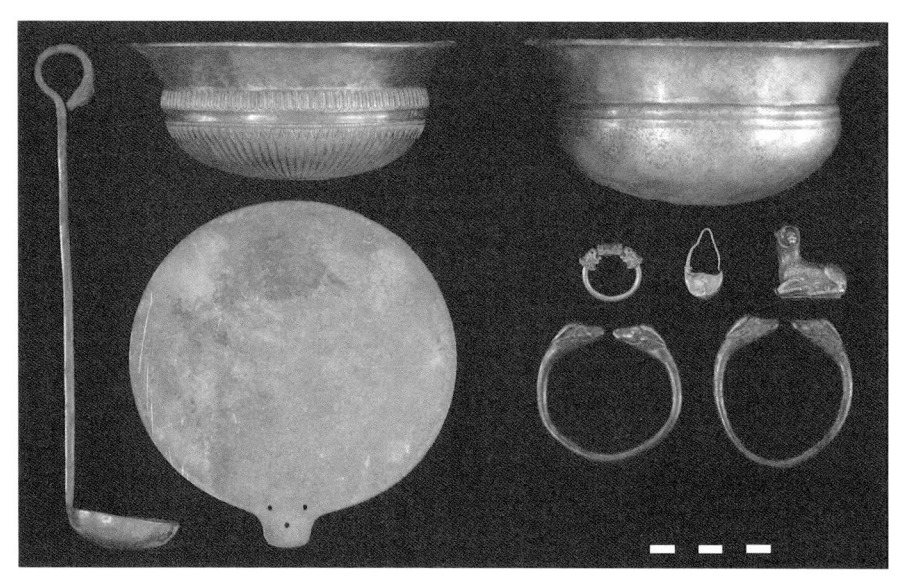

75. Selected items from Gökçeler. MM4611–16, 5288–90. After Roosevelt 2009: fig. C.20
Courtesy Christopher Roosevelt.

Achaemenid Anatolia as a whole – often chose to bury their dead in ways that continued or even celebrated local tradition, but the artifacts with which they buried the dead, the realia that reflected the living society, the accoutrements of living behavior, were defined not by geographic locale or ethnicity but by status. Elite people signaled their allegiance to and identification with Achaemenid imperial hegemonic vision. Mortuary inclusions from Sardis make this point abundantly clear.

Mortuary Inclusions from Sardis

Some 160 of the tombs excavated at Sardis contained objects, generally in disturbed contexts. The mortuary assemblages are largely partial, due to plundering and preservation. Furthermore, in many cases the tombs were used for reinterment and do not represent closed or single-use deposits. The occupants of the tombs were generally missing at the time of twentieth-century excavation, although recent excavation of a rock-cut tomb with a kline shaped like the Greek letter pi, wrapping around the back and side walls, revealed skeletons on the side benches with their heads toward the door.[33] The original arrangement of inclusions can in most cases not be reconstructed, but certain patterns are clear and add to our sense of elite behaviors gained from elsewhere in Lydia.[34]

Sardian elite mortuary inclusions are remarkably consistent from one grave to the next, regardless of whether the tomb was rock-cut, a cist, or a tumulus. They demonstrate the preponderance of Achaemenid authority-laden iconography and the visual performance of linked styles that signaled membership

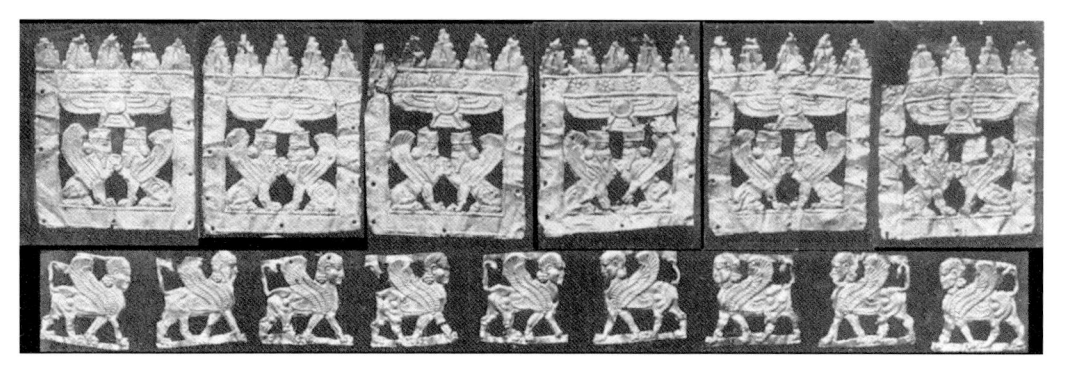

76. Gold foil clothing appliqués from Sardis. After C. Curtis 1925 : pl. I,1 and 2.

in the elite.[35] It is important to note that most of the objects were highly visible: jewelry, personal seals, stamped gold foil ornaments, and banqueting paraphernalia.[36]

Despite the emphasis in the preceding chapter on silver vessels and in addition to the silver wine-drinking assemblages from Sardis's tombs described there, grave goods made of clay as well as precious metals emphasize and underscore the importance of banqueting at Sardis. The overwhelming majority of ceramic vessels from tombs are drinking vessels – cups (skyphoi, Achaemenid bowls), storage vessels (amphorae, hydriae), mixing vessels (kraters), and pouring vessels (oenochoae) – as well as wine-serving or -flavoring implements such as ladles, and frequent unguentaria such as lekythoi, alabastra, and lydions.[37] Of the more than 250 vessels recovered from tombs at Sardis, at least 100 are drinking vessels and another 100 or so are unguent vessels. Perhaps funerary rituals included a feast or it was thought appropriate to provide the dead with the paraphernalia for an eternal feast; or perhaps this emphasis had less to do with funerary ritual than with the living behaviors of the elite, who in death perpetuated their elite status by including the accoutrements of feasting.[38]

Gold clothing appliqués were frequent inclusions in Sardian tombs. The ornaments were made by stamping gold foil with a cut stone or metal stamp bearing an image in intaglio.[39] This technique and some of the repertoire of compositional formats also apply to personal sealstones; the same artisans may have cut both sealstones and the stamps used to make the clothing ornaments. These were apparently sewn to cloth or possibly leather, as the perforations or small loops for attachment to clothing indicate. The artifacts designed for the behavioral signaling of Achaemenid authority were objects in full public sight, designed to make a statement about the social identity and status of an individual. They share iconographic traits with strongly Achaemenid overtones, made in a variety of styles that have unifying features of rendition.[40] Bearded sphinxes, winged man-bulls, crenellations, and the figure emerging from the winged disk all form part of this symbolically significant repertoire.

77. Beaded necklace from Sardis. IAM 4570. Courtesy Yapı Kredi Yayınları.

Gold appliqués would have been immediately discernible indicators of authority – not only the authority of the person wearing them, but also that of the imperial administration and the associated status that made people want to wear them.[41] At this point we do not know whether people were buried in specifically funerary attire or in their living finery, but the association of the garments with banqueting vessels in the tombs suggests a gorgeous display in a context of public drinking. The popularity and uniformity of the style and theme of the appliqués recovered from the tombs of Achaemenid Lydia demonstrate that the elite affiliated themselves with a particular hegemonic iconographic code.[42]

The jewelry found in Sardian tombs conveys much the same message. Necklaces and earrings combine craft traditions to form a new idiom of imperial authority.[43] That a koine in authority-signaling jewelry existed among the Achaemenid elite is also demonstrated by the statue of the Egyptian Udjahorresne, who wears Achaemenid-style jewelry, or that of Ptah-hotep, probably from Memphis, who sports a striking Achaemenid animal-headed torque.[44] Jewelry mattered and was noticed; earrings similar to ones actually found are shown being worn by a small ivory head from an Achaemenid-period tomb at Sardis, a fact that

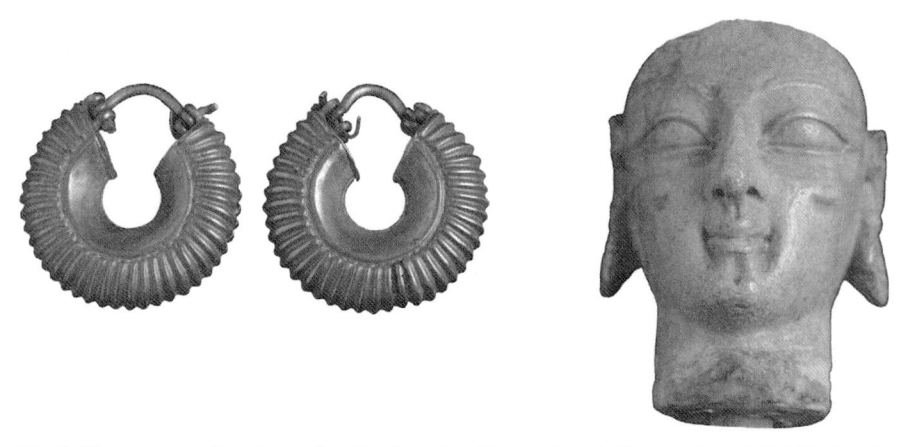

78. Gold earrings and an ivory figurine from Sardis wearing similar earrings. IAM 5148 and 4657. Courtesy Yapı Kredi Yayınları.

79. Seals with Neo-Babylonian and Greek imagery from Sardis. IAM 5133 and 4518. Courtesy Yapı Kredi Yayınları.

highlights their perceived significance. Neither the production nor ownership and use of these objects can be attributed to people of one particular ethnic background; their display seems rather to convey a message of wealth, status, and authority rather than an ethnically specific statement linking them to a given heritage. In this way the portable elite culture of the empire conveys a very different message than the continuity of ethnically Lydian tumulus tombs into the Achaemenid period.

For the most part, the styles of Sardian seals reflect the same koine as the appliqués and the jewelry and suggest a network of visual expression that united the polyethnic elite. In some cases, a seal may be linked with a particular tradition; thus IAM 5133 from Tomb 1005 is carved in the style and with the iconography traditionally associated with Neo-Babylonian glyptic, while IAM 4518 from Tomb A1 is carved in a Greek style.[45] On IAM 5133, a winged disk in one of the common Achaemenid styles of Sardis was added to the space before

80. Gold seal ring from Sardis, apparently that of a seventeen-year-old girl. IAM 4585. Courtesy Yapı Kredi Yayınları.

81. Two seal rings from Sardis, Tomb S 16. IAM 4634 and 4637. Courtesy Yapı Kredi Yayınları.

the worshiper's head, the space that on such seals is most frequently occupied by a crescent moon (sign of the god Sin). The Fortification Archive displays the popularity of Babylonian worship scenes at Persepolis and demonstrates that they bore no connection to ethnicity there.[46] I find it fascinating that this one was altered to make it look more Achaemenid in iconography even as it was being used at the very edge of the empire. The addition of the winged disk makes the same claims of cohesion and authority for its owner as other seals from Sardis, carved with explicitly Achaemenid iconography in a recognizably related collection of apparently local styles.

In some cases, seals provide insights into society at Achaemenid-period Sardis that run counter to traditional expectations. The inhabitant of one of the sarcophagi in Tomb 381, the "Tomb of the Bride," was described by Butler as a young woman of about seventeen years. She was decked out with gold hair fillets, a necklace, earrings, anklets, clothing appliqués, and two seals, of which

82. Gold seal ring and pyramidal stamp seal from Sardis, Tomb 811. IAM 4636 and 4641. Courtesy Yapı Kredi Yayınları.

83. Two seals and a pendant from Sardis, Tomb 18. IAM 4523, 4524, and 4577. Courtesy Yapı Kredi Yayınları.

one, a gold seal ring, was found by the Butler expedition; the other (of glass?) disintegrated, leaving behind a suspension device in the form of ducks' heads.[47]

The seal ring this young woman wore showed a lion advancing, snarling, with tail held aloft. Perhaps the use of lions as seal images by women is to be expected in an area well known for its worship of Cybele, where people lived who may also have been familiar with worship of Ishtar-Anahita; it certainly acts as a warning against making too hasty an assumption about the gender of seal users based on modern associations with a given image.[48] Such an association of lions with women may also be suggested by the two seals found in Tomb S 16, IAM 4634 and IAM 4637, which show, respectively, a snarling lion and a robed woman seated on a chair with curved back and legs, in front of whom are carved two small crescents.

Dealing with the Dead

Because multiple interments might occur, multiple seals from the same tomb need not have belonged to a single individual. They nonetheless sometimes provide interesting pairings. Tomb 1005, for instance, from which came the chalcedony Neo-Babylonian-type pyramidal stamp seal IAM 5133, also produced a chalcedony pyramidal stamp held by silver ducks' heads showing a winged lion-griffin advancing to the right. This lion-griffin is carved in an Achaemenid koine style. Whether the two seals belonged to one individual or two people interred in the same tomb, their shared findspot demonstrates the multicultural associations embraced by the elite at Sardis.

A different scenario of cultural interaction is revealed by Tomb 811. Both seals from Tomb 811, IAM 4636 and IAM 4641, are carved with unifying Achaemenid iconography and styles.[49] They show a lion with an abbreviated sun disk symbol and a wonderful winged human-headed goat-sphinx with a symbol above it.

In Tomb 18 was found a single body, with no evidence recorded for more than one interment.[50] On the forehead of the skeleton was a broad strip of gold; with it were a gold and carnelian necklace, a rock crystal pendant with lion's-head suspension (IAM 4577), two large silver earrings, and a small gold one. Also found were two sealstones. One (IAM 4523) is of agate cut into a squat cylinder with a heavy silver mounting, showing a lion and bull in combat, with a sun disk, a circle of stars, and a crescent moon above their backs. The other (IAM 4524), an oval of dark mottled stone now missing its mounting, shows a bearded crowned figure in a long robe seated on a high-backed throne with his feet on a footstool, holding in one hand something resembling a globe and in the other hand an uncertain object. These are images drawn straight from Persepolitan iconography of authority, both rendered in Achaemenid koine styles.

The seals from the tombs of Sardis in the Achaemenid period thus corroborate the social organization suggested by other grave goods. The elite at Sardis comprised a body of people with diverse tastes, who in the living society differentiated themselves from those of lesser status through adaptive referencing to Achaemenid expressions rather than from each other on the basis of ethnic background.

It is clear: style does not equal ethnicity. For instance, a seal from Kertch in Crimea, now in St. Petersburg, was carved in an Achaemenid koine style with two bearded crowned sphinxes and inscribed in Lydian "Manelim," or "of Manes."[51] The presence of this Lydian name – in Lydian – and Achaemenid imagery on a seal buried north of the Black Sea shows the versatility of prestige indicators and their dissociation from modern notions of geographically generated ethnicity. At Persepolis and Dascylium, impressions demonstrate that seal owners of a particular ethnic identity did not necessarily use seals that conform to our notions of ethnically based visual culture.[52] So, too, the tombs at Sardis suggest that artistic style and iconography were status indicators, signaling membership in the polyethnic elite of Achaemenid Anatolia.

84. Doorstones from İkiztepe. Courtesy Yapı Kredi Yayınları.

Grave Markers

Visible, external grave markers add to the complex weave of identities and behaviors signified by mortuary remains. The sculpted funerary monuments of Lydia come in five primary forms: "phallic markers," symbolic doors, stelae topped with anthemia, stelae with additional relief sculpture, and sculpted lions. They have been found in association with rock-cut tombs and tumulus tombs; some of them may also have accompanied cist graves.

The "phallic markers," stone pillars with a swollen rounded top, have been found only in connection with tumuli. These markers, or *ouroi*, may have been used not to distinguish the grave but to commemorate the efforts of those who contributed to the construction of the tumulus.[53] The symbolism and function of the phalli thus remain unclear, but their origin certainly harks back to pre-Achaemenid Lydia. They provide a clear example of a local funerary marker associated with local traditions that persisted in the new imperial age.

Burial tumuli and rock-cut tombs were both marked at times by stelae carved in imitation of doors.[54] These doors may have symbolized "the passage to the underworld, the household, and/or perhaps the house-like conception of the tomb itself."[55] Mark Waelkins suggests that the symbolic doorstone originated in Phrygia, maybe around the second half of the sixth century, when

85. Anthemion stele fragments from Sardis. After Ratté 1994: fig. 14. © Archaeological Exploration of Sardis.

the symbolic door panel became the most important part of a tomb.[56] During the Achaemenid period, the notion of a house for the dead expanded across Anatolia, with the symbolic doorstone a crucial element not only of the tomb but of its expression in the minds of local inhabitants.[57] Doorstones are found primarily in association with tumuli; one type perhaps dating to pre-Achaemenid times as well as into the Achaemenid period draws on the ornamental architectural vocabulary of Phrygia and Ionia, while another type dating exclusively to the Achaemenid period also incorporates anthemion stelae on either side of the door.[58] A version possibly restricted to the Cayster valley includes door panels elaborately ornamented with eight-petaled rosettes resembling those at Persepolis.[59]

Anthemion stelae are topped with floral embellishment, often plain but sometimes with inscriptions or relief carving. Some may have been painted. They are common grave markers from Achaemenid-period Lydia and the western seaboard. At least ten are known from Sardis alone, and they have been found in Greece, the Aegean Islands, and western Anatolia as well.[60] Lydian anthemion stelae all postdate the Persian conquest of the area and testify to the interactions between European and insular Greece with western Anatolia; they appear in Lydia almost immediately after their appearance on the Aegean seaboard and signify the wealthy.[61]

The anthemion stelae from Sardis are clearly associated with rock-cut chamber tombs. Three other anthemion stelae from Lydia may therefore share a similar context.[62] A number of those from greater Lydia were inscribed, generally in Lydian but sometimes in Aramaic or bilingual Lydian–Aramaic. They warn would-be vandals away from the tomb, paralleling their counterparts at the satrapal center.[63]

The funerary inscriptions found at Sardis, all apparently dating to the Achaemenid period and later, follow a standard form: they name the person interred and his father and invoke the wrath of the gods on anyone who violates the mortuary arrangements.[64] Most are inscribed in Lydian, and one is a bilingual Lydian–Aramaic.[65] Another few inscriptions in Greek demonstrate that this language could be inscribed, too. In this way the use of language in mortuary inscriptions becomes a rich iteration of multiple ethnic heritages serving to express status-laden behaviors and of written language demonstrating the broadly inclusive sweep of authority within the Achaemenid elite.

The bilingual Lydian–Aramaic funerary inscription, found on the northern slope of the Necropolis, is one of the lengthiest. Although its use of Aramaic as well as Lydian is unique, it is otherwise typical of the funerary inscriptions from Sardis:

Lydian text:
[missing at least one line]
in the beginning of the month of Bakkhos. This stele and this [grave chamber]
and this dromos and the property which to this grave chamber
belongs, now [they are] of Manes, son of Kumli, son of Siluka. And if anybody
to this stele or this grave chamber or this dromos or this land belonging to this grave chamber
and also if anybody to the land does damage, then may Artemis
of Ephesus and Artemis of Coloe his holding and his house
and his soil and water and everything of his destroy.

Aramaic text:
On the 5th of Marheswan [of the] 10th year of King Artaxerxes,
in the fortress of Sardis. This stele and the cavern [and] the wall (?),
the piece of land (?) and the forecourt which is the forecourt of this grave chamber (?), [are]
of Mani, son of Kumli, son of Siruka (?). And if anybody against this stele or
the cavern or the or wall (?) or (?) or against the land in front of this cavern,
that is to say, if anybody destroys or breaks anything, then
may Artemis of Coloe and of Ephesus his holding, his house,
his land, soil and water, and everything that is his, destroy him and crush him (or destroy him and his heir(s)).[66]

86. Banquet stele from Sardis. NoEx 77.15. Note raised rhyton, elaborate garments and upholstery, flower and footstool, and Lydian inscription. © Archaeological Exploration of Sardis.

Because there are no pre-Achaemenid funerary inscriptions from Lydia, we cannot know whether cursing a destroyer was a local tradition, but it has a lengthy history in Mesopotamia and Elam. Artemis of Ephesus is frequently mentioned in the Sardian texts, along with several other apparently Lydian deities. Thus these stelae both marked the presence of a grave and the elite status of the person(s) buried within, and they had an apotropaic function, preserving the tomb and its contents from ill-wishers or robbers.

The Achaemenid date of Sardis's stelae and their association with rock-cut tombs are interesting in connection with the rock-cut tombs of the Persian kings from Darius onward at Naqsh-i Rustam and (later) on the mountainside overlooking the Persepolis terrace, embellished with sculpted reliefs and multilingual inscriptions.[67] The rock of the necropolis and acropolis hills at Sardis is too soft and crumbly to withstand sculpting. It is possible that the funerary stelae found in association with these tombs at Sardis recalled the royal tombs,

87. Grave stelae from Ödemiş and Hayallı. İzAM4344 and MM6255. After Roosevelt 2009: figs. 6.20 and 6.21. Courtesy Christopher Roosevelt.

88. (*left*) Grave stele from Manisa, now in Bergama. BM4394. Author's drawing, after Roosevelt 2009: fig. 6.28.

89. (*above*) Grave stele from Tire. 25.6. After Roosevelt 2009: fig. 6.29. Courtesy Christopher Roosevelt.

90. Grave stele from Gökçeler. MM9156. After Roosevelt 2009: fig. 6.25. Courtesy Christopher Roosevelt.

a practical way to link those buried at Sardis to Achaemenid imperial authority through tomb display.[68]

Most of the sepulchral sculptures from Sardis show banqueting men, with women and usually also servants attending them; they reiterate the emphasis of mortuary inclusions.[69] The idea of funerary banquets probably was current in Lydia before the conquest by Cyrus; the preponderance of drinking vessels included in grave assemblages of the Lydian Kingdom suggests as much. But it is only in the Achaemenid period that people began to represent banquets in funerary art at Sardis.

Grave stelae with relief figures are common in Lydia; in addition to Sardis, they have been found at Ödemiş, Hayallı, Manisa, Incesu, Haliller, Gökçeler,

Musacali, Tire, and Kiraz.[70] The repertoire of images is limited. Banquet scenes include a male figure reclining on a kline and holding a drinking vessel in his right hand, often with a veiled female seated at his feet with her feet on a footstool.[71] Some variations occur; on a relief from Ödemiş, for instance, the seated figure at the banqueter's feet plays a kithara, while a veiled figure with a footstool sits at his head.[72] Often the central figures are accompanied by one or more attendants, usually equipped with drinking vessels. Another common theme emphasizes elite masculinity: hunting and fighting, usually atop a galloping horse.[73]

These stelae mirror those from Sardis and show images of Achaemenid Anatolian elite behaviors, including virile activities pursued on horseback. Two examples from Lydia of seated females without reclining males, with their feet on a footstool and an attendant before them, fit into the "mistress and maid" theme so common in late-fifth- and fourth-century Athens.[74] A final two stelae from Lydia simply show standing figures in low relief, one of which portrays a man wearing the garb of a horseman and should perhaps be considered part of the equine group. The other comes from Gökçeler and warrants further comment.

The Achaemenid-period settlement at Gökçeler, below Şahankaya, has produced a striking grave stele of the early fifth century that may have been associated with the tumulus burial and other grave goods found nearby and illustrated earlier.[75] It was carved in a style and with a theme unusual in Lydia. On it a person of ambiguous gender, ethnicity, and status holds a dove or cock and another item, perhaps a bud. The figure has short, close-cropped, thickly curling hair and wears a simple cloth shift, sandals, and anklets; burly thighs and biceps are clearly shown.[76] No females are shown in Persian relief sculpture, but the muscularity and peculiarly shaped breasts of females in early-fifth-century Greek vase painting and sculpture should make us shy away from assuming anatomical accuracy in female portrayals.[77] Perhaps this figure with his (?) unusual clothing, exotic gift, and close-curled hair is a rendition of a foreign slave, an imported and lovely acquisition. The very ambiguity of gender, ethnicity, objects held, garments, hairdo, and status provides a glimpse into just how much we do not know about Achaemenid Lydia.

A last grave marker type deserves mention here: freestanding sculpted lions, generally couchant with open mouths roaring. These were common in Lydia; indeed, they were the most common type of grave marker there. Lions dated on stylistic grounds to the Achaemenid period have been found at thirteen sites, as has a lion-griffin.[78] This type of marker has pre-Achaemenid Lydian precedents and should be considered a continuation into the Achaemenid period of a local tradition, although lions were used to convey messages of power and legitimacy in Persia as well. Thus "continuity" can involve a mix of ancient phenomena injected with new meanings into the old form, yielding a powerful cocktail of associations.

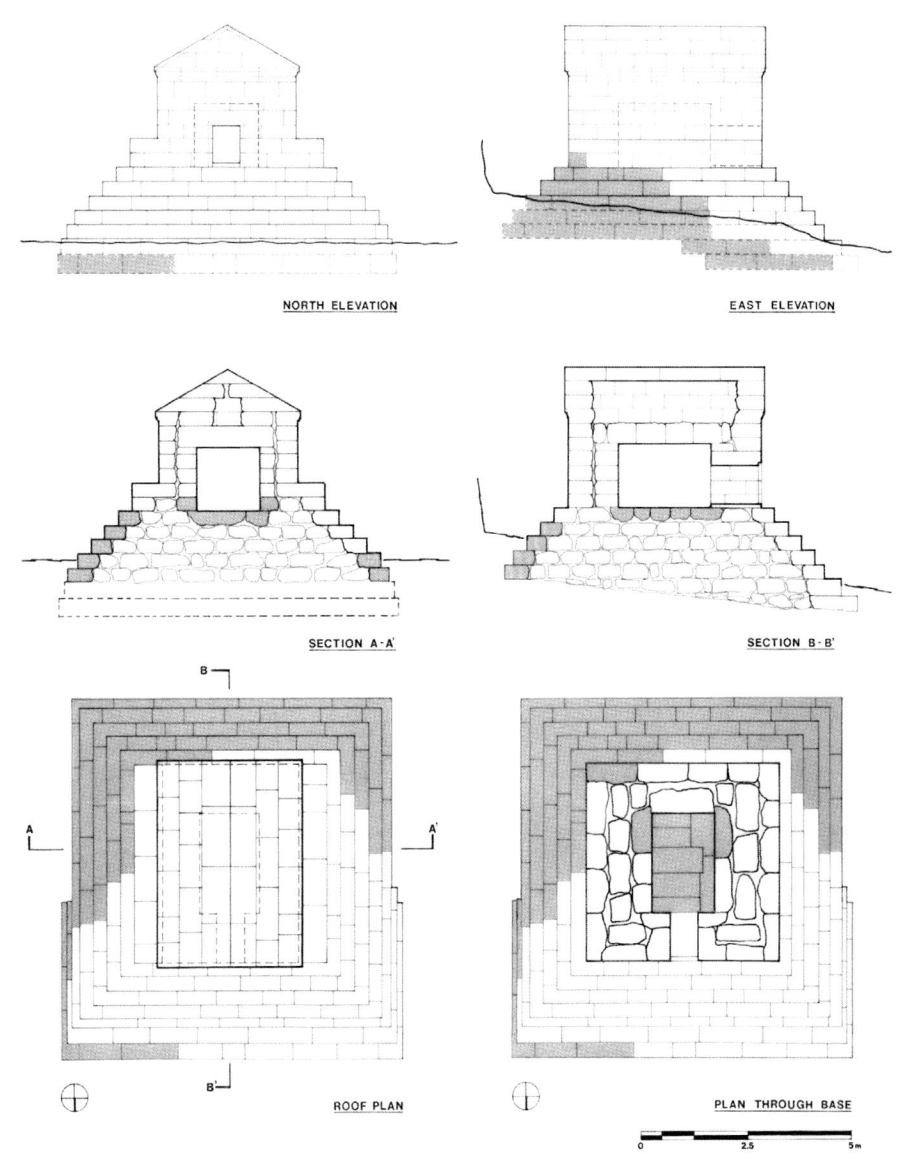

91. Pyramid Tomb at Sardis. © Archaeological Exploration of Sardis.

Unique Structures

This survey of mortuary evidence from Lydia ends with three monuments so far unique in the area. The Pyramid Tomb at Sardis probably dates to the second half of the sixth century, while the chamber tomb at Taş Kule near Phocaea is probably slightly later. A pediment sculpted with a relief banquet from Sardis attests to the presence of a temple tomb there. It dates to the second half of the fifth century, making it the oldest version of a temple tomb known yet.

92. Taş Kule. Author's photo.

Pyramid Tomb

Located east of the Pactolus River, on the north side of a ridge that runs down from the Acropolis, the Pyramid Tomb as preserved consists of a stepped platform of which six limestone steps survive, laid around a core of earth and rubble.[79] The burial chamber has disappeared except for two displaced wall blocks and several floor blocks; the positions of all four walls of the chamber are marked by incised lines. The entrance to the chamber was probably centered in the front (north) wall, perhaps at a higher level than the floor. The tomb has been convincingly reconstructed to bear a close resemblance to the Tomb of Cyrus at Pasargadae (ca. 530).[80] The masonry techniques used in the construction of the Tomb of Cyrus and the Pyramid Tomb are strikingly similar.[81] The Sardian tomb's date is somewhat unclear, but it is thought to have been built after the conquest of Lydia and after the Tomb of Cyrus, between the mid–sixth and early fifth centuries.[82] We cannot discern the ethnicity of the person for whom this tomb was constructed.

Taş Kule

About 7 km east of Phocaea, with no known settlement closer, a freestanding tomb called Taş Kule was cut from a single outcrop of limestone bedrock jutting

93. Banqueting pediment from Sardis. NoEx 69.14, NoEx 78.1. © Archaeological Exploration of Sardis.

above the valley floor around.[83] Although Taş Kule conveys certain Achaemenid architectural elements and perhaps aspects of ritual, the tomb is not a Persian type. It is unique. It dates to the second half of the sixth or earlier fifth century. A large lower block-shaped element contains a chamber hollowed out within, with an unadorned cube above that has no chamber. A false door on its front is its only major embellishment, a matter that draws attention to the symbolic function of this feature.[84] Taş Kule's closest architectural parallels are the Pyramid Tomb and the Tomb of Cyrus at Pasargadae; the architectural moldings above its door link it to two reliefs from Dascylium showing rites and sacrifices performed by people in Persian dress before a tomb door (see Chapter 6) as well as the Tomb of Cyrus.[85] A bowl-like hollow in front of the false door has been interpreted as a fire bowl used in Zoroastrian funerary ritual.[86] This tomb thus seems to proclaim Persian connections in its stepped pedestal and its moldings as well as its fire bowl, with perhaps a nod to local flavor in its symbolic door. It gives an idea of the range of possibility and flexibility open to people in tomb design.

Temple Tomb

One last tomb type in Lydia is suggested by a pedimental relief that shows a bearded figure banqueting. It is the earliest sculpture portraying a funeral banquet found at Sardis, dating to ca. 430–420. The relief sculpture shows a bearded male at center, reclining on a banqueting couch, or kline, with his left elbow on cushions and his right hand holding a rhyton aloft. Three females are seated at the left. A servant at the right brings a vessel to the reclining figure, while another, smaller servant at the right stands by a laden table.[87]

The pediment has been reconstructed as coming from a temple-shaped mausoleum.[88] It is uncertain what the form of the mausoleum might have been; reconstructions are varied but in general follow types known from Caria and Lycia.[89] This pediment, however, predates the very temple tombs that have been used in proposing its reconstruction, and it is possible that the type originated at Sardis.[90] The pediment thus demonstrates again the degree of spectacular, obvious, creative display that might be associated with elite mortuary structures in Achaemenid Lydia.

Although there are variations and distinctive forms, the overarching sense of mortuary behaviors gained from this consideration of Lydia applies to Anatolia as a whole. Thus a variety of tomb markers or tomb types is to be seen, but local burial customs clearly might continue into the Achaemenid period, demonstrating local autonomy and an apparent desire to associate with specifically local, pre-Achaemenid pasts. Where we can reconstruct mortuary assemblages, conversely, they show great conformity and display of authority in specifically Achaemenid terms. Imperial authority and reciprocal obligations were signaled and cemented by standardized elite behaviors. It is impossible to tell the ethnicity of people on the basis of their grave goods. Their grave types, however, may tell another story and assert potent memories of an autonomous past.

The Western Seaboard: Ionia and Mysia

The city-states along the Aegean coast provide a unique challenge to the study of Achaemenid Anatolia, for some of them seem to have been depopulated at one time or another and it is not clear to what extent they functioned as part of the Achaemenid Empire – perhaps even at the same time as they were paying tribute to Athens.[91] This ambiguity and flux in political/military allegiance cannot be isolated from the fact of Achaemenid imperial authority in the region; this was real, however tempered or poorly understood it may remain to us in detail. Some sites were abandoned perhaps temporarily. Clazomenae, for instance, seems to have moved from a mainland setting onto an island sometime at the beginning of the fifth century.[92] Smyrna, thought to have been sacked by the Lydian king Alyattes at the end of the seventh century, was repopulated by the mid-sixth century but may not have been functioning as an independent polis and was apparently more or less abandoned by the middle of the fifth century.[93] Nonetheless, graves and grave markers provide an indication of cultural milieux and interchanges along the western seaboard of Achaemenid Anatolia.

Clazomenian Sarcophagi

The best-known grave markers from Ionia are terracotta sarcophagi with a flat foot so that they can stand upright as well as be laid flat. The rims of many of them were painted with motifs ranging from simple wavy lines to elaborate scenes of animals and humans. They range in date from ca. 550 to sometime after 450 and thus correspond to the first century of the Achaemenid Empire, a time when most of Ionia was under Persian hegemony. Most of them date between 530 and 470 (about fifty between 530 and 500, more than seventy between 500 and 470).[94] Painted sarcophagi have been found at Clazomenae, Smyrna, Teos,

94. Clazomenian Sarcophagus, ca. 480–470. 77.AD.88. J. Paul Getty Museum, Villa Collection, Malibu, CA.

Lebedus, and the eastern side of the Erythraea, with additional examples from "Larisa" and from Pitane. They were probably created by craftspeople who also made tiles and revetments.[95]

Few goods were found within the sarcophagi – indeed, it has been suggested that sumptuary laws existed and/or that the sarcophagi themselves constituted adequate mortuary offerings – and we should consider the paintings on their rims to be primary indications of social status and values.[96] Their iconography is striking. In addition to "orientalizing" motifs like braided guilloches or bud-and-lotus friezes, and Greek motifs like egg-and-dart friezes, they include emblems that closely resemble the "lyre" motifs of Lydia's anthemion stelae.[97]

Animal combat scenes featuring lions and boars, lions and stags, or lions and bulls are common, as are heraldic animals confronting each other – across the corpse within the sarcophagus or with a floral element. These animals are occasionally male and female of the same species rather than only male, a feature that links them to Near Eastern rather than Greek tradition. Deities with double sets of wings hold lions and other animals aloft. Images featuring humans most frequently show battle scenes and/or hunting scenes, usually with horses prominently displayed.

To my knowledge, not a single banquet scene is shown on a Clazomenian sarcophagus, and even the occasional erotic scenes lack drinking vessels. The absence of banqueting motifs and of grave goods associated with drinking suggests a series of funerary rituals and elite signals that are wholly different from those that defined the graves of Achaemenid Lydia. Another set of behaviors pertained to those dwelling in these cities of Ionia.

The painted sarcophagi of Ionia show a mix of Greek and Near Eastern ornamental ideas. Fertility is suggested by vegetal emblems and confronting male and female animals. The visual language of masculine power is paramount on these sarcophagi, however, with their repeated themes of animal combat, divine control, and battle. The iconography thus links Ionian notions of power and status to those prevalent across the rest of Achaemenid Anatolia, emphasizing male power through hunting and fighting rather than that associated with banqueting. Theirs is a message of masculine elite authority embedded in horses and armor. The concepts of manhood and authority shown here connect the men of Ionia to the men of the rest of Achaemenid Anatolia. The sense of community, however, is not portrayed.

Grave Stelae

In addition to the sarcophagi, a number of sculpted monuments mark the graves of Ionia. The array and range of grave stelae known from Athens are lacking in the cities of Anatolia: Möbius and Pfuhl include four fragments from Pergamum and one each from Cyzicus, Ephesus, and Miletus.[98] The two Pergamene examples showing women – one head, one lower half of a standing figure – date to the latter half of the fourth century, and both are works by Attic sculptors.[99] Another Pergamene fragment shows a bearded male head, made in Athens in the first quarter of the fourth century and imported to Pergamum at some later date.[100] The last, a seated male figure in high relief with a hound under his chair, is "strongly atticizing, but an East Greek work of the first quarter of the fourth century."[101] The stele from Cyzicus, made from Pentelic marble in an Athenian style in the first quarter of the fourth century, shows a standing male and a seated female; it is a standard Attic grave stele.[102] The fragments from Ephesus and Miletus are also of Pentelic marble; the Ephesian stele, showing a woman and her maid in low relief, was an Attic work of the late fourth century (possibly post-Achaemenid), while that from Miletus is so badly worn that its style is uncertain, but it has been argued that it is an Attic work of sometime after 412.[103] Thus all postdate the Clazomenian sarcophagi.

These sculptures have been assigned an ethnic origin based on the style in which they were carved. This may be correct, but "Attic"-style sculptures need not have been carved in Athens by an Athenian but could have been carved by a foreign metic working in Athens or by a sculptor working elsewhere who had been trained in an Athenian school or was adept at copying.

Several interesting things emerge. The first is that fragments of grave stelae associated by style or iconography with European Greek sculpture are few and are found in only a few cities. The second is that most are carved in a style imported from Athens, rather than reflecting a local style; this demonstrates a desire to mark graves with specifically Attic style, sometimes using recognizably Attic marble. The "Attic" monuments also demonstrate a cosmopolitan and powerful ability to acquire those works and use them elsewhere. Interestingly, the only sculpture Möbius and Pfuhl assert was made in a local East Greek style rather than an Athenian one depicts a man of European Greek manner and with indicators of manliness, Greek style – but they are also indicators of elite manliness in Achaemenid Anatolia. Draped in rich cloth and with a hunting hound under his seat, the figure from Pergamum neatly incorporates cultural and stylistic accoutrements of wealth and virility from multiple backgrounds. This surely reflects the multicultural milieu of fourth-century Pergamum itself.

Hellespontine Phrygia

Extensive work in the Granicus River valley and elsewhere in Hellespontine Phrygia shows a great variety of mortuary strategies and memorials. A few unplundered tombs give a sense of the kinds of grave goods included. This discussion will not provide a complete list of all funerary monuments discovered but will instead seek to explore the options exploited by the inhabitants of the area in the Achaemenid period.

Roughly a hundred burial tumuli have been mapped and recorded in the Granicus valley alone, the place where Alexander first defeated the Persians in 334.[104] These tumuli were heaped over stone sarcophagi or built stone chambers that often had gabled roofs and stone burial couches within and that sometimes included painted decorations.[105] As was the case in Lydia, the situation of tumuli on high ridges or along major waterways made them prominent landmarks in a setting of large estates ruled by the polyethnic Achaemenid elite.[106] Their size and visibility gave these tumuli multiple functions: "In one sense they served as territorial markers of the estate, yet the number and size of the tumuli also

95. Polyxena Sarcophagus, Çanakkale Archaeological Museum. Author's drawing, after Sevinç 1996b: fig. 9.

symbolized the wealth of the Hellespontine Phrygian elite.... By virtue of their size they also functioned as observation platforms and were used as such in times of war."[107] The tumuli were overt statements of wealth and power. As their publisher comments, the tombs and their inclusions demonstrate that the people of the region "embraced both Greece and Persia, yet chose to identify exclusively with neither."[108]

Granicus Valley Tumuli

Two sarcophagi of Proconnesian marble were discovered in the mound of Kızöldün, one of the largest tumuli in the area. The earlier, the so-called Polyxena Sarcophagus, dates stylistically to ca. 500, making it the earliest relief sarcophagus known in Asia Minor. Its low-relief images show the murder of the Trojan (i.e., local) princess Polyxena at the grave of Achilles, celebrations involving women exchanging gifts and soldiers dancing the "Pyrrhic" dance, and women feasting.[109] The imagery departs from Greek iconography of symposia or weddings (the most common situation in which women are featured in European Greece); its closest parallel is that of the Harpy Tomb at Xanthus in Lycia.[110] The sarcophagus had not been completed at the time it was buried under the tumulus. Terracotta tiles were placed all around its exterior sides, covering the reliefs and separating them from the dirt. Leaning against its west side were the remains of a cart, presumably that used to draw the sarcophagus to its burial.[111]

A surprising feature of this burial is that the sarcophagus emphasizes women – indeed, more than three-quarters of the figures represented on it are female – yet the person buried within it was a forty-year-old man.[112] It may have been intended for a woman but used before it was finished to encase the body of a prematurely dead male.[113] Richard Neer suggests, however, that it may have been intended for the man buried within – in which case its iconography, showing a warlike invader slaying a local princess at a specific local site, with a dance named in his honor performed on the other side of the sarcophagus, takes on particular significance in the context of the Achaemenid Troad.[114]

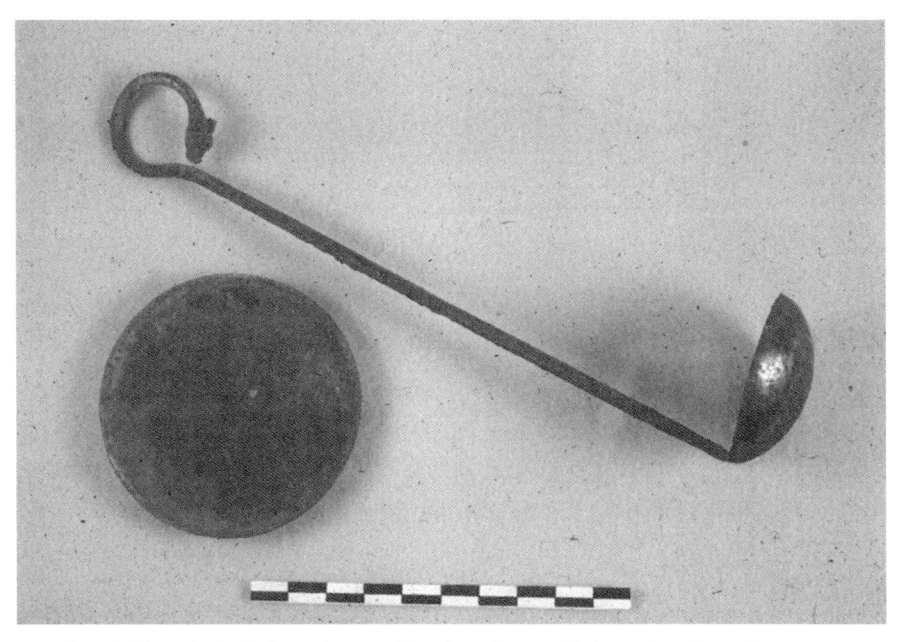

96. Silver ladle and phiale from the Kızöldün burial, Çanakkale Archaeological Museum. Courtesy C. Brian Rose.

The other sarcophagus found in the same tumulus was only two-thirds the size of the Polyxena Sarcophagus and had no reliefs. It was buried directly in the earth without tiles or tomb chamber around it. It held the bones of a girl, aged eight or nine, and her grave goods.[115] These included on either side of her pelvis a silver phiale and ladle with a calf's-head terminus, perhaps originally held in her hands, a wooden bust of a female – a doll? – and a wooden pyxis and glass aryballos (dating to the late sixth or fifth century) that probably once lay on the girl's garment. She wore gold bracelets with antelope-head terminals and two gold and red-glass necklaces, and she had eight boat-shaped earrings arranged around her head. The necklaces and much of the other jewelry showed significant wear and were probably heirlooms. They link her, despite her youth, into the network of elite status and prestige.

Another tumulus of the Granicus valley is that at Dedetepe, located about 6 km from Kızöldün and probably part of the same estate.[116] It was constructed between 480 and 460; like the two sarcophagi, its entire tomb chamber is Proconnesian marble. Two painted marble klinae stood against the walls, and in front of them were two wooden tables. Remains of drinking vessels and musical instruments, including an aulos and pieces of hippopotamus ivory that formed part of a stringed instrument, were recovered from within the tomb chamber.[117] Even supplementary banqueting vessels such as the oil-holding alabastra were embellished: "One especially exciting feature of the alabastra found within the tomb is that their exteriors are stained with patches of Tyrian purple, an indigo

Empire, Authority, and Autonomy in Achaemenid Anatolia

97. Sarcophagus from Çan in the Granicus valley, Çanakkale Archaeological Museum. Courtesy C. Brian Rose.

dye often used to color textiles. In the course of the funeral service, these alabastra were probably tied with freshly-dyed fillets of the same type as those that figure among the gifts in the reliefs on the Polyxena sarcophagus."[118] Thus the funerary ceremony here included aspects of banqueting.[119]

A final tumulus from the Granicus valley covered a circular chamber with a corbeled roof that enclosed a sarcophagus with relief carvings on two sides.[120] The Çan Sarcophagus dates to the first quarter of the fourth century and shows on one short side a battle scene in which a mounted figure wearing Persian military garb spears a fallen Greek soldier in the eye. One long side is carved with two mounted hunt scenes, separated by a tree: a stag hunt at the left with a blue painted background and a boar hunt at the right with a green background. The man buried in the sarcophagus died in his twenties, having suffered a severe fall from his horse apparently during battle.[121] The portrayal of elite manly pursuits on the sarcophagus, hunting and fighting from horseback, therefore may accurately reflect aspects of his life.

Grave Stelae

Hellespontine Phrygia is well known for its grave stelae. Dozens of these have now been found and published.[122] There is variety in the imagery, but for the most part they include banqueting scenes and/or scenes of funeral processions, with hunting or other imagery. Enough of them are inscribed with names of various ethnicities that we can be sure their iconography spanned ethnic bounds – or, since we cannot be certain that a man with, say, a Semitic name was himself a Semitic language speaker, we can say that their iconography included people with varied identities.[123]

To my knowledge, none of these stelae was found in situ or associated with a particular grave, but the similarity of their iconography to the sarcophagi and their persistent emphasis on death and ritual support their link to graves and

98. Two examples of grave stelae from Hellespontine Phrygia. Courtesy Istanbul Archaeological Museums.

suggest that they served as a reminder of funerary rites. Indeed, they might have functioned as less expensive iterations of the banquets and funeral processions that the finds from the Granicus tumuli suggest the very wealthy staged as part of mortuary ritual. The link to masculine pursuits of the elite, hunting and fighting from horseback, forms another parallel connecting the owners of these funerary markers to those buried in tumuli. The art of death in Hellespontine Phrygia creates a clear sense of behavioral bonds linking the Achaemenid elite, regardless of ethnic background.

Pillar Tomb

A recent analysis of reliefs from Dascylium in the Istanbul Archaeological Museums showing men and women on horseback (men astride, women side-saddle) reconstructs them as part of a pillar tomb.[124] Pillar tombs, as known from examples in Achaemenid-period Lycia, present a tomb chamber atop a pillar, often, if not always, with the exterior walls decorated in some fashion. If the reconstruction of the Dascylium reliefs in Istanbul is correct, it means the presence in Hellespontine Phrygia of a single example of this type of tomb and reiterates the connections between this area and Lycia seen in the link between the Polyxena Sarcophagus and the Harpy Tomb mentioned already.

Hellespontine Phrygia thus provides evidence for four or five elite mortuary structures during the Achaemenid period: (1) sarcophagi buried within tumuli; (2) built tomb chambers within tumuli; (3) sarcophagi within tomb chambers within tumuli; (4) some sort(s) of grave marked by stelae carved in relief; and (5) possible pillar tombs. The imagery on the sarcophagi and stelae, and the finds within the tumuli, suggest that the funerary *rites* associated with these different structures and the emphases of the elite on prestige-laden pastimes were similar. Thus the funerary rituals apparently included a procession, with the body of the deceased carried by a horse-drawn cart to the spot of burial. Either a funeral banquet was held, or the deceased was shown enjoying the bibulous and culinary pleasures, including conversation, of a permanent feast – perhaps both the real and the implied eternal formed part of mortuary ritual. At least one person was bedecked with gold and accompanied by wine-flavoring implements, though she was but a young girl. Those implements link her to the evidence for banqueting from the Dedetepe tumulus, as well as the visual evidence of sarcophagi and stelae, and proclaim her hereditary wealth. The iconography and apparent cause of death associated with the young man in the Çan Sarcophagus provide clear evidence for the high-prestige pursuits of an elite male and connect the activities of the man to his mortuary art and the various funerary stelae of the area as well. Thus we see the Achaemenid elite linked by activity, ritual, and self-portrayal in clear and close ways. The variety of mortuary monuments demonstrates the degree of choice exercised by the members of that elite in disposing of the dead, even while the continuity of content and representation demonstrate the cohesiveness of power and prestige.

Central Anatolia: Highland Phrygia, Cappadocia

Three highland Phrygian tombs will represent the variety of tomb types in this region. Tumulus A at Gordion is erected over an Achaemenid-period cremation burial.[125] The excavation Web site states:

> The continuation of tumulus burials into the early Achaemenid period is another indication of continuity from the Iron Age at Gordion, and again indicates the presence of powerful elites. Although it is difficult to assign some of the sixth century Gordion tumuli to either side of the Persian conquest, one of the most striking, Tumulus A, is datable ca. 540–530. This was a very wealthy female cremation burial with a dismantled vehicle (hearse) and harness fittings, as well as a striking quantity of precious metalwork, including a silver mirror and a gold necklace. The practice of depositing vehicles within elite burials finds close parallels from the same period in the western parts of the Hellespontine Phrygian satrapy (e.g. at Üçpınar).[126]

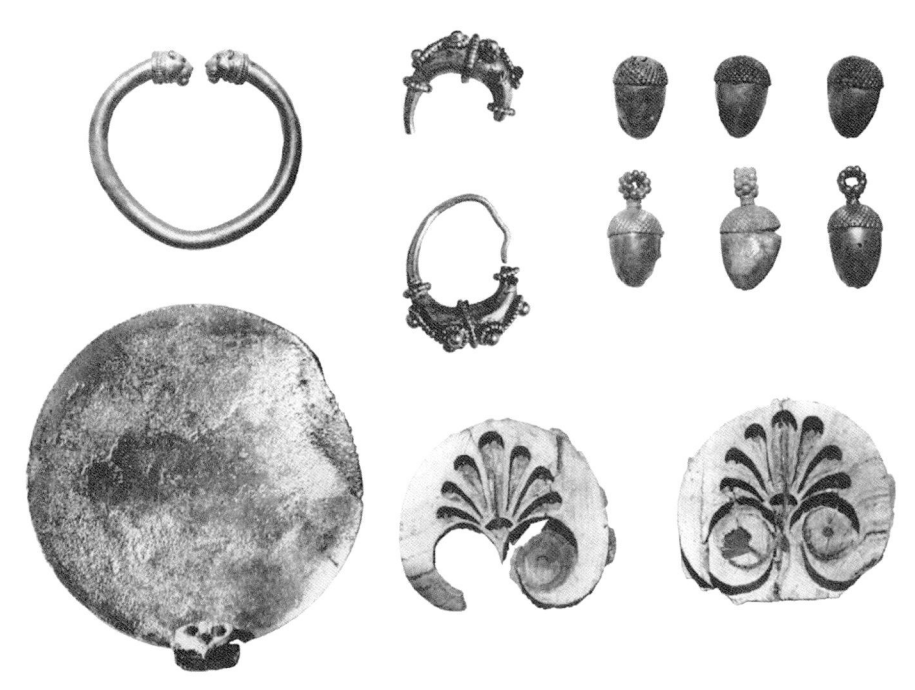

99. Items from Tumulus A at Gordion. After R. Young 1951: pls. 8 and 9. © Gordion Archaeological Project.

The body had been burned elsewhere and the ashes brought to an area floored with fine white clay; a pit near the center contained the bones and teeth of the deceased, while the remaining ashes were strewn over the floor.[127] Most of the gold and electrum jewelry was found in the pit with the bones, some pieces "preserved in almost perfect condition, while others were badly fused or damaged by heat."[128] Perhaps the jewelry was interred with the bones after cremation but while they were still hot, for it would have melted more in the fire had it, too, been cremated.

The jewelry included a gold bracelet with lion's-head terminals, boat-shaped earrings with granulated decoration, and a necklace with acorn pendants. Ivory inlays, themselves inlaid with colored glass, show that furniture or caskets formed part of the grave offerings, while ceramic lydions and an East Greek vase in the form of a girl clutching a bird to her bosom as well as an alabaster alabastron suggest perfumed oils.[129] The gold pendants of the Gordion necklace parallel glass ones from Uşak and silver ones from Tumulus B4 (dated 530–510) at Bayındır in northern Lycia; burial of the funeral cart, as mentioned, has parallels in western Anatolia. This tumulus thus draws on the Phrygian past for its form but its contents join its occupant to members of the Anatolian elite.

A grave stele from Altıntaş also links the deceased to (Hellespontine) Phrygian funerary markers and to Achaemenid Anatolian elite status. It is carved in a flat relief that may have been intended as is, may have been unfinished, or may

100. Stele from Altıntaş, Afyon Archaeological Museum. After Karagöz 2007: fig. 18. Courtesy Şehrazat Karagöz.

have been intended to have details painted. Here confronted winged sphinxes gesture reverently to a central vegetal element; the lower register reiterates the banqueting theme. Although the flat style of this stele differs from the style of others, its imagery links it emphatically to elite mortuary signaling.[130] Other anthemion stelae from Phrygia connect this highland area to western and northwestern Anatolia as well.[131]

The painted wooden tomb chamber once covered by a tumulus at Tatarlı, near modern Afyon and ancient Celaenae, is the sole known example of a mortuary form that was probably more common in Achaemenid Anatolia than the archaeological record implies.[132] The wooden tomb chamber corresponds to pre-Achaemenid Phrygian antecedents at Gordion; the images painted on the beams show a battle scene between Persians and Scythians, two funeral processions, weapon dances, crouching felines, and a few other scenes that are "hardly recognizable" at this point.[133] Paint in red, blue, white, and gray is preserved.

101. Painted beams from Tatarlı. Courtesy Lâtife Summerer.

Tatarlı demonstrates another context in which tomb design draws on long-standing local tradition, while the images used to adorn it situate it squarely in the context of the Anatolian Achaemenid elite. Persians are portrayed in military and equestrian costume – as archers, cavalry, and a charioteer – while Scythians with pointed hats gallop in on comparatively diminutive horses. The corpses strewn about show that the Persians are winning. Lâtife Summerer suggests that the scene depicts no historical battle and points out that the presence of Scythians distinguishes this battle from other Anatolian versions with defeated Greeks: the frieze reflects a tradition preserved otherwise in glyptic.[134] Reference to a banquet is missing from the extant paintings; perhaps such a scene covered one of the beams removed in antiquity for secondary burials or more recently by looters, or perhaps this tomb included no such depiction. The tomb's contents were not preserved, and thus our understanding of the concerns preoccupying the living society responsible for its construction remains incomplete, but its remarkable paintings demonstrate those people's participation in particularly defined types of authority.

Black Sea Coast

The central Black Sea region probably formed part of the satrapy of Cappadocia.[135] Achaemenid-period mortuary structures from Paphlagonia include tumulus tombs over built stone chambers and local specialties as well.[136] Rock-cut tombs in this region reflect local wooden domestic architecture, complete with pillars at the front. In form, they are quite distinct from the rock-cut tombs of Achaemenid Lydia or Persia.[137] Relief sculpture adorns some tombs with lions, bulls, and other creatures, reflecting the influence of both Greek and Achaemenid art. It has been argued that the simpler tombs are earlier and reflect an indigenous burial form, while the more ornate ones reflect the cosmopolitan artistic environment of the Achaemenid Empire and should be dated to the fifth and fourth centuries.[138] The form of these rock-cut tombs is thus distinctive and local, growing from local architecture and taking on embellishments that link the tombs to Achaemenid power iconography.

A few grave stelae have also been found in the central Black Sea area. One, a cubical stele from near Daday, shows a banquet scene with participants dressed in Persian garb.[139] Its type distinguishes it from the stelae of Hellespontine Phrygia or Lydia, but its imagery links it to that iconographic repertoire. Another stele, found near Tosya, is shaped like those of Dascylium, but its imagery is quite distinct: its four registers show what may be different phases of the same man's life.[140] The bottom register shows a child with a goose; the primary register above it shows a man dressed as a horseman leaning on a staff and smelling a flower; the next shows a mounted horseman; and the uppermost shows armed men dancing. The stele is topped off with a tree of life.[141] In this instance the stele's shape resembles Achaemenid elite mortuary markers elsewhere, and although the arrangement of imagery sets it apart, the content and expressions of elite masculinity connect it to the rest of Anatolia.

Illicit excavations at Sinope and Ünye have produced silver artifacts demonstrating that the grave goods of the wealthy linked them in practice and display to the Achaemenid elite elsewhere.[142] An omphalos phiale from Ünye with five gadrooned lobes and appliqué ibexes on it seems to be a local product, with certain stylistic aspects that link it to local tradition at the same time that its overall appearance most closely resembles the metal vessels of the Lydian Treasure.[143] Two graves near Sinope produced a series of silver vessels – seven from one tomb and two from the other – that demonstrate this cohesiveness of shape and style even more clearly; indeed, they provide the closest parallels known to date for the Uşak material.[144] Found together were a silver omphalos phiale with ten lobes and a trefoil oenochoe with a handle terminating in an antelope head. Other finds from the same grave include a silver alabastron decorated with bands and maeanders, plus two duck heads; two ladles with duck's-head termini; a bowl; and another shallow phiale.[145] From the other grave came a silver trefoil oenochoe with an ornate handle and bead-and-reel decoration at the join of neck to body, as well as a square flat silver plate with concentric circles engraved in it that correspond to the base of the oenochoe – surely a stand for that vessel.[146] Although no parallels exist for the square plate, the close parallels between the other vessels and the Lydian Treasure suggest a date of ca. 500 for these burials.[147]

The mortuary remains of the central Black Sea coast again show great variety in mortuary structures, with distinctive local forms represented. Although the iconography of the funerary stelae on occasion displays unique features, the imagery emphasizes themes similar to those that predominate in the rest of Anatolia: prestige activities such as banqueting and expensive manly pursuits involving horses and armor. The finds from within tombs are telling. Some of them, at least, are clearly made locally. They demonstrate local adaptation and expression of Achaemenid elite behaviors and ways of signaling prestige, including not only the paraphernalia of feasting but dishes particular to performative

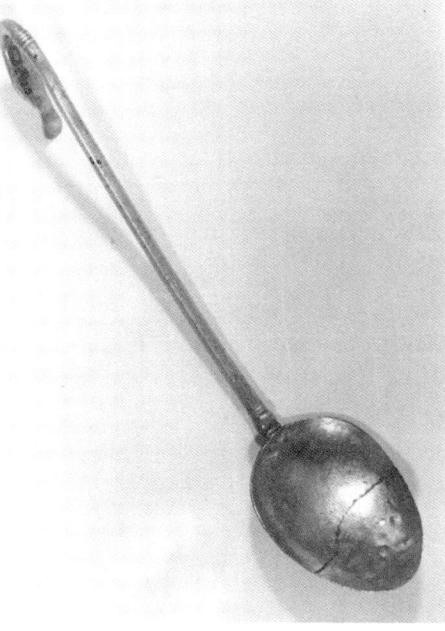

102. Silver from Sinope. St 213, 216. National Archaeological Museum, Athens. © Hellenic Ministry of Culture and Tourism/Archaeological Receipts Fund.

aspects of drinking that included ladles, shallow bowls, and elaborate jugs for pouring. The exquisite Achaemenid decorative style provides an additional link to the elite across the empire.

Armenia

Excavations at the Urartian capital, Tushpa, 5 km to the west of modern Van, show that the western part of the mound that had once formed the northern quarters of the lower city was used in the Achaemenid period for burials.[148] These graves constitute some of the few examples of non-elite Achaemenid-period mortuary remains in Anatolia. They fall into two major categories: simple pit graves and cist graves lined with stone or mudbrick. The ceramic sequences are still unclear, but graves have been identified as "Median" or "Achaemenid" based on the introduction of new shapes (bowls reflecting Persian traditions, including the Achaemenid bowl) and decorative styles (especially Triangle and Festoon Wares), as well as different techniques that fire clay buff instead of gray or dark. Grave 140 contained the bones of a forty-seven-year-old woman buried with three bronze rings near her ears, as well as a double-handled amphora and two bowls, one with a carinated lip; about the amphora, the excavators comment that "this type of vessel appears frequently at most of the centres in northwestern Iran throughout the Achaemenid period."[149] Even in this non-elite grave, then, the grave goods show a connection to wine drinking in a way that links the grave and the cultural system it represents to the rest of the empire.

Two rock-cut tombs at the Rock of Van are significant not only because they demonstrate continuity with the Urartian elite practice of constructing articulated rock-cut tombs of "fine simplicity," but because they may recall the arrangement of the royal tombs at Naqsh-i Rustam.[150] The excavators note the presence of niches along one wall in one of the tombs, akin to the tomb of Darius I, and connect the layout of the other tomb to that of Xerxes. The tombs are prominently situated on the Rock, one just above the monumental rock-cut tomb of the Urartian king Argisti I and the other directly under the Grand Platform that afforded access to the elaborate tombs of several generations of kings, including Sarduri I and Ispuini.[151] Their placement is significant: they are in exceptionally visible spots, associated with some of Van's most elaborate tombs commemorating some of Urartu's most famous kings. Indeed, their situation symbolically connects them to the Urartian past even as their visibility and careful location, higher than the one tomb and as if shoring up the others, suggest that the Achaemenid-period occupants were more important than the earlier kings.

Although these rock-cut tombs draw on ancient Urartian practice in certain ways, their physical inaccessibility to the public is similar to that of the Achaemenid royal tombs but quite foreign to local tradition. The excavators at Van comment that Armenia during the Achaemenid period experienced "a time of cultural decline, if not of a reversion to barbarism." They suggest that the Urartian system "totally collapsed; the culture completely changed, and the region turned into what it had once been: the land of villages and peasants."[152] The presence of these rock-cut tombs at Van, with their allusion to the glories of the Urartian royal past and contemporary Achaemenid royal tombs, indicates that Armenia as a whole may not have suffered the same decline in fortunes as Tushpa itself. Indeed, the continued use of the palace at Altıntepe may explain where the Achaemenid elite were concentrated at this time – this makes the decision to cut explicitly elite tombs into the Rock at Van with its rich royal history all the more telling.[153] The combination of these tombs with the inscription of Xerxes discussed earlier truly would have delivered the coup de grâce, expressing the military might and cultural superiority of the Achaemenid Empire over that of the Urartians and Assyrians alike. Together, they form a powerful expression of imperial authority at this most charged site of eastern Anatolia.

Once again, the contents of tombs link the elite of Achaemenid Armenia to those elsewhere. Here we are hindered by the fact that the well-known silver vessels of this area came into the public eye through the activities of looters and/or very early explorations rather than recent scientific excavations. The silver beaker "from Erzurum," now in Oxford, and the silver rhyton and eight other examples of banqueting paraphernalia in silver "from Erzincan," now in

103. Silver vessels "from Erzincan." ME 124081, ME 123256, and ME 124082. © Trustees of the British Museum.

London, nonetheless demonstrate the cohesiveness of mortuary inclusions that united the Achaemenid elite in Armenia.[154] This cohesion, indeed, spread well outside Anatolia; its impact as a visual language of prestige was clearly readily understood and profound.[155]

Southeast

Hacınebi, a site in the Euphrates River valley just north of Birecik at the Syrian border, has a six-thousand-year history of settlement. It is at the northernmost extent of the reliably navigable portion of the Euphrates, in an area with adequate rainfall and sufficiently fertile soil; it overlooks the eastern bank of the river at the spot where the Royal Road crossed it during the Achaemenid period.[156] At this time Achaemenid architecture has not been found, but burials of the fifth century demonstrate occupation:

> Two richly furnished 5th century Achaemenid burials in area B provide the earliest evidence for this occupation phase. Op. 7 burial 28 was a stone and mudbrick walled single burial whose grave goods included ceramics, silver and bronze jewelry, bronze arrowheads, a bronze mirror, and Egyptian artifacts such as a scarab seal with a griffin motif and two alabastra. An Achaemenid style silver signet ring with a griffin motif helped date the burial to the fifth century BC. Op. 13 burial 38 consisted of a single burial placed in an oval "bathtub-shaped" ceramic coffin, set inside a covered mudbrick chamber. The associated grave goods included ceramic vessels, a bronze mirror with pieces of leather still adhering to it, silver jewelry, alabastra, and assorted bronze artifacts.[157]

Bracelets with animal-head terminals and numerous terracotta rider figurines are also to be included in this list.[158] Hacınebi has thus produced recognizably Achaemenid materials in two different types of burial at the southeastern edge of Anatolia. The mortuary assemblages emphasize public drinking and prestige behaviors; the number of imports suggests a degree of artifact movement and imperial openness paralleled by the ceramic assemblages of Gordion and elsewhere.

Deve Hüyük is at the border between the modern Turkish Republic and Syria. Described as the cemetery of an Achaemenid military outpost, its stone-lined cist burials demonstrate Achaemenid identity constructions manifested in a non-elite echelon of society. The tomb type was identified as ethnically Persian by Moorey, based on the excavator's description and comparanda found in western Iran; this assignation has been challenged by Oren Tal, who suggests that the tomb structure reflects not ethnicity but rather the wealth of those who could afford a stone-lined cist rather than a simple hole, and Miller most recently clarifies that the ethnicity of the tomb's occupants cannot be determined on the basis of the tomb structures.[159] In the context of the present discussion, that lack of ethnic clarity is not only interesting but fits the patterns observed elsewhere in Anatolia. Nowhere can a tomb's occupant be typed by ethnicity. Rather, people buried their dead with the paraphernalia of Achaemenid ideology and lifestyle regardless of their own ethnic heritage or identity. Deve Hüyük provides another example of this, in graves of the non-elite.

As mentioned in Chapter 3, the graves at Deve Hüyük included vessels made of bronze, clay, faience, glass, and stone, as well as weapons and remnants of horse harnesses.[160] Seals came as cylinders and stamps in a variety of shapes and materials, many with Achaemenid connections in shape and iconography. Personal adornments included bracelets and anklets (some with animal-head terminals), fibulae and earrings, finger rings and pins, beads and amulets of shell and glass paste among other materials, hair rings, and pendants. Various toiletries were found, including tweezers, a number of bronze mirrors, and kohl tubes with sticks. Terracotta figurines and relief plaques included handmade and mold-made varieties.

It is astonishing that Moorey was able to piece together the finds belonging to fully twenty-four distinct grave assemblages from the artifacts and records remaining to him.[161] Certain features unite them. Twenty assemblages include a bronze drinking bowl, either an Achaemenid bowl or a mesomphalic phiale. Most of them include further signifiers of Achaemenid imperial behaviors and the infusion of Achaemenid hegemonic ideas: additional banqueting vessels, seals, and/or Achaemenid-type jewelry. Perhaps also to be associated with banquets are the numerous oil flasks. Egyptian-influenced items, including faience amulets or seals (sometimes imported) and Egyptian-type vessels, turn up in some of the graves; some Attic imports are also present. Cosmetics, jewelry, and weapons may all be buried in the same grave.

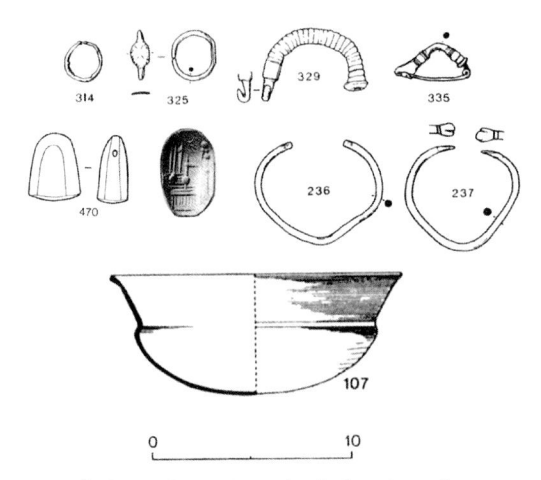

104. Deve Hüyük Grave Group 1. Author's drawing, after Moorey 1980a.

Deve Hüyük provides a non-elite comparison to the spectacular elite finds of elsewhere. Like the grave at Tushpa, those of Deve Hüyük demonstrate that the paraphernalia of Achaemenid living – seals, personal adornments, drinking vessels – and possibly some of their attendant behaviors – manners of sealing, styles of drinking – were used not only by the elite and wealthy but also by those of different wealth and prestige. I have compiled illustrations of the contents of three of those graves here, selecting them because they were particularly well illustrated by Moorey in his magisterial work of 1980. They display neither more nor less wealth than other grave groups described by Moorey.[162] They do not illustrate the full range of items in all the graves, but they do give a sense of their type and variety.

One difficulty of interpretation has to do with gender, a particularly knotty issue with no skeletal material to corroborate or countermand our own gender assumptions. Moorey pointed out that the toiletry articles of the Deve Hüyük graves and some of the jewelry conform to types common throughout Syro-Palestine and suggested that the cemetery preserves the remains of members of a garrison force who married local girls.[163] This is problematic, as it is certain that men as well as women wore kohl and jewelry. The presence of weapons and horse bells in Grave Groups 15 and 20 suggest that these are the graves of men. There is clear evidence from elsewhere, however, for double interments in sarcophagi, so we cannot assume that all items from a grave belonged to a single individual.[164] It is not impossible that Grave Group 15 indicates a female as well as a male, even a husband–wife pair; and for that matter, might the presence of a "feeder" indicate a family group with a child? Or might the so-called feeder be a beer mug with a strainer to filter bits of detritus from a microbrew recently fermented in a nearby jar? Perhaps, indeed, we see here the assemblage of but a single person, and we should think of gender in a more fluid manner. It is quite possible that a

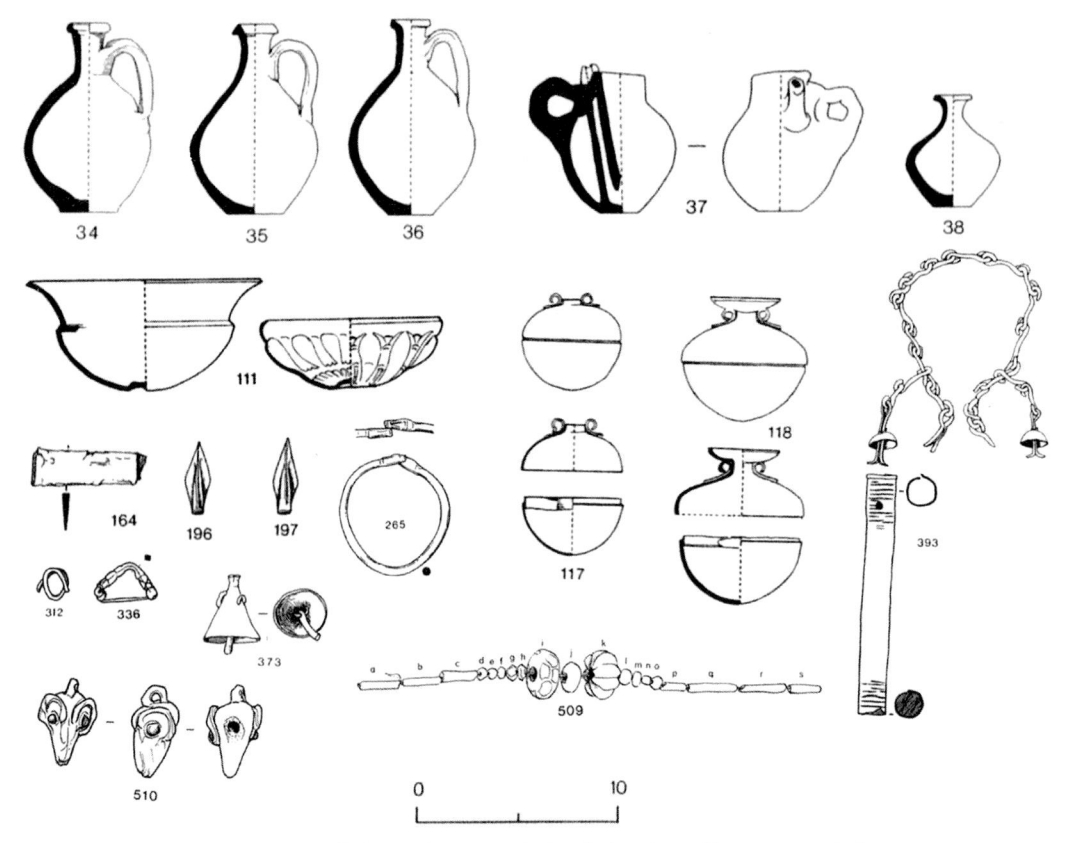

105. Deve Hüyük Grave Group 15. Author's drawing, after Moorey 1980a.

man would buy his jewelry or makeup from a local vendor as enthusiastically as would a woman. For that matter, women might offer some of their own personal or intimate belongings to their male deceased. The contents of Grave Group 15 thus highlight the ambiguity of gender signaling.

The large number of drinking vessels reminds us that the banqueting imagery of most Achaemenid Anatolian mortuary art includes both men and women: their sitting/reclining and drinking behaviors distinguish them by gender, but banqueting was apparently not a gender-segregated activity. Similarly, as we have seen, the iconography and use of sealstones were not gendered.[165] The gender ambiguity of mortuary assemblages at Deve Hüyük highlights the active participation of women even in a society whose visual imagery was largely male-dominated.

The presence here of seals and bronze Achaemenid bowls, banqueting vessels and unguentaria, jewelry in recognizably Achaemenid forms as well as recognizably local ones, weapons, and horse bells connects this non-elite military cemetery at the edge of modern Turkey to mortuary assemblages and expressions of the elite across the rest of the peninsula. The activities that united

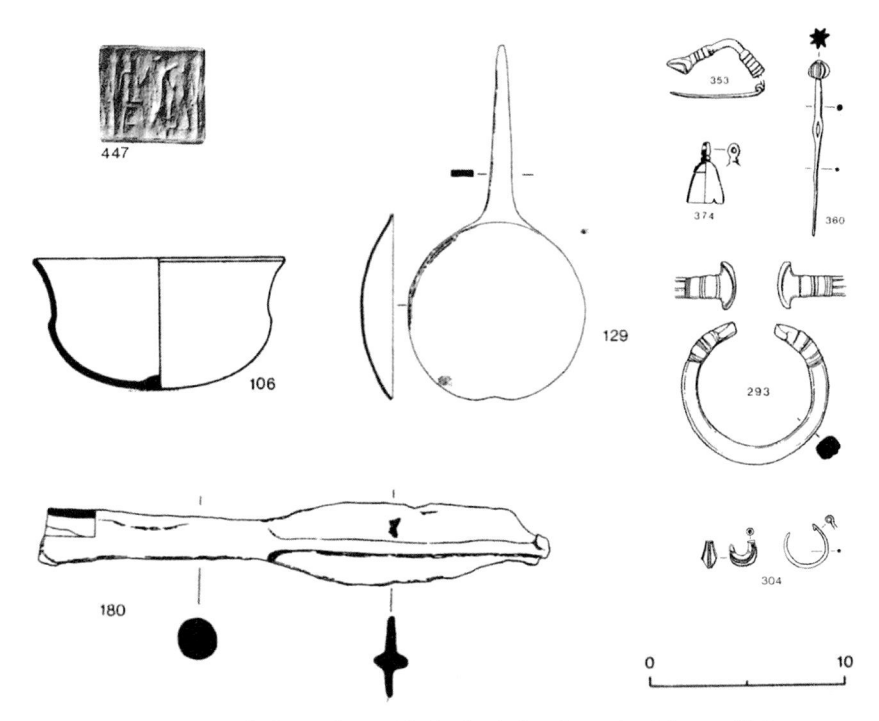

106. Deve Hüyük Grave Group 20. Author's drawing, after Moorey 1980a.

men in imperially charged ways – fighting, working with horses, drinking wine together in a particular manner using particular cups – formed part of the behaviors attested in these grave groups. Although the bodies here were not buried in gold-encrusted garments, their jewelry and sealstones demonstrate public expression of imperially condoned actions and authority. The tombs of Deve Hüyük thus help fill out our understanding of the cohesion that characterized behavior in Achaemenid Anatolia. They afford us a glimpse of a particular category of non-elite that allows us to see here, too, a unifying emphasis on particular expressions of masculine authority within an imperial context.

CILICIA

In the past two decades alone, Cilicia has produced six grave stelae inscribed in Aramaic.[166] Most of these date to the fourth century; they were found at various places around Cilicia, particularly in the eastern part of the province, and were made for individuals from a variety of linguistic backgrounds. The inscriptions name the deceased and, sometimes, family members; a number of them invoke curses on those who would violate the tombs. Three are crowned with relief carvings of a crescent moon and star. They demonstrate that Aramaic was used in nonsatrapal circles, at least in some circumstances. In this sense they parallel the Aramaic funerary stelae from Dascylium, Sardis, and other sites and link the

107. Gold foil clothing appliqué from Silifke, Silifke Archaeological Museum. After Karagöz 2007: fig. 20. Courtesy Şehrazat Karagöz.

occupants of the graves to those buried elsewhere in Achaemenid Anatolia. The star and crescent moon may point to a local cult of the dead, but more evidence is needed before this can be ascertained.[167] Indeed, given the popularity of this imagery in Babylon, the association of crescent and star with Aramaic may point to a locally expressed idea that found its origins in Mesopotamia. This suggestion perhaps finds support in the stele that calls on the gods Sahar and Shamash to see to justice should anyone violate the tomb.[168]

A gold foil clothing appliqué from Silifke, a city on the coast at the mouth of the Calycadnus River in westernmost Cilicia, links Cilician elite mortuary signaling to that elsewhere.[169] The appliqué, with facing seated bearded winged sphinxes and walking winged sphinxes, rendered within an articulated square topped with granulated crenellations, very closely resembles appliqués from Lydia. Once again, the variety of mortuary markers in Cilicia is offset by the uniformity of the authority-laden grave inclusions of the elite.

Pisidia

A tumulus over a built stone chamber with a dromos and a single room at Delipınar, near the ancient city of Tymandus in Pisidia, was excavated after illicit looting in the 1970s and 1980s; the modern excavations uncovered three

108. Stele from Delipınar. Author's drawing, after Özsait and Özsait 2007: fig. 4.

grave stelae that are now in the Isparta Museum.[170] Two of these are unadorned (perhaps once painted?) anthemion stelae that the excavators link stylistically to Dascylium.[171] The third is crowned with a pediment, with an egg-and-dart and bead-and-reel border at its base; the stele is carved in relief with a winged sphinx that has no clear parallels in sculpture but seems a hybrid of East Greek, western Anatolian, and Achaemenid impulses.[172] Thus Delipınar shows the admixture of unique forms and cohesive parallels in its mortuary art that we have seen characterize Achaemenid Anatolia.

Lycia

The tombs of Lycia are some of the best-known monuments of Anatolia, thanks to their spectacular relief sculptures and detailed publication record over the course of the past century and more. This discussion cannot address all of them or do justice to the nature of the work that has come before; it attempts only to point out a few of the ways in which Lycia adds to our understanding of mortuary treatment in Anatolia.[173] Lycia demonstrates two things that depart from and add to our understanding of mortuary signaling. Greek iconography plays a much greater role in Lycian artistic development than it does in other parts of the peninsula, and sometimes the mortuary monuments may have been used to signal not only explicitly Lycian but possibly also anti-Persian identity.

The latter suggestion, made by Bruno Jacobs, is based in part on the rise of Theseus in some areas and aspects of Lycian relief sculpture; Jacobs links these developments to political tensions between eastern and western Lycia and suggests that the elite of west Lycia were so firmly identified with the Achaemenid Empire that it was beneficial for the eastern rulers to dissociate themselves from Persia and make conscious reference to Athens instead.[174] Such finesse in visual association demonstrates the impact those designing the tombs expected their mortuary monuments to have: they believed viewers would (1) see them; (2) recognize different myth and image repertoires; (3) connect the person interred with the images, the stories, and the cultural associations of their tombs; and (4) associate with those people the power and the authority of the referent cultures. The people designing these tombs and other visual material expected them to convey a clear message to viewers, and they manipulated imagery accordingly.

Lycian emphasis on monumental tomb architecture decorated with figural relief sculpture sets the area apart from the other regions of Anatolia considered so far. Some Lycian monuments predate the Achaemenid period, and certain mortuary structures refer to a local tradition in their form.[175] Their imagery is rich and fascinating, offering tremendous statements of power and identity. Although no intact Achaemenid-period tombs have revealed their contents, the iconographic record of Achaemenid Lycian tombs provides us with valuable information.

Pillar Tombs

A distinctively Lycian tomb type consisted of a square limestone box perched atop a tall pillar, sometimes decorated with relief sculptures.[176] The body was placed inside the upper chamber through a small opening on the side. The pillar on which the tomb rested might be inscribed or left plain; it is not clear if any of the pillars were painted in antiquity. At least thirty-three pillar tombs are known, and there may be as many as forty-three; they range in date from the mid–sixth to the mid–fourth century and were probably made for local elites, most likely erected during the owner's lifetime.[177]

The Harpy Tomb, erected around 480, is an ornate example of such a pillar monument; the sculpted slabs that formed the tomb chamber atop the pillar are now in the British Museum. It receives its name from the female-headed

109. Reconstructed pillar tomb at Xanthus. Courtesy Peter Sommer Travels Ltd.

birds at the corners of each side (probably neither harpies nor sirens, but perhaps connected to the Egyptian ba birds that symbolized the soul). They carry small figures that may represent souls of the dead in localized idiom. Above the doorway on the west side is a cow suckling her calf, a strongly Assyrianizing image and one that may have been widely disseminated through the export of ivory-inlaid furniture.[178] The four sides all show scenes of seated figures receiving gifts from standing figures; that on the east side is arranged like the famous audience scenes at Persepolis.[179] This tomb may have been built for Kybernis, who led the Lycian contingent of forty to fifty ships for the Persians at Salamis.[180] He was succeeded by Kuprlli, who minted coins at Xanthus ca. 480–440 and erected Buildings F, G, and H at Xanthus around 470–460, after a fire that was perhaps started by the Athenian Cimon. Kuprlli was succeeded by his grandson Kheriga, for whom the so-called Inscribed Pillar may have been erected.[181]

Certain details of the Harpy Tomb add to its elite authority. The audience scene's close resemblance to that of the Persepolitan reliefs provides an obvious reference to Persian kingly might, and it may be that the Assyrian cow and calf held similar meaning for a Lycian viewer. The arms of the throne supporting one figure have animal-head terminals, another reference to Achaemenid luxury items that were redolent with associations of authority and power. Definitions of specifically masculine authority are to be found in the Greek-style warrior, with helmet and panoply. The person who commissioned this mortuary sculpture thus drew on the iconography and artistic styles of multiple traditions to

110. East side of the Harpy Tomb. GR 1848.10-20.1. © Trustees of the British Museum.

demonstrate authority here.[182] The Harpy Tomb's local type meshes with its internationally sophisticated message of power.

A recent discussion of Achaemenid-period pillar tomb reliefs clearly outlines their significance.[183] Catherine Draycott argues for two distinct phases in the self-image of Lycian elite, with the Harpy Tomb serving as the pivotal point: "An initial phase starting around the time of the Persian conquest, characterised by a spate of remarkably ostentatious tomb building, and a subsequent period when out of the preceding mixed discourse, a powerful dynastic identity emerged."[184] The development of an explicitly "royal" iconography, designed to claim for local rulers a status that might rival that of the Persian king of kings, was part of the development of a Lycian elite identity – especially that of particular rulers.[185] This is important because the situation of these rulers is not entirely clear: there seems to have been a certain dynastic hope, so that some of the men passed on power from father to son. The rulers of Lycia and their jockeying for power provide us with a variation on the notion and mechanics of leadership in Achaemenid Anatolia.

The Inscribed Pillar at Xanthus is apparently the funerary marker of a dynastic satrap. It demonstrates a different emphasis and manner of displaying status and ideas than do the sculpted reliefs. Perhaps the most elaborate example of the Lycian pillar tomb, it is important for the battle reliefs, now in London and Istanbul, that adorned its tomb chamber, and for the long historical inscription in Lycian that covers the south, east, and half of the north side of the pillar shaft. This is followed on the north side by a twelve-line epigram in Greek and a moderately long inscription on the rest of the north and entire west side in Lycian B or Milyan.[186] The date of the pillar is probably ca. 400, based on the style of the relief and analysis of the inscription.

The Lycian language is still not fully understood, but this inscription is a historical narrative detailing various exploits of the Lycian ruler (including the fact

111. Audience scene from Persepolis. P57121. Courtesy of the Oriental Institute of the University of Chicago.

that he acted as a mediator in an agreement between Sparta and Tissaphernes). The words of the Greek epigram reflect the military scenes shown also in the reliefs that once accompanied it:

> Since the time when the ocean separated Europe from Asia, no Lycian has ever yet raised such a stele to the Twelve Gods in the holy temenos of the agora, this immortal monument to his victories in war (?). It was [Kheriga/Kherei?], the son of Harpagos, having excelled in all respects the youth of his day in his prowess at wrestling, who conquered many acropoleis with (the support of) Athene, sacker of cities, and distributed part of his kingdom amongst his kin. In recognition of this, the immortal (gods) made him just recompense. He killed seven Arkadian hoplites in a single day, he who of all mankind set up the most numerous trophies to Zeus and garlanded by his illustrious exploits the family of Karika.[187]

This inscription takes the power statements of Achaemenid imperial authority and translates them into a Lycian context in interesting ways.[188] Darius's inscriptions of a hundred years earlier at Bisitun, Persepolis, and Naqsh-i Rustam frequently provide three related texts in different languages; this one, with three different texts in different languages, most closely resembles the inscription on the south wall of the terrace at Persepolis that stood next to the formal entrance to the terrace at this side.[189] Darius's monument at Bisitun, like this one, includes a visual representation of the verbal version of events. The Lycian one departs from that at Bisitun, however: Lycia had a highly developed tradition of Achaemenid-period funerary monuments that deployed Assyrianizing city siege imagery of a sort systematically eschewed in heartland Achaemenid imperial tradition.[190] Even in seals, as diverse as were the options under the Achaemenids, there is little warfare imagery from Persia as opposed to symbolic heroic imagery and animal combat imagery. Thus the city siege imagery of the Lycians provides a powerful statement of military authority, expressed in a manner strongly assertive of local autonomy.

112. The Inscribed Pillar at Xanthus. Courtesy Peter Sommer Travels Ltd.

The inscription takes the form of a historical narrative that resonates with the Assyrian literary tradition of war annals. It assigns personal credit for the conquests of subject peoples symbolized by individual rulers to the tomb's occupant. It claims a particularly close relationship with the gods, in terms of both the favor they showed the ruler and the honor the ruler showed them. It reflects the inscription of Darius on his own tomb at Naqsh-i Rustam, asserting the excellence of the ruler in pursuits considered appropriate for young men. And it reflects Darius's inscription on the terrace at Persepolis, claiming this to be the first time someone has set up such a monument in this spot. The Inscribed Pillar is the only monument of its kind to bear an inscription praising its owner.[191] It creates a remarkable claim to legitimate kingship and kinship with the king of kings in Persia, both in what it actually says and in the ways it mimics the words and approaches of Darius I himself, apparently underscored by what seems to be a specifically Lycian resonance with Assyrian military ideas.

113. The Sarcophagus of Payava. GR 1848.10-20.142. © Trustees of the British Museum.

The pillar tombs of Xanthus are visually striking and culturally significant. They take a local tomb form and ornament it with sophisticated and nuanced language in words and images. The message they convey is one of great authority, situated locally but drawing on multiple other traditions for tremendously powerful expression. The emphases of the rest of Achaemenid Anatolia are seen here too, but these tombs make such explicit connections not only to imperial authority but also to the very authority of kingship in Persia that the dynastic desires of their occupants cannot be ignored. They are expressions of authority in the idiom of local autonomy, drawing on manly and kingly power to magnify their impact.

Sarcophagi

Distinctively Lycian are sarcophagi, often set atop pillars or on pedestals, with high arching roofs.[192] These may reflect domestic architecture, with rush

114. The theater group at Myra. Courtesy Peter Sommer Travels Ltd.

thatching and articulated panels. They continue to be used throughout the Achaemenid period, sometimes carved in relief and sometimes left plain – perhaps painted originally.

The British Museum has on display one of the most ornate of all Lycian sarcophagi.[193] The occupant, Payava, is named in an inscription. The figures carved on the walls of the sarcophagus combine elements in a manner characteristic of Achaemenid Anatolia; particularly characteristic of Lycia is the uniting of Greek and Persian elements.[194] On one short side are an athlete and a bearded companion who reflect Greek portrayals, while one of the longer sides boasts an audience scene with a seated figure in Persian dress receiving a delegation.[195] The two other sides portray battle scenes. The uppermost level has two friezes, one showing a bear hunt and the other a battle between horsed and unhorsed warriors. From the curved roof project lion protomes; the roof itself is decorated with a chariot scene. The ends of the gabled roof feature a seated couple in Persian dress, while pairs of sphinxes sit in the pediment above them. This sarcophagus is quintessentially Lycian in its form and combination of styles and themes. Once more we see the emphases on horses, hunting, fighting, and images of political power familiar from Achaemenid-period tombs across Anatolia. The audience scene makes explicit claims to power and elite ideas and expressions that prevailed particularly in Lycia.

115. Kızılbel southwest corner, departure scene. Courtesy Robert A. Bridges, Jr.

Rock-Cut Tombs

Particularly striking are the rock-cut tombs of Lycia, often painted and usually carved in cliffs above and separate from the settlements with which they are presumably associated.[196] Notoriously difficult to date, the rock-cut tombs were probably carved for the most part in the third century and later, but some of them may date to the Achaemenid period or even earlier. Most of the putatively early ones draw on the woodworking patterns of local domestic architecture for their form.[197]

A few inscriptions associated with Lycian tombs link them to the international world: one from eastern Lycia, in Greek, comments on the righteousness of the grave's occupant, a feature that reflects Achaemenid royal practice and also finds parallels in Greek epitaphs.[198] Limyra's rock-cut tombs include one with a bilingual Greek–Aramaic inscription from the middle of the fourth century that names its occupant and his father (Artimas son of Arzapias).[199] Here the languages link the tomb to Achaemenid and Greek practice, while the meaning of the inscription cannot be associated with any single culture. These two funerary inscriptions demonstrate the cosmopolitan, international associations of the Lycian elite even as the form of the tombs connects them explicitly to Lycia itself.

Tumulus Tombs

Two tumulus tombs have been excavated at Kızılbel and Karaburun in the plain of Elmalı in northwestern Lycia.[200] They demonstrate that this very widespread

Empire, Authority, and Autonomy in Achaemenid Anatolia

116. Kızılbel south wall, Gorgons and Pegasus. Courtesy Robert A. Bridges, Jr.

Achaemenid Anatolian tomb type was present in Lycia, along with the various indigenous types. The tomb at Kızılbel is earlier than that at Karaburun, dating probably to the third quarter of the sixth century.[201] It consists of a stone-built tomb chamber with gabled roof, within which were a stone kline and pedestal. The interior walls of the tomb were painted with figural decoration in a style the excavators argue was local, incorporating as it does aspects of Greek, Urartian, and Assyrian techniques.[202] It includes images from Greek mythological and epic traditions of Gorgons, Pegasus (steed of that native Lycian son, Bellerophon), and the murder of the Trojan prince Troelus by Achilles (a common scene in the figural representation of western Anatolia); figures of uncertain identity who have been linked to now unknown Lycian mythology; a seated figure with a staff, receiving suppliants and attended by numerous figures behind his throne; a departure scene in which a warrior mounts a chariot and a banquet scene directly above the kline; and portrayals of manly endeavor such as boxing, wrestling, and hunting boars, lions, and stags.[203]

While local flavor is clear in the highlighting of Troelus and Pegasus, the emphasis of the paintings links us to the concerns of the Achaemenid elite elsewhere in Anatolia: horses, fighting and hunting, an audience scene, and banqueting with appropriate paraphernalia (an Achaemenid-style metal vessel with horizontal ridges on the table in front of the kline). The emphasis on Troelus in the imagery of western Anatolia acquires greater significance in the face of real non-Greek hegemony and frequent Greek invasion; the dastardly assassination of a local prince by a Greek would have particular resonance here.

Dealing with the Dead

Tomb II at Karaburun is slightly later than that at Kızılbel (ca. 470) and also comprises a painted stone chamber with gabled roof, surmounted by a tumulus. A banquet scene on the west wall, opposite the symbolic door at the east, provides important links to the Achaemenid elite elsewhere – not least in the clearly rendered cord for seal suspension and the symbolically significant manner in which the banqueter holds his drinking cup (see Figure 65). Miller has analyzed the tomb's painting and its significance, touched on already in Chapter 4:

> [The banqueter] is flanked at the head by a woman with ribbons, and at the foot by two male attendants wearing Persian attire and handling Persian implements (a fan- and towel-bearer; a cup-bearer). The most strikingly non-Anatolian element is how the dynast balances his drinking bowl on three fingers; his red-garbed attendant at far left does the same.
>
> The mannered method of holding the bowl is surely that described by Xenophon in an authorial aside, in the context of an imaginary discussion between the young Cyrus the Great and his grandfather Astyages, king of the Medes (Xen. *Cyrop*. 1.3.8): "The cup-bearers of these kings do their task elegantly and they pour the wine and hand it over neatly. They carry the phiale about on their three fingers, and they present it in such a way as to put it in the most convenient fashion into the hand of the person who is about to drink."
>
> ... Whoever commissioned the painting insisted on painstaking accuracy on points of detail relating to the banqueting style of the Persian elite in Anatolia. The Karaburun dynast is portrayed engaged in an act of distinguishing himself from his fellow Lycians and associating himself with Persians. The manner of drinking declares an adoption of lifestyle, a level of emulation beyond the mere ownership of vessels in the Persian manner: it declares cultural identity in terms of affiliation.[204]

Karaburun II, like Kızılbel, shows the cosmopolitan nature of elite culture in Achaemenid Lycia. The paintings inside the tomb chambers provide a glimpse into the kind of concerns the living society faced: situating themselves as elite in this context included adopting certain aspects of overtly Persian accoutrements and manners, while also maintaining local Lycian ideas and traditions and incorporating Greek ideas and those of western Anatolia in visual portrayals and notions of living.[205]

Temple Tombs

One of the best-known Lycian tombs is the Nereid Monument, the sculptures of which were removed from Xanthus and taken to the British Museum in the nineteenth century. It is thought to have been the tomb of the Lycian ruler Erbbina (Arbinas, in Greek), son of that Kherei who may have erected the Inscribed Pillar. His tomb reflects the great authority he wielded over Lycia, for he reconquered

117. The Nereid Monument, reconstructed Room 17. © Trustees of the British Museum.

Xanthus, Telmessus, and Pınara after those cities had been annexed by a leading figure of Limyra, one Pericles (a name that itself bore resonance in the world of Greek and Persian usable pasts).[206] Thus Erbbina reunited Lycia under one authority, an authority that he makes certain through visual means is to be connected to the imperial hegemony of Persia, not to the Greeks implied by his foe's name. The Nereid Monument dates to the early fourth century, perhaps 390–380.[207]

The Nereid Monument serves as an ending point for our discussion of Lycian mortuary monuments because of its overt use of different kinds of structures and iconographies. Erbbina was not Greek, but he chose to have his tomb look like an Ionic Greek temple, a statement of grandeur and self-image. It made a clear impression on contemporary Lycian elites: the heroön at Limyra, thought

118. Erbbina (?) under a parasol, from the Nereid Monument. GR 1848.10-20.62. © Trustees of the British Museum.

to be constructed for Erbbina's rival Pericles, follows the Nereid Monument in creatively adapting the form of a Greek temple – this time one fully equipped with caryatids as well as relief sculptures and freestanding statues.[208] Self-aggrandizement on the Nereid Monument is seen in the relief sculpture that adorns the pedestal on which the temple-shaped tomb chamber is set. Typical manly pursuits such as mounted battle and mounted hunt (in this case, of a bear) connect the Lycian to Achaemenid elite elsewhere.

Particularly important, perhaps, is the relief showing an audience scene, in which the elite occupant of the tomb is seated under a parasol, an image that links him as directly to portrayals of the Persian king as the tomb's form links him to Greek divinities.[209] Indeed, the fact that the seated figure is shown wearing Persian military dress, while the suppliants appearing before him wear Greek garb, may refer specifically to the Apadana reliefs at Persepolis. This is underscored by the figures bearing Persian riding habits as a gift to the seated figure – just as is the case on the Apadana.[210] In an era when western Lycia made claims to Persia in its iconography and style while eastern Lycia joined itself with Greece, the scene on the Nereid Monument takes on additional significance. It demonstrates the reunification of Lycia as a province under the hegemony of its western elite.

CARIA

Caria is home to many rock-cut tombs that, like their Lycian counterparts, draw on wooden architecture for inspiration.[211] The distribution of tombs is independent of any geographic distinction between Caria and Lycia but rather extends across those political boundaries.[212] Unfortunately, their dating is all but impossible at this point; the earliest ones to which a date can be assigned (at Caunus) are largely

119. Mausoleum at Halicarnassus, reconstruction. Photo: author.

120. Two slabs of the Amazonomachy frieze, from the Mausoleum. GR 1857.12-20.235. © Trustees of the British Museum.

fourth century, but their publisher considers them Hellenistic – and indeed most tombs are apparently Roman.[213] The few inscriptions associated with the tombs are primarily in Greek, but a few Carian inscriptions demonstrate the continuity of local language use at least in this highly charged mortuary context.[214]

121. Artemisia II (?) and Mausolus (?). GR 1857.12-20.233, 260, GR 1857.12-20.232. © Trustees of the British Museum.

Caria's most famous tomb, by contrast, is solidly Achaemenid in date and most important for our understanding of Achaemenid Anatolian mortuary treatments. The Mausoleum at Halicarnassus, one of the seven wonders of the ancient world according to Antipater of Sidon, was a vast temple tomb with freestanding sculptures atop an enormous pedestal, perhaps a stepped pillar with sculpted reliefs.[215] It was built between 353 and 350 for the ruling couple, Mausolus and Artemisia II, who were siblings as well as spouses. The building was said to have been built by Greek architects, Satyrus and Pythius, and the reliefs to have been carved by the four greatest Greek sculptors of the age, Leochares, Bryaxis, Scopas of Paros, and Timotheus, each of whom was responsible for one side of the pedestal. It represents the apogee of the Achaemenid Anatolian temple tomb and of the pillar tomb.[216]

Significant in the context of this discussion are several things. One is the fact that famous, named Greek artists were brought to work on this mortuary

122. Rhodian silver didrachm of 400–333. 1941.153.870. © American Numismatic Society.

monument; so strong was the statement it was expected to make that even the renown of the artists mattered, not just the excellence of their work. That the fame gained was felt to be a reciprocal benefit is clear from a story in Pliny according to which the artists agreed to continue working after the death of Mausolus and Artemisia, each "considering that it was at once a memorial of his own fame and of the sculptor's art."[217] This all makes very clear the impact mortuary monuments could have – especially if they were vast and impressive.

The second significant point here has to do with the self-image and self-portrayal of Mausolus himself. It is significant that beneath the Mausoleum at Halicarnassus were discovered a number of alabaster jars (in fragments), one with the quadrilingual cuneiform and hieroglyphic inscription "Xerxes, the Great King."[218] Mausolus included in his mortuary monument unguent vessels useful for banqueting and bearing direct reference to the great king in order to serve as an important symbol of the connections uniting the two. His expressions of power may have been stronger than this, however, if the identifications are accurate of the greater than life size statues generally called Mausolus and Artemisia that stood with the gods and goddesses between the thirty-six pillars of the temple tomb atop the pedestal.

Perhaps the most immediately apparent aspect of these statues is the clothing they wear: emphatically draped with extra folds and textures to highlight their opulence, the garments embody the figures within. In the context of fourth-century Greek sculpture, this is surprising. In the context of Achaemenid Anatolia, however, where garments and cloth were held in tremendous esteem and bestowed prestige on the wearer, where cloth and clothing were considered gifts fit for a king – both to give and to receive – the emphasis on clothing takes on new meaning. These elaborately draped figures, clothed so that the drapery itself is the most important visual aspect of the statue, were situated in the uppermost echelons of the Achaemenid elite. A fragmentary, colossal seated statue, clothed entirely in purple, is also generally identified as Mausolus and reiterates the point. The inclusion in the tomb of the heirloom stone vessels inscribed with the great king's name in languages from distant parts of the

123. Mausolus (?). GR 1857.12-20.232. © Trustees of the British Museum.

empire makes Mausolus's aspirations all the more apparent. Here is a man who would be king – or at least who fashioned himself on the model of a king, with the apparent sanction of the imperial court.

But perhaps this is not all. This is, after all, a tomb shaped like a temple, and Mausolus's portrayal of himself apparently extends to the freestanding sculptures arranged between the columns of the temple-like structure itself. The other statues are of gods and heroes; including Artemisia and Mausolus among them is suggestive, to say the least. I wonder, indeed, if the very arrangement of hair and features makes a claim for divinity as well. Caria fronts on the island of Rhodes, and Artemisia II had successfully waged a naval battle against that island's formidable warships. Rhodes was dedicated to Helios, the sun god, whose face adorned the coins of Rhodes in the fourth century.

The portrayal of this statue, with long streaming locks springing from a high brow, a furrow across the forehead that accentuates the large deep-set eyes, the slight tilt to one side of the head, may be intended as an explicit reference to Helios. Indeed, it may equate the figure with the god.[219] Retaining a Persian beard, with the short cut that would allow it to fit readily under a military helmet, Mausolus has nonetheless had himself represented in such a way that he closely resembles the Greek sun god. In an Achaemenid context, that sun god is the god of light, truth, and justice, the direct protector of the king. In the polyethnic context of Achaemenid Anatolia, Mausolus makes a very strong statement indeed.[220] As Anne Marie Carstens puts it, "Even if [the Mausoleum] was not a temple, it was presented like one – and Maussollos was the god to worship."[221]

Empire, Authority, and Autonomy in Achaemenid Anatolia

Summary

The overview presented in this chapter makes certain things clear. The manner in which people disposed of their dead seems not to have mattered to the imperial authority, and this was an area in which residents of the empire could exert considerable autonomy. Regional traditions often continued into the Achaemenid period and in some cases seem to have become a citation of geographically specific identity. The similarity of grave goods and funerary art that united the elite across Anatolia is remarkable and demonstrates similar behaviors on the part of the living population. That aspects of non-elite mortuary assemblages reflect those of the elite is perhaps not surprising, but it is nonetheless striking. Certain kinds of actions, manners, public behaviors, and definitions of social identity were highly standardized in Achaemenid Anatolia, as indicated by the mortuary inclusions that resulted from these activities.

Graves could become citations of power. We see this reiteratively across Anatolia, from the embellished tombs of Lydia or Hellespontine Phrygia to the rock-cut statements of Armenia. Nowhere is it as obvious as in Lycia and Caria. The grandiose statements Mausolus conveyed through his tomb at Halicarnassus are thus shown not to be singular but a direct outgrowth of mortuary expression in Achaemenid Anatolia as a whole. Mortuary structure, art, and inclusions all served as potent and nuanced expressions of identity, authority, and autonomy.

SIX

WORSHIPING THE DIVINE

Cultic practice and religious belief in Fars remain notoriously difficult to study, but it is essential to provide at least a brief glimpse of Persian religious expression in Persia before we can consider the impact of Persian presence on the cults of Anatolia.[1] "Achaemenid religion," as I use the expression, means the official religion of the Achaemenid dynasty within the court circle of Fars, as gleaned from imperial texts and representations. Achaemenid religion was surely not static across the longue durée of the empire, and ample evidence demonstrates a diversity of religious expression practiced at the court itself. Mark Garrison's new discussion of religion in Iran demonstrates how little of what has previously been said about Achaemenid religion stems from contemporary evidence; most earlier treatments use texts of other cultures or time periods to try to re-create the belief system and practices of the Persians. Garrison draws on the extensive written records of the late sixth and early fifth centuries and the vast visual corpus provided by the seal impressions on the Persepolis Fortification Archive to begin constructing a notion of early Achaemenid religion that is attested in early Achaemenid documents. He summarizes his findings as follows:

> One of the principal observations to have emerged from this preliminary analysis is the very existence of a rich and detailed iconography for the depiction of the divine and numinous in the early Achaemenid period. This imagery was permeated, moreover, by anthropomorphic, theriomorphic, and aniconic depictions of deities. The existence of this imagery would seem to complement the evidence, documented in the texts from the Fortification archive, that shows the existence of a wide array of deities whose worship was sponsored by the state. Both the textual and pictorial evidence stand in direct contrast to the two most generally perceived notions about religious imagery and the Achaemenid Persians: first, that

they did not depict deities in anthropomorphic form (the "Herodotean" perspective); second, that the prevailing religious belief was Zoroastrianism (the "Avestan" perspective).

Of the imagery itself, it is clear that the grammar, syntax, and vocabulary of the depiction of the divine and the numinous in the early Achaemenid period was deeply embedded in traditional Assyro-Babylonian and Elamite representational imagery.... [W]e may hazard two general observations. First, one aspect of the syntax of the depiction of the numinous seems repeatedly emphasized. This phenomenon, for lack of a better term, I have articulated as "ascension" or "upliftedness." We have repeatedly seen the numinous expressed through the concept of movement upward by the use of winged figures, atlantids, partial figures emerging from winged symbols, partial figures in various other guises, astral symbolism, and figures standing on animals/stands and pedestal creatures. This concept permeates the visual imagery in both glyptic and monumental relief. Indeed, it seems so deeply embedded in the Persian consciousness that it is expressed not only in the visual arts, but also in the very architecture at Naqsh-i Rustam and Persepolis....

Second, king and kingship are intimately connected to/interwoven within this visual grammar and syntax. Through the use of crowns, Persian court robes, inscriptions, bows, archers, date palms, pedestal creatures and, in some cases, what can only be the very figure of the king himself, the centrality of king/kingship is constantly reiterated and/or reformulated. "Ascension," then, may be the defining characteristic of the numinous, the divine, and the royal.[2]

As in Persia, religion in Anatolia was tremendously eclectic. At various places we see Persian, local, and syncretized gods and rituals. Once more I have used behavioral categories to organize this discussion: instances where local cults continued fundamentally unaltered through the Achaemenid period; instances of syncretism of different deities; the introduction of new cults; and a consideration of hero worship. The role of temples as upholders of authority is briefly examined, after which the chapter ends by considering the possible introduction of a royal cult.

Much material relating to religion in Achaemenid Anatolia has been published, particularly from western and central regions. Architectural remains such as temples and altars allow us to consider tensions and interplay between local and imported deities. Numismatic and glyptic evidence provides visual means of examining religious belief and practice. The discussion here will, I hope, raise questions and introduce nuance into the authority–autonomy model.

The consideration of Achaemenid imperialism and authority in this chapter is necessarily complicated. Local autonomy was exercised in the continuation from pre-Achaemenid periods of local cults. On occasion other gods, including Anatolian but also specifically Persian ones such as Anahita, were introduced – it is not clear whether this was the result of Persian will, foreign immigration, or local emulation. Some people used religion to further their own power or ideological ends, whether by co-opting a religious hierarchical structure or syncretizing local gods with Achaemenid ones to solidify their own power. Priests of certain cults held tremendous authority, financial as well as religious. Thus this chapter raises a few questions and suggests directions in which the evidence points, rather than struggling to tie everything into a neat package.

I am not sure if the geographic differences to be observed here result from the nature of the evidence preserved or reflect actual practices of antiquity. At this point we know but little about cultic practice and worship in Achaemenid Armenia. In the rest of Anatolia, we see evidence for the continuity of local cults. We also see the spread of particular Anatolian cults, perhaps resulting from increased communication across the regions of the empire that overrode the political boundaries defining earlier (often rival) kingdoms. Western and southwestern Anatolia show marked openness to adopting aspects of new cults into their local practices, with an emphasis on aspects of the mother goddess, and there is evidence for the adoption of Persian cultic practice as well. Cilicia and Cappadocia introduced Persian and Syrian deities as primary figures into the pantheon, either expressing manifestations of those gods in a mix of hellenizing imagery and the use of Aramaic (as in Cilicia) or expressing worship using Aramaic in a manner that differed from its use in the Persian heartland (as in Cappadocia). Sealstones from across Anatolia demonstrate a widespread iconography laden with religious symbolism and focused on the king himself.

The Achaemenid administration clearly did not require local adoption of foreign gods. Certain important cults such as that of Artemis at Ephesus, however, came under Persian influence, with priests either themselves Persian or taking a Persian name. The importance of religion and belief was clear to the Achaemenid administration. Its incorporation of particular influential cults, the lack of imposition of Persian cultic practice, and the emphasis on the image of the "king ascendant" made for powerful but subtle expressions of power and authority in Anatolia.

Continuity of Cults

Mother Goddess

Various cults continued in more or less their pre-Achaemenid form through the two centuries of Persian hegemony in Anatolia. Of those, I have selected a few examples as case studies. The first is the Phrygian mother goddess, called Matar, Meter, Mama, Kubaba, or Cybele in different parts of Anatolia. The Mother is the only Phrygian goddess depicted in anthropomorphic form. Given our limited knowledge of Phrygian language and the kind of Phrygian texts available

124. Relief of Matar from Ankara. 114-594–68. © Museum of Anatolian Civilizations.

for study, we do not know what the Phrygians thought about the divine, and with only the physical remains of rituals we cannot be certain about the nature of religious practices.[3] Made extensively of natural materials and set in sacred monuments, Phrygian relief facades carved onto rock outcrops or cliff faces and Phrygian rock-cut shrines and votive spaces were often rural but could also be found in urban contexts.[4] Some relief sculptures were freestanding; most depict a single humanoid form, but in a few instances more than one figure is shown and several examples of aniconic stelae or figures are schematically anthropomorphic.[5] Stelae with relief figures of the goddess are usually articulated as architecturally embellished niches: the goddess appears as if standing in the open doorway of a building with a central door. She may hold a drinking vessel or a bird of prey and be accompanied by a lion or composite lion-human figure, or in one case by two young male musicians.[6]

The elaborate architectural facades of the Phrygian highlands, with niches sometimes including the goddess or sometimes left blank but with cuttings that suggest something could have been placed within the doorway, are well known and generally thought to date to between the eighth or seventh centuries and the middle of the sixth century, the main period of Phrygian hegemony over central Anatolia. Phrygian inscriptions on several of the facades identify the deity as Matar, sometimes with an adjective that at least twice is "Kubeliya." Of these rock-cut facades, the Midas Monument at Midas City is not only the most

125. Midas Monument. Courtesy G. Kenneth Sams.

impressive but also the only one associated with a datable context; even it has been assigned dates as dramatically different as the eighth century and the first half of the sixth century.[7]

The monument has two inscriptions, the principal of which appears to have been carved at the same time as the facade and is a dedication to Midas. Lynn Roller suggests that this implies the monument was dedicated after Midas's death, as there is no evidence for Phrygian worship of a living king; however, since the monument is now generally agreed to be a shrine to the goddess, the reference to a king need not imply his prior death.[8] It is almost certainly pre-Achaemenid, in any case. A second inscription may suggest activity at the site over a prolonged period; it runs vertically along the right side of the monument and may be dated on the basis of orthography to the sixth century – indeed, Roller implies in her discussion that it is to be dated to the second half of the sixth century.[9] If so, it demonstrates the numinous significance of the monument even after the Persian conquest of Anatolia. This most famous Phrygian religious marker thus may provide the first clue for the continuity of cults into the Achaemenid period.

The site of Midas City includes an unusually large number of sacred monuments, and this makes it all the more interesting that the excavated architectural remains all belong to a single settlement datable to the Achaemenid period.[10] Evidence for habitation, social activity, and construction of new religious installations during the Achaemenid period is clear. Still ambiguous is the degree to which we can assign evidence for cult activity related to Matar to the Achaemenid period rather than later. Votive altars dedicated to the mother goddess continued to be placed at Midas City as late as the third century C.E. There is clear evidence for dedications during the Hellenistic period and after, but due to the difficulties of chronological typology it is unclear whether any of the Phrygian cult artifacts connected with worshiping the mother goddess can be dated to the Achaemenid period.[11] It is clear, however, that the cult retained essential features of its traditional practice, for the Hellenistic shrine on the high point of the older Phrygian settlement at Midas City demonstrates the continued link between the Matar cult and high places of Phrygia.[12] Similar continuity in cultic practice can be observed at Gordion:

> This form of the Mother's cult, as it is illustrated by the early Phrygian material, apparently lasted until the Hellenistic period. The succeeding fifth and fourth centuries BC have yielded much less information, but those objects from this period which can be ascribed to the cult of the Mother suggest that the basic forms of this cult remained constant. The continuing prominence of her principal attribute, a bird of prey, is attested through a number of scattered finds of votive birds of prey from mixed fifth and fourth century contexts, although images of the goddess herself are disappointingly few. There is, however, one possible exception which should be introduced, a small alabaster figurine, discovered in a fourth century BC context which also included earlier material.
>
> ... Thus this small figurine of the seated goddess is clearly connected with the early Phrygian tradition. Its pose was probably derived, not directly from a Greek model, but through the indirect influence of seated statuettes from other parts of Phrygia. Taken together with the votive birds of prey, the work supports the contention that the cult of the goddess retained its earlier forms until the third century BC.[13]

During the time of Achaemenid hegemony in Anatolia, the Matar cult spread and the iconography used to portray her developed. The second half of the sixth century saw the introduction of a new typology into the Anatolian plateau, a series of seated sculptures showing the mother goddess, which may supersede the earlier typology. This portrayal may have emerged from the seated Meter renditions of mid-sixth-century Ionia and demonstrates an increase in visual communication during the Achaemenid period in Anatolia.[14] A series of reliefs showing a seated figure appears at this time in the cities of the western coast. Found at Smyrna, Erythrae, Clazomenae, Miletus, Ephesus, and Cyme, these sculptures show the goddess seated on a throne, wearing a long gown and a low headdress with a veil.[15] She is framed within an architectural niche, usually with a pointed gable, and she often holds an object in her lap, which in a few cases has been preserved well enough to be identified as a lion.[16] Interestingly, six sculptures from Cyme were found in graves, and it may be that Meter had certain cult functions associated with death.[17]

The spread of Phrygian cultic activity during the Achaemenid period is demonstrated by shrines in the hinterlands of western Anatolia. Near Phocaea, a set of rock-cut stairs leads up to a cliff carved with almost a hundred votive niches; most of these were empty, but at least two of them retain traces of a female figure carved in relief, one holding a tympanum and one seated, without other attributes.[18] The earliest phases of this sanctuary probably date to the late sixth or fifth century, making it perhaps the earliest example of rock-cut niches associated with a Meter sanctuary in western Anatolia.[19] Other examples followed, however, including ones at Fındık near Kütahya, at Ephesus, and at Erythrae.[20]

While the cult of Meter may have spread to the western seaboard of Anatolia from the central highlands, in the Achaemenid period the iconography of her portrayal moved in the other direction as well. Two examples from south central Anatolia near Konya, one from Gordion, one from Takmaköy near modern Eskişehir, and one from Zonguldak on the Black Sea coast have been found so far; they show the goddess seated on a formal throne, sometimes framed in a niche.[21] Greek influence is particularly apparent in the statuette from Takmaköy: the goddess wears a garment like a Greek chiton and holds animals (a lion and a hare) in her lap in a manner that first appears after the introduction of the seated goddess into Greek iconography.[22] The other figures, in contrast, adopt the Greek pose but retain Phrygian costume; the statuette from Gordion continues to hold a traditional bird of prey in her arms.[23] The cultural contact between Greece and Phrygia so well attested in the ceramic record of the Achaemenid period thus also included the visual expression of cultic practice.[24]

Another explicitly Phrygian cult marker is the stepped monument, sometimes with one or two idols on top and cup cuttings that may have been designed for liquid offerings.[25] The idols often have thronelike arms framing them; at least one of these monuments is inscribed to Matar, while those with two idols may be dedicated to a mother goddess and her male counterpart, perhaps a version of the Anatolian thunder god. Most are dedicated to unknown deities or to those of uncertain identity. The idols often have a disk or a semicircular disk at their top, often framed by curling tails that have been identified as hair. They are found not only in extramural or rural sanctuaries but also within cities; indeed, no fewer than nine monumental idols have been recovered from the approach to the Palace Complex at Kerkenes Dağ.[26] It is almost impossible to date the stepped

126. The main step monument at Midas City, surmounted with a double idol. Courtesy G. Kenneth Sams.

monuments or idols. Some may date to the Early Phrygian period, while some definitely date to the Middle Phrygian period (800–550).[27] Although dates in the Achaemenid period cannot be ruled out for their construction, much less for their use, at this point it remains impossible to determine whether the stepped monuments of Phrygia continued in use as cult foci during the Achaemenid period.

In Cilicia, the cult of the mother goddess Kubaba continued into the Achaemenid period with much activity.[28] Particularly interesting is the fourth-century Aramaic inscription on a basalt stele found in Bahadırlı, 6 km north of Karatepe, claiming the goddess's protection over a tract of land.[29] She is clearly to be equated with the goddess of Hierapolis Castabala: "This is the border of KRBJL and KRŠJ, the city (or cities?) that belong to Kubaba of PWŠD/R, who is in Kastabala. And anyone who crosses this border before Kubaba of PWŠD/R or another ... " Here a localized version of the ancient form of the goddess is invoked in the language used by the Achaemenid administration, calling on all of her traditional protective powers. She is thus woven into the new authority even as her own might apparently remains undiminished.

The cult of the mother goddess in western Anatolia demonstrates a combination of continuity and development. In addition to her manifestations as Meter, we see her in the form of the goddesses Cybele and Artemis (a very different goddess in Anatolia, it seems, than the chaste huntress of Athens).[30] These goddesses have a pre-Achaemenid history; by the time of the Achaemenid period, their worship was codified and architecturally articulated with such ornaments as vast temples and altars.

The cult of Cybele at Sardis forms the beginning of discussion here. A few sculptural representations provide all the evidence available so far for Achaemenid-period temples at Sardis. None has been excavated, and there are no literary references or epigraphic sources beyond Herodotus's mention of a temple to Kybebe. This silence parallels that of the Lydian period, for which we also have as yet no information on temple architecture or indeed much information on cultic practice – a gap in our knowledge that is made all the more obvious because of the vast Temple of Artemis at Ephesus, at which Croesus dedicated columns inscribed with his name.[31] Construction on the Artemisium at Ephesus continued into the Achaemenid period, and we may imagine that temple construction to local gods also continued at Sardis under Achaemenid hegemony.

A marble model of a temple from Sardis dates to ca. 540–530. It is probably of the Ionic order (the tops of the columns are broken off), with a detached or semiattached peripteros. The cella walls are decorated with discrete groups of individuals in bands like those on the Ishtar Gate at Babylon, apparently mythological figures in separate but related action groups.[32] The temple model is the earliest Achaemenid-period sculpture at Sardis that shows a goddess. A draped female figure apparently holding snakes emerges from one of its narrow ends, as in the Phrygian stelae. The model has been identified as a temple of Cybele,[33] and it may suggest that an equivalently grand edifice was to be found in contemporary Sardis. Indeed, it has been suggested that the model is a literal representation of a temple at Sardis dating to ca. 570–560, about thirty years before the proposed date of the model's sculpting.[34] If this is the case, it demonstrates the continuity of the Cybele cult from pre-Achaemenid into Achaemenid times.

Cybele is represented in a different form at Sardis by the next century, perhaps in response to the immensely popular and influential image by Agoracritus (?) in Pheidian style showing the goddess with a tympanum and two lions at her sides, and certainly in keeping with the developing portrayals of Matar across Anatolia.[35] The relief from Sardis NoEx 58.27 indicates a shallow naiskos with a pitched roof and three acroteria, supported by pilasters on the sides. Cybele sits on a square throne, a lion lying in her lap and another seated at her side. She holds a tympanum and a small round bowl, which she extends over the head of the seated lion. This relief demonstrates the ability of sculptors in the fourth century to meld influences from disparate areas: the archaic image is known in dozens of reliefs and certainly also circulated at Sardis. But the sculptor of this image incorporated the additional lion that brought his relief into line with contemporary notions in European Greece.

Cybele may not have been the most important goddess of Achaemenid-period Sardis: the common reference in inscriptions to Artemis of Sardis and an

127. Marble temple sculpture from Sardis. S63.51:5677. ©
Archaeological Exploration of Sardis.

apparently local cult of Artemis of Ephesus show that Artemis was key. A stele from Sardis dating to ca. 430–420 shows two goddesses holding animals and being approached by small worshipers; it gives a sense of multiple manifestations of the Anatolian mother goddess worshiped in tandem. As one of the goddesses holds a deer and the other a lion, with a tympanum hanging behind her, they have been identified as Artemis and Cybele. Cybele is slightly smaller than Artemis. The form of the stele recalls the Phrygian relief portrayals of Matar within her architectural setting.

This is important for understanding cults at Sardis in the later fifth century. It suggests that Cybele and Artemis were worshiped as two separate goddesses, although their connection may have been perceived as so great that they shared a temple.[36] Artemis recalls the Ephesian type with her hinds, although Artemis of Ephesus is generally flanked by a deer on either side, whereas this Artemis cradles hers in her arms. The relief may represent the cult of the goddess at Sardis that had stemmed from Ephesus.[37]

The most famous example of continuity of cults in Achaemenid Anatolia is provided by the Artemisium at Ephesus. The site was the locus of cult perhaps as early as the Bronze Age; the archaic temple was the largest building ever made of marble. This temple was begun in the sixth century and enjoyed the royal sponsorship of Croesus.[38] Ulrike Muss has shown that the priesthood at Ephesus was hereditary in the aristocratic classes and that structural changes in early versions of the temple may be linked to reorganizations of Ephesian clan

128. Stele from Sardis with Artemis and Cybele. S68.6, MM3937.
© Archaeological Exploration of Sardis.

structure and hence festivals at the site. Various historically attested ceremonies at the temple seem to have been conducted by different branches of the aristocracy, the differing clans being responsible for different festivals.[39] She has also demonstrated that the original cult at Ephesus was not of Artemis but rather her mother, Leto; evidence for a cult of Eleusinian Demeter also points to original worship of a mother goddess at Ephesus.[40] Indeed, she argues, the cult of Artemis at Ephesus as it existed in the mid–sixth century was a syncretism of several earlier mother goddess cults.[41]

Ephesus, a city with a strong Greek and Lydian presence before the Achaemenid period and with an apparently strong Persian presence during the time of Achaemenid hegemony, thus provides an interesting example of the sorts of hybrids that formed. This is demonstrated not only by cult behaviors but also by the Temple of Artemis itself, with its Ionic frieze along the parapet sima and the famous (Egyptianizing?) *columnae caelatae* probably begun

129. Silver coin of Ephesus, fifth century, with bee and incuse, Australian Centre for Ancient Numismatic Studies, Macquarie University. Courtesy Kenneth Sheedy.

by Croesus and finished in the Achaemenid period, as well as its bulls modeled in high relief like Assyrian and Achaemenid guardian colossi, either on its antae or on a propylon before the temple.[42] Moreover, fifth-century silver coins of Ephesus portray a bee on the obverse, the head of which has curling tendrils that resemble both the "hair" on the Phrygian idols and the "tail" on the Achaemenid winged disk.

The cult of Artemis of Ephesus shows continuity from pre-Achaemenid to Achaemenid times. Its incorporation of multiple artistic traditions demonstrates the iconographic communication that characterized religious landscapes of Achaemenid Anatolia. The co-option of the cult's leadership by the Persians, as we shall see, demonstrates their ability and desire to retain authority over this most powerful religious institution. Apparently Artemis of Ephesus was so mighty that her worship could be allowed little autonomy, even if its new leaders showed no desire to alter its ancient traditions. This perhaps relates to the role of Artemis of Ephesus as an upholder of rectitude and finance, for in Achaemenid Anatolia, religion also encompassed the law, which was underwritten by divine justice and punishment.[43]

At Ephesus, a priest named Megabyzus performed essential financial services in the late fifth and early fourth centuries to keep deposits safe and oversee bequests to the temple and its cult.[44] "Megabyzus" may have been a hereditary office and name.[45] It is a Persian name: this most important priesthood was held by someone with Persian identity by the end of the fifth century. This demonstrates a degree of Achaemenid authority over religion and finance and highlights the importance of the cults. Such functions and aspects of cultic practice were not limited to Ephesus.

Two legal decrees in Lydian set up by one Mitridastas near the site of the Hellenistic temple to Artemis at Sardis show a similar interplay of responsibilities and authority.[46] The first deals with the dedication of a temple to Qλdãns and Artemis (by Mitridastas?) and the establishment of a trust fund entailing all of Mitridastas's belongings, to be held by the association of the temple (apparently a council of priests) to maintain the temple. The second, missing its final lines, records the transmittance of Mitridastas's possessions to the association of the temple. Artemis of Ephesus and Qλdāns the mighty are held responsible for the conduct of the overseers and proper use of the trust, as well as the property itself: if anyone damaged Mitridastas's property or interfered with its oversight, the gods were to destroy him and his property. Artemis was also to destroy those who tampered with Mitridastas's decree. It seems that Artemis herself was the highest punitive body in Sardis at the time the decrees were set up.

Artemis of Ephesus and her cult thus served as financial guarantor and as bank. This was an ethnically mixed function at Sardis that in some ways paralleled that of the cult at Ephesus itself. Mitridastas is a Persian name, but at Sardis he put his wealth in the safekeeping of Artemis of Ephesus and specified how it was to be used in maintaining her cult. Similarly, at Ephesus the cult included a priest with a Persian name guarding the wealth of others under the protection of the goddess. Apparently this version of the Anatolian mother goddess would safeguard material riches, certainly during the Achaemenid period and perhaps earlier, too.

Lycia provides another example of the mother goddess showing hybridization within various cultic functions. The cult of Leto demonstrates patronage by Persian-appointed rulers for a local cult. Considered "by far the most important sanctuary in Lycia," the sanctuary of Leto at Xanthus, or Letoön, was of great antiquity according to literary sources, with archaeological evidence dating at least to the sixth century, possibly the seventh, and epigraphic evidence attesting to a full-scale temple within the Letoön.[47] This cult was dedicated to Leto and her children (only once explicitly named, as Apollo and Artemis, in the Aramaic version of the Letoön Trilingual Inscription), and it was promoted in the early fourth century by the kings of Lycia at Xanthus as part of their dynastic ambitions.[48] The deity takes here the name of the Greek goddess; the continuity of her cult from pre-Achaemenid through Achaemenid times parallels that of the mother goddess elsewhere in Anatolia.

A different aspect of the mother goddess and her cult in Lycia is seen in the goddess Ertẽme/i- or Erteme/i. Erbbina foregrounds her name in the inscriptions on his statue base, and she is mentioned frequently in inscriptions from Telmessus as well as a votive from Trysa.[49] Because the name of the Lydian goddess was Artimu, the deity may be an Anatolian one.[50] She may be a late arrival "since Artimu at Ephesus was another aspect of the same Anatolian mother-goddess already represented in Lycia by Eni Mahanahi," but Sardis demonstrates that multiple aspects of the goddess might be worshiped in the same place at the same time under different names.[51] In any case it is certain that the mother goddess was worshiped in various guises in Lycia, some of which are attested in the most ancient times and some of which might be the result of increased communication between cultures and cult sites in more recent times.

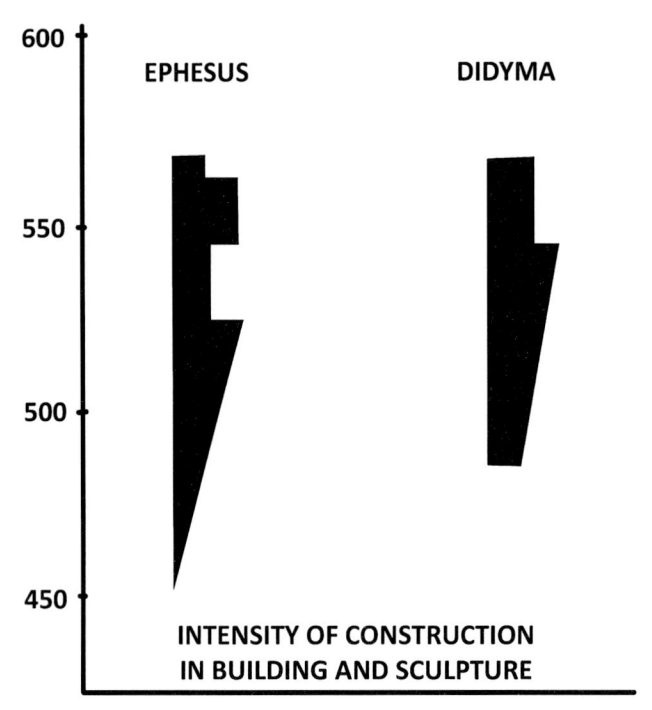

130. Construction at Ephesus and Didyma. Author's drawing, after Muss 1994: 98.

Apollo

Miletus and its oracular temple to Apollo at nearby Didyma provide another example of cultic continuity and demonstrate the degree to which local cults might thrive under Achaemenid hegemony. Didyma, a cult site on a limestone outcrop connected to Miletus by a sacred way, may have been founded as early as the second millennium; certain evidence of activity at the site dates to as early as the eighth century.[52] Early textual sources for the mother goddess in her aspect as Leto also mention an oracle here, while archaic inscriptions mention Artemis and Hecate; Tuchelt suggests that the cult and its oracle enjoyed continuity of function from the end of the Bronze Age into much later times.[53] Apollo may have been a newcomer to the site, but he predated the Persian arrival in western Anatolia. An early small temple (naiskos) and references to a sacred laurel tree were succeeded by a major expansion phase between 700 and 550, characterized by construction in limestone and increasing offerings at the sanctuary, the codification of the sacred naiskos in the sanctuary, and perhaps the cult statue of Apollo.[54]

With the beginning of Achaemenid hegemony came a flurry of new construction at Didyma. The temple was first expanded and then built anew, no earlier than 550; this included construction of new terrace walls and treasuries, as well as work on the temple itself.[55] Tuchelt comments: "Certainly the cultic

131. Statue from Achaemenid-period Didyma. GR 1859.12-26.9.
© Trustees of the British Museum.

and oracular functioning would have been affected by the work, but they were in no way interrupted."[56] The impetus for expansion may have begun before the Persian arrival in Ionia, but it is certain that the great building phase continued through the rest of the sixth century, perhaps even until the Ionian Revolt was put down in 494.[57] The Achaemenid imperial authority may have taken over patronage of this cult and its enormous construction projects; if this is true, it demonstrates something far more than simple cultic continuity – active, engaged support. Of the life-size seated statues of male and female figures flanking the sacred way from Miletus to Didyma, some date to the second quarter of the sixth century, but the majority date to the years after 550.[58] Indeed, the blossoming of work on the temple was paralleled by a floruit in production of these statues during the early Achaemenid period.

It is thus clear that the temple at Didyma with its oracular shrine of Apollo saw not only continuity of cults into the Achaemenid period, but an initial time under the Persians when the sanctuary flourished mightily. New construction at the temple seems to have ended with the Ionian Revolt, and no monumental structures can be dated between 494 and 300.[59] Significantly, though, the sanctuary continued to be used, and although the oracle was silent during the Achaemenid period, the cult of Apollo clearly retained importance.[60]

Anatolian Storm God

Less clear is the example of the Lycian god Trqqas.[61] The name derives from a stem Trqqñt-, which was pronounced either "Tarkunt" or "Trokont," and is obviously the same as the name of the ancient Anatolian storm god Tarhunt. It indicates a deity of great antiquity, but his presence in Lycia itself is not attested before Achaemenid-period inscriptions; whether we see here an ancient cult continuing in situ or an ancient cult practiced in Lycia during the Achaemenid period but not before remains uncertain.

Malija

Much clearer is the Lycian deity Malija, a goddess of considerable antiquity. She is mentioned in Achaemenid-period Lycian inscriptions found at Tlos, Xanthus, the Letoön, Tyberissus, and Arneae.[62] Although she is not to be equated with the Greek goddess Athena, the iconography of Malija's portrayal drew on Greek visual vocabulary for her rendering in the fifth and fourth centuries. As Antony Keen remarks, "They are representing the Lycian cult of Malija in the Greek-derived media of coinage and Greek-language epigraphy through the established vocabulary of those media."[63] This Anatolian goddess, then, provides another example of continuity of definition and practice of cultic forms during the Achaemenid period combined with an expanded sense of expression.

Hero Cults

The hero cults attested in Lycia and Hellespontine Phrygia show some continuity as well, interesting in light of the fact that mythical or epic histories can function as usable pasts in specific political contexts. In the Troad, for instance, literary evidence mentions a monument to Achilles and Patroclus at the end of the Achaemenid period, at which Alexander and Hephaistion are said to have offered garlands.[64] Alcock has argued that the increase in cult activity associated with Bronze Age heroes in Greece during the Late Classical and Hellenistic periods resulted from the pressures of political and institutional change within the polis.[65] In particular, she has suggested, hero cult activity in European Greece reflected elites' need to announce and legitimate their increasingly dominant role in civic life. Indeed, myths and hero cults can readily be reworked to

132. Relief from Building G at Xanthus. GR 1848.10-20.18. © Trustees of the British Museum.

emphasize particular aspects that underscore the legitimacy and might of current leaders.[66]

We cannot trace a similar upswing in elite cultic activity during the late Achaemenid period – elite dominance was apparently an ongoing feature of life in Achaemenid Anatolia. It seems the impetus for hero cults was different in Anatolia than in Greece. I suggest that such cults provided an opportunity to associate with specifically local, non-Persian heroes. Perhaps the continuity of heroes worshiped in Achaemenid Anatolia is not, therefore, a direct example of the continuity of cultic forms from pre-Achaemenid to later times. It may rather reflect people's desire to claim cultural connections to larger-than-life figures of the distant past who shared links to local people rather than Persians. Hero cults might have allowed ethnically non-Persian members of the Achaemenid elite to assert and legitimate their role in administration. At the same time, if ethnic Persians were seen to pay homage to local heroes, it could have demonstrated their openness to local cults and vicariously accrued to them some of that sense of deep-rooted tradition and responsibility. The hero cults thus provide an example of local autonomy that establishes local authority in nuanced ways depending on who is responsible for worship: they might create authority in the teeth of imperial might, or they might co-opt locally based authority into the overarching umbrella of imperium. They tie into the processes described in the preceding chapter, the authoritative autonomy of monumental tombs that selectively utilize ideas from a variety of sources, including Persian and Greek as well as local.

Lycia provides archaeological and epigraphic evidence for hero cult activity. The iconography of sculptures associated with the various heroa might incorporate Persian and Greek motifs and ideas – even as the monuments apparently venerate local Lycian figures. Most heroa include similar elements: the place where the hero's grave either was or was thought to be, a strongly built stone pedestal with a niche for liquid offerings, and a temple or temple-like open hall that reminded others of the presence of a superhuman being.[67] Some of the Lycian heroa were designed by and for still-living kings. In connection with the palaces nearby, these would symbolize the might and staying power of the ruler; this is perhaps the case for certain heroa at Trysa and Xanthus, including

133. Xanthus Building G detail (© Trustees of the British Museum) and the king's horse from the Apadana at Persepolis (courtesy of the Oriental Institute of the University of Chicago).

the older ones at the south of the site, built to resemble houses rather than temples (Buildings F, G, and H), as well as the pillar monuments to the north.[68]

Building G is an example of the type at Xanthus. A tower monument with architectural features imitating timber constructions, it was flat-topped with a pillared interior and a sculpted frieze. Some of that frieze showed horses and men. The horses display Persian conformation, treatment of forelocks and tails, and trappings, and were walked in-hand like the horses on the Apadana at Persepolis; at the same time they are shown with prominent veins and pulling manned chariots in a manner reflecting Greek notions of equine portrayal. A nice detail is that the forward-stepping front leg of a horse at Xanthus is bent at the knee, something seen at Persepolis only among the king's horses. Perhaps this provides a visual reworking of local cultic practice to provide legitimacy and authority through connection to the king.

The heroön at Limyra in eastern Lycia, built by/for Pericles ca. 370–350, may also have dynastic pretensions. Interestingly, the heroön shows Greek stylistic influence on its imagery, which is strongly pro-Persian in iconographic impact.[69] It was built on a rock-cut platform at the southernmost rim of the town's upper fortifications and looked out over the residential town. It followed the usual pattern for Lycian heroa: a stone pedestal topped by a temple-shaped monument, in this case with columns at back and caryatids at front; these have been interpreted as divine supporters of the hero cult.[70] A marble frieze showed the ruler's leadership, supported and abetted by Persian might, with scenes of a four-horse chariot, the ruler and his entourage, cavalry, and infantry bearing shields and spears. Many figures wear Persian garments and headgear, including one horseman wearing the tiara.[71] The acroteria at the heroön's peak include an image of

Perseus that legitimates the dead hero and creates links between himself and the mythological past. This figure is clearly Perseus the Assyrian, who became the first Greek; as Keen describes it, "The implication is that, just as Pericles himself was claiming to be the heir of Bellerophon, so he was implying that the Persian King was the heir of Perseus and therefore had a right to claim dominion over both Persia and the Greek world."[72]

The tomb is of particular interest in the context of hero cults. Built by a living local dynast operating within the embrace of Achaemenid hegemony to monumentalize his death, it creates the same sort of numinous atmosphere demonstrated by the earlier temple tomb, the Nereid Monument, and by the later Mausoleum. It connects the local Lycian dynastic ruler to Persian kingship and ruling. But it also connects him to a hero with links to Lycia, one with local geographic resonance as well as overarching political significance.

The cult of Sarpedon at Xanthus contributes to our sense of multivalenced symbolism. The great Lycian hero who died at Troy and figures so prominently in Homer was supposedly buried in Xanthus, and by the Hellenistic period a deme had been named after him there and another at Tlos.[73] By the fifth century, a major cult complex had been built at Xanthus on the acropolis, and games were held in the hero's honor. In the Achaemenid period, some offerings were left at the tombs even of normal people, and scholars suggest that "regular offerings would be made at the Sarpedoneion."[74] Here is clear evidence for the sort of hero worship also seen in Hellespontine Phrygia, emphasizing Bronze Age heroes with local importance who were distinctively non-Persian but whose worship flourished during the period of Persian hegemony even as local elites connected themselves as well with Achaemenid-approved notions of rulership and self-portrayal. Perhaps, indeed, the fact that Sarpedon fought for the Trojans against the Greeks made him of particular interest to local elites in Achaemenid Lycia. Hero cults became powerful citations of authority, with a flavor of local autonomy that must have made them particularly palatable to the local population.

Accretion of Cults

Deities were very seldom syncretized, that is, multiple deities were rarely combined into one, but aspects of their cults were much more fluid and show significant accretion of ritual. Thus we can at no point say definitively that, for instance, Zeus and Ahuramazda are one and the same, but we can say that aspects of worship and ritual might be adapted from one cult and incorporated into another.[75] This observation relates to the iconographies of Malija and Athena, but it is clear that hybridization could include practice as well as portrayal. Actual cultic syncretism is different from the fluidity of iconography seen in mother goddess cults. It implies that the practices of worshiping two different deities are meshed into one, or at least that aspects of their cults are – apparently similarities between gods or goddesses of different cultural heritage might suggest that they could be worshiped as one, or sometimes two deities of similar traditional background might be amalgamated in the manner of their worship. They were not, it seems, thought to be the same god. Their cultic practice and associated behaviors might more readily be hybridized, however. Achaemenid authority in Anatolia allowed not only communication between areas, but also increased fluidity in rendering and enacting cultic practice. As will emerge, it is seldom clear whether religious accretions were encouraged by the imperial authority as a mechanism for social identity elision or whether they were locally generated.

Artemis at Sardis and Ephesus

Literary sources provide a particular kind of information about cult places dedicated to Artemis in Lydia. Pausanias, describing events of ca. 323–322, mentions one Adrastus, who evidently died in the Lamian War: "The Lydians erected a bronze statue of Adrastus himself in front of the sanctuary of Persian Artemis, and wrote an epigram saying that Adrastus met his end fighting against Leonnatus on behalf of the Greeks" (7.6.6). An altar to Artemis at Sardis was held in respect by the Persians, as demonstrated by Xenophon's account of Cyrus the Younger quizzing one Orontas, who was engaged in treachery against him: "Is it not the case," said Cyrus, "when again you learned your real [lack of] power, that you went to the altar of Artemis and said that you repented, and did you not persuade me, giving me tokens of faith again and receiving them from me?" (Anab. 1.6.7).

An altar has been excavated at the west end of the Hellenistic temple to Artemis at Sardis, in the sanctuary of Artemis on the east bank of the Pactolus River.[76] It is built of calcareous tufa blocks; as preserved, it consists of three steps on top of a single-course euthynteria, and setting marks show that there was originally at least one more step above the three preserved. The excavators believed the altar was faced in marble and reconstructed it to resemble the oblong altar of Poseidon at Cape Monodendri.[77]

The dating of this monument is securely Achaemenid.[78] It is at the site of the Hellenistic temple to Artemis, and the likelihood of continuity of cultic practice suggests that the Achaemenid-period altar was sacred to Artemis. Perhaps the cult was an offshoot of Ephesian Artemis.[79] The identification of the deity worshiped as a version of Artemis is borne out by local inscriptions that mention Artemis of Sardis. This was an important goddess of the city; she figures in many Lydian-language Achaemenid-period inscriptions from Sardis. It seems reasonable to suppose that this altar was sacred to Artemis in the Achaemenid period.

134. The altar to Artemis at Sardis. © Archaeological Exploration of Sardis.

The monument helps us consider the social situation at Sardis. This large and elaborate altar, perhaps faced in marble, was built in the Achaemenid period to a local goddess. It is not a Persian shape or, as far as we know, a Lydian one, but rather reflects the religious architectural traditions of the Ionian Greek cities. The addition of steps is a key point, however: steps of this nature are a feature of Persian fire altars and tie into the notion of "ascension" described by Garrison.[80] The Artemis altar is thus a hybrid form.[81] Achaemenid authority allowed considerable autonomy in religious practice and expression, creating an environment that would certainly have allowed for hybridization of behavior and performance of cults as well as architectural or artistic rendering.

Inscriptional evidence adds to our sense of Artemis in western Anatolia. The cult of Artemis of Ephesus was introduced to Sardis at some early point, and Lydian inscriptions at Sardis make clear that Artemis of Sardis and Artemis of Ephesus were not thought to be one and the same.[82] They do seem to have been considered different manifestations of the same deity, however, and they are often mentioned together in Lydian inscriptions. The well-known Sacrilege Inscription from Ephesus reads as follows:

> The judges for the goddess brought in
> the sentence of death on account of the accusation
> of the following crime: when sacred messengers
> had been sent by the city to
> the Chitons for Artemis according to the cus-
> toms of our ancestors and the sacred objects and

the sacred messengers had arrived at Sar-
dis and the Sanctuary of Artemis
founded by the Ephesians, the
sacred objects they profaned and the sacred messengers they assaulted.
The punishment for the crime is death.
The following were sentenced:
Tuios son of Manes son of Saplous,
Strombos son of Manes son of Saplous,
Mousaios son of Herakleidos, Paktyes
son of Karous son of Herakleidos, ...
son of Karous, Miletos son of Karous,
Pytheas son of Karous, Paktyes son of
Atis, Saplous son of Pilos,
Herakleidos son of Artymas son of Manes
the bathman, Herakleidos
of the son of Artymas son of Manes the bathman
son of his brother Ilos, Maneas son of Atis
son of Ariotes, Moxos son of Atas
the shoe seller,
Moxos son of Atas
the shoe seller his brother,
Moxos son of Oilos son of Saplas the
sandal seller, Moschion and
Hermolaos brothers, Pilos son of Kar-
os son of Boukopos (or "the bull slayer"), Artymas son of S...
mos son of Boukopos (or "the bull slayer"), Strombos son of
Karous son of Kondas, Strombos
son of Pakyos son of Manes, Strombous [son of]
Herakleidos the goldsmith, Saplous
son of Strombos, Tamatis son of Strombos, Zakrores son of Kados son of Manes,
Strombos son of Manes son of Ephesos,
Artymas son of Daos, Tuios son of Pytheas,
Artymas son of Manes son of Kotylos,
Sisines son of Eumanes from Hiera
Kome, Pytheas son of Strombos son of . . .
stes, Paktyes son of Atis the priest,
Paktyes son of Manes the oil seller [, ...?]
son of Karous, Papes son of Ephesos [son of]
Karous, Mithradates son of Tuios [son of]
Manes the slave of Attis, Strombos
son of Karous son of Kotylos, Strombos
son of Karous, Pytheas son of Strombous
son of Kados son of Babas, Paktyes son of
Manes <Karos>, Moxos son of Strombos son of

> Pytheas, Spelmos son of Tuios, Baga[da?]-
> tes the sacred herald, Batopates (?) son of
> Papas, Karous son of Manes son of Atas
> from Ibis Kome, Atas who has [as wife?]
> the daughter of Paktyes son of Atis,
> Samatikes son of Potas. [83]

This clarifies several aspects of cultic practice: Ephesus was responsible for guarding the branch of its cult at Sardis; religious transgressions carried tremendous penalties; young men of all ethnic identities might participate in vandalism against serious matters such as cultic practice and expression; and likenesses between the goddesses might extend as far as worship behaviors but did not mean that the two aspects of the deity were thought to be identical. Thus we see here the export of a cult and its adoption at another site. The "Sanctuary of Artemis founded by the Ephesians" at Sardis was one of paramount importance, but the emphasis in Lydian epitaphs on Artemis of Ephesus and Artemis of Sardis shows that these were different aspects of the goddess. The cult and sacred objects mentioned in the inscription demonstrate the open religious atmosphere in Achaemenid Sardis, one paralleled by the mixed ethnicities shown in naming patterns within families. They do not indicate the co-option of one cult by another. The combined evidence of the altar and the inscription at Sardis attests to the fluidity of religious expression and behavior.

Greek literary, epigraphic, and numismatic evidence also refers to "Artemis Persike" and "Artemis Anaitis" in Lydia, and scholars have tended to take these as identifying the Persian goddess Anahita.[84] It is possible that Anahita remained separate from Artemis in western Anatolia, while the cult of Artemis became "Persianized."[85] This notion perhaps parallels that concerning the altar to Artemis at Sardis: we have no evidence that Artemis and Anahita were equated, but evidence suggests that expressions of worship devoted to one deity might be subsumed into the cult expressions of another.[86]

Evidence for Persian engagement with Greek beliefs and practices is widespread; for example, in 409 Tissaphernes sought the protection of Artemis at Ephesus; a statue was donated to the local cult of Zeus at Sardis by Droaphernes, son of Barakes, *hyparchos* of Lydia; and a formal civic decree was found at Amyzon integrating two men with Persian names, Bagadates and his son Ariaramnes, into the city's structure as the *neokoros* of Artemis.[87] The Droaphernes Inscription may demonstrate a Persian family cult of the Greek god Zeus.[88] In the Hellenistic period, Persian cults were seen by Greek authors as distinct because their rites were performed by Persian priests speaking an unintelligible language.[89] These are not incompatible occurrences and demonstrate the variety of religious expression found in western Anatolia as Persians engaged with Greek and local cults. Greek engagement with Persian cults, in turn, seems to have

135. Coin of Mausolus. Author's drawing.

recognized similarities among various deities that allowed for the assimilation of notions, practices, and/or epithets, without leading to an equation of gods or goddesses.[90]

We should not blithely assume that the inhabitants of Achaemenid Anatolia relinquished their own deities or renamed them to give them a new spin. Instead, we see an open-minded approach to adapting aspects of worship or rendition from other cults or cultures in order best to express the manifestation of the deity known locally. This process manifests visually as well: we have observed it in renditions of the Phrygian mother goddess, and we shall see that it typifies early Lycian renditions of deities on coins.[91]

The Sanctuary of Zeus at Labraunda

The sanctuary of Zeus at Labraunda predated the Persian arrival in Caria, so that according to Herodotus some Carians sought refuge in the sanctuary of "Zeus of Armies" there, characterized by its great grove of plane trees.[92] The earliest evidence for the cult of Zeus Labraundus dates to the middle of the seventh century.[93] I include the cult here not because it assimilated specific aspects of other deities' worship, but because it demonstrates associations between worshiping the god and paying homage to the king, a blend of actions and iconography that brings the Hecatomnid dynasts of Caria into the notion of "ascension" at Persepolis. In this way, Labraunda forms a link to numinous aspects of kingship as well as the god.

The Hecatomnids were official, Persian-appointed governors of Caria.[94] In the fourth century the Hecatomnid family took advantage of its ruling position to sponsor the sanctuary of Zeus; proclaiming this abroad are the silver coins minted by the family showing Zeus Labraundus with his characteristic double-bladed ax. The Hecatomnids sponsored most of the buildings at Labraunda, including the terraced sanctuary itself, the Temple of Zeus, buildings for feasting, and the "oikoi" behind the temple.

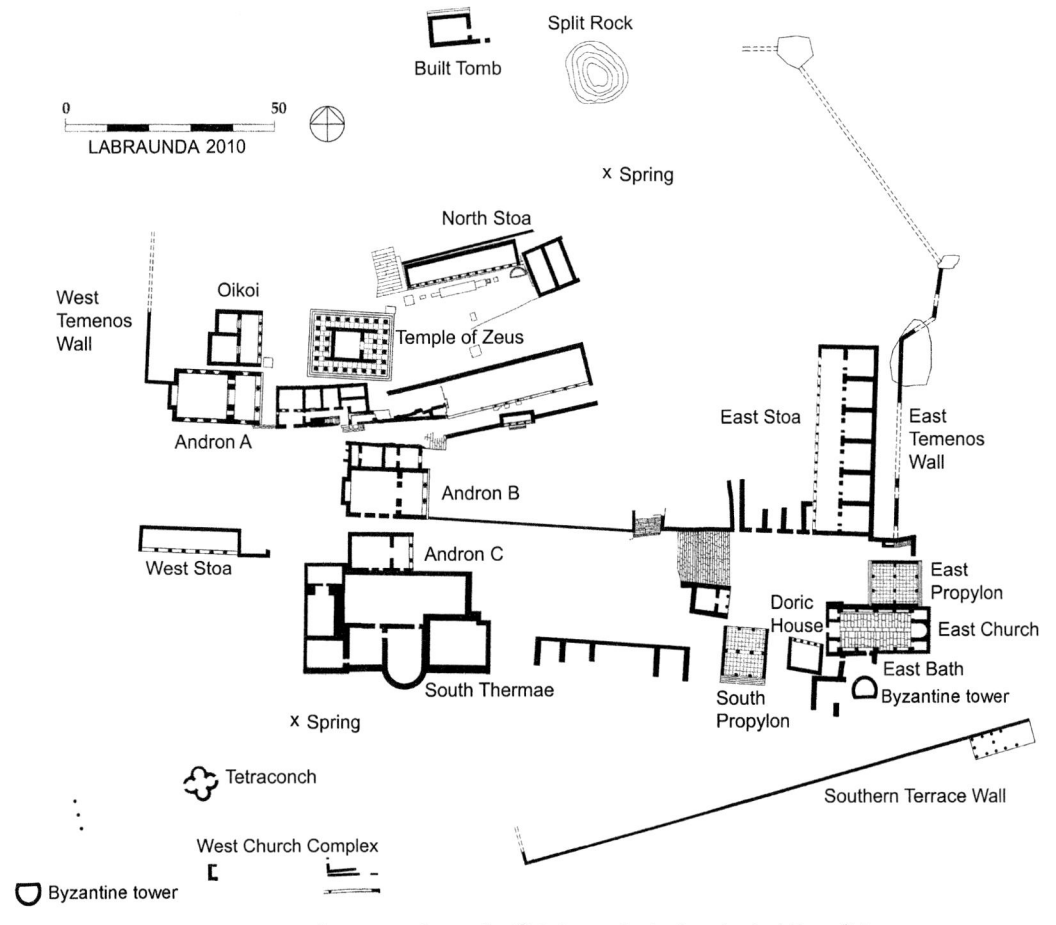

136. Sanctuary of Zeus at Labraunda. © Labraunda Archaeological Expedition.

The fourth-century Temple of Zeus was built over a precursor that dated to the end of the sixth century (thus already during the Achaemenid period).[95] It is shorter than most contemporary temples and thought to have been built by Pythius before he built the Temple of Athena at Priene or embarked on the Mausoleum; it was probably constructed before Idrieus (351–344) dedicated the curious "Oikoi" behind the temple. The excavators comment, "The function of the Oikoi Building is not evident.... A main purpose of the Oikoi Building may, however, have been as a treasury for the safe-keeping of valuable gifts to the god."[96]

Andron B, a temple-shaped building with a marble facade, including two Ionic columns at the front and richly sculpted anta capitals, was built by Mausolus. The edifice combines Ionic columns with a Doric entablature and includes a massive inscription naming Mausolus as dedicator of the building. Within the well-lit main room of the andron were twenty dining couches, arranged around the back and sides of the room. The back wall included a large niche, which the

137. Andron B at Labraunda. © Labraunda Archaeological Expedition.

excavators suggest would have held three statues: Zeus in the middle and the ruling couple (Mausolus and his sister-wife Artemisia) on the sides.[97]

Sacred banquets had long formed part of ritual in Greek sanctuaries – and indeed probably in all religions to whose deities animals were sacrificed.[98] They were of particular import, both because of the connection to the divine and because of the opportunity to consume meat.[99] Here, where the sanctuary had been built by the ruling family, where the elaborate andron – as large as the Temple of Zeus – could hold so many diners, and where the room displayed statues of Zeus and the local ruler together, it must have been obvious both who provided the feast and that his status was godlike. Moreover, if proximity implied status, the permanent juxtaposition of Mausolus and Artemisia with Zeus, with other diners arranged at increasing distance, would have made the point all the more clear. Outside, the andron was topped at its acroteria by two marble sphinxes that drew on the iconography of Persepolis, where sphinxes

138. Sphinx from Labraunda. Courtesy Pontus Hellstrøm.

were associated with kingly responsibility for righteous harmony and peace, with added western Anatolian elements such as locks of hair behind the ears.[100] Ann Gunter explains: "The range and richness of the sphinxes' meaning and context in Achaemenid court art, the art of a Lydian elite, the religious and funerary architecture of western Asia Minor, and the official art of the dynasty, seem to have been evoked intentionally on the *andron* of Mausolus."[101]

In this sanctuary of Zeus at Labraunda, then, Mausolus made explicit connections between himself and kingship, himself and righteousness, himself and divinity. The sanctuary became a locus not only for worship of the god but for homage to the local ruler; Mausolus adapted the association between ruler and god that was so strong at Persepolis and assimilated it into the ritual practices of Caria at Labraunda.[102] Such ability to function on this scale must have been sanctioned by the imperial authority – just as worship of local gods was sanctioned.

Mausolus's brother Idrieus, who succeeded him, probably built Andron A in addition to the Oikoi. Its plan is identical to that of Andron B, except that it is even larger and has even more windows. Like Andron B, this was used for banqueting, as was the East Stoa.[103] Evidence from the Hellenistic period suggests political meetings by members of a Carian league at Labraunda; it is possible that the architectural evidence for banqueting at the site during the Achaemenid period links it to political meetings and discussions as well.[104] In any case, the diners at the site would have been reminded of the link between Zeus Labraundus and the rulers of Caria in the last century of Achaemenid hegemony over Anatolia. We see here not syncretism between the cults of one traditional god and another, but association between practices connected with paying homage to the king of gods, the king of kings, and the king of local lands.

Conversion of Cult? The Altar to Cybele at Sardis

A different, and apparently rare, approach is perhaps to be seen in one part of Sardis.[105] On the eastern bank of the Pactolus River, about half a kilometer to the north of the Artemis altar, a gold refinery prospered in Lydian times.[106] It had small ovens and cupels for smelting, loosely grouped about an open space. In the middle of this industrial zone was a small, freestanding, rectangular altar with a limestone lion atop each corner, apparently sacred to the goddess Cybele.[107] There is no evidence that the gold refinery continued to be used after the Persian conquest of the city.[108] The altar in its center underwent major reconstruction, apparently in the Achaemenid period: the lions were removed from the corners and carefully placed in the interior of the altar, perhaps as a kind of pious decommissioning. The altar was built up higher, and the top showed clear traces of burning with layers of ash and clay.[109] Here we see the reconstruction of a pre-Achaemenid Lydian altar to Cybele, in which the lions were hidden within the newly heightened superstructure to provide an area for repeated burning.

It has been suggested that this represents the conversion of the structure to a fire altar.[110] A fire altar might conform to the practices of Mazdaism; although there is mention in the excavators' reports of bone in the uppermost layer of burning, the seals of Persepolis show that burnt sacrifice might be associated with fire altars in the Achaemenid period, and burnt animal bones have been found in a shrine context in Iran at Dahan-i Gulaman.[111] This altar, if indeed it was converted from a local form to a fire altar, would form a telling contrast to the continuation of local practices otherwise seen in Anatolia. Rather than continuity of religion, here we may perhaps see the co-option and conversion of a sacred monument. If this interpretation is correct, it demonstrates an unusually heavy hand of authority exerted over local cultic practice. One wonders just what it was that made this site different from the others.

Introduction of Non-Anatolian Cults

The freedom to worship particular gods or to worship in a particular way has already been indicated by the presence at Sardis of the seal IAM 5133 with its Neo-Babylonian worship scene. This seal, of course, does not prove that its owner worshiped Neo-Babylonian gods in the Neo-Babylonian manner, but it is not impossible that such was the case. A large number of Neo-Babylonian worship seals were carved in various styles and impressed on the Persepolis Fortification tablets; some were certainly new productions rather than heirloom curiosities and demonstrate a particular clientele who wanted that imagery.[112] References to Babylonians at Persepolis in the Persepolis Fortification texts also suggest that Babylonians continued their religious traditions under the Achaemenids. They may, perhaps, even have continued them when they moved to other areas of the empire.[113] Certainly there is evidence for the introduction of new, non-Anatolian cults into parts of Anatolia during the Achaemenid period.[114]

Documenting such an introduction are the Aramaic inscriptions on two stones from Arebsun near Nevşehir in Cappadocia, now in Istanbul. These stelae date to the third century but are generally held to pertain to the Achaemenid period because of the strong Persian influence they demonstrate.[115] They are sculpted in low relief with scenes that include floral vistas, animal processions, waterfowl and fish, trouser-clad humans, and a chariot racing at full tilt with Achaemenid-style studs on its wheel.[116] Although their grammar does not conform to the norms of Imperial Aramaic orthography, the gods they name are clearly Persian and Mesopotamian in origin.[117] The first of the two stelae, Stele A, mentions Bel and, perhaps, Ahuramazda by name:

Arebsun 1: Stele A (no. 7754)

1. ZRZ 'BYD BHTḤTN BYL RB' MLK'
2. 'HWRMZD?YM'/YB?D/RQ/M'MTR?BD/R
3. MW'TR *DDY* MW['/]TR *DDY* MW'TR *DDY*

1. *Monument* (?) made for the marriage of Bel, the great, the king
2. Ahuramazda..........
3. Abundant *blessings*, beloved! Abundant *blessings*, beloved! Abundant *blessings*, beloved![118]

Stele B includes multiple inscriptions; these mention Mazda and an uncertain divinity (?), Daenamazdayasnish, as well as Bel. The moon and the month of Tammuz (the first of the summer months) figure in them as well, as does a "seer" named Abbas, who performs certain kinds of rituals that seem to include dedicating fire:

Arebsun 2: Stele B, side A, inscription 1 (no. 7753, = RES 1785E)

1. ? MZD W*DYNMZDYSN*/MŠ ?
2. [MLK]T' ' ḤTH W'NTTH ZY BYL
3. KN 'MR 'NH 'NTT ZY BYL MLK'
4. ḤR BYL KN 'MR L*DYNMZDYSNŠ*
5. 'NT ḤTY ŠGY' ḤKYM
6. WŠPYR' 'NT MN 'LHN
7. W'L ZK 'NH ŠWYT LKY
8. 'NTT *ZY L*
9. BY

Empire, Authority, and Autonomy in Achaemenid Anatolia

1. ? Mazda *and* Daenamazdayas*n*ish ?
2. *[the queen?]* the sister and wife of Bel
3. has said "I am the wife of Bel, the king."
4. Then Bel spoke thus to Daenamazdayas*n*ish
5. "My sister, you are very wise
6. and (more) beautiful than the gods,
7. and because of that I have established you as
8. the woman *of my*
9. heart."

Arebsun 3: Stele B, side A, inscription 2 (= RES 1785F)

1. B XX III III LTMWZ ḤḤT*D/R/K*S*T*R Q*Y*MN QRYBN LWT
2. BYL 'LHY "L QDM BYL ḤḤNY*K/N/P* "L ḤYW'/*H*
3. QRYBN LWT YRḤ LTMWZ ŠGY' ṬBYN 'ḤR YRḤ/*BH*
4. ṬB' ḤY' WŠLM' 'ḤR BYL ŠGY' ṢBY
5. QDMWH 'ḤR BYL *N*PQ MN ŠMY'
6. *[WQR]B*YH ḤY' ṬB' <W>Š{W}LM[']

1. On the 26th of Tammuz [...] *were held* offerings to
2. Bel *my* god, *on behalf of* Bel. He *dedicated* for *his* life
3. *the offerings* to the Moon of Tammuz, very good. Then *she will increase(?)*
4. happiness, life and peace, then Bel is strongly desired
5. *by her*, then Bel emerges from heaven
6. *along with his offerings*: life, happiness, and peace.

Arebsun 4: Stele B, side A, inscription 3

1. [Z]RZ 'BYD BḤTḤ*T*N

1. *Monument(?)* for marriage

Arebsun 5: Stele B, side B, inscription 1 (= RES 1785A)

1. 'B' *PT[WR]*' ḤKYM' QYM QDM
2. BYL W'LHYN WMḤ*N*Y*K* H*W*
3. 'ŠT' W'ṬYN WKTYB ???
4. WBṢBWT' ZY BYL *W*ZMN'
5. L'LHYN *K*N

1. *Abbâ, the sage, inter[prets dreams]*, stands before
2. Bel and the gods, and *dedicated*
3. fire and ...? ...and he wrote???
4. and in accordance with *the desire* of Bel *and* the time
5. (belongs) to the gods *as well*.

Arebsun 6: Stele B, side B, inscription 2 (= RES 1785B)

1. *[.....................?]* TMWZ 'ḤR NḤŠ' *'B'* ṬB'
2. *[.....................?]* 'MR LBYL ḤḤT*RN/S[TR]* QYMN

3. *[QRYBN ? BY]L* NPQ MN ŠMY' WḤZH B'RQ' Z' ḤLY
4. *[...............?]* HW *ZY* NḤŠ' MLY' 'LH MLYL
5. *[...............?]* B'RQ' WḤDH HW' *B*H WŠM*Y*N
6. ?

1. [.............] Tammuz. Then the good seer *Abbâ*
2. [.............] said to Bel...? ... they held
3. *[the offerings? Be]l* has emerged from heaven and enjoyed the view of this *pleasant* land
4. [.............] *He*, the seer, spoke these words
5. [.............] on earth and he rejoices *over this and the heavens*
6. ?[119]

These inscriptions are puzzling, to say the least.[120] Whatever the nature of the cultic practices or religious beliefs they describe, however, this much is clear: by the third century, the non-Anatolian god Bel had been introduced into Cappadocia and was worshiped there.[121] Ahuramazda may also have been worshiped, although the meaning of this text is still unclear. Life, happiness, and peace were among the blessings these gods dispersed, as were fertility and abundance. Observing these blessings caused the gods joy when they emerged from the heavens. This concept of divinity is radically different from that related to the Anatolian storm god, or even the mother goddess with her birds of prey.

The nature of rites performed and offerings dedicated by the priests of Persian-introduced cults have sparked a great deal of debate, most of which, as Garrison has pointed out, is founded in a desire to apply either Herodotus or the Avestas to Persian cultic practice.[122] The Greek sources are notoriously vague; Herodotus does not even mention fire worship. It does seem that certain cults introduced by Persians included rituals that were carried out in non-Greek languages, and some scholars have made a case for exclusivity of cult on the basis of this feature.[123] It is true that regulating the language of cultic practice can affect who is initiated into its innermost secrets or its ministration. I am not convinced that religion practiced in a language other than that spoken by the local populace need be exclusive in its appeal, however; consider, for instance, the example of the Catholic Church, which conducted Mass in Latin for more than a millennium and a half before introducing the vernacular. Sometimes the beauty of a concept can be enhanced rather than diminished by a lack of perfect understanding.

The kind of beatific vision inherent in the Arebsun inscriptions may explain why these cults remained popular in Anatolia, sometimes in the original languages, well into the Hellenistic period and beyond. To name but a few of many examples, in addition to the Arebsun inscriptions, we find a mid-fourth-century Aramaic inscription in Lydia that mentions the god Mên.[124] A bilingual Greek–Aramaic inscription from Faraşa, in southeastern Cappadocia, records a Magian sacrifice to Mithras in the Hellenistic period. A Greek inscription found near Aksaray in Cappadocia invokes the "great goddess Anahita," described as

139. Persian ritual: left, Cappadocia; middle and right, Dascylium. © Museum of Anatolian Civilizations, Istanbul Archaeological Museums.

"barzochara," or "of the high mountain" – this inscription dates to the Roman imperial period and demonstrates the longevity of worship. Indeed, Strabo describes rites that were held in Cappadocia apparently in his lifetime:

> In Cappadocia – for there the sect of the Magians, who are also called fire kindlers, is large – they have fire temples, noteworthy enclosures; and in the midst of these is an altar, on which there is a large quantity of ashes and where the Magians keep the fire ever burning. And there, entering daily, they make incantations for about an hour, holding before the fire their bundle of rods and wearing round their heads high turbans of felt, which reach down their cheeks far enough to cover their lips.[125]

The existence of such worshipers was not limited to Cappadocia, as demonstrated not only by the literary evidence but also by the visual record of Cappadocia, Phrygia, and Hellespontine Phrygia.

Archaeological evidence for the kind of fire cult mentioned by Strabo and implied in the Arebsun inscriptions is problematic not only in Anatolia but also in Persia itself, as Garrison has demonstrated.[126] If the fire basin at Şahankaya is not a fire altar but rather the base for a fire signal, the only possible physical remains for fire altars in Anatolia are the converted altar of Cybele at Sardis and the cuttings before the false door of the tomb at Taş Kule, neither of which are wholly unproblematic.

The visual evidence provided by sculpted stelae should urge us not to be too surprised by this dearth of excavated fire altars, however. The sculpture in Ankara may conceivably show a fire bowl atop a stele, with the ball of fire

140. Tarsus stater, struck under Pharnabazus (379–374). Author's drawing.

141. Tarsus stater. 1967.152.501. © American Numismatic Society.

flaming within it – would we recognize such a thing as a fire altar if we were to find it?[127] The two in Istanbul urge even further caution in interpreting Persian ritual: one shows a door resembling symbolic doors on tombs, and the other is very unclear in its form and interpretation. Garrison's work on fire altars represented in the Persepolis Fortification Archive demonstrates the tremendous variety of form found in both the shapes of the altars themselves and the kinds of worship that may have taken place before or on them.[128] Persian worship was complex and varied in Persia itself, and the ways it may have developed as it was practiced in Anatolia are at the moment beyond our ken. This makes the identification of something as specific as a fire altar all the more difficult.

Non-Anatolian cults were enthusiastically adopted not only in Cappadocia and Phrygia, however. Baal became the patron god of Tarsus in Cilicia and is shown on Cilician coins as both Baal and Baaltar. Between 413 and 370, a common type of silver stater in Cilica had Baal seated left on the obverse, while the reverse showed a helmeted male head facing left.[129]

From 361 to 333, several series of silver staters minted at Tarsus show on the obverse the god seated left, holding a grape cluster, a grain ear, and a scepter, while on the reverse a lion attacks a stag. On one version of this coin, Aramaic

239

142. Tarsus stater. Author's drawing.

legends proclaim BLTRZ on the obverse and MZDI on the reverse: Baaltars and Mazdaios. Baal of Tarsus was the patron god of the city; the name Mazdaios is clearly related to (Ahura)Mazda.

The type was popular and continued in use during the last generation of Achaemenid hegemony in Cilicia.[130] Even more popular, and minted at the same time and place, was a series of silver staters showing on the obverse Baaltar seated left, holding an eagle, a grape cluster, a grain ear, and a scepter, while on the reverse was a lion attacking a bull rather than a stag.[131]

The manner in which this non-Anatolian god was portrayed is interesting. Lacking a traditional artistic vocabulary for the deity, the Cilicians used Greek art for stylistic and iconographical inspiration: Baal/Baaltar looks for all the world like Olympian Zeus. The image may also draw on Persian notions of the king enthroned, like those shown on the Apadana reliefs and reiterated on at least one seal from Sardis. The lion and stag or bull show a mixture of Greek style with the iconographic repertoire that circulated throughout the Achaemenid Empire via sealstones.[132] The Fortification Tablet shown in Figure 143 preserves the impression left by the large and elegant stamp seal used by Darius's right-hand man, Gobryas – a man who chose to have his seal made not in the usual cylinder shape but as a stamp.[133] Although lions hunting stags were common in the seals impressed on the Fortification Archive, this stamp arranges them differently and in a way that links it to seals found as far afield as that on the right, excavated from a tomb at Sardis, showing similarly imperially laden imagery of a lion attacking a bull with celestial symbols above them.[134] This, combined with the Aramaic legends, demonstrates the ingenuity of the Cilicians in finding a verbal and artistic métier for displaying and realizing the non-Anatolian manifestation of Tarsus's patron god.

An even more complex synthesis of visual representation is found on a coin of Cilician Issus at the beginning of the third century. Here we see Baaltar standing on the obverse, while on the reverse is a half-figure emerging from a winged disk. The coin's imagery provides a curious combination of Persepolitan iconography and Greek sculptural style, affect, and nudity.

143. Seal of Gobryas, impressed on Persepolis Fortification Tablet 688 (courtesy Mark Garrison and Margaret Root); and seal IAM 4523 from Sardis (after Dusinberre 2003a).

144. Issus stater, struck under Tiribazus. Author's drawing.

These coins demonstrate the intricacies of expressing and practicing newly introduced cults. The behaviors of religious authority, when not rooted in local tradition, were fluid and open to innovation of expression in Achaemenid Anatolia.

Royal Cult

There is still insufficient evidence to demonstrate conclusively the existence of a royal cult in Anatolia during the Achaemenid period, but enough circumstantial evidence exists to be highly suggestive at the very least. Garrison has shown the interwoven nature of portrayals of the royal and the divine at Persepolis, and indeed it is clear that the Achaemenid kings systematically and deliberately adapted long-established iconographies across the empire to replace figures of deities with that of the king in imperial art.[135] Thus in the western reaches of the

145. Stater of Myriandrus (left) and obol (right), both 361–334. Author's drawing.

empire, as described in Chapter 2, we see coins that replace the traditional Greek head of a divinity on the obverse with the head of the Persian king dressed as if for war.[136] These tiarate head coins appropriated Greek iconography and artistic style to equate the king with the divine.

The series of coins minted under the Cilician satrap Mazdaeus at Myriandrus between 361 and 334 also makes the connection clear. The staters have on their obverse an image of Baaltar in Greek style, seated and holding a lotus-tipped scepter, while on the reverse a lion paces left. The obols retain the pacing lion on the reverse but display on their obverse an image in Achaemenid koine style of the king seated and holding a lotus-tipped scepter. The king of kings and the king of gods inhabit the same space and embody the same functions on these coins.

This kind of visual statement equating king with god was certainly effective, as its reception demonstrates. Aeschylus's play *Persians* affords our best literary evidence for the impact of the message and the way Greeks consequently conceived Persian perceptions of kingship. As Mark Munn has summarized, "Throughout the *Persians*, prosperity (*ploutos, olbos*) for the realm, which is repeatedly described as 'all of Asia,' is signified by the stability of divine kingship. The Persians of the play repeatedly refer both to Xerxes and to his deceased father, Darius, as divinities; nowhere else in the extant fifth-century Attic tragedy is a king called a god (*theos*). Atossa, the wife of Darius and mother of Xerxes, is referred to as the 'consort of a god,' 'mother of a god,' and 'mistress of this land.'"[137] Much has been said to the effect that *Persians* is not a reflection of actual Persian behaviors or beliefs but rather an Athenian creation of the Other.[138] I agree with this. But it is significant that, as Munn has pointed out, the prosperity of the realm is signified by the stability of divine kingship, for this is the central theme of the entire program of Achaemenid imperial art.[139] That fifth-century Athenians should have recognized and repeated this notion makes it all the more plausible that the portrayal of king as god in *Persians* also reflects explicit Achaemenid ideology.

146. Cylinder seals from Gordion (Seal 100) and Sardis (IAM 4581). After Dusinberre 2003a, 2005.

The nuances of kingly ascension in Anatolia are rich. Although they do not necessarily demonstrate the practice of a royal cult, they strongly suggest such. Two sealstones serve to make the point. The first of these is Gordion's Seal 100, mentioned in connection with the Mosaic Building at Gordion, and the second is a seal excavated from Tomb 813 at Sardis, IAM 4581.

Gordion's Seal 100 is a complex rendition of worship at three primary religious symbols: the figure emergent from a winged disk, a fire altar, and a half-figure in the celestial disk.[140] The central element of the scene is a combination of images that represent the sun, fire, and the moon; the celestial figures face in opposite directions, one toward each of the heraldic king figures, who make worshipful gestures toward them.[141] Those kings are supported by sphinxes, powerful symbols of the Light at Persepolis.[142] The beards and hairstyles of all human heads on the seal equate them visually with each other, as do the crowns they wear; the kings themselves become divine through their representation. The seal from Sardis is less explicit but makes the same point. The king ascendant, poised on the heads of sphinxes that are symbols of the Light, serves as the central element toward which they raise their worshiping paws. That king grapples with and holds at bay the ferocious forces of evil in the form of lion-griffins. In both cases, the imagery of the seals suggests that it is the Achaemenid king, a figure with divine power, who maintains harmony and balance. Interestingly, the artistic style and the Aramaic inscription with Persian names on the seal from Gordion intimate that it is the Achaemenid elite who disseminate this harmony and balance to the various regions of the empire.[143]

With these recognitions of divine kingship expressed in Anatolia – the king ascendant like any other deity – the sculptural dedications at Labraunda and the role of Mausolus in planning the andron fall into place. The sphinxes that serve as acroteria, symbols of the Light with beards that equate them with royalty and locks of hair that situate them locally, are not just decoration. They link Mausolus to the divine imagery of the Persian king. Their situation atop the roof of the banqueting hall associated with feasting in honor of the god connects them to the animal-protome capitals of Persepolis: these divine symbols of local kingship hold aloft the heavens. It was only a small step from here to the divine pretensions of the Mausoleum itself. Mausolus provides an instance of a local dynast following the example of the Persian king, linked to Achaemenid Persian notions of numinous kingship, the king ascendant, and the king as representative of the Light, just like the sun, the moon, fire, or sphinxes. The iteration of this feature of ruling and worship in Achaemenid Anatolia suggests that it was this that mattered to the Achaemenid authority, more than the worship of any specific pantheon.

SEVEN

EDUCATING THE YOUNG AND OLD

What constitutes education? Some forms of education are obvious – for instance, that of an apprentice by a master. Others, such as farming techniques learned by children from their parents, are implicit. Some are gender-specific, while others are class-specific. This chapter does not attempt to trace particular instances of education; rather, it presents a preliminary outline of approaches. In the absence of schoolrooms, textbooks, or copybooks or of any overt discussion of education remaining to us, how might we begin to think about what education entailed in Achaemenid Anatolia and how knowledge was passed on or learning fostered? This discussion explores several aspects of authority–autonomy interactions in the filtering of imperially charged notions of education and educational values at the top tier (the king himself) to tiers of nobles, including people who became satraps and members of satrapal courts. It also considers the sorts of authority inherent in education, where one more knowledgeable or skilled guides another in learning.

Educating the Persian Elite

Greek authors described the education of Cyrus the Great, although his youth is so shrouded in mystery and legend that it is unclear what, if anything, in their accounts reflects reality. They share several significant features: from the youngest age, Cyrus possessed natural authority and curiosity about how best to manage human resources; he took on various tasks readily and mastered them quickly. Thus Herodotus has him at the age of ten organizing the other boys into groups to perform specific tasks, while Ctesias tells us he attached himself first to one man and then another at the royal palace to learn different aspects of courtly life and become closer to the king.[1] Xenophon says of his early education, "He showed himself to be better than all others of his age, both in learning all that was required and in carrying out each task efficiently and with courage."[2]

Certain aspects of Greek descriptions are perhaps reflected in Persian sources as well. Herodotus tells us of the elite: "The period of a boy's education is between the ages of five and twenty, and they are taught three things only: to ride, to use the bow, and to speak the truth."[3] These virtuous educational missions have to do either literally or metaphorically with "straightness." They resonate in Darius's imperial inscriptions, which emphasize his horror of the Lie, his ability as a horseman, a bowman, and a spearman, and his wisdom and justice. Thus the Bisitun Inscription emphasizes that Darius had the support of Ahuramazda and the other gods "because I was not disloyal, was no traitor, was no wrong-doer, neither I nor my family, (but) adhered to righteousness and did no wrong to the weak nor to the powerful."[4] Those who are wicked lie; and when the Lie comes upon the land terrible things ensue.[5] In one of the inscriptions on his tomb at Naqsh-i Rustam, Darius proclaims that he was "a friend to right, not a friend to wrong," and Ahuramazda bestowed "wisdom and strength" on him so that he excelled: "As a horseman I am a good horseman; as a bowman I am a good bowman, both on foot and on horse; as a spearman I am a good spearman, both on foot and on horse."[6] These phrases demonstrate a value system that resembles the education described by Greek sources. The emphasis on straightness – straight shooting, straight talking, and straight riding – was a feature of the king's education and virtue, and indeed it seems to have been a feature of educating virtuous elite men in general.

Herodotus and Xenophon would have seen many members of the Persian elite in Anatolia, and their impressions of Persians were probably founded largely on their Anatolian experiences. Xenophon's description of the Persian educational system as it applied to the sons of the elite is interesting but must be read with caution.[7] As Kuhrt remarks, it "has similarities to that practised in Sparta, a state much admired by Xenophon."[8] He claims that the royal palace and government buildings were in a separate square, from which merchants were barred, and here elite males gathered in separate areas, one part set aside for boys, one for youths, one for adults, and one for the elderly. Boys and youths were educated by elders and adults. Xenophon says, "The boys go to school and spend their time in learning justice," as well as self-control, temperance, and obedience to their superiors.[9] He adds that along with learning justice and moderation, boys learn to shoot and to throw the spear.[10] Their training continues as they grow, when the king himself takes them hunting in all kinds of weather, through which they become accustomed to the hardships of war and to following their leader, to riding and shooting – skills they also practice when they are not hunting.[11]

Of interest in Xenophon's description is the notion of a common educational system headed by public teachers, available to the sons of the elite and a sine qua non of acquiring a position of status and rank.[12] Education can be a powerful tool for security and for reproducing or altering the status quo.[13] This makes the uniformity of descriptions of Persian male elite education all the more interesting. Strabo also provides a description: "From age five to twenty-five they are trained to shoot with the bow, handle the spear, ride on horseback and speak the truth."[14] Like Xenophon, Strabo describes an official schooling system with educators who "interweave their teachings with the mythical element, thus reducing that element to a useful purpose, and rehearse both with song and without song the deeds both of the gods and of the noblest men."[15] Thus educators were entrusted with passing on oral traditions. This is supported by Xenophon, who speaks "of tales and songs still heard today.... In them, Cyrus is [presented as] having received from nature a very beautiful figure, a very generous soul, a passion for study and for glory."[16]

The emphasis on truth in Greek sources is probably a reflection of the Old Persian word *arta-*, which means "order," "righteousness," or "justice" and encapsulates "the duties of subject to king and with them the maintenance of the social, political and moral order."[17] The connection in Darius's inscriptions between this notion and the favor of Ahuramazda demonstrates that the concept also had religious underpinnings. Thus speaking the truth can be seen as an ethical, even religious principle that was part of Persian noble education. It is clear from Greek sources that it was understood to be a principle with applicability no matter what formal or traditional religious persuasions were the operative norm in a given locality. The notion of straightness underlay all aspects of elite male Persian education.

This issue of ethical doctrine, malleable to local realities, is important in considering the education of governing elites. What, for instance, was the role of the dog-eared copy of an Aramaic version of the Bisitun text found in Elephantine? Certainly, it was consulted over and over not for its solutions to specific legal problems, but rather for its statements of principles of good governance and good leadership.[18] In this context, Greek fascination with Cyrus the Great's childhood and precocity in justice and governing takes on new meaning. Writing a hundred years and more after Cyrus, the foreign authors must have drawn on Persian narratives of virtue in a king, narratives that demonstrated the embodiment of good leadership. The fact that Elephantine in Egypt produced a version of the Bisitun Inscription and that Greek authors encountering Persians in Anatolia were drawn to Cyrus demonstrates that these virtues were proclaimed not only in Fars itself but across the empire. The principles of straightness that formed the foundations for Persian elite male education would also have formed the foundations for governance.

ART AND EDUCATION

Skilled craftspeople as well as unskilled laborers were employed at and around Persepolis, and were moved from one place to another as their expertise was demanded. They included masons, sculptors, blacksmiths, makers of mail shirts, goldsmiths, and makers of parchment.[19] Specialists such as these are all skilled and require years of training in their professions to become adept. In the Achaemenid Empire, we have little direct evidence for apprenticeship, although Babylonian sources suggest that there may have been such formal arrangements.[20] Although the notion of guilds and guild structures in Babylonia has now largely been discarded, it is nonetheless clear from textual sources that intergenerational groups worked together in associations resembling what we might think of as workshops, with expert artisans instructing novices over a sometimes lengthy period.[21]

The notion of workshops, where ideas could be spread among craftspeople and the skilled could educate the young, forms the springboard for the next part of this chapter. In workshops we can see education – training in techniques and sharing of ideas – in the production of craftspeople. The following discussion focuses on seal carvers, sculptors, and potters. It begins with this aspect of education as a direct, hands-on example of education as we experience it today.

At Persepolis, as we have seen, seals carved in different styles were impressed on the tablets of the Fortification Archive.[22] Some of these involved hybrids; thus the Persepolitan modeled style relates to the earlier Assyrian-Babylonian modeled styles but introduces new elements. So, too, the two "mixed styles" defined at Persepolis combine various stylistic elements. The continuities across time and styles demonstrate communication among seal carvers, and indeed Garrison has defined stylistic workshops at Persepolis in a way that suggests carvers were trained through apprenticeship to a master.[23] The kind of obedience to higher authority that apparently formed part of Persian elite male education was reflected in the training of craftspeople as well.

Several finds suggest visual education in the form perhaps of circulating "copybooks." At Ur, a cache of impressions made by earlier and contemporary seals, coins, and metal wares from a great geographic range was found in a Hellenistic burial; these were pieces of clay that had been impressed by various artifacts and then baked to preserve the images.[24] It seems their owner was a seal carver who kept on hand a reference (or inspiration?) collection for himself and his patrons.

The late-fourth-century Alexander Sarcophagus, from Sidon, may also suggest the existence of copybooks. In the battle and hunting scenes carved in relief on its sides Alexander appears twice, once in a battle against Persians and once in a lion hunt engaged jointly by Persians and Greeks/Macedonians.

The sarcophagus preserves traces of painted imagery on the interior of two shields held by Persians. These display versions of authority-laden imagery drawn directly from the palace reliefs at Persepolis: the king in heroic combat with an animal and the king holding audience.[25] The iconographic similarity of these scenes to their prototypes suggests that some sort of copybook must have been used – a suggestion given greater weight by the much earlier DS 4 from Dascylium with its Persepolitan audience scene.[26] Versions of the imagery of kingship circulated widely and served as a means of educating artists in the visual language of authority. With this backdrop, the visual expressions of Achaemenid hegemony we see in the sealstones of Anatolia fall into place as a visual performance of authority.

The fact of a koine Achaemenid hegemonic iconographic language, couched in visually related artistic styles, demonstrates shared ideas and techniques among seal carvers. We have seen such seals at Sardis, Dascylium, İkiztepe, and Gordion. Relevant glyptic iconography and styles were also found at places as widely dispersed as Troy, Patara (the harbor of Xanthus on the south coast), Kaman-Kalehöyük in Cappadocia, and Dülük Baba Tepesi in the southeast, as well as outside Anatolia at such places as Kertch and Nymphaeum in the Crimea.[27]

Training craftspeople in elements of style and iconography is an essential feature of education, and it is very important that Achaemenid authority-laden seals are so widely spread in Anatolia (and beyond). We do not see here a simple example of an individual seal carver training an apprentice, or a single workshop that trains several people in a particular technique, for there are too many seals for this to be the case. Some broader education ranged across time or geographic region. Indeed, the conformity of visual culture supports the notion that copybooks were passed on from one seal carver to another. Also significant is the educational impact these seals would have had on their owners and viewers – the ways they helped to shape the thoughts of those associated with their use or observing the people who used them.

Similar observations can be made about the carving of grave stelae, with their continuity of visual language, and the creation of drinking vessels in both metal and clay. The similarity of clay Achaemenid bowls shows shared notions of fabrication, just as do the silver and gilt vessels and ladles. This is important: it is common to talk about these connections in terms of ideology or acculturation, but an essential element in the process is educational. What makes something meaningful? How do you craft something in the "right" way? What are the nuances that make it say what you want it to? And what are the logistics of physical craftsmanship that allow you to do so? All of this is linked to education, whether specifically conducted by a master or self-taught by an observant learner. Manufacturing items in a specific style or with a particular collection of iconographic elements required an attentive eye, an engaged mind, and an artisan educated in the niceties of production.

Ideology

Education in an empire can involve teaching people about local or other pre-imperial traditions. Thus examples of resistance or retained earlier traditions demonstrate a particular form of education.[28] Education can also involve teaching imperial desiderata. The assumption of overtly imperial iconography or ideas is the result of education. These aspects of imperial education must be handled very delicately, however, as many other things are involved: positioning oneself politically and socially was likely the primary motivation of people adopting or resisting imperial propaganda, so conscious education in these matters would have been a tool but not the goal of this behavior.

Aspects of Achaemenid ideology were adopted wholesale throughout Anatolia. These include certain drinking behaviors, adopted throughout all classes of society. They include the cohesive, semiotically charged signaling of the elite via seals, dress, and grave goods. Thus the outwardly visible manifestations of Achaemenid ideology were an important part of Achaemenid Anatolia. How was this system of ideas disseminated? What aspect of it can be considered the result of education?

We know that the dissemination of imperial ideology mattered to Darius, so that he had versions of the Bisitun Inscription and relief distributed about the empire. Surely the materially manifested cohesiveness of the elite in Anatolia originated in a specific visual program like that which Darius and his successors created at Persepolis. The reliefs at Meydancıkkale demonstrate knowledge of central Persian imperial art and message. Their iteration in Anatolia highlights the education of the artists and those who observed the work.

More evidence can be found in the iconography chosen for sealstones. Many of the seals from Sardis emphasize kingly images known from Persepolis: the king enthroned, the king as archer shooting a rampant lion, the king stabbing a lion-griffin, or the Persian hero figure stabbing a lion. The lion-and-bull combat on the seal from Sardis is rare in glyptic art at Persepolis but figures prominently on the staircases of the Apadana.[29] Single animals, such as the lions or lion-griffins on the Sardian seals, or double animals such as the seated sphinx and lion-griffin illustrated in Figure 147, find parallels in Persepolitan glyptic as well as the relief sculptures or column capitals of the Apadana. The visual language of authority demonstrated in these seals shows that artists were well educated in imperial renditions of power.

Thus sealstones can demonstrate the dissemination of ideas, a significant form of education. The point is made clearly by the bullae of Dascylium. As discussed in Chapter 2, some bear impressions of trilingual royal name seals (of which no language is local) and combinations of imagery common on the Persepolis Fortification Archive, including the royal audience scene on DS 4. This is a superb example of a courtly motif, rendered through a different artistic

147. Impression of a rock-crystal pyramidal stamp seal from Tomb 5(A) at Sardis. IAM 4579. Courtesy Sir John Boardman.

vehicle but with equally authority-laden meaning. The adherence of seals at Dascylium to the imperially charged iconography of Persepolis, carved in a variety of styles that includes one linked intimately to seal-carving workshops at Persepolis, leads me to suspect a top-down imposition of ideology by the Achaemenid authority rather than simple emulation by local elites. The seals at this satrapal capital form part of an educational and visual system. They reflect a social environment that made possible multiple manifestations of visual culture that was resonant with power, expressions of authority that bound people to the same expressive system across the empire.

This is of importance for the authority–autonomy model. Educating the elite in the ideology of imperial authority would be paramount: it was this group of local and/or transplanted people of influence on whom the success, well-being, and continuation of the empire depended. To mark the tools of administration – seals – with imagery of authority emphasizes the cohesion of the elite and their loyalty both to each other within Anatolia or a smaller region and to the central authority and its ideology. Sending versions of imperial writings out from Persepolis to other parts of the empire, including versions in local languages, was certainly important. The seals of Anatolia demonstrate knowledge and awareness of imperial visual symbols and strategies, which like the inscription could be rendered in locally accessible visual languages and styles.[30] This aspect of education mattered to the imperial authority.

Once people had internalized these symbols, so that the notions and representations became deeply acculturated, personal choice and possibly local autonomy played a role as well. Choice of glyptic style and iconography existed at Persepolis not only for those of lower social echelons but also for the elite. We see such choices available to the seal users of Achaemenid Anatolia, too, in the multiple options found at Sardis and Dascylium as well as the nonsatrapal site of Gordion. The Gordion seals demonstrate a wider range of materials, styles, and imagery than do those from Sardis, but like the Sardian seals these draw enthusiastically on the imagery of the Achaemenid heartland.[31] The seal owners of Sardis seem to have preferred semiprecious stones for their seals, and many of the seals reiterate authority-laden iconographic messages, but even within this iconographic grouping there is some variety of style, and the presence at Sardis of at least one seal carved in overtly Greek style and iconography demonstrates the degree of choice available. Dascylium's seals, too, provide evidence for a wide variety of choice in the visual presentation of self. Thus the "educational" aspect of seal design was not overly didactic but allowed for personal preference.

The regional variety of mortuary customs and the continuation of pre-Achaemenid traditions demonstrate different ideologies and educational strategies at play in Achaemenid Anatolia. Thus the increase in burial tumuli in Lydia, for instance, may demonstrate an increasing number of people who wished to and could associate themselves with the elite, but it may also reflect a specifically *local* tradition, adhered to as a non-Persian manifestation of elite status.[32] It certainly demonstrates education through the generations about what pre-Achaemenid Lydian traditions might have entailed. The pillar tombs of Lycia seem also to be a regional phenomenon and are perhaps to be interpreted as representing specifically local resistance to Persian ideas – although in this case, the enthusiastic assumption of Achaemenid ideology through images makes the scenario more complicated. In either instance, local mortuary traditions attest to local educational norms. The fact that they are so very different, both from each other and from Persian practice, suggests that they may result from education counter to a central imperial notion, education in which people might exercise considerable autonomy.

Religion

The role of education in religion is profound. Priests and priestesses had to learn how to perform a complicated series of rites. Unfortunately, we know very little of these rituals or the education of young novices; for instance, although we are told that the priestesses of Artemis of Ephesus were called melissai, or "bees," and coins of Ephesus bear an image of a bee, we do not know how the priestesses were chosen, for how long they served, what their training entailed, or the nature of the rites they performed.[33] Needless to say, if a royal cult was introduced at this time, worship of the king would demonstrate one of the most authority-charged and divergent forms of education possible in Achaemenid Anatolia. Berossus's statement about the introduction of statues to Anahita's cult in Susa, Ecbatana, Persia, Bactria, Damascus, and Sardis suggests that cults were established in satrapal centers to unite ethnic Persians and provide an opportunity for polyethnic demonstration and practice of authority through religion.[34] Certainly such cults would have required constructing shrines, creating statues, and performing the appropriate rites. Perhaps the best evidence we have for education in religion comes from the imported religions said by Greeks of the Hellenistic period to be "Persian." Here the Greek sources claim that religious rites were performed in a foreign language, and indeed the Arebsun inscriptions demonstrate that this aspect of religious observation might be significant. Educating people to perform rites in one language but to interact with local people in a different language would have been an important aspect of this, so the use of Aramaic and/or other "Persian" languages in cultic practice demonstrates significant education in multiple aspects of religious practice and performance.

Language

Language provides us with a possible avenue for learning about education. Monumental inscriptions in Anatolia during the Achaemenid period include those in Greek, Aramaic, Phrygian, Lydian, Carian, and Lycian, as we have seen, as well as the Trilingual Inscription of Xerxes at Van.[35] Retaining a local language or adopting a new one requires thought, effort, and learning. When, as seems to be the case at Sardis, Aramaic is inscribed only on mortuary or religious monuments but does not turn up scratched into everyday ceramic sherds as the local Lydian letters do, we learn that non-elite people did not learn Aramaic or did not use it for quotidian purposes; we also learn that some members of the elite did learn Aramaic and that it served as a "power language" inscribed on silver or stone. This may therefore provide evidence for different kinds of education for elite and non-elite – indeed, education perhaps helped differentiate the two. Once again I want to emphasize that we cannot distinguish gendered behaviors in this regard: we do not know if language instruction was a gendered phenomenon.

Changes in language may also provide information on education. The inscriptions from Lydia and Lycia span a length of time and deal with several aspects of the living societies. Unfortunately, our understanding of these languages is still insufficient to provide much information about language shifts; even our understanding of letter forms is rudimentary. This is an exciting avenue for further research.[36]

It is possible that naming patterns reflect education. Many inscriptions in western Anatolia follow the Greek norm of naming child and parent; some, like the Sacrilege Inscription, may delineate multigenerational lineages. Most interesting in this context is the evidence the Sacrilege Inscription provides for children with names of different ethnic background than those of their fathers.[37] Does this suggest a mother of a different ethnicity? Does it indicate that certain names enjoyed increased popularity at particular times? Does it suggest that parents were trying to gain favor for a child with a particular name, or perhaps trying to avoid lack of favor? Perhaps names were given with an understanding of their meaning in the original language; this would suggest a significant degree of education and social memory. Although we still cannot answer these questions, we can state with assurance that conforming to traditional naming patterns demonstrates education in those traditions, while adopting new naming patterns demonstrates a degree of choice and an awareness of other options that also attests to new knowledge and education.

Gender Matters

Another form of education can be seen in the army. Military men were educated in warcraft, teamwork, and loyalty to the Achaemenid Empire. This training was charged with meaning for masculine Achaemenid elites; as we have seen, Darius's notions of educational and skillful straightness were passed on to men in Anatolia. The success of this education and the shared values of the masculine elite are demonstrated conclusively by the iconography of mortuary monuments that emphasize these characteristics. The army provided a place for men to be educated in skills that linked them to each other across boundaries of class, ethnicity, and background.

Whether spinning and weaving were women's work in Achaemenid Anatolia is unknown. Arguing that this might have been the case is the likelihood that men were at least sometimes conscripted for military duty. Arguing against it is the possibility that cloth manufacture was sufficiently high status to have been performed by men. Arguing for it again is the complete silence of Greeks on the matter, who most likely would have commented on it as yet another example of Oriental effeminacy had men been working the loom in Anatolia under Persian hegemony – but even in Athens, sometimes men did the weaving.[38] Who did the work of cloth production probably depended on the type of textiles and the kind of production system involved.[39] Spinning seems generally in human history to be done by women, while carding and combing (very heavy work) are done by men. Men have historically been responsible for much of industrial-level weaving, as well as fulling. Thus a number of processes, as well as context, quantity, and level of production, must be considered. Cloth mattered, though, and was apparently sent around the empire. Sardis evidently continued to be a source of high-quality textiles in the Achaemenid period, while a mass of fine textiles was said to have been found in the Susa Treasury, and the Apadana reliefs show cloth and clothing as some of the most frequent gifts brought to the king.[40]

It is essential to mention cloth manufacture in the context of education, for this was a skilled, labor-intensive task of utmost importance in both practical and symbolic terms, and girls would have been educated in the art of spinning from the time they were old enough to drop a spindle. Those responsible for weaving, too, would have needed to learn their craft – including, perhaps, loom construction – from a young age. Such lengthy training was necessary if as adults they were to be able to spin an even thread, weave elegant or sturdy cloth, and sew a fine seam. There is much evidence demonstrating the value of cloth in Persia itself and in Achaemenid Anatolia. This means we should recognize the value that must also have been attached to skilled, educated, and accomplished textile workers – probably of both sexes.

Another way in which education may have figured in fabrics has to do with their patterning. Insufficient material evidence exists to determine regional or familial patterns. Greek sources, however, suggest that at least sometimes cloth presented visual narratives that could be elaborate indeed – and we should not forget that Arachne, who wove the illicit loves of the gods into her cloth, was a Lydian.[41] Weavers would need to be educated in counting, reproducing, and creating patterns and, of course, if figural narrative was an element of textile design, in the stories that those textiles represented.

Ideas might be shared by textile workers in a great variety of ways. These include parents training children or masters training apprentices in a workshop. They might also include cross-cultural marriages or the taking of captives who brought their native cultural traditions of craft and lifeways with them into a new situation.[42]

Crop and animal husbandry are also matters that require intensive education. Despite the English word "husbandry," these are not solely the bailiwick of men. Indeed, in many areas it is women who do the lion's share of work in the fields. Gardening was a value-laden subject in the Achaemenid Empire; the "king as gardener" was an aspect of ideology in royal education insisted upon in Classical sources.[43] Tending animals was probably a slightly different story: in an era before sedatives, large-animal veterinary medicine required great strength on the part of its practitioners, and even such tasks as shearing sheep might call for more strength than the average woman boasts. Children could be useful almost as soon as they could walk for such tasks as gleaning the fields or keeping an eye on the geese, and by the time they reached adulthood some individuals would certainly have learned sufficient skill in particular areas to specialize to a certain extent. In both agriculture and animal tending, we should expect to see families educating their children in slightly different ways that had been found to work best for them over the generations or on a particular plot of land. The daily demands of living required extensive education.

One aspect of this for which we have no direct evidence in Anatolia but that may well have existed is the movement of particular groups of people. The Fortification Archive documents groups of workers being moved from one place to another during the Achaemenid period, some with particular skills such as the blacksmiths brought to Fars from Sardis attested on PF 873.[44] If imperial strategies in Anatolia also involved such movement of skilled workers or field laborers, in addition to the military movement discussed already, this would be an avenue for broadening education and sharing ideas across various geographic bounds that might previously have been impermeable.

Accounting

Archives provide information on accounting and the kind of education necessary to keep accounts. Scribes were trained in their work; the Fortification Archive mentions Persian "boys" copying texts at least twice (PF 871 and 1137), while Aramaic follows a standard form across the empire, from the Arshama documents from Egypt of the late fifth century through the Fortification and Treasury Archives of Persepolis to the Bactrian documents of the 340s–320s.[45] The best example of an Achaemenid-period archive excavated so far from Anatolia is that from Dascylium. It has the disadvantage of including no texts, but the seals that were used to ratify the bullae have been well published, and methodologies for understanding archiving practices through seals have been developed for the Persepolis Fortification Archive.[46] This makes the study of the Dascylium archive as such possible.

Kaptan, quoted in Chapter 2, describes the Dascylium system as having dealt with local bureaucratic and economic issues. She suggests that its archives included "copies of documents on regional bureaucratic activities, petitions sent to the satrap and his decisions on the local issues."[47] Payments and deliveries made to and from the local treasury, including rations and taxes, were documented; the sealed bullae of Dascylium originally enclosed these receipts, written on papyrus or parchment.[48] Such an elaborate accounting system, with records and receipts kept neatly archived, would have required intensive training and oversight. It demonstrates extensive education in a specialized skill, as well as a careful selection of students to be entrusted with such responsibility.

Education in understanding seal impressions is implied by the very different system existing at Seyitömer Höyük in Phrygia, near modern Kütahya.[49] Several tags have been excavated from this site that bear seal impressions, but unlike the Dascylium bullae these are small, flat, round or ovoid disks with a seal impression on each side. Two of them have string holes, while the other two do not. Kaptan suggests that they might have functioned as tokens for accounting purposes, left with an official when an item was brought in or removed, or as an authorization device accompanying an oral message. These tags provide evidence of accounting practices even at nonsatrapal sites, sites without extensive archival systems but with a need to track goods or interactions. They demonstrate that this aspect of accountability must have extended far deeper into the social echelons than had previously been suspected. They show the need for education in this area at a much more widespread array of sites than just the satrapal capitals.

Evidence for accountability is also found at sanctuaries in western Anatolia. Temples might serve as banks, and their walls might be used to record lengthy contracts. Thus the temples must have been places where people practiced (and were educated in) not only religious behaviors but also behaviors to do with banking and accounting. Xenophon left his finances in charge of the Temple of Artemis at Ephesus:

> There they divided the money received from the sale of the booty. And the tithe, which they set apart for Apollo and for Artemis of the Ephesians, was distributed among the generals, each taking his portion to keep safely for the gods.... As for Xenophon, he caused a votive offering to be made out of Apollo's share of his portion and dedicated it in the treasury of the Athenians at Delphi.... The share which belonged to Artemis of the Ephesians he left behind, at the time when he was returning from Asia with Agesilaus to take part in the campaign against Boeotia, in charge of Megabyzus, the sacristan of Artemis, for the reason that his own journey seemed likely to be a dangerous one; and his instructions were that in case he should escape with his life, the money was to be returned to him, but in case any ill should befall him, Megabyzus was to cause to be made and dedicated to Artemis whatever offering he thought would please the goddess.[50]

It is clear from this passage that Artemis of Ephesus was considered an appropriate guardian of worldly goods. This has great educational implications. Accounts must have been kept, and deposits guarded and kept track of so that they could be returned to their owners. Some kind of accounting system must have been in place, and those responsible would have to have been educated in maintaining accounts as well as in physically tending deposits. A similar situation pertained at the Temple of Artemis at Sardis, as the two Mitridastas decrees demonstrate.

The Mnesimachus Inscription at Sardis provides another example of accountability connected with the cult of Artemis and the education that would have been required to go with it. It was carved in two columns on a white marble block that formed part of the south face of the north anta to the Hellenistic Temple of Artemis.[51] The inscription preserves the middle and final clauses detailing a mortgaged property: it describes the handing over of Mnesimachus's lands and their appurtenances to pay back a loan of 1,325 gold staters he had borrowed from the Temple of Artemis but was unable to repay in specie. This inscription is generally thought to be a recarving of an original decree dating to the end of the fourth century, just after the Achaemenid Empire came to an end.[52] It concludes:

> And if the king because of Mnesimachus should take away from Artemis the *komai* or the *kleroi* or any of the other things mortgaged, then the

principal in gold of the deposit-loan, the 1325 gold staters, we ourselves, I Mnesimachus and my descendants, will immediately pay to the treasury of Artemis, and the value of the building and of the planting done by Artemis, we will immediately pay that value whatever it may be worth; and concerning the produce and the fruits, if they do not receive fruits in that year, we will pay into the treasury of Artemis as much gold as these things are worth; and as long as we shall not have paid, the debt shall constitute a deposit-loan to me and my descendants until we shall have paid the whole to the treasury of Artemis; and the transaction, so long as it is not yet had from us, is to be enforceable.

The Mitridastas Inscriptions and the Mnesimachus Inscription demonstrate the importance of Artemis's cult at Sardis as a financial and legal institution. The temple treasury clearly functioned as a kind of bank, offering loans and serving as the executor of trusts – perhaps in much the same way as the cult of Artemis at Ephesus. We recognize the expense of temple and cult upkeep, suggested by the properties being given by Mitridastas to support these costs. The savvy of the executive body called the Council of Priests is suggested by the formal language of the Mnesimachus Inscription and its terms, which seem by no means unfavorable to the goddess. The temple association was apparently a powerful and wealthy body that wielded great juridical might backed up by the persuasive measure of the divine curse. Its members would have had to be educated in financial, legal, record-keeping, and religious matters to ensure its capability.

Summary

Although we have no schoolrooms or texts from Achaemenid Anatolia, or any explicit discussion of pedagogy, rich sources remind us of multiple sorts of education. Whether in the context of farming and the household's requirements for cooked food and clothing, the creative workshops of artisans, or the accounting practices of official archivists and priest-bankers, young people and adults were being educated at all times. Sometimes this education was turned toward subsistence; other times it was used to emphasize or resist imperial authority. Local traditions played a great role in the education of the young, but the overarching education in imperial ideology permeated all levels of society. We cannot say anything conclusive at this point about literacy rates, but the widespread nature and tremendous cohesion of authority-laden iconography across Achaemenid Anatolia attests to a high rate of literacy in visual culture at any rate. The many avenues for ideological dissemination and adoption certainly played a role in the success of this education.

EIGHT

EMPIRE AND IDENTITY IN ACHAEMENID ANATOLIA

"Identity" has become such a catchall buzzword in the past fifteen years that I am almost ashamed to bring it into play in this discussion. One of the interesting things to emerge from this study, however, is a recognition of different kinds of identity expressed in Achaemenid Anatolia and the ways they operated within the constructs of an authority–autonomy model. Perhaps most interesting to me are the ways in which individual people, or categories of people, defined themselves in multiple ways at various times – among other things, in opposition to particular kinds of ideology. Indeed, the selective deployment of discrete types and aspects of identifiers means that we can trace the same individuals or groups emphasizing different aspects of their identity under different circumstances. I hope to provide a brief overview of some of those identities, including status-related, ethnic, religious, and administrative ones. As is generally the case in Achaemenid Anatolia, the evidence is clearer for the western, central, and southern parts of the peninsula, while the nature of the evidence means that we have only glimpses into Achaemenid Armenia or Paphlagonia. Fortunately, those glimpses include clear indications of certain kinds of identity being foregrounded and enable us to weave together at least some aspects of behavioral expression in the entire peninsula.

Identity and Status

One expression of imperial authority in Achaemenid Anatolia is the overarching cohesion of the elite: it seems that when individuals signaled membership in the Achaemenid elite, this was their primary identity. Masculine elite identity enjoyed extra identifiers; thus men on horseback, whether hunting or fighting, wear the trousers and cap of the Persian soldier, while their fine steeds, caparisoned with Persian riding blankets and with forelocks and tails tied up in the Persian manner, leap forward with forelegs in the air and noses tucked to their chests. Male banqueters recline, raising rhyta or phialae, often with one or more female companions seated at their feet or head. Being elite was a matter of importance.

The sealstones that the elite used to identify themselves in an official capacity, as well as to adorn their daily dress, add nuance to our understanding. They had a great variety of shapes and uses: for instance, the cylinder seals and pyramidal stamp seals of Sardis include fastenings for suspension and may have been looped on a string/thong/ribbon or pinned to a garment, while the gold seal rings of Sardis were worn on the finger with the sealing surface out. The seal rings of İkiztepe have an inscribed stone on a swivel, so that they could be worn with the flat sealing surface facing in against the finger, but they could have the stone turned so the sealing surface faced out for use. The ways these sealstones were worn differed greatly and would have had an impact on the ease of seal use. Their shapes, including cylinders, pyramidal stamps, scarabs, and scaraboids, show an equal degree of variety. Although many of the stones from which they were made are semiprecious versions of cryptocrystalline quartz (chalcedony, agate, rock crystal, etc.), many of them are not. Even the styles in which they are carved show variation; these include overtly foreign styles such as Greek, Persepolitan Court Style, and Neo-Babylonian. This makes the cohesion of iconography that characterizes so many seals, particularly those carved in the family of styles that seems to be associated explicitly with the Achaemenid Anatolian elite, all the more interesting. The members of the elite had many options in their choice of seal shapes, materials, styles, iconographies, and use patterns. Many chose seals proclaiming their participation in imperial authority, a fact that demonstrates their concern with signaling their status, their identity as members of the Achaemenid elite.

Identity and Ethnicity

Within this rubric of "elite identity" there was room for play, however – room to signal individual preferences and identity. One thing that demonstrates this very clearly is the use of names. Several sealstones were carved with Achaemenid hegemonic iconography and inscribed in Lydian with Lydian names claiming ownership.[1] Others were carved with a similar collection of images linking their users to Achaemenid authority and in styles situated, it seems, in Anatolia; but they were inscribed in Old Persian cuneiform naming the kings Xerxes and Artaxerxes, in Aramaic with Persian names, or in Aramaic with names of another ethnicity altogether.[2] Thus these individuals signaled membership in the elite by their use of an Achaemenid iconographic system of visual authority, but they differentiated themselves within that category by the languages deployed on their sealstones and the ethnic backgrounds of their own names or those of the kings to whom they proclaimed allegiance.[3]

What makes this particularly interesting is the evidence that names might be selectively deployed. The Sacrilege Inscription shows that sometimes families named their children according to differing ethnicities. Thus a name of a particular ethnicity need not indicate a person of that ethnicity. When a person has a name of an obvious ethnic background, we must assume that name was assigned as a matter of choice by the parents, not as a codified and automatic corollary based on the ethnicity of the father. That the elite of Achaemenid Anatolia used seals carved with the unifying visual language of Achaemenid authority but named their children according to a variety of ethnic options demonstrates different aspects of identity being articulated within the overarching identity of the elite. This is not surprising, but it is exciting and unusual to be able to trace it so clearly.

Ethnic identity was clearly a matter of great importance at times.[4] This adds nuance to our understanding of elite unity and ties into central imperial authority and ideology in key ways. Imperial texts and reliefs accentuate notions of ethnicity as distinctive indicators of identity, within a framework of universal empire: like the U.S. motto, Achaemenid ideology emphasizes a sense of *e pluribus unum*. Metaphorical layering characterizes the visual presentation of ethnically distinct delegates on the Apadana reliefs, but the overarching import is a rhetorical trope of unity in diversity.[5] The strength of the empire is both reflected and created by the notion of unifying imperial authority over diverse peoples and cultures: imperial ideology emphasizes the unity of many rather than any notion of ethnic identities in isolation. The Apadana presents a strong metaphor for marriage and many instances in which gifts seem if anything to mute idiosyncrasy and to create subgroups within imperial cohesion.[6]

In this context, it can be seen as a demonstration of imperial strength, as well as of regional autonomy, for the different peoples of the realm to speak different languages and maintain widely differing social customs. In Anatolia we see this in different mortuary practices, religions, and languages: cultural continuity, or regionally determined cultural shifts that have to do with increased communication across geographic boundaries that are the result of the new imperium but that have no direct reflection of Persian notions, are common. Indeed, the great variety of costumes and offerings displayed in symbolic ways on the Apadana reliefs at Persepolis suggests that the central authority may not only have delighted in the diversity of the empire but even have encouraged it.

The emphatic use of Lydian and Lycian in mortuary texts during the Achaemenid period is related to this. At this point there is no clear evidence that these languages were deployed in mortuary contexts before the Persian conquest of Anatolia, but during the Achaemenid period the use of these local languages, written on stone to mark graves in specifically local ways, exploded.

Indeed, the "epigraphic habit" manifested in Achaemenid Anatolia may itself have been a result of Achaemenid presence. Perhaps originally North Syrian, this epigraphic habit may reflect the greater presence in the region of foreign populations and ways.[7] The names associated with these mortuary inscriptions express ethnic identity in the same language: Lydian names in Lydian language and Lycian names in Lycian language. This cannot be accidental but rather demonstrates a strong local and ethnic identity, expressed in visible terms.

Although imperial ideology emphasized ethnic identity, within the imperial scheme there is no rubric for "being Anatolian" – that is, for a broader geographic category. We see this nuance of imperial ideology reflected in archaeological remains. Anatolia is remarkable for its diversity of geography and climate, as well as the diversity of cultures and peoples inhabiting it. The dwellings of the non-elite sometimes continued in traditional form through the Achaemenid period, if Xenophon's description of houses in Armenia is to be believed; at Sardis, too, non-elite houses continue as before. Gordion provides an alternative to this observation, with the introduction of pit houses in the Achaemenid period, an observation that demonstrates the complexity of the situation.[8] The peninsula shows wide diversity in aspects of local identity and wide cohesion in aspects of elite identity. It provides no evidence whatsoever for a sense of broader Anatolian, or western Anatolian, or higher-altitude Anatolian, or all-of-us-Anatolians-together-against-the-Greeks identity.

Some mortuary treatments suggest explicit reference to local habit in the face of Persian hegemony – an example of autonomy in the teeth of authority, perhaps. Thus the hundreds of Achaemenid-period tumuli identified in Lydia spread throughout the region and are situated in highly visible locations: they are an overt reminder of Lydian heritage and Lydian kingly glory that predated Persian hegemony.[9] And yet it is clear that the grave goods buried with the elite link them to each other rather than to a localized pre-Achaemenid inheritance. This does not seem to be limited to Anatolia: finds from Pasargadae and the artifacts of the Oxus Treasure demonstrate the cohesion of the elite across the empire. They might pick and choose between elements of local ethnic indicators, but in fact for the elite there seems not to have been a localized emphasis *despite* imperial rhetorical tropes that lean on rubrics of ethnicity.

Certain regional variety in this picture can perhaps be seen, however. The mountainous and relatively isolated regions of Lycia and Caria, which unlike Lydia, Phrygia, or Urartu had no clear history of monarchy or even confederation, seem to demonstrate internal dynastic jockeying for position that could be couched in ethnic terms. The Persianizing emphasis of western Lycia, the Hellenizing emphasis of eastern Lycia, and the all-inclusive approach of the Hecatomnids – culminating in the Mausoleum – are the result of internal politics and local dynastic ambition. The emphasis in Lycia on the emphatically Lycian pillar tomb and its elaborated successor, the temple tomb, and on recognizable shapes such as the Lycian sarcophagus takes on particular localized ethnic meaning in this context of local conflict, with local leaders asserting an evident right to rule the region.

Identity and Religion

Religious cult is possibly also tied to ethnic identity. The Anatolian storm god and mother goddess continued to be worshiped in various manifestations during the Achaemenid period, and this doubtless tied into people's sense of tradition and identity. Specific local gods and goddesses also seem to have formed a key part of identity, however. In some cases, this was as straightforward as the patron god of a city being "Bel of Tarsus" or Baaltar. The Sacred Way connecting Miletus to the Temple of Apollo at Didyma was such a focus of sculptural adornment that we can be certain that the link to the god and his cult formed an important part of elite identity in this Greek colony turned piece of the Achaemenid Empire.

The glorious Temple of Artemis at Ephesus surely formed a focus of local identity as well, but here we have a bit more information to shed light on the multivalent nature of such a definition: the sacristan of the goddess at the end of the fifth century had the Persian name Megabyzus, and it has even been argued that this was a hieratic name taken on by those assuming the position. Similarly, at Sardis a priest of Artemis had a Persian name, Mitridastas. In instances where cult had clearly been introduced, the picture is varied: the seer mentioned by name at Arebsun, Abbas, has a non-Anatolian name and quite clearly a non-Anatolian religious identity, but all we can say about the priests of Persian cults in western Anatolia in later times is that they spoke unusual languages. Perhaps the use of Aramaic was a key part of religious identity for certain cults introduced into Anatolia under the Persians. The interface between ethnicity and religion, and the impact these features had on identity as perceived both by individuals practicing those religions and by those observing them, were complex to say the least.

Identity and Administration

The right to rule was a large part of identity for the polyethnic Achaemenid elite who governed Anatolia. Administrative identity was signaled through material means, particularly in the form of palaces and bureaucratic practices. Few palaces have been excavated in Anatolia, of course, but those that have demonstrate the phenomenon. Subtle but powerful are the palatial remains at Dascylium. Overtly Ionian in their architectural moldings, they assert the power of Achaemenid authority over the craftspeople of the western seaboard. They also link this satrapal capital at the far western end of the empire to the overtly

148. Glass Seals 56, 188, 44, 90, 112, 192, 205, and 75 from Gordion. After Dusinberre 2010a: fig. 31.8.

Ionian work at Pasargadae itself, in the heart of Fars at the east–west geographic center of the empire. The connection between Dascylium and the Persian heartland is seen also in the royal name seals impressed on the archive at Dascylium, as well as in the archiving practices of this capital.

The impact of Achaemenid authority on seals and seal usage, those essential indicators of individual identity, was profound. We have seen already the variety of choices at Sardis, where as yet no seals have been found that predate the Achaemenid period. But Achaemenid authority affected the administrative identities of more than those in satrapal cities, as the seals from the second-tier but still large and important site of Gordion demonstrate.

One material, glass, may serve as a case study for the importance surrounding this observation.[10] Workshops across the empire produced not only seals of hard stone but also examples in glass. More than a fifth of the Achaemenid seals from Gordion are made of glass, and they show that the artists drew on overtly Achaemenid imagery and Near Eastern shapes as well as Greek. They include a cylinder, pyramidal stamp seals, and scaraboids; Achaemenid imagery is found on all shapes, while three scaraboids bear iconography reflecting Greek myth and visual rendition. The glass is of different colors, including blue, green, and clear. Whether they were purchasing seals hot off the glass press at Gordion

149. Glass seals from Dülük Baba Tepesi. After Facella 2009: fig. 16. © Forschungsstelle Asia Minor, Westfälische Wilhelms-Universität Münster.

itself, using imports from elsewhere, or traveling to distant lands to bring seals back, people at Gordion had a range of options in glyptic shape and image, even within this one material category.

The iconography of the Achaemenid-period seals varied. Instead of the striations and nondescript imagery that characterize many seals from pre- and post-Achaemenid periods, the seals dating to the Achaemenid period at Gordion have recognizable and often idiosyncratic imagery. These seals see parallels elsewhere in the Achaemenid Empire and situate Gordion in the middle of glyptic practice throughout the empire. They give an idea of an Achaemenid administration at Gordion, a taste for Achaemenid imagery. Even those who were not members of the highest social and administrative echelon adopted the accoutrements of Achaemenid administrative identity. The exact parallel of this situation found at Dülük Baba Tepesi in eastern Anatolia near Gaziantep demonstrates the widespread nature of the phenomenon.[11]

Authority and Autonomy in Achaemenid Anatolia

The question of identity and its interface with an authority–autonomy approach to imperialism is complex. Miller comments:

> Clearly we need more evidence for certainty ... but at present all indicators are pointing to a comparatively rapid process of acculturation to the Persian model throughout western Anatolia owing to the wide-spread residence of prominent Persians (and their native Anatolian deputies) in the countryside as required for military purposes. "Rapid" acculturation was not sought by the Persians; it was a by-product of social and military functions. And "rapid" does not mean universal nor does it mean consistent. Anatolian cultures continued on their own track, with a new overlay of cultural ideas added to the pre-existing mix.[12]

This discussion of acculturation illuminates the study of authority, autonomy, and identity. Acculturation is one way in which identities could be forged and signaled, a way in which people could respond to imperial or to local authority. It could be a way of adapting behaviors; for instance, the assumption by people in the Phrygian highlands of what had been western seaboard iconographies of the mother goddess shows a kind of acculturation in the Achaemenid period that responds to religious authority and expression. Specifically "Persian" expressions of ethnic identity could be linked to authority, too; naming patterns make us realize we should not assume that a Persian expression necessarily indicates a Persian person but rather a Persian identity. Local or traditional expressions of identity, the sort of thing that might be seen as defying acculturative processes, can be understood as manifestations of autonomy.

In its simplest terms, the authority–autonomy model anticipates a good deal of cohesion in aspects of behavior that mattered to the central authority, while great variability might reflect areas that were of lesser importance and thus could be less carefully regulated. Autonomy could be exercised by individuals or by groups of people; as we have seen, autonomy could be local but might also extend across behavioral categories rather than be simply defined by regional traditions. This study of Achaemenid Anatolia helps us understand the priorities and workings of the Achaemenid Empire and, perhaps, sheds light on imperial workings in general.

Empire and Identity in Achaemenid Anatolia

In Anatolia, the army was a complex and sophisticated mechanism with some flexibility but more obvious cohesion across the peninsula. Steps were taken to ensure loyalty to cohort and commanders rather than to the local populace, and a clear top-down hierarchy stemmed ultimately from the Persian king himself. The sculpted reliefs at Meydancıkkale demonstrate that the army could be a conduit for spreading imperial ideology, reinforcing the strength of the central authority in a more subtle manner, as well as the overt human manifestation that was the army itself. Although certain Persian satraps and/or nobles (such as Cyrus the Younger) could muster troops in their own name, their ultimate subordination to imperial authority was clear and the tasks they might ask such troops to perform were limited. This was crucial to the central authority. When people (such as Cyrus the Younger) exerted autonomous authority, the cost could be great. Thus the army's identity had to be cohesive and firmly associated with the imperial authority.

It is likely that the manly identity signaled on so many mortuary reliefs formed part of this concept of military authority. Training men, from boyhood up, in the "proper" manner of hunting and fighting – which ideally included expensive Persian-style horses, trousers, and headdresses – would form an important part of maintaining a standing army. If elite males identified themselves via particular behaviors that coupled them to other elite males, the Achaemenid army, and Persian notions of manhood, then the likelihood of autonomous armed uprisings would dwindle. The tombs of the Anatolian elite and that of the Persian king unite these men in definitions of manhood, definitions that ultimately tie the men of Achaemenid Anatolia to the identity and goals of Achaemenid military authority.

Such unity was an essential element of governance. In creating a cohesive sense of administrative authority, the elite of Achaemenid Anatolia strengthened their imperial hold and ability to rule. Administrative structures such as palaces that referred overtly to Achaemenid hegemony through varied and sophisticated architectural forms could make the claim of unified authority clearly and quickly. An administrative apparatus reflecting that in Persia not only had an ideological impact on the local populace, but materially benefited the record keepers who had to account to satraps and their representatives. Thus archiving practices and the introduction of particular types of personal signifiers in the form of sealstones could become a way to demonstrate authority and ensure its longevity.

Conspicuous consumption was a crucial element of unified authority in Achaemenid Anatolia. Rich clothes, gold jewelry and clothing ornaments, and sealstones of semiprecious stones announced the wealth of the person they adorned. The cohesion of visual expression in these personal items made the point even stronger: across Anatolia, people used the symbols of Achaemenid authority to augment and underscore their own importance and authority. Fathom the impact of such behavior. Imagine if all government officials today dressed fundamentally alike, wearing clothes that instantly and recognizably set them apart from others, while those at the top of the echelon carried, say, smart phones of a particular style and color, which they might ostentatiously whip out of a pocket and use at any moment. Lesser officials or other people wishing to accrue some of that prestige and authority to themselves would no doubt make use of less expensive versions of these outward manifestations of power. It is perhaps this kind of behavior that was associated with the glass seals of Gordion.

The evidence for banqueting and the specific paraphernalia for elite banqueting preserved in mortuary contexts of Achaemenid Anatolia demonstrate that what the elite used for signaling power was not limited to clothing and seals, however. The continuity of the vessels in elite graves and the evidence of mortuary relief sculpture and painting attest to the importance of drinking and dining in the "right" way. Members of the elite apparently performed this essential behavior in a similar manner, with similar vessels, across Anatolia. That so many of these vessels bear an obvious relation to imperially charged iconographies and styles underscores their importance in the context of imperial authority.

What matters is not just that some people could afford silver vessels, but that these objects overtly signaled their membership in the Achaemenid elite. That this signaling should have taken place in the context of banqueting is of great importance. We cannot be certain of the makeup of a dinner or drinking party; we do not know whether the Greek model, in which men regularly dined together in small groups, pertained in Anatolia. If so, this would provide another opportunity to create a firm bond between elite men in a manner similar to that suggested by the mortuary reliefs. If dining groups included both sexes, as the frequent presence of seated females near the reclining males on funerary reliefs may suggest, the implications are if anything more profound. Here was a way for men and women to share an elite identity, for family or other groups to meld within the constructs of Achaemenid authority.

Dining behaviors that connected people of Anatolia to Achaemenid authority included not only the elite but also the non-elite. Ceramic Achaemenid bowls have been found in every region of Anatolia where Achaemenid-period deposits have been excavated, usually next to traditional drinking cups. The introduction of Achaemenid bowls into the standard ceramic assemblage implies not just a new cup shape but a new manner of drinking, one that joined not just the elite but *everybody* to the Achaemenid authority. This is a profound new twist to local identities during the Achaemenid period in Anatolia.

In addition to this fundamental change in daily practice, permanent reminders of Achaemenid authority were to be found in more specialized arenas as well. The power statements of Xerxes formed one such reminder, from the inscription in the east to the plane tree in the west. The Achaemenid road system would have had an impact not only on trade and communication, but also on those who lived near enough to a road to use it, see it, or hear about it (surely most people). Moreover, the trade and communication facilitated would certainly have required local participation; someone had to feed and water the horses kept at the way stations, for instance, keep them groomed and pick their feet, see to their veterinary needs, muck out their living quarters, and keep them sufficiently exercised that they could be of use when their services were required. All those involved in growing hay and grain and transporting these crops, as well as grooms, stable hands, and exercise riders, would have been reminded regularly of the authority of the empire. Thus imperial authority was enacted by the elite and the non-elite, with powerful reminders of its presence manifested not only in behaviors and individual expressions, but also through its impact on the landscapes and livelihoods of entire regions.

Various aspects of life were open to considerable expression of individual or local autonomy, however. This is an essential element of keeping an empire: too restrictive or authoritarian an expression of imperial might, without opportunity for individual expression or decision making, is doomed to failure. Mortuary monuments illuminate a meaningful aspect of identity. Treating the dead with appropriate respect and ritual is charged and important. Different cultures, sometimes different families within different cultures, have their own approaches and priorities. Feelings often run high about such matters. For one person, exposing the body of a loved one to dogs and carrion birds is an appalling thought, for another the thought of worms in the flesh of the interred is nauseating, while for another the notion of a body burning to a curling crisp during cremation is anathema. Whereas Achaemenid authority created coherence in the physical manifestation of elite status and behavior, as well as corresponding continuity in grave goods across Anatolia, autonomy was exhibited by those dealing with corpses. The decision by the imperial administration not to regulate burial customs accounts for the diversity of mortuary monuments in Achaemenid Anatolia, even as the mortuary inclusions of those same graves show similarity.

Religion, too, was an area where people might define themselves according to a great diversity of approach. Persians took interest in the varied cults of Anatolia and became involved in worship, as inscriptions from Sardis and the presence of Megabyzus at Ephesus demonstrate. At no point do we see evidence for an attempt to co-opt one of these major sites or its administration. If the altar at Sardis was converted to a fire altar, as suggested when it was first excavated, it is the only Anatolian example of a change of cult in the Achaemenid period. It may be that in fact a process other than forcible Persian imposition of foreign cult underlay its reconstruction. We do, however, see numerous examples of hybridizing cults and different cults adopting and adapting aspects of other rituals and expressions. Indeed, religious autonomy seems to have been so great and communication among different areas to have increased so much during the Achaemenid period that religious expressions could spread freely from one region or one cult to another. This is clear in expressions of worship of the Phrygian mother goddess, the importance of "Artemis of Ephesus" at Sardis, the Letoön at Xanthus, and the iconography used to express Baaltar. Particular cults may suggest ethnic enclaves, as the use of Aramaic to worship Bel and others at Arebsun may indicate, but I want to emphasize that there is no evidence for this beyond the name Abbas – and it has already been shown that ethnic names are not necessarily an indication of ethnic heritage. Clearly we see at Arebsun an expression of a particular religious identity, and it is a religious identity strongly felt and expressed. It is not an ethnic identity. It attests to an autonomy of cultic practice and expression within the imperial system, not to ethnic ghettoizing.

It has been much harder to trace educational practices in Achaemenid Anatolia, but certainly in some aspects of education, too, we see considerable autonomy. Such is suggested by the selective deployment of names, which show neither slavish adherence to a single ethnic group nor a trend toward Persianizing names. Instead, parents had freedom of choice, it seems, in the names they gave their children – and the very fact that they could learn of various names demonstrates shared knowledge. Continuity of cultic practice demonstrates autonomy of education at sanctuaries, where priests and priestesses were trained in their duties and maintained the practices of yore. Sculptors and seal carvers must have had autonomy in education as well, as the variety of styles executed in these art forms demonstrates. The emphasis in education on less-skilled people being guided by experts finds an interesting parallel, though, in the hierarchical arrangement of the Persian elite who were apparently taught obedience to superiors as part of an overarching notion of straightness and order. The education of the king was reflected in the education of the elite in its emphasis on riding, shooting, and justice. The education of the elite was reflected in the education of all in its emphasis on following a superior leader. The authority inherent in any educational system reflected imperial structures even as that same education allowed for exercise of autonomy in many personal areas.

This brings us to one last important aspect of autonomy: the freedom to express personal taste. The variety of artistic styles represented in Achaemenid visual culture shows that patrons as well as artists could make individual choices based on their personal taste and personal identity as well as any number of other factors. The range of styles found in grave stelae, even those found in the same area, is as profound as that in seals. Achaemenid Anatolia was a place where imperial authority could be and was expressed powerfully, but it was also a place where individuals exercised some types of autonomy, mostly in

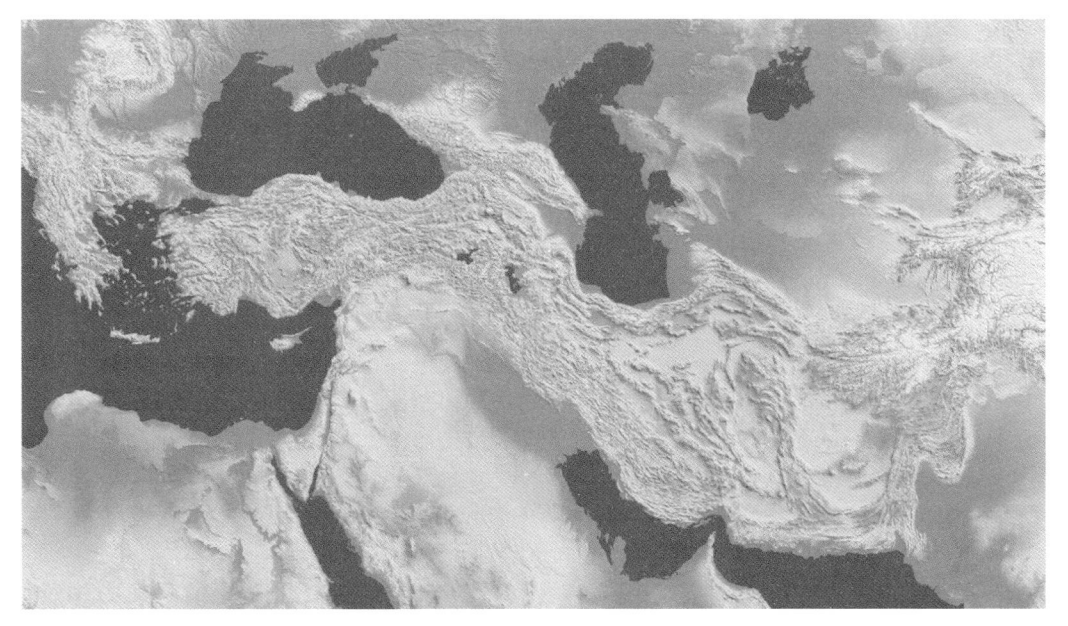

150. Achaemenid Empire. Courtesy Karl Mueller.

ways that allowed them to express their individual identity within the rubric of administrative authority.

When Cyrus conquered Anatolia in the mid–sixth century, he suddenly had to incorporate a large number of people with very different traditions into the new empire. He and the subsequent Achaemenid kings had to implement an imperial system that would consolidate and keep the empire, one that would allow for diverse populations and cultural backgrounds but still unite the people into a stable whole. Finding the areas in which authority had to be exerted and those in which autonomy could be allowed was a complex and nuanced task. Ultimately, it was not only the elite and the military that expressed and reified imperial authority, but also the eating and drinking behaviors of the people of Anatolia as a whole, the assumption of new patterns of administrative authority deep in the social ranks, and an entirely different system of trade and communication. Personal expressions of identity saw great autonomy, from religious belief and cult through mortuary customs to educational practices and priorities. Through the flexible combination of authority and autonomy, the Achaemenid administration saw to the successful enactment and ultimate longevity both of individual identity and of empire.

NOTES

One: Introduction

1. For Cyrus's accession to power, see Hdt. 1.107–30, as well as Ctesias and a few brief passages in Diodorus and Justin. For a discussion of these and other texts, see Briant 1996a: 910, 2002: 14–32. See also Mallowan 1972; Dusinberre 2003a: ch. 2; Rollinger 2008. All dates are B.C.E. unless otherwise indicated.
2. Hdt. 1.71, 1.73. Rollinger 2003 casts doubt on the reality of the Halys frontier.
3. Hdt. 1.53; Arist. *Rhet.* 3.1047a 5.4; Cic. *Poet. frag.* 90.
4. Debord 1999 examines Asia Minor in the fourth century, rather than the whole peninsula during the entire Achaemenid period.
5. For authority, see, e.g., Green 1989; Buchanan 2003; Shapiro 2002. Definitions of authority vary widely from field to field; here I consider it to be the potential or actual exercise of power with a sense of justification and legitimacy shared at least to some extent by wielder and recipient.
6. Beran 1987; Mommsen 1992: 46. For a relatively recent overview of discussions concerning authority that focuses on political authority, see Christiano 2004.
7. See Simmons 2001. Studies of power have formed a primary focus in the social sciences, anthropology, psychology, and other fields. Since Gramsci 1971 and Foucault 1980, it has become common to consider power to be not only a force that permeates the "capillaries" of social interaction, but also a collusive system of "hegemony" in which those being dominated participate in their domination as much as the dominating force itself. See Williams 1977: 110; Comaroff 1991: 23; Bourdieu 1977; Stoler 1997. For the relation of this to notions of nationalism, see B. Anderson 1991. For a revisionist approach to cognition and power, see McIntosh 1997.
8. Just as important are the circumstances of their writing: Herodotus, born during the reign of Xerxes to a Greek father and Carian mother at Halicarnassus in southwest Anatolia, wrote for the Athenians and other Greeks after the unsuccessful Persian invasions of Greece. Thucydides laid the blame for Athenian defeat in the war with Sparta at the end of the fifth century partly on the Persian gold that supported the Spartans. Xenophon encountered the empire within the sphere of Cyrus the Younger as he sought to legitimize his attempt to take the throne from his brother Artaxerxes II at the end of the fifth century. Ctesias, a Cnidian from Caria, served as

Artaxerxes II's doctor and wrote a treatise on Persians that was full of spicy orientalizing anecdotes for a Greek audience. Berossus was a priest of Bel-Marduk in the Hellenistic period, who wrote a little-used work about Babylonian history and more famously about astrology – both works known, like those of Ctesias, only through other ancient authors' citations. Diodorus Siculus wrote in the Augustan age for a courtly milieu that was fashioning itself as the new avenger of the Persian sack of Athens – this time, Rome vs. the Parthians. Strabo, a historian, geographer, and philosopher, was born in Amaseia in Anatolia near the Black Sea and wrote in Greek during the time of Augustus. Arrian lionized Alexander in the early second century C.E. The role of social memory and social construct in these histories was great and had an impact on the events related and on narrative construction. We have few texts on which to base a narrative history that addresses regions east of Persepolis, even though many of these regions were rich in resources and strategic interest for the Achaemenid kings. See Briant 1994b, 1994c. For a thorough political overview, see Dandamaev 1989.

9   See Dusinberre 2003a: 1. Throughout this work, I use "Persian" to signify only "ethnic" Persians. "Achaemenid" refers not so much to a discrete family line of Persians as to the ideological umbrella created by the imperial hegemony. See Root 1979. For the Medes, see, e.g., Ghirshman 1963b; Schmitt 1967; Muscarella 1980; Lewis 1980; Brown 1986, 1988; Tuplin, 1994; Roaf 1995, 2004; Dusinberre 2002; Rollinger 2003, 2008; Razmjou 2005a.

10 Studying Achaemenid history is difficult not only because of the empire's size but because sources include texts from disparate origins, texts in many languages, and texts that postdate the empire sometimes by significant amounts of time. Kuhrt 2007 provides translations of Greek, Old Persian, Akkadian, Hebrew, Aramaic, Egyptian, and Latin sources; see also Kuhrt 1995a; Briant 1997, 2001, 2002; Waters 2004; Azzoni, forthcoming. For thoughtful articles on the nature of the sources, see Sancisi-Weerdenburg and Kuhrt 1987. For heartland Persian inscriptions, see Kent 1953; Lecoq 1997; Schmitt 1991, 2000. For the Persepolis Treasury Archive that records government payments in silver, see Cameron 1948, 1958, 1965; Hallock 1960. For the Fortification Archive, see later in this chapter. For recent archaeological contributions, see Garrison and Root 2001; Briant and Boucharlat 2005; Magee, Petrie, Knox, and Khan 2005; Callieri 2007.

11 The date is contested. The Nabonidus Chronicle, perhaps to be dated to ca. 500, mentions Cyrus's campaigns in the west before the conquest of Babylon. For Cyrus, see Waters 2004. For the Nabonidus Chronicle, see Grayson 1975; Beaulieu 1989; Glassner 2004; Lecoq 1997: 181–3; S. Smith 1924: 116. For the chronology of the event, see Cargill 1977; Rollinger 2008. For a translation and notes on the problems, see Kuhrt 2007: 50. See also the Marmor Parium (*FGrH* 239 F42); Segal 1971; Mallowan 1972; Erbse 1979; Balcer 1984: 33; Greenewalt 1992; 1995a.

12 For Pasargadae, see D. Stronach 1978, 1989b, 1990, 1994a, 1994b; for Achaemenid imperial rhetoric, see Root 1979. The inscriptions at Pasargadae date to the reign of Darius, not Cyrus, and they form no part of the current discussion. See Borger and Hinz 1959; Nylander 1967: 170–3.

13 Illustrated in *Iran* 10 (1972), pls. IIa, b; see also Kawami 1972.

14 See D. Stronach 1978: 55.

15 All the references in the statue's text are to the temple of Neith at Sais; the statue was transported to Hadrian's villa at Tivoli and is now in the Vatican. Udjahorresne's tomb was discovered at Abusir by Polish excavators in the 1990s.

16 See Kuhrt 1995a: 662–4; for Udjahorresne, see Lloyd 1982; Bresciani 1985; Baines 1996; Bares 1996, 1999.

17 For the date, see Briant 2002: 105. For Darius's legitimacy, see Waters 1996.
18 The Bisitun Inscription is reiterated in Elamite, Babylonian, and Old Persian. For the inscription, see Hinz 1974; Luschey 1974; von Voigtlander 1978; Borger 1982; Greenfield and Porten 1982; Schmitt 1990a, 1990b; 1991a. For the relief, see King and Campbell Thompson 1907; Luschey 1968; Root 1979; Börker-Klähn 1982.
19 Hdt. 3.88. For the results, see Corsarso 1985.
20 See Kurke 1999: 68–89; also Fehling 1989; Dillery 1992; Descat 1994; Asheri 1996; Waters 1996.
21 See Root 1979; also Dusinberre 2003b, 2004.
22 Kent 1953.
23 Dieulafoy 1893; De Mecquenem 1938, 1947; Ghirshman 1963a; Amiet 1972a, 1972b, 1974, 1980, 1994; Haerinck 1973; Perrot 1974, 1981; Pillet 1914; Boucharlat 1990a, 1990b, 1997. For the statue of Darius made in Egyptian style that was found at Susa, see, e.g., Kervran, Stronach, Vallat, and Yoyotte 1972; Yoyotte 1974; Razmjou 2002.
24 See esp. Root 1979, 2007; see also Schmidt 1953; Roaf 1983; Adams 1992.
25 For the Fortification Archive, see esp. Hallock 1950, 1969, 1973, 1978; Hinz 1960; Koch 1990; Garrison and Root 2001; Razmjou 2004b; Briant, Henkelman, and Stolper 2008. Henkelman 2008: ch. 2 offers the most comprehensive and clearest introduction to the archive. Its discovery is mentioned in Herzfeld 1934: 231. An Elamite archive found at Susa, which may date to the mid–sixth century and has most of the features of the Persepolis system, suggests that Darius may have continued and adapted a local system; see Greenfield 1986; Brosius 2003. See also Berg 1979 for an archive kept during the time of Cyrus that could be consulted later in case of need. Nonimperial archives include Babylonian business or temple documents; see Stolper 1985. The multilingual aspect of the Fortification Archive has parallels elsewhere; see Abraham 1995.
26 Garrison 1988, 1991, 2000; Garrison and Root 2001. For the importance, see Bourdieu 1984.
27 For Egypt, see Cruz-Urribe 1980; Hdt. 7.1, 7.7. For Babylonia, see Briant 1992; Waerzeggers 2003–4.
28 Kuhrt and Sherwin-White 1987; Sherwin-White and Kuhrt 1993; Kuhrt 1995a: 670; Stolper 1989.
29 Petit 1990: 181–6.
30 Thuc. 1.100.
31 Kuhrt 1995a: 671.
32 Thuc. 1.104.
33 Thuc. 1.110; Kuhrt 1995a: 671–2; Wuttmann and Marchand 2005.
34 For Ezra and Nehemiah, see Hoglund 1992; against that, Grabbe 1994; and now Briant 2002: 583–7. For the possibility of the Peace of Callias, see, e.g., Badian 1987; Briant 2002: 579–80.
35 For Athens, see M. Miller 1992, 1997. For the Cadusians, see Briant 2002: 730–3; also *FGrH* 688 F5, F9; Xen. *Hell.* 2.1.13; Justin 10.3.2–5; Arr. 3.19.4–5; Plut. *Artax.* 24.1–3, 10–11, cited in Kuhrt 2007. For Pazyryk, see Rudenko 1970; Lerner 1991.
36 Kuhrt 1995a: 673.
37 Thuc. 8.
38 Xen. *Hell.* 1.4.3.
39 It took until 400/399 for Upper Egypt to join; see Kuhrt 2007: 391.
40 Kent 1953: A2 Ha-c; Vallat 1989. For the progress of the Persian kings from one capital to another during the year, see Briant 1988b; Tuplin 1998.
41 See Kuhrt 2007: 566–7. For the role religion can play in cementing relations in permeable borderlands, see, e.g., Conrad and Demarest 1984; Millett 1995; McIntosh 2009.

42 Henkelman 2008.
43 Plut. *Artax.*
44 Kuhrt 1995a: 675 points out that Artaxerxes III's reputation for harshness may be as undeserved as that of Cambyses.
45 Schmidt 1970.
46 Calmeyer and Shahbazi 1976; Tilia 1978.
47 Diodorus's story about poisoning is contradicted by a cuneiform tablet in the British Museum, BM 71537; see Kuhrt 2007: 423.
48 For the reasons Alexander was able to conquer the Achaemenid Empire, see Briant 2002: ch. 18, 2010.
49 See, e.g., Kuhrt and Sherwin-White 1994.
50 Turkish Ministry of Tourism 2005: Geography of Turkey (http://www.turizm.net/turkey/info/geography.html); NASA Earth Observatory: Mount Ararat (http://earthobservatory.nasa.gov/IOTD/view.php?id=1515).
51 University of Southern California Department of Civil Engineering, "Brief Seismic History of Turkey" (http://www.usc.edu/dept/civil_eng/structural_lab/eq-rp/seismicity.html). I am grateful to Karl Mueller for explaining Turkey's exceptionally complex geology and shifting plates to me.
52 Turkish State Meteorological Service: "Climate of Turkey" (http://www.meteor.gov.tr/2006/english/eng-climateofturkey.aspx; see also http://www.dmi.gov.tr/tahmin/turkiye.aspx).
53 For Urartu, see Zimansky 1985, 1995a; Kuhrt 1995a: 548–62; and refs.
54 Kuhrt's discussion of the Assyrian sources and the ways they may bias our understanding of Urartu is cogent and concise (1995a: 554–62).
55 Kuhrt 1995a: 554.
56 TCL 3 ll. 203–26.
57 Xen. *Anab.* 4.24–6, trans. Jona Lendering (www.livius.org). For continuities from Urartian into Achaemenid times, see Zimansky 1995b.
58 Rollinger 2008 reads the Nabonidus Chronicle as referring to Urartu rather than Lydia, but this is uncertain. If it does indeed read "Urartu," it probably refers to a geographic region rather than a separate state (A. Kuhrt, personal communication, 2010).
59 The Hittites were a major Bronze Age civilization with significant interactions and impact: Beal 1995; Beckman 1995; Hoffner 1995; Imparati 1995; Macqueen 1995. We know much less about the Neo-Hittites at this juncture, but see Hawkins 1995.
60 Voigt 1994: 267–72; Sams and Voigt 1995: 370–4; see also Gunter 1991. The following discussion in the text of Gordion and Phrygia is drawn from Dusinberre 2005: 8–12.
61 Sams 1997: 245. See also Voigt 1993; Henrickson and Voigt 1998; Voigt and Henrickson 2000a, 2000b.
62 For the Early Phrygian period, see Sams 1994, 1995, 2005; Voigt 2005; Voigt and Henrickson 2000b. For architecture and contents of the megarons, see DeVries 1980: 34ff., Sams 1995.
63 J. Jones 2005.
64 For the date, see Voigt 1994: 272–3; DeVries, Kuniholm, Sams, and Voigt 2003; DeVries 2005; Dusinberre 2005: 3–4. Arguing for a date of 700 instead, see Muscarella 2003; Keenan 2004.
65 For the Middle Phrygian period, see Voigt and Young 1999: 198–220; Voigt 2005.
66 Voigt and Young 1999: 205.
67 Voigt and Young 1999: 205.

68 Recent exploration has demonstrated that the New Citadel (and possibly the Old Citadel) saw the Citadel Mound divided into two parts, with the Eastern Mound continuing to support the palace area, which was laid out on the same plan as before. Meanwhile, the Western Mound served as quarters for wealthy families, "perhaps minor officials associated with the Phrygian court or independent merchants" (Voigt and Young 1999: 210; see also Voigt 2005). In addition to the Citadel Mound itself, Gordion in the Middle Phrygian period had a Lower Town (see Voigt 2005 and refs.). The area to the south of the Citadel Mound was fortified, with the Küçük Höyük forming a tall mudbrick fortress at the southeast to protect the Middle Phrygian levels that had been raised above the level of the surrounding plain with a fill (see Voigt and Young 1999: 211; for the Küçük Höyük, see R. Young 1953: 26–29, 1957: 324, 1958: 140–1; Glendinning 1996).

69 As Mustafa Metin of the Museum of Anatolian Civilizations in Ankara corroborates, personal communication, 2004. For the pots, see Henrickson 1993, 1994, 2005; Henrickson and Voigt 1998; Henrickson, Vandiver, and Blackman 2002: 391. It is an interesting contradiction that these achievements saw no counterpart in the seals of the Middle Phrygian period from Gordion, although certainly some sort of administration was required to govern Phrygian territories. For Gordion's seals, see Dusinberre 2005.

70 Kerkenes was initially thought to be Median but is now generally considered a Phrygian construction; see, e.g., Rollinger 2003: 321–6; Summers 1997, 2000; yearly newsletters to be found at http://www.kerkenes.metu.edu.tr/kerk2/index.html. See also the discussion and references collected at http://www.kerkenes.metu.edu.tr/kerk1/index.html.

71 For the "tumulus of Midas," see Liebhart and Johnson 2005.

72 Richard Liebhart, personal communication, 2004; see Roller 1983; Sams 1995, 1997; Liebhart and Johnson 2005.

73 I am grateful to Robert Henrickson (personal communication, 2004, Henrickson 2005) for information about imports and local responses at the end of the Middle Phrygian period. Interestingly, the only Lydian shape copied in local gray ware was the "fruitstand," a shallow bowl or deep plate on a high pedestal foot. Roof tiles also demonstrate connections with Lydia (Glendinning 2005: 98–9).

74 Herodotus's Lydian stories (1.6–94) are an excellent read but of limited historical value. Literary sources on Sardis are gathered in Pedley 1972; and see also Briant 1991. For a recent historical overview of Lydia, see Roosevelt 2009.

75 Roosevelt 2009: 13–19; see also Bryce 2003.

76 See Dusinberre 2003a: 31–5.

77 This point is important for the modern scholar trying to understand from contemporary Greek accounts events and underlying causes in the ancient Near East. Important discussions of Greek perceptions of Persians and the way these have skewed our impressions include Momigliano 1975: 123–50; C. Starr 1975: 40–2, 1977; Orlin 1976; Root 1979: 40–2; Briant 1989a. See also Schmitt 1967; Hartog 1988. For visual manifestations of this world view, see Gunter 1990, 2009.

78 Archilochus 15; Alcman 16; Sappho F 218, 219; Mimnermus F 13; Alcaeus F 116; Hipponax F 42.

79 Hom. *Il.* 2.864–6, 5.43–4, 20.382–5, 20.389–92 for beauty and wealth; 4.141–5 describes one of its specialty crafts: staining ivory with purple to make cheek pieces for horses.

80 The Rassam Cylinder (644–636), Cylinder B (648), Cylinder E (640s), and a building tablet concerning the reconstruction of the Temple of Sin at Harran (third quarter of seventh century) mention the Lydian king. For the Rassam Cylinder, Cylinder B,

and the Sin Temple tablet, see Luckenbill 1927: 297–8, 323, 351–2. For Cylinders B and E, see Piepkorn 1933: 47, 17.

81 Hdt. 7.30. For the boundaries, see Greenewalt 1995a: 1175; Kuhrt 1995a: 56; Rollinger 2003; Roosevelt 2009:25. The conquest of Smyrna by Croesus's father, Alyattes (Hdt. 1.16), has been confirmed archaeologically (*CAH* 3/2: 647–8; Doğer and Gezgin 1997), and the conquest of Phrygia and construction of the fortress at Gordion seem to have happened under his rule (Hanfmann 1983: 71).

82 Hdt. 1.50–1.

83 A brief discussion of these is provided in *CAH* 3/2: 650, 654–5; see also Dusinberre 2002.

84 Bryce 1995:1162; see also Radt 1970; Peschlow 2002.

85 Bryce 2003. For ongoing ethnic tensions and interactions well into the Achaemenid period, see Keen 2002; Schweyer 2002.

86 Ray 1995:1187; see also Kolb 1993, 1995, 1996, 1998, 2000a, 2000b, 2003; des Courtils and Marksteiner 1997, 1999, 2000. For its continued appearance into the Achaemenid period, see Schweyer 1996; Thomsen 2002.

87 The pirates of Lycia, Pamphylia, and Cilicia were legendary; Carian soldiers are among the bodyguards of the king maker Jehoiada of Judah (ca. 837–800) in 2 Kings 11:4, 19 and figure prominently in the inscriptions and archaeology of Egypt during the reign of Psammetichus II and after (593–411). See Ray 1995: 1190–92. For the social and political situation of Lycia, see Marksteiner 2002a.

88 Sevin 1976.

89 Meriç 1982; Dominguez 2000; Greaves 2010: 225–7. For the importance, see Bal, Crewe, and Spitzer 1999.

90 D. Miller 1987; Mills 1999, 2004.

91 Alcock 1989, 1993; Sinopoli 1994; Sinopoli and Morrison 1995.

Two: Governing Anatolia

1 See Ahn 1992.

2 A necessary element in many empires; see, e.g., Brunt 1976; Adams 1979; Barber and Joyce 2007. See also Briant 1988a.

3 See Balcer 1993; Dusinberre 2003a: chs. 1, 2, passim.

4 For the extent and nature of the Anatolian satrapies, see, e.g., Briant 1996a: 75–80 and refs.; Sekunda 1988, 1991; Petit 1990; Weiskopf 1982, 1989; Casabonne 2004, 2007. Following Western scholarly convention, I call the satrapies here by their Greek rather than Persian names.

5 Thus Zenis and Mania are called "satraps" by Xenophon, although they are clearly subject to Pharnabazus, the "satrap" or governor of Hellespontine Phrygia. Herodotus uses "hyparchus" for governor of a province. See Schmitt 1976; Tuplin 1987a; see also Bivar 1961; Weiskopf 1982.

6 See Kuhrt 1995a: 690–701 and refs.; see also Dandamaev 1999. For the Romans, also faced with incorporating disparate regions during an expansionist phase, see, e.g., Gruen 1984a, 1984b. For a regional capital and the complexities of "center–periphery" models, see Invernizzi 1996.

7 One well-documented example is the satrapy of Egypt; see Dandamaev and Lukonin 1989: 103–4 and refs. For a particular example of Egyptian practices maintained in the Achaemenid period, see Verger 1964.

8 For taxes, see, e.g., Salonen 1972; Balcer 1988; Descat 1997; Potts 1999: 320 and refs.; Descat 1989; Koch 1989; Briant 1982.

9 Kuhrt 1995a: 691.

10 For satrapal archives, see Briant 1986b: 434–7; a copy of a royal decree kept in various capitals is described in Ezra 5:17–6:2. For evidence that the satrapal capitals had a bureaucracy similar to that of Persepolis, see Helms 1982. For the bullae that demonstrate the existence of a satrapal archive in Dascylium, seat of Hellespontine Phrygia, see Balkan 1959; Kaptan 1990, 1996, 2002, 2007; and the discussion later in this chapter. For the administration of the eastern regions of the empire, see Briant 1984; for the Bactrian parchments, see Shaked 2004. For the controversial "King's Eye," see Balcer 1977.

11 Hdt. 5.52–4, 5.8.98. Extensive documentation of the road system is to be found in the Persepolis Fortification Archive, e.g., PF 1318, 1351, 1361, 1501, 1544, 1550, 1555 (Hallock 1969). The Arshama passport, written in Aramaic on leather and now in Oxford, provides authorization to draw supplies for a journey (Driver 1957: 6). The way stations may have been used on occasion as a tracking mechanism; see Root 1997b, 2008. See also Razmjou 2005b.

12 For Mania, see Xen. *Hell.* 3.1.10; Kuhrt 1995a: 697–8. For Artemisia the elder at Salamis, see Hdt. 8.87–8; for Artemisia the younger, see Chapter 5.

13 See Hallock 1969. For Irtashduna, see Hdt. 3.87; Garrison and Root 2001: PFS 38. For Irdabama, see Henkelman 2009, 2010; Garrison and Root 2001: intro., forthcoming a: PFS 51. For women in the Achaemenid Empire, see Brosius 1996.

14 Neh. 3:7. See also al-Masudi 1863/1977.

15 See Dusinberre 2003a: 4.

16 Cf. the story of Themistocles and the Andrians (Hdt. 8.111); see also Gallant 1991 for the potential pitfalls.

17 Sancisi-Weerdenburg 1989, 1998 discusses the significance of the objects coming into the imperial treasuries.

18 See Tuplin 2007; Dönmez 2007; Johnson 2010; Nieling and Rehm 2010; Summerer and von Kienlin 2010.

19 Ps.-Arist. *Oec.* 2.1.1–4; trans. Kuhrt 2007: 672–3. For the text and a commentary, see van Groningen 1933; Aperghis 2004: ch. 7.

20 Cf. Kuhrt 2007: 669, 673–7 for the tribute described by Herodotus (3.89–97) and two later accounts of Darius as a generous king, who halved the amount of tribute others suggested exacting from the various provinces (Plut. *Mor.* 172–3; Polyaen. 7.11.3).

21 See discussions in Briant 2002: 388–421; Kuhrt 2007: 669–75. For a case study, see Thompson 1981.

22 Descat 1989: 82.

23 Bivar 1885; see also Levi 1976; Descat 1985.

24 See also Briant 1973b, 1985a. Lydian tribute may also have been paid in coined money as croesids and/or archers. Archer coins are discussed later in the chapter. For the complex relations between the types, see, e.g., Cahill and Kroll 2005; Sheedy 2009.

25 Dusinberre 2003a: 123–5.

26 Roosevelt 2009: 113–14.

27 Roosevelt 2009: 114. For Achaemenid estates, see Briant 1974, 1985a; Kuhrt 2007: 820–5.

28 Roosevelt 2009:114.

29 Plut. *Alex.* 36.1–2.

30 Strabo 15.3.21; cf. BE X 97 Nippur, x/19/4, Darius II (420/19); Kuhrt 2007: 680.

31 Kuhrt 2007: 670, 706–7; 679 is a text of Aelian describing an Indian pigment brought to the king that produced a dye the Persians preferred even to those they got from Sardis.

32 For transport, see Joannès 1989: 142–53, 156. For canals, BM 74463, BM 61330. For roadwork, BM 79746; Ael., *De nat. anim.* 15.26. For work duty, BM 49718; cited in Kuhrt 2007: 708–11.
33 For the king's table, see Briant 1989b; Kuhrt 2007: 604–14, 711–12; Henkelman 2010.
34 Kuhrt 2007: 670, 681–703.
35 Kuhrt 2007: 704–6.
36 Kuhrt 2007: 672.
37 See Dusinberre 2003a: 35–44.
38 Hdt. 1.153.3. For the satraps and their ethnicities, see, e.g., Petit 1990.
39 Hdt. 1.153. For Pactyes' uprising, see Briant 1996a: 47–8.
40 Hdt. 1.154–7; 3.120.1; Briant 1996a: 134–5.
41 See Hdt. 3.120–7 for the deeds of Oroetes.
42 Herodotus's narrative structure gives the impression that Darius I's first act on seizing the throne was to remove Oroetes, but we do not know when this occurred – sometime before the Scythian campaign, whenever that was (see, e.g., Balcer 1972; Borger 1982). The suggestion that Darius would move to cement his power in the area is consistent with the Bisitun text, however.
43 Artaphernes was appointed perhaps in the 510s (Hdt. 5.25, 6.42). Who had governed Lydia in the interim is not known. For the Ionian Revolt, see Hdt. 5, 6; Thuc. 3.65, 82; Wardman 1961; Hegyi 1966; Chapman 1972; Tozzi 1978; Lateiner 1982; Balcer 1984: 227; 1997. The Persepolis Fortification Archive documents the journey from Sardis to Persepolis of one Datiya in 494; this was probably Datis the Mede, who later commanded the Persian expedition at Marathon, perhaps bringing to the king at Persepolis an account of the quelled rebellion (PF Q 1809, discussed in Lewis 1980).
44 For Artaphernes, see Hdt. 6.42–3; Briant 1987.
45 Agricola 1900; Murray 1966; Balcer 1984: 204–5.
46 Hdt. 7.60.
47 Hdt. 6, 7.
48 Hdt. 8.116; 9.108–9 for the date. For the "secondary wall" at Sardis, see Dusinberre 2003a: 47–56. For the phenomenon and its importance, see Bedon, Chevallier, and Pinon 1988.
49 For an excellent overview of the problems, see Bosworth 1990.
50 Thuc. 1.115–17. See also Balcer 1984: 168, 176.
51 Tissaphernes appears in the Lycian A version of the Xanthus Inscribed Pillar as "son of Hydarnes" (Kuhrt 2007: 339).
52 See Schmitt 1983.
53 See Briant 1996a: 608–29 for the information in the following paragraph; also Lewis 1977; Greenewalt 1995b. The move may have been intended to circumvent an uprising in the area in protest against Tissaphernes' politics. Briant 1996a: 611–12.
54 Kuhrt 2007: 356–8.
55 Xen. *Anab.* 1.1–2; Plut. *Artax.* For a different chronology of events, probably drawn from Ephorus, see Dio. Sic. 14.11; Nepos *Alc.* 9; Plut. *Alc.* 37–9. See also Briant 1996a: 635.
56 Plut. *Artax.* 2 says quite clearly that Darius II appointed Artaxerxes his successor (difficult to do after his death). For the date, see Stolper 1983. It is important to realize that Egypt rose in simultaneous revolt against the king (Briant 1996a: 633–7).
57 Xen. *Hell.* 3.1; see also Briant 1996a: 649. For Artaxerxes II's clemency, see Dio. Sic. 14.35, 80; Polyaen. 7.11; Hell. Oxy. 14; Xen. *Hell.* 14.1.

58 Dio. Sic.14.27, 35; Xen. *Hell*. 3.1. Tissaphernes seems at no point to have had control over the Greek coastal cities.
59 See Lewis 1977: 137. For Pharnabazus at Dascylium and Tissaphernes at Sardis, see Xen. *Anab*. 7.6, 7. For the actions of the first Spartan general, Thibron, at Magnesia and Tralles, see Dio. Sic. 14.36. For Dercyllidas, see Xen. *Hell*. 3.1, 2. See also Lewis 1977: 140. After Cnidus, the navy could be used against Egypt as well. Xen. *Hell*. 3.4; Philochorus 328 F 144–5; Isoc. 4.142; Hell. Oxy. 19; Dio. Sic. 14.35, 79. For Tithraustes' succession after Tissaphernes' defeat, see Dio. Sic. 14.80; Xen. *Hell*. 3.4. Dio. Sic. 14.80 and Plut. *Artax*. 23 suggest that the royal mother, Parysatis, may have instigated punishment of Tissaphernes as her own revenge for her son Cyrus – a tale that smacks of Greek bias.
60 His position is rather unclear; see Kuhrt 2007: 374 n. 2. For the battle, see J. Anderson 1974.
61 Xen. *Hell*. 4.8; Xen. *Anab*. 4.4; Dio. Sic. 14.85; Plut. *Artax*. 7.
62 See Lewis 1977: 145 for this treaty.
63 Xen. *Hell*. 5.1.
64 Dio. Sic. 15.90; Briant 1996a: 675–94.
65 Weiskopf 1989.
66 For decisions referred to the king, see, e.g., Kuhrt 2007: 369, 378–80.
67 C. Gates 2005: 50. See also Ramsay 1920; Edwards 1987; Durugönül 1989, 1990, 2001; Desideri and Jasink 1990; Casabonne 1996; Blanton 2000; Durugönül, Durukan, and Aydınoğlu 2003; Ehling, Pohl, and Sayar 2004. For trade and the economy, see esp. Vann 1992; Laflı 2001a, 2001b. For Kelenderis, west on the coast near Silifke and significant, inter alia, for its role as a trade center, see Zoroğlu 1994, 1996, 2000; Zoroğlu, Arslan, Tekocak 2001.
68 Casabonne 2004: 101–80, 237.
69 Casabonne 2004: 188–223.
70 Casabonne 2004: 237.
71 Syennesis was forced to join Cyrus but immediately sent a secret message to Artaxerxes assuring him of his support (Kuhrt 2007: 360).
72 The degree of control exerted over mountain people in the empire was often significantly less than that over plains dwellers; see Briant 1982; Kuhrt 2007: 826–7.
73 Hdt. 5.52–3; Kuhrt 2007: 733–6.
74 According to Herodotus 5.52–3, between Sardis and Susa were 111 staging posts, guarding a distance of 450 parasangs. For the parasang, see Dusinberre 2003a: 13–14; see also Levi 1976; Descat 1985; Bivar 1985: 638; Tuplin 1997: 404–21. Suggested lengths of the parasang vary, but Bivar's suggestion that it was roughly 3 miles is a good average; this would mean there were way stations about every 12.2 miles. A way station of the sort described by Herodotus has been excavated next to the main road leading past Bisitun to Ecbatana in Media (Mousavi 1989). For the road between Susa and Persepolis, see Koch 1986, 1990. For possible routes in Anatolia, see Calder 1925; S. Starr 1963; Winfield 1977; Debord 1994; D. Graf 1994; French 1998. For predecessors, see Birmingham 1961; French 1997. For successors, see French 1980, 1981.
75 Briant 2002: 360–1.
76 Briant 2002: 361–4; Kuhrt 2007: 746–7.
77 Briant 2002: 364–9.
78 Kuhrt 2007: 730–1; see also 739–41, 778–82.
79 Hdt. 7.115.
80 See, e.g., Claessen and Skalnik 1978: 628; Kurtz 1981: 182.
81 For local versions of the Bisitun monument, see Kuhrt 1995a: 666–7. That from Babylon is the most striking, with its pictorial representation and local linguistic

version publicly set up (Seidl 1976, 1999, who points out that this version replaces Ahuramazda with Bel-Marduk; von Voigtlander 1978). Only an Aramaic version has been found in Egypt, which may therefore have been intended for Achaemenid chancelry usage rather than public Demotic comprehension; its discovery among the Elephantine papyri shows that the text was still being copied as late as the end of the fifth century (Sayce 1906; Greenfield and Porten 1982). For symbolic value, see Root 1991: 4, Root, forthcoming a.

82 See, e.g., DeMarrais, Castillo, and Earle 1996; M. Marcus 1995.

83 Root 1979: 309–11 explores the impact of Achaemenid artistic programs. Kuhrt 1990 explores Cyrus's exploitation of Mesopotamian iconographic and textual traditions; and see Kuhrt 1996 for the Seleucids. Exploring "top down" vs. "bottom up" ideologies are, e.g., Hays 1993; Brumfiel 1996; Alt 2001.

84 Sancisi-Weerdenburg 1990: 265.

85 Kent 1953: XV; Lecoq 1997: 263–4; Brosius 2000: no. 64; Kuhrt 2007: 301; Khatchadourian 2008: 442–5; Root 2010.

86 D. Stronach 1978, 2000 demonstrates that the inscriptions naming Cyrus at Pasargadae were in fact carved by Darius.

87 For the possibility of worshiping multiple gods, see Schmitt 2000. For the "Daiva" Inscription of Xerxes, XPh, see Abdi 2006; Kuhrt 2007: 304–6 and refs.; for the meaning of "Daiva," see Kellens 1991a, 1991b; cf. Lecoq 1997: 154–5.

88 Xerxes made a material mark on earth and water in a similarly forceful and symbolic way beyond the far end of Anatolia when he cut a canal through Mt. Athos in Chalcidice. This was such an overt power statement, rather than a necessary venture, that it elicited a furor of comment in antiquity (Hdt. 7.22–4).

89 Hdt. 7.31; Kuhrt 2007: 256; Sancisi-Weerdenburg 1994; Sancisi-Weerdenburg and Henkelman 2003. For kings and trees, see Briant 2002: 234–7.

90 Sancisi-Weerdenburg 1994; Kuhrt 2007: 251–2, 256. It is this action that also inspired Handel's aria "Ombra mai fu" that opens the opera *Serse*.

91 Hdt. 7.43. See Kuhrt 2007: 256 for the connection to Herodotus's suggestion that the Persians claimed to be invading Greece to avenge the destruction of Troy. See also T. Harrison 2002: 553 and refs.; Lenfant 2004, cited in Kuhrt 2007: 256.

92 For the alabastra, see Newton 1862–3; Moorey 1980a, 1980b. For the inscription, see Weissbach 1911: xxvi, 118–19; Posener 1936: no. 51; Lecoq 1997: XVS.

93 For royally inscribed prestige items, see Gunter and Root 1998.

94 DS 2 and DS 3 are royal name seals of Xerxes (DS 2 is bilingual in Akkadian and Old Persian; DS 3 is monolingual in Old Persian). DS 4 is a royal name seal of Artaxerxes, in Old Persian. See Kaptan 2002, 2007: 280. For royal name seals at Persepolis, see Garrison and Root 2001: 69. Garrison suggests that royal name seals at Persepolis may have indicated a type of social contract between the king and a class of administrators/individuals that was somewhat lower than the uppermost echelons (Garrison, personal communication, 2011). The importance of sealings at Dascylium is underscored by Xenophon, describing Pharnabazus's reception of Cyrus the Younger in 407 – Cyrus's assumption of military power was authorized by a sealed document from the king (Xen. *Hell.* 1.4.1–7).

95 Garrison and Root 2001: 7 n. 21, 10.

96 Kaptan 2007: 280.

97 Xen., *Anab.* 1.2.7–9; fieldwork conducted by Lâtife Summerer is contributing greatly to our understanding of this site and its role in the empire (see Summerer, Ivantchik, and von Kienlin 2011). Ceramic evidence demonstrates an earlier settlement in the Phrygian tradition, with significant Lydian influence as well; thus Xerxes augmented the site rather than founded a new one.

98 For Dascylium, see Xen. *Hell.* 4.1.15–16; Bakır 1991, 1995, 2001b, 2007; Bakır, Demir, and Tanrıver 2003; Bakır, Erdoğan, Bulut, and Yıldızhan 2004; Ateşlier 1997, 1999, 2001; Akurgal 1956. For Sardis, see Plut. *Alc.* 24.7; Dio. Sic. 14.83.4–7; Descat 1992. Magnesia on the Maeander is suggested by the letter of Darius to Gadatas, if it is not a forgery (Fried 2004: 108–18; see also Lochner-Hüttenbach 1964; Boffo 1978; Hansen 1986; Wiesehöfer 1987). The existence of other paradeisoi is extrapolated from their apparent frequency in Persia. See Briant 2002: 201–2, 441–6; Kuhrt 2007: 510–14 (including PFa 33, describing fruit seedlings to be planted in a garden in Elam), 806–8; D. Stronach 1978; Dandamaev 1984a.
99 Briant 2002: 201–2; see also Clermon-Ganneau 1921.
100 Oppenheim 1965.
101 Briant 2002: 202; Kuhrt 2007: 510–14, 806–8.
102 See Dusinberre 2003a: 70–2.
103 Although some formal gardens may have been laid out within the city's confines, that of Tissaphernes certainly lay outside the city walls. In the time of Tiribazus's satrapy, Agesilaus ravaged the paradeisos (Dio. Sic. 14.80.2): "Coming into the country as far as Sardis, he destroyed the garden and the paradeisos of Tissaphernes, which had been carefully and expensively laid out with plants and all other things that contribute to luxury and the peaceful appreciation of good things." Cyrus the Younger planned gardens at Sardis and worked on them in person, as well as showing them off to distinguished guests such as the Spartan Lysander. See Xen. *Oec.* 4.20–2; see also Cic. *De senect.* 59.
104 D. Stronach 1994a.
105 See the discussion of gardens in Briant 1996a: 98–9, 245–51, 456–9; D. Stronach 1989b, 1990. See also Tuplin 1996: 80–131.
106 Only one throne base was excavated at Pasargadae, in the Palace P portico.
107 D. Stronach 1994a: 3. For landscaping, see Boucharlat and Atai 2009: nn. 1–6.
108 D. Stronach 1994a: 9, after Weiskopf 1989: 14; see also Briant 1996a: 98–9, 245–51, 456–9.
109 Erdoğan 2007: 177–8.
110 Erdoğan 2007: 177.
111 Erdoğan 2007: 178–9.
112 For the treatment of the mound, see Erdoğan 2007: 178–9; Ateşlier 1999: 62.
113 Erdoğan 2007: 178, drawing on Ateşlier 1999: 61–4, pl. 41; Bakır 2001b: 169–70; Benli 2002: 9–13, figs. 1–5, pls. 1–7; Bakır, Demir, and Tanrıver 2003: 492–3, pl. 4; Bakır, Erdoğan, Bulut, and Yıldızhan 2004: 311–12, pls. 1–3; Coşkun 2005: 368–75.
114 Ateşlier 1999: 65–82; Erdoğan 2007: 179–80.
115 Ateşlier 1999: 65–70. Erdoğan 2007: 180 mentions an acroterion, a small Ionic votive capital, and an Ionian cyma decorated with a lotus-and-palmette frieze that may have belonged to various administrative buildings of the city.
116 For the links to Miletus and Didyma, see Bakır 1995: 274; Ateşlier 1999: 68. See also Boardman 1959 for Ionic architecture. For assertively Ionian workmanship at Pasargadae, see Nylander 1970. The Persepolis Fortification Archive includes various references to craftspeople from Lydia traveling from Lydia to Persepolis at this time (509–494) or of Lydians in the center of the empire (PF 873, 1321, 1401, 1409). For other mobile craftspeople at Persepolis, see PF 1049 (Lycians), 1799 (Assyrian), 1559 (Egyptians), 1137 (Persians), 1947 (Bactrians), 1118 (Sogdians); PT 15 (Syrians, Egyptians, and Ionians); see also DSf. Moving subject populations is, of course, a common feature of consolidating empires. For the role of colonization in moving people, see, e.g., G. Cohen 1983. For foreign populations at work in the Achaemenid Empire, see, e.g., Dandamaev 1963, 1975; Uchitel 1988, 1991.

117 Erdoğan 2007: 180–1 suggests that this was after Dascylium became the administrative center of its own province, Hellespontine Phrygia.
118 For the archive building, see Coşkun 2005: pls. 19, 22, 23; tables 4, 6. For remnants of buildings reused in a (Hellenistic?) terrace wall, see Ateşlier 1999: 85–109; Coşkun 2005: 340–4.
119 For the suggestion, see Erdoğan 2007: 183. For the fragments, Ateşlier 1999: 113; Coşkun 2005: 360–1. For mention of Dascylium's satrapal residences, see Xen. *Hell.* 4.1.15, 4.1.33; Hell. Oxy. 22.3.
120 For nonmonumental (and non-elite) structures, see Erdoğan 2007: 183–5 and Chapter 4, this volume.
121 Halim Korucu, personal communication, 2011; Karaosmanoğlu 2009; Karaosmanoğlu and Korucu, forthcoming. Paintings continued to be discovered in 2007; for earlier publications and their similarity to the Achaemenid painted hall at Arin-Berd, see Özgüç 1963: 44–5, 1966: 46.
122 Karaosmanoğlu 2009: 353.
123 Summers 1993: 94.
124 Summers 1993: 96.
125 Summers 1993: 96; for the "Erzincan" material, see Dalton 1964: nos. 178–86.
126 Summers 1993: 96. For the bars (ingots?), see Barnett and Gökçe 1953: 121.
127 For the pots, see Summers 1993: 87–88 and Chapter 4, this volume.
128 See, e.g., DeVries 1996: 447, 2005: esp. 36, 44; Voigt and Young 1999: 220–36.
129 R. Young 1953: 11–14, fig. 10; Dusinberre 2005: no. 33; see also Dusinberre 2008a.
130 R. Young 1953: 11, 14, fig. 10.
131 For tiles and potsherds, see Gordion Fieldbook 30: 133 and Glendinning 1996: 23–5. For the building's date, see Glendinning 1996: 23; Sams 1994: 825; Roller 1991: 134 n. 37. For the seal, see Dusinberre 2005: cat. no. 33; Gordion Fieldbook 30: 133.
132 Glendinning 1996: 23–4.
133 Glendinning 1996: 24.
134 Gordon Fieldbook 30: 133.
135 Dusinberre 2010a.
136 Dusinberre 2008a: 92. For Persian names, see, e.g., Mayrhofer 1973.
137 Dusinberre 2005: 12–14, 24–6.
138 Dusinberre 2008a; see also Chapter 7, this volume.
139 For the Attic pottery at Gordion, see DeVries 1977, 1988, 2000, 2005; Sams 1979. For local production, see Henrickson 1994, Kohler 1980. For the status of Gordion during the Achaemenid period, see Voigt and Young 1999.
140 Facella 2009: 397–8.
141 Facella 2009: 398–9.
142 Lemaire, http://www.achemenet.com/cappadoce13.pdf, with refs.
143 Kuhrt 2007: 859–63.
144 Note, too, the Pherendates correspondence from fifth-century Egypt, which is in Demotic but shows underlying Aramaic usage (Kuhrt 2007: 853); other evidence from Egypt also demonstrates people familiar with local vernaculars working in satrapal offices (Kuhrt 2007: 727–9).
145 For Dascylium seals, see Kaptan 2002; for Sardis, Dusinberre 2003a; for Seyitömer, Kaptan 2005; for Gordion, Dusinberre 2005; for İkiztepe, Özgen and Öztürk 1996; for Patara, Işın 2007; for Dülük Baba Tepesi, Facella 2009.
146 Kaptan 2002: 14; see also Balkan 1959; Kaptan 1990, 1996, 2007.
147 E.g., DS 68 (thirteen impressions with smooth backs, two impressions with papyrus impressions on the back) and DS 85 (all four impressions with smooth backs).

148 Kaptan 2002: 22–3.
149 Kaptan 2007: 280, fig. 1.
150 For the options, see Dusinberre 1997 and refs.; see also Leith 1990, 1997; Bregstein 1993, 1997; Kaptan 2002. For similar issues in Assyria, see Herbordt 1992.
151 See Chapter 8; M. Miller 2011, drawing on Röllig 2002: 209. The ethnicities represented by inscriptions on the Dascylium sealings include Iranian, Semitic, and Babylonian. See Gusmani and Polat 1999; Lemaire 2001 for these inscriptions and those on the stelae from the area.
152 Kaptan 2001: 58. For the languages, see Schmitt 2002. See also Bakır and Gusmani 1991, 1993.
153 Kaptan's "Achaemenid Persian *koine*," Kaptan 2005. For the difficulties with what used to be called "Graeco-Persian," see esp. J. Gates 2002. See also Maximova 1928; Richter 1949, 1952; Nikoulina 1971; Dusinberre 1997.
154 M. Miller 2011.
155 M. Miller 2011, drawing on Kaptan 2002: 36, 113; Schmitt 2002: 197.
156 For the Sardian tombs of the Achaemenid period, see Dusinberre 2003a: 128–57, 239–63; Roosevelt 2009: 135–84. For the tombs in general, see McLauchlin 1985.
157 As of 2011, only one seal has been found at Sardis that might predate the Achaemenid period, from a mixed context in the city itself. Whether these numbers mean few seals were used previously or that Lydians chose not to be buried with them, this change is significant. That the seals were used by the elite is demonstrated not only by their material but by associated grave goods; see Dusinberre 2003a.
158 Pyramidal stamp seals: IAM 4521, 4522, 4525, 4527, 4528, 4578, 4579, 4580, 4589, 4591, 4592, 4641, 4642, 5133, 5134; weight-shaped seals: 4523, 4524, 4590; cylinder seals: 4532, 4581, 4643; rings with gold bezels: 4548 (bezel undecorated), 4585, 4636, 4637; rings with stone bezels: 4519, 4520, 4632, 4633 (sealing surface of scarab undecorated), 4634, 4635, 4639; bracelet: 4518; necklace: 4640. Materials include blue chalcedony, carnelian, and gold (C. D. Curtis 1925).
159 For the status of at least one seal user at Sardis, see Dusinberre 1997; for the impact of the style, see Dusinberre 1997: 109–15, 2003a: 158–71, 264–83. Not all high-status people at Persepolis used seals with Achaemenid court imagery, including Parnaka (PFS 9* and 16*, Garrison and Root 2001) and Gobryas (Garrison and Root, forthcoming b). For early roots of Achaemenid visual styles, see, e.g., Amiet 1972b, 1973a, 1973b; Calmeyer 1973, 1975, 1976, 1978, 1992, 1996; Bollweg 1988.
160 For these seals, see Özgen and Öztürk 1996: 95–103, 198–9; Kaptan 2007. For follow-up excavations in the tumuli, see Akbıyıkoğlu 1991, 1993, 1994a, 1994b, 1996.
161 Kaptan 2007: 280, fig. 1.
162 See, e.g., Işın 2007; Kaptan 2005.
163 See Dusinberre 1997, 2010a, 2010b for discussion and bibliography; see also Kaptan 2002, 2007.
164 This phenomenon was not limited to the Achaemenid Empire; see Gorelick and Gwinnett 1990.
165 See discussion and overview in Dusinberre 2005, 2008a and refs.
166 It is important to note that most of the Achaemenid-period seals from Gordion were found in Hellenistic-period deposits – the number is probably too great to be accounted for by residuals and suggests that a number of Achaemenid tombs may have been found and looted during the Hellenistic period.
167 For the mobility of craftspeople, see, e.g., Zaccagnini 1983.
168 See Root 1997a; Garrison and Root 2001; Garrison 2008.

169 See Dusinberre 2003b.
170 For Lydia, see Cahill and Kroll 2005; Günther 2006; Wallace 1988, 2006. For Ephesus, see Weissl 2002, 2005; Wallace 2006. These are primarily electrum coins, but Cahill and Kroll demonstrate that pre-Achaemenid purified metal coins existed in Lydia before the Achaemenid period saw widespread distribution of gold and silver coins.
171 Thus C. Harrison 2002; see also Sheedy 2009 and cf. Kolata 1992.
172 For darics, see Carradice 1987b. See also Babelon 1893; Hill 1922; Kraay 1976; Vickers 1986a, 1986b; Seyrig 1959; Noe 1956; E. Robinson 1947, 1958, 1960; Schlumberger 1953; Descat 1989; Naster 1962; Price 1989; Root 1988, 1989; D. Stronach 1989a.
173 Plut. *Artax.* 20.
174 For an analysis of these artifacts as tokens of royal esteem, see Nimchuk 2002.
175 For a discussion of the archer types and the possible figures they may portray, see C. Harrison 1982: 14–38; see also D. Stronach 1989a. The identification of the figure in the winged disk is disputed; it may represent Chvarnah, or Fate, rather than Ahuramazda. See overview in Garrison, forthcoming.
176 Carradice 1987a: 93.
177 The coins are thought to have been minted in Anatolia because of inscriptions on some of them naming western satraps as well as their preponderance in coin hoards found in Anatolia. See Carradice 1987b. They have sometimes been considered evidence of satrapal autonomy: Imhoof-Blumer 1885; Babelon 1893; Schwabacher 1957, 1968; Mørkholm 1959, 1974; Seyrig 1959b; Richter 1965; Thompson 1965; Metzler 1971; Mørkholm and Zahle 1972, 1976; Cahn 1975, 1985; Bodenstedt 1976; Kraay 1976; Hurter 1979; C. Harrison 1982a, 1982b. For their use, see Thompson 1965.
178 Hdt. 1.132.1, 3.12.4, 5.49.3, 7.66.2, 8.120; Xen. *Cyr.* 8.3.13; Strabo 15.3.15, 3.19. Most of the heads are in profile; an issue of the Lycian dynast Kherei shows the head in three-quarter view. See Erhart 1979; Cahn 1975.
179 Debate has raged for years about the identity of the individual(s) represented on the tiarate coins. See, e.g., Imhoof-Blumer 1885: 4–5, 24; G. Jenkins 1959, 1972; Schwabacher 1968; Olçay and Mørkholm 1971; Mørkholm and Zahle 1972; Cahn 1975; Kraay 1976: 271; Mørkholm and Zahle 1976: 85; Hurter 1979; C. Harrison 1982a; Cahn 1985. C. Harrison 1982a: 81–96 includes a detailed summary and discussion of scholarship on these issues.
180 Mørkholm and Zahle 1976.
181 Schwabacher 1968: 116.
182 See Casabonne and Gabrielli 2007.
183 Kraay 1966: pl. 184, nos. 621, 622, 623. For the impact of these and related coins, see, e.g., Vismara 1996, 1999, 2007.
184 See Root 1979: 227–84, esp. 279–82, on "Median" garb.
185 See Dusinberre 2003b.
186 Sekunda 1988; his extension draws on the comprehensive explanation of Persian land-grant systems in Briant 1985a; see also Briant 1985b.
187 Mentioned also in M. Miller 2011. For Pythius, see Hdt. 7.28; for Zenis and Mania, Xen. *Hell.*, 3.1.10–15. Miller also cites Maffre 2007b: 119–21.
188 "Proskynesis" means to kiss the hand before, not to prostrate. See Frye 1972. It is illustrated on the Treasury reliefs from Persepolis (the original central panels of the Apadana facades); Oriental Institute P 57121.
189 For horses at Persepolis, see Gabrielli 2006; Tuplin 2010; Azzoni and Dusinberre, forthcoming.

190 M. Miller 2011, citing Mellink, Bridges, and di Vignale 1998: pl. XXI, Guide sheet B; Borchhardt and Bleibtreu 2008: 178 (saddle cloths); Waldbaum 1983: cat. no. 86; Bakır 1995: 276; Curtis and Tallis 2005: cat. no. 387 (bridles); Metzger 1963: pl. 38.2; Zahle 1991: 151 (in-hand); Nollé 1992: stele 1; Sevinç, Rose, and Strahan 1999; Roosevelt 2009: figs. 6.27, 6.28 (hairstyle).

191 For Lydian horsemanship, see Greenewalt 2010b. Greenewalt 1971 published a "trick vase" from Sardis, shaped like a rider with a phallus-shaped spout, that probably dates to the Achaemenid period.

192 For bits, see Moorey 1980a: nos. 227, 228, 229 (and comparanda from across the empire); for bell, no. 233 (with comparanda).

193 Although some evidence suggests that by the second or third quarter of the sixth century western Anatolian horsemanship might have included a similar positioning of the head, it is certain that Achaemenid-period representations regularly do. For an architectural terracotta showing a horse rearing up with its nose tucked from Düver in Pisidia, dating to sometime around the middle of the sixth century, see Greenewalt 2010b: fig. 5; Glendinning 1996: 114; see also Hostetter 1994.

194 For the speed of adoption, see M. Miller 2011.

195 See, e.g., Hdt. 7.134–7, 8.5, 9.18, etc.; Xen. *Oec.* 4.7, 4.8; Xen. *Anab.* 1.9.14–22. See also Mauss 1966; Briant 2002: 304–7.

196 Cahill 1985; Sancisi-Weerdenburg 1989, 1998.

197 Xen. *Cyr.* 8.2.7–8; translation from Briant 2002: 305.

198 For drinking cups, see Gunter and Root 1998; for dress, see, e.g., Hdt. 3.84; for horses with golden brides, gold jewelry, and a gold dagger, see Xen. *Anab.* 1.2.27; for the hierarchy of royal gifts, see Briant 2002: 305.

199 Kuhrt 2007: 641.

200 Briant 2002: 305–7.

201 Root 1979: 279–82.

202 For the weight, see Aelian *VH* 1.22; for the significance, see Appadurai 1986; Gunter and Root 1998.

Three: Controlling Anatolia, Guarding the Empire

1 Providing familiar food is another aspect of helping people feel at home, and I believe we see this not only in the stores of U.S. military bases abroad, where such items as Cornflakes®, Pop-Tarts®, and Oreos® can be purchased, but also in the regularized diet consumed by Roman soldiers. For the Roman military diet, see, e.g., Davies 1971; Knights et al. 1983; King 1984; Groenman-van Waateringe 1989; Bowman et al. 1990. R. Curtis 1991 and the Vindolanda tablets emphasize a common military diet different from, and differentiated from, local norms (see http://vindolanda.csad.ox.ac.uk). For the role of diet in assimilation, see, e.g., Meadows 1994. I am grateful to Jacob Morton, graduate student at the University of Pennsylvania, for these references. I have been unable to learn anything about the diet of the Achaemenid army in Anatolia, but this is an important subject for future study.

2 For this site see Roosevelt 2009: 118–22 and refs., 240–2 and refs.

3 Roosevelt 2009: 119–20. For northeastern Lydia in general, see Debord 1985.

4 Roosevelt 2009: 121.

5 Roosevelt 2009: 121.

6 It is largely thanks to Tuplin 1987b, 1988, 2010 that this chapter is possible at all.

7 Tuplin 1987b: 168.

8 Xen. *Cyr.* 8.6.14. See Tuplin 1987b: 170, passim; Briant 2002: 67.

9. Tuplin 1987b: 170 clarifies: "In *akrai* both the commander *and his men* belonged to the King, whereas in the *khora* the most that one could say was that the chiliarchs were 'of the King' in that they were directly appointed by him" (emphasis in original).
10. Tuplin 1987b: 170.
11. For this suggestion, see Tuplin 1987b: 171; see also Briant 1986a.
12. For the cavalry's importance, see Tuplin 2010. Horses eat between 1.5 and 3% of their body weight daily, of which 75% or more must be forage – this equals roughly 9,000 lb. of hay per year for a 1,000-lb. horse. See Azzoni and Dusinberre, forthcoming.
13. Xen. *Anab.* 1.1–3.
14. Most extensively studied in Tuplin 1987b, 1988.
15. Tuplin 1987b: 172.
16. Tuplin 1987b: 173.
17. Tuplin 1987b: 174.
18. Stolper 1985; Briant 2002: 405; Kuhrt 2007: 715–17.
19. Kuhrt 2007: 716 n. 5.
20. Babylonian tablet, Dar. 253; Joannès 1982: 18; Briant 2002: 405; Kuhrt 2007: 715. For cress, see Stol 1985.
21. Babylonian tablet, BE X, no. 61. Joannès 2000: 150; Kuhrt 2007: 716.
22. Babylonian tablet, BM 33928. Abraham 2004: no. 75; Kuhrt 2007: 716.
23. See, e.g., Cowley 1923: 2.5. 24.39, 43.8, 2.16, 11.6.
24. See, e.g., Cowley 1923: 80.5; Tuplin 1987b: 225.
25. Cowley 1923: 5.9, 13.10, 20.10, 46.6.
26. Stein, forthcoming.
27. For Mysia and Paphlagonia, see Briant 2002: 643. For literary and epigraphic evidence, see Xen. *Anab.* 7.8.8–22; Dittenberger 1903–5: 264, ll. 6–9.
28. Briant 2002: 643.
29. M. Miller 2011.
30. Hdt. 5.102. Amélie Kuhrt (personal communication, 2010) suggests that these were not necessarily ethnic Persians, but people settled by the regime on land subject to military duties.
31. For the *phrouria*, see Strabo 12.2.2–7; for the *castella*, see Nepos *Dat.* 4.2. For the existence of seventy-five Hellenistic forts, see Briant 1978–9: 62; Balcer 1984: 201; for a caution about extending their existence earlier, see Tuplin 1987b: 212.
32. I do not consider here the well-known ethnic multiplicity of the army that invaded Greece under Xerxes (see, e.g., Briant 2002: 533–542; Sekunda 1992). Here I focus rather on those troops regularly available for service in Anatolia. For Persian presence in the western satrapies, M. Miller 1997: 91–97.
33. E.g., Xen. *Anab.* 1.2.
34. This is ambiguous in sources such as Xen. *Anab.* 1.3.
35. E.g., Xen. *Anab.* 1.2.
36. Tuplin 1987b: 220. See also Marek 2006.
37. Stein, forthcoming.
38. For these, see Tuplin 1987b: 219–20, with evidence for more Iranians at Eion, Byzantium, Gaza, and Memphis.
39. Briant 2002: 352.
40. Babylonian officers at Elephantine include, e.g., Nabukudduri and Iddinabu; see Cowley 1923: 7.35, 20. For the Persian conquest of Elephantine, see, e.g., Burkard 1995; see also Briant 1996b.
41. For these, see Tuplin 1987b: 221 and refs.

42 Briant 2002: 507. Similarly, the peoples at Elephantine include Persians, Medes, Caspians, Khwarezmians, Egyptians, Jewish Aramaeans, and Babylonians. For interesting religious interactions, see Briant 1996b.
43 Xen. *Anab.* 7.8.8–22. The passage is discussed in detail in Tuplin 1987b: 213, 219–22.
44 For Comania, see Sekunda 1985: 5; Tuplin 1987b: 213.
45 Tuplin 1987b: 222 suggests that the Assyrians and Hyrcanians represent a special class of mercenary soldier with a particular relation to the king, while the other troops consist of mercenaries of a different sort.
46 For Tissaphernes, see Thuc. 8.85.1–2; for Pigres, see, e.g., Xen. *Anab.* 1.2. Other resources for the presence and role of interpreters are collected in Kuhrt 2007: 847–9.
47 If so, it might be an element in the discovery at Dascylium of three Semitic names on stelae: Elnap, Adda, and Pedaya. See Gilliam 1965 for the role of the army in Romanizing the Greek East; doubtless the Achaemenid army also played a role in acculturation.
48 Hdt. 8.98.
49 Xen. *Anab.* 7.8.7–22; see also Hinz 1979: 146; Briant 2002: 500.
50 Arist. *De mundo* 398.
51 Strabo 15.3.18.
52 Briant 2002: 371.
53 Tuplin's interpretation, although slightly different from mine, forms its foundation; see Tuplin 1987b: 174–5.
54 See discussion in Lewis 1977; Briant 1982; Hornblower 1982; Tuplin 1987b, 1988.
55 For this, see, e.g., Briant 1973a: 80–3, 1973b: 97–8, 1982: esp. 211; Hornblower 1982: esp. 1–34; Balcer 1984: 211–12; Tuplin 1987b.
56 Tuplin 1987b: 207 collects instances from Hellespontine Phrygia and Lycia, as well as Cappadocia; he concludes his extensive discussion, "The Iranian element in the local military establishments of Western Anatolia extended beyond a small social elite." See also Gabrielli 2006; Casabonne and Gabrielli 2007; Baughan, forthcoming, with refs.
57 See Garrison and Root 2001; Dusinberre 2008a.
58 For images on the Persepolis Fortification Archive, see Garrison 2000; Garrison and Root, forthcoming a. For the Persepolis Treasury Tablets, see Schmidt 1957: PTS 28–31. The "archer" coins, both darics and sigloi, are well known, and to these we may add those of Tarsus, Phaselis (considering an armored prow to signify the military), the tiarate head coins discussed earlier, and the coins of Lycian Antiphellus (indeed, the change of these from the tiarate heads to the fighting warriors on the coins of Pericles lends support to the interpretation of the tiarate heads suggested in the text). The seals are also common; for a selection, see Boardman 1970a: 881–3; Casabonne and Gabrielli 2007: figs. 1–5.
59 Hdt. 1.136. See also Briant 1998b.
60 DNb §2h, 2i; XPl; Kuhrt 2007: 505.
61 See, e.g., Dolunay 1967; Nollé 1992: nos. S3, S4, S5, S6 (?), S7, S8, FI, FII, FIV, FV; Mellink, Bridges, and di Vigale 1998: pls. 16, 27, 28, 30, 31; Maffré 2007a: 229–33; Rose 2007: figs. 12, 13, 14; Summerer 2006b, 2007a, 2007b, 2010; Roosevelt 2009: figs. 6.27, 6.28, 6.29, 6.30.
62 See Mierse 1983: 46–47; Dusinberre 2003a: 47–56; Ratté 2011.
63 Hdt. 1.91.
64 Xen. *Ages.* 1.33.
65 Discussed in a talk delivered in April 2009 by Nicholas Cahill, director of excavations at Sardis. I am grateful to Cahill for sharing the transcript of his talk with me. The contrast with Lydian-era houses is great; see Cahill 2002.

66. Hdt. 1.152–3.
67. Hdt. 5.100–1 for Artaphernes; 5.102 for the reserves.
68. Arist. *Analyt. post.* 94a.
69. For Hamadan/Ecbatana, see Sarraf 1997: 40–1; Brown 1997; Boucharlat 1998, 2005. For Persepolis, see Mousavi 1999.
70. Arr. 1.17.
71. Dusinberre 2003a: 46–57 and refs.
72. Briant 1993, 2002: 843.
73. For the stronghold, see Hell. Oxy. 22.3; for the garrison, see Arr. 1.17.2.
74. Erdoğan 2007.
75. For the increase in habitable area, see Ateşlier 1999: 62; for defensibility, see Erdoğan 2007: 179.
76. Erdoğan 2007: 181–2.
77. Erdoğan 2007: 179.
78. For Meydancıkkale, see esp. Davesne and Laroche-Traunecker 1998; Briant 2001: 47–51; Casabonne 2004: 151–65; C. Gates 2005: 62–3.
79. Davesne, Lemaire, and Lozachmeur 1987: 379–81; Davesne and Laroche-Traunecker 1998: 280; C. Gates 2005: 63.
80. Davesne, Lemaire, and Lozachmeur 1987; Laroche-Traunecker 1993; Casabonne 1998: 200–8; Davesne and Laroche-Traunecker 1998; C. Gates 2005: 63.
81. Casabonne 2004: 153–7, drawing on Laroche-Traunecker 1993: 19, 21; Wuttmann, Laroche-Traunecker, and Courtois 1998: 118–19; Davesne and Laroche-Traunecker 1998. For the date of the gate, see Casabonne 2004: 154–5; for the magazines, which may be post-Achaemenid, see 156–7.
82. Kirshu appears in the Neo-Babylonian Neriglissar Chronicle as a fortified city with a palace belonging to Appuashu, king of Pirindu; it was burned by Neriglissar in 557, but Appuashu managed to escape. See Grayson 1975: no. 6; Laroche and Davesne 1981; Davesne, Lemaire, and Lozachmeur 1987: 377, 379; Casabonne 2004: 153; C. Gates 2005: 63.
83. Casabonne 2004: 161 n. 655; for the palace at Vouni on Cyprus, see Nielsen 1994: 58; Buitron-Oliver and Herscher 1997.
84. For the sculptures, see Davesne and Laroche-Traunecker 1998: 295–306; Casabonne 2004: 157–8.
85. Casabonne 2004: 158.
86. Davesne, Lemaire, and Lozachmeur 1987; Laroche and Davesne 1981; also Hermary 1984; Casabonne 2004: 157–8. For audience scenes, see, e.g., Gabelmann 1984; Kaptan 1996; D. Stronach 2002. For the gesture and its meaning, see Root 2007.
87. For the suggestion, see Roosevelt 2009: 121.
88. Roosevelt 2009: 121.
89. Habicht 1975: 73; Robert 1982, 371–3; Sekunda 1985: 25; Malay 1992: 118; Şahin 1998: 86; Roosevelt 2009: 120.
90. Foss 1975; Roosevelt 2009: 120, 199, 242, fig. C.21, and refs.
91. For the finds, see Roosevelt 2009: 240–2 and Chapter 5, this volume.
92. Roosevelt 2009: 271 n. 43; parallel published in D. Stronach 1966: 226, fig. 19.
93. D. Stronach 1966 published physical examples; Moorey 1979 published illustrations of fire altars on Achaemenid seals, now augmented by the Fortification sealings. For a comprehensive overview, see Garrison 1999.
94. Quote from Roosevelt 2009: 120.
95. Described by C. L. Woolley and T. E. Lawrence in various letters and publications, summarized in Moorey 1980a: 1–4. Finds were sold to a Madame Koch, to various dealers in Aleppo, and to Woolley and Lawrence, who were working at nearby

Carchemish. They purchased and sent artifacts from Deve Hüyük to England, where they were distributed among five museums and collectors. See Moorey 1980a: i–ii, 1–10.
96 Moorey 1980a: 8.
97 E.g., Tuplin 1987b: 204. See Chapter 5, this volume, for further discussion of ethnicity.
98 Moorey 1980a: 10. For imported pots and their significance, see Carter and Parker 1995.
99 Roosevelt 2009: 117. See also Lane 1975; Foss 1979, 1982, 1987, 1993; Meriç 1985, 1986, 1987a, 1987b, 1988, 1989a, 1989b, 1991, 1993; Meriç and Nollé 1985; Malay 1987, 1994, 1999; Bengisu 1994, 1996; Bingol 1998. For the importance of the landscape, see, e.g., Cosgrove 1984; Cosgrove and Daniels 1988; Bekker-Nielsen 1989; Basso 1996. Textual sources include Hdt. 5.35; Xen. *Anab.* 1.9.13, 4.6.11, 5.6.7; Strabo 13.4.5; and see the epigraphic evidence published by Littmann 1916; Herrmann 1970, 1986, 1991, 1996, 1997; Petzl 1976, 1978, 1985, 1994, 1996, 1998; Ihnken 1978; Petzl and Pleket 1979; Herrmann and Keil 1981, 1989; Naour 1981; Malay and Nalbantoğlu 1996.
100 Marksteiner 2005: 37. See also Marksteiner 1997a: 187–91, 1999: 317–21.
101 Fuensanta and Charvat 2005: for Sultantepe, 162; for Altıntepe, 164.
102 Marksteiner 2005: 37–8; for the Greeks' discussion of tower houses, see Balcer 1984: 211–12, 1985: 31–5 Tuplin 1987b: 176.
103 Marksteiner 2005: 38.
104 For the "Persian habitation," see Aston 1999. For the "Aramaean quarter," see von Pilgrim 1998; Vittmann 2003. For the site in general, see Grelot 1964, 1972; Kaiser et al. 1975, 1990; Aston 1999; Briant 1996b; Porten 1998; von Pilgrim 1998; Chauveau 1999; Azzoni 2000, forthcoming; Vittmann 2003. The Kharga Oasis, with its temple supported by Darius I, was surely garrisoned in Achaemenid times, as it was both earlier and later, although at this point there is no archaeological evidence for it.
105 Wuttmann and Marchand 2005: 103.
106 Wuttmann and Marchand 2005: 105, 114.
107 Achaemenid fortresses have been excavated at Shiqmona (Elgavish 1968), Tel Michal (Herzog 1989), and Ashdod (Porath 1974). See Tal 2005: 81–2, fig. 7.
108 Francfort 1979, 1985, 2005: 328–34; see also Knauss 2006.
109 Xen. *Anab.* 7.8.12–15, trans. Perseus Project.
110 Tuplin 1987b: 235–6: "The Hell. Oxy. text is an important corrective to Xen. *Hell.* 4,1,15–40, where the description of Daskyleion and the account of Pharnabazos' 'nomadic' response to Agesilaos' incursions does nothing to suggest that Daskyleion was a stronghold. The claim of M. Weiskopf, Achaemenid Systems of Governing in Anatolia, Berkeley [Diss.] 1982, 50 that the oikemata in Xen. *Hell.* 4,1,33 could be fortified strongpoints in the Dascylium region is not particularly attractive."
111 Tuplin 1987b: 236: "Ilion, Skepsis and Kebren are also, in Dem. 23,154 f. and Ps.-Arist. *Oec.* 1351b19 f., *khoria* held, and perhaps garrisoned, at various times from the late 360s until (?) late 350s by Memnon and Mentor as agents of Artabazos, sometimes loyal to the King."

Four: Eating and Drinking with Class and Style

1 Douglas and Isherwood 1978; Weissner and Schiefenhövel 1996; Garnsey 1999; see esp. Bray 2003: 3.
2 See also Brewer and Porter 1993; Kistler 2010.

3. See, e.g., Lewis 1987: 80. The meals of Alexander are said by Athenaeus to have cost as much as those of the Persian king: Lewis 1987: 81.
4. Polyaen. *Strat.* 4.3.32, trans. Kuhrt 2007; he was a second-century Macedonian author best known for his work on military tactics. For the likely overall veracity of this list, see Lewis 1987; Briant 2002: 286–92. See Henkelman 2010 for a discussion based largely on the Fortification Archive.
5. Ath. 4.145e.
6. Hdt. 1.118 (cf. 7.83).
7. Briant 1994a.
8. Sancisi-Weerdenburg 1997a, 1997b.
9. I am indebted to Jacob Morton for drawing my attention to the following features of the Greek accounts.
10. PF 298 (Hallock 1969).
11. E.g., PF 337, 338, 339, 353, 767, 769 (Hallock 1969). Henkelman 2010: 685–6 points out that the differences between the ingredients given in Greek sources and those we can understand from the Fortification Archive reflect the concentration of the archive on cultured products (including honey), whereas the Classical sources also list wild or gathered ingredients.
12. Henkelman 2010: 671, 673 n. 14.
13. Morton (personal communication, 2009) suggests that the meats might have been an either/or option rather than a gourmande extravaganza that included all of the varieties every day. Even if cows were smaller in antiquity, Morton points out, so that a yearling weighed only about 600 lb., they would provide 300 lb. of edible meat apiece, or 30,000 lb. altogether – enough for each of the 15,000 people Athenaeus mentions (4.146c) to have consumed 2 lb. of meat from the cattle alone on a daily basis. It was Morton who created a scrumptious "Persian Duck" meal from the ingredients listed by Polyaenus (http://ancientfoodstoday.blogspot.com).
14. Henkelman 2010: 678–82, 685; for differences in quantity, 686–9.
15. Ath. 13.608a.
16. Ath. 4.145b.
17. Henkelman 2010: 671–2 reiterates this point as underscored in the Persepolis Fortification Archive. See also Briant 2002: 293.
18. Thus Polyaenus, as quoted earlier, says the king fed his soldiers; Athenaeus (4.146c) reported, "Every day the royal table fed 15,000 people"; Herodotus (7.119) differentiates between those who ate with Xerxes in his tent and those who remained without. See also Henkelman 2010: 670–2.
19. Hdt. 9.82; Briant 2002: 294–7.
20. Henkelman 2010: 686 (emphasis in original).
21. E.g., Ar. *Acharn.* 72–3: "And those pitiless Persian hosts! They compelled us to drink sweet wine, wine without water, from gold and glass cups." See also Hdt. 1.188, 7.190, 9.80; Xen. *Cyr.* 5.2.7; Xen. *Anab.* 4.2.27, 4.4.21. See discussion in Simpson 2005: 104.
22. Simpson 2005: 105–7.
23. Simpson 2005: 108. For the processes used by Anatolians in purification and the techniques used to create the vessels, see Toker and Öztürk 1992: 15–18; Greenewalt 2010a.
24. Ctes. *FGrH* 688 F 40.
25. Hdt. 7.119; trans. A. de Sélincourt.
26. Wiessner 1996: 6.
27. Hdt. 1.133.
28. Cahill 1985; Gunter and Root 1998.

Notes to Pages 120–126

29 Razmjou 2004a argues that these are ritual items.
30 Lewis 1990: 1; Henkelman 2010.
31 For Gobryas, see Lewis 1977: 4–5, 1984: 595; for Parnaka, see Lewis 1990: 2; Garrison and Root 2001: 92–4, 404–6. For the logistics involved in transporting this kind of quantity of food, see Hunt 1987.
32 Against redistribution, see Lewis 1990: 2; cf. Heracleides of Cumae (*FGrH* 689 F2), a fourth-century historian, who comments on the large amounts of food that served as wages and prestige markers at the Persian court, and the number of personal retainers each recipient was supposed to support via his payments in food. Quoted in Kuhrt 2007: 610–11. When the wealthy stop feeding those under their care, awful things can happen; see Clarkson and Crawford 2001.
33 Hallock 1969: 5.
34 Hallock 1969: 6.
35 Lewis 1990: 2.
36 This was not unique to Persia in the ancient Near East; Damerow 1996: 149 shows that in Uruk rations "were deliberately scaled to rank, and that rationing had economic and power dimensions."
37 See Dietler 1996: 91–2 for this role of hospitality; see also Spielman 2004.
38 Dietler 1990, 1996; see also Wiessner 1996.
39 Dietler 1996: 89.
40 See, e.g., Wiessner 1996: 8; Hayden 1996: 129–30.
41 See Halstead and Barrett 2004: 7.
42 Halstead and Barrett 2004: 8.
43 Wills and Crown 2004: 163.
44 Vickers and Gill 1994; Vickers 1999.
45 Potter and Ortman 2004: 174.
46 Halstead and Isaakidou 2004.
47 Gero 2003: 285.
48 Halstead and Barrett 2004: 8.
49 Bray 2003: 5; see also Counihan 1999: 9.
50 See Goody 1982; van Keuren 2004. Bray 2003: 6 suggests that this may be due to the time women spent in food preparation and presentation, time that could therefore not be invested in other social activities such as political or ceremonial events where power and status were negotiated.
51 See Dietler and Hayden 2001: 10 for instances of gender distinction in feasting behaviors, including those of a spatial, quantitative, qualitative, and social nature.
52 Jellinek 1977; Jennings and Bowser 2009: 1, 3; Douglas 1987: 4.
53 McGovern 2009: xiii.
54 Murray 1991: 83.
55 Murray 1991: 86.
56 Burkert 1991: 7.
57 See Spycket 1980; Cannon 1989, 1991.
58 See Henrickson 1993, 1994, 2005; Sams 1979, 1994; deVries 1977, 1980, 1988, 2000.
59 Henrickson 1993: 132–3.
60 Henrickson 1993: 133–9.
61 Henrickson 1993: 139.
62 Henrickson 1993: 141.
63 Henrickson 1993: 144–7, nn. 173 and 174, with extensive refs.; Henrickson 1994: 113.
64 Henrickson 1994: 113; Henrickson 1993: 147–8, n. 188.

65 Dusinberre 1999, 2003a.
66 There is not yet evidence to confirm that these cooking pots – of the Lydian or Achaemenid periods – were made at Sardis. This point is significant: perhaps people obtained their cooking pots from a different source in the Achaemenid period. See Berlin 1998.
67 Dusinberre 2003a: ch. 8.
68 T. C. Young, personal communication, 1994; see also Young 1965.
69 T. C. Young, personal communication, 1996, 1997; see also Young 1969. At Pasargadae, 142 of the total 340 vessel shapes from the Achaemenid and Hellenistic periods are bowls (D. Stronach 1978). For Median Baba Jan, see Meade 1969; Goff 1977, 1978. For Nush-i Jan, see Roaf and Stronach 1973, R. Stronach 1978.
70 Henrickson 1994; deVries 1977, 1988, 2005.
71 See, e.g., Gürtekin 1996; Görkay 1999; Tuna-Nörling 1999; Gürtekin-Demir 2002, 2003. For imported wares at Sardis, see Schaeffer, Ramage, and Greenewalt 1997.
72 Summers 1993.
73 Dietler 2003: 271–2.
74 Hdt. 1.133.
75 For beer, see, e.g., PF 353, Xen. *Anab.* 4.5.
76 Garrison and Root, forthcoming a. Garrison counts thirty-two seals on the Elamite tablets published by Hallock with figures holding drinking cups; he estimates that twice as many were impressed on the rest of the archive (personal communication, 2011). Note that banqueting scenes in Persepolitan glyptic show seated rather than reclining drinkers; see Lissarrague 1990. For royal banqueting in the post-Achaemenid period, see Nielsen 1998.
77 See Calmeyer 1993, who contrasts distinction of dress with conformity of vessels. See also Melikian-Chirvani 1993; Simpson 2005: 104–6; M. Miller 2007: 68–9. Sideris 2008: 339 discusses the difficulty of defining a specific "court toreutic" as opposed to elite style. This difficulty is all the more important in the current discussion, as it highlights the similarity of elite metal wares. The importance of shape as a signifier of elite status is made amply clear in the tomb paintings of Petosiris, which show high-value vessels in use in a high-status context; see Lefebvre 1924. For the importance of consistent imagery in Achaemenid Palestine, see Nunn 1996.
78 See, e.g., Collon 1992.
79 Ebbinghaus 2005.
80 See Ebbinghaus, 1999, 2000, 2005, 2008a, 2008b; Summerer 2003. See also Santrot 1996 for examples from Armenia and Marazov 1998 for examples from Thrace.
81 Simpson 2005: 107.
82 PFS 535* is one of the best illustrations of an animal-protome rhyton at Persepolis; see Garrison and Root, forthcoming a. Ebbinghaus 2000 explores one of the most famous examples from Anatolia and its connotations.
83 The various bowl shapes have been a subject of extensive study. See, e.g., Iliffe 1935; Fossing 1937; Matz 1937; Luschey 1939; Dohen 1941; Gjerstad 1953; Hamilton 1966; Hestrin and Stern 1973; Moorey 1988; M. Miller 1993; Yağcı 1995; Dusinberre 1999.
84 An extensive bibliography exists on glass bowls of the Achaemenid period. See, e.g., Hogarth 1908; Fossing 1937; van Saldern 1959, 1975; Barag 1968; Oliver 1970; Vickers 1972; Roos 1974; Goldstein 1980; Grose 1989; Stein and Schlick-Nolte 1994; Ignatiadou 2002, 2005. For the bowl from Ephesus, see Hogarth 1908; for two clear glass phialae from Mylasa, see Yağci 1995. For examples from Iran, see Gunter and Root 1998; Curtis and Tallis 2005: no. 113.

85 By "cups" I mean all three shapes. The inscription on the Artaxerxes phiale in the British Museum specifically refers to it as a wine-drinking cup; see Gunter and Root 1998.
86 M. Miller 2007 offers the best discussion of the phenomenon; the wine cups from İkiztepe show specific combinations and variations of imagery that demonstrate Anatolian provenance for their manufacture and, she argues, the origin of their users. "[I]t is now clear that emulation of the Persian model caused them to adopt these signifiers of wealth and status in their own lives. Yet their imitation admitted creative innovation and reciprocity: interculturation perhaps rather than acculturation" (69). See also M.-H. Gates 1994, 1999, 2001; Clark 2004.
87 M. Miller 2009.
88 The presence of precious-metal vessels in tombs is, of course, partly a matter of archaeological recovery of behavioral deposit. It need not mean that silver vessels were used only as grave goods. It does, however, show that drinking paraphernalia were considered appropriate for burial, perhaps as part of a commensal ceremony for the dead.
89 Waldbaum 1983: nos. 963–9; see also Greenewalt, Ratté, and Rautman 1993: 35–7.
90 Oliver 1971. For the tombs, see McLauchlin 1985; Dusinberre 2003a.
91 Dusinberre 1999: table 2.
92 M. Miller 2009. Silver and bronze long-handled ladles with animal-head terminals were also part of the banqueting repertoire; as collected by M. Miller 2009, these include examples from Hellespontine Phrygia (Sevinç, Rose, and Strahan 1999; Özgen and Öztürk 1996: fig. 125) and from Lydia, including Sardis (Waldbaum 1983: no. 965), Gökçeler Köyü (Özkan 1991: 133), İkiztepe (Özgen and Öztürk 1996: nos. 24–31), and Aydın (Amandry 1963: 264). See also Moorey 1980b, Simpson 2005: 106 and refs. For the shock of outlandish behavior at banquets, see M. Miller 1991.
93 See Simpson 2005: 104–6 for the point that the cups become especially precarious if filled with wine above the point of carination.
94 These cups are illustrated and discussed, along with issues of provenance, in Chapter 5. The examples from Lydia are probably best known at this time; see Özgen and Öztürk 1996, Özkan 1991: 132–3; Roosevelt 2009. The appeal these vessels held for the elite, and their use by the elite, extended beyond the borders of the empire; Ignatiadou 2008: 337–8 discusses their discovery in elite Achaemenid-period tombs in Macedon and Thrace; findings include silver or glass examples from Sindos, Vergina, Chalcidice, and Archontiko (all late sixth century), Cozani (fifth century), Nikesiane, Derveni, and "many rich burials" (Late Classical).
95 For klinae, see Baughan 2004, 2008, forthcoming. For banqueting assemblages from Lydian tombs, see Baughan 2008: 287–92. For the suggestion that drinking vessels in tombs are the result of cultic activity, see Carstens 2001. For Mesopotamian antecedents, see Reade 1995.
96 Karaburun II; see Mellink 1971: 250–5, 1972: 263–9, 1973: 297–301, 1974: 355–9, 1978: 805–9, 1979a: 484–95. Stella Miller-Collett is completing the final publication of the tomb and its paintings.
97 See Chapter 5; the image of reclining is widely spread in western Anatolia in the Achaemenid period, being found at Karaburun near Elmalı in Lycia, on funerary stelae from Dascylium and Ödemiş, and at Altıntaş and Çavuşköy to the east, as well as to the south on the "satrap sarcophagus" from Sidon. For Dascylium, see Chapter 5. For other sites in Anatolia, see Dentzer 1969, 1971, 1982. For the Satrap Sarcophagus, see Winter 1894; Kleemann 1958. See also Booth 1991.
98 See Khatchadourian 2008: 452 for the suggestion that conviviality that makes use of specifically charged objects connected the subjects of a "unifying imperial world, while at the same time serving instrumental ends for local leaders."

99 Dusinberre 1999: table 2, 2003a: 190–1. Bowls, rather than rhyta, were generally used for drinking wine in Achaemenid Sardis. Like the silver Achaemenid bowls, metal ware rhyta were copied in local clays in other areas, however; see, e.g., Iranian examples in Kawami 1992: nos. 141–4; Ebbinghaus 2000, 2005, 2008a. An early discussion of the phenomenon in Iran and the northeastern parts of the empire can be found in Cattenat and Gardin 1977. See also the discussion of Athenian adoption and adaptation of Iranian ceramics in Miller 1997: 135–53 for rhyta.
100 Costin 1991.
101 Dusinberre 1999: 78, 2003a: 189 n. 42. For the continued production of the cups into the third century even in the face of an overarching shift to new Hellenistic ideas, see Rotroff and Oliver 2003: 60–2.
102 M. Miller 2011, citing Özgen and Öztürk 1996: fig. 67; Roosevelt 2008: 21; Mellink 1971: 250; Toteva 2007: 120.
103 Dusinberre 1999.
104 For Dascylium, see Bakır 2001b: 174; for Gordion, Henrickson 1993, 1994 and author's observation; for Karaçallı in Pamphylia, Çokay-Kepçe and Recke 2007. For southeast Turkey, see Facella 2009: 393–4.
105 Sagona and Sagona 2004.
106 Xen. *Anab.* 4.5.
107 Sagona and Sagona 2004: fig 118, nos. 8 and 9.
108 Summers 1993: figs. 6, 7 for "Triangle Ware" and cups; fig. 6.3 has a characteristically carinated rim, while figs. 4 and 6 most resemble the Achaemenid bowls from western Anatolia.
109 *BMCR* 2004.02.21, review of Dusinberre 2003a.
110 J. Butler 1999.
111 J. Butler 1999: 135–63.
112 In this, Butler uses Derrida's theory of iterability; J. Butler 1993: 95.
113 J. Butler 1999: 171–90.

Five: Dealing with the Dead

1 Binford 1971; Wiessner 1996: 4–5.
2 A careful consideration of "Persianness" in western Anatolia has recently been undertaken in M. Miller 2006, 2011.
3 Opened in 1910–14 and 1922; Greenewalt 1972: 115 n. 5. Information about the form of these graves comes from brief descriptions on object cards written by G. H. Chase in 1914 and T. L. Shear in 1922. For a recent discussion, see Baughan 2010; see also McLauchlin 1985; Dusinberre 2003a; Baughan 2004.
4 Baughan (2002–4, 2004) has shown that my earlier suggestion, that tombs with benches necessarily dated to the Achaemenid period rather than earlier, is wrong; for the Achaemenid date of multiple-interment tombs, see Baughan 2010.
5 Dusinberre 1997.
6 See H. Butler 1922: nos. 43, 23A, 720; McLauchlin 1985: 55–78, 97–108, 215–25; Ratté 1989: 94 n. 3; Roosevelt 2009: 139.
7 Roosevelt 2009: 140.
8 Roosevelt 2009: 140.
9 See Dusinberre 2003a; Baughan 2010. For terracotta sarcophagi, see Evren 1985. For bronze sarcophagi from Assyria, see J. Curtis 1983.
10 Tallon 1992; Harper, Arus, and Tallon 1992. For the significance of the bathtub sarcophagus at Hacınebi, see Stein, forthcoming.

11 Baughan 2010: 299.
12 Roosevelt 2009: 148. See also Duyuran 1973; Dedeoğlu 1991, 1992, 1994, 1996; Bilgin, Dinç, and Önder 1996.
13 Kökten 1998; Baughan 2010: 279. For wheeled vehicles, see Littauer and Crouwel 1979; Nagel 1986.
14 Roosevelt 2006, 2009: 142–8.
15 Baughan 2010.
16 Roosevelt 2009: 149.
17 See in general McLauchlin 1985: 126–39. For the Tomb of Alyattes at Bin Tepe, see Greenewalt, Rautman, and Meriç 1986: 20–2. Roosevelt 2009: 153 notes that six phalli have been found atop tumuli, and the findspots of another thirty-seven are consistent with original siting on a tumulus.
18 For the Tomb of Alyattes, see Greenewalt 1972: 128 n. 12; von Olfers 1858: 547; Hanfmann 1963: 55; McLauchlin 1985: 171–4; Ratté 1989b: 157–62, 2011. For BK 71.1, see Ramage 1972: 11–15; McLauchlin 1985: 197–200; Ratté 1989: 189–95, 2011. See also Baughan 2004.
19 McLauchlin 1985: 156–8. Another example of ash above the chamber of a tumulus tomb is found at İkiztepe: Özgen and Öztürk 1996.
20 MM6277 and MM5225, respectively.
21 Kökten 1998; Baughan 2010: 280.
22 Roosevelt 2008; Stinson 2008; Baughan 2008.
23 Roosevelt 2008.
24 Stinson 2008.
25 Baughan 2008: 58.
26 For Harta, see Özgen and Öztürk 1996: 36–9.
27 Özgen and Öztürk 1996: 38.
28 See Root 2007.
29 Özgen and Öztürk 1996; Özgen 2010. See also http://www.smithsonianmag.com/history-archaeology/Loot-Chasing-the-Lydian-Hoard.html; Tezcan 1979; Akbıyıkoğlu 1991, 1993, 1994a, 1994b, 1996.
30 Stein, forthcoming.
31 For this sarcophagus and its contents, see Roosevelt 2009: 209–10 and bibliography.
32 M. Miller 2007.
33 Baughan 2010: 283.
34 Any attempts to interpret the symbolic or actual use of these objects must be made with caution; this discussion is prefatory.
35 Pasztory 1989.
36 Illustrated in C. D. Curtis 1925.
37 For the lydion, see Greenewalt 1972: 132–33; for its contents, see Rumpf 1920: 165–7; Roebuck 1959: 56. The association of scented oils with banqueting in Greece is clear, and it is likely they were associated in Anatolia also.
38 For the latter suggestion, see Baughan 2010: 296.
39 For examples of such stamps, see Özgen and Öztürk 1996.
40 For the rosette-and-lotus motif, see Dusinberre 2003a. For the suggestion that Sardis was the first locus of appliqué production in western Anatolia, see Meriçboyu 2010: 163. For the significance of appliqués, see Oppenheim 1949; Roos 1970.
41 The appliqués are probably inadvertent mortuary inclusions, there not for their own sake but because of the cloth to which they were attached. For the importance of this, see, e.g., Weiss 1996.
42 Of the seventy-nine tombs listed in Dusinberre 2003a, fully eleven, or 14%, included gold clothing appliqués. This number is certainly an underrepresentation,

as tomb robbers would have removed a disproportionate amount of gold from the graves. Appliqués from the Uşak tombs, illustrated in Özgen and Öztürk 1996, show the same styles and themes: Baughan 2010; Özgen 2010. For dress codes as identity markers, see, e.g., Wobst 1977: 317.

43 See, e.g., C. D. Curtis 1925; Özgen and Öztürk 1996; Öztürk 1998; Meriçboyu 2010.
44 For Udjahorresne, see Chapter 2, this volume; for Ptah-hotep, see Kuhrt 2007: fig. 13.5; Cooney 1953; Bothmer 1961: no. 64; Posener 1986; Jansen-Winkeln 1999: 163–72.
45 Many "Neo-Babylonian" stamp seals were impressed on the Persepolis Fortification tablets, deep into the reign of Darius, and there is a strong likelihood that many of those used at Persepolis are *new* products, not holdovers from before 539. The complexity of stylistic deployment among people at Persepolis shows that it is over-simplifying to call these seals "Neo-Babylonian." See Root 1998; Garrison and Root, forthcoming a.
46 For "Neo-Babylonian" seals at Persepolis, see Root 1998.
47 For duck's-head finials on jewelry and dining implements from Pasargadae and Persepolis, see D. Stronach 1978; Sami 1955; Schmidt 1957.
48 See also the association of lion-shaped pins with women at Hasanlu: M. Marcus 1990, 1993, 1994. At Persepolis, aggressively masculine imagery is deployed on the royal woman Irdabama's seal (PFS 51) with its hunting scene, while that of the queen Irtashduna (PFS 38) shows the royal hero controlling human-headed quadrupeds. For PFS 38, see Garrison and Root 2001: 83–85; for PFS 51, see Garrison and Root, forthcoming a.
49 A third stone, IAM 4633, with a silver mounting over its base, may have been carved in intaglio, but the silver is now too corroded to be certain.
50 Dusinberre 2003a: 244.
51 Boardman 1970b: 39, pl. 5.
52 See Garrison 1991; Garrison and Root 2001.
53 McLauchlin 1985: 115–16; Roosevelt 2009: 153.
54 See esp. Waelkens 1986; Roosevelt 2006.
55 Roosevelt 2009: 153.
56 Waelkens 1986: 14, 15, 18.
57 Büsing-Kolbe 1978; Waelkens 1986: 24–6; Roosevelt 2006.
58 Roosevelt 2009: 153, fig. 6.18 (a), (b). Examples come from İkiztepe, Sardis, Ertuğrul, and Kennez, among other places.
59 Three examples have been published: one in the Ödemiş Museum and two in the Tire Museum. Roosevelt 2009: cat. nos. 18.8, 25.3–4; see also Roosevelt 2006.
60 See Hanfmann 1976, 1978; Ratté 1994a; Roosevelt 2009: 155–6. For one from Miletus, see von Graeve 1989, who also includes a general bibliography on anthemion stelae; see also Kurtz and Boardman 1971: 220. "East Greek" anthemion stelae are collected in Pfuhl and Möbius 1977 (esp. nos. 3, 12, 20); cf. Buschor 1933; Comstock and Vermeule 1976: 15–16.
61 Ratté 1994a: 15–16.
62 Roosevelt 2009: 155.
63 Dusinberre 2003a: Ch. 5, App. 2; Roosevelt 2009: 155. For Sardis, see, e.g., Buckler 1924.
64 Dusinberre 2003a: Ch. 5. Use of the masculine gender here is a generalization.
65 See Dusinberre 2003a: App. 2.
66 Gusmani 1986: no. 1; Kahle and Sommer 1927; Donner and Röllig 1966–9: no. 264; Dusinberre 2003a: no. 9. The Lydian inscriptions are collected in Gusmani 1964, 1979, 1985, 1986. For Artemis of Coloe, see Merkelbach 1991.

67　For inscriptions of Darius I at Naqsh-i Rustam and Artaxerxes III at Persepolis, see Schmidt 1970.

68　Actual representations on the royal tombs are different and very specific; see B. Anderson 2002 for royal resonances in Nabataea. No physical evidence exists at this point for nonroyal elite burials in Fars, but the Fortification Archive provides evidence for ceremonies at the tombs of Hystaspes, Phaedyme, and Cambyses, as well as of someone called Zišunduš (Henkelman 2003). Given the lack of any burials of Persian aristocrats in the center of the empire, we cannot assess how mortuary treatment at Sardis may parallel or diverge from those.

69　The earliest funeral stele does not conform to the type of the later sculptures. It is an inscribed stele with a proposed date of 520–500 and shows a man seated at a table, holding writing implements (Manisa 1: Hanfmann and Ramage 1978: 55–56). The inscription names the owner of the stele one Atrastas, son of Sakardas. The portrayal of a seated man is unique at Sardis. Banquet stelae include NoEx 77.15 and IAM 4030.

70　Roosevelt 2009.

71　For funerary banqueting, see Dusinberre 2003a; Baughan 2004. Three examples of reclining banqueters are known from rural Lydia; see Roosevelt 2009: 157–8.

72　Roosevelt 2009: fig. 6.20.

73　Fully five stelae show such scenes: Roosevelt 2009: 161–4. Note that Roosevelt 2009: fig. 6.20 shows the quintessentially Achaemenid animal combat with lions hunting an ibex. Roosevelt 2009: fig. 6.26 shows a man standing to the right, wearing a cloak over the garb of a horseman: knee-length tunic, trousers, and boots. For the importance of hunting in Greece, see, e.g., J. Anderson 1975; Andronikos 1984.

74　From Incesu and Haliller; see Roosevelt 2009: 158–9. Those with standing figures are from Gökçeler and Musacalı in the middle Hermus valley (Roosevelt 2009: 160).

75　See Roosevelt 2009: 241–2 and bibliography for the grave(s), looted in 1968 and again in 1970.

76　Roosevelt 2009: 160 suggests the figure is male. He points out a similarly composed stele in Boeotia, as well as similarities in artistic style both to Ionian sculptural workshops and to the Apadana reliefs at Persepolis.

77　No garment on the Apadana looks like that worn by this figure. Glyptic examples show elegant, fully clothed females.

78　Lions have been found at Birgi, Akselendi, Soma, Turgutlu, Sivrice, Beyoba, Lâle Tepe, Manisa, Hierakome, Akhisar, Selçikli, Soma-Altınlı, and Gördes, with the lion-griffin found at Kula. See Strocka 1977; Anabolu 1979; Roosevelt 2009. For lions from near Pergamum, see Radt 1996. For the lion-griffin, see von Gall 1999.

79　H. Butler 1922: 167–70; Hanfmann 1961: 31, 1962: 28–30; Hanfmann and Waldbaum 1970: 36–38; Ratté 1989: 206–15, 1992.

80　Ratté 1989: 212–14, 1992, 2011.

81　D. Stronach 1978: 17; Nylander 1970.

82　Ratté 1992: 152–4.

83　For Taş Kule, see Cahill 1988 and refs.

84　Cahill 1988: 496–8. See also Tritsch 1943; Roos 1971; Mellink 1979b; Waelkins 1980a, 1980b. See Waelkins 1986 for a full collection and study of Anatolian doorstones as funerary monuments that appear during the Achaemenid period; their meaning is debated (Waelkins 1986: 17–19). Most recently, see Roosevelt 2006.

85　Cahill 1988: 492–3.

86　Cahill 1988: 495.

87　Hanfmann 1974: 299; Hanfmann and Erhart 1981. See also N. Ramage 1979.

88　Hanfmann and Erhart 1981: 89.

89 Hanfmann and Erhart 1981: 86, 89.
90 Hanfmann and Erhart 1981: 89.
91 For the Athenian tribute lists, see IG³ and Meritt, Wade-Gery, and McGregor 1939–53. For an essential updated edition of the tribute lists, see Paarmann 2007; see also Greaves 2010.
92 For Clazomenae, see R. Cook 1981: 142.
93 R. Cook 1974, 1981: 142.
94 Johansen 1942; Byvanck 1948; R. Cook 1966, 1974, 1981: 148.
95 Rumpf 1933: 67; Johansen 1935: 182–8; Åkerström 1966: 129–30, 208, 231–2; R. Cook 1981: 150. See also Böhlau and Schefold 1940. For the building identified as a palace at Larisa, probably rather a hestiatorion, see Schefold 1978.
96 R. Cook 1981: 153–4.
97 E.g., R. Cook 1981: pl. 22. The notion that the sarcophagi suggest different identities and priorities from those of the inland inhabitants does not mean there was no Achaemenid impact on the Greek colonies, of course; see, e.g., Baslez 1986.
98 Their other "Ionian" examples are largely of uncertain provenance or are from across the Bosphorus or the Aegean Islands.
99 Möbius and Pfuhl 1977: nos. 82, 84. Another Attic creation of ca. 330 was found at Sinope: Möbius and Pfuhl 1977: no. 80.
100 Möbius and Pfuhl 1977: no. 97.
101 Möbius and Pfuhl 1977: no. 92. For mixed identities in Athens itself, see Allen 2003.
102 Möbius and Pfuhl 1977: no. 93.
103 For Ephesus, see Möbius and Pfuhl 1977: no. 94; for Miletus, see Möbius and Pfuhl 1977: no. 95. For the Attic origin and date of the Milesian head, see Kleiner 1968:127.
104 For the tumuli, see Rose 2007; for settlement patterns in general, see Sekunda 1988. For estates, see Rose 2007: nn. 7, 8.
105 For burial couches, see Baughan 2004. For sarcophagi, see, e.g., Sevinç 1996b; Sevinç, Rose, and Strahan 1999; Sevinç et al. 2001; Rose 2007. For a chamber with painted decoration, see Sevinç et al. 1998.
106 For the estates, see Özgen and Öztürk 1996: 19–35; Roosevelt 2003. For the siting and significance, see Ramage and Ramage 1971; Roosevelt 2009. For ethnicity, see, e.g., Rose 2007.
107 Rose 2007: 248.
108 Rose 2007: 249.
109 Sevinç 1996a, 1996b; Geppert 2006; Rose 2007. See also Hitzl 1991; Steuernagel 1998. For other graves in the Troad, see, e.g., Seeher 1998.
110 For Greek imagery, see Oakley and Sinos 1993, cited in Rose 2007: 251.
111 Rose 2007: 249; for the type of cart, see Kökten-Ersoy 1998.
112 Rose 2007: 252.
113 See Rose 2007: 256.
114 Neer, personal communication, 2011.
115 As Rose 2007: 252 notes, this child "suffered from Cribra Orbitalia, a syndrome possibly connected to anemia brought on by malaria (Stuart-Macadam 1992)." For the contents of the sarcophagus, see Rose 2007: 252–3.
116 Rose 2007: 253. For this tumulus, see also Sevinç et al. 1998.
117 Rose 2007: 253.
118 Rose 2007: 254.
119 Rose 2007: 254.
120 Rose 2007: 254.

121 Rose 2007: 255.
122 See, e.g., Akurgal 1966, 1974, 1990; Dolunay 1967; Bernard 1969; Möbius 1971; Altheim-Stiehl, Metzler, and Schwertheim 1983; Cremer 1984; Altheim-Stiehl and Cremer 1985; von Gall 1989; Nollé 1992; Polat 1994, 2001, 2007. For two anthemion stelae from Perinthus and one from Dascylium, see Bruns-Özgan 1989: pl. 32.1–2, Akurgal 1986: pl. 86; For Dascylium, see Pfuhl and Möbius 1977: no. 5; Metzler, Altheim-Stiehl, and Schwertheim 1983. For another stele from the Troad, see Comstock and Vermeule 1976: no. 23. A stele in the Bergama museum is published in Radt 1983. See also L'vov-Basirov 2001.
123 For the names, see Röllig 2002; Schmitt 2002; and refs.
124 Karagöz 2007.
125 Kohler 1980. For additional Phrygian tumulus burials, see, e.g., Atasoy 1974; Dörtlük 1977, 1988, 1989, 1990; Aslan 1989; and esp. Kohler 1995. For a Cappadocian tumulus, see Coindoz 1985. For the phenomenon of cremation across Anatolia, see Buluç 1993.
126 http://sites.museum.upenn.edu/gordion/history/achaemenid.
127 R. Young 1951: 17.
128 R. Young 1951: 17.
129 R. Young 1951: 19.
130 For other flat reliefs, see, e.g., Polat 2007.
131 For Ankara, see Koenigs and Philipp 1987; for Dorylaeum, Pfuhl and Möbius 1977: no. 2.
132 For Tatarlı, see Summerer 2007a and refs.; the beams of the tomb are in Afyon and Munich. See also Uçankuş 1979, 2002.
133 Summerer 2006b: 17.
134 Summerer 2007b: 21.
135 Dönmez 2007: 107.
136 For the most recent comprehensive discussions of Paphlagonia in the Achaemenid period, see Glatz and Matthews 2009; Johnson 2010. See also Summerer 2005 for a specific artifact and the intercultural connections it demonstrates.
137 Dönmez 2007: 108. Waelkens 1986: 26 believes that this notion of an eternal house as grave began in Phrygia and suggests that the Paphlagonians elaborated on that tradition.
138 Dönmez 2007: 109 and refs.
139 Donceel-Vôute 1984: 101–8, pl. 5, 2.3.4, cited in Summerer 2003: 20.
140 Durugönül 1994: 1–14; Summerer 2003: 20. See the latter's n. 34, in which she argues contra Durugönül that the register with armed men shows a Pyrrhic dance rather than a combat.
141 Durugönül 1994: 17 suggests that these reliefs may reflect the paintings that once adorned the inner walls of tumulus tombs, of which there are many in the area.
142 Amandry 1953, 1959; Akurgal 1967. One unanswered question is whether cities like Sinope, founded by Greeks, were themselves part of the satrapy; for an overview of this problem, see Summerer 2003: 17–20.
143 For Ankara 57-1-66, see Akurgal 1967; Summerer 2003: 22 connects it also to the Oxus Treasure, at the eastern edge of the empire.
144 First published Amandry 1953–4: 11–19. Summerer 2003: 21 compares them to the Lydian Treasure and describes their sale to the collector Hélène Stathatos in 1935 by the onetime conservator at the Istanbul Archaeological Museums, Théodor Macridy. The vessels are now in the National Museum in Athens.
145 Summerer 2003: 21–4.
146 Summerer 2003: 24–5.

147 Other examples of Achaemenid metalwork nominally from the central Black Sea area, including animal-protome rhyta, amphora-rhyta, and amphorae with animal handles, are known through the art market; see Summerer 2003, 2006a.
148 Belli 1989; Tarhan 2007:119 and refs.
149 Tarhan 2007: 120. See also Tarhan and Sevin 1994: 848–9, figs. 7, 11, 12; Tarhan 1994: 40–1, 42, 53. For continuities from the Urartian into the Achaemenid period, see Seidl 1994.
150 Tarhan 2007: 122–3 and refs.
151 Ussishkin 1994; Burney 1995; Çevik 1997; Tarhan 2007: fig. 1.
152 Burney and Lang 1971: 182; Sevin 2005: 92: both quoted in Tarhan 2007: 124.
153 For Altıntepe, see Forbes 1983: 59; Summers 1993: 85–96; Dönmez 2007: 110.
154 For the Oxford beaker, AN 1967.819, see Vickers 2000: 263, fig. 2. For the Erzincan material, see Curtis and Tallis 2005: nos. 104, 106, 107, 108, 109, 119 and refs.
155 Treister 2007.
156 http://faculty-web.at.northwestern.edu/anthropology/stein/HNoverview.html.
157 http://faculty-web.at.northwestern.edu/anthropology/stein/HNexcavationsHell.html; see also Stein, forthcoming.
158 McMahon 1996, 1997; see also http://faculty-web.at.northwestern.edu/anthropology/stein/HNfindsHellenistic.html.
159 Moorey 1980a: 7–9; Tal 2005: 87–8; M. Miller 2011. See also Bonatz 2000.
160 For a complete catalogue, see Moorey 1980a: vessels, 11–49; weapons and harness, 50–73; seals, 105–27; ornaments, 74–93; toiletries, 94–9; terracottas, 100–4. For comparanda from Palestine, see Amiran 1972, 1981; and cf. Howes Smith 1986.
161 Moorey 1980a: 160–3; he draws primarily on Woolley's records (Woolley 1914–15: 117–20) and points out that Woolley did not record a "grave group 12" – hence, the numbers 1–25 preserve information for twenty-four graves. There were, of course, far more graves excavated at Deve Hüyük; these grave groups indicate those Moorey could isolate, not all those that originally existed.
162 Moorey 1980a: 160–3. Figure 104 includes all objects from Grave Group 1 illustrated in Moorey 1980a. The full description of the group is as follows: "Bronze bowl, type 2, Pl. XXI, found under the head; two fibulae, types D and K, Pl. XXIII; two bronze rings, one plain, with flat inscribed bezel; two bronze bracelets with tripartite heads; suspended from the neck a chalcedony conoid seal of Late Mesopotamia type, pl. XXIX; two very rough clay pots, one of bottle shape, one squat with almost straight sides slightly turned out to the rim" (Moorey 1980a: 160, quoting Woolley). Figure 105 includes all objects from Grave Group 15 illustrated in Moorey 1980a. The full description of the group is as follows: "Small bronze bowl (diameter 0.12 m) of unusual type, a gadrooned base being soldered on to an already complete vessel of type 2, giving effect of type 1, Pl. XXI; two small bronze aryballoi (broken), Pl. XXII, 1; a bronze kohl-stick; a small bronze bell, complete with clapper, Pl. XXII, 27; several bronze bracelets, plain; a silver bracelet and a decorated pin, Pl. XXII, 13; a few beads of mosaic glass; a ram's head in glass of different colours, Pl. XXIX, 1; five small plain clay vases, viz., a feeder (Pl. XXVII, 13), an aryballos, and two oenochoae (Pl. XXVII, 9)" (Moorey 1980a: 162, quoting Woolley). Figure 106 includes all objects from Grave Group 20 illustrated in Moorey 1980a. The full description of the group is as follows: "Plain bronze bowl, type 2, Pl. XXI; fragments of second bronze bowl, apparently a patera; large bronze spoon, Pl. XXII, 8; large fibula, type G, Pl. XXIII; three bronze rings, corroded together; plain bronze anklet; small bronze bell, cf. Pl. XXII, 27; bent bronze rod; three plain bronze kohlsticks; two plain bronze rings; a bronze pin; iron spearhead, type E, Pl. XXV; silver earring (broken) with granouillé work;

steatite spindle-whorl; a few mixed beads; the lower part of an Attic b.f. lecythus, with design of cross hatching and fine wreath in black on a white ground; a black cylinder, engraved; a plain scaraboid" (Moorey 1980a: 163, quoting Woolley).

163 Moorey 1980: 10, passim.
164 Baughan 2010: 298.
165 PFS 38 (Irtashduna) and PFS 51 (Irdabama) are discussed earlier in the chapter. By the same token, PFS 77* depicting a seated courtly female is used by a man on the Fortification tablets (Garrison and Root, forthcoming a).
166 Lemaire 1993, 1994, 2004; Sayar 2000, 2007; see also http://www.achemenet.com.
167 For local cults, see Sayar 2007. Moons and stars are also popular on Babylonian stelae and are found on almost all "Neo-Babylonian" seals of the Fortification Archive; see Root 2008.
168 Gibson 1975: no 33; Hanson 1968: 3–5; Donner and Röllig 1966–9: no. 258; Lipinski 1975b: 146–7; Teixidor 1986: 452–3; Torrey 1915: 370–4.
169 Karagöz 2007: 201, fig. 20.
170 Özsait and Özsait 1990, 2007.
171 Özsait and Özsait 2007: 160.
172 Özsait and Özsait 2007: 160–2. Sphinx-type figures moving to the right in stately and magnificent isolation are known in seal impressions on the Fortification Archive as well as the glyptic of Anatolia; see Garrison and Root, forthcoming b; Dusinberre 2010a.
173 I will not treat here the gnarled question of "influence" but will instead consider these monuments in the context of what they might tell us about Achaemenid Lycia. For influence as a unidirectional cultural modality, see, e.g., Richter 1959; for stylistic influence wielded as a power tool, see Jacobs 1987.
174 Jacobs 1987: 65–7, 70. Jacobs includes nonmortuary reliefs in his analysis, but even mortuary remains alone make his point clear.
175 The dating of all Lycian monuments is disputed, as illustrated by a single example. The Lion Tomb has been assigned a date of 600 (Pryce 1928; Richter 1959), 560 (Demargne 1958), and 540 (Akurgal 1941; Rudolph 2003). The later dates are based on the notion that a lag existed between the time particular stylistic features appeared in Athens and the time they showed up in Lycia. Akurgal's magisterial discussion remains the most extensive discourse on the tomb, and Rudolph supports the Achaemenid date.
176 Two fairly recent books deal extensively with these tombs: Marksteiner 2002b: 246–91; Rudolph 2003. Earlier discussions include Akurgal 1941; Tritsch 1942; Zahle 1975b, 1983. Most recently, see the excellent discussion in Draycott 2007.
177 Keen 1992: 53. The more recently suggested dating of the pillar tomb at Isında to ca. 550 places this monument potentially before the Achaemenid period (Özhanlı 2002); if correct, it shows that pillar tombs are explicitly pre-Achaemenid Lycian in type.
178 For ivory furniture inlays with animal scenes from Nimrud, see, e.g., Mallowan 1966; Barnett 1982; G. Herrmann 1986, 1992, 1996. For models of furniture, see Cholidis 1992.
179 For the date, see Rudolph 2003. For the monument, see Tritsch 1942: pls. 1–4; Berger 1970: l. 148; Zahle 1975b: fig. 7; Boschung 1979: figs. 2–3. For the reliefs and their interpretation, see Jacobs 1987: 45–7; Rudolph 2003. Most recently, see Froning 2004. For the furniture on which figures sit, see, e.g., Kyrieleis 1969; Himmelmann 1986; Jamzadeh 1996; Nunn 2000; see Paspalas 2000a for related furniture in Macedon. The meaning of the audience scenes is much debated, but they indisputably recall those at Persepolis. See esp. Jacobs 1987: pl. 6, 2.

180 Rudolph 2003: 34; I. Jenkins 2006: 155.
181 This is disputed, and many think it was erected for his successor Kherei; see I. Jenkins 2006: 155.
182 For Lycia as "south Ionia," see Rudolph 2003: 8, passim.
183 Draycott 2007.
184 Draycott 2007: 128.
185 See also Borchhardt 1976, 1999; Rudolph 2003: 42–53.
186 Childs 1979: 97; Gygax 2001; Gygax and Tietz 2005.
187 I. Jenkins 2006: 155–6.
188 For the inscription from a Persian perspective, see Herrenschmidt 1985.
189 DPd-g.
190 Childs 1978.
191 See I. Jenkins 2006: 156, n. 32.
192 See Demargne 1974.
193 A. Smith 1900; Slatter 1994.
194 Jacobs 1987.
195 Curtis and Tallis 2005: 46 interpret this figure as "probably the satrap Autophradates," but it is possible the enthroned personage was Payava.
196 The famous tombs of Myra, for instance, are in two groups: one above the theater and the other in the so-called river necropolis at the east side of the town. See Borchhardt 1975; Kjeldsen and Zahle 1975; Bryce 1979. For the importance of size, style, and siting, see Keen 1995.
197 Already demonstrated by the nineteenth century; see Benndorf and Niemann 1884: 110; also Roos 1989. Waelkens 1986: 25 includes a discussion of those that reflect domestic architecture, and see Işık 1996; Cavalier 2002.
198 Marksteiner 2005: 36; Wörrle 1996–7: 27.
199 Hanson 1968: 3–5; Donner and Röllig 1966–9: no. 262; Lipinski 1975b: 162–71; Kuban 1996: 133. See also Blakolmer 1988, 1993, 1999; and contributions to Blakolmer et al. 1996.
200 Investigation of these tombs started in 1970. See Mellink 1971, 1972, 1973, 1974, 1975, 1978, 1979a; Mellink, Bridges, and di Vignale 1998. Stella Miller-Collette is overseeing the final publication of Karaburun II. For additional Lycian tumulus tombs, see, e.g., Zahle 1975a; Marksteiner 1994.
201 Mellink, Bridges, and di Vignale 1998: 55.
202 Mellink, Bridges, and di Vignale 1998: esp. 57, 63.
203 Mellink, Bridges, and di Vignale 1998: 57–64; for Troelus, see 58.
204 M. Miller 2011.
205 Briant 2002: 672–3 stresses that much of this is about local competition.
206 As detailed in the trilingual Letoön inscription from Xanthus, for which see http://www.achemenet.com. For dedications made by Erbbina, with geographic and historical background, see Rhodes and Osborne 2003: 58–63.
207 Although it has been suggested that it may be the earliest tomb with a temple facade (Roos 1989: 68), the banquet pediment from Sardis certainly predates it.
208 For the Heroon at Limyra, see, e.g., Borchhardt and Schiele 1976; Borchhardt 1996–7. For the Nereid Monument and other relief sculptures, see esp. Coupel and Demargne 1969; Childs and Demargne 1989; see also British Museum 1900; Borchhardt 1968, 1980, 1983; R. Martin 1971; Demargne 1976; Nieswandt 1995; T. Robinson 1999; Ebbinghaus 2000.
209 For the parasol and its importance, see M. Miller 1992; Muscarella 1999.
210 Root 1979. See also Borchhardt 1997, 2004; for the importance of costume, see Borchhardt 2007.

211 Roos 1985: 8, passim, 1989, 2006; Carstens 1999.
212 Roos 1985: 50. For the shifting nature of that boundary, see, e.g., Lohmann 1999; Behrwald 2000.
213 Roos 1972, 1985: 51, 2006: 64–5. "I know of no Carian rock-cut chamber-tomb that must be dated before 400 B.C." (Roos 1989: 63). See also Bean 1978, 1979, 1989.
214 See, e.g., Roos 1972: 36, 93, 1985: 50–1.
215 Its reconstruction is uncertain and contested; for a version with a stepped pedestal that resembles the Tomb of Cyrus, see Waywell 1978. For excavation reports, see Danish Archaeological Expedition, 1981–1997. For a recently discovered and spectacular tomb, see Özet 1994; Prag and Neave 1994.
216 For the Mausoleum, see Jeppesen et al. 1981–2004.
217 Pliny *NH* 36.5.
218 See Chapter 2, this volume; Moorey 1980b; Kuhrt 2007: fig. 7.4.
219 If this is true, it helps illuminate Alexander's choice to have himself portrayed in a very similar manner a few decades later.
220 We do not know how the Persian king might have responded to local dynasts setting themselves up as gods. Certainly no action seems to have been taken against Mausolus.
221 Carstens 2002: 403.

Six: Worshiping the Divine

1 The essential nature of religion as a system of values and behaviors that define a society is outlined in Geertz 1973.
2 Garrison, forthcoming: summation. For earlier approaches to Achaemenid religion, see, e.g., Boyce 1975, 1982; Briant 1980, 1990; Boucharlat 1984; Kellens 1989, 1991a, 1991b, 2006–7; Boyce and Beck 1991; Bedford 1996. See also Mitchell 1993.
3 An excellent summary is to be found at http://sites.museum.upenn.edu/gordion/articles/myth/34-cultpractice; see also Roller 1988; Işık 1999.
4 All examples of images found on the Gordion settlement mound were discovered in reused contexts, so their original use context remains unknown. See http://sites.museum.upenn.edu/gordion/articles/myth/34-cultpractice.
5 See, e.g., Işık 2001.
6 From Boğazköy, Ankara 138-3-64. Kulaçoğlu 1992: fig. 160. For the town, see Bittel 1970.
7 Roller 1999: 100: eighth or seventh century; http://sites.museum.upenn.edu/gordion/articles/history/31-midascity: first half of sixth century.
8 See Roller 1999: 100 for the posthumous dedication.
9 Roller 1999: 100.
10 http://sites.museum.upenn.edu/gordion/articles/history/31-midascity. See also Gabriel 1965; Berndt 1994.
11 See Roller 1991: 131–2; Roller 1999: 102; for votive altars from Midas City, see Haspels 1971: 295–302.
12 Roller 1999: 192; for the conservatism of the cultic practice at Midas City, see Haspels 1971: 154–5. For similar processes elsewhere, see, e.g., Blagg 1985, 1986.
13 Roller 1991: 131 and n. 15.
14 Naumann 1983: 19–20; de la Genière 1985: 704; Roller 1999: 105.
15 Möbius 1916: 166 n. 2; Roller 1999: 131–2 and n. 47, citing F. Graf 1985: 318 (Erythrae), 388–9 (Clazomenae), 419–20 (Phocaea), and in general 108, as well as Naumann 1983: 124–36, nos. 48–68. Roller adds a work from Didyma, Tuchelt 1970: L 87.

16 Roller 1999: 132.
17 Reinach 1889.
18 Roller 1999: 138, citing Langlotz 1969: 383–5, Naumann 1983: 153–5; F. Graf 1985: 419–20. See also Akşit 1983; Arel 1992; Roosevelt 2009: 129.
19 Roller 1999: 138.
20 Haspels 1971: 92; Roller 1999: 138.
21 Naumann 1983: 122–4, pl. 15, figs. 2, 3, nos. 44–7; Roller 1991: fig. 3b, 1999: 105.
22 Roller 1999:105–6.
23 Naumann 1983: 118–22, pl. 14, figs. 3, 4; Roller 1991: 121–32, pl. 3b.
24 For Greek–Phrygian contacts in northwestern Anatolia that may have smoothed exchanges of religious ideas and forms, see Naumann 1983: 137; Rein 1996; Roller 1999: 106. For the essential conservatism of cultic practice at Gordion, despite its Hellenizing trappings, see Roller 1999: 192. For Pessinous, see Devreker and Vermeulen 1991; Devreker 1994; Roller 1999: 192.
25 For the information in this paragraph, see Berndt-Ersöz 2006, 2007.
26 Summers and Summers 2006.
27 Berndt-Ersöz 2006: 20 and refs.
28 Casabonne 2004; see also Bean 1970.
29 Lemaire, http://www.achemenet.com/, "cilicie07.pdf" under "textes épigraphiques d'Anatolie – araméens." See also A. Dupont-Sommer 1961, 1965; Dupont-Sommer and Robert 1964: 7–15; Donner and Röllig 1966–9: no. 278; Gibson 1975: 156–7, no. 36.
30 For the complexities, see Roller 1999.
31 The Lydian ritual dinners including puppies constitute a clear exception to this; see Greenewalt 1976.
32 See Koldewey 1918; for related Achaemenid-period friezes in colored brick, see Muscarella 1992.
33 For the Cybele cult, see Rein 1993.
34 Hanfmann and Ramage 1978; see also Asgari 1979.
35 For statues of Cybele at Sardis, see Hanfmann and Polatkan 1959; Hanfmann and Balmuth 1965; Hanfmann and Waldbaum 1969.
36 Hanfmann and Waldbaum 1969.
37 As described in the "Sacrilege Inscription." Hanfmann and Waldbaum 1969: 265; Hanfmann 1987.
38 Hdt. 1.92. Fragmentary inscriptions on some columns have been restored to read "*basileus Kroisos anetheken*," but all the signed columns are otherwise undecorated; the sculpted columns may be dated to shortly after 560. See also Kerschner 1997a, 1997b.
39 Muss 1983: 88–91.
40 Muss 1983: 92.
41 Muss 1983: 92–4.
42 Lethaby 1908: 12–13 suggests that the bulls were attached to the antae. For sima and columns, see Bookidis 1967: 276, 281. For Assyrian prototypes, see, e.g., Reade 1983. For the *columnae caelatae*, see, e.g., Muss 1983, 1994; Rugler 1988: 24–6. See also Bammer 1982.
43 Clear from numerous inscriptions; the cult of Artemis of Ephesus serves as a case study. Although sacred justice most likely had a secular arm, inscriptions mention only the divine – but religion and law were inextricably connected in the epigraphic record.
44 Thus a young Athenian could entrust his savings to the priest at Ephesus and expect them not only to be kept safe but actually delivered to him in European Greece! Xen. *Anab.* 5.3.4–6. See Chapter 7, this volume.

NOTES TO PAGES 218–222

45 See Munn 2006: 227. For Megabyzus, see also Bremmer 2008.
46 Dusinberre 2003a:119.
47 Keen 1998: 194–5; *SEG* 39 1414.27, in honor of Erbbina, indicates the presence of a temple. See also Bourgarel, Metzger, and Siebert 1992; Bryce 1996. For the relief sculptures, see, e.g., Metzger 1971, 1979, 1980. For the role of Persian presence in Lycian religion, see Raimond 2007.
48 For the triad of Leto, Apollo, and Artemis, see Keen 1998: 196; for a link between king and cult, see Bryce 1983. For the inscription, see Metzger, Laroche, and Dupont-Sommer 1974; Metzger, Laroche, Dupont-Sommer, and Mayrhofer 1979.
49 Keen 1998: 200: Erbbina's inscription is *SEG* 39 1414.53; the Telmessus inscriptions include the decrees *TAM* ii 1.37 and 2.18 and a series of dedications, *TAM* ii 4; the votive from Trysa is Metzger 1952: 17, no. 6.
50 For Artimu, see Nilsson 1955: 481; Hanfmann 1958: 65, 81 n. 4, cited in Keen 1998: 200.
51 Keen 1998: 201.
52 Tuchelt 1970: 190–203; for Artemis and Hecate, 207. For the significance of siting and sacred paths, see, e.g., A. Joyce 2004.
53 Tuchelt 1970: 190–8.
54 Fontenrose 1988: 11 puts the date of the statue at the end of the sixth century.
55 Tuchelt 1970: 203–4.
56 Tuchelt 1970: 204.
57 There is no archaeological evidence that Miletus was ever sacked; see Mitchell 1989–90. Tuchelt 1970: 206 dates architectural fragments as follows: fragments of volute acroteria, ca. 550; four small column capitals, ca. 535; volute fragments, 525–500; fragment of a corner acroterion, 510–500; corner acroterion, 525–500; three large column capitals, ca. 500.
58 Tuchelt 1970: 210; for the floruit, see esp. 210–17.
59 Fontenrose 1988: 12 summarizes the Greek literary sources and their conflicting information about when and how badly the temple at Didyma was plundered and burned. For the importance, see Barthel 1996.
60 Fontenrose 1988: 14–15.
61 Keen 1998: 201, citing Melchert 1993: 79. For the pronunciation, see Laroche 1980: 3. As Keen 1998: 201 n. 64 points out, the name appears in Greek as Tarkondas/Trokondas in Pamphylia, Pisidia, and Isauria (*FHG* IV 619; *TAM* ii 925.2–3). See also Kretschmer 1896: 363; Cousin 1899: 287; Wilhelm 1909: 224; Sundwall 1913: 269; all cited by Keen 1998. For epigraphic insights into Lycian deities, see also Laroche 1979, 1980; Lebrun 1992.
62 As Keen 1998: 202 and nn. 74, 75 points out, she is attested in Hittite texts (Laroche 1980: 4), and her name often forms the root of second- and first-millennium names (Neumann 1967: 34–5, 1970: 54–5; Barnett 1974: 900–1). For Tlos: *TAM* i 26.12; Xanthus: *TAM* i 44.a.43, c.5, 7–8; Tyberissus: *TAM* i 75.6, 86.5; Arneae: *TAM* i 80; all cited in Keen 1998: 202. See also Hawkins 1974.
63 Keen 1998: 202–3, also citing Mørkholm and Zahle 1976: 75–9.
64 For sacrifice at the tomb of Achilles, see Arr. 1.12 and the Polyxena Sarcophagus. Similar in geography and import is the cult site of Protesilaus, across the Hellespont in the Thracian Chersonese (Hdt. 9.116–20, 7.23; Arr. 1.11). For continuity of cult and settlement at Ilium through the Achaemenid period, see Berlin 2002; note also the magi accompanying Xerxes, who performed cult for heroes there in 480 (Hdt. 7.43).
65 Alcock 1991. For the importance of retaining and building social memory in times of violent unrest, see, e.g., Berry and Berry 1999.

66 See, e.g., Morris 1992: 318–61 for remaking the Theseus myth in archaic Athens.
67 Borchhardt 1976: 17.
68 Borchhardt 1976: 19 suggests that Trysa and Xanthus were built by rulers whose ancestors had served as vassals of the great king between 546 and 538.
69 Childs 1981, 1983; Keen 1998: 158.
70 For the caryatids, frieze, and acroteria, see Borchhardt 1976: 117–25. For the form, see Işık 1998. For the heroön at Trysa, see Oberleitner 1994.
71 For the burial site, Hom. *Il.* 16.681–3; Arist. fr. 641.58. For the demes, see Keen 1998: 158, citing Borchhardt 1976: 49–79, 121–3, 1993: 49–50; the figure with the tiara is Borchhardt 1976: 53 no. 22. For Persian armor, see Bernard 1964.
72 Keen 1998: 158. For Bellerophon and his Lycian cult, see Keen 1998: 211.
73 Keen 1998: 210; for the Xanthian deme, see *TAM* ii 264.2, 265.2; note also *SEG* 37 1234.12; for Tlos, see *TAM* ii 597a.2.
74 Keen 1998: 210. For evidence, he draws on *TAM* ii 245, 636, 637, 715 (Roman); *TAM* i 74.b, 84.5–6; N 304 (Classical). For archaeological evidence of offerings found in tombs at Xanthus and Limyra, see Bryce 1980, 1986: 126–7; Zhuber-Okrog 1990: 58–59; all cited in Keen 1998: 210 n. 143. See also Strathmann 2002.
75 That gods *may* have been syncretized is suggested by Hellenistic inscriptions of Antiochus IV in Commagene, which mention four deities: Zeus–Oromasdes, Apollo–Mithra–Helios–Hermes, Artagnes–Herakles–Ares, and the goddess Commagene. See Facella 2009: 382.
76 Ratté 1989: 216–17 and refs.
77 Ratté 1989: 217–18.
78 Based on architectural resemblance to the Pyramid Tomb and Tomb 813 and the discovery within it of an Achaemenid bowl sherd and the nozzle of an Achaemenid-period lamp.
79 See Hanfmann 1987.
80 For fire altars, see D. Stronach 1985; Schippmann 1971; Erdmann 1941; Garrison 1999. For Taş Kule, see Cahill 1988.
81 The importance of assuming architectural features from another culture is explored in Dodge 1990.
82 Discussion based on Dusinberre 2003a.
83 Ephesus 1631, dating to ca. 334–281. See Knibbe 1961–3.
84 Brosius 1998: 227, 228–32 and refs.; see 233–4 for a discussion, and dismissal, of a hellenized Persian cultic practice.
85 Brosius 1998: 227, 232–3, 234–8; sharply criticized by Briant 2001: 179.
86 Also Anahita and Aphrodite: Munn 2006: 227–30.
87 For Tissaphernes, see Xen. *Hell.* 1.2.6. For Droaphernes, see Chaumont 1990; Briant 1998a, 2002: 677–8; Brosius 1998: 234. For Bagadates and Ariaramnes, see Robert 1953: 410–11; Briant 1985b: 169–71, 1986b: 435; Brosius 1998: 234; Fried 2004: 129–36. For Persian devotion to local cults, see also the statue of Ariobarzanes at Ilium described by Dio. Sic. 17.17.6. For Athena Oreia, see Sayar 2004 and refs.
88 Briant 2002: 678; Greenewalt 1978c; Robert 1975.
89 Briant 1985b.
90 "Artemis Anaitis" is known in Hellenistic inscriptions from Sardis, Kula, Divlit, and Hypaepa. See Brosius 1998: 234. For Artemis Persike, see Robert 1982: 372; for Artemis Anaitis, Buckler and Robinson 1932: 97. For Sardis, see Buckler and Robinson 1912: 95; for Koula, Brosius 1998: 236; for Divlit, Reinach 1885: 107; for Hypaepa, *OGIS* 470. Brosius 1998: 236–7 argues that these are Greek adaptations of western Anatolian cults, incorporating aspects of the Persian goddess, rather than actual syncretism of deities.

91. Bryce 1996: 44 suggests that the "Greek" deities on Lycian coinage in the fifth century are artistic motifs, implying no necessary identification with Lycian deities. Cited by Keen 1998: 193 n. 4. Keen also points out that the Lycians may have adapted aspects of Egyptian religious expression in their translation of the name Apollodotus as Natrbbijẽmi. See Keen 1998: 199.
92. Hdt. 5.119–20.
93. http://www.labraunda.org/.
94. For discussions of Hecatomnid Caria within the eastern Mediterranean, see Ruzicka 1992; Isager 1994.
95. Hellstrøm and Thiele 1982.
96. http://www.labraunda.org/Labraunda.org/Oikoi_Building_eng.html.
97. http://www.labraunda.org/Labraunda.org/Andron_B_eng.html.
98. See, e.g., Hellstrøm 1989. Hellstrøm suggests that the andrones may not have been used for banqueting, although he is convinced that the Oikoi and East Stoa were, but the excavators now accept banqueting as a main activity in the two buildings. See http://www.labraunda.org/.
99. For meat eating, see, e.g., Jameson 1988.
100. See Gunter 1989, 1995: 21–31. For the meaning of sphinxes, see Dusinberre 1997.
101. Gunter 1995: 30.
102. The cult of "Basileus Kaunios" at Xanthus in the final years of the Achaemenid period may display a similar association of ruler and god; Keen 1998: 10; Fried 2004: 140–53. Briant 1998c argues against the interpretation.
103. Hellstrøm 1989: 104 n. 22.
104. For Hellenistic leagues at Labraunda, see Hellstrøm 1989: 103–4.
105. This discussion is drawn from Dusinberre 2003a.
106. Ramage and Craddock 2000; Ramage 1987: 10–12; Greenewalt 2010a.
107. Ramage and Craddock 2000: 72–81.
108. Ramage and Craddock 2000: 78–80; Hanfmann 1983: 37.
109. Ramage and Craddock 2000: 74; Hanfmann 1983: 37.
110. Ramage and Craddock 2000: 74. For fire altars, see Garrison 1999. For the kind of religious toleration that more generally characterized the Achaemenid Empire, see Garnsey 1984.
111. See Herrenschmidt 1980. For seals and fire altars, see Garrison, forthcoming; for PFS 75, which demonstrates the complexity of religious practice at Persepolis, see Garrison and Root, forthcoming a. For Dahan-i Gulaman, I am indebted to Amélie Kuhrt, personal communication, 2010.
112. Root 1998.
113. For people carrying gods and cult elements with them as documented in the Fortification Archive, see Henkelman 2008; the Jewish temple at Elephantine is an Egyptian example.
114. M. Miller 2011 synthesizes the scanty evidence for "manifestly intrusive religious practice" in parts of western Anatolia, pointing out that the so-called Achaemenid cult place at Dascylium is Achaemenid in date rather than character and that the so-called palace at "Larisa" is more likely a sanctuary hestiatoreion than a Persian or Persianizing building. For different cults at Persepolis, see, e.g., Root 1998.
115. See, e.g., the discussion at cappadoce01.pdf, on http://www.achemenet.com/, and Lemaire 2003.
116. Lemaire 2003: figs. 1–14.
117. Annalisa Azzoni, personal communication, 2010. I am also grateful to Azzoni for assistance with translations; in general I have followed the transliterations and

translations (into French) offered by Lemaire on http://www.achemenet.com/. For Aramaic elsewhere, see, e.g., Lidzbarski 1902; Sayce 1906; S. Cook 1917; Torrey 1917–18; Cuny 1920, 1921; Cowley 1921, 1923; Elderkin 1925; Kahle and Sommer 1927; Driver 1957; A. Dupont-Sommer 1961, 1965; Dupont-Sommer and Robert 1964; Verger 1964; Cross 1966; M. Dupont-Sommer 1966; Donner and Röllig 1963, 1966–9; Hanson 1968; Bowman 1970; Bogoliubov 1971; Grelot 1972; Kornfeld 1973; Gibson 1975; Lipinski 1975a, 1975b; Greenfield and Porten 1982; Altheim-Stiehl and Cremer 1985; Lemaire 1993, 1994, 2001, 2002, 2003, 2004; Lemaire and Lozachmeur 1996; Lecoq 1997; Kwasman and Lemaire 2002; Röllig 2002; Shaked 2004; Azzoni and Dusinberre, forthcoming.

118 Lemaire 2003: 141–4. Numbering after Lemaire, http://www.achemenet.com/. See also Smirnow 1896: 444–6; Clermont-Ganneau 1898, 1900: 69–70; Lidzbarski 1902: 72–4; Chabot 1918:no. 1785; Donner and Röllig 1966–9: no. 263; Bogoliubov 1971. For the date of Stele A, see Lemaire 2003: 144–6.

119 For the inscriptions of Stele B, see Lemaire 2003: 146–64; Lemaire, http://www.achemenet.com/. See also Clermont-Ganneau 1898: 635–8, 1900: 64–7; Lidzbarski 1902: 59–74, 319–26, 322–4; Chabot 1918: nos. 1785A, 1785B, 1785E, 1785F; Russell 1990: 2687, pl. 2; Donner and Röllig 1966–9: no. 264.

120 Lemaire 2003: 162–4 offers four possible interpretations of the marriage: a fusion between the worship of Bel and that of "Mazda"; a sacred marriage between a king and a priestess; a mortal marriage between two humans bearing the names of divinities; or a mortuary belief equating death (possibly of Bel, the great, the king) with marriage to the divine.

121 Bel is, it seems, the same as the Syrian god Baal.

122 See Garrison, forthcoming. Much debate has centered on the question of whether Persians worshiped statues; as Garrison, forthcoming, n. 13, says, Jacobs 2001 and Briant 2002: 240–54, 676–7, 915–17, 998–9 provide much evidence and bibliographic information.

123 See, e.g., Brosius 1998, who also summarizes the evidence for Persian cultic activity in Lydia in the Hellenistic period.

124 Manisa Museum 73 Etütlük; see Lemaire 2002; Roosevelt 2003: 677, 2009: 244–5. For Faraşa, see Lipinski 1975b: 173–85 and refs. See also Boyce, Grenet, and Beck 1991: 272. For Anahita barzochara at Aksaray, see Harper 1967; Schmitt 1970; Wikander 1972. Bivar 1992: 266 comments, "Eastwards of Sardis also, attestations of Anaitis are numerous, at Philadelphia and present-day Kula and Gölde. While, in the spirit of Zoroastrianism, she is invoked as a water-goddess at Silandos. Again in Phrygia, at Celaenae-Apameia (modern Dinar), source of four rivers, coins attest an Artemis of the Hypaipa type, thus presumably Iranian." See also Wikander 1946: 79–101; Rigsby 1995.

125 Strabo *Geo.* 15.3.15.

126 Garrison, forthcoming. See also D. Stronach 1966; Cahill 1988; Garrison 1999; Roosevelt 2009.

127 The style of this stele has local antecedents; see Alkım 1974.

128 Garrison, forthcoming.

129 Illustrated, e.g., by American Numismatic Society coins, nos. 1944.100.54355, 1944.100.54356, 1944.100.54358, 1961.179.77, and 1977.158.551. For Cilician coinage, see, e.g., Casabonne 2000 and the excellent work of Koray Konuk on www.achemenet.com.

130 Further examples of the type include ANS 1944.100.54395, 1944.100.54396, 1944.100.54397, 1944.100.54400, 1944.100.54401, 1944.100.54403, 1944.100.54404, 1954.185.32, 1977.158.564, and 1978.64.193.

NOTES TO PAGES 240–248

131 Examples include ANS 1912.36.1, 1936.140.4, 1944.100.54405, 1944.100.54406, 1944.100.54407, 1944.100.54408, 1944.100.54411, 1944.100.54412–1944.100.54427, 1954.185.33, 1968.57.131, 1977.158.569, and 1984.65.97–1984.65–101.
132 For the lion and bull in Iran, see Root 2002.
133 For the ratios, see Dusinberre 2008b.
134 For the seal of Gobryas, see Garrison and Root, forthcoming b; for the Sardis seal, see Dusinberre 2003a.
135 Garrison, forthcoming; Dusinberre 2003b.
136 Dusinberre 2003b: 168–71; for the significance, see T. Martin 1985.
137 Munn 2006: 232; for wealth and prosperity, see *Persians*, ll. 163–4, 250–2, 751; for "all Asia," ll. 56–7, 61, 249, and cf. ll. 12, 73, 270, 549, 584, 763, 929; for the divinity of Darius, ll. 157, 620, 634, 641–2, 643, 651, 711, 856; for the queen as wife or mother of a god, ll. 157, 623.
138 See, e.g., Said 1978: 21, 56–67; E. Hall 1989: 86; Griffith 1998; T. Harrison 2000: 43, 44, 87; Briant 2002: 516–17; cited also in Munn 2006: 233.
139 Root 1979; Dusinberre 2003b. For another example of Athenian recognition and use of Achaemenid imperial rhetoric, in this case visual, see Bivar 1970.
140 Dusinberre 2008a. The bud-and-lotus friezes at top and bottom find their closest parallel in a sealing found at Memphis: Petrie, Mackay, and Wainwright 1910: no. 46.
141 After Dusinberre 2008a: 98.
142 For the symbolism of sphinxes and lion-griffins, see Dusinberre 1997.
143 See also Dusinberre 2008a: 98.

Seven: Educating the Young and Old

1 Hdt. 1.114; Ctes. *FGrH* 90 F66 (1–7).
2 Xen. *Cyr.* 1.3.1.
3 Hdt. 1.136.
4 DB 4.61–65. See also Schmitt 1983a.
5 Thus DB and also DPd.
6 DNb 6–8, 3, 41–45; see also Chapter 3.
7 Xen. *Cyr.* 1.2.2–1.3.1.
8 Kuhrt 2007: 99.
9 Xen. *Cyr.* 1.2.6.
10 Xen. *Cyr.* 1.2.8.
11 Xen. *Cyr.* 1.2.9–12.
12 Xen. *Cyr.* 1.2.15.
13 See Kuhrt 2007: 629–30 for (fabricated?) connections between Classical authors' descriptions of Persian education and Spartan; see also Briant 2002: 328–30. For its lasting effects in the Roman Empire see, e.g., Blázquez 1989.
14 Xen. *Cyr.* 15.3.18.
15 Xen. *Cyr.* 15.3.18.
16 Xen. *Cyr.* 1.2.1, quoted in Briant 2002:330.
17 Kuhrt 2007: 629. For *arta*- see Kent 1953; Briant 2002: 329–30.
18 I am grateful to Margaret Cool Root for this example (personal communication, 2010).
19 Briant 2002: 429–31.
20 For apprenticeship contracts from Babylonia of this period, see Dandamaev 1984b.
21 Weisberg 1967.
22 Garrison and Root 2001: 16–21.

23 Garrison 1991.
24 Collon 1996.
25 von Graeve 1970: 105, 110.
26 Kaptan 2002. The similarity of the stag hunt on the Alexander Sarcophagus to that of the Pella mosaics may also imply circulating copybooks.
27 For Troy, see Miller-Collett and Root 1997; for Patara, see Işın 2007; for Kaman-Kalehöyük, see notice at Yıldırım and Gates 2007 and refs., as well as Omura 1992, 1995, 1996; for Kertch, see Boardman 1970b: no. 5; for Nymphaeum, see Boardman 1970a: no. 838; for Olbia, see Bats 1988. See also Boardman 1976, 1998, 1999, 2000; Sorokina and Zhuraviyov 1997. For mechanisms that made such trade possible, see Gill 1988.
28 See, e.g., Bowersock 1986; Scott 1987, 1992; D. Miller 1989; Pauketat 2000; Carstens 2006; see also Joyce and Weller 2007 for the role that religion in particular may play in resistance.
29 The two-animal emblem of lion and bull as known on the palace facades is attested in only two (pyramidal stamp) seals on the Fortification Archive seals studied by Garrison and Root (Root, personal communication, 2010).
30 Royal texts beyond that at Bisitun were circulated: part of Darius's text DNb and Xerxes's text XPl appear at the end of the Aramaic version of the Bisitun text DB found at Elephantine in Egypt. Xenophon's evocation of Persian kingship (*Anab.* 1.9) mirrors royal statements and may be based on disseminated versions. I am grateful to Amélie Kuhrt for pointing these instances out to me (personal communication, 2010).
31 Dusinberre 2010b.
32 See Roosevelt 2009.
33 For the melissai, see *Inschriften von Ephesos* 2109; they were directed by a "king bee," or *essên*. Paus. 8.13.1 says that the essenes were priests who served a yearlong term under strict rules of purity, but we do not know what this entailed.
34 *FGrH* 680 F11, cited in Kuhrt 2007: 566–7.
35 Seal inscriptions also provide much information, of course, and are discussed in Chapter 8.
36 See, e.g., Borchhardt et al. 1997–9; Kloekhorst 2011.
37 Thus "Paktyes (L) the son of Karous (L) the son of Herakleidos (G)," "Mithridates (P) the son of Tuios (L) the son of Manes (L), the slave of Attis (L?)," and "Pythes (L) the son of Strombos (G) the son of Kadodos (P) the son of Babados (P)." See commentary in Hanfmann 1987: 2–3, 6–7; Dusinberre 2003a. See also Benveniste 1965; Neumann 1996.
38 High-tier professional male weavers had a key role in weaving the gigantomachy peplos for Athena; see Mansfield 1985; Barber 1992: ch. 13.
39 I am indebted to Amélie Kuhrt for the observations in the remainder of this paragraph (personal communication, 2010). For important comparanda in Central America, see Brumfiel 1983, 1987, 1996; Berdan 1982, 1986, 1987; R. Joyce 1993.
40 For Sardis, Ael. *NA* 4.46; for Susa, Plut. *Alex.* 36.1–2. There are in addition a group of Nabonidus dated texts from Uruk, which refer to purple wool "from Ionia" (Kuhrt, personal communication, 2010).
41 For Arachne and links to weaving in Greece, see Weinberg and Weinberg 1956.
42 See, e.g., C. Cameron 2008.
43 Briant 2003.
44 Hallock 1969: 252; see also Briant 2002: 431–7.
45 Babylonian learning, too, shows great continuity in the period; see Gesche 2000. For the Persepolis Treasury Archive, see esp. G. Cameron 1948, 1958, 1965.

46 For Dascylium, Kaptan 1990, 1996, 2001, 2002, 2007, 2008. For Persepolis, see Root 1990, 1997a, 1997b; Garrison and Root 1996/8, 2001; Garrison 2008.
47 Kaptan 2002: 22.
48 Kaptan 2002: 23.
49 Kaptan 2005, 2010. It is certainly the case that nonsatrapal archives existed in the empire, and their seal impressions demonstrate the sophisticated understanding people had of visual rhetoric; an excellent example of this is the Murashu archive in Bablyonia. See, e.g., Cardascia 1951; Stolper 1985, 1992; Bregstein 1993, 1997.
50 Xen. *Anab.* 5.3.4–6. Trans. http://www.perseus.tufts.edu. Xenophon continues: "In the time of Xenophon's exile and while he was living at Scillus, near Olympia, where he had been established as a colonist by the Lacedaemonians, Megabyzus came to Olympia to attend the games and returned to him his deposit. Upon receiving it Xenophon bought a plot of ground for the goddess in a place which Apollo's oracle appointed."
51 Buckler and Robinson 1912, 1932: 1–7; Atkinson 1972: 45.
52 For the date, see Debord 1972, 1982; for reinscription on the temple wall, see Hanfmann 1983: 119, 125. For letter forms, see Descat 1985: 98. See also Roosevelt 2009: 112–15.

Eight: Empire and Identity in Achaemenid Anatolia

1 E.g., Boardman 1970b: nos. 3, 4, 5, 8.
2 For the royal name seals in Old Persian, Dascylium Seals DS 3, 4 (Kaptan 2002); for Persian names in Aramaic, Gordion Seal 100, Dascylium Seal DS 16; for other ethnicities written in Aramaic, Dascylium Seals DS 18 (Sogdian?), 24 (a Babylonian name). Interestingly, no seals carved with such imperially charged images have yet been found inscribed in Greek; see Boardman 1970b: 21.
3 Although the royal name seals used at Dascylium were not used by Xerxes and Artaxerxes themselves, as signifiers of imperial authority they gain great weight by the use of the languages and names. See also Barth 1969.
4 For the importance of this much-studied aspect of identity, see, e.g., Moerman 1965, 1968; Barth 1969; de Vos 1975; Lockwood 1984; Hanfmann 1987; Goudriaan 1988; Pasztory 1989; J. Hall 1995, 1997, 2002; Ricoeur 1996, 2004; S. Jones 1997; J. Gates 2002; Roudometov 2002; Clark 2004; Ma 2008.
5 Root 1990; see also Clifford and Marcus 1986.
6 Root, forthcoming b.
7 I am grateful to Margaret Miller for this suggestion (personal communication, 2011).
8 Xen. *Anab.* 4.24–6; for Sardis, see Dusinberre 2003a: 58–9; for Gordion, see Voigt and Young 1999.
9 M. Miller 2011; Roosevelt 2006, 2009: 195.
10 Dusinberre 2010a.
11 Facella 2009: 402, 403.
12 M. Miller 2011.

BIBLIOGRAPHY

Abdi, K. 2006. "The Daiva Inscription Revisited." *IJAIS* 11/12: 45–74.

Abraham, K. 1995. "The Egibis in Elam." In *Languages and Cultures in Contact: Programme and Abstracts of the 42e Rencontre Assyriologique Internationale*. Leuven. Unpaginated.

    2004. *Business and Politics under the Persian Empire: The Financial Dealings of Marduk-nasir-apli of the House of Egibi (521–487 BC)*. Bethesda, MD.

Adams, R. McC. 1979. "Late Hispanic Empires of the New World." In M. T. Larsen, ed., *Power and Propaganda: A Symposium on Ancient Empires*: 59–73. Copenhagen.

    1992. "Ideologies: Unity and Diversity." In A. A. Demarest and G. W. Conrad, eds., *Ideology and Pre-Columbian Civilizations*: 205–22. Santa Fe, NM.

Agricola, E. F. M. 1900. *De Aristidis censu*. Berlin.

Ahn, G. 1992. *Religiöse Herrscherlegitimation im achämenidischen Iran. ActIr* 31. Leiden.

Akbıyıkoğlu, K. 1991. "Güre Basmacı Tümülüsleri Kurtarma Kazısı." *MKKS* 1: 1–23.

    1993. "Güre Velişin Tepe Tümülüsleri Kurtarma Kazısı." *MKKS* 3: 53–63.

    1994a. "Güre 'Basmacı Tümülüsü' Kurtarma Kazısı." *AS* 64–5: 2–8.

    1994b. "Kayaağıl Tümülüsü Kurtarma Kazısı." *MKKS* 4: 69–82.

    1996. "1994 Güre İkiztepe Tümülüsü Kazısı." *MKKS* 6: 163–76.

Åkerström, Å. 1966. *Die Architektonischen Terrakotten Kleinasiens*. Lund.

Akşit, O. 1983. *Manisa Tarihi Magnesia ad Sipylum*. Istanbul.

Akurgal, E. 1941. *Griechische Reliefs des VI. Jahrhunderts aus Lykien. Schriften zur Kunst des Altertums* 3. Berlin.

    1956. "Recherches faites à Cyzique et à Ergili." *Anatolia* 1: 15–24.

    1966. "Griechisch-Persische Reliefs aus Daskyleion." *IrAnt* 6: 147–56.

    1967. "Eine Silberschale aus dem Pontus." *AntK* 10: 32–8.

    1974. "Zur Datierung der Grabstelen aus Daskyleion." *Mansel'e Armağan. Mélanges Mansel*: 967–70. Ankara.

    1986. "Neue archaische Skulpturen aus Anatolien." In H. Kyrieleis, ed., *Archaische und klassische griechische Plastik*: 1: 1–14. Mainz.

    1990. *Ancient Ruins and Civilizations of Turkey*. 7th ed. Istanbul.

Alcock, S. E. 1989. "Archaeology and Imperialism: Roman Expansion and the Greek City." *JMA* 2: 87–135.

Bibliography

1991. "Tomb Cult and the Post-Classical Polis." *AJA* 95: 447–67.

1993. *Graecia Capta: The Landscapes of Roman Greece*. Cambridge.

Alkım, U. B. 1974. *Yesemek Taşocağı ve Heykel Atelyesinde yapılan Kazı ve Araştırmalar* [Excavation and research in the Yesemek Quarry and Sculpture Workshop]. Ankara.

Allen, K. H. 2003. "Becoming the 'Other': Attitudes and Practices at Attic Cemeteries." In C. Dougherty and L. Kurke, eds., *The Cultures within Ancient Greek Culture: Contact, Conflict, Collaboration*: 207–36. Cambridge.

Al-Masudi. 1863, 1977. *Les prairies d'or II*. Trans. C. B. de Meynard and P. de Courteille. Paris.

Alt, S. M. 2001. "Cahokian Change and the Authority of Tradition." In T. R. Pauketat, ed., *The Archaeology of Traditions: Agency and History before and after Columbus*: 141–56. Gainesville, FL.

Altheim-Stiehl, R., and M. Cremer. 1985. "Eine gräko-persische Türstele mit aramäischer Inschrift aus Daskyleion." *EA* 6: 1–16.

Altheim-Stiehl, R., E. Metzler, and E. Schwertheim. 1983. "Eine neue gräko-persische Grabstele aus Sultaniye Köy und ihre Bedeutung für die Geschichte und Topographie von Daskyleion." *EA* 1: 1–23.

Amandry, P. 1953. *Collection Hélène Stathatos: le bijoux antiques*. Strasbourg.

1953–4. "Vaesselles d'argent de l'époque achéménide." *ArchEph*: 11–19.

1959. "Toreutique achéménide." *AntK* 2: 38–56.

1963. "Argenterie achéménide." *Collection Hélène Stathatos* 3: 260–72. Strasbourg.

Amiet, P. 1972a. "Les ivoires achéménides de Suse." *Syria* 49: 167–91.

1972b. *Glyptique susienne des origines à l'époque des perses achéménides*. MDAFI 43. Paris.

1973a. "La glyptique de la fin de l'Elam." *ArsAsia* 28: 3–45.

1973b. "Glyptique Élamite, à propos de nouveaux documents." *ArsAsia* 26: 364.

1974. "Quelques observations sur le palais de Darius à Suse." *Syria* 51: 65–73.

1980. *Art of the Ancient Near East*. New York.

1994. "Un étage au palais de Darius à Suse?" In M. Dietrich and O. Loretz, eds., *Beschreiben und Deuten in der Archäologie des Alten Orients: Festschrift für Ruth Mayer-Opificius*: 1–5. Münster.

Amiran, R. 1972. "Achaemenian Bronze Objects from a Tomb at Kh. Ibsan in Lower Galilee." *Levant* 4: 135–8.

1981. "Persian-Achaemenid Impact on Palestine." In A. U. Pope and P. Ackerman, eds., *Survey of Persian Art*: 14: 3017–23. Ashiya.

Anabolu, M. U. 1979. "Yayınlanmamış olan birkaç arslanlar heykeli." *TTK* 8/1: 415–18.

Anderson, B[enedict]. 1991. *Imagined Communities: Reflections on the Origin and Spread of Nationalism*. Rev. ed. London.

Anderson, B[jörn]. 2002. "Imperial Legacies, Local Identities: References to Achaemenid Persian Iconography on Crenelated Nabataean Tombs." *ArsOr* 32: 163–207.

Anderson, J. K. 1974. "The Battle of Sardis in 395 B.C." *CSCA* 7: 27–53.

1975. *Hunting in the Ancient World*. Berkeley, CA.

Andronikos, M. 1984. *Vergina: The Royal Tombs and the Ancient City*. Athens.

Aperghis, G. G. 2004. *The Seleukid Royal Economy: The Finances and Financial Administration of the Seleukid Empire*. Cambridge.

Appadurai, A., ed. 1986. *The Social Life of Things: Commodities in Cultural Perspective*. Cambridge.

Arel, A. 1992. "Soma yakınlarında eski bir dağ yerleşmesi – Tırhala Köyü." *AST* 9: 119–30.

Asgari, N. 1979. "Anadolu'da antik mermer ocakları." *TTK* 8/1: 451–6.

Bibliography

Asheri, D. 1996. "L'ideale monarchico di Dario: Erodoto III.80–82 e DNb Kent." *AASA* 3: 99–106.

Aslan, M. 1989. "Mama Deresi Frig Tümülüsü Kurtarma Kazısı." *Müze* 1: 62–6.

Aston, D. A. 1999. *Pottery from the Late New Kingdom to the Early Ptolemaic Period*. Elephantine 19. Mainz.

Atasoy, S. 1974. "The Kocakızlar Tumulus in Eskişehir, Turkey." *AJA* 78: 255–63.

Ateşlier, S. 1997. "Daskyleion'da Satraplık Dönemine Ait Erken Klasik Bir Yapı Üzerine Düşünceler." Paper presented at the First International Symposium on Anatolia in the Achaemenid Period, Bandırma, 15–18 August.

― 1999. "Daskyleion Buluntuları Işığında Batı Anadolu'da Akhaemenid Dönemi Mimarisi." Ph.D. dissertation, Ege Üniversitesi, Sosyal Bilimler Enstitüsü, Klasik Arkeoloji Bilim Dalı.

― 2001. "Observations on an Early Classical Building of the Satrapal Period at Daskyleion." In T. Bakır, ed., *Achaemenid Anatolia: Proceedings of the First International Symposium on Anatolia in the Achaemenid Period, Bandırma, 15–18 August 1997*: 147–68. Leiden.

Atkinson, K. T. C. 1972. "A Hellenistic Land Conveyance: The Estate of Mnesimachus in the Plain of Sardis." *Historia* 21: 45–74.

Azzoni, A. 2000. "Un giuramento ebraico ad Elefantina d'Egitto.". *Annali della Facoltà di Lettere e Filosofia dell'Università degli Studi di Milano* 53/2: 265–71.

― Forthcoming. The Private Life of Women in Persian Egypt.

Azzoni, A., and E. R. M. Dusinberre. Forthcoming. "Persepolis Fortification Aramaic Tablet Seal 2 and the Keeping of Horses: An Offering in Honor of Matthew W. Stolper." In W. Henkelman, C. Jones, M. Kozuh, and C. Woods, eds., *Extraction and Control: Studies in Honor of Matthew W. Stolper*. Chicago.

Babelon, E. 1893. *Les Perses Achéménides*. Paris.

Badian, E. 1987. "The Peace of Callias." *JHS* 107: 1–39.

Baines, J. 1996. "On the Composition and Inscriptions of the Vatican Statue of Udjahorresnet." In P. der Manuelian, ed., *Studies in Honor of W. K. Simpson*: 1: 83–92. Boston.

Bakır, T. 1991. "Daskyleion." *Höyük* 1: 75–84.

― 1995. "Archäologische Beobachtungen über die Residenz in Daskyleion." In P. Briant, ed., *Dans les pas de Dix-Mille*. Pallas 43: 269–85. Paris.

― ed. 2001a. *Achaemenid Anatolia: Proceedings of the First International Symposium on Anatolia in the Achaemenid Period, Bandırma, 15–18 August 1997*. Leiden.

― 2001b. "Die Satrapie in Daskyleion." In T. Bakır et al., eds., *Proceedings of the First International Symposium on Anatolia in the Achaemenid Period, Bandırma, 15–18 August 1997*: 168–80. Leiden.

― 2007. "Auswertung der Keramik für eine Relative Chronologie im perserzeitlichen Daskyleion." In *Achaemenid Impact*: 167–76. Istanbul.

Bakır, T., and R. Gusmani. 1991. "Eine neue phrygische Inschrift aus Daskyleion." *EA* 18: 157–64.

― 1993. "Graffiti aus Daskyleion." *Kadmos* 32: 135–44.

Bakır, T., A. Erdoğan, H. Bulut, and H. Yıldızhan. 2004. "Daskyleion 2002 Kazıları." *25. KST* 1, Ankara, 26–31 May 2003: 311–18. Ankara.

Bakır, T., G. Demir, and C. Tanrıver. 2003. "Daskyleion 2001 Kazıları." *24. KST* 1, Ankara, 27–31 May 2002: 491–500. Ankara.

Bakır-Akbaşoğlu, T. 1997. "Phryger in Daskyleion." In *Frigi e Frigio. Atti del 1o Simposio Internazionale, Roma, 1995*: 229–38. Rome.

Bal, M., J. V. Crewe, and L. Spitzer. 1999. *Acts of Memory: Cultural Recall in the Present*. Hanover, NH.

Bibliography

Balcer, J. M. 1972. "The Date of Herodotus IV: 1. Darius' Scythian Expedition." *HSCP* 76: 99–132.

1977. "The Athenian Episkopos and the Achaemenid 'King's Eye.' " *AJPh* 391: 252–63.

1984. *Sparda by the Bitter Sea: Imperial Interaction in Western Anatolia*. Chico, CA.

1985. "Fifth Century B.C. Ionia: A Frontier Redefined." *REA* 87: 31–42.

1988. "Ionia and Sparda under the Achaemenid Empire – The Sixth and Fifth Century B.C.: Tribute, Taxation and Assessment." In P. Briant and C. Herrenschmidt, eds., *Le tribut dans l'empire perse*: 2–24. Paris.

1993. "The Ancient Satrapies and Satraps of Western Anatolia." *AMI* 26: 81–90.

1997. "The Liberation of Ionia: 478 B.C." *Historia* 46/3: 374–7.

Balkan, K. 1959. "Inscribed Bullae from Daskyleion-Ergili." *Anatolia* 4: 123–8.

Bammer, A. 1982. "Forschungen im Artemision von Ephesos von 1976 bis 1981." *AnatSt* 32: 61–87.

Barag, D. 1968. "An Unpublished Achaemenid Cut Glass Bowl from Nippur." *JGS* 10: 17–20.

1985. *Catalogue of Western Asiatic Glass in the British Museum I*. London.

Barber, E. J. W. 1992. *Prehistoric Textiles: The Development of Cloth in the Neolithic and Bronze Ages with Special Reference to the Aegean*. Princeton, NJ.

Barber, S. B., and A. A. Joyce. 2007. "Polity Produced and Community Consumed: Negotiating Political Centralization in the Lower Rio Verde Valley, Oaxaca." In E. C. Wells and K. L. Davis-Salazar, eds., *Mesoamerican Ritual Economy*: 221–44. Boulder, CO.

Bares, L. 1996. "Foundation Deposits in the Tomb of Udjahorresnet at Abusir." *ZÄS* 123: 1–9.

1999. *Abusir IV: The Shaft Tomb of Udjahorresnet at Abusir*. Prague.

Barnett, R. D. 1974. "A Silver Head-Vase with Lycian Inscriptions." In A. Akurgal and U. B. Alkim, eds., *Mansel'e Armağan: Mélanges Mansel*: 893–901. Ankara.

1982. *Ancient Ivories in the Middle East*. QEDEM, Monographs of the Institute of Archaeology 14. Jerusalem.

Barnett, R. D., and N. Gökçe. 1953. "The Find of Urartian Bronzes at Altın Tepe, Near Erzincan." *AnatSt* 3: 121–9.

Barth, F. 1969. *Ethnic Groups and Boundaries: The Social Organisation of Cultural Difference*. London.

Barthel, D. L. 1996. *Historic Preservation, Collective Memory, and Historical Identity*. New Brunswick, NJ.

Baslez, M. F. 1986. "Présence et traditions iraniennes dans les cités de l'Egée." *REA* 87/1–2: 137–55.

Basso, K. H. 1996. *Wisdom Sits in Places: Landscape and Language among the Western Apache*. Albuquerque, NM.

Bats, M. 1988. *Vaisselle et alimentation à Olbia de Provence v. 350–50 av. J. C.: modèles culturels et catégories céramiques*. RAN suppl. 18. Paris.

Baughan, E. P. 2002–4. Review of E. R. M. Dusinberre, *Aspects of Empire in Achaemenid Sardis*. *JFA* 29: 225–8.

2004. "Anatolian Funerary Klinae: Tradition and Identity." Ph.D. dissertation, University of California at Berkeley.

2008. "Lale Tepe: A Late Lydian Tumulus near Sardis. 3. The Klinai." In N. D. Cahill, ed., *Love for Lydia: A Sardis Anniversary Volume Presented to Crawford H. Greenewalt, Jr.*: 49–78. Cambridge, MA.

2010. "Lydian Burial Customs." In N. D. Cahill, ed., *The Lydians and Their World*: 273–304. Istanbul.

BIBLIOGRAPHY

Forthcoming. "Persian Riders in Lydia? The Painted Frieze of the Aktepe Kline." *Proceedings of the XVII International Congress of Classical Archaeology*.Rome.

Beal, R. H. 1995. "Hittite Military Organization." *CANE*: 545–54. New York.

Bean, G. E. 1970. *Journeys in Rough Cilicia, 1964–1968*. Vienna.

———. 1978. *Lycian Turkey: An Archaeological Guide*. London.

———. 1979. *Turkey's Southern Shore: An Archaeological Guide*. 2d ed. London.

———. 1980. *Turkey beyond the Maeander: An Archaeological Guide*. 2d ed. London.

Beaulieu, P.-A. 1989. *The Reign of Nabonidus, King of Babylon, 556–539 BC*. New Haven, CT.

Beckman, G. 1995. "Royal Ideology and State Administration in Hittite Anatolia." *CANE*: 529–44. New York.

Bedford, P. R. 1996. "Early Achaemenid Monarchs and Indigenous Cults: Towards the Definition of Imperial Policy." In M. Dillon ed., *Religion in the Ancient World: New Themes and Approaches*: 17–39. Amsterdam.

Bedon, R., R. Chevallier, and P. Pinon. 1988. *Architecture et urbanisme en Gaule romaine*. Paris.

Behrwald, R. 2000. *Der Lykische Bund, Untersuchungen zu Geschichte und Verfassung*. Antiquitas Reihe 1, Band 48. Bonn.

Bekker-Nielsen, T. 1989. *The Geography of Power: Studies in the Urbanisation of Roman North-west Europe*. BAR International Series 477. Oxford.

Belli, O. 1989. *The Capital of Urartu: Van, Eastern Anatolia*. Istanbul.

Bengisu, R. L. 1994. "Torrhebia Limne." *TürkAD* 2: 22–43.

———. 1996. "Lydian Mount Karios." In *Cybele, Attis, and Related Cults: Essays in Memory of M. J. Vermaseren*: 1–36. Leiden.

Benli, E. 2002. "Daskyleion Teras-Sur Yapısı." Ph.D. dissertation, Adnan Menderes University.

Benndorf, O., and G. Niemann. 1884. *Reisen in Lykien und Karien*. Vienna.

Benveniste, E. 1965. "Termes de parenté dans les langues indo-européennes." *L'Homme* 5: 5–16.

Beran, H. 1987. *The Consent Theory of Political Obligation*. London.

Berdan, F. F. 1982. *The Aztecs of Central Mexico: An Imperial Society*. Orlando, FL.

———. 1986. "Enterprise and Empire in Aztec and Early Colonial Mexico." In B. L. Isaac, ed., *Research in Economic Anthropology: Economic Aspects of Prehispanic Highland Mesoamerica*: 281–302. Greenwich, CT.

———. 1987. "The Economics of Aztec Luxury Trade and Tribute." In E. H. Boone ed., *The Aztec Templo Mayor*: 161–83. Washington, DC.

Berg, S. B. 1979. *The Book of Esther: Motifs, Themes and Structure Society of Biblical Literature*. Dissertation Series 44. Missoula, MT.

Berger, E. 1970. *Studien zum griechischen Grab- und Votivrelief um 500 v. Chr. und zur vorhippokratischen Medizin*. Veröffentlichungen des Antikenmuseums Basel I. Basel.

Berlin, A. 1998. "Tel Anafa, Vol. II: The Persian, Hellenistic and Early Roman Plainwares." *JRA* Suppl.

———. 2002. "Ilion before Alexander: A Fourth Century B.C. Ritual Deposit." *StTroica* 12: 131–66.

Bernard, P. 1964. "Une pièce d'armure perse sur un monument lycien." *Syria* 41: 195–212.

———. 1969. "Les bas-reliefs gréco-perses de Dascylion a la lumière de nouvelles découvertes." *RA* 1969: 17–28.

Berndt, D. 1994. "Langsam stirbt Kybele. Fortschreitende Zerstörung phrygischer Felsdenkmäler." *AW* 25: 166–71.

Bibliography

Berndt-Ersöz, S. 2006. *Phrygian Rock-Cut Shrines: Structure, Function, and Cult Practice.* Leiden.

———. 2007. "Phrygian Rock-Cut Step Monuments: An Interpretation." In A. Çilingiroğlu and A. Sagona, eds., *Anatolian Iron Ages 6: The Proceedings of the Sixth Anatolian Iron Ages Colloquium Held at Eskişehir, 16–20 August 2004*: 19–40. Paris.

Berry, J. A., and C. P. Berry. 1999. *Genocide in Rwanda: A Collective Memory.* Washington, DC.

Bilgin, A. I., R. Dinç, and M. Önder. 1996. "Lydia'daki İki Tümülüs'de Temizlik Kazısı Çalışmaları." *TürkAD* 4: 207–22.

Binford, L. R. 1971. "Mortuary Practices: Their Study and Potential." *AmAnt* 36/3.2: 6–29.

Bingöl, O. 1998. *Magnesia ad Maeandrum: Magnesia on the Meander.* Ankara.

Birmingham, J. M. 1961. "The Overland Route across Anatolia in the Eighth and Seventh Centuries B.C." *AnatSt* 11: 185–95.

Bittel, K. 1970. *Hattusha: The Capital of the Hittites.* Oxford.

Bivar, A. D. H. 1961. "A 'Satrap' of Cyrus the Younger." *NC*, Series 7/1: 119–27.

———. 1970. "A Persian Monument at Athens, and Its Connections with the Achaemenid State Seals." In M. Boyce and I. Gershevitch, eds., *W. B. Henning Memorial Volume*: 43–61. London.

———. 1985. "Achaemenid Coins, Weights and Measures." In I. Gershevitch, ed., *The Cambridge History of Iran: The Median and Achaemenian Periods*: 610–39. Cambridge.

———. 1992. Review of M. Boyce, R. Grenet, and R. Beck, *A History of Zoroastrianism 3: Zoroastrianism under Macedonian and Roman Rule*. *JRS* 82: 265–7.

Blagg, T. F. C. 1985. "Cult Practice and Its Social Context in the Religious Sanctuaries of Latium and Southern Etruria: The Sanctuary of Diana at Nemi." In C. Malone and S. Stoddart, eds., *Papers in Italian Archaeology* IV. Part iv: Classical and Medieval Archaeology. BAR International Series 246: 33–50. Oxford.

———. 1986. "Roman Religious Sites in the British Landscape." *Landscape History* 8: 15–25.

Blakolmer, F. 1988. "Limyra 3. Die Grabung in der Nekropole V." *KST* 10/2: 125–39.

———. 1993. "Die Grabung in der Nekropole V von Limyra – Vorläufige Ergebnisse." *Akten des II. Internationalen Lykien-Symposions*: 2: 149–62. Vienna.

———. 1999. "Zum Grab des Ploutiades in der Nekropole V von Limyra." In H. Scherrer and H. Thür Taeuber eds., *Steine und Wege. Festschrift für D. Knibbe*. Vienna.

Blakolmer, F., K. R. Krierer, F. Krinzinger, A. Landskrom-Dinstl, H. D. Szemethy, and K. Zhuber-Okrog, eds. 1996. *Fremde Zeiten. Festschrift für Jürgen Borchhardt zum sechzigsten Geburtstag am 25. Februar 1996.* Vienna.

Blanton, R. E. 2000. *Hellenistic, Roman and Byzantine Settlement Patterns of the Coast Lands of Western Rough Cilicia.* Oxford.

Blázquez, J. M. 1989. "¿Romanización o asimilación?" In J. M. Blázquez, ed., *Nuevos Estudios sobre la Romanización*: 99–145. Madrid.

Boardman, J. 1959. "Chian and Early Ionic Architecture." *AntJ* 39: 170–218.

———. 1970a. *Greek Gems and Finger Rings: Early Bronze Age to Late Classical.* London.

———. 1970b. "Pyramidal Stamp Seals in the Persian Empire." *Iran* 8: 19–45.

———. 1976. "Greek and Persian Glyptic in Anatolia and Beyond." *RA* 1976: 45–54.

———. 1998. "Seals and Signs: Anatolian Stamp Seals of the Persian Period Revisited." *Iran* 36: 1–13.

———. 1999. *The Greeks Overseas.* 4th ed. London.

———. 2000. *Persia and the West: An Archaeological Investigation of the Genesis of Achaemenid Persian Art.* London.

———. 2001. *Greek Gems and Finger Rings.* 2d ed. London.

Bodenstedt, F. 1976. "Satrapen und Dynasten auf Phokäischen Hekten." *SM* 26: 69–75.

Bibliography

Boffo, L. 1978. "La lettera di Dario I a Gadata: i privilegi del tempio di Apollo a Magnesia sul Meandro." *Bulletino dell'Istituto di Diritto Romano 'Vittorio Scialoja'* 81: 267–303.

Bogoliubov, M. H. 1971. "An Old Iranian Prayer to Ahuramazda in Aramaic Characters on the Undeciphered Inscription from Cappadocia." In V. Gafurov, ed., *Istoriya Iranskogo Gosudarstra i Kul'turî*: 277–85, 347. Moscow.

Böhlau, J., and K. Schefold. 1940. *Larisa am Hermos I. Die Bauten*. Berlin.

Bollweg, J. 1988. "Protoachämenidische Siegelbilder." *AMI* 21: 53–61.

Bonatz, D. 2000. *Das syro-hethitische Grabdenkmal. Untersuchungen zur Entstehung einer neuen Bildgattung in der Eisenzeit im nordsyrisch-südostanatolischen Raum*. Mainz.

Bookidis, N. 1967. "A Study of the Use and Geographical Distribution of Architectural Sculpture in the Archaic Period." Ph.D. dissertation, Bryn Mawr College.

Booth, A. 1991. "The Age for Reclining and Its Attendant Perils." In W. J. Slater, ed., *Dining in a Classical Context*: 105–20. Ann Arbor, MI.

Borchhardt, J. 1968. "Epichorische, gräko-persische beeinflußte Reliefs in Kilikien." *IstMitt* 18: 161–211.

  ed. 1975. *Myra. Eine lykische Metropole in antiker und byzantischer Zeit*. IstForsch 30. Berlin.

  1976. *Die Bauskulptur des Heroons von Limyra. Das Grabmal des lykischen Königs Perikles*. Berlin.

  1980. "Zur Deutung lykischer Audienzszenen." In H. Metzger, ed., *Actes du Colloque sur la Lycie Antique, Istanbul 1977*: 7–12. Paris.

  1983. "Bildnisse achaimenidischer Herrscher." *AMI Ergänzungsband* 10: 207–23.

  1993. *Die Steine von Zêmuri. Archäologische Forschungen an den verborgenen Wassern von Limyra*. Vienna.

  1996–7. "Zur Politik der Dynasten Trbbenimi und Perikle von Zemuri." *Lykia* 3: 1–23.

  1997. "Gedanken zur lykischen Gesellschaftsstruktur unter attischer und persischer Herrschaft." In G. Arsebük, M. J. Mellink, and W. Schirmer eds., *Light on Top of the Black Hill, Festschrift Halet Çambel*: 155–169.

  1999. "Die Bedeutung der lykischen Königshöfe für die Entstehung des Porträts." In H. von Steuben, ed., *Antike Porträts. Zum Gedächtnis von Helga von Heintze*: 53–84. Möhnsee.

  2004. "Das Fürstentum von Myra/Trysa in der Klasik." In H. Heftner and K. Tomaschitz, eds., *Ad Fontes: Festschrift für Gerhard Dobesch*: 379–406. Vienna.

  2007. "Der Gürtel als Zeichen der Gefolgschaft." In *Achaemenid Impact*: 33–58. Istanbul.

Borchardt, J., and E. Bleibtreu. 2008. "Von der Pferdedecke zum Sattel. Antike Reitkunst zwischen Ost und West." In I. Delemen, S. Çokay-Kepçe, A. Özdizbay, and Ö Turak, eds., *Euergetes. Festschrift für Prof. Dr. Haluk Abbasoğlu zum 65. Geburtstag*: 167–215. Antalya.

Borchhardt, J., H. Eichner, M. Pesditschek, and P. Ruggendorfer. 1997–9. "Archäologisch sprachwissenschaftliches Corpus der Denkmäler mit lykischer Schrift." *AnzWien* 134: 11–96.

Borchhardt, J., and W. Schiele. 1976. *Die Bauskulptur des Heroons von Limyra. Das Grabmal des lykischen Königs Perikles*. Berlin.

Borger, R. 1982. "Die Chronologie des Darius-Denkmals am Behistun Felsen." *Nachrichten der Akademie der Wissenschaften in Göttingen, philosophische-historische Klasse* 3. Göttingen.

Borger, R., and W. Hinz. 1959. "Eine Dareios-Inschrift aus Pasargadae." *ZDMG* 109: 117–27.

BIBLIOGRAPHY

Börker-Klähn, J. 1982. *Altvorderasiatische Bildstelen und Vergleichbare Felsreliefs*. Mainz.

Boschung, D. 1979. "Ein Dämon und drei Götter. Zur Deutung des Harpyien-Monumentes." *Hefte des Archäologischen Seminars der Universität Bern* 5: 10–15.

Bosworth, A. B. 1990. "Plutarch, Callisthenes and the Peace of Callias." *JHS* 110: 1–13.

Bothmer, B. V. 1961. *Egyptian Sculpture of the Late Period, 700 B.C. to 100 A.D.* New York.

Boucharlat, R. 1984. "Monuments religieux de la Perse achéménide: état des questions." In G. Roux, ed., *Temples et sanctuaires*: 119–35. Lyon.

— 1990a. "La fin des palais achéménides de Suse: une mort naturelle." In F. Vallat, ed., *Contribution à l'histoire de l'Iran: mélanges offerts à Jean Perrot*: 225–33. Paris.

— 1990b. "Suse et la Susiane à l'époque achéménide: données archéologiques." In H. Sancisi-Weerdenburg and A. Kuhrt, eds., *AchHist 4. Centre and Periphery*: 149–75. Leiden.

— 1997. "Susa under Achaemenid Rule." In J. Curtis, ed., *Mesopotamia and Iran in the Persian Period: Conquest and Imperialism, 539–331 B.C.*: 54–67. London.

— 1998. "A la recherche d'Ecbatane sur Tepe Hegmataneh." In R. Boucharlat, J. E. Curtis, and E. Haerinck, eds., *Neo-Assyrian, Median, Achaemenian and Other Studies in Honor of David Stronach 1: IrAnt*: 33: 173–86. Gent.

— 2005. "Iran." In *L'archéologie de l'empire achéménide*: 221–92. Paris.

Boucharlat, R., and M. T. Atai. 2009. "An Achaemenid Pavilion and Other Remains in Tang-i Bulaghi." *ARTA* 2009.005: 1–33.

Bourdieu, P. 1977. *Outline of a Theory of Practice*. Trans. R. Nice. Cambridge.

— 1984. *Distinction: A Social Critique of the Judgement of Taste*. London.

Bourgarel, A., H. Metzger, and G. Siebert. 1992. *La région nord du Letoon. Fouilles de Xanthos* 9. Paris.

Bowersock, G. W. 1986. "The Mechanics of Subversion in the Roman Provinces." In A. Giovannini, ed., *Opposition et résistance à l'empire d'Auguste à Trajan*. Entretiens Hardt 33: 291–320.

Bowman, A., et al. 1990. "Two Letters from Vindolanda." *Britannia* 21: 33–52.

Bowman, R. A. 1970. *Aramaic Ritual Texts from Persepolis*. Chicago.

Boyce, M. 1975. *A History of Zoroastrianism 1*. Leiden.

— 1982. *A History of Zoroastrianism 2*. Cologne.

Boyce, M., F. Grenet, and R. Beck. 1991. *A History of Zoroastrianism 3*. Leiden.

Bray, T. L. 2003. "The Commensal Politics of Early States and Empires." In T. L. Bray, *The Archaeology and Politics of Food and Feasting in Early States and Empires*: 1–16. New York.

Bregstein, L. 1993. "Seal Selection and Seal Usage in Fifth Century B.C. Nippur, Iraq: A Study of the Murashu Archive." Ph.D. dissertation, University of Pennsylvania.

— 1997. "Sealing Practice in the Fifth Century B.C.: Murashu Archive from Nippur, Iraq." In M.-F. Boussac and A. Invernizzi, eds., *Archives et sceaux du monde hellénistique. Archivi et sigilli nel monde ellenistico BCH*, Suppl. 29: 53–63. Paris.

Bremmer, J. 2008. "Priestly Personnel of the Ephesian Artemision: Anatolian, Persian, Greek and Roman Aspects." http://theol.eldoc.ub.rug.nl/FILES/root/2008/Priestly_1/Bremmer-Priests.pdf.

Bresciani, E. 1985. "Ugiahorresnet a Menfi." *Egitto e Vicino Oriente* 8: 1–6.

Brewer, J., and R. Porter, eds. 1993. *Consumption and the World of Goods*. London.

Briant, P. 1973a. *Antigone le Borgne*. Paris.

— 1973b. "Remarques sur 'laoi' et esclaves en Asie Mineure hellénistique." *Actes du Colloque 1971 sur l'esclavage*: 93–133. Paris.

— 1974. "Villages et communautés villageoises d'asie achéménide et hellénistique." *JESHO* 18: 165–88.

1978–9. "Contrainte militaire, dépendence rurale et exploitation des territoires en Asie achéménide." Index. *Quaderni camerti di studi romanistici* 8: 48–98.

1980. "Forces productives, dépendance rurale et idéologies religieuses dans l'empire achéménide." *Table ronde de Besançon 1977*: 1–42.

1982. *Rois, Tributs et Paysans*. Paris.

1984. *L'Asie Centrale et les royaumes proche-orientaux du premier millénaire*. Paris.

1985a. "Dons de terres et de villes: l'Asie Mineure dans le contexte achéménide." *REA* 87: 53–72.

1985b. "Les Iraniens d'Asie Mineure après la chute de l'empire achéménide." *DHA* 11: 167–95.

1986a. "Guerre, tribut et forces productives dans l'empire achéménide." *DHA* 12: 33–48.

1986b. "Polythéisme et empire unitaire. Remarques sur la politique religieuse des Achéménides." *Les Grand Figures Religieuses: fonctionnement pratique et symbolique dans l'antiquité, Besançon, 25–26 avril 1984*. Centre de Recherches d'Histoire Ancienne 68: 425–43. Paris.

1987. "Pouvoir central et polycentrisme culturel dans l'empire achéménide: quelques réflexions et suggestions." In H. Sancisi-Weerdenburg, ed., *AchHist 1. Sources, Structures and Synthesis*: 1–32. Leiden.

1988a. "Ethno-classe dominante et populations soumoises dans l'empire achéménide: le cas d'Egypte." In A. Kuhrt and H. Sancisi-Weerdenburg, eds., *AchHist 3. Method and Theory*: 137–74. Leiden.

1988b. "Le nomadisme du Grand Roi." *IrAnt* 23: 252–73.

1989a. "Histoire et idéologie: les greces et la 'décadence perse.' " In M. M. Mactoux and E. Gery, eds., *Mélanges P. Léveque*: 2: 33–47. Paris.

1989b. "Table du roi, tribut et redistribution chez les Achéménides." In P. Briant and C. Herrenschmidt, eds., *Les Tributs dans l'empire perse: Actes de la Table Rond de Paris, 12–13 décembre 1986*: 35–44. Paris.

1990. "The Seleucid Kingdom, the Achaemenid Empire and the History of the Near East in the First Millennium B.C." In P. Bilde et al., eds, *Religion and Religious Practice in the Seleucid Kingdom*: 40–65. Aarhus.

1991. "De Sardes à Suse." In H. Sancisi-Weerdenburg and A. Kuhrt, eds., *AchHist 6. Asia Minor and Egypt: Old Cultures in a New Empire*: 67–82. Leiden.

1992. "La date des revoltes babyloniennes contre Xerxés." *StIr* 21: 7–20.

1993. "Alexandre à Sardes." In *Alexander the Great: Myth and Reality* ARID Suppl. 21: 1–15. Rome.

1994a. "L'eau de Grand Roi." In L. Milano, ed., *Drinking in Ancient Societies: History and Culture of Drinks in the Ancient Near East – Papers of a Symposium Held in Rome, May 17–19, 1990*: 45–65. Padova.

1994b. "L'histoire achéménide: sources, methodes, raisonnements et modeles." *Topoi* 4: 109–30.

1994c. "Sources gréco-hellenistiques, institutions perses et institutions macédoniens: continuités, changements et bricolages." In H. Sancisi-Weerdenburg, A. Kuhrt, and M. C. Root, eds., *AchHist 8. Continuity and Change*: 283–310. Leiden.

ed. 1995. *Dans le pas des Dix-Mille: peuples et pays du Proche-Orient vus par un Grec – Actes de la Table Ronde Internationale Toulouse, 3–4 fevrier 1995*. Toulouse.

1996a *AchHist 10. Histoire de l'empire perse de Cyrus à Alexandre*. Leiden.

1996b. "Une curieuse affaire à Éléphantine en 410 av. J.-C.: Widranga, le sanctuaire de Khnum et le temple de Yaweh." *Méditerranées* 6/7: 115–38.

1997. "Bulletin d'histoire achéménide BHAch I." In J. Andreau, M.-F. Boussac et al., eds., *Recherches récentes sur l'empire achéménide. Topoi* Suppl. 1: 5–127. Paris.

BIBLIOGRAPHY

    1998a. "Droaphernès et la statue de Sardes." In P. Briant et al., eds., *AchHist 11. Studies in Persian History: Essays in Memory of David M. Lewis:* 205–26. Leiden.

    1998b. "War, Persian Society and the Achaemenid Empire." In K. Raaflaub and N. Rosenstein, eds., *Soldiers, Society and War in the Ancient and Medieval Worlds*: 105–28. Cambridge, MA.

    1998c. "Cités et satrapes dans l'empire achéménide: Xanthos et Pixôdaros." *CRAI* 305–40.

    2001. *Bulletin d'histoire achéménide BHAch II.* Paris.

    2002. *From Cyrus to Alexander: A History of the Persian Empire.* Winona Lake, IN.

    2003. "À propos du roi-jardinier: remarques sur l'histoire d'un dossier documentaire." In W. F. M. Henkelman and A. Kuhrt, eds., *AchHist 13. A Persian Perspective: Essays in Memory of Heleen Sancisi-Weerdenburg*: 33–49. Leiden.

    2010. *Alexander the Great and His Empire.* Trans. A. Kuhrt. Princeton, NJ.

Briant, P., and R. Boucharlat, eds. 2005. *L'archéologie de l'empire achéménide: nouvelles recherches.* Persika 6. Paris.

Briant, P., W. F. M. Henkelman, and M. W. Stolper, eds. 2008. *L'archive des Fortifications de Persépolis: état des questions et perspectives de recherches.* Persika 12. Paris.

Briant, P., and C. Herrenschmidt, eds. 1989. *Le tribut dans l'empire perse.* Paris.

British Museum, Department of Greek and Roman Antiquities. 1900. *The Nereid Monument and Later Lycian Sculpture.* London.

Brosius, M. 1996. *Women in Ancient Persia, 559–331 B.C.* Oxford.

    1998. "Artemis Persike and Artemis Anaitis." In M. Brosius and A. Kuhrt, eds., *AchHist 11. Studies in Persian History: Essays in Memory of David M. Lewis*: 227–38. Leiden.

    2000. *The Persian Empire from Cyrus II to Artaxerxes I.* London.

    ed. 2003. *Ancient Archives and Archival Traditions: Concepts of Record-Keeping in the Ancient World.* Oxford Studies in Ancient Documents. Oxford.

Brown, S. C. 1986. "Media and Secondary State Formation in the Neo-Assyrian Zagros." *JCS* 38: 107–19.

    1988. "The Mêdikos Logos of Herodotus and the Evolution of the Median State." In A. Kuhrt and H. Sancisi-Weerdenburg, eds., *AchHist 3. Method and Theory:* 71–86. Leiden.

    1997. "Ecbatana." *EncIr* 8/1: 80a–84a.

Brumfiel, E. M. 1983. "Aztec State Making: Ecology, Structure and the Origin of the State." *AmAnth* 85: 261–84.

    1987. "Elite and Utilitarian Crafts in the Aztec State." In E. M. Brumfield and T. K. Earle, eds., *Specialization, Exchange and Complex Societies*: 102–18. Cambridge.

    1996. "Figurines and the Aztec State: Testing the Effectiveness of Ideological Domination." In R. Wright, ed., *Gender and Archaeology*: 143–66. Philadelphia.

Bruns-Özgan, C. 1987. *Lykische Grabreliefs des 5. und 4. Jahrhunderts v. Chr.* IstMitt 33. Tübingen.

    1989. "Grabstelen gebildeter Jünglinge." In H.-U. Cain, H. Gabelmann, and D. Salzmann, eds., *Festschrift für Nikolaus Himmelmann*: 183–90. Mainz.

Brunt, P. A. 1976. "The Romanization of the Local Ruling Classes in the Roman Empire." In D. M. Pippidi, ed., *Assimilation et résistance à la culture gréco-romaine dans le monde ancien*: 161–73. Paris.

Bryce, T. R. 1979. "Lycian Tomb Families and Their Social Implications." *JESHO* 23: 296–313.

    1980. "Sacrifices to the Dead in Lycia." *Kadmos* 19: 41–9.

    1983. "The Arrival of the Goddess Leto in Lycia." *Historia* 32: 1–13.

    1986. *The Lycians in Literary and Epigraphic Sources. The Lycians: A Study of Lycian History and Civilisation to the Conquest of Alexander the Great* 1. Copenhagen.

1995. "The Lycian Kingdom in Southwest Anatolia." *CANE*: 1161–72. New York.

1996. "The Gods and Oracles of Ancient Lycia." In M. P. J. Dillon, ed., *Religion in the Ancient World: New Themes and Approaches*: 41–50. Amsterdam.

2003. "The Luwians in Their Iron Age Context." In H. C. Melchert, ed., *The Luwians*: 93–123. Leiden.

Buchanan, A. 2003. *Justice, Legitimacy and Self-Determination*. Oxford.

Buckler, W. H. 1924. *Sardis* VI/2: *Lydian Inscriptions*. Leiden.

Buckler, W. H., and D. M. Robinson. 1912. "Greek Inscriptions from Sardis I." *AJA* 16: 11–18.

1932. *Sardis* VII/1: *Greek and Latin Inscriptions*. Leiden.

Buitron-Oliver, D., and E. Herscher. 1997. "The City-Kingdoms of Early Iron Age Cyprus in Their Eastern Mediterranean Context." *BASOR* 308: 5–7.

Buluç, S. 1993. "Anadolu'da Kremasyon – Ölü Yakma – Geleneği." *1992 Yılı Anadolu Medeniyetleri Müzesi Konferansları*: 83–101. Ankara.

Burkard, G. 1995. "Literarische Tradition und historische Realität. Die persische Eroberung Ägyptens am Beispiel Elephantine." *ZÄS* 122/1: 31–7.

Burkert, W. 1991. "Oriental Symposia: Contrasts and Parallels." In W. J. Slater, ed., *Dining in a Classical Context*: 7–24. Ann Arbor, MI.

Burney, C. A. 1995. "Urartian Funerary Customs." In S. Campbell and A. Green, eds., *The Archaeology of Death in the Ancient Near East*. Oxbow Monograph 51: 205–8. Oxford.

Burney, C. A., and D. M. Lang. 1971. *The Peoples of the Hills: Ancient Ararat and Caucasus*. London.

Buschor, E. 1933. "Altsamische Grabstelen." *AthMitt* 58: 22–46.

Büsing-Kolbe, A. 1978. "Frühe griechische Türen." *JdI* 93: 66–174.

Butler, H. C. 1922. *Sardis* I: *The Excavations*. Leiden.

Butler, J. 1993. *Bodies That Matter: On the Discursive Limits of "Sex."* New York.

1999. *Gender Trouble: Feminism and the Subversion of Identity*. New York.

Byvanck, A. W. 1948. "Some Remarks on Clazomenian Sarcophagi." *AntCl* 93–100.

Cahill, N. D. 1985. "The Treasury at Persepolis: Gift-Giving at the City of the Persians." *AJA* 89: 373–89.

1988. "Taş Kule: A Persian-Period Tomb near Phokaia." *AJA* 92: 481–501.

2002. "Lydian Houses, Domestic Assemblages, and Household Size." In D. C. Hopkins, ed., *Across the Anatolian Plateau*. *AASOR* 57 2000: 173–85. Boston.

Cahill, N. D., and J. H. Kroll. 2005. "New Archaic Coin Finds at Sardis." *AJA* 109: 589–617.

Cahn, H. 1975. "Dynast oder Satrap?" *SM* 25: 84–91.

1985. "Tissaphernes in Astyra." *AA* 587–94.

Calder, W. M. 1925. "The Royal Road in Herodotus." *CR* 39: 7–11.

Callieri, P. 2007. *L'archéologie du Fars à l'époque achéménide: quatre leçons au Collége de France, 8, 15, 22 et 29 mars 2007*. Persika 11. Paris.

Calmeyer, P. 1973. *Reliefbronzen in babylonischen Stil. Eine westiranische Werkstatt des 10. Jahrhunderts v. Chr.* Munich.

1975. "Zur Genese altiranischer Motive III. Felsgräber." *AMI* 8: 99–113.

1976. "Zur Genese altiranischer Motive IV. 'Persönliche Krone' und Diadem." *AMI*, new ser., 9: 45–95.

1978. "Das Grabrelief von Ravansar." *AMI* 11: 73–85.

1992. "Zwei mit historischen Szenen bemalte Balken der Achaimenidenzeit." *MJBK* 43: 7–18.

1993. "Die Gefässe auf den Gabenbringer-Reliefs in Persepolis." *AMI* 26: 147–60.

1996. "Achaimenidische Möbel un Kussu Sa Sarrute." In G. Herrmann, ed., *The Furniture of Western Asia, Ancient and Traditional: Papers of the Conference Held at the Institute of Archaeology, University College London, June 28 to 30, 1993*: 223–31. Munich.

Calmeyer, P., and A. S. Shahbazi. 1976. "The Persepolis 'Treasury Reliefs' Once More." *AMI*, new ser., 9: 151–6.

Cameron, C. M., ed. 2008. *Invisible Citizens: Captives and Their Consequences*. Salt Lake City, UT.

Cameron, G. G. 1948. *Persepolis Treasury Tablets*. OIP 65. Chicago.

———. 1958. "Persepolis Treasury Tablets Old and New." *JNES* 17: 161–76.

———. 1965. "New Tablets from the Persepolis Treasury." *JNES* 24: 167–92.

Cannon, A. 1989. "The Historical Dimension in Mortuary Expressions of Status and Sentiment." *CAnth* 30: 437–58.

———. 1991. "Gender, Status, and the Focus of Material Display." In D. Walde and N. D. Willows, eds., *The Archaeology of Gender: Proceedings of the 22nd Annual Chacmool Conference*: 144–49. Calgary, ON.

Cardascia, G. 1951. *Les archives de Murashu: une famille d'hommes d'affaires babyloniens à l'époque perse 455–403 av. J.-C*. Paris.

Cargill, J. 1977. "The Nabonidus Chronicle and the Fall of Lydia." *American Journal of Ancient History* 2/2: 97–116.

Carradice, I. 1987a. *Coinage and Administration in the Athenian and Persian Empires*. BAR International Series 343. Oxford.

———. 1987b. "The 'Regal' Coinage of the Persian Empire." In I. Carradice, ed., *Coinage and Administration in the Athenian and Persian Empires*. BAR International Series 343: 73–95. Oxford.

Carstens, A. M. 1999. "Survey of Ancient Tombs on the Halikarnassos Peninsula." *16. AST*: 330–33. Ankara.

———. 2001. "Drinking Vessels in Tombs: A Cultic Connection." In C. Scheffer, ed., *Ceramics in Context: Proceedings of the Internordic Colloquium on Ancient Pottery, Stockholm, 13–15 June 1997*: 127–38. Stockholm.

———. 2002. "Tomb Cult on the Halikarnassos Peninsula." *AJA* 106: 391–409.

———. 2006. "Cultural Contact and Cultural Change: Colonialism and Empire." In T. Bekker-Nielsen, ed., *Rome and the Black Sea Region: Domination, Romanisation, Resistance*. Black Sea Studies 5: 119–31. Aarhus.

Carter, E., and A. Parker. 1995. "Pots, People, and the Archaeology of Death in Northern Syria and Southern Anatolia in the Latter Half of the Third Millennium BC." In S. Campbell and A. Green, eds, *The Archaeology of Death in the Ancient Near East*. Oxbow Monograph 51: 96–115. Oxford.

Casabonne, O. 1996. "Présence et influence perses in Cilicie à l'époque achéménide. Iconographie et représentations." *AnatAnt* 4: 121–45.

———. 1998. "La Cilicie à l'époque achéménide." Ph.D. dissertation, University of Toulouse-Le Mirail.

———. 2000. "Conquête perse et phénomène monétaire: l'exemple cilicien." In O. Casabonne, ed., *Mécanismes et innovations monétaires dans l'Anatolie achéménide: numismatique et histoire*. Varia Anatolica 12: 21–93. Paris.

———. 2004. *La Cilicie à l'époque achéménide*. Persika 3. Paris.

———. 2007. "The Formation of Cappadocia: Iranian Populations and Achaemenid Influence." In *Achaemenid Impact*: 103–6. Istanbul.

Casabonne, O., and M. Gabrielli. 2007. "A Note on Persian Armours." In *Achaemenid Impact*: 265–70. Istanbul.

Cattenat, A., and J.-C. Gardin. 1977. "Diffusion comparée de quelques genres de poterie caractéristiques de l'époque achéménide sur le Plateau Iranien et en Asie Centrale."

BIBLIOGRAPHY

In *Le Plateau Iranien et l'Asie Centrale des origines a la conquête islamique: colloques internationaux du Centre National de la Recherche Scientifique*: 567: 225–48. Paris.

Cavalier, L. 2002. "Remarques sur les techniques de construction lyciennes." *AnatAnt* 10: 227–34.

Çevik, N. 1997. "Urartu Kaya Mezarlarında Ölü Kültüne İlişkin Mimari Elemanlar." *TürkAD* 31: 419–59.

Chabot, J. B. 1918. *Répertoire d'épigraphie sémitique 3*. Paris.

Chapman, G. A. H. 1972. "Herodotus and Histiaeus' Role in the Ionian Revolt." *Historia* 21: 546–68.

Chaumont, M. L. 1990. "Un nouveau gouverneur de Sardes à l'époque achéménide d'après une inscriptions récemment découverte." *Syria* 57/3: 579–608.

Chauveau, M. 1999. "Ordre chronologique des lettres démotiques d'Éléphantine." RdÉ 50:269–71.

Childs, W. A. P. 1978. *The City Reliefs of Lycia*. Princeton, NJ.

1979. "The Authorship of the Inscribed Pillar of Xanthos." *AnatSt* 29:97–102.

1981. "Lycian Relations with Persians and Greeks in the Fifth and Fourth Centuries Re-examined." *AnatSt* 31:55–80.

1983. "Lycian Art of the Classical Period." *AJA* 87:229.

Childs, W. A. P., and P. Demargne. 1989. *Fouilles de Xanthos VIII: Le monument des Néréides. Le décor sculpté*. Paris.

Cholidis, N. 1992. *Möbel in Ton. Untersuchungen zur archäologischen un religiongeschichtlichen Bedeutung der Terrakottamodelle von Tischen, Stühlen und Betten aus dem Alten Orient*. Altertumskunde des Vorderen Orients 1. Münster.

Christiano, T. 2004. "The Authority of Democracy." *JPolPhil* 12/3: 245–70.

Claessen, H. J. M., and P. Skalnik, eds. 1978. *The Early State*. The Hague.

Clark, J. J. 2004. "Tracking Cultural Affiliation: Enculturation and Ethnicity." In B. J. Mills, ed., *Identity, Feasting, and the Archaeology of the Greater Southwest: Proceedings of the 2002 Southwest Symposium*: 42–73. Boulder, CO.

Clarkson, L. A., and E. M. Crawford. 2001. *Feast and Famine: Food and Nutrition in Ireland, 1500–1920*. Oxford.

Clermont-Ganneau, S. 1898. "Inscription araméenne de Cappadoce." *CRAI* 1898: 630–40, 808–10.

1900. "Inscription araméenne de Cappadoce." *Recueil d'archéologie orientale* 3: 59–70.

1921. "Le paradeisos royal achéménide de Sidon." *RBibl* 30: 106–9.

Clifford, J., and G. E. Marcus, eds. 1986. *Writing Culture: The Poetics and Politics of Ethnography*. Berkeley, CA.

Cohen, G. M. 1983. "Colonization and Population Transfer in the Hellenistic World." In E. van Dack, P. van Dessel, and W. van Gucht, eds., *Egypt and the Hellenistic World*: 63–74. Leuven.

Coindoz, M. 1985. "Recherches archéologiques dans la région d'Avanos Cappadoce: le Tumulus du Cec." *Anatolica* 12:1–28.

Çokay-Kepçe, S., and M. Recke. 2007. "Achaemenid Bowls in Pamphylia." In *Achaemenid Impact*: 83–96. Istanbul.

Collon, D. 1992. "Banquets in the Art of the Ancient Near East." In R. Gyselen, ed., *Banquets d'Orient*. Res Orientales 4: 23–9. Bures-sur-Yvette.

1996. "A Hoard of Sealings from Ur." In M.-F. Boussac and A. Invernizzi, eds., *Archives et sceaux du monde hellénistique: archivi et sigilli nel monde ellenistico*. BCH Suppl. 29: 65–84. Paris.

Comstock, M. B., and C. C. Vermeule. 1976. *Sculpture in Stone: The Greek, Roman, and Etruscan Collections of the Museum of Fine Arts, Boston*. Boston.

BIBLIOGRAPHY

Conrad, G. W., and A. A. Demarest. 1984. *Religion and Empire: The Dynamics of Aztec and Inca Expansionism*. Cambridge.
Cook, R. M. 1966. "Painted Sarcophagi from Pitane." *Anadolu* 10:179–92.
— 1974. "Old Smyrna: The Clazomenian Sarcophagi." *BSA* 69: 55–60.
— 1981. *Clazomenian Sarcophagi*. Kerameus 3. Mainz.
Cook, S. A. 1917. "A Lydian–Aramaic Bilingual." *JHS* 37: 77–87, 219–31.
Cooney, J. D. 1953. "The Portrait of an Egyptian Collaborator." *Brooklyn Museum Bulletin* 15:1–16.
Corsaro, M. 1985. "Tassazione regia e tassazione cittidina dagli achemenidi ai re ellenistici: alcune osservazioni." *REA* 87: 73–95.
Cosgrove, D. E. 1984. *Social Formation and Symbolic Landscape*. London.
Cosgrove, D. E., and S. Daniels, eds. 1988. *The Iconography of Landscape: Essays on the Symbolic Representation, Design and Use of Past Environments*. Cambridge.
Coşkun, G. 2005. "Daskyleion'da Orta Akhaemenid Dönem." Ph.D. dissertation, Ege Üniversitesi, Sosyal Bilimler Enstitüsü, Klasik Arkeoloji Bilim Dalı.
Costin, C. L. 1991. "Craft Specialization: Issues in Defining, Documenting, and Explaining the Organization of Production." *AMT* 3: 1–56
Counihan, C. 1999. *The Anthropology of Food and Body: Gender, Meaning, and Power*. London.
Coupel, P., and P. Demargne. 1969. *Fouilles de Xanthos* III: *Le monument des Néréides. L'architecture*. Paris.
Cousin, G. 1899. "Inscriptions de Termessos de Pisidie." *BCH* 23: 280–303.
Cowley, A. E. 1921. "L'inscription bilingue araméo-lydienne de Sardes." *CRAI* 1922: 7–14.
— 1923. *Aramaic Papyri of the 5th Century B.C.* Oxford.
Cremer, M. 1984. "Zwei neue gräko-persische Stelen." *EA* 3: 87–99.
Cross, F. M. 1966. "An Aramaic Inscription from Daskyleion." *BASOR* 184: 7–10.
Cruz-Urribe, E. 1980. "On the Existence of Psammeticus IV." *Serapis* 5/2: 35–9.
Cuny, A. 1920. "L'inscription lydo-araméenne de Sardes I." *REA* 22: 259–72.
— 1921. "L'inscription lydo-araméenne de Sardes II." *REA* 23: 1–27.
Curtis, C. D. 1925. *Sardis* XIII: *Jewelry and Gold Work*. Rome.
Curtis, J. 1983. "Late Assyrian Bronze Coffins." *AnatSt* 33: 85–95.
Curtis, J., and N. Tallis, eds. 2005. *Forgotten Empire: The World of Ancient Persia*. London.
Curtis, R. I. 1991. *Garum and Salsamenta: Production and Commerce in Materia Medica*. Leiden.
Dalton, O. M. 1964. *The Treasure of the Oxus with Other Examples of Early Oriental Metal-Work*. 3d ed. London.
Damerow, P. 1996. "Food Production and Social Status as Documented in Proto-Cuneiform Texts." In P. Wiessner and W. Schiefenhövel, eds., *Food and the Status Quest: An Interdisciplinary Perspective*: 149–169. Providence, RI.
Dandamaev, M. A. 1963. "Foreign Slaves on the Estates of the Achaemenid Kings and Their Nobles, II." *International Congress of Orientalists, XXV, Moscow 1960*: 147–54. Moscow.
— 1975. "Forced Labour in the Palace Economy of Achaemenid Iran." *Altorientalische Forschungen* 2: 71–78.
— 1984a. "Royal *Paradeisoi* in Babylonia." *ActIr* 23: 113–17. Leiden.
— 1984b. *Slavery in Babylonia: From Nabopolassar to Alexander the Great*. De Kalb, IL.
— 1989. *A Political History of the Achaemenid Empire*. Leiden.
— 1999. "Achaemenid Imperial Policies and Provincial Governments." In *Neo-Assyrian, Median, Achaemenian and other Studies in Honor of David Stronach 2*. *IrAnt* 34: 269–82.

Dandamaev, M. A., and V. G. Lukonin. 1989. *The Culture and Social Institutions of Ancient Iran*. Cambridge.

Danish Archaeological Expedition to Bodrum. 1981–97. *The Maussolleion at Halikarnassos: Reports of the Danish Archaeological Expedition to Bodrum* 1–3. Copenhagen.

Davesne, A., and F. Laroche-Traunecker. 1998. *Gülnar I: Le site de Meydancıkkale. Recherches enterprises sous la direction d'Emmanuel Laroche, 1971–1982*. Paris.

Davesne, A., and G. Le Rider. 1989. *Le trésor de Meydancıkkale. Gülnar II*. Paris.

Davesne, A., A. Lemaire, and H. Lozachmeur. 1987. "Le site archéologique de Meydancikkale Turquie: du royaume Pirindu à la garnison ptolémaïque." *CRAI* 1987: 365–77.

Davies, R. W. 1971. "The Roman Military Diet." *Britannia* 2: 122–42.

Debord, P. 1972. *Actes due Colloque 1971 sur l'esclavage*. Besançon.

——— 1982. *Aspects sociaux et économiques de la vie reliegieuse dans l'Anatolie gréco-romaine*. Études préliminaires aux religions orientales dans l'empire romain 88. Leiden.

——— 1985. "La Lydie du Nord-Est." *REA* 87: 345–56.

——— 1994. "Les routes royales en Asie Mineure Occidentale." *Pallas* 43: 89–97.

——— 1999. *L'Asie Mineure au IV siècle*. Paris.

Dedeoğlu, H. 1991. "Lydia'da bir tümülüs kazısı." *MKKS* 1: 119–49.

——— 1992. "Yabızlar Tepesi Tümülüsü." *MKKS* 2: 65–79.

——— 1994. "Lydia'da bir kilise kazısı ön rapor." *MKKS* 4: 185–97.

——— 1996. "Harta Abidintepe tümülüsü kazı çalışmaları." *TürkAD* 4: 197–206.

Degani, H. 1983. *Hipponactis Testimonia et Fragmenta*. Leipzig.

de la Genière, J. 1985. "De la Phrygie à Locres Épizéphyrienne: le chemins de Cybèle." *Antiquité* 97: 693–717.

Demargne, P. 1958. *Fouilles de Xanthos I: Les piliers funéraires*. Paris.

——— 1974. *Fouilles de Xanthos V: Tombes-maisons, tombes rupestres et sarcophages*. Paris.

——— 1976. "L'iconographie dynastique au Monument des Néréides de Xanthos." *Recueil Plassart, Études sur l'antiquité grecque offertes à André Plassart par ses collègues de la Sorbonne*. Paris.

DeMarrais, E., L. J. Castillo, and T. Earle. 1996. "Ideology, Materialization, and Power Strategies." *CAnth* 37: 15–31.

de Mecquenem, R. 1938. "The Achaemenid and Later Remains at Susa." In A. U. Pope, ed., *A Survey of Persian Art:* 1: 321–29. Oxford.

——— 1947. *Contribution à l'étude du palais achéménide de Suse*, MDP 30. Paris.

Dentzer, J. M. 1969. "Reliefs au banquet dans l'Asie Mineure du Ve siècle av. J.-C." *RA* 2: 195–224.

——— 1971. "Aux origines de l'iconographie du banquet couché." *RA* 4: 215–58.

——— 1982. *Le motif du banquet couché dans le Proche-Orient et le monde grec du VII au IV siècle avant J.C.* Rome.

Descat, R. 1985. "Mnésimachos, Hérodote et le système tributaire achéménide." *REA* 87: 97–112.

——— 1989. "Notes sur la politique tributaire de Darius Ier." In P. Briant and C. Herrenschmidt, eds., *Le tribut dans l'empire achéménide*: 77–93. Paris.

——— 1992. "Le paradis de Tissapherne." *DATA* (Achaemenid History Newsletter) 1.

——— 1994. "Darius, le roi kapelos." In H. Sancisi-Weerdenburg, A. Kuhrt, and M. C. Root, eds., *AchHist 8. Continuity and Change*: 161–66. Leiden.

——— 1997. "Le tribut et l'économie tributaire dans l'empire achéménide." *Topoi* Suppl. 1: 253–62.

des Courtils, J., and T. Marksteiner. 1997. "Un établissement fortifié au voisinage de Xanthos." *AnatAnt* 5: 87–100.

——— 1999. "Le long mur au nord de Xanthos." *AnatAnt* 7: 89–104.

2000. "Gölbent, un nouveau site en Lycie méridionale." *AnatAnt* 8: 143–58.
Desideri, P., and A. M. Jasink, 1990. *Cilicia. Dall'età di Kizzuwatna alla conquista macedone*. Turin.
de Vos, G. 1975. "Ethnic Pluralism: Conflict and Accommodation." In G. de Vos and Ramanucci-Ross, eds., *Ethnic Identity: Cultural Continuities and Change*: 5–42. Stanford, CA.
Devreker, J. 1994. "The New Excavations at Pessinus." In E. Schwertheim, ed., *Forschungen in Galatien*. AMS 12: 105–30. Bonn.
Devreker, J., and F. Vermeulen. 1991. "Phrygians in the Neighbourhood of Pessinus Turkey." In H. Thoen, J. Bourgeois, F. Vermeulen, P. Crombé, and K. Verlaeckt, eds., *Liber Amicorum Jacques A. E. Nenquin*. Studia Archaeologica: 109–18. Gent.
DeVries, K. 1977. "Attic Pottery in the Achaemenid Empire." *AJA* 81: 544–48.
1980. "Greeks and Phrygians in the Early Iron Age." In K. DeVries, ed., *From Athens to Gordion: The Papers of a Memorial Symposium for Rodney S. Young*: 33–49. Philadelphia.
1988. "Gordion and Phrygia in the Sixth Century B.C." *Source: Notes in the History of Art*, 7/3–4: 51–9.
1996. "The Attic Pottery from Gordion." In J. H. Oakley, W. D. Coulson, and O. Palagia, eds., *Athenian Potters and Painters*: 447–55. Oxford.
2000. "The Nearly Other: The Attic Vision of Phrygians and Lydians." In B. Cohen, ed., *Not the Classical Ideal: Athens and the Construction of the Other in Greek Art*: 338–63. Leiden.
2005. "Greek Pottery and Gordion Chronology." In L. Kealhofer, ed., *The Archaeology of Midas and the Phrygians: Recent Work at Gordion*: 36–54. Philadelphia.
DeVries, K., P. I. Kuniholm, G. K. Sams, and M. M. Voigt. 2003. "New Dates for Iron Age Gordion." *Antiquity* 77: 296. http://antiquity.ac.uk/ProjGall/devries/devries.html.
Dietler, M. 1990. "Exchange, Consumption, and Colonial Interaction in the Rhône Basin of France: A Study of Early Iron Age Political Economy." Ph.D. dissertation, University of California at Berkeley.
1996. "Feasts and Commensal Politics in the Political Economy: Food, Power, and Status in Prehistoric Europe." In P. Wiessner and W. Schiefenhövel, eds., *Food and the Status Quest: An Interdisciplinary Perspective*: 87–126. Providence, RI.
2003. "Clearing the Table: Some Concluding Reflections on Commensal Politics and Imperial States." In T. L. Bray, ed., *The Archaeology and Politics of Food and Feasting in Early States and Empires*: 271–84. New York.
Dietler, M., and B. Hayden. 2001. "Digesting the Feast – Good to Eat, Good to Drink, Good to Think: An Introduction." In M. Dietler and B. Hayden, eds., *Feasts: Archaeological and Ethnographic Perspectives on Food, Politics, and Power*: 1–22. Washington, DC.
Dieulafoy, M. 1893. *L'acropole de Suse, d'après les fouilles exécutées en 1884, 1885, 1886, sous les auspices du Musée du Louvre*. Paris.
Dillery, J. 1992. "Darius and the Tomb of Nitocris Hdt. 1.187." *CP* 87/1: 30–8.
Dittenberger, W. 1903–5. *Orientis Graeci Inscriptiones Selectae*. Lipsiae.
Dodge, H. 1990. "The Architectural Impact of Rome in the East." In M. Henig, ed., *Architecture and Architectural Sculpture in the Roman Empire*: 108–20. Oxford.
Doğer, E., and İ. Gezgin. 1997. "Arkaik ve Klasik Dönemde Smyrna'nın Dış Savunması Üzerine Gözlemler." *İzmir Araştırmaları Dergisi* 1997: 7–30.
Dohen, E. H. 1941. Review of H. Luschey, *Die Phiale*. *AJA* 45: 125–7.
Dolunay, N. 1967. "Daskyleion'da bulunan Kabartmalı Steller." *IAMY* 13–14: 19–33, 97–111.

BIBLIOGRAPHY

Dominguez, A. J. 2000. "Phocaeans and Other Ionians in the Western Mediterranean." In F. Krinzinger, ed., *Die Ägäis und das westliche Mittelmeer. Beziehungen und Wechselwirkungen, 8. Bis 5. Jhr. v. Chr.*: 507–13. Vienna.

Donceel-Voûte, P. 1984. "Un banquet funéraire perse en Paphlagonie." In R. Donceel and R. Lebrun, eds., *Archéologie et religions de l'Anatolie ancienne: mélanges en l'honneur du professeur Paul Naster*: 101–18. Louvain-la-Neuve.

Dönmez, Ş. 2007. "The Achaemenid Impact on the Central Black Sea Region." In *Achaemenid Impact*: 107–16. Istanbul.

Donner, H., and W. Röllig. 1963. *Kanaanäische und aramäische Inschriften 2*. Wiesbaden.

— 1966–9. *Kanaanäische und aramäische Inschriften 3*. Wiesbaden.

Dörtlük, K. 1977. "1975 Uylupınar Kazı Rapor." *TürkAD* 24: 9–32.

— 1988. "An Excavation That Will Change the Historical Geography of the Phrygians: The New Phrygian Tumuli Excavated in Antalya." *Image of Turkey* 14: 22–4.

— 1989. "Elmalı Bayındır Tümülüsleri Kurtarma Kazısı." *KST* 10/1: 171–4.

— 1990. "Bayındır: I Tresori dei Frigi." *Archaeo. Attualita del Passato* 65: 41–7.

Douglas, M. 1987. "A Distinctive Anthropological Perspective." In M. Douglas, ed., *Constructive Drinking: Perspectives on Drink from Anthropology*: 3–15. Cambridge.

Douglas, M., and B. Isherwood. 1978. *The World of Goods: Towards an Anthropology of Consumption*. London.

Draycott, C. 2007. "Dynastic Definitions: Differentiating Status Claims in the Archaic Pillar Tomb Reliefs of Lycia." In A. Çilingiroğlu and A. Sagona, eds., *Anatolian Iron Ages 6: The Proceedings of the Sixth Anatolian Iron Ages Colloquium Held at Eskişehir, 16–20 August 2004*. ANES Suppl. 20: 103–34. Leuven.

Driver, G. R. 1957. *Aramaic Documents of the Fifth Century BC*. Oxford.

Dupont-Sommer, A. 1961. "Une inscription araméenne inédite de Cilicie et la déesse Kubaba." *CRAI* 1961: 19–22.

— 1965. "Une inscription araméenne inédite de Bahadirli (Cilicie)." *Jahrbuch für kleinasiatische Forschung* 4: 200–9.

Dupont-Sommer, A., and L. Robert. 1964. *La déesse de Hiérapolis Castabala*. Paris.

Dupont-Sommer, M. A. 1966. "Une Inscription Araméenne inédite d'époque perse trouvée a Daskylíon." *CRAI* 21/1: 44–57.

Durugönül, S. 1989. *Die Felsreliefs im Rauhen Kilikien*. Oxford.

— 1994. "Grabstele eines 'Adlingen' aus Paphlagonien der dritten Satrapie." In *Forschungen in Galatien*. AMS 12: 1–14.

— 1998. *Türme und Siedlungen im Rauhen Kilikien. Eine Untersuchung zu den archäologischen Hinterlassenschaften im Olbischen Territorium*. Bonn.

— 2001. "Nagidos'un Tarihteki Yer [The place of Nagidos in history]." In É. Jean, A. M. Dinçol, and S. Durugönül, eds., *La Cilicie: espaces et pouvoirs locaux 2e millénair av. J.-C. – IVc siècle ap. J.-C.. Actes de la Table ronde internationale d'Istanbul, 2–5 novembre 1999*: 429–43. Istanbul.

Durugönül, S., M. Durukan, and Ü. Aydınoğlu. 2003. "2001 Yılı Nagidos Bozyazı Kazısı." *KST* 24/1: 243–8.

Dusinberre, E. R. M. 1997. "Imperial Style and Constructed Identity: A 'Graeco-Persian' Cylinder Seal from Sardis." *ArsOr* 27: 99–129.

— 1999. "Satrapal Sardis: Achaemenid Bowls in an Achaemenid Capital." *AJA* 103: 73–102.

— 2002. "An Excavated Ivory from Kerkenes Dağ, Turkey: Transcultural Fluidities, Significations of Collective Identity, and the Problem of Median Art." *ArsOr* 32: 17–54.

— 2003a. *Aspects of Empire in Achaemenid Sardis*. Cambridge.

2003b. "King or God? Imperial Iconography and the 'Tiarate Head' Coins of Achaemenid Anatolia." In D. Hopkins, ed., *Across the Anatolian Plateau*. *AASOR* 57: 157–71. Boston.

2004. "Western Asia, 500–300 BC." In J. Onians, ed., *Atlas of World Art*: 78–9. London.

2005. *Gordion Seals and Sealings: Individuals and Society*. Philadelphia.

2008a. "Circles of Light and Achaemenid Hegemonic Style in Gordion's Seal 100." In N. D. Cahill, ed., *Love for Lydia, Festschrift for C. H. Greenewalt*: 87–98. Cambridge, MA.

2008b. "Seal Impressions on the Persepolis Fortification Aramaic Tablets: Preliminary Observations." In P. Briant, W. F. M. Henkelman, and M. W. Stolper, eds., *L'archive des Fortifications de Persépolis: état des questions et perspectives de recherches*. Persika 12: 239–52. Paris.

2010a. "Anatolian Crossroads: Achaemenid Seals from Sardis and Gordion." In J. E. Curtis and St. J. Simpson, eds., *The World of Achaemenid Persia: Diversity of Ancient Iran*. London.

2010b. "Lydo-Persian Seals from Sardis." In N. D. Cahill, ed., *Lydia and the Lydians*: 177–90. Istanbul.

Duyuran, R. 1973. "Akhisar Tepe Mazarlığında yapılan arkeolojik araştırmalar: II." *TürkAD* 20/2: 17–27.

Ebbinghaus, S. 1999. "Between Greece and Persia: Rhyta in Thrace from the Late 5th to the Early 3rd Centuries BC." In G. R. Tsetskhladze ed., *Ancient Greeks West and East*: 385–425. Leiden.

2000. "A Banquet at Xanthos: Seven Rhyta on the Northern Cella Frieze of the 'Nereid Monument.'" In G. R. Tsetskhladze, A. J. N. W. Prag, and A. M. Snodgrass, eds., *Periplous: Papers on Classical Art and Archaeology Presented to Sir John Boardman*: 99–109. London.

2005. "Prestige Drinking: Rhyta with Animal Foreparts from Persia to Greece." Paper presented at the conference "The World of Achaemenid Persia," British Museum, London.

2008a. "Of Rams, Women, and Orientals: A Brief History of Attic Plastic Vases." In K. Lapatin, ed., *Papers on Special Techniques in Athenian Vases*: 145–60. Los Angeles.

2008b. "Patterns of Elite Interaction: Animal-Headed Vessels in Anatolia in the Eighth and Seventh Centuries BCE." In B. J. Collins, M. Bacharova, and I. Rutherford, eds., *Anatolian Interfaces: Hittites, Greeks and Their Neighbours*: 181–90. Oxford.

Edwards, R. 1987. *The Fortifications of Armenian Cilicia*. Washington, DC.

Ehling, K., D. Pohl, and M. H. Sayar. 2004. *Kulturbegegnung in einem Brückenland. Kulte als Indicatoren von Akkulturationsprozessen im Ebenen Kilikien*. AMS 53. Bonn.

Elderkin, G. W. 1925. "The Lydian Bilingual Inscription." *AJA* 29: 87–9.

Elgavish, J. 1968. *Archaeological Excavations at Shiqmona: The Levels of the Persian Period*. Haifa.

Erbse, H. 1979. "Über Herodots Kroisoslogos." *Ausgewahlte Schriften zur klassischen Philologie*: 180–202. Berlin.

Erdmann, K. 1941. *Das iranische Feuerheiligtum*. Leipzig.

Erdoğan, A. 2007. "Beobachtungen zur achämenidischen Architektur Daskyleions." In *Achaemenid Impact*: 177–94. Istanbul.

Erhart, K. P. 1979. *The Development of the Facing Head Motif on Greek Coins and Its Relation to Classical Art*. New York.

Evren, A. 1985. *Terracotta Sarcophagi from Tire and Its Environs*. Istanbul.

Facella, M. 2009. "Darius and the Achaemenids in Commagene." In P. Briant and M. Chauveau, eds., *Organisation des pouvoirs et contact culturels dans les pays de l'empire achéménide*. Persika 14: 379–414. Paris.

Fehling, D. 1989. *Herodotus and His 'Sources': Citation, Invention and Narrative Art*. Trans. J. G. Howie. Liverpool.

Fontenrose, J. E. 1988. *Didyma: Apollo's Oracle, Cult, and Companions*. Berkeley, CA.

Forbes, T. B. 1983. *Urartian Architecture*. BAR International Series 170. Oxford.

Foss, C. 1975. "A Bullet of Tissaphernes." *JHS* 95: 25–30.

   1979. "Explorations in Mount Tmolus." *CSCA* 11: 21–60.

   1982. "A Neighbor of Sardis: The City of Tmolus and Its Successors." *CA* 1/2: 178–205.

   1987. "Sites and Strongholds of Northern Lydia." *AnatSt* 37: 81–101.

   1993. "New Discoveries on Mount Tmolus." *AJA* 97: 318.

Fossing, P. 1937. "Drinking Bowls of Glass and Metal from the Achaemenian Time." *Berytus* 4: 121–9.

Foucault, M. 1980. *Power/Knowledge: Selected Interviews and Other Writings*. Ed. Colin Gordon. New York.

Francfort, H.-P. 1979. *Les fortifications en Asie Centrale de l'âge du bronze à l'époque kouchane*. Paris.

   1985. "Fortifications et sociétés en Asie Centrale protohistorique." *Indus* 379–88.

   2005. "Asie Centrale." In *L'archéologie de l'empire achéménide*: 315–52. Paris.

French, D. H. 1980. "The Roman Road-System of Asia Minor." In H. Temporini and W. Haase, eds., *Aufstieg und Niedergang der römischen Welt*: 2/7.2: 698–729. Berlin.

   1981. *Roman Roads and Milestones of Asia Minor*. Part 1. BAR International Series 105. Oxford.

   1997. "Pre- and Early-Roman Roads of Asia Minor: A Stadion-Stone from Ephesos." *TürkAD* 5: 189–96.

   1998. "Pre- and Early-Roman Roads of Asia Minor: The Persian Royal Road." *Iran* 36: 15–43.

Fried, L. S. 2004. *The Priest and the Great King: Temple–Palace Relations in the Persian Empire*. Winona Lake, IN.

Froning, H. 2004. "Das sogenannte Harpyien-Monument von Xanthos. Überlegungen zur Form und Funktion sowie zur Interpretation des Reliefschmucks." In *Anadolu'da doğdu. 60 yaşında Fahri Işık'a armağan. Festschrift für Fahri Işık zum 60. Geburtstag*: 315–60. Istanbul.

Frye, R. N. 1972. "Gestures of Deference to Royalty in Ancient Iran." *IrAnt* 9: 102–7.

Fuensanta, J. G., and P. Charvat. 2005. "Birecik achéménide et l'âge du Fer IIIB dans le Sud-Est anatolien." In *L'archéologie de l'empire achéménide*: 151–73. Paris.

Gabelmann, H. 1984. *Antike Audienz- und Tribunalszenen*. Darmstadt.

Gabriel, A. 1965. *La Cité de Midas: Architecture. Phrygie*. Exploration archéologique IV. Paris.

Gabrielli, M. 2006. *Le cheval dans l'empire achéménide*. Istanbul.

Gallant, T. W. 1991. *Risk and Survival in Ancient Greece: Reconstructing the Rural Domestic Economy*. Stanford, CA.

Garnsey, P. D. A. 1984. "Religious Toleration in Classical Antiquity." In W. J. Scheils, ed., *Persecution and Toleration*: 1–27. Oxford.

   1999. *Food and Society in Classical Antiquity*. Cambridge.

Garrison, M. B. 1988. "Seal Workshops and Artists at Persepolis: A Study of Seal Impressions Preserving the Theme of Heroic Encounter Preserved on the Persepolis Fortification and Treasury Tablets." Ph.D. dissertation, University of Michigan.

   1991. "Seals and the Elite at Persepolis: Some Observations on Early Achaemenid Persian Art." *ArsOr* 21: 1–29.

   1996. "A Persepolis Fortification Seal on the Tablet MDP 11 308 Louvre Sb 13078." *JNES* 55: 15–35.

1998. "The Seals of Asbazana Aspathines." In M. Brosius and A. Kuhrt, eds., *AchHist 11. Studies in Persian History: Essays in Memory of David M. Lewis*: 115–131. Leiden.

1999. "Fire Altars." *EncIr*. http://www.iranicaonline.org/articles/fire-altars/.

2000. "Achaemenid Iconography as Evidenced by Glyptic Art: Subject Matter, Social Function, Audience and Diffusion." In C. Uehlinger, ed., *Images as Media*. OBO 175: 115–63. Freiburg.

2001. "Anatolia in the Achaemenid Period: Glyptic Insights and Perspectives from Persepolis." In T. Bakır et al., eds., *Proceedings of the First International Symposium on Anatolia in the Achaemenid Period, Bandırma, 15–18 August 1997*: 65–82. Leiden.

2008. "The Uninscribed Tablets from the Fortification Archive: A Preliminary Analysis." In P. Briant, W. F. M. Henkelman, and M. W. Stolper, eds., *L'archive des fortifications de Persépolis: état des questions et perspectives de recherches*. Persika 12: 149–238. Paris.

Forthcoming. "Visual Representation of the Divine and the Numinous in Early Achaemenid Iran: Old Problems, New Directions." In C. Uehlinger and F. Graf, eds., *Iconography of Ancient Near Eastern Religions I: Pre-Hellenistic Periods: Introductory Essays*. Leiden.

Garrison, M. B., and M. C. Root. 1996/8. *AchHist 9. Persepolis Seal Studies: An Introduction with Provisional Concordances of Seal Numbers and Associated Documents on Fortification Tablets 1–2087*. Leiden.

2001. *Seals on the Persepolis Fortification Tablets 1: Images of Heroic Encounter*. OIP 117. Chicago.

Forthcoming a. *Seals on the Persepolis Fortification Tablets 2: Images of Human Activity*. Chicago.

Forthcoming b. *Seals on the Persepolis Fortification Tablets 3: Animals, Creatures, Plants, and Geometric Devices*. Chicago.

Gates, C. 1999. "Kinet Höyük, 1992–1997: The Achaemenid Persian and Hellenistic Periods." *Olba* 2: 323–32.

2005. "The Place of the Achaemenid Persian Period in Archaeological Research in Cilicia and Hatay Turkey." In *L'archéologie de l'empire achéménide*: 49–69. Paris.

Gates, J. 2002. "The Ethnicity Name Game: What Lies behind 'Graeco-Persian'?" *ArsOr* 32: 105–32.

Gates, M.-H. 1994. "1992 Excavations at Kinet Höyük Dörtyol/Hatay." *KST* 15/1: 193–200.

1999. "Kinet Höyük in Eastern Cilicia: A Case Study for Acculturation in Ancient Harbors." *Olba* 2: 303–12.

2001. "1999 Excavations at Kinet Höyük Yeşil-Dörtyol, Hatay." *KST* 22/1: 203–22.

Geertz, C. 1973. "Religion as a Cultural System." Reprinted in C. Geertz, *The Interpretation of Cultures: Selected Essays*: 87–125. London.

Geppert, K. 2006. "Überlegungen zum Polyxena-Sarkophag von Çanakkale." In N. Kreutz and B. Schweizer, eds., *Tekmeria: Archäologische Zeugnisse in ihrer kulturhistorischen und politischen Dimension. Beiträge für Werner Gauer*: 89–102. Münster.

Gero, J. M. 2003. "Feasting and the Practice of Stately Manners." In T. L. Bray, ed., *The Archaeology and Politics of Food and Feasting in Early States and Empires*: 285–8. New York.

Gesche, P. D. 2000. *Schulunterricht in Babylonien im ersten Jahrtausend vor Christus*. AOAT 275. Münster.

Ghirshman, R. M. 1963a. "L'Apadana de Suse." *IrAnt* 3: 148–54.

1963b. *Perse: proto-iraniens, medes, achéménides*. Paris.

Bibliography

Gibson, J. C. L. 1975. *Textbook of Syrian Semitic Inscriptions* 2: Aramaic Inscriptions. Oxford.

Gill, D. J. W. 1988. "The Distribution of Greek Vases and Long Distance Trade." In J. Christiansen and T. Melander, eds., *Proceedings of the 3rd Symposium on Ancient Greek and Related Pottery, Copenhagen, August 31–September 4, 1987*: 175–85. Copenhagen.

Gilliam, J. F. 1965. "Romanization of the Greek East: The Role of the Army." *BASP* 2:65–73.

Gjerstad, S. 1953. *Swedish Cyprus Expedition* IV/2. Stockholm.

Glassner, J.-J. 2004. *Mesopotamian Chronicles*. Atlanta.

Glatz, C., and R. Matthews. 2009. *At Empire's Edge: Project Paphlagonia Regional Survey in North-Central Turkey*. Ankara.

Glendinning, M. R. 1996. "A Mid-Sixth Century Roof Tile System at Gordion." *Hesperia* 65/1: 99–119.

—— 2005. "A Decorated Roof at Gordion: What Tiles Are Revealing about the Phrygian Past." In L. Kealhofer, ed., *The Archaeology of Midas and the Phrygians: Recent Work at Gordion*: 82–100. Philadelphia.

Goff, C. 1977. "Excavations at Baba Jan: The Architecture of the East Mound, Levels II and III." *Iran* 15: 103–40.

—— 1978. "Excavations at Baba Jan: The Pottery and Metal from Levels III and II." *Iran* 16: 29–66.

Goldstein, S. M. 1980. "Pre-Persian and Persian Glass: Some Observations on Objects in the Corning Museum of Glass." In D. Schmandt-Besserat, ed., *Ancient Persia: The Art of an Empire*. Malibu, CA.

Goody, J. 1982. *Cooking, Cuisine, and Class: A Study in Comparative Sociology*. Cambridge.

Gorelick, L., and A. J. Gwinnett. 1990. "The Ancient Near Eastern Cylinder Seals as Social Emblem and Status Symbol." *JNES* 49: 45–56.

Görkay, K. 1999. "Attic Black-Figure Pottery From Daskyleion." *AMS* 34: 1–100.

Goudriaan, K. 1988. *Ethnicity in Ptolemaic Egypt*. Amsterdam.

Grabbe, L. 1994. "What Was Ezra's mission?" In T. C. Eskenazi and K. H. Richards, eds., Second Temple Studies 2: *Temple Community in the Persian Period*. JSOT Supplementary Series 173: 286–99. Sheffield.

Graf, D. F. 1994. "The Persian Royal Road System." In H. Sancisi-Weerdenburg, A. Kuhrt, and M. C. Root, eds., *AchHist 8. Continuity and Change*: 167–89. Leiden.

Graf, F. 1985. *Nordionische Kulte. Religionsgeschichtliche und epigraphische Untersuchungen zu den Kulten von Chios, Erythrai, Klazomenai und Phokaia*. Bibliotheca Helvetica Romana 21. Vevey.

Gramsci, A. 1971. *Selections from the Prison Notebooks*. Ed. and trans. Q. Hoare and G. Nowell Smith. New York.

Grayson, A. K. 1975. *Babylonian Historical-Literary Texts*. TSTS 3. Toronto.

Greaves, A. M. 2010. *The Land of Ionia: Society and Economy in the Archaic Period*. Oxford.

Green, L. 1989. *The Authority of the State*. Oxford.

Greenewalt, C. H., Jr. 1971. "An Exhibitionist from Sardis." In D. G. Mitten, J. G. Pedley, and J. A. Scott eds., *Studies Presented to George M.A. Hanfmann*: 29–46. Mainz.

—— 1972. "Two Lydian Graves at Sardis." *CSCA* 5: 114–45.

—— 1976. *Ritual Dinners in Early Historic Sardis*. UCPCS 17. Berkeley.

—— 1978c. "The Seventeenth Campaign at Sardis (1974)." *AASOR* 43: 61–71.

—— 1992. "When a Mighty Empire Was Destroyed: The Common Man at the Fall of Sardis, ca. 546 B.C." *PAPHS* 136/2: 247–71.

1995a. "Croesus of Sardis and the Lydian Kingdom." *CANE*: 1173–83. New York.

1995b. "Sardis in the Age of Xenophon." In P. Briant, ed., *Dans les pas des Dix-Mille. Pallas* 43: 125–45.

2010a. "Gold and Silver Refining at Sardis." In N. D. Cahill, ed., *The Lydians and Their World*: 135–42. Istanbul.

2010b. "Horsemanship." In N. D. Cahill, ed., *The Lydians and Their World*: 217–24. Istanbul.

Greenewalt, C. H., Jr., N. D. Cahill, and M. L. Rautman. 1987. "The Sardis Campaign of 1984." *BASOR Suppl.* 25: 13–54.

Greenewalt, C. H., Jr., C. Ratté, and M. L. Rautman. 1993. "The Sardis Campaigns of 1988 and 1989." *AASOR* 51: 1–43.

Greenewalt, C. H., Jr., M. L. Rautman, and N. D. Cahill. 1987. "The Sardis Campaign of 1985." *BASOR Suppl.* 25: 55–92.

Greenewalt, C. H., Jr., M. L. Rautman, and R. Meriç. 1986. "The Sardis Campaign of 1983." *BASOR Suppl.* 24: 1–30.

Greenfield, J. C. 1986. "Aspects of Archives in the Achaemenid Period." In K. R. Veenhof, ed., *Cuneiform Archives and Libraries, Papers Read at the 30th RAI*: 291–5. Leiden.

Greenfield, J. C., and B. Porten. 1982. *The Bisitun Inscription of Darius the Great, Aramaic Version*. London.

Grelot, P. 1964. "Huile de ricin à Éléphantine." *Semitica* 14: 63–70.

1972. *Documents Araméens d'Égypte*. Paris.

Griffith, M. 1998. "The King and Eye: The Rule of the Father in Greek Tragedy." *PCPS* 44: 20–84.

Groenman-van Waateringe, W. 1989. "Food for Soldiers, Food for Thought." In J. C. Barrett, A. P. Fitzpatrick, and L. Macinnes, eds., *Barbarians and Romans in Northwest Europe from the Later Republic to Late Antiquity*. BAR 471: 96–107. Oxford.

Grose, D. F. 1989. *The Toledo Museum of Art: Early Ancient Glass*. New York.

Gruen, E. S. 1984a. *The Hellenistic World and the Coming of Rome*. Berkeley, CA.

1984b. "Material Rewards and the Drive for Empire." In W. V. Harris, ed., *The Imperialism of Mid-Republican Rome*: 59–88. Rome.

Gunter, A. C. 1989. "Sculptural Dedications at Labraunda." *Boreas 17: Architecture and Society in Hecatomnid Caria*: 91–8. Uppsala.

1990. *Investigating Artistic Environments in the Ancient Near East*. Washington, DC.

1991. *The Bronze Age*. Gordion Excavations Final Reports 3. Philadelphia.

1995. *Labraunda II/5: Marble Sculpture*. Stockholm.

2009. *Greek Art and the Orient*. Cambridge.

Gunter, A. C., and M. C. Root. 1998. "Replicating, Inscribing, Giving: Ernst Herzfeld and Artaxerxes' Silver *Phiale* in the Freer Gallery of Art." *ArsOr* 28: 3–40.

Günther, L.-M. 2006. "Alkaios und die Statere des Lyderkönigs." In R. Rollinger and B. Truschnegg, eds., *Altertum und Mittelmeerraum. Die antike Welt diesseits und jenseits der Levante, Festschrift P.W. Haider. HZ* 285: 43–52. Stuttgart.

Gürtekin, R. G. 1996. "Wild Goat Style Pottery from Daskyleion." *TürkAD* 4: 87–95.

Gürtekin-Demir, R. G. 2003. "Imported Painted Pottery from Asia Minor to Daskyleion." In W. F. M. Henkelman and A. Kuhrt, eds., *AchHist 13. A Persian Perspective: Essays in Memory of Heleen Sancisi-Weerdenburg*: 203–26. Leiden.

Gusmani, R. 1964. *Lydisches Wörterbuch. Mit grammatischer Skizze und Inschriftensammlung*. Heidelberg.

1979. "Lydische Epigraphik." *Kadmos* 18/1: 76–9.

1985. "Anthroponymie in den lydischen Inschriften." In Y. Arbeitman, ed., *Gedenkschrift B. Schwartz*: 179–96. New York.

1986. *Lydisches Wörterbuch*. Ergänzungsband I. Heidelberg.

Gusmani, R., and G. Polat. 1999. "Manes in Daskyleion." *Kadmos* 38: 137–62.

Gygax, M. D. 2001. *Untersuchungen zu den lykischen Gemeinwesen in klassischer und hellenistischer Zeit*. Antiquitas Reihe 1, Band 49.

Gygax, M. D., and W. Tietz. 2005. "'He Who of All Mankind Set Up the Most Numerous Trophies to Zeus: The Inscribed Pillar of Xanthos Reconsidered." *AnatSt* 55: 89–98.

Habicht, C. 1975. "New Evidence on the Province of Asia." *JRS* 65: 53–6.

Haerinck, E. 1973. "Le palais achéménide de Babylone." *IrAnt* 10: 108–32.

Hall, E. 1989. *Inventing the Barbarian: Greek Self-Definition through Tragedy*. Oxford.

Hall, J. 1995. "Approaches to Ethnicity in the Early Iron Age of Greece." In H. Spencer, ed., *Time, Tradition, and Society in Greek Archaeology: Bridging the 'Great Divide.'* London.

1997. *Ethnic Identity in Greek Antiquity*. Cambridge.

2002. *Hellenicity: Between Ethnicity and Culture*. Chicago.

Hallock, R. T. 1950. "New Light from Persepolis." *JNES* 9: 237–52.

1960. "A New Look at the Persepolis Treasury Tablets." *JNES* 19: 90–100.

1969. *The Persepolis Fortification Tablets*. Chicago.

1973. "The Persepolis Fortification Archive." *Orientalia* 92: 320–3.

1978. "Selected Fortification Texts." *CDAFI* 8: 109–36.

Halstead, P., and J. C. Barrett. 2004. "Introduction: Food, Cuisine and Society in Prehistoric Greece." In P. Halstead and J. C. Barrett, eds., *Food, Cuisine and Society in Prehistoric Greece*: 1–15. Oxford.

Halstead, P., and V. Isaakidou. 2004. "Faunal Evidence for Feasting: Burnt Offerings from the Palace of Nestor at Pylos." In P. Halstead and J. C. Barrett, eds., *Food, Cuisine and Society in Prehistoric Greece*: 136–54. Oxford.

Hamilton, R. W. 1966. "A Silver Bowl in the Ashmolean Museum." *Iraq* 28: 1–17.

Hanfmann, G. M. A. 1958. "Lydiaka." *HSCP* 63: 65–88.

1961. "The Third Campaign at Sardis (1960)." *BASOR* 162: 8–49.

1962. "The Fourth Campaign at Sardis (1961)." *BASOR* 166: 1–57.

1963. "The Fifth Campaign at Sardis (1962)." *BASOR* 170: 1–65.

1974a. "A Pediment of the Persian Era from Sardis." In E. Akurgal and B. Alkım, eds., *Mélanges Mansel*: 289–302. Ankara.

1976. "On Lydian and East Greek Anthemion Stelai." *RA* 1976: 35–44.

1978. "Lydian Relations with Ionia and Persia." *Proceedings of the Xth International Congress of Classical Archaeology* 1: 25–35.

1983. *Sardis from Prehistoric to Roman Times*. Cambridge, MA.

1987. "The Sacrilege Inscription: The Ethnic, Linguistic, Social and Religious Situation at Sardis at the End of the Persian Era." *BAI* 1: 1–8.

Hanfmann, G. M. A., and M. S. Balmuth. 1965. "The Image of an Anatolian Goddess at Sardis." *Anadolu Araştırmaları* 2/1–2: 261–9.

Hanfmann, G. M. A., and K. P. Erhart. 1981. "Pedimental Reliefs from a Mausoleum of the Persian Era at Sardis: A Funerary Meal." In W. K. Simpson and W. M. Davis, eds., *Studies in Ancient Egypt, the Aegean, and the Sudan*: 82–90. Boston.

Hanfmann, G. M. A., and K. Z. Polatkan. 1959. "Three Sculptures from Sardis in the Manisa Museum." *Anatolia* 4: 55–65.

Hanfmann, G. M. A., and N. H. Ramage. 1978. *Sculpture from Sardis: The Finds through 1975*. Cambridge, MA.

Hanfmann, G. M. A., and J. C. Waldbaum. 1969. "Kybebe and Artemis: Two Anatolian Goddesses at Sardis." *Archaeology* 22/4: 264–9.

1970. "The Eleventh and Twelfth Campaigns at Sardis 1968, 1969." *BASOR* 199: 7–58.

Hansen, O. 1986. "The Purported Letter of Darius to Gadates." *RhM* 129: 95–6.
Hanson, R. S. 1968. "Aramaic Funerary and Boundary Inscriptions." *BASOR* 192: 3–11.
Harper, P. O., J. Arus, and F. Tallon. 1992. *The Royal City of Susa: Ancient Near Eastern Treasures in the Louvre*. New York.
Harper, R. P. 1967. "A Dedication to the Goddess Anaitis at Ortaköy, North of Aksaray (Nitalis?)." *AnatSt* 17: 193.
Harrison, C. M. 1982. "Coins of the Persian Satraps." Ph.D. dissertation, University of Pennsylvania.
  2002. "Numismatic Problems in the Achaemenid West: The Undue Modern Influence of 'Tissaphernes.' " In V. B. Gormann and E. W. Robinson, eds., *Oikistes: Studies in Constitutions, Colonies, and Military Power in the Ancient World Offered in Honor of A. J. Graham. Mnemosyne* 232: 301–19. Leiden.
Harrison, T. 2000. *The Emptiness of Asia: Aeschylus' Persians and the History of the Fifth Century*. London.
  2002. "The Persian Invasions." In E. J. Bakker, I. J. F. de Jong, and H. van Wees, eds., *Brill's Companion to Herodotus*: 551–578. Leiden.
Hartog, F. 1988. *The Mirror of Herodotus: The Representation of the Other in the Writing of History*. Berkeley, CA.
Haspels, C. H. E. 1971. *The Highlands of Phrygia: Sites and Monuments*. Princeton, NJ.
Hawkins, J. D. 1974. "The Attestations of Malija (Athena) in Lycian." In E. Akurgal and U. B. Alkim, eds., *Mansel'e Armağan: Mélanges Mansel*: 902–3. Ankara.
  1995. "Karkamish and Karatepe: Neo-Hittite City-States in North Syria." *CANE*: 1295–1308. New York.
Hayden, B. 1996. "Feasting in Prehistoric and Traditional Societies." In P. Wiessner and W. Schiefenhövel, eds., *Food and the Status Quest: An Interdisciplinary Perspective*: 127–48. Providence, RI.
Hays, K. 1993. "When Is a Symbol Archaeologically Meaningful? Meaning, Function, and Prehistoric Visual Arts." In N. Yoffee and A. Sherratt, eds., *Archaeological Theory: Who Sets the Agenda?* 81–92. Cambridge.
Head, B. V. 1911. *Historia Numorum*, 2d ed. Oxford.
Hegyi, D. 1966. "The Historical Background of the Ionian Revolt." *AJAH* 14: 285–6.
Hellstrøm, P. 1989. "Formal Banqueting at Labraunda." In T. Linders and P. Hellstrøm, eds., *Architecture and Society in Hecatomnid Caria*. Acta Universitatis Uppsaliensis. *Boreas* 17: 99–104. Uppsala.
Hellstrøm, P., and T. Thiele. 1982. *Labraunda I/3: The Temple of Zeus*. Uppsala.
Helms, S. W. 1982. "Excavations at 'the City and the Famous Fortress of Kandahar.'" *Afghan Studies* 3/4: 1–24.
Henkelman, W. F. M. 2008. AchHist 14. *The Other Gods Who Are: Studies in Elamite-Iranian Acculturation Based on the Persepolis Fortification Texts*. Leiden.
  2009. "Exit Atossa, Enter Irdabama: Royal Women in the Fortification Archive." Paper presented at American Oriental Society convention, 13–16 March, Albuquerque, NM.
  2010. " 'Consumed Before the King': The Table of Darius, That of Irdabama and Irtaštuna, and That of His Satrap, Karkiš." In B. Jacobs and R. Rollinger, eds., *Der Achämenidenhof / The Achaemenid Court*: 667–775. Basel.
Henrickson, R. C. 1993. "Politics, Economics, and Ceramic Continuity at Gordion in the Late Second and First Millennium B.C." In W. D. Kingery, ed., *Social and Cultural Contexts of New Ceramic Technologies*: 89–176. Westerville, OH.
  1994. "Continuity and Discontinuity in the Ceramic Tradition of Gordion During the Iron Age." In A. Çilingiroğlu and D. H. French, eds., *Anatolian Iron Ages 3: The*

Proceedings of the Third Anatolian Iron Ages Colloquium held at Van, 6–12 August 1990: 95–129. Ankara.

    2005. "The Local Potter's Craft at Phrygian Gordion." In L. Kealhofer, ed., *The Archaeology of Midas and the Phrygians: Recent Work at Gordion*: 124–36. Philadelphia.

Henrickson, R. C., P. B. Vandiver, and M. J. Blackman. 2002. "Lustrous Black Fine Ware at Gordion, Turkey: A Distinctive Sintered Slip Technology." In P. B. Vandiver, M. Goodway, and J. Mass, eds., *MIAA* 6: 391–9.

Henrickson, R. C., and M. M. Voigt. 1998. "The Early Iron Age at Gordion: The Evidence from the Yassıhöyük Stratigraphic Sequence." In N. Tuna, Z. Aktüre, and M. Lynch, eds., *Thracians and Phrygians: Problems of Parallelism*: 79–108. Ankara.

Herbordt, S. 1992. *Neuassyrische Glyptik des 8. –7. Jh. v. Chr. unter besonderer Berücksichtigung der Siegelungen auf Tafeln und Tonverschlüssen*. Helsinki.

Hermary, A. 1984. "Un nouveau relief 'greco-perse' en Cilicie." *RA* 1984: 289–300.

Herrenschmidt, C. 1980. "La religion des Achéménides: état de la question." *StIr* 9: 325–9.

    1985. "Une lecture iranisante du poème de Symmachos dedié à Arbinas, dynaste de Xanthos." *REA* 87: 125–36.

Herrmann, G. 1986. *Ivories from Room SW 37 Fort Shalmaneser: Commentary and Catalogue*. London.

    1992. *The Small Collections from Fort Shalmaneser (Ivories from Nimrud* V). London.

    1996. "Ivory Furniture Pieces from Nimrud: North Syrian Evidence for Regional Traditions of Furniture Manufacture." In G. Herrmann, ed., *The Furniture of Western Asia: Ancient and Traditional*: 153–66. Mainz.

Herrmann, P. 1970. "Zur Geschichte der Stadt Iulia Gordos in Lydien." *Anzeiger* 107: 92–103.

    1986. "Zwei Ortsnamen in Lydien: Agatheira und Tibbai." *EA* 7: 17–20.

    1991. "E Naeitenon katoikia. Ein Beitrag zur historischen Landeskunde des südöstlichen Lydien." *TürkAD* 1: 77–85.

    1996. "Mystenvereine in Sardeis." *Chiron* 26: 315–41.

    1997. "Grabepigramm aus Büyükbelen in Lydien." *TürkAD* 5: 171–4.

Herrmann, P., and J. Keil. 1981. *Tituli Asiae Minoris* V. *Tituli Lydiae* 1. *Regio septentrionalis ad orientem vergens*. Vienna.

    1989. *Tituli Asiae Minoris* V. *Tituli Lydiae* 2. *Regio septentrionalis ad occidentem vergens*. Vienna.

Herzfeld, E. 1934. "Recent Discoveries at Persepolis." *JRAS*: 226–32.

Herzog, Z. 1989. "Persian Period Stratigraphy and Architecture (Strata XI–VI)." In Z. Herzog, G. Rapp Jr., and O. Negbi, eds., *Excavations at Tel Michal, Israel*: 88–114. Minneapolis.

Hestrin, R., and E. Stern. 1973. "Two 'Assyrian' Bowls from Israel." *IEJ* 23: 152–5.

Hill, J. N. 1977. *Explanation of Prehistoric Change*. Albuquerque, NM.

Himmelmann, N. 1986. "Ostionische Thronfiguren." In H. Kyrieleis, ed., *Archaische und klassische griechische Plastik* 1: 15–20. Mainz.

Hinz, W. 1960. "Zu den Persepolis Täfelchen." *ZMDG* 110: 236–51.

    1974. "Die Behistun-Inschrift des Darius in ihrer ursprünglichen Form." *AMI* 7: 121–34.

    1979. *Darius und die Perser* II. Baden-Baden.

Hitzl, I. 1991. *Die griechischen Sarkophage der archaischen und klassischen Zeit*. Jonsered.

Hoffner, H. A., Jr. 1995. "Legal and Social Institutions of Hittite Anatolia." *CANE*: 555–70. New York.

BIBLIOGRAPHY

Hogarth, D. G. 1908. *Excavations at Ephesus: The Archaic Artemisia.* London.

Hoglund, K. G. 1992. *Achaemenid Imperial Administration in Syria-Palestine and the Missions of Ezra and Nehemiah.* Society of Biblical Literature Dissertation Series 125. Atlanta.

Hornblower, S. 1982. *Mausolus.* Oxford.

Hostetter, E. 1994. *Lydian Architectural Terracottas: A Study in Tile Replication, Display, and Technique.* Atlanta.

Howes Smith, P. H. G. 1986. "A Study of Ninth-Seventh Century Metal Bowls from Western Asia." *IrAnt* 21: 1–88.

Hunt, R. C. 1987. "The Role of Bureaucracy in the Provisioning of Cities: A Framework for Analysis of the Ancient Near East." In M. Gibson and R. D. Biggs, eds., *The Organization of Power: Aspects of Bureaucracy in the Ancient Near East*: 161–92. Chicago.

Hurter, S. 1979. "Der Tissaphernes-Fund." In O. Mørkholm and N. M. Waggoner, eds., *Greek Numismatics and Archaeology: Essays in Honor of Margaret Thompson*: 97–108. Wetteren.

Ignatiadou, D. 2002. "Colorless Glass in Late Classical and Early Hellenistic Macedonia." *JGS* 44: 11–24.

2005. "Achaemenid and Greek Colourless Glass." Paper presented at the conference "The World of Achaemenid Persia," British Museum, London 29 September–1 October.

Ihnken, T. 1978. *Die Inschriften von Magnesia am Sipylos.* Bonn.

Iliffe, J. H. 1935. "A Tell Fara Tomb Group Reconsidered." *QDAP* 4: 182–6.

Imhoof-Blumer, F. 1885. *Porträtsköpfe auf antiken Münzen hellenischer und hellenisierter Völker.* Leipzig.

Imparati, F. 1995. "Private Life Among the Hittites." *CANE*: 571–86. New York.

Invernizzi, A. 1996. "Seleucia on the Tigris: Centre and Periphery in Seleucid Asia." In P. Bilde et al., eds., *Centre and Periphery in the Hellenistic World*: 230–50. Aarhus.

Isager, J., ed. 1994. *Hekatomnid Caria and the Ionian Renaissance.* Odense.

Işık, F. 1996. "Zum Ursprung lykischer Felsheiligtümer." K. Blakolmer, R. Krierer, F. Krinzinger, A. Landskrom-Dinstl, H. D. Szemethy, and K. Zhuber-Okrog, eds., *Fremde Zeiten. Festschrift für Jürgen Borchhardt zum sechzigsten Geburtstag am 25. Februar 1996* 1: 51–64. Vienna.

1998. "Zum Typus des Temenosgrabes in Lykien." *IstMitt* 48: 157–72.

1999. *Doğa Ana Kubaba. Tanrıçaların Ege'de Buluşması* [Mother Nature Kubaba. Meeting of the goddesses in the Aegean]. Suna-İnan Kıraç Akdeniz Medeniyetleri Araştırma Enstitüsü Monografi Dizisi I. Istanbul.

2001. "Die anthropomorphe Halbstatue der 'Eni Mahanahi' aus Letoon." In N. Birkle et al., eds., *Macellum: Culinaria Archaeologica – Festschrift Robert Fleischer*: 143–151. Mainz.

Işın, G. 2007. "An Achaemenid Stamp Seal from Patara." In *Achaemenid Impact*: 75–82. Istanbul.

Jacobs, B. 1987. *Griechische und persische Elemente in der Grabkunst Lykiens zur Zeit der Achämenidenherrschaft.* SIMA 78. Jonsered.

2001. "Kultbilder und Gottesvorstellung bei den Persern. Zu Herodot, Historiae 1.131 und Clemens Alexandrinus, Protrepticus 5.65.3." In T. Bakır et al., eds., *Achaemenid Anatolia: Proceedings of the First International Symposium on Anatolia in the Achaemenid Period, Bandırma, 15–18 August 1997*: 83–90. Leiden.

Jameson, M. H. 1988. "Sacrifice and Animal Husbandry in Classical Greece." In C. R. Whittaker, ed., *Pastoral Economies in Classical Antiquity*. PCPS Suppl. 14: 87–119. Cambridge.

Jamzadeh, P. 1996. "The Achaemenid Throne-Leg Design." *IrAnt* 31: 101–46.

Jansen-Winkeln, K. 1999. "Drei Denkmäler mit archaisierender Orthographie." *Orientalia* 67: 155–72.

Jellinek, E. M. 1977. "The Symbolism of Drinking: A Culture-Historical Approach." *JSA* 38/5: 849–66.

Jenkins, G. K. 1959. "Recent Acquisitions of Greek Coins by the British Museum." *NC* 38–9.

——— 1972. *Ancient Greek Coins*. New York.

Jenkins, I. 2006. *Greek Architecture and Its Sculpture*. Cambridge, MA.

Jennings, J., and B. J. Bowser. 2009. "Drink, Power, and Society in the Andes: An Introduction." In J. Jennings and B. J. Bowser, eds., *Drink, Power, and Society in the Andes*: 1–27. Gainesville, FL.

Jeppesen, K., et al. 1981–2004. *The Maussolleion at Halikarnassos*. 7 Vols. Aarhus.

Joannès, F. 1982. *Textes économiques de la Babylonie récente*. Étude des textes TBER 6. Paris.

——— 1989. *Archives de Borsippa – la famille Ea-ilûta-bâni: étude d'un lot d'archives familiales en Babylonie di VIIe au Ve siècle av. J.-C.* Écoles Pratiques des Hautes Études, IVe Section, Sciences Historiques et Philologiques II. Hautes Études Orientales 25. Geneva.

——— 2000. *La Mésopotamie au 1er millénaire avant J.-C*. Collection U, Histoire. Paris.

Johansen, K. F. 1935. "Fragmente klazomenischer Sarkophage in der Ny Carlsberg Glyptotek." *ActArch* 6: 167–213.

——— 1942. "Clazomenian Sarcophagus Studies: The Earliest Sarcophagi." *ActArch* 14: 1–64.

Johnson, P. A. 2010. "Landscapes of Achaemenid Paphlagonia." Ph.D. dissertation, University of Pennsylvania.

Jones, J. D. 2005. "Glass Vessels from Gordion: Trade and Influence Along the Royal Road." In L. Kealhofer, ed., *The Archaeology of Midas and the Phrygians: Recent Work at Gordion*: 101–16. Philadelphia.

Jones, S. 1997. *The Archaeology of Ethnicity: Constructing Identities in the Past and Present*. New York.

Joyce, A. A. 2004. "Sacred Space and Social Relations in the Valley of Oaxaca." In J. Hendon and R. Joyce, eds., *MesArch*: 192–216. Oxford.

Joyce, A. A., and E. T. Weller. 2007. "Commoner Rituals, Resistance, and the Classic-to-Postclassic Transition in Ancient Mesoamerica." In N. Gonlin and J. C. Lohse, eds., *Commoner Ritual and Ideology in Ancient Mesoamerica*: 143–184. Boulder, CO.

Joyce, R. A. 1993. "Women's Work: Images of Production and Reproduction in Pre-Hispanic Southern Central America." *CAnth* 34/3: 255–74.

Kahle, P., and F. Sommer. 1927. "Die lydisch-aramäische Bilingue." *KF* 1/1: 18–86.

Kaiser, W., et al. 1975. "Stadt und Tempel von Elephantine." *MDAIK* 31/1: 39–80.

——— 1990. "Stadt und Tempel von Elephantine. 17.118 Grabungsbericht." *MDAIK* 46: 185–249.

Kaptan, D. 1990. "A Group of Seal Impressions on the Bullae from Ergili/Daskyleion." *EA* 16: 15–27.

——— 1996. "The Great King's Audience." In K. Blakolmer, R. Krierer, F. Krinzinger, A. Landskrom-Dinstl, H. D. Szemethy, and K. Zhuber-Okrog, eds., *Fremde Zeiten. Festschrift für Jürgen Borchhardt zum sechzigsten Geburtstag am 25. Februar 1996* 1:259–71. Vienna.

——— 2001. "On the Satrapal Center in Northwestern Asia Minor." In T. Bakır, ed., *Achaemenid Anatolia: Proceedings of the First International Symposium on Anatolia in the Achaemenid Period, Bandırma, 15–18 August 1997*: 57–64. Leiden.

Bibliography

2002. *AchHist* 12. *The Daskyleion Bullae: Seal Images from the Western Achaemenid Empire*. Leiden.

2005. "Seal Impressions on Clay Tags from Phrygia." Paper presented at "The World of Achaemenid Persia," 29 September–1 October, British Museum, London.

2007. "A Channel of Communication: Seals in Anatolia during the Achaemenid Period." In *Achaemenid Impact*: 275–90. Istanbul.

2008. "Sketches on the Archaeology of the Achaemenid Empire in Western Turkey." In I. Delemen, S. Çokay-Kepçe, A. Özdizbay, and Ö. Turak, eds., *Euergetes. Festschrift für Prof. Dr. Haluk Abbasoğlu zum 65. Geburtstag*: 653–60. Antalya.

2010. "Clay Tags from Seyitömer Höyük in Phrygia." In J. E. Curtis and St. J. Simpson, eds., *The World of Achaemenid Persia: Proceedings of a Conference Held at the British Museum*: 361–8. London.

Karagöz, Ş. 2007. "Neue Überlegungen zu einem freistehenden Grabmonumenten aus Daskyleion." In *Achaemenid Impact*: 195–214. Istanbul.

Karaosmanoğlu, M. 2009. "İkinci Dönem Kazıları Işığında Altıntepe Apadanası." In *Altan Çilingiroğlu'na Armağan: Yukarı Denizin Kıyısında Urartu Krallığı'na Adanmış Bir Hayat*: 353–7. Istanbul.

Karaosmanoğlu, M., and H. Korucu. Forthcoming. "The Apadana of Altıntepe in Light of the Second Season Excavations." *Anatolian Iron Ages Symposium VII*. Ankara.

Kawami, T. S. 1972. "A Possible Source for the Sculptures of the Audience Hall, Pasargadae." *Iran* 10: 146–8.

1992. *Ancient Iranian Ceramics from the Arthur M. Sackler Collections*. New York.

Keen, A. G. 1992. "The Dynastic Tombs of Xanthos: Who Was Buried Where?" *AnatSt* 42: 53–63.

1995. "The Tombs of Lycia: Evidence for Social Stratification?" In S. Campbell and A. Green, eds., *The Archaeology of Death in the Ancient Near East*. Oxbow Monograph Series 51: 221–5. Oxford.

1998. *Dynastic Lycia*, *Mnemosyne* Suppl. 178. Leiden.

2002. "The Poleis of the Southern Anatolian Coast (Lycia, Pamphylia, Pisidia) and Their Civic Identity: The Interface Between the Hellenic and the Barbarian Polis." In G. R. Tsetskhladze and A. M. Snodgrass, eds., *Greek Settlements in the Eastern Mediterranean and the Black Sea*. BAR/Archaeopress: 27–40. Oxford.

Keenan, D. J. 2004. "Radiocarbon Dates from Gordion." *AWE* 3: 100–3.

Kellens, J. 1989. "Avesta." *EncIr* 3: 35–44.

1991a. "Questions préalables." In J. Kellens, ed., *La réligion iranienne à l'époque achéménide*: 81–6. Ghent.

1991b. *Zoroastre et l'Avesta ancien*. Paris.

2006–7. *Études avestiques et mazdéennes* 1 and 2. Persika 8 and 10. Paris.

Kent, R. 1953. *Old Persian: Grammar, Texts, Lexicon*. New Haven, CT.

Kerschner, M. 1997a. "Ein Kessel der früheren Tierfriesstiles aus den Grabungen unter der Tetragonos-Agora in Ephesos." *ÖJh* 66: 9–27.

1997b. "Ein stratifizierter Opferkomplex des 7. Jhs. v. Chr. aus dem Artemision von Ephesos." *ÖJh* 66: Suppl. 84–226.

Kervran, M., D. Stronach, F. Vallat, and J. Yoyotte. 1972. "Une statue de Darius découverte à Suse." *JA* 260: 235–66.

Khatchadourian, L. 2008. "Social Logics under Empire: The Armenian 'Highland Satrapy' and Achaemenid Rule, ca. 600–300 BC." Ph.D. dissertation, University of Michigan.

King, A. 1984. "Animal Bones and the Dietary Identity of Military and Civilian Groups in Roman Britain, Germany and Gaul." In T. F. C. Blagg and A. C. King, eds., *Military and Civilian in Roman Britain: Cultural Relationships in a Former Province*. BAR 126: 187–217. Oxford.

Bibliography

King, L. W., and R. Campbell Thompson. 1907. *The Sculptures and Inscription of Darius the Great on the Rock of Behistûn in Persia*. London.

Kistler, E. 2010. "Achämenidischer Becher und die Logik kommensaler Politik im Reich der Achämeniden." In B. Jacobs and R. Rollinger, eds., *Der Achämenidenhof / The Achaemenid Court*: 411–57. Wiesbaden.

Kjeldsen, K., and J. Zahle. 1975. "Lykische Gräber. Ein vorläufiger Bericht." *AA*: 312–50.

Kleemann, I. 1958. *Die Satrapen-Sarkophag aus Sidon*. IstForsch 20. Berlin.

Kleiner, G. 1968. *Die Ruinen von Milet*. Berlin.

Kloekhorst, A. 2011. "The Opening Formula of Lycian Funerary Inscriptions: *Meti* vs. *Mene*." *JNES* 70: 13–23.

Knauss, F. 2006. "Ancient Persia and the Caucasus." *IrAnt* 41: 79–118.

Knibbe, D. 1961–3. "Ein religiöser Frevel und seine Sühne. Ein Todesurteil hellenistischer Zeit aus Ephesos." *ÖJh* 46: 175–82.

Knights, B. A., et al. 1983. "Evidence Concerning the Roman Military Diet at Bearsden, Scotland, in the 2nd c. AD." *JAS* 10: 139–52.

Koch, H. 1986. "Die achämenidische Poststrasse von Persepolis nach Susa." *AMI* 19: 33–47.

— 1989. "Tribut und Abgaben in Persis und Elymais." In P. Briant and C. Herrenschmidt, eds., *Le tribut dans l'empire perse*: 121–8. Paris.

— 1990. *Verwaltung und Wirtschaft im persischen Kernland zur Zeit der Achämeniden*. Wiesbaden.

Koenigs, W., and H. Philipp. 1987. "Die Löwensäule von Ankara." *Anadolu* 21: 157–73.

Kohler, E. L. 1980. "Cremations of the Middle Phrygian Period at Gordion." In K. DeVries, ed., *From Athens to Gordion: The Papers of a Memorial Symposium for Rodney S. Young*: 65–89. Philadelphia.

— 1995. *Gordion Excavations, 1950–1973: Final Reports* II: *The Lesser Phrygian Tumuli*, pt. I: The Inhumations. Philadelphia.

Kökten, H. 1998. "Conservation and Reconstruction of Phrygian Chariot Wheels from Mysia." In N. Tuna, Z. Aktüre, and M. Lynch, eds., *Thracians and Phrygians* 1998: 131–46. Ankara.

Kökten-Ersoy, H. 1998. "Two Wheeled Vehicles from Lydia and Mysia." *IstMitt* 48: 107–33.

Kolata, A. L. 1992. "Economy, Ideology and Imperialism in the South-Central Andes." In A. A. Demarest and G. W. Conrad, eds., *Ideology and Pre-Columbian Civilizations*: 65–86. Santa Fe, NM.

Kolb, F., ed. 1993. *Lykische Studien* 1. *Die Siedlungskammer von Kyaneai in Lykien*. AMS 9.

— 1995. *Lykische Studien* 2. *Die Siedlungskammer von Kyaneai in Lykien*. AMS 18.

— ed. 1996. *Lykische Studien* 3. *Die Siedlungskammer von Kyaneai in Lykien*. AMS 24.

— ed. 1998. *Lykische Studien* 4. *Feldforschungen auf dem Gebiet von Kyaneai*. AMS 29.

— 2000a. "Von der Burg zur Polis. Akkulturation in einer kleinasiatischen Provinz." *Jahrbuch des Historischen Kollegs*: 39–83. Munich.

— ed. 2000b. *Lykische Studien* 5. *Die Siedlungskammer des Yavu-Berglandes*. AMS 41.

— ed. 2003. *Lykische Studien* 6. *Feldforschungen auf dem Gebiet der Polis Kyaneai*, AMS 44.

Koldewey, R. 1918. *Das Ischtar-Tor in Babylon*. Leipzig.

Konuk, K. 1998. "The Early Coinage of Kaunos," in R. Ashton and S. Hurter, eds., *Studies in Greek Numismatics in Memory of Martin Jessop Price*: 197–222. London.

Kornfeld, W. 1973. "Jüdisch-aramäische Grabinschriften aus Edfu." *AnzWien* 110: 123–37.

Bibliography

Kraay, C. M. 1976. *Archaic and Classical Greek Coins*. Berkeley, CA.

Kretschmer, P. 1896. *Einleitung in die Geschichte der griechischen Sprach*. Göttingen.

Kuban, Z. 1996. "Ein Astodan in Limyra?" In K. Blakolmer, R. Krierer, F. Krinzinger, A. Landskrom-Dinstl, H. D. Szemethy, and K. Zhuber-Okrog, eds., *Fremde Zeiten. Festschrift für Jürgen Borchhardt zum sechzigsten Geburtstag am 25. Februar 1996* 1: 133–44. Vienna.

Kuhrt, A. 1990. "Achaemenid Babylonia: Sources and Problems." In A. Kuhrt and H. Sancisi-Weerdenburg, eds., *AchHist 4. Centre and Periphery*: 177–94. Leiden.

——— 1995a. *The Ancient Near East, c. 3000–330 BC*. Cambridge.

——— 1995b. "The Assyrian Heartland in the Achaemenid Period." *Pallas* 43: 239–45.

——— 1996. "The Seleucid Kings and Babylonia: New Perspectives on the Seleucid Realm in the East." In P. Bilde et al., eds., *Aspects of Hellenistic Kingship*: 41–54. Aarhus.

——— 2007. *The Persian Empire: A Corpus of Sources from the Achaemenid Period*. London.

Kuhrt, A., and S. M. Sherwin-White. 1987. "Xerxes' Destruction of Babylonian Temples." In H. Sancisi-Weerdenburg and A. Kuhrt, eds., *AchHist 2. The Greek Sources*: 69–78. Leiden.

——— 1994. "The Transition from Achaemenid to Seleucid Rule in Babylonia: Revolution or Evolution?" In H. Sancisi-Weerdenburg, A. Kuhrt, and M. C. Root, eds., *AchHist 8. Continuity and Change*: 311–27. Leiden.

Kulaçoğlu, B. 1992. *Museum of Anatolian Civilizations: Gods and Goddesses*. Ankara.

Kurke, L. 1999. *Coins, Bodies, Games, and Gold: The Politics of Meaning in Archaic Greece*. Princeton, NJ.

Kurtz, D. V. 1981. "The Legitimation of Early Inchoate States." In H. J. M. Claessen and P. Skalnik, eds., *The Study of the State*: 177–200. The Hague.

Kurtz, D. V., and J. Boardman. 1971. *Greek Burial Customs*. London.

Kwasman, T., and A. Lemaire. 2002. "An Aramaic Inscription from Kemaliye (Lydian Philadelpheia)." *EA* 34: 185–7.

Kyrieleis, H. 1969. *Throne und Klinen. Studien zur Formgeschichte altorientalischer und griechischer Sitz- und Liegemöbel vorhellenistischer Zeit*. Berlin.

Laflı, E. 2001a. "Ceramiche in Cilicia tra XIIe-VIe secolo a. C." *Quaderni fiulani di archeologia* 11: 155–91.

——— 2001b. "Geschichte und Perspektiven der archäologischen Erforschung des eisenzeitlichen Kilikien." In G. Wilhelm, ed., *Akten des IV Internationalen Kongresses für Hethitologie, Würzburg, 4. –8. October 1999* Studien zu den Boğazköy-Texten 45: 308–25. Wiesbaden.

Lane, E. N. 1975. "Two Notes on Lydian Topography." *AnatSt* 25: 105–10.

Langlotz, E. 1969. "Beobachtungen in Phokaia." *AA* 84: 377–85.

Laroche, E. 1979. "L'inscriptions lycienne. In H. Metzger et al., eds., *Fouilles de Xanthos VI: La stèle trilingue du Létôon*: 49–127. Paris.

——— 1980. "Les dieux de la Lycie classique d'après les textes lyciens." In H. Metzger, ed., *Actes du colloque sur la Lycie antique, Bibliothèque de l'Institut Français d'Études Anatoliennes d'Istanbul*: 27: 1–6. Paris.

Laroche, E., and A. Davesne. 1981. "Les fouilles de Meydandjik près de Gülnar Turquie et le trésor monétaire hellénistique." *CRAI* 1981: 356–70.

Laroche-Traunecker, F. 1993. "Les édifices d'époque archaique et gréco-perse de Meydancıkkale Gülnar." In J. des Courtils and J.-C. Moretti, eds., *Les grand ateliers d'architecture dans le monde égéen du VIe siècle av. J.-C. Actes du colloque d'Istanbul, 23–25 mai 1991*: 13–28. Paris.

Lateiner, D. 1982. "The Failure of the Ionian Revolt." *Historia* 31: 129–60.

Bibliography

Lebrun, R. 1992. "De quelqes cultes lyciens et pamphyliens." In H. Otten, E. Akurgal, H. Ertem, and A. Suelm, eds. *Hittite and Other Near Eastern Studies in Honour of Sedat Alp: Sedat Alp'a Armağan: Festschrift für Sedat Alp, Anadolu Medeniyetleri Araştırma ve Tanıtma Vakfı Yayınları* 1: 357–63. Ankara.

Lecoq, P. 1997. *Les inscriptions de la Perse achéménide: traduit du vieux perse, de l'élamite, du babylonien et de l'araméen, présenté et annoté par Pierre Lecoq*. Paris.

Lefebvre, M. G. 1924. *Le tombeau de Petosiris*. Cairo.

Leith, M. J. W. 1990. "Greek and Persian Images in Pre-Alexandrine Samaria: The Wâdi ed-Dâliyeh Seal Impressions." Ph.D. dissertation, Harvard University.

⸻ 1997. *Wadi Daliyeh, 1: The Wadi Daliyeh Seal Impressions*. DJD 24. Oxford.

Lemaire, A. 1993. "Deux nouvelles inscriptions araméennes d'époque perse in Cilicie orientale." *EA* 21: 9–14.

⸻ 1994. "Deux nouvelles stèles funéraires araméennes de Cilicie orientale." *EA* 23: 91–8.

⸻ 2001. "Les Inscriptions Araméennes de Daskyleion." In T. Bakır et al., eds., *Achaemenid Anatolia: Proceedings of the First International Symposium on Anatolia in the Achaemenid Period, Bandırma, 15–18 August 1997*: 21–35. Leiden.

⸻ 2002. "Nouvelle inscription araméenne d'époque achéménide provenant de Kenger (Lydie)." *EA* 34: 179–84.

⸻ 2003. "Les pierres et inscriptions araméennes d'Arebsun, nouvel examen." In S. Shaked and A. Netzer, eds., *Irano-Judaica*: 5: 138–64. Jerusalem.

⸻ 2004. "Nouvelle inscription araméenne de Cilicie orientale: Aigeai." *EA* 37: 88–90.

Lemaire, A., and H. Lozachmeur. 1996. "Remarques sur le plurilinguisme en Asie Mineure à l'époque perse." In R. Briquel-Chatonnet, ed., *Mosaïque de langues, mosaïque culturelle. Le bilinguisme dans le Proche-Orient ancien*: 91–123. Paris.

Lenfant, D. 2004. "L'amalgame entre les Perses et les Troyens chez les Grecs de l'époque classique: usages politiques et discours historiques." In J. M. Candau Morón, F. J. Gonzales Ponce, and G. Cruz Andreotti, eds., *Historia y mito: el pasado legendario como fuente de autoridad*: 77–96. Málaga.

Lerner, J. 1991. "Some So-Called Achaemenid Objects from Pazyryk." *Source: Notes in the History of Art* 10/4: 8–15.

Lethaby, W. R. 1908. *Greek Buildings Represented by Fragments in the British Museum*. London.

Levi, M.-A. 1976. "Au sujet des Laoi et des inscriptions de Mnésimachos." In *Actes du Colloque 1973 sur l'esclavage: Annales Littéraires de l'Université de Besançon 182*. Centre de Recherche d'Histoire Ancienne: 18: 259–271. Paris.

Lewis, D. M. 1977. *Sparta and Persia*. Leiden.

⸻ 1980. "Datis the Mede." *JHS* 100: 194–5.

⸻ 1987. "The King's Dinner (Polyaenus IV 3.32)." In H. Sancisi-Weerdenburg and A. Kuhrt, eds., *AchHist 2. The Greek Sources*: 79–87. Leiden.

⸻ 1990. "The Fortification Texts." In H. Sancisi-Weerdenburg and A. Kuhrt, eds., *AchHist 4. Center and Periphery*: 1–6. Leiden.

Lidzbarski, M. 1902. Aramäische Inschriften aus Kappadokien. *Ephemeris für semitische Epigraphik* I. Giessen.

Liebhart, R. F., and J. S. Johnson. 2005. "Support and Conserve: Conservation and Environmental Monitoring of the Tomb Chamber of Tumulus MM." In L. Kealhofer, ed., *The Archaeology of Midas and the Phrygians: Recent Work at Gordion*: 191–203. Philadelphia.

Lipinski, E. 1975a. "La stèle égypto-araméenne de Tumma', fille de Bokkorinif." *Chronique d'Egypte* 50: 93–104.

Bibliography

1975b. *Studies in Aramaic Inscriptions and Onomastics* I. Leuven.
Lissarrague, F. 1990. *The Aesthetics of the Greek Banquet*. Princeton, NJ.
Littauer, M. A., and J. H. Crouwel. 1979. *Wheeled Vehicles and Ridden Animals in the Ancient Near East*. Leiden.
Littmann, E. 1916. *Sardis* VI.I: *Lydian Inscriptions*. Leiden.
Lloyd, A. B. 1982. "The Inscription of Udjahorresnet: A Collaborator's Testament." *JEA* 68: 166–80.
Lochner-Hüttenbach, F. 1964. "Brief des Königs Darius an den Satrapen Gadatas." In W. Brandenstein and M. Mayrhofer, eds., *Handbuch des Altpersischen*: 91–8. Wiesbaden.
Lockwood, W. G., ed. 1984. *Beyond Ethnic Boundaries: New Approaches to Ethnicity*. Ann Arbor, MI.
Lohmann, H. 1999. "Zwischen Kaunos und Telmessos. Reisenotizen aus dem karisch-lykischen Grenzgebiet." *Orbis Terrarum* 5: 43–83.
Luckenbill, D. D. 1927. *Ancient Records of Assyria and Babylonia* II. Chicago.
Luschey, H. 1939. *Die Phiale*. Beicherode am Herz.
  1968. "Studien zu dem Darius-Relief von Bisutun." *AMI* 1: 63–94.
  1974. "Bisutun: Geschichte und Forschungsgeschichte." *AA* 89: 114–49.
L'vov-Basirov, O. P. V. 2001. "Achaemenian Funerary Practices in Western Asia Minor." In T. Bakır, ed., *Achaemenid Anatolia: Proceedings of the First International Symposium on Anatolia in the Achaemenid Period, Bandırma, 15–18 August 1997*: 101–7. Leiden.
Ma, J. 2008. "Mysians on the Çan Sarcophagus? Ethnicity and Domination in Achaemenid Military Art." *Historia* 39: 1–16.
Macqueen, J. G. 1995. "The History of Anatolia and of the Hittite Empire: An Overview." *CANE*: 1085–1106. New York.
Maffré, F. 2007a. "Example of the Persian Occupation in the Satrapy of Phrygia through the Study of the Population from the Asian Provinces in the Achaemenid Empire (Semites/Iranians)." In *Achaemenid Impact*: 225–46. Istanbul.
  2007b. "Indigenous Aristocracies in Hellespontine Phrygia. In C. Tuplin ed., *Persian Responses: Political and Cultural Interaction within the Achaemenid Empire*: 117–41. Swansea.
Magee, P., C. Petrie, R. Knox, and F. Khan. 2005. "The Achaemenid Empire in South Asia and Recent Excavations at Akra (NWFP, Pakistan)." *AJA* 109: 711–41.
Malay, H. 1987. "Lydia araştırmaları." *AST* 5: 379–81.
  1992. *Hellenistik Devirde Pergamon ve Aristonikos Ayaklanması*. Izmir.
  1994. *Greek and Latin Inscriptions in the Manisa Museum*. Vienna.
  1999. *Researches in Lydia, Mysia and Aiolis*. Vienna.
Malay, H., and C. Nalbantoğlu. 1996. "The Cult of Apollo Poeurenos in Lydia." *TürkAD* 4: 75–81.
Mallowan, M. E. L. 1966. *Nimrud and Its Remains* II. New York.
  1972. "Cyrus the Great, 558–529 B.C." *Iran* 10: 7–12.
Mann, M. 1986. *Sources of Social Power*. Cambridge.
Marazov, I., ed. 1998. *Ancient Gold: The Wealth of the Thracians*. New York.
Marcus, M. I. 1990. "Centre, Province and Periphery: A New Paradigm from Iron-Age Iran." *Art History* 13/2: 129–50.
  1993. "Incorporating the Body: Adornment, Gender, and Social Identity in Ancient Iran." *CAJ* 3: 157–78.
  1994. "Dressed to Kill: Women and Pins in Early Iran." *OAJ* 17/2: 3–15.
  1995. "Art and Ideology in Ancient Western Asia." *CANE*: 2487–2505. New York.
Marek, C. 2006. *Die Inschriften von Kaunos*. Vestigia 55. Munich.

Bibliography

Marksteiner, T. 1994. "Brand- und Körperbestattung; Tumulus- und Fassadenkammergräber. Überlegungen zu einem Wechsel der Bestattungsbräuche im vorhellenistischen Lykien." *Lykia* 1: 78–88.

——— 1996. "Ein klassisches Turmgehöft bei Asar Önü." In K. Blakolmer, R. Krierer, F. Krinzinger, A. Landskrom-Dinstl, H. D. Szemethy, and K. Zhuber-Okrog, eds., *Fremde Zeiten. Festschrift für Jürgen Borchhardt zum sechzigsten Geburtstag am 25. Februar 1996* 1: 85–93. Vienna.

——— 1997. *Die befestigte Siedlung von Limyra. Studien zur vorrömischen Wehrarchitektur und zur Siedlungsentwicklung Lykiens unter besonderer Berücksichtigung der klassischen Periode*. Vienna.

——— 1999. "Überlegungen bezüglich einer strukturellen Verwandtschaft achämenidenzeitlicher Gipfelbefestigungen des südwestlichen Kleinasien." *Olba* 2/2: 313–22.

——— 2002a. "Städtische Strukturen im vorhellenistischen Lykien." In M. H. Hansen ed., *A Comparative Study of Six City-State Cultures*. Historisk-filosofiske Skrifter 27, Det Kongelige Danske Videnskabernes Selskab: 57–72. Copenhagen.

——— 2002b. *Trysa, eine zentrallykische Niederlassung im Wandel der Zeit*. Wiener Forschungen zur Archäologie 5. Ed. J. Borchhardt and F. Krinzinger. Vienna.

——— 2002c. "Untersuchungen an den westlichen Stadtmauern von Xanthos." *AnatAnt* 10: 197–216.

——— 2005. "Das achämenidenzeitliche Lykien." In *L'archéologie de l'empire achéménide*: 27–48. Paris.

Martin, R. 1971. "Le Monument des Néréides et l'architecture funéraire." *RA* 1971: 327–7.

Martin, T. R. 1985. *Sovereignty and Coinage in Classical Greece*. Princeton, NJ.

Matz, F. 1937. "Altitalische und vorderasiatische Riefelschalen." *Klio* 30: 110–17.

Mauss, M. 1966. *The Gift: Forms and Functions of Exchange in Archaic Societies* [1925]. Trans. I. Cunnison. London.

Maximova, M. 1928. "Griechisch-persische Kleinkunst in Kleinasien nach den Perserkriegen." *AA* 648–77.

Mayrhofer, M. 1973. *Onomastica Persepolitana. Das altiranische Namengut der Persepolis-Täfelchen*. Vienna.

McGovern, P. E. 2009. *Uncorking the Past: The Quest for Wine, Beer, and Other Alcoholic Beverages*. Berkeley, CA.

McIntosh, J. 1997. "Cognition and Power." Paper delivered at the Society for Literature, Science, and the Arts Meetings 30 October–2 November 1997, Pittsburgh.

——— 2009. *The Edge of Islam: Power, Personhood, and Ethnoreligious Boundaries on the Kenya Coast*. Durham, NC.

McLauchlin, B. K. 1985. "Lydian Graves and Burial Customs." Ph.D. dissertation, University of California at Berkeley.

McMahon, A. 1996. "The Achaemenid-Hellenistic Occupation at Hacınebi." In G. Stein et al., eds., "Uruk Colonies and Anatolian Communities: An Interim Report on the 1992–1993 Excavations at Hacınebi, Turkey." *AJA* 100: 222–29.

——— 1997. "Achaemenid-Hellenistic Remains at Hacınebi, 1996 Interim Report." In G. Stein et al., eds., "Excavations at Hacınebi, Turkey – 1996: Preliminary Report." *Anatolica* 23: 121–4.

Meade, C. G. 1969. "Excavations at Baba Jan, 1967." *Iran* 7: 115–30.

Meadows, K. 1994. "You Are What You Eat: Diet, Identity and Romanization." In S. Cottam, D. Dungworth, S. Scott, and J. Taylor, eds., *TRAC 94: Proceedings of the Fourth Annual Theoretical Roman Archaeology Conference, Durham, 1994*: 132–40. Oxford.

Melchert, H. C. 1993. *Lycian Lexicon* (2d ed.), *Lexica Anatolica 1*. Chapel Hill, NC.

Melikian-Chirvani, A. S. 1993. "The International Achaemenid Style." *BAI* 7: 111–30.

Mellink, M. J. 1971. "Excavations at Karataş-Semayük and Elmalı, Lycia, 1970." *AJA* 75: 245–55.

1972. "Excavations at Karataş-Semayük and Elmalı, Lycia, 1971." *AJA* 76: 257–69.

1973. "Excavations at Karataş-Semayük and Elmalı, Lycia, 1972." *AJA* 77: 293–303.

1974. "Excavations at Karataş-Semayük and Elmalı, Lycia, 1973." *AJA* 78: 351–9.

1975. "Excavations at Karataş-Semayük and Elmalı, Lycia, 1974." *AJA* 79: 349–55.

1978. "Mural Paintings in Lycian Tombs." In E. Akurgal, ed., *Proceedings of the Xth International Congress of Classical Archaeology*: 805–9. Ankara.

1979a. "Fouilles d'Elmalı, en Lycie du Nord (Turquie): découvertes préhistoriques et tombes à fresques." *CRAI* 1979: 476–96.

1979b. "The Symbolic Doorway of the Tumulus at Karaburun, Elmalı." *TTK* 8/1: 383–7.

Mellink, M. J., R. A. Bridges, Jr., and F. C. di Vignale. 1998. *Kızılbel: An Archaic Painted Tomb Chamber in Northern Lycia*. Philadelphia.

Meriç, R. 1982. *Metropolis in Ionien. Ergebnisse einer Survey-Unternehmung in den Jahren 1972–75*. Königstein.

1985. "1984 yılı İzmir ve Manisa illeri yüzey araştırmaları." *AST* 3: 199–208.

1986. "1985 yılı İzmir ve Manisa illeri yüzey araştırmaları." *AST* 4: 301–10.

1987a. "1985 yılı Alaşehir kazı çalışmaları." *KST* 8/2: 259–71.

1987b. "1986 yılı İzmir ve Manisa illeri yüzey araştırmaları." *AST* 5: 247–56.

1988. "1987 İzmir-Manisa-Aydın illeri yüzey araştırması." *AST* 6: 385–92.

1989a. "1987 yılı Alaşehir kazısı." *KST* 10/1: 157–70.

1989b. "1988 yılı İzmir, Manisa illeri Arkeolojik yüzey araştırması." *AST* 7: 361–6.

1991. "Doğu Lydia'dan bir mezar steli." *TürkAD* 1: 121–2.

1993. "Neue ostgriechische Grabreliefs aus Ionien und Lydien; mit einem historisch-topographischen Exkurs." *ÖJh* 62: 57–75.

Meriç, R., and J. Nollé. 1985. "Neue Inschriften aus der Umgebung von Philadelphia in Lydien: Badınca." *EA* 5: 19–26.

Meriçboyu, Y. A. 2010. "Lydian Jewelry." In N. D. Cahill, ed., *The Lydians and Their World*: 157–76. Istanbul.

Meritt, B. D., H. T. Wade-Gery, and M. F. McGregor. 1939–53. *The Athenian Tribute Lists*. Cambridge, MA.

Merkelbach, R. 1991. "Ein Orakel des Apollon für Artemis von Koloe." *ZPE* 88: 70–2.

Metzger, H. 1952. *Catalogue des monuments votifs du Musée d'Adalia*. Études Orientales 11. Paris.

1963. Fouilles de Xanthos II: *L'Acropole Lycienne*. Paris.

1971. "Sur deux groupes de reliefs 'gréco-perses' d'Asie Mineure." *L'antiquité classique* 40: 505–25.

1979. "La base d'Arbinas au Létôon de Xanthos. In *VIII Türk Tarih Kongressi*: 471–5. Ankara.

1980. "Deux sanctuaires des eaux d'époque perse ou héllenistique ancienne au Létôon de Xanthos." In H. Metzger, ed., *Actes du colloque sur la Lycie antique, Bibliothéque de l'Insititut Français d'Études Anatoliennes d'Istanbul* 27: 21–8. Paris.

Metzger, H., E. Laroche, and A. Dupont-Sommer. 1974. "La stèle trilingue récemment découverte au Létôon de Xanthos." *CRAI* 82–149.

Metzger, H., E. Laroche, A. Dupont-Sommer, and M. Mayrhofer. 1979. *Fouilles de Xanthos VI: La stèle trilingue du Létôon*. Paris.

Metzler, D. 1971. *Porträt und Gesellschaft. Studien über die Entstehung des griechischen Porträts*. Munich.

Metzler, D., R. Altheim-Stiehl, and E. Schwertheim. 1983. "Eine neue gräko-persische Grabstele aus Sultaniye Köy und ihre Bedeutung für die Geschichte und Topographie von Daskyleion." *EA* 1: 1–23.

Mierse, W. E. 1983. "The Persian Period." In G. M. A. Hanfmann, ed., *Sardis from Prehistoric to Roman Times: Results of the Archaeological Exploration of Sardis 1958–1975*: 100–8. Cambridge, MA.

Miller, D. 1987. *Material Culture and Mass Consumption*. Oxford.

— 1989. "The Limits of Dominance." In D. Miller, M. Rowlands, and C. Tilley, eds. *Domination and Resistance*: 73–9. London.

Miller, M. C. 1991. "Foreigners at the Greek Symposium?" In W. J. Slater, ed., *Dining in a Classical Context*: 59–82. Ann Arbor, MI.

— 1992. "The Parasol: An Oriental Status-Symbol in Late Archaic and Classical Athens." *JHS* 112: 91–105.

— 1993. "Adoption and Adaption of Achaemenid Metalware Forms in Attic Black-Gloss Ware of the Fifth Century." *AMI* 26: 109–46.

— 1997. *Athens and Persia in the Fifth Century BC*. Cambridge.

— 2006. "Betwixt and Between: Western Anatolia in the Persian Period." In C. Mattusch, A. Donohue, and A. Brauer, eds., *Common Ground: Archaeology, Art, Science and Humanities: Proceedings of the XVI International Congress of Classical Archaeology, Boston, 2003*: 255–70. Oxford.

— 2007. "The Poetics of Emulation in the Achaemenid World: The Figured Bowls of the 'Lydian Treasure.'" *AWE* 6: 43–72.

— 2009. "Diacritical Drinking in Achaemenid Anatolia." Paper presented at the colloquium "Formen von Prestige in Kulturen des Altertums," Munich. Forthcoming as "'Manners Makyth Man': Diacritical Drinking in Achaemenid Anatolia." In E. Gruen, ed., *Cultural Identity in the Ancient Mediterranean*: 97–134. Los Angeles, CA.

— 2011. "Town and Country in the Satrapies of Western Anatolia: The Archaeology of Empire." In L. Summerer, A. Ivantchik, and A. von Kienlin, eds., *Kelainai-Apameia Kibotos: Développement urbain das le context anatolien. Actes du colloque international Munich, 2–4 Avril 2009*: 319–44. Bordeaux.

Miller-Collett, S., and M. C. Root. 1997. "An Achaemenid Seal from the Lower City." *StTroica* 7: 355–62.

Millett, M. 1995. "Re-thinking Religion in Romanization." In J. Metzler, M. Millett, N. Roymans, and J. Slofstra, eds., *Integration in the Early Roman West: The Role of Culture and Ideology*: 93–100. Luxembourg.

Mills, B. J. 1999. "Ceramics and Social Contexts of Food Consumption in the Northern Southwest." In J. M. Skibo, ed., *Pottery and People: A Dynamic Interaction*: 99–114. Salt Lake City.

— 2004. "Identity, Feasting, and the Archaeology of the Greater Southwest." In B. J. Mills, ed., *Identity, Feasting, and the Archaeology of the Greater Southwest: Proceedings of the 2002 Southwest Symposium*: 1–26. Boulder, CO.

Mitchell, S. M. 1989–90. "Archaeology in Asia Minor, 1985–89." *JHS* 36: 83–131.

— 1993. *Anatolia: Land, Men and Gods in Asia Minor* I. Oxford.

Möbius, H. 1916. "Form und Bedeutung der sitzenden Gestalt." *AthMitt* 41: 119–219.

— 1971. "Zu den Stelen von Daskyleion." *AA* 86: 442–55.

Moerman, M. 1965. "Who Are the Lue?" *AmAnth* 67: 1215–30.

— 1968. "Being Lue: Uses and Abuses of Ethnic Identification." In J. Helm, ed., *Essays on the Problem of Tribe*: 153–69. Seattle.

Momigliano, A. 1975. *Alien Wisdom: The Limits of Hellenization*. Cambridge.

Mommsen, W. J. 1992. *The Political and Social Theory of Max Weber: Collected Essays*. Chicago.

Moorey, P. R. S. 1979. "Aspects of Worship and Ritual on Achaemenid Seals." *Akten des VII. Kongress für iranische Kunst und Archäologie*. Munich.

1980a. *Cemeteries of the First Millennium B.C. at Deve Hüyük, Near Carchemish, Salvaged by T. E. Lawrence and C. L. Woolley in 1913.* BAR International Series 87. Oxford.

1980b. "Metal Wine-Sets in the Ancient Near East." *IrAnt* 15: 181–97.

1988. "The Technique of Gold-Figure Decoration on Achaemenid Silver Vessels and Its Antecedents." *IrAnt* 23: 231–45.

Mørkholm, O. 1959. "A South Anatolian Coin Hoard." *ActArch* 30: 184–201.

1974. "A Coin of Artaxerxes III." *NC* 1–4.

Mørkholm, O., and J. Zahle. 1972. "The Coinage of Kuprlli: A Numismatic and Archaeological Study." *ActArch* 43: 57–113.

1976. "The Coinages of the Lycian Dynasts Kheriga, Kherêi and Erbbina: A Numismatic and Archaeological Study." *ActArch* 47: 47–90.

Morris, S. P. 1992. *Daidalos and the Origins of Greek Art*. Princeton, NJ.

Mousavi, A. 1989. "The Discovery of an Achaemenid Station at Deh-Bozan in the Asadabad Valley." *AMI* 22: 135–8.

1999. "La ville de Parsa: quelques remarques sur la topographie et le système défensive de Persépolis." In *Neo-Assyrian, Median, Achaemenian and Other Studies in Honor of David Stronach* 2. *ActIr* 34: 145–56.

Munn, M. H. 2006. *The Mother of the Gods, Athens, and the Tyranny of Asia: A Study of Sovereignty in Ancient Religion*. Berkeley, CA.

Murray, O. "Ο ΑΡΧΑΙΟΣ ΔΑΣΜΟΣ." *Historia* 15:142–56.

1991. "War and the Symposium." In W. J. Slater, ed., *Dining in a Classical Context*: 83–104. Ann Arbor, MI.

1996. "Hellenistic Royal Symposia." In P. Bilde et al., eds., *Aspects of Hellenistic Kingship*: 15–27. Aarhus.

Muscarella, O. W. 1980. "Excavated and Unexcavated Achaemenian Art." In D. Schmandt-Besserat, ed., *Ancient Persia: The Art of an Empire*: 23–42. Malibu, CA.

1992. "Achaemenid Brick Decoration." In P. O. Harper, J. Aruz, and F. Tallon, eds., *The Royal City of Susa: Ancient Near Eastern Treasures in the Louvre*: 223–41. New York.

1999. "Parasols in the Ancient Near East." *Source: Notes in the History of Art* 18/2: 1–7.

2003. "The Date of the Destruction of the Early Phrygian Period at Gordion." *AWE* 2: 225–52.

Muss, U. 1983. *Studien zur Bauplastik des archaischen Artemisions von Ephesos*. Bonn.

1994. *Die Bauplastik des archaischen Artemisions von Ephesos*. Vienna.

Nagel, W. 1986. "Die Entwicklung des Wagens im frühen Vorderasien." *Achse, Rad, und Wagen. Fünftausend Jahre Kultur- und Technikgeschichte*: 9–34. Göttingen.

Naour, C. 1981. "Inscriptions du moyen Hermos." *ZPE* 44: 11–44.

Naster, P. 1962. "Les sicles persiques à la demi-figure dans leur contexte numismatique et archéologique." *BSFN* 17/6: 170–71.

Naumann, F. 1983. *Die Ikonographie der Kybele in der phrygischen und der griechischen Kunst*. IstMitt. Suppl. 28. Tübingen.

Neumann, G. 1967. "Beiträge zum Lykischen III." *Sprache* 13: 31–8.

1970. "Beiträge zum Lykischen IV." *Sprache* 16: 54–62.

1996. "Griechische Personennamen in lykischen Texten." In K. Blakolmer, R. Krierer, F. Krinzinger, A. Landskrom-Dinstl, H. D. Szemethy, and K. Zhuber-Okrog, eds., *Fremde Zeiten. Festschrift für Jürgen Borchhardt zum sechzigsten Geburtstag am 25. Februar 1996* 1: 145–51. Vienna.

Newton, C. T. 1862–3. *A History of Discoveries at Halicarnassus, Cnidus and Branchidae*. London.

Nieling, J., and E. Rehm eds. 2010. *Black Sea Studies 11: Achaemenid Impact in the Black Sea – Communications in Power*. Aarhus.

Nielsen, I. 1994. *Hellenistic Palaces: Tradition and Renewal*. Studies in Hellenic Civilization 5. Aarhus.

   1998. "Royal Banquets: The Development of Royal Banquets and Banqueting Halls from Alexander to the Tetrarchs." In I. Nielsen and H. S. Nielsen, eds., *Meals in a Social Context: Aspects of the Communal Meal in the Hellenistic and Roman World*: 102–33. Aarhus.

Nieswandt, H.-H. 1995. "Zur Herrschaftsrepräsentation am Nereidenmonument." *Lykia* 2: 115–44.

Nikoulina, N. M. 1971. "La glyptique 'grecque-orientale' et 'gréco-perse.' " *AK* 14/2: 90–106.

Nilsson, M. 1955. *Geschichte der griechischen Religion*. 2d ed. Munich.

Nimchuk, C. L. 2002. "The 'Archers' of Darius: Coinage or Tokens of Royal Esteem?" *ArsOr* 32: 55–79.

Noe, S. P. 1956. *Two Hoards of Persian Sigloi*. ANSNNM 136. New York.

Nollé, M. 1992. *Denkmäler vom Satrapensitz Daskyleion. Studien zur graeco-persischen Kunst*. Berlin.

Nunn, A. 1996. *Kontinuität und Wandel im Motivschatz Phöniziens, Syriens und Transjordaniens vom 6. bis zum 4. Jahrhundert v. Chr. Vorderasiatische, ägyptische und griechische Bilder im Widerstreit*. Munich.

   2000. "Zur Architektur in Westvorderasien während der Achämenidenzeit." In R. Dittmann et al., eds., *Variatio Delectat. Iran und der Westen. Gedenkschrift für Peter Calmeyer*: 502–38. Münster.

Nylander, C. 1967. "Who Wrote the Inscriptions at Pasargadae?" *Orientalia Suecana* 16: 135–80.

   1970. *Ionians in Pasargadae*. Uppsala.

Oakley, J., and R. Sinos. 1993. *The Wedding in Ancient Athens*. Madison, WI.

Oberleitner, W. 1994. *Das Heroon von Trysa. Ein lykisches Fürstengrab des 4. Jahrhunderts v. Chr.*, Zaberns Bildbände zur Archäologie 18. Mainz.

Olçay, N., and O. Mørkholm. 1971. "The Coin Hoard from Podalia." *NC* 1–29.

Oliver, A. 1970. "Persian Export Glass." *JGS* 12: 9–16.

   1971. "A Bronze Mirror from Sardis." In D. G. Mitten, J. G. Pedley, and J. A. Scott, eds., *Studies Presented to George M. A. Hanfmann*: 113–20. Mainz.

Omura, S., ed. 1992. *Kaman-Kalehöyük*: 1: 1–74. Tokyo.

   1995. "A Preliminary Report on the Ninth Excavation at Kaman-Kalehöyük, 1994." In S. Omura, ed., *Kaman-Kalehöyük*: 4: 1–48. Tokyo.

   1996. "A Preliminary Report on the Tenth Excavation at Kaman-Kalehöyük, 1995." In S. Omura, ed., *Kaman-Kalehöyük*: 5: 1–69. Tokyo.

Oppenheim, A. L. 1949. "The Golden Garments of the Gods." *JNES* 8: 172–93.

   1965. "On Royal Gardens in Mesopotamia." *JNES* 24: 328–33.

Orlin, L. L. 1976. "Athens and Persia ca. 507 B.C.: A Neglected Perspective." In L. L. Orlin, ed., *Michigan Oriental Studies in Honor of George G. Cameron*: 255–66. Ann Arbor, MI.

Özet, M. A. 1994. "The Tomb of a Noble Woman from the Hekatomnid Period." In J. Isager, ed., *Hekatomnid Caria and the Ionian Renaissance*: 88–96. Odense.

Özgen, I. 2010. "Lydian Treasure." In N. D. Cahill ed., *The Lydians and Their World*: 305–38. Istanbul.

Özgen, İ., and J. Öztürk. 1996. *Heritage Recovered: The Lydian Treasure*. Istanbul.
Özgüç, T. 1963. "Altıntepe'de Urartu Mimarlık Eserleri: The Urartian Architecture on the Summit of Altıntepe." *Anatolia* 7: 43–9.
    1966. *Altıntepe*. TTK 5/24. Ankara.
Özhanlı, M. 2002. "Isinda: The Isinda Pillar Tomb." *ADALYA* 5: 73–106.
Özkan, T. 1991. "Lydia'da ele geçen bir greko-pers buluntu grubu." *TürkAD* 1: 131–5.
Özsait, M., and N. Özsait. 1990. "1987 ve 1988 Yılı Senirkent Çevresi Tarihöncesi Araştırmaları." *7. AST*, Antalya, 18–23 May 1989: 381–9. Ankara.
    2007. "Delipınar Mezar Stelleri." In *Achaemenid Impact*: 159–66. Istanbul.
Öztürk, J. 1998. "Lydian Jewelry." In D. Williams, ed., *Art of the Greek Goldsmith*: 41–7. London.
Paarmann, B. 2007. "A Revised Edition of the Athenian Tribute Lists." Ph.D. dissertation, University of Fribourg.
Paspalas, S. A. 2000a. "On Persian-Type Furniture in Macedonia: The Recognition and Transmission of Forms." *AJA* 104: 531–60.
    2000b. "A Persianizing Cup from Lydia." *OJA* 19/2: 135–74.
Pasztory, E. 1989. "Identity and Difference: The Uses and Meanings of Ethnic Styles." In S. J. Barnes and W. S. Melion, eds., *Cultural Differentiation and Cultural Identity in the Visual Arts*: 15–39. Washington, DC.
Pauketat, T. R. 2000. "The Tragedy of the Commoners." In M.-A. Dobres and J. E. Robb, eds., *Agency in Archaeology*: 113–29. London.
Pedley, J. G. 1972. *Sardis M2: Ancient Literary Sources on Sardis*. Cambridge, MA.
Perrot, J. 1974. "Le palais de Darius le Grand à Suse." In *Proceedings of the Second Annual Symposium on Archaeological Research in Iran*: 94–107. Tehran.
    1981. "L'architecture militaire et palatiale des Achéménides à Suse." In *150 Jahre Deutsches Archäologisches Institut, 1829–1979*: 79–94. Mainz.
Peschlow, A. 2002. "Die Arbeiten des Jahres 2000 in Herakleia am Latmos und dem zugehörigen Territorium Beşparmak." *AST* 19/1: 255–62.
Petit, T. 1990. *Satrapes et satrapies dans l'empire achéménide de Cyrus le Grand à Xerxès Ier*. Paris.
Petzl, G. 1976. "Antike Zeugnisse aus der Umgebung von Thyateira." *ZPE* 23: 244–50.
    1978. "Inschriften aus der Umgebung von Saittai." *ZPE* 30: 249–76.
    1985. "Epigraphische Funde aus Lydien." *EA* 15: 49–72.
    1994. "Zuweisungsprobleme." *TürkAD* 2: 137–48.
    1996. "Neue Inschriften aus Lydien I." *EA* 26: 1–29.
    1998. "Neue Inschriften aus Lydien III." *EA* 30: 19–46.
Petzl, G., and H. W. Pleket. 1979. "Inschriften aus Lydien." *ZPE* 34: 281–95.
Pfuhl, E., and H. Möbius. 1977. *Die ostgriechischen Grabreliefs* 1. Mainz.
Piepkorn, A. C. 1933. *Historical Prism Inscriptions of Assurbanipal*. Chicago.
Pillet, M. L. 1914. *Le palais de Darius Ier à Suse*. Paris.
Polat, G. 1994. "Eine Neuerwerbung des Uşak-Museums. Eine anatolisch-persische Grabstele." *TürkAD* 2: 61–6.
    2001. "Das Grabdenkmal des Autophradates." In T. Bakır et al., eds., *Achaemenid Anatolia: Proceedings of the First International Symposium on Anatolia in the Achaemenid Period, Bandırma, 15–18 August 1997*: 123–33. Leiden.
    2007. "Daskyleion'dan Yeni bir Anadolu-Pers Steli." In *Achaemenid Impact*: 215–24. Istanbul.
Porath, J. 1974. "A Fortress of the Persian Period." *'Atiqot* 7: 43–55.
Porten, B. 1998. *Archives from Elephantine: The Life of an Ancient Military Colony*. Berkeley, CA.

Posener, G. 1936. *Première domination perse en Égypte*. Cairo.

    1986. "Du nouveau sur Kombabos." *RdÉ* 37: 91–6.

Potter, J. M., and S. G. Ortman. 2004. "Community and Cuisine in the Prehispanic American Southwest." In B. J. Mills, ed., *Identity, Feasting, and the Archaeology of the Greater Southwest: Proceedings of the 2002 Southwest Symposium*: 173–91. Boulder, CO.

Potts, D. T. 1999. *The Archaeology of Elam: Formation and Transformation of an Ancient Iranian State*. Cambridge.

Prag, A. J. N. W., and R. A. H. Neave. 1994. "Who Is the Carian Princess?" In J. Isager, ed., *Hekatomnid Caria and the Ionian Renaissance*: 97–109. Odense.

Price, M. 1989. "Darius I and the Daric." *REA* 91: 9–14.

Pryce, F. N. 1928. *Catalogue of Sculpture in the Department of Greek and Roman Antiquities of the British Museum* I/1: Prehellenic and Early Greek. London.

Radt, W. 1970. *Siedlungen und Bauten auf der Halbinsel von Halikarnassos unter besonderer Berücksichtigung der archaischen Epoche*. IstMitt 3. Tübingen.

    1983. "Eine gräko-persische Grabstele im Museum Bergama." *IstMitt* 33: 53–68.

    1996. "Archaische Löwen aus der Umgebung von Pergamon." *IstMitt* 46: 83–92.

Raimond, E. 2007. "Persian Power and Lycian Religion." In *Achaemenid Impact*: 69–74. Istanbul.

Ramage, A. 1987. "Lydian Sardis." In E. Guralnick, ed., *Sardis: Twenty-Seven Years of Discovery*: 6–16. Chicago.

Ramage, A., and P. Craddock. 2000. *King Croesus' Gold: Excavations at Sardis and the History of Gold Refining*. AES 11. Cambridge, MA.

Ramage, A. and N. Ramage. 1971. "The Siting of Lydian Burial Mounds." In *Studies Presented to G. M. A. Hanfmann*: 143–60.

Ramage, N. H. 1979. "A Lydian Funerary Banquet." *AnatSt* 29: 91–5.

Ramsay, W. M. 1920. "Military Operations on the North Front of Mount Tarsus." *JHS* 40: 89–112.

Ratté, C. J. 1989. "Lydian Masonry and Monumental Architecture at Sardis." Ph.D. dissertation, University of California at Berkeley.

    1992. "The 'Pyramid Tomb' at Sardis." *IstMitt* 42: 135–61.

    1994a. "Anthemion Stelae from Sardis." *AJA* 98: 593–607.

    1994b. "Not the Tomb of Gyges." *JHS* 114: 157–61.

    2011. *Lydian Architecture: Ashlar Masonry Structures at Sardis*. Cambridge, MA.

Ray, J. D. 1995. "Soldiers to Pharaoh: The Carians of Southwest Anatolia." *CANE*: 1185–94. New York.

Razmjou, S. 2002. "Assessing the Damage: Notes on the Life and Demise of the Statue of Darius from Susa." *ArsOr* 32: 81–104.

    2004a. "Lan Ceremony and other Ritual Ceremonies in the Achaemeni Period: Persepolis Fortification Tablets." *Iran* 42: 103–17.

    2004b. "Project Report of the Persepolis Fortification Tablets in the National Museum of Iran." ARTA 2004.004. http://www.achemenet.com/ressources/enligne/arta/pdf/2004.004-Razmjou.pdf.

    2005a. "In Search of the Lost Median Art." *IrAnt* 40: 271–314.

    2005b. "Notes on a Forgotten Achaemenid Site at Farmeshgan: Iran." In *L'archéologie de l'empire achéménide*: 293–312. Paris.

Reade, J. E. 1983. *Assyrian Sculpture*. London.

    1995. "The Symposion in Ancient Mesopotamia: Archaeological Evidence." In O. Murray and M. Tecusan, eds., *In Vino Veritas*: 35–56. Rome.

Rein, M. J. 1993. "The Cult and Iconography of Lydian Kybele." Ph.D. dissertation, Harvard University.

1996. "Phrygian *Matar*: Emergence of an Iconographic Type." In E. N. Lane, ed., *Cybele, Attis and Related Cults: Essays in Memory of M. J. Vermaseren*: 223–37. Leiden.

Reinach, S. 1885. "Chronique d'Orient." *RA* 5: 87–116.

1889. "Statues archäiques de Cybèle." *BCH* 13: 543–60.

Rhodes, P. J., and R. Osborne. 2003. *Greek Historical Inscriptions, 404–323 BC*. Oxford.

Richter, G. M. A. 1949. "The Late 'Achaemenian' or 'Graeco-Persian' Gems." *Hesperia* Suppl. 8: 291–98.

1952. "Greek Subjects on 'Graeco-Persian' Seal Stones." In G. C. Miles, ed., *Archaeologica Orientalia in Memoriam Ernst Herzfeld*: 189–94. Locust Valley, NY.

1959. Review of *Fouilles de Xanthos*, I, *Les Piliers Funéraires* by P. Demargne. *AJA* 63/4: 400–1.

1965. *The Portraits of the Greeks* I. London.

Ricoeur, P. 1996. *Memory and Cultural Politics: New Approaches to American Ethnic Literatures*. Boston.

2004. *Memory, History, Forgetting*. Chicago.

Rigsby, K. 1995. "The Royal Letter from Sarıçam." *Forschungen in Lydien*, AMS 17: 77–83.

Roaf, M. 1983. *Sculptures and Sculptors at Persepolis*. Iran 21. London.

1995. "Media and Mesopotamia: History and Architecture." In J. Curtis, ed., *Later Mesopotamia and Iran*: 54–66. London.

2004. *Cultural Atlas of Mesopotamia and the Ancient Near East*. Amsterdam.

Roaf, M., and D. Stronach. 1973. "Excavations at Tepe Nush-i Jan: Second Interim Report." *Iran* 11: 129–40.

Robert, L. 1953. "Le sanctuaire d'Artémis à Amyzon." *CRAI* 1953: 403–15.

1982. "Documents d'Asie Mineure XXI: Au Nord de Sardes." *BCH* 106: 334–78.

Robinson, E. S. G. 1947. "A Hoard of Persian Sigloi." *NC* 173–4.

1958. "The Beginnings of Achaemenid Coinage." *NC* 187–93.

1960. "Two Greek Coin Hoards." *NC* 31–6.

Robinson, T. 1999. "Erbbina, the 'Nereid Monument' and Xanthus." In G. R. Tsetskhladze, ed., *Ancient Greeks: West and East. Mnemosyne* Suppl. 196: 361–78. Leiden.

Roebuck, C. 1959. *Ionian Trade and Colonization*. New York.

Roller, L. E. 1983. "The Legend of Midas." *CA* 2: 299–313.

1988. "Phrygian Myth and Cult." *Source* 7: 43–50.

1991. "The Great Mother at Gordion: The Hellenization of an Anatolian Cult." *JHS* 111: 128–43.

1999. *In Search of God the Mother: The Cult of Anatolian Cybele*. Berkeley, CA.

Röllig, W. 2002. "Appendix II: Aramaic Inscriptions." In D. Kaptan, *AchHist 12. The Daskyleion Bullae: Seal Images from the Western Achaemenid Empire*: 198–210. Leiden.

Rollinger, R. 2003. "The Western Expansion of the Median 'Empire'." In G. Lanfranchi et al., eds., *Continuity of Empires(?)*: 305–13. Tehran.

2008. "The Median 'Empire': The End of Urartu and Cyrus the Great's Campaign in 547 BC (Nabonidus Chronicle II 16)." *AWE* 7: 51–65.

Roos, P. 1970. "An Achaemenian Sketch Slab and the Ornaments of the Royal Dress at Persepolis." *EW* 20: 51–9.

1971. "The Rock-Tomb Doors of the Lyco-Carian Borderland." *OpAth* 10: 25–30.

1972. *The Rock Tombs of Caunus*. SIMA 34. Göteborg.

1974. *The Rock Tombs of Caunus: The Finds*. Studies in Mediterranean Archaeology 34/2. Göteborg.

- 1985. *Survey of Rock-Cut Chamber Tombs in Caria I: South-Eastern Caria and the Lyco-Carian Borderland*. SIMA 72/1. Göteborg.
- 1989. "Rock-Tombs in Hecatomnid Caria and Greek Architecture." In T. Linders and P. Hellstrøm, eds., *Architecture and Society in Hecatomnid Caria*. Proceedings of the Uppsala Symposium 1987, Boreas 17. Uppsala.
- 2006. *Survey of Rock-Cut Chamber Tombs in Caria II: Central Caria*. SIMA 72/2. Göteborg.

Roosevelt, C. H. 2003. "Lydian and Persian Period Settlement in Lydia." Ph.D. dissertation, Cornell University.
- 2006. "Symbolic Door Stelae and Graveside Monuments in Western Anatolia." *AJA* 110/1: 65–91.
- 2008. "Lale Tepe: A Late Lydian Tumulus near Sardis. 1. Introduction, Excavation, and Finds." In N. D. Cahill ed., *Love for Lydia: A Sardis Anniversary Volume Presented to Crawford H. Greenewalt, Jr.*: 1–24. Cambridge, MA.
- 2009. *The Archaeology of Lydia, from Gyges to Alexander*. Cambridge.

Root, M. C. 1979. *The King and Kingship in Achaemenid Art: Essays on the Creation of an Iconography of Empire*. ActIr 19. Leiden.
- 1985. "The Parthenon Frieze and the Apadana Reliefs at Persepolis." *AJA* 89: 103–20.
- 1988. "Evidence from Persepolis for the Dating of Persian and Archaic Greek Coinage." *NC* 1–12.
- 1989. "The Persian Archer at Persepolis: Aspects of Chronology, Style, and Symbolism." *REA* 91: 33–50.
- 1990. "Circles of Artistic Programming: Strategies for Studying Creative Process at Persepolis." In A. C. Gunter, ed., *Investigating Artistic Environments in the Ancient Near East*: 115–42. Washington, DC.
- 1991. "From the Heart: Powerful Persianisms in the Art of the Western Empire." In H. Sancisi-Weerdenburg and A. Kuhrt, eds., *AchHist 4. Asia Minor and Egypt: Old Cultures in a New Empire*: 1–29. Leiden.
- 1997a. "Cultural Pluralisms on the Persepolis Fortification Tablets." *Topoi* Suppl. 1: 229–52.
- 1997b. "The Persepolis Fortification Tablets: Archival Issues and the Problem of Stamps versus Cylinder Seals." In M.-F. Boussac and A. Invernizzi, eds., *Archives et sceaux du monde hellénistique / Archivi et sigilli nel monde ellenistico*: 3–27. Paris.
- 1998. "Pyramidal Stamp Seals: The Persepolis Connection." In M. Brosius and A. Kuhrt, eds., *AchHist 11. Persepolis Studies: Memorial Volume in Honour of Professor David M. Lewis*: 257–89. Leiden.
- 2002. "Animals in the Art of Ancient Iran." In B. J. Collins, ed., *A History of the Animal World in the Ancient Near East*. Handbook of Oriental Studies 64: 169–209. Leiden.
- 2007. "Reading Persepolis in Greek: Gifts of the Yauna." In C. Tuplin, ed., *Persian Responses: Political and Cultural Interaction with(in) the Achaemenid Empire*: 177–224. Swansea.
- 2008. "The Legible Image: How Did Seals and Sealing Matter in Persepolis?" In P. Briant, W. F. M. Henkelman, and M. W. Stolper, eds., *L'archive des Fortifications de Persépolis: état des questions et perspectives de recherches*: 87–148. Paris.
- 2010. "Palace to Temple – King to Cosmos: Achaemenid Foundation Texts in Iran." In M. J. Boda and J. R. Novotny, eds., *From the Foundations to the Crenellations: Essays on Temple Building in the Ancient Near East*: 165–210. Münster.
- Forthcoming a. "Defining the Divine in Achaemenid Persian Arts of Kingship." In L. Mitchell and C. Melville, eds., *Every Inch a King: From Alexander to the King of Kings*. Leiden.

Forthcoming b. "Medes in the Imperial Imagination." In K. Abdi, ed., *Festschrift for Alireza Shapour Shahbazi*. Tehran.

Rose, C. B. 2007. "The Tombs of the Granicus Valley." In *Achaemenid Impact*: 247–64. Istanbul.

Rotroff, S. I., and A. Oliver. 2003. *Sardis M12: The Hellenistic Pottery from Sardis*. Cambridge, MA.

Roudometov, V. 2002. *Collective Memory, National Identity, and Ethnic Conflict: Greece, Bulgaria, and the Macedonian Question*. Westport, CT.

Rudenko, S. I. 1970. *Frozen Tombs of Siberia: The Pazyryk Burials of Iron-Age Horsemen*. Berkeley, CA.

Rudolph, C. 2003. *Das 'Harpyien-Monument' von Xanthos – Seine Bedeutung innerhalb der spätarchaischen Plastik*. BAR International Series 1108. Oxford.

Rugler, A. 1988. *Die Columnae Caelatae des jüngeren Artemisions von Ephesos*. IstMitt Suppl. 34.

Rumpf, A. 1920. "Lydische Salbgefässe." *AthMitt* 45: 163–70.

———. 1933. "Zu den Klazomenischen Denkmälern." *JdI* 48: 55–83.

Russell, J.-R. 1990. "Pre-Christian Armenian Religion." In W. Haase, ed., *Aufstieg und Niedergang der römischen Welt 2*, 18/4: 2679–92. Berlin.

Ruzicka, S. 1992. *Politics of a Persian Dynasty: The Hecatomnids in the Fourth Century B.C.* Norman, OK.

Sagona, A. G., and C. Sagona. 2004. *Archaeology at the North-east Anatolian Frontier I: An Historical Geography and a Field Survey of the Bayburt Province*. ANES Suppl. Series 14. Herent.

Şahin, I. 1998. "Lydia'da Küçük Yerleşimler." Ph.D. dissertation, Ege University.

Salonen, E. 1972. *Über den Zehnten im alten Mesopotamien. Ein Beitrag zur Geschichte der Besteuerung*. Helsinki.

Sami, A. 1955. *Persepolis Takht-i-Jamshid*. Trans. R. N. Sharp. Shiraz.

Sams, G. K. 1979. "Imports at Gordion: Lydian and Persian Periods." *Expedition* 21/4: 6–17.

———. 1994. *The Gordion Excavations, 1950–1973: Final Reports* IV – The Early Phrygian Pottery. Philadelphia.

———. 1995. "Midas of Gordion and the Anatolian Kingdom of Phrygia." *CANE*: 1147–59. New York.

———. 1997. "Gordion and the Kingdom of Phrygia." In R. Gusmani, ed., *Frigi e Frigio: Atti del 1° Simposio Internazionale Roma, 16–17 ottobre 1995*: 239–48. Rome.

———. 2005. "Gordion: Exploration over a Century." In L. Kealhofer, ed., *The Archaeology of Midas and the Phrygians: Recent Work at Gordion*: 10–21. Philadelphia.

Sams, G. K., and M. M. Voigt. 1995. "Gordion Archaeological Activities, 1993." *KST* 16/1: 369–92.

Sancisi-Weerdenburg, H. 1989. "Gifts in the Persian Empire." In P. Briant and C. Herrenschmidt, eds., *Le tribut dans l'empire Perse*: 129–46. Paris.

———. 1990. "The Quest for an Elusive Empire." In H. Sancisi-Weerdenburg and A. Kuhrt, eds., *AchHist 4. Centre and Periphery*: 263–74. Leiden.

———. 1994. "Xerxes en de plataan: vier variaties op een motief." *Lampas* 27: 213–29.

———. 1997a. "Crumbs from the Royal Table: Foodnotes on Briant, pp. 297–306." *Topoi* Suppl. 1: 333–45.

———. 1997b. "Persian Food: Stereotypes and Political Identity." In J. Wilkins et al., eds., *Food in Antiquity*. Exeter.

———. 1998. "Baji." In M. Brosius and A. Kuhrt, eds., *AchHist 11. Studies in Persian History: Essays in Honour of David M. Lewis*: 23–4. Leiden.

Sancisi-Weerdenburg, H., and W. F. M. Henkelman. 2003. "Xerxes Anno 1918: The Persian Wars as l'Art pour l'Art." In M. Haagsma, P. den Boer, and E. M. Moormann, eds., *The Impact of Classical Greece on European and National Identities*. Proceedings of an International Colloquium Held at the Netherlands Institute at Athens, 2–4 October 2000: 181–213. Amsterdam.

Sancisi-Weerdenburg, H., and A. Kuhrt, eds. 1987. *AchHist 2. The Greek Sources*. Leiden.

Santrot, J., ed. 1996. *Arménie: trésors de l'Arménie ancienne des origines au VI siècle*. Nantes.

Sarraf, M. R. 1997. "Ecbatane, capitale des Mèdes, capitale achéménide." *Archéologia* 339: 40–41.

Sayar, M. H. 2004. "Athena Oreia." In H. Heftner and K. Tomaschitz, eds., *Ad Fontes. Festschrift für Gerhard Dobesch*: 455–65. Vienna.

———. 2007. "Eskiçağ'da Çukurova'da Hilal ve Yıldızın Kullanımı." In *Achaemenid Impact*: 97–102. Istanbul.

Sayce, A. H. 1906. *Aramaic Papyri Discovered at Assuan*. London.

Schaeffer, J. S., N. H. Ramage, and C. H. Greenewalt, Jr. 1997. *The Corinthian, Attic, and Lakonian Pottery from Sardis*. AES 10. Cambridge, MA.

Schefold, K. 1978. "Die Residenz von Larisa am Hermos im Licht neuer Forschungen." In E. Akurgal, ed., *The Proceedings of the Tenth International Congress of Classical Archaeology, 1973*: 549–64. Ankara.

Schippmann, K. 1971. *Die iranischen Feuerheiligtümer*. Berlin.

Schlumberger, D. 1953. "L'argent grec dans l'empire Achéménide." In R. Curiel and D. Schlumberger, eds., *Trésors monétaires d'Afghanistan*: 3–62. Paris.

Schmidt, E. F. 1953. *Persepolis I: Structures, Reliefs, Inscriptions*. OIP 68. Chicago.

———. 1957. *Persepolis II: Contents of the Treasury and Other Discoveries*. OIP 69. Chicago.

———. 1970. *Persepolis III: The Royal Tombs and Other Monuments*. OIP 70. Chicago.

Schmitt, R. 1967. "Medisches und persisches Sprachgut bei Herodot." *ZDMG* 117: 119–45.

———. 1970. "BARZOCHARA. Ein neues Anahita-epitheton aus Kappadokien." *ZVS* 84: 207–10.

———. 1976. "Der Titel 'Satrap.'" In A. Morpurgo-Davies and W. Meid, eds., *Studies in Greek, Italian and Indo-European Linguistics offered to L. R. Palmer*: 373–90. Innsbruck.

———. 1983. "Achaemenid Dynasty. i. The Clan and Dynasty." *EncIr*, online ed., available at http://www.iranica.com/articles/achaemenid-dynasty.

———. 1990a. "Bisotun III. Darius's Inscriptions." *EncIr* 4:299–305.

———. 1990b. "Epigraphisch-exegetische Notizen zu Dareios' Bisutun-Inschriften." *AnzWien* Sitzungsberichte 286: 3–88.

———. 1991. *The Bisutun Inscriptions of Darius the Great: Old Persian Text*. London.

———. 2000. *The Old Persian Inscriptions of Naqsh-i Rustam and Persepolis* (CII I/1, 2). London.

———. 2002. "Appendix I: Cuneiform Inscriptions." In D. Kaptan, *AchHist 12. The Daskyleion Bullae: Seal Images from the Western Achaemenid Empire*: 194–7. Leiden.

Schwabacher, W. 1957. "Satrapenbildnisse. Zum neuen Münzporträt des Tissaphernes." In K. Schauenburg, ed., *Charites: Studien zur Altertumswissenschaft*. Festschrift Ernst Langlotz: 27–32. Bonn.

———. 1968. "Lycian Coin-Portraits." In C. M. Kraay and G. K. Jenkins, eds., *Essays in Greek Coinage Presented to Stanley Robinson*: 111–24. Oxford.

Schweyer, A.-V. 1996. "Le pays lycien, une étude de géographie historique aux époques classique et héllenistique." *RA* 1996: 3–68.

———. 2002. *Les Lyciens et la mort: une étude d'histoire sociale*. Varia Anatolica 14. Paris.

Scott, J. C. 1987. *Weapons of the Weak: Everyday Forms of Peasant Resistance*. New Haven, CT.

1992. *Domination and the Arts of Resistance: Hidden Transcripts*. New Haven, CT.
Seeher, J. 1998. "Die Necropole von Demircihüyük – Sarıket im 7. bis 4. Jahrhundert v. Chr." *IstMitt* 48: 135–55.
Segal, C. 1971. "Croesus on the Pyre: Herodotus and Bacchylides." *Wiener Studien* 84: 39–51.
Seidl, U. 1976. "Ein Relief Dareios' I. in Babylon." *AMI* 9: 125–30.
  1994. "Achaimenidische Entlehnungen aus der urartaischen Kultur." In H. Sancisi-Weerdenburg, A. Kuhrt, and M. C. Root, eds., *AchHist 8. Continuity and Change*: 107–29. Leiden.
  1999. "Ein Monument Darius' I. aus Babylon." *ZA* 89: 101–14.
Sekunda, N. V. 1985. "Achaemenid Colonization in Lydia." *REA* 87: 7–29.
  1988. "Persian Settlement in Hellespontine Phrygia." In A. Kuhrt and H. Sancisi-Weerdenburg, eds., *AchHist 3. Method and Theory*: 175–96. Leiden.
  1991. "Achaemenid Settlement in Caria, Lycia, and Greater Phrygia." In A. Kuhrt and H. Sancisi-Weerdenburg, eds., *AchHist 6. Asia Minor and Egypt: Old Cultures in a New Empire*: 83–143. Leiden.
  1992. *The Persian Army*. London.
Sevin, V. 1976. "Kroisos ve Pamphylia." *Belleten* 40: 185–93.
  2005. "Urartu Devleti." *ArkeoAtlas* 4: 62–78, 80–2, 84, 86–8, 91–2, 94.
Sevinç, N. 1996a. "Çanakkale – Gümüşçay Tümülüsleri 1994 Yılı Kurtarma Kazıları Ön Raporu." *MKKS* 6: 443–49.
  1996b. "A New Sarcophagus of Polyxena from the Salvage Excavations at Gümüşçay." *StTroica* 6: 251–64.
Sevinç, N., et al. 1998. "The Dedetepe Tumulus." *StTroica* 8: 305–27.
Sevinç, N., R. Korpe, M. Tombul, C. B. Rose, D. Strahan, H. Kiesewetter, and J. Wallrodt. 2001. "A New Painted Graeco-Persian Sarcophagus from Çan." *StTroica* 11: 383–420.
Sevinç, N., C. B. Rose, and D. Strahan. 1999. "A Child's Sarcophagus from the Salvage Excavations at Gümüşçay." *StTroica* 9: 489–509.
Seyrig, H. 1959. "Le roi de Perse." *Syria* 36: 52–6.
Shaked, S. 2004. *Le satrape de Bactriane et son gouverneur: documents araméens du IVe s. avant notre ère provenant de Bactriane*. Paris.
Shapiro, S. 2002. "Authority." In J. Coleman and S. Shapiro, eds., *The Oxford Handbook of Jurisprudence and Philosophy of Law*. Oxford.
Sheedy, K. A. 2009. "Asia Minor in the Archaic and Classical Periods." In M. Amandry and D. Bateson, eds., *Survey of Numismatic Research, 2002–2007*: 65–75. Glasgow.
Sherwin-White, S., and A. Kuhrt. 1993. *From Samarkhand to Sardis: A New Approach to the Seleucid Empire*. London.
Sideris, A. 2008. "Achaemenid Toreutics in the Greek Periphery." In S. M. R. Darbandi and A. Zournatzi, eds., *Ancient Greece and Ancient Iran: Cross-Cultural Encounters*: 339–54. Athens.
Simmons, A. J. 2001. *Justification and Legitimacy: Essays on Rights and Obligations*. Cambridge.
Simpson, S. 2005. "The Royal Table." In J. E. Curtis and N. Tallis, eds., *Forgotten Empire: The World of Ancient Persia*: 104–31. London.
Sinopoli, C. M. 1994. "The Archaeology of Empires." *ARA* 23: 159–80.
Sinopoli, C. M., and K. D. Morrison. 1995. "Dimensions of Imperial Control." *AmAnth* 97/1: 83–96.
Slatter, E. 1994. *Xanthus: Travels of Discovery in Turkey*. London.
Smirnow, Y. J. 1896. *Zapisky Imperatorskoe Russkoe archeologicheskoe Obshchesevo*. Petersburg.

Bibliography

Smith, A. H. 1900. *A Catalogue of Sculpture in the British Museum* 2. London.

Smith, S. 1924. *Babylonian Historical Texts*. London.

Sorokina, N. P., and D. V. Zhuravlyov. 1997. "Collections of Artefacts from Classical Centres on the North Coast of the Black Sea in the Collection of the State Historical Museum Moscow." *ACSS* 4: 158–85.

Spielman, K. A. 2004. "Communal Feasting, Ceramics, and Exchange." In B. J. Mills, ed., *Identity, Feasting, and the Archaeology of the Greater Southwest: Proceedings of the 2002 Southwest Symposium*: 210–32. Boulder, CO.

Spycket, A. 1980. "Women in Persian Art." In D. Schmandt-Besserat, ed., *Ancient Persia: The Art of an Empire*: 43–5. Malibu, CA.

Starr, C. G. 1975. "Greeks and Persians in the Fourth Century B.C.: A Study in Cultural Contacts before Alexander, Part I." *IrAnt* 11: 39–99.

—— 1977. "Greeks and Persians in the Fourth Century B.C. (Part II)." *IrAnt* 12: 49–116.

Starr, S. F. 1963. "Mapping Ancient Roads in Anatolia." *Archaeology* 16/3: 162–9.

Stein, G. J. Forthcoming. "Persians on the Euphrates? Two Achaemenid Burials from Hacınebi, Southeast Turkey." In W. Henkelman, C. Jones, M. Kozuh, and C. Woods, eds., *Extraction and Control: Studies in Honor of Matthew W. Stolper*. Chicago.

Stern, E. M., and B. Schlick-Nolte. 1994. *Early Glass of the Ancient World, 1600 B.C–A.D. 50: Ernesto Wolf Collection*. Ostfildern.

Steuernagel, D. 1998. "Ein spätarchaischer Sarkophag aus Gümüşçay im Museum von Çanakkale. Ikonographische Beobachtungen." In R. Rolle and K. Schmidt, eds., *Archäologische Studien in Kontaktzonen der antiken Welt*: 165–77. Göttingen.

Stinson, P. T. 2008. "Lale Tepe: A Late Lydian Tumulus near Sardis: 2. Architecture and Painting." In N. D. Cahill, ed., *Love For Lydia: A Sardis Anniversary Volume Presented to Crawford H. Greenewalt, Jr.*: 25–48. Cambridge, MA.

Stol, M. 1985. "Cress and Its Mustard." *JEOL* 28/1983–4: 24–32.

Stoler, A. 1997. "On political and psychological essentialisms." *Ethos: Journal of the Society for Psychological Anthropology* 25/1: 101–6.

Stolper, M. W. 1983. "The Death of Artaxerxes I." *AMI* 16: 223–36.

—— 1985. *Entrepreneurs and Empire: The Murašu Archive, the Murašu Firm, and Persian Rule in Babylonia*. Leiden.

—— 1989. "The Governor of Babylon and Across-the-River in 486 BC." *JNES* 48: 283–305.

—— 1992. "The Murashu Texts from Susa." *RA* 86: 69–77.

Strathmann, C. 2002. "Grabkultur im antiken Lykien des 6. bis 4. Jhr. v. Chr." *Europäische Hochschulschriften* Reihe 38, Band 75.

Strocka, V. W. 1977. "Neue archaische Löwen in Anatolien." *AA* 1977: 481–512.

Stronach, D. 1966. "The Kuh-i Shahrak Fire Altar." *JNES* 25: 217–27.

—— 1978. *Pasargadae: A Report on the Excavations Conducted by the British Institute of Persian Studies from 1961 to 1963*. Oxford.

—— 1985. "On the Evolution of the Early Iranian Fire Temple." *Papers in Honour of Professor Mary Boyce*: 605–27. Leiden.

—— 1989a. "Early Achaemenid Coinage: Perspectives from the Homeland." *IrAnt* 24: 255–79.

—— 1989b. "The Royal Garden at Pasargadae: Evolution and Legacy." In L. de Meyer and E. Haerinck, eds., *Archaeologia Iranica et Orientalis, Miscellanea in Honorem Louis van den Berghe*: 475–502. Ghent.

—— 1990. "The Garden as a Political Statement: Some Case Studies from the Near East in the First Millennium B.C." *BAI* 4: 171–80.

—— 1994a. "Parterres and Stone Watercourses at Pasargadae: Notes on the Achaemenid Contribution to Garden Design." *Journal of Garden Studies* 14/11: 3–12.

—— 1994b. "Patterns of Prestige in the Pazyryk Carpet: Notes on the Representational Role of Textiles in the First Millennium B.C." *OCTS* 4: 19–34.

Bibliography

2000. "Of Cyrus, Darius, and Alexander: A New Look at the 'Epitaphs' of Cyrus the Great." In R. Dittmann, B. Hrouda, U. Löw, P. Matthiae, R. Mayer-Opficius, and S. Thürwächter, eds., *Variatio Delectat: Iran und der Westen. Gedenkschrift für Peter Calmeyer*: 681–702. Münster.

2002. "Icons of Dominion: Review Scenes at Til Barsip and Persepolis." *IrAnt* 37: 373–402.

Stronach, R. 1978. "Excavations at Tepe Nush-i Jan: Part 2, Median Pottery from the Fallen Floor in the Fort." *Iran* 16: 11–24.

Stuart-Macadam, P. 1992. "Anemia in Past Human Populations." In P. Stuart-Macadam and S. Kent, eds., *Diet, Demography, and Disease: Changing Perspectives on Anemia*: 151–70. New York.

Summerer, L. 2003. "Achämenidische Silberfunde aus der Umgebung von Sinope." *ACSS* 9: 17–42. Leiden.

2005. "Achämeniden am Schwarzen Meer. Bemerkungen zum spätarchaischen Marmorkopf aus Herakleia Pontike." *ANES* 42: 224–49.

2006a. "Bemerkungen zum silbernen Kalbskopfrhyton in der Ermitage." In F. Pertemes and A. Furtwängler, eds., *Pontos Euxeinos. Beiträge zur Archäologie und Geschichte des antiken Schwarzmeer- und Balkanraumes. Festschrift für Manfred Oppermann*: 135–44. Langenweißbach.

2006b. "From Tatarlı to Munich: The Recovery of a Painted Wooden Tomb Chamber in Phrygia." Abstract, International Conference, Ancient Greece and Ancient Iran: Cross-Cultural Encounters, Athens, 11–14 November 2006.

2007a. "From Tatarlı to Munich: The Recovery of a Painted Wooden Tomb Chamber in Phrygia." In *Achaemenid Impact*: 131–58. Istanbul.

2007b. "Picturing Persian Victory: The Painted Battle Scene on the Munich Wood." In A. Ivantchik and V. Licheli, eds., *Achaemenid Culture and Local Traditions in Anatolia, Southern Caucasus and Iran: New Discoveries*: 3–30. Leiden.

2010. *Tatarlı. Renklerin Dönüşü*. Istanbul.

Summerer, L., A. Ivantchik, and A. von Kienlin, eds. 2011. *Kelainai-Apameia Kibotos: développement urbain dans le contexte anatolien. Actes du colloque international Munich, 2–4 Avril 2009*. Bordeaux.

Summerer, L., and A. von Kienlin. 2010. "Achaemenid Impact in Paphlagonia: Rupestral Tombs in the Amnias Valley." In J. Nieling and E. Rehm, eds., *Black Sea Studies 11: Achaemenid Impact in the Black Sea – Communications in Power*: 195–221. Aarhus.

Summers, G. D. 1993. "Archaeological Evidence for the Achaemenid Period in Eastern Turkey." *AnatSt* 43: 85–108.

1997. "The Identification of the Iron Age City on Kerkenes Dağ in Central Anatolia." *JNES* 56: 81–94.

2000. "The Median Empire Reconsidered: A View from Kerkenes Dağı." *AnatSt* 50: 57–73.

Summers, G. D., and M. E. F. Summers. 2006. "The Kerkenes Project in 2006." *Anatolian Archaeology*. British Institute at Ankara Research Reports 12. Ankara.

Sundwall, J. 1913. *Die einheimlischen Namen der Lykier nebst einem Verzeichnisse kleinasiatischer Namenstamme*. Klio Suppl. 11. Leipzig.

Tal, O. 2005. "Some Remarks on the Coastal Plain of Palestine under Achaemenid Rule: An Archaeological Synopsis." In *L'archéologie de l'empire achéménide*: 71–96. Paris.

Tallon, F. 1992. "The Achaemenid Tomb on the Acropole." In P. O. Harper, J. Aruz, and F. Tallon, eds., *The Royal City of Susa: Ancient Near Eastern Treasures in the Louvre*: 242–52. New York.

Bibliography

Tarhan, M. T. 1994. "Recent Research at the Urartian Capital Tushpa." *Tel Aviv* 21/1: 22–57.

———. 2007. "Median and Achaemenid Periods at Tushpa." In *Achaemenid Impact*: 117–30. Istanbul.

Tarhan, M. T., and V. Sevin. 1994. "Van Kalesi ve Eski Van Şehri Kazıları 1990 Yılı Çalışmaları." *Belleten* 220: 843–61.

Teixidor, J. 1986. *Bulletin d'épigraphic sémitique* 131. Paris.

Tezcan, B. 1979. "İkiztepe Kazısı." *TTK* 8/1: 391–7.

Thompson, W. E. 1965. "Tissaphernes and the Mercenaries at Miletos." *Philologus* 109: 294–7.

———. 1981. "The Carian Tribute." *AnatSt* 31: 95–100.

Thomsen, A. 2002. *Die lykische Dynastensiedlung auf dem Avşar Tepesi*. Antiquitas Reihe 3, Band 43.

Tilia, A. B. 1978. *Studies and Restorations at Persepolis and Other Sites of Fars*. Rome.

Toker, A., and J. Öztürk. 1992. *Museum of Anatolian Civilizations: Metal Vessels*. Ankara.

Torrey, C. C. 1915. "An Aramaic Inscription from Cilicia in the Museum of Yale University." *JAOS*: 370–4.

———. 1917–18. "The Bilingual Inscription from Sardis." *AJSemL* 34: 185–98.

Toteva, G. D. 2007. "Local Cultures of Late Achaemenid Anatolia." Ph.D. dissertation, University of Minnesota.

Tozzi, P. 1978. *La rivolta ionica*. Pisa.

Treister, M. Y. 2007. "The Toreutics of Colchis in the 5th–4th Centuries BC: Local Traditions, Outside Influences, Innovations." *ACSS* 13: 67–107.

Tritsch, F. J. 1942. "The Harpy Tomb at Xanthos." *JHS* 62: 39–50.

———. 1943. "False Doors on Tombs." *JHS* 63: 113–15.

Tuchelt, K. 1970. *Die archaischen Skulpturen von Didyma*. IstForsch 27. Berlin.

Tuna-Nörling, Y. 1999. "Die attisch schwarzfigürige und rotfigürige Keramik." http://daskyleion.tripod.com/112A_Keramik.html.

Tuplin, C. 1987a. "The Administration of the Achaemenid Empire." In I. Carradice, ed., *Coinage and Administration in the Athenian and Persian Empires*. BAR International Series 343: 119–66.

———. 1987b. "Xenophon and the Garrisons of the Achaemenid Empire." *AMI* 20: 167–245.

———. 1988. "Persian Garrisons in Xenophon and Other Sources." In A. Kuhrt and H. Sancisi-Weerdenburg, eds., *AchHist 3. Method and Theory*: 67–70. Leiden.

———. 1994. "Persians as Medes." In H. Sancisi-Weerdenburg, A. Kuhrt, and M. C. Root eds., *AchHist 8. Continuity and Change:* 235–56. Leiden.

———. 1997. "Achaemenid Arithmetic: Numerical Problems in Persian History." *Topoi* 365–421.

———. 1998. "The Seasonal Migration of Achaemenid Kings: A Report on Old and New Evidence." In M. Brosius and A. Kuhrt, eds., *AchHist 11. Studies in Persian History: Essays in Memory of David M. Lewis*: 63–114. Leiden.

———. 2010. "All the King's Horse: In Search of Achaemenid Persian Cavalry." In G. G. Fagan and M. Trundle, eds., *New Perspectives on Ancient Warfare*: 101–82. Leiden.

Uçankuş, H. T. 1979. "Afyon'un Tatarlı Kasabasında Bulunan Phryg Tümülüsü Kazısı." *TTK* 8/1: 305–34.

———. 2002. "Afyon'un Tatarlı Kasabasında Bulunan Phryg Tümülüsü Kazısı." *AS* 106: 23–42.

Uchitel, A. 1988. "Organization of Manpower in Achaemenid Persia." *ActSum* 11: 225–38.

1991. "Foreign Workers in the Fortification Archive." In L. de Meyer and H. Gasche, eds., *Mesopotamie et Elam: Actes de la XXXVIème Recontre Assyriologique Internationale: Gand, 10–14 juillet 1989*: 127–35. Ghent.

Ussishkin, D. 1994. "The Rock-Cut Tombs at Van and Monumental Tombs in the Near East." In A. Çilingiroğlu and D. H. French, eds., *Anatolian Iron Ages III: Proceedings of the Third Anatolian Iron Ages Colloquium, Van, 6–12 August 1990*: 253–64. London.

Vallat, F. 1989. "Le palais d'Artaxerxès II à Babylone." *NAPR* 2: 3–6.

van Groningen, B. A. 1933. *Aristote: le second livre de l'Économique*. Leiden.

van Keuren, S. 2004. "Crafting Feasts in the Prehispanic Southwest." In B. J. Mills, ed., *Identity, Feasting, and the Archaeology of the Greater Southwest: Proceedings of the 2002 Southwest Symposium*: 192–209. Boulder, CO.

Vann, R.L. 1992. "A Survey of Ancient Harbors in Rough Cilicia: The 1991 Preliminary Survey." *AST* 10: 29–40.

van Saldern, A. 1959. "Glass Finds at Gordion." *JGS* 1: 22–49.

——— 1975. "Two Achaemenid Glass Bowls and a Hoard of Hellenistic Glass Vessels." *JGS* 17: 37–46.

Verger, A. 1964. "L'amministrazione della giusticia nei papiri aramaici di Elefantina." *Rendiconti dell'Accademia Nazionale dei Lincei. Classe di scienze morali* 8/19: 75–94.

Vickers, M. 1972. "An Achaemenid Glass Bowl in a Dated Context." *JGS* 14: 15–16.

——— 1986a. "Early Greek Coinage, A Reassessment." *NC* 1–44.

——— 1986b. "Persepolis, Athenes, et Sybaris: Questions de monnayage et de chronologie." *REG* 99: 248–53.

——— 1999. *Skeuomorphismus, oder die Kunst aus wenig viel zu machen*. Mainz.

——— 2000. "Lapidary Shock: Meditations on an Achaemenid Silver Beaker 'from Erzerum' in the Ashmolean Museum, Oxford." *AMIT* 32: 261–73.

Vickers, M., and D. Gill. 1994. *Artful Crafts: Ancient Greek Silverware and Pottery*. Oxford.

Vismara, N. 1996. *Monetazione arcaica della Lycia III: le prime emmissioni de Wedri*. Milan.

——— 1999. *Ripostigli d'epoca prehellenistica VI–IV sec. ac. con monete della Lycia arcaica*. Milan.

——— 2007. "Some Reflections on Iconographic Motifs in Lycian Coinage: The Central Achaemenid Empire's Powerful Political Presence in a Border Region." In *Achaemenid Impact*: 59–68. Istanbul.

Vittmann, G. 2003. *Ägypten und die Fremden im ersten vorchristlichen Jahrtausend*. Mainz.

Voigt, M. M. 1993. "The Bronze Age–Iron Age Transition at Gordion (1200–800 B.C.)." *AJA* 97: 302–3.

——— 1994. "Excavations at Gordion, 1988–1989: The Yassıhöyük Stratigraphic Sequence." In A. Çilingiroğlu and D. H. French, eds., *Anatolian Iron Ages 3: The Proceedings of the Third Anatolian Iron Ages Colloquium Held at Van, 6–12 August 1990*: 265–93. Ankara.

——— 2005. "Old Problems and New Solutions: Recent Excavations at Gordion." In L. Kealhofer, ed., *The Archaeology of Midas and the Phrygians: Recent Work at Gordion*: 22–35. Philadelphia.

Voigt, M. M., K. DeVries, R. C. Henrickson, M. Lawall, B. Marsch, A. Gürsan-Salzmann, and T. C. Young, Jr. 1997. "Fieldwork at Gordion, 1993–1995." *Anatolica* 23:1–59.

Voigt, M. M., and R. C. Henrickson. 2000a. "The Early Iron Age at Gordion: The Evidence from the Yassıhöyük Stratigraphic Sequence." In E. D. Oren, ed., *The Sea Peoples and Their World: A Reassessment*: 327–60. Oxford.

2000b. "Formation of the Phrygian State: The Early Iron Age at Gordion." *AnatSt* 50: 37–54.

Voigt, M. M., and T. C. Young, Jr. 1999. "From Phrygian Capital to Achaemenid Entrepot: Middle and Late Phrygian Gordion." *IrAnt* 34: 191–242.

von Gall, H. 1989. "Zum Bildgehalt der graeco-persischen Grabstelen." *Anatolia* 22: 143–65.

——— 1999. "Der achämenidische Löwengreif in Kleinasien." *AMI* 31: 149–60.

von Graeve, V. 1970. *Der Alexandersarkophag und seine Werkstatt*. Berlin.

——— 1989. "Eine spätarchaische Anthemienstele aus Milet." *IstMitt* 39: 143–51.

von Olfers, J. F. M. 1858. "Über die lydischen Königsgräber bei Sardes und den Grabhügel des Alyattes." *AbhBerl*: 539–56.

von Pilgrim, C. 1998. "Tetzeugnis und archäologischer Befund. Zur Topographie Elephantines in der 27. Dynastie." In H. Guksch and D. Polz, eds., *Stationen. Beiträge zur Kulturgeschichte Ägyptens Rainer Stadelmann gewidmet*: 485–97. Mainz.

von Voigtlander, E. 1978. *The Bisitun Inscription of Darius the Great, Babylonian Version*. London.

Waelkens, M. 1980a. "The Doorstones of Phrygia." *Yayla* 3: 12–16.

——— 1980b. "Das Totenhaus in Kleinasien." *AW* 11/4: 3–12.

——— 1986. *Die kleinasiatischen Türsteine. Typologische und epigraphische Untersuchungen zu kleinasiatischen Grabreliefs mit Scheintür*. Mainz.

Waerzeggers, C. 2003–4. "The Babylonian Revolts against Xerxes and the 'End of Archives.'" *AfO* 50: 150–73.

Waldbaum, J. C. 1983. *Metalwork from Sardis: The Finds from 1958–1974*. AES 8. Cambridge, MA.

Wallace, R. W. 1988. "WALWE. and .KALI." *JHS* 108: 203–7.

——— 2006. "KUKLAIM, WALWET, and the Artemision Deposit: Problems in Early Anatolian Electrum Coinage." In P. G. van Alfen, ed., *Agoranomia: Studies in Money and Exchange Presented to John H. Kroll*: 37–48. New York.

Wardman, A. E. 1961. "Herodotus on the Cause of the Greco-Persian Wars." *AJPh* 82: 133–50.

Waters, M. 1996. "Darius and the Achaemenid Line." *AHB* 10/1: 11–18.

——— 2004. "Cyrus and the Achaemenids." *Iran* 42: 91–102.

Waywell, G. B. 1978. *The Free-Standing Sculptures of the Mausoleum at Halicarnassus in the British Museum*. London.

Weinberg, G. D., and S. S. Weinberg. 1956. "Arachne of Lydia at Corinth." In S. S. Weinberg, ed., *The Aegean and the Near East: Studies Presented to Hetty Goldman*: 262–67. Locust Valley, NY.

Weisberg, D. B. 1967. *Guild Structure and Political Allegiance in Early Achaemenid Mesopotamia*. New Haven, CT.

Weiskopf, M. N. 1982. "Achaemenid Systems of Governing in Anatolia." Ph.D. dissertation, University of California at Berkeley

——— 1989. *The So-Called 'Great Satraps' Revolt,' 366–360 B.C.: Concerning Local Instability in the Achaemenid Far West*. Historia 63. Stuttgart.

Weiss, B. 1996. "Dressing at Death: Clothing, Time, and Memory in Buhaya, Tanzania." In H. Hendrickson, ed., *Clothing and Difference: Embodied Identities in Colonial and Post-Colonial Africa*: 133–54. Durham, NC.

Weissbach, F. H. 1911. *Die Keilinschriften der Achämeniden*. VAB 3. Leipzig.

Weissl, M. 2002. "Grundzüge der Bau- und Schichtenfolge im Artemision von Ephesos." *ÖJh* 71: 313–46.

——— 2005. "Zur Datierung des 'Foundation-Deposit' aus dem Artemision von Ephesos." In *Synergia 1. Festschrift Friedrich Krinzinger*: 363–70. Vienna.

Wiessner, P. 1996. "Introduction: Food, Status, Culture, and Nature." In P. Wiessner and W. Schiefenhövel, eds., *Food and the Status Quest: An Interdisciplinary Perspective*: 1–18. Providence, RI.

Wiessner, P., and W. Schiefenhövel. 1996. *Food and the Status Quest: An Interdisciplinary Perspective*. Providence, RI.

Wikander, S. 1946. *Feuerpriester in Kleinasien und Iran*. Lund.

— 1972. "BARZOCHARA." *Acta Orientalia* 34: 13–15.

Wilhelm, A. 1909. *Beiträge zur griechischen Inschriftenkunde mit einem Anhange über die öffentliche Aufzeichnung von Urkunden*. Vienna.

Williams, R. 1977. *Marxism and Literature*. New York.

Wills, W. H., and P. L. Crown. 2004. "Commensal Politics in the Prehispanic Southwest: An Introductory Review." In B. J. Mills, ed., *Identity, Feasting, and the Archaeology of the Greater Southwest: Proceedings of the 2002 Southwest Symposium*: 153–72. Boulder, CO.

Winfield, D. 1977. "The Northern Routes across Anatolia." *AnatSt* 27: 151–66.

Winter, F. 1894. "Die Sarkophage von Sidon." *AA* 1–23.

Wobst, M. 1977. "Stylistic Behavior and Information Exchange." In C. Cleland, ed., *For the Director: Research Essays in Honor of James B. Griffin*. UMMAA Papers 61: 317–342. Ann Arbor, MI.

Woolley, C. L. 1914–15. "A North Syrian Cemetery of the Persian Period." *LAAA* 7: 115–29.

Wörrle, W. 1996–7. "Die Inschriften am Grab des Apollonios am Asartaş von Yazır in Ostlykien." *Lykia* 3: 24–38.

Wuttmann, M., F. Laroche-Traunecker, and J.-Cl. Courtois. 1998. "Les états d'occupation du secteur Nord [de Meydancıkkale]." In A. Davesne and F. Laroche-Traunecker, eds., *Gülnar I: le site de Meydancıkkale. Recherches enterprises sous la direction d'Emmanuel Laroche, 1971–1982*: 107–65. Paris.

Wuttmann, M., and S. Marchand. 2005. "Égypte." In *L'archéologie de l'empire achéménide*: 97–128. Paris.

Yağcı, E. E. 1995. "Akhaemenid Cam Kaseleri ve Milas Müzesinden Yayınlanmamış İki Örnek." *Anadolu Medeniyetleri Müzesi 1995 Yıllığı*: 312–326.

Yıldırım, B. and M.-H. Gates. 2007. "Archaeology in Turkey, 2004–2005." *AJA* 111: 275–356.

Young, R. S. 1951. "Gordion – 1950." *University Museum Bulletin* 16/1: 3–20.

— 1953. "Progress at Gordion, 1951–1952." *University Museum Bulletin* 17/4: 3–40.

— 1957. "Excavations at Gordion." *AJA* 61: 319–31.

— 1958. "Excavations at Gordion." *AJA* 62: 139–54.

Young, T. C. 1965. "A Comparative Ceramic Chronology for Western Iran, 1500–500 B.C." *Iran* 3: 53–87.

— 1969. *Excavations at Godin Tepe: First Progress Report*. Toronto.

Yoyotte, J. 1974. "Les inscriptions hiéroglyphiques de la statue de Darius à Suse." *CDAFI* 4: 181–3.

Zaccagnini, C. 1983. "Patterns of Mobility among Ancient Near Eastern Craftsmen." *JNES* 42/4: 245–64.

Zahle, J. 1975a. "Archaic Tumulus Tombs in Central Lycia Phellos." *ActArch* 46: 77–94.

— 1975b. *Harypienmonument i Xanthos. En lykisk pillegrav*. Studier fra Sprog- og Oldtidsforskning. Copenhagen.

— 1983. *Arkaeologiske studier i lykiske klippgrave og deros reliéffer fra c. 550–300 f. Kr. Sociale og religiøse aspekter*. Copenhagen.

1991. "Achaemenid Influences in Lycia (Coinage, Sculpture, architecture): Evidence for Political Changes during the 5th Century B.C." In H. Sancisi-Weerdenburg and A. Kuhrt, eds., *AchHist 6. Asia Minor and Egypt: Old Cultures in a New Empire*: 145–60. Leiden.

Zhuber-Okrog, K. 1990. "Die Terrakotten von Limyra." *ÖJh* 60 Suppl.: 53–120.

Zimansky, P. E. 1985. *Ecology and Empire: The Structure of the Urartian State*. SAOC 41. Chicago.

1995a. "The Kingdom of Urartu in Eastern Anatolia." *CANE*: 1135–46. New York.

1995b. "Xenophon and the Urartian Legacy." *Pallas* 43: 255–68.

Zoroğlu, L. 1994. *Kelenderis I: Kaynaklar, Kalıntılar, Buluntular* [Kelenderis I: sources, remains, finds]. Ankara.

1996. "Tarsus Cumhuriyet Alanı 1994 Yılı Çalışmaları [Cumhuriyet Square, Tarsus: work in 1994]." *KST* 17/2: 245–63.

2000. "Kelenderis Nekropolü [The Necropolis of Kelenderis]." *Olba* 3: 115–33.

Zoroğlu, L., N. Arslan, and M. Tekocak. 2001. "Kelenderis Kazısı 1999 Yılı Çalışmaları [The Kelenderis excavations: work in 1999]." *KST* 22/2: 311–24.

INDEX

Abbas, 235–7, 263, 270
accounting practices. *See* finance
Achaemenid (meaning), 274
Achaemenid
    bowl, 125, 127, 129, 132, 134–5, 136–40,
        150–1, 181, 184–7, 295, 296, 308;
        *Figs. 58, 59, 61, 62, 64, 66, 67, 73,
        75, 103, 104, 105, 106*
    Empire, extent of, 8
    imperial rhetoric. *See* Truth/Lie
    institutions, longevity of, 14
    religion, 207–8. *See also* ascension
    style
        Achaemenid Anatolian, 69
        Achaemenid koine, 69, 157
Achilles, 307
administrative
    centers, 34
    regions, 16, 32, 33, 278
adoption of Persian luxury ideas outside the
        empire, 12–13
Adrastus, 226
Aegean, 15
Aeolis, 89, 90, 91, 109
Aeschylus, 242, 311
Afghanistan, 71
Afyon, 19, 178
Ağaca Kale, 64
Agesilaus, 95, 283, 291
Agoracritus, 215
Ahuramazda, 10–11, 13, 51, 52, 73, 225, 235–8,
        240, 246, 282, 286, 308, 310
Aksaray, 237
alabastron, 53, 173, 180, 183, 204, 282
Alaca Höyük, 21
Alcmeon, 23
alcohol, 122–3, 129 et passim
Alexander of Macedon (the Great), 14, 39, 45, 95,
        96, 117, 171, 248, 274, 276, 292
Alexander Sarcophagus, 248–9, 312

Alişar, 21
altars, 28, 85, 212, 226–7, 234, 308; *Fig. 134*
Altıntaş, 177–8; *Fig. 100*
Altıntepe, 32, 59–60, 81, 106, 138, 302; *Fig. 32*
Alyattes, 145, 168, 278, 297
Amanus Mountains, 46
Amaseia, 274
Amyrtaeus, 13
Amyzon, 229
Anahita, 13, 229, 237–8, 252, 308, 310
Anatolia, as region of the empire, 1–2, 15–16
Antalcidas, Peace of, 45
anthemion stelae. *See* stelae, anthemion
Antioch, 46
Antipater of Sidon, 203
Aramaic, 11, 39, 41, 62, 64, 88, 98, 106, 160,
        187–8, 197, 214, 235–7, 239–40, 243,
        253, 256, 260, 270, 282, 289, 309–10,
        312; *Fig. 61*
Ararat, Mount, 15; *Fig. 12*
Aras River, 15
archers, 73, 94, 246, 279, 286, 289
architectural style and power, 57–60, 63, 81
archives, 29, 33, 34, 53–4, 58, 64, 65–9, 81, 256,
        279, 284, 313
Arebsun, 235–7, 263, 270, 309–10
Ariaramnes, 229, 308
Arin-Berd, 284
Aristophanes, 292
Aristotle, 95, 289, 290
Armenia, 17, 33, 51, 91, 106, 112–13, 128, 135,
        137–9, 181–3, 262
army, 27, 46, 83–5, 86–8, 267
    communication in. *See* communication
    ethnicity of, 43, 89, 90–1, 92–3, 107,
        288–9; *Fig. 46*
    maintenance of, 87–9
    sites with evidence for (catalogue), 108–13
Arneae, 222, 307
Arrian, 274, 275, 290, 307

Index

Arses. *See* Artaxerxes II
Arshama, 48, 279
Arslankaya, 19
Artabazus I, 59
Artapates, 80
Artaphernes, 43, 44, 95, 280, 290
Artaphernes II, 44
Artaxerxes I, 12, 66, 260, 313
Artaxerxes II, 13, 44, 46, 80, 87, 273, 281
Artaxerxes III, 13–14, 276, 299
Artaxerxes IV, 14
Artemis, 214–9, 220, 226–30, 257–8, 298, 307; *Figs. 127(?), 128*
Artemis Anaitis, 229, 308, 310
Artemis of Ephesus, 161, 215, 216–9, 226–30, 252–3, 257, 263, 270, 306, 312
Artemis Perasia, 47
Artemis Persike, 229, 308
Artemisia, 34, 202–6, 232, 279
Artimas, 197
Aryaramna, 64
ascension, in Achaemenid religion, 208, 227, 230, 243; *Fig. 146*
Asidates, 89, 107
Assur, 73
Assurbanipal, 18
Assyria, 16, 17–18, 138
Assyrians, 90, 91, 182, 191, 276
Astyages, 8, 200
Athena, 53, 193, 222, 225, 308
Athenaeus, 116, 118, 292
Athens, 12, 13, 43, 44, 75, 79, 170–1, 254, 273, 300, 303; *Fig. 42*
Atossa, 242
authority-autonomy model, 2, 3–4, 4–8, 26–7, 29, 30–1, 45, 47, 59, 63, 72, 76, 81–2, 107–8, 114, 128, 130, 136, 140, 141, 150–1, 153, 193, 195, 201, 206, 208–9, 218, 224–5, 243–4, 249, 251–2, 258, 266–71, 273
Autophradates, 304
Aydın, 295

Baal. *See* Bel
Baba Jan, 294
Babylon, 9, 13, 33, 41, 86, 91, 188, 215, 223, 274
Babylonia, 11, 14, 23, 44
Babylonian, 51, 53, 89, 288
Bactria, 8, 91, 256, 279
Bagadates, 229, 308
Balawat, 17
banking. *See* finance
banqueting. *See* feasts
banqueting vessels, 53
Barakes, 229
Bardiya, 9
Bayındır, 177
Bel, 237–41, 263, 270, 310; *Figs. 140, 141*
Berossus, 252, 274
Bin Tepe, 145, 297; *Fig. 70*
Birecik, 63, 183
birthdays, 119–20, 121
Bisitun, 9, 49, 193–4, 246, 247, 275, 280, 281; *Fig. 27*
Bisitun Inscription, Babylonian version, 19, 49, 250, 281–2

Black Sea, 15, 35, 179–81, 274, 302
Bosphorus, 15, 57, 300
bowls. *See* Achaemenid, bowl; round-bottomed bowl

Cadusians, 12
Caecus River, 89, 91, 143
Calycadnus River, 188
Cambyses, 9, 276, 299
Çan Sarcophagus, 174, 176; *Fig. 97*
canals, 41, 280
Cappadocia, 19, 33, 35, 43, 44, 64, 112, 179, 235–8, 249, 289
Carchemish, 12, 291
Caria (Carian), 16, 24–5, 33, 34, 35, 44, 81, 91, 111–12, 167, 202–5, 230–4, 262, 273, 309
  language, 202, 253
  league, 233
Castabala, 47, 214
Caunus, 90, 91, 202
Cayster River, 106, 143, 159
Celaenae, 51, 54, 90, 91, 137, 178, 282
Chalcidice, 75
Choaspes River, 117, 128
Cicero, 283
Cilicia, 16, 24–5, 32, 33, 35, 46–7, 48, 81, 89, 91, 112, 187–8, 214, 239–41, 278
Cimin Tepe, 59, 138
Cimmerian invasion, 23, 276
Cimon, 191
cist tombs, 144–5, 158, 181–2, 184
Clazomenae, 168–9, 213, 300
Clazomenian sarcophagi. *See* sarcophagi
cloth production, 254–5, 312
clothing, 67, 75, 79, 80, 94, 101, 148–50, 152, 153, 188, 201, 204, 208, 224, 254, 259, 267, 286, 294, 297, 298, 299, 304
Cnidus, 273, 281
coins, 28, 33, 38, 46, 72–6, Table 3, 222, 230, 252, 279, 286, 289, 310–11; *Figs. 41, 42, 122, 129, 135, 140, 141. See also* Tiarate head coins
Comania, 91, 107, 289
communication, 47, 48, 85, 90–2, 101–4, 245, 248
copybooks, 28, 245, 248–9, 256, 312
core-periphery model, 2, 3, 34
courier system, 48
Cranaspes, 43, 57
Croesus, 1, 22, 24, 25, 43, 215, 216, 278, 306
crowns, 73; *Figs. 140, 141, 146*
Ctesias, 245, 273, 292, 311
cult
  continuity of, 28, 209–25
  conversion of, 28, 234, 269
  hero, 222–5, 307–8
  introduction of, 28, 53, 234–41, 252, 270, 309; *Fig. 139*
  Matar, 209–19, 230, 270, 305–6; *Fig. 124*
  power statements in, 53
  royal, 28, 73–6, 205, 208, 241–4, 252; *Fig. 145*
  syncretism/hybridization of, 28, 225–34, 308, 309
Cunaxa, battle of, 13, 44, 80
Cybele, 23, 47, 209–19, 234, 238, 306; *Fig. 128*

368

Index

Cyme, 45, 213
Cyprus, 12, 98, 290
Cyrus II (the Great), 1, 8–9, 25, 26, 42, 57, 79, 80, 86, 95, 163, 200, 245–6, 271, 273, 274, 282, 305, 311–12
Cyrus the Younger, 13, 44, 47, 54, 79, 80, 87, 91, 226, 267, 273, 281, 282, 283
Cyzicus, 57, 170

Daday, 180
Daenamazdayasnish, 235–6
Dahan-i Gulaman, 234, 309
Darics, 73, 75, 286, 289
Darius I, 8, 9–11, 34, 38, 43, 44, 49, 51, 52, 65, 67, 94, 120, 182, 193, 242, 246, 250, 275, 279, 280, 283, 291, 299
Darius II, 12–13, 44, 280
Darius III, 14
Darius, inscriptions
    DB, 246, 280, 282, 311
    DNb, 94, 289
    DPd, 10–11, 304
    at Elephantine, 312
    in general, 193–4, 299
Dascylium, 32, 42, 43, 51, 53–4, 55, 56–9, 64, 65–7, 81, 83, 96–7, 127–8, 137, 157, 167, 175, 180, 187, 250–1, 256, 263, 279, 281, 283, 284, 290, 291, 296, 309, 313; *Fig. 31*
Daskylitis, Lake, 57
Datiya (Datis the Mede), 280
decision-making, 129
Dedetepe, 173–4, 176
Delian League, 12, 43
Delipınar, 188–9; *Fig. 108*
Delphi, Temple of Apollo, 1, 24
Demus, 79
Dercyllidas, 281
Deve Hüyük, 78, 83, 103–5, 132, 135, 184–7, 290–1, 302–3; *Fig. 104, 105, 106*
Didyma, 57, 220–2, 263, 283, 307; *Fig. 130*
diet, 124, 127, 287
dining. See eating behaviors; feasts
Diodorus Siculus, 90, 273, 274, 276, 280, 281, 283, 308
doorstones, from tombs, 145, 146, 158–9, 299; *Fig. 84*
Dorginarti, 106
Doriscus, 90
dress. See clothing
drinking behaviors, 27, 80, 114, 128, 131–2, 133–4, 135, 139–40, 150–1, 163, 173–4, 186, 199, 249, 250, 260, 268, 294, 295, 296, 297, 299; *Figs. 61, 65, 86, 87*
drinking vessels
    clay, 27, 122, 125–8, 133, 136–40, 146, 152, 181, 182, 184, 268, 296; *Figs. 58, 64, 66, 67*
    glass, 125, 132, 292, 294; *Fig. 62*
    metal, 27, 59, 79–80, 118–19, 120, 122, 130–3, 132, 133, 147–8, 150, 152, 173, 180, 184–7, 199, 267, 284, 292, 294, 295, 302; *Figs. 59, 60, 61, 71, 75, 86, 87, 96, 102, 103, 104, 105, 106*

Droaphernes, 229, 308
Dülük Baba Tepesi, 249, 266; *Fig. 149*

eating behaviors, 114, 117–20, 121–2, 122–4, 163, 268, 292, 293, 295; *Fig. 57*. See also feasts
Ecbatana, 13, 91, 95, 281, 290
education, 28
Egypt, 9, 11, 12, 13, 14, 23, 41, 45, 71, 88, 91, 106–7, 183, 184, 191, 256, 275, 278, 280, 281, 282, 284, 291, 293, 298, 309
Eion, 90
Elamite, 1, 51, 53, 275
Elephantine, 41, 88, 90, 106, 247, 282, 289, 309, 312
elites
    education of, 28–9, 77, 94
    ethnicity of, 33, 76, 132, 142, 150–1, 171, 200, 206, 250, 280
    mortuary inclusions, 27–8, 141–2, 148–50, 152–6, 168, 171–4, 176, 177, 180, 206, 250; *Fig. 65*
    portable elite culture, 76, 141–2, 153–4, 168, 250
    role in governing, 27, 32, 33, 66–70, 76–9, 81–2, 186–7, 247, 250, 260, 263–6, 267
Elmalı, 197
Eni Mahanani, 219
Ephesus, 125, 170, 213, 269, 300; *Figs. 129, 130*
    Sacrilege Inscription. See Sacrilege Inscription from Ephesus
    Temple of Artemis, 24, 132, 306
Erbbina, 201, 219, 304, 307; *Fig. 118*
Erythraea, 169, 213
Erzincan, 59, 132, 135, 284, 302; *Fig. 103*
estates, 39, 279, 300
ethnicity. See identity, ethnicity
Euphrates River, 1, 12, 15, 63, 103, 135, 183
Eurymedon River, 12, 44
Ezra, 12, 275, 279

feasts, 122–4, 135, 147–8, 150, 152, 153, 161, 163–4, 167, 170, 172, 173–4, 176, 180, 182, 230–4, 243–4, 268, 292, 309; *Figs. 93, 98, 100*. See also eating behaviors
finance, 218, 256–8
fire altars, 85, 101–2, 167, 227, 234, 238–9, 269, 290, 309
foodstuffs allotted to travelers, 48–9
fortifications, 59–60, 85, 94–103, 280, 288
fortresses, 105–7, 291
funerary rites, 135–6, 145, 147, 150, 152, 160, 163, 167, 169, 174, 176, 177, 179, 182, 295, 297, 299; *Fig. 98*

Gadatas, 283
garrisons, 12, 83, 85, 86–7, 88, 89, 91, 92, 94–103, 290, 291
Gaza, 90
gender roles, 28–9, 60, 78–9, 81, 94, 104, 120–1, 123, 124, 131, 132, 139, 155–6, 160, 163–4, 167, 170, 171, 172, 174, 175, 180, 185–7, 191, 198, 203–6, 246–7, 254–6, 259–60, 267, 268, 293, 298, 299, 300, 303; *Figs. 86, 87, 88, 89, 90, 93, 97, 98*

369

Index

gifts, 33, 79–81, 120, 131, 204, 218–19, 282, 287
Gobryas, 120, 240, 285, 293, 311; *Fig. 143*
Gökçeler, 150, 163–4, 295, 299; *Figs. 75, 90*
gold, 23, 24
Gordion, 16, 19–22, 32–3, 60–3, 65, 125–6, 127, 137, 176–7, 178, 184, 243, 262, 276, 277, 278, 296, 305, 313; *Figs. 14, 58, 99*
Graeco-Persian style, 68
Granicus River, 89, 171–4
grave markers, 158–64 et passim
Greek
    language, 64, 75, 89, 101, 159, 192, 197, 227–9, 253, 261, 300
    lyric poets, 277
    mercenaries, 89–90
greetings, 77; *Fig. 43*
guides, 49
Gyges, 22, 23

Hacımusalar, 137
Hacınebi, 183–4, 296
Halicarnassus, 51, 53, 273
Haliller, 161
Halys River, 1, 19, 23, 89
Hamadan, 9
Harpagus, 26, 193
Harpy Tomb, 172, 175, 190–2; *Fig. 110*
Harta, 137, 146–7, 297; *Fig. 72*
Hasanlu, 298
Hayallı, 161
Hecatomnids, 230, 262
Helios, 204; *Fig. 122*
Hellenica Oxyrhynchia, 280, 281, 290, 291
Hellespont, 15, 57
Hellespontine Phrygia, 12, 33, 35, 55, 57, 77, 81, 90, 91, 108–10, 137, 171–6, 279, 284, 289, 295
Hermus River, 23, 89, 106, 143, 299
hero cult, 222–5, 307
Herodotus, 9, 10, 18–19, 23, 39, 43, 48, 49, 53, 89, 90, 94, 106, 116–17, 119, 121, 129, 215, 237, 245–6, 273, 275, 277, 278, 279, 280, 281, 282, 287, 288, 289, 290, 291, 292, 293, 306, 311
Hieroglyphs, 53, 204
Hittites, 19, 276
horses, 39, Table 2, 46, 48, 78–9, 83, 87, 88, 93, 104, 105, 107, 133, 145, 147, 164, 170, 174, 175, 175, 176, 180, 185, 246–7, 259–60, 267, 269, 286–7, 288, 299; *Figs. 20, 23, 44, 46, 63, 87, 88, 97, 98, 101, 115, 132, 133*
Hydarnes, 280
Hyrcanian plain, 106, 143
Hyrcanians, 90, 91, 107
Hystaspes, 299
Hystaspes II, 44

iconography and power, 33, 49, 62, 67–72, 75, 81, 129, 147–8, 150–1, 154, 163, 167–8, 170, 172, 179, 184, 190, 191, 192, 196, 200–1, 206, 224, 233, 242, 249, 250, 251–2, 260–1, 264–6, 282

identity
    ethnicity, 28, 33, 54, 55–6, 64, 77, 89, 90–1, 129, 130, 132, 150–1, 154, 155, 157, 158, 160, 166–8, 171, 172, 174, 178, 183, 184, 190, 192, 194, 197, 198, 199–201, 206, 218, 219, 223, 248–9, 252, 253–4, 260–3, 266, 285, 295, 296, 300, 303, 312
    religion, 263, 269–70, 305, 307
    status, 28, 33, 76–7, 79–81, 119–20, 121, 122–3, 129–36, 137, 142, 148, 150–1, 152, 155, 158, 160, 161, 172, 176–7, 178, 180, 182, 186–7, 191–2, 199–201, 204–5, 206, 223, 246–7, 250, 252, 259–60, 268, 295
ideology, 49–50, 250–2
Idrieus, 231, 233–4
İkiztepe tombs, 65, 132, 147–8, 150, 295; *Figs 37, 73*
Iliad, 23, 277
Ilium, 53, 249, 307, 312
Incesu, 163
India, 39, 279
Inscribed Pillar, 192–3, 201, 280; *Fig. 112*
Ionia, 9, 25–6, 44, 45, 76, 90, 105, 108, 159, 168–71, 189, 202, 212, 221, 263, 281, 283, 299, 312
Ionian Revolt, 43, 89, 95, 280, 307
Irdabama, 34, 279, 298, 303
Irtashduna (Artystone), 34, 279, 298, 303
Issus, 240; *Fig. 144*
ivory, 99, 176–7, 303

Jerusalem, 12
jewelry, 79–80, 142, 145, 147–8, 148–50, 153–4, 155, 176–7, 183–4, 260, 267, 298; *Figs. 74, 75, 76, 77, 78, 80, 81, 82, 83, 99*
Justin, 273, 275

Kaman-Kalehöyük, 249, 312
Karaburun, 135, 137, 197–9, 295, 304; *Fig. 65*
Kel Dağ, 106
Kelenderis, 281
Kerkenes Dağ, 21, 213, 277
Kertch, 157, 249, 312
Kharga Oasis, 291
Kheriga/Kherei, 191, 193, 201, 304
King's Dinner, 114–19, 122, 280, 292
King's Eye, 279
King's Peace, 13
Kiraz, 161
Kızılbel, 197–8; *Figs. 115, 116*
Kızöldün, 172–3; *Fig. 96*
klinae, 135–6, 142, 145, 146, 146–7, 171, 173, 176–7, 295, 296, 300; *Figs. 65, 71, 99*
Konya, 16
Kubaba, 214
Kuprlli, 191
Kybebe, 215
Kybernis, 191

labor obligations and control, 41, 81
Labraunda, 230–4, 309; *Figs. 135, 136, 137, 138*
Lâle Tepe, 137, 146; *Fig. 71*
land granting systems, 27, 38, 218–19, 257–8
language and power, 33, 52, 53, 62, 63–4

INDEX

Larisa, so-called, 169, 300, 309
Latmus, 106
law. *See* legal institutions
Lebedus, 169
legal institutions, 39, 218–19
Leto, 219, 220
Limyra, 106, 197, 200–1, 224–5, 304, 308
lions, 146, 147, 155–7, 164, 179, 196, 210, 213, 215, 234, 240–1, 250, 298, 299, 303, 311, 312; *Figs. 36, 80, 81, 82, 83, 87, 141, 142, 143, 145*
Lycia (Lycian), 16, 24–5, 33, 35, 64, 75, 106, 111–12, 132, 167, 172, 175, 177, 189–202, 222, 223, 262, 278, 289, 289, 303
   language, 192–3, 253, 261, 280, 307
Lycus River, 143
Lydia (Lydian), 1, 8, 12, 16, 22–4, *23*, 28, 32, 33, 35, 39, 42–6, 53, 55, 76, 77, 81, 95–6, 100–3, 105–6, 110–11, 126–7, 132, 135, 142–68, 188, 262, 276, 277, 278, 279, 295
   crafts, 23, 283
   language, 158–60, 226, 253, 260, 298
   pottery, 126–7, 294; *Fig. 67*
lyric poets, Greek, 277

Maeander River, 54, 89
Maebazanoe, 101
Magnesia ad Sipylum, 105
Magnesia on the Maeander, 283
Magians, 238; *Fig. 139*
Malatya, 16
Malija, 222, 225
Mallus, 47
Mania, governor of Hellespontine Phrygia, 34, 77, 278, 279
Manisa, 163
many-columned hall, 59–60
Marathon, 9, 280
Marmara, Sea of, 57
marriage, to secure allegiances, 45
Marsyas River, 54
Matar cult, 209–19, 230, 270, 305–6; *Fig. 124*
Mausoleum at Halicarnassus, 53, 203–6, 231, 262, 305; *Figs. 119, 120, 121, 122*
Mausolus, 34, 53, 203–6, 231–3, 243, 305; *Figs. 135, 137*
Mazaca, 47
Mazdaism, 13, 207–8, 234
Megabazus, 12
Megabyzus, 218, 257, 263, 269, 307, 313
Memphis, 90, 153
Mên, 237
Mermnad kings, 22
Meydancıkkale, 83, 98–9, 250, 267, 290; *Figs. 51, 52, 53*
Midas City, 19, 210–12, 305; *Figs. 125, 126*
Miletus, 57, 90, 170–1, 213, 221, 263, 283, 300, 307
mints, Table 3
Mita of Mushki, 21
Mithradates, 80
Mithras, 13, 237, 308
Mithrenes, 96

Mitridastas, 218–19, 257, 263, 269
Mitrobates, 43, 57
Mnesimachus Inscription, 39, 257–8, 269
models. *See* authority-autonomy model; core-periphery model
Monodendri, Cape, 226
monuments. *See* stepped monuments
mortuary
   inclusions, 27–8, 74, 75, 103–5, 132–3, 141–2, 145, 147–8, 148–50, 151–7, 163, 167–8, 173–4, 176, 177, 180, 181–3, 183–7, 188, 213, 269, 295; *Figs. 62, 63, 76, 77, 78, 79, 80, 104, 105, 106, 107*
   inscriptions, 160, 174, 197, 202, 261–2, 298
   structures or types, 27–8, 103, 135, 141, 142–51, 165–8, 171–4, 175–6, 179, 181–2, 183, 184, 190–202, 262–3, 269; *Figs. 68, 69, 70, 91, 92, 93*
Mosaic Building at Gordion, 60–2, 284
mother goddess. *See* Matar cult
movement of work forces, 283, 285
multilingualism, 51, 64, 156, 158–9, 174, 187–8, 192–4, 197, 202, 204, 229, 235–8, 243, 253, 260–1, 270, 275, 282, 284, 304, 313; *Figs. 28, 112*
Musacali, 164
Mylasa, 125; *Fig. 62*
Myra, 304; *Fig. 114*
Myriandrus, 242; *Fig. 145*
Mysia, 89, 107, 109, 168–71, 288
Mytilene, 90

Nabataea, 299
Nabonidus Chronicle, 274, 276
Nabopolassar, 18
Naqsh-i Rustam, 13, 101, 160, 182, 193–4, 246, 299
Nebuchadnezzar, 9
Nehemiah, 12, 275, 279
Neo-Assyrian Empire, 23, 52
Neo-Babylonia, 16
Neo-Hittite principalities, 16, 276
Nereid Monument, 75, 199–201, 304; *Figs. 117, 118*
Nile River, 106
Notion, 90
numismatic evidence. *See* coins
Nush-i Jan, 294
Nymphaeum, 249, 312

Ödemiş, 161
Old Persian, 51, 53, 260
Oroetes, 43, 280
Oxus Treasure, 262, 301

Pactolus River, 23, 166, 226
Pactyes, 43, 95, 280
palace
   at Altıntepe, 59–60, 81, 284
   at Celaenae, 54
   at Dascylium, 56–9, 81, 263, 283, 284
   at Persepolis, 13
   at Tille Höyük, 63
Palestine, 107, 291, 293

371

INDEX

Pamphylia, 12, 16, 24–5, 46, 137, 278
Paphlagonia, 89, 135, 179–81, 288, 301
Paradeisoi, 32, 54–6, 283
parasang, 281
parasols, 202, 304
Parmenion, 117–18
Parnaka (Pharnaces), 120, 285, 293
Parysatis, 281
Pasargadae, 8–9, 33, 51, 55–6, 57, 166, 167, 262, 264, 282, 283, 294, 305; *Fig. 30*
passports, 48, 279
Patara, 249, 312
Pausanias, 226
Payava, 195–6, 304; *Fig. 113*
Pazyryk, 12–13, 275
Peace of Callias, 12, 44, 275
Pergamum, 170–1
Pericles, 224–5
Perikle. *See* Pericles
Persepolis, 11, 13, 33, 51, 52, 53, 65, 67, 71, 95, 101, 114, 132, 147, 150, 155, 157, 159, 193, 195, 231, 232, 250, 290, 299
    Apadana, 11, 39, 99, 106, 120, 130, 132, 147, 191, 202, 240, 250, 254, 261, 286, 294, 299; *Figs. 7, 23, 43, 44, 60, 111, 133*
    Fortification Archive, 11, 34, 48–9, 117, 120–2, 129, 130, 154, 156, 207–8, 235, 239, 240, 248, 250, 255–6, 274, 275, 279, 280, 282, 283, 285, 289, 292, 293, 294, 298, 299, 303, 309, 311; *Figs. 61, 143*
    Palace of Darius, 13
    Treasury Archive, 274, 312
    treasury relief, 13, 67, 193, 286; *Figs. 43, 111, 118*
Persian luxury ideas outside the empire, adoption of, 12–13
Petosiris, tomb of, 293
Phaedyme, 299
Pharnabazus, 45, 90, 278, 281, 282, 291
Phaselis, 289
phiale, 129, 130, 132, 173, 182, 184; *Figs. 59, 62, 65, 73, 96, 103*
Philip of Macedon, 14
Phocaea, 165, 213
Phoenicia, 13
Phraortes, 9
Phrygia (Phrygian), 16, 19–22, 33, 44, 48, 53, 110, 125–6, 135, 157, 176–9, 209–12, 262, 276, 278
    language, 209, 210–12, 253, 276
    pottery, 20, 21, 22, 125–6, 127, 276, 277, 282; *Fig. 58*
Phrygius River, 143
Pigres, 91
pillar tombs, 175–6, 190–5, 203, 224, 303; *Fig. 109*
pirates, 25, 278
Pisidia, 44, 112, 188–9
Pissouthnes, 44
Pitane, 169
Pınara, 201
plane tree of Xerxes, 51, 53, 282
Plataea, battle of, 11
Pliny, 305

Plutarch, 13, 80, 275, 276, 280, 281, 286, 312
Polyaenus, 115, 280, 292
Polycrates, 43
Polyxena Sarcophagus, 172, 307; *Fig. 95*
portable elite culture, 76, 141–2, 153–4, 168, 250
power. *See* architectural style and power; cult, power statements in; iconography and power; language and power; religion and power; visual record and power
Priene, 231
Proconnesus, 57, 172, 173
proskynesis, 77, 286; *Fig. 43*
Psammetichus II, 278
Ptah-hotep, 153, 298
Pyramid Tomb at Sardis, 165–6, 308; *Fig. 91*
Pythius of Lydia, 77
Pythius the architect, 203, 231

Rassam Cylinder, 277–8
religion, Achaemenid, 207–8. *See also* ascension
religion and power, 33, 63–4, 275
Rhodes, 205
rhyton, 129, 130, 131–2, 294, 296; *Figs. 59, 61, 103*
roads, 27, 32, 34, 35, 41, 47–9, 57, 81, 91, 113, 183, 269, 280, 281; *Fig. 26*
rock-cut tombs, 142–4, 157, 179, 182, 197, 202; *Figs. 68, 114*
round-bottomed bowl, 129; *Figs. 59, 61(?)*
royal cult. *See* cult, royal
royal name seals. *See* seals, royal name

Sacrilege Inscription from Ephesus, 77, 227–9, 261, 306, 312
Şahankaya, 83, 85, 99–103, 150, 238, 290; *Figs. 55, 56*
Sais, 9
Salamis, battle of, 34, 191, 279
Samos, 13, 43, 44, 90
sarcophagi, 97, 142–5, 148, 149, 155, 168–70, 172–4, 176, 181, 195–6, 296, 297, 300, 307; *Figs. 69, 94, 95, 113*
Sardis, 1, 16, 22–4, 43–6, 48, 55, 65, 67–8, 83, 85, 89, 90, 95–6, 100, 132, 133, 136–8, 142–3, 144, 145, 151–7, 187, 215–16, 226–7, 229, 234, 238, 256, 257–8, 269, 270, 277, 281, 283, 289, 293, 295, 308, 312; *Figs. 16, 48, 134*
Sargon II, 18, 21
Sarıkız, 148–50; *Fig. 74*
Sarpedon, 225
satrap, 32, 33, 35, Table 1, 43–6, 66, 76, 87, 90, 229, 230, 245, 267, 278, 280
satrapies, 32, 33, 35, Table 1, 44, 278, 301
satraps' revolt, so-called, 13, 45
schoolrooms, 28, 245
Scythia, 9
seals, 28, 33, 65, 65–72, 184, 248–9, 260, 267, 289, 298; *Figs. 61, 104, 106*
    from Dascylium, 53–4, 65–7, 249, 250, 251–2, 282, 284–5; *Fig. 35*
    from Gordion, 60–3, 65, 71–2, 243, 249, 251–2, 264–5, 267, 277, 285–6; *Fig. 40, 146, 148*
    from İkiztepe, 68–9, 249, 260; *Fig. 37*

Index

from Sardis, 67–8, 152, 154–7, 234, 240, 243, 249, 250, 251–2, 260, 285, 311; *Figs. 1, 36, 38, 39, 79, 80, 81, 82, 83, 143, 146, 147*
    royal name, 51, 53–4, 66–7, 282, 313; *Fig. 35*
    sealing behaviors and practices, 54, 65–7, 71–2, 81, 199, 264–6, 282, 284
Sevan, Lake, 17
Seyitömer Höyük, 256–7
Shalmaneser III, 17
Sicily, 13
Sidon, 248, 295
sigloi, 73, 75, 289
Silifke, 188, 281
Sin Temple, 277–8
Sinai, 106
Sinope, 132, 135, 180, 301; *Fig. 102*
slaves, 41
Smyrna, 168, 213, 278
Social War (Athens), 13
Sogdiana, 8
soldiers, 34, 35, 93–4, 123, 278, 288; *Fig. 46*
Solon, 24
sovereignty. *See* tempered sovereignty
Sparta, 23, 44, 45, 193, 246, 273
sphinxes, 146–7, 157, 188, 189, 232–3, 243–4, 250, 303, 309, 311; *Figs. 34, 35, 37, 74, 76, 100, 107, 108, 137, 138, 146, 147*
staters, 240, 257; *Figs. 136, 140, 141, 142, 144, 145*
stelae
    anthemion, 143, 156, 159–60, 298, 301; *Fig. 85*
    inscribed, 160, 187, 289, 303, 306, 309–10
    relief, 150, 156, 160–2, 170–1, 174–5, 177–8, 180, 189, 210, 249, 267, 295, 299–300, 301; *Figs. 86, 87, 88, 89, 90, 98, 100, 108, 124*
stepped monuments, 213–14; *Fig. 126*
Strabo, 238, 247, 274, 289
style (visual) and meaning, 66–72, 75, 81, 152–7, 159, 170–1, 189, 190, 196, 198, 199–200, 224, 234–5, 240–1, 242, 249, 251–2, 260, 263, 285, 298, 300. *See also* Achaemenid Empire, style; architectural style and power; visual styles
Sultantepe, 106
Susa, 11, 33, 39, 48, 71, 91, 144, 254, 275, 281, 312
syennesis, 46, 281
Syllion, 91
Syria, 9, 103, 183, 184, 262
Syrian Gates, 91
Syro-Palestine, 12

Tabalus, 43, 95
Tarsus, 46, 263, 289; *Figs. 140, 141*
Taş Kule, 165–7, 238, 308; *Fig. 92*
Tatarlı, 178–9, 301; *Fig. 101*
Taurus Mountains, 15, 46
taxes and taxation, 26, 27, 32, 34, 35–42, Table 2, 46, 47, 49, 81, 83, 218–19, 256, 257–8, 278, 279, 300
    Darius'/Artaphernes' organization of, 9, 43, 279
Tell Defenneh, 106
Tell el-Herr, 106
Tell Kedoua, 106
Telmessus, 201, 219, 307
tempered sovereignty, 3
temple tombs, 163, 167–8, 200–2, 203, 224, 304
temples, 28, 29
Teos, 168
Thibron, 281
Thrace, 20, 49, 57, 119, 295
Themistocles, 279
Thucydides, 44, 273, 275, 280
tiarate head coins, 73–6, 286, 289; *Figs. 41, 42*
Tigris River, 1, 15
Tilbes Höyük, 63
Tille Höyük, 63
Tire, 164
Tiribazus, 45
Tissaphernes, 44–5, 85, 91, 101, 193, 229, 280, 281, 283, 308
Tithraustes, 45, 281
Tlos, 222, 225, 307
Tmolus mountain range, 23, 106, 143
Tomb of Cyrus, 166, 167, 305
tombs. *See* cist tombs; doorstones; mortuary; pillar tombs; rock-cut tombs; tumuli
Tosya, 180
towers, 106, 107, 291
Troad, 109, 172, 222, 301
Troelus, 198
Troy. *See* Ilium
Trqqas, 222
Truth/Lie, in Achaemenid imperial rhetoric, 10, 94, 246–7, 311
Trysa, 219, 223, 308
tumuli, 21, 144, 145–8, 150, 158, 164, 171–4, 176–7, 179, 188, 197–9, 277, 297, 300, 301, 304
Tumulus A at Gordion, 176–7; *Fig. 99*
Tushpa, 181
Tyberissus, 222, 307
Tymandus, 188

Udjahorresne, 9, 10, 153, 274, 298; *Fig. 5*
Ulhu, 18
Ünye, 180
Ur, 248
Urartu, 16, 17–19, 51–3, 59, 137, 181, 182, 262, 276
Urmia, Lake, 17
Uşak, 135, 147–9, 150, 177, 298; *Fig. 73*

value, 122–3, 128, 295
Van
    Lake, 15, 17, 181
    the Rock at, 51–2, 182; *Fig. 29*
    Xerxes' inscription, 51–2; *Fig. 28*
vandalism, 229
vessels. *See* banqueting vessels; drinking vessels
visual record and power, 33, 49–50, 62, 65–72, 282. *See also* iconography and power
visual styles, 54, 62, 66, 129, 309. *See also* style (visual) and meaning

way stations, 34, 48, 279, 281; *Fig. 26*
weapons, 86, 87–8, 91, 92, 101, 103–5, 107, 183, 185, 224, 246; *Figs. 46, 97, 105, 106*

373

Index

Xanthus, 24, 64, 75, 106, 172, 191, 199–201, 219, 222, 223, 223, 225, 249, 270, 280, 304, 307, 308, 309; *Figs. 132, 133*
Xenophon, 18, 54, 79, 80, 85–8, 89, 91, 92, 107, 137, 200, 226, 245–6, 257, 262, 273, 275, 278, 279, 280, 281, 282, 283, 287, 288, 289, 291, 292, 293, 296, 306, 308, 311, 312, 313
Xerxes, 11–12, 32, 43, 44, 49, 50–4, 66, 94, 182, 204, 242, 260, 269, 273, 282, 283, 307, 312, 313

inscription, 51–2; *Fig. 28*
invasion of Greece, 43, 54, 119, 191, 279
plane tree of, 51, 53, 282
progress through Anatolia, 50–4, 282

Yarıkkaya, 106
Yılan Kalesi, 106

Zagros Mountains, 8, 9
Zenis, 77, 278
Zeus, 225, 229, 230–4, 240, 308; *Figs. 135, 136*